Acknowledgements

Project Director	Margo R. Friedman
Editor	Mary S. Gordon
Consulting Editor	Arthur S. Levine
Graphics Production Coordinator	Gibby Edwards
Writers	Susan Antigone Barbi Baker Melanie Stockdell
Contributing Writers	Anthony J. Anastasi Margaret Carlson Robert C. Czapiewski Carl H. Kaplan Mary Dixon Trullinger John Zarafonetis
Research	Madeleine Adamson Gibby Edwards Richard Kazis Arch Parsons Robert Schur
Resources Coordinator	William Caldwell
Editorial Assistants	Dottie Akinleye Connie Smith
Illustrator	Nathan Davies
Special Thanks to	Anna Barnes, Mary Brayboy, Anne Chapman, Gail Chipman, Marion Ciaccio, Richard Cuffe, Cathy Floyd, R. Benjamin Johnson, Harry Judd, Lyla Krayenhagen, Robin Lee, Frank R. Marvin, Juanita Micas, Kim Mitchell, Martha Myers, Linda Nicoletti, Freeman Palmer, Dale Rampell, Dan Rumelt, Gina Sammis, Howard Seltzer, Carolyn Smith

The efforts of many others, too numerous to acknowledge, who generously gave their time and expertise have made the production of PEOPLE POWER possible. We are greatly appreciative and extend special thanks to each of them.

Table of Contents

People Power:

What Communities are Doing to Counter Inflation

Published by
U.S. Office of Consumer Affairs
Esther Peterson, Director

Produced by
Consumer Information Division
Midge Shubow, Director

Esther Peterson,
Director of the
U.S. Office of Consumer Affairs and
Special Assistant to the President
for Consumer Affairs

General Introduction

It's the sorry truth that each year American families pay more and more of their incomes for the basic necessities. That's because spiraling inflation hits hardest at food, housing, energy and health care. In 1979 they rose collectively by 18.2 percent while nonessentials — everything from flower vases to liquor — rose by 7.0 percent. Not surprisingly, energy led the way, leaping by 37.4 percent. Housing followed with an increase of 17.4 percent. Food and health care trailed but still rose significantly by 10.2 and 10.1 percent respectively.

People's Movement Taking Hold

But something special is happening that makes our country's economic picture a good deal brighter. There is a new movement — an exciting cooperative spirit — making itself felt everywhere from rural towns to big city neighborhoods. The movement has no single leader nor does it have a national platform. Rather, consumers are taking concrete steps to beat inflation on the local level. They are forming partnerships with businesses, governments, unions, private foundations and, most importantly, with each other. The movement varies in form but the spirit is the same whether it's manifested in a Detroit housing renovation program or a free health clinic in Wisconsin.

The successes of the almost 100 local groups we describe provide exciting proof of how much consumers can do to fight spiraling costs and provide their neighbors with low-cost, needed services. In addition, we briefly mention hundreds of other projects and organizations which have set examples that you can follow.

At first glance the groups may not seem to have much in common. Some serve poor whites in Appalachia or middle-class families in Seattle. Others help central Nebraska farmers or inner-city blacks in Los Angeles. Some of the groups operate on tiny budgets using the help of a few volunteers; others have multimillion dollar budgets and large paid staffs.

Common Goals

But these groups do share common goals. Most notably they are working to serve the needs of their neighbors and, directly or indirectly, save consumers money. They ultimately promote self-reliance. They share a spirit of commitment and cooperation. And they've succeeded because the organizers have won community support and have found and used available resources.

Some of the programs we feature are saving families hundreds of dollars annually. For instance, we see how several groups are promoting community and backyard gardening—which pays off in big savings. In 1979, according to Gardens For All, a national gardening clearinghouse and one of our featured groups, backyard and community gardening projects nationwide produced a staggering $13 billion worth of produce. Another example, a corporate-sponsored ridesharing program in California, saves commuters $4 million in commuting costs and an estimated two million gallons of gasoline each year.

Other groups have found less tangible ways to save while making life more enjoyable for those they serve. For example, some organizations are giving residents a new sense of pride by revitalizing their neighborhoods. In St. Louis, a dynamic inner-city group has renovated $15 million worth of housing, created jobs for 450 residents by luring a shoe factory into the area and opened a low-cost medical clinic. Add the group's two day care centers and their programs for youth and the elderly and you have a portrait of an organization making a real contribution to their neighbors' quality of life. And by boosting their local economy they have decreased the welfare and unemployment rolls and increased personal spending power.

Innovative Programs

Many groups are fighting inflation by finding alternatives to the traditional marketplace. They've used innovative and practical programs to promote medical self-care, food co-ops, self-help home repairs—anything that works. In New York City, for example, a homelike childbearing center offers residents an alternative to traditional hospitals which often charge as much as three times more for deliveries and aftercare.

Citizen Participation

Still other groups have gained citizen power, becoming high-powered advocates, winning reforms in many different fields from established institutions. These groups are using old-fashioned political methods to achieve their goals. For example, in Cape Cod, Massachusetts a citizens coalition successfully lobbied a local hospital to adhere to a Federal law and provide emergency care for poor people. Community organizing also paid off for the group when their coalition-backed slate won election to an influential health planning council. The consumer-oriented board then used its power to win new community health services such as a needed medical clinic for area women.

Similarly, groups around the country are striving to educate their neighbors about Federal programs for which they might qualify. In Nashville, Tennessee, for example, a determined group convinced the local school board to implement a Federal school breakfast program. Through research and lobbying, the group showed that the fully subsidized program could provide nutritious meals to thousands of children at little cost to the school system.

Helping the Needy

Many of the organizations in this book are especially committed to helping those most in need—the poor, the elderly and those on fixed incomes. For them, rising costs mean more than pinching pennies or switching from steak to hamburgers. It takes its toll in real human suffering—poor nutrition, decaying homes and untreated illnesses.

Spreading the Word

Those of us at the United States Office of Consumer Affairs wanted people around the country to learn and benefit from the achievements of local organizations. The best way to reach that goal, we decided, was to share our knowledge — and theirs — through a book. We envisioned our audience to be thousands of active community leaders and groups across the nation as well as citizens wishing to begin action in their own neighborhoods.

We began a search for representative organizations in the fall of 1978. We sent thousands of questionnaires to consumer and citizen groups, some of which in turn passed them on to others. Through the questionnaires and word of mouth, we learned about the valuable work of hundreds of organizations.

Our search, of course, wasn't meant to be exhaustive. Rather, we wanted to provide readers with a sampling of cost-cutting activities that are underway around the country. The groups mentioned in this book may not be the best in their field and a few of their programs may have ended by the time this book is published. But they've all had important successes that help illustrate the various approaches others can take to fight inflation.

Forging Partnerships — Anywhere and Everywhere

In looking at the groups that are chronicled in this book, it becomes clear that forging workable partnerships is a key ingredient of success. Often the Federal government plays a role in those partnerships. But Federal grants and assistance programs do have limits. For instance, there is stiff competition for them and qualifying often involves considerable paperwork. Also, much of the funding is short-term. These limits often apply to state and local government programs as well.

So most of our featured groups have also become adept at garnering funds and assistance from other sources — neighbors, churches, foundations, unions and area businesses. In fact, their successes are marked by a willingness to use whatever resources they can — from the help of a few volunteers to a Federal grant — to reach their goals. To do so requires hard work, imagination and commitment, but as you'll see throughout this book, these virtues pay off!

It's Up To You

In this book you'll learn about the triumphs of many groups as well as obstacles they overcame. You'll meet their leaders and will hear from the people they have helped. You'll discover that despite differences in income, geographical location, occupation and race, the people involved are much like you and your neighbors. We hope that you will be so inspired by their efforts that you too will take action.

The United States Office of Consumer Affairs views this upsurge of consumer action as one of the most refreshing developments in our national life.

The "people's movement" is truly worth celebrating!

Esther Peterson

How to Use This Book

We hope this book will be a valuable resource for those wishing to take the kind of consumer action that has meant a better life for thousands of Americans who have been touched by our featured groups.

To help you get the most from it, we've prepared a brief explanation of how the book is organized. We hope you take time to read it.

Text

The book is divided into five sections. First, *Basic Tools* provides the nuts and bolts of launching a community project. It contains helpful hints on organizing a group, raising funds and attracting needed publicity.

The next four sections, *Food, Housing, Energy* and *Health,* profile the projects of dynamic groups around the country that have successfully cut costs or provided neighbors with essential services. Their stories are full of innovative, exciting ideas and resources. Also, the *Energy Section* contains two glossaries to help you better understand energy terms and utility jargon.

Resources

Following each section are *Resources,* which list useful organizations and publications. The organizations are eager to help consumer groups nationwide by providing published materials, technical assistance or — in some cases — funding. The publications include how-to manuals, directories and newsletters which can help you start neighborhood programs or expand existing ones.

Appendices

At the end of the book are two Appendices. *Appendix I* contains information on Federal programs that have provided assistance to our featured groups. Sometimes we've placed the details of the programs in footnotes. But in all cases, asterisks (*) lead you to *Appendix I* where brief program descriptions are listed under the administering department or agency. Also, addresses and phone numbers of national and, where appropriate, regional Federal offices are provided so you can get more detailed information about the programs highlighted as well as others for which your group might qualify.

Appendix II outlines the structure of the National Consumer Cooperative Bank, a valuable new source of technical and financial assistance for citizens wishing to launch cooperatively owned, nonprofit ventures.

Finally, the *Index* contains a complete listing of our featured groups as well as page numbers where they appear.

Cape Cod
Nursing
Home Council
PIONEER
PIONEER

Basic Tools

An Organizing Strategy

Introduction

The point of this book is to show that individuals working together can make a difference—a big difference—in the type, quality and price of the food, housing, health care and energy they receive.

As the success stories in this book demonstrate, problems too complex to be solved by one can often be solved by many. Institutions too large to heed one voice might be moved by a chorus of voices. Their stories show that Americans possess immeasurable quantities of creativity, energy and generosity of human spirit, and those qualities are easily tapped when basic rights are threatened or fundamental needs are not being met.

This chapter is all about creatively tapping those qualities and channeling them toward a common goal. At the heart of this book are the dynamic groups which have, through successful organizing, tackled food, housing, health care and energy problems. We hope their stories will challenge and inspire you.

Please use this section as a *tool* to guide you in your organizing efforts. It doesn't cover everything, but it does contain basic tips on marshaling support; conducting meetings; raising funds; winning publicity; merging with other groups; and finally, deciding if and when to incorporate.

We hope it will help you and your group get off to a good beginning.

Identifying Community Concerns

Every American community has a unique blend of people and problems. Yet all have the need for workable systems that deliver to residents essential services at affordable costs. Lack of those services is reason enough to organize your friends and neighbors and successfully overcome your community's problem.

Whether the problem is big or small, capable of being resolved in a month or only after years of hard work, the first steps to a solution are always the same—identify the problem and get organized.

Narrowing the Issues

It usually isn't too difficult to identify community needs or problems. If you don't already know, a survey of friends, neighbors, co-workers and community leaders should reveal the areas of most serious concern. Is it lack of health care? High energy costs? Inadequate housing? Poor quality and expensive food?

Narrow your issues to one area—such as food—where the need for services is greatest and where you have the best chance of making a difference. Always remember that your group can expand to other areas later.

As you survey, collect the names of those who express interest in working with you. And keep written notes—safely filed—on all conversations as well as information you gather. They will come in handy later. After surveying, you should have:

- several descriptions of the problem;
- a variety of causes and culprits;
- differing opinions on what, if any, action can be successfully taken; and
- a good indication of how many people are interested enough in the issue to work with you toward a solution.

Exploring the Problem/ Assessing Your Resources

You've identified the problem. Now it's time for some basic research.

- Read as many pertinent articles, pamphlets and other materials as you can find on your chosen issue. Interview key players on both sides. For instance, if your issue is high-priced, low-quality food, compare prices at local grocers and find out if they sell local produce. If not, why? Talk to farmers. Find out what their outlets are—and prices.

- Check to see if all existing laws that relate to your issue are being enforced. And while you're at it, learn everything you can about local, state and Federal programs that relate to your area of need and might be a potential source of technical and/or financial assistance.

Learning from Others

Remember you don't have to "reinvent the wheel." Learn from the experiences of others who have tackled similar problems.

- Locate other groups that may have formed for similar reasons. If local, plan to work with these groups. If not, don't hesitate to contact them for guidance on how to get started and what to do next.

- Don't forget to tap the expertise of local, state and Federal agency officials who are involved with your issue.

- Write to national clearinghouses, some of which are listed in the Resource Sections throughout this book. They are likely to have valuable information.

- Look in this book under the section dealing with your issue, and read the stories of groups profiled to give you ideas on how to tackle the problem and where to look for funds and assistance.

Getting Together

After you are familiar with the issue and feel comfortable talking about it, call a meeting of those who have expressed interest in helping. Remember that new groups don't have to be created every time a new problem arises. Chances are that a group or two already exist that share an interest in your issue. So publicize the meeting (date, time, place and purpose) on community bulletin boards, in supermarkets, local laundries and perhaps in the meeting section of your local newspaper. If you already belong to a club or organization, ask that your proposal be placed on the agenda for the next meeting. And ask your friends to announce the meeting to their clubs and organizations.

At the meeting:

• tell what you have learned and the results of your survey;

• describe the problem as you see it;

• discuss some possible solutions;

• discuss how much effort might be involved in finding and pursuing the right course of action.

Keys to a Successful Issues Meeting

• **Follow an agenda.**

• **Get feedback.**

• **Encourage debate** on how to tackle the problem; others might come up with a better idea.

• **Listen to others.**

• **Be open to compromise;** disagreements will arise.

• **Assess group interest** to determine how many are willing to volunteer for the basic tasks necessary to get the project underway.

Chart 1

With a successful, lively meeting, you're on your way! Now to harness your group's energy and enthusiasm and plot your goal-reaching strategy.

Make It a Team Effort

First, tasks should be assigned so no one member bears the brunt of the work. Based on goals and group size, determine what committees are needed to tackle various tasks. Research, fundraising and budget, publicity, newsletter, membership and community liaison are among those your group might want to establish.

Step-By-Step Approach to Problem Solving

Plan your strategy carefully—step-by-step. The completion of each step toward reaching the overall goal is cause for celebration, regrouping and moving ahead.

Perhaps the best way to illustrate the step-by-step approach to reaching a goal is by example. Our first example deals with launching a community project; the second with providing a service for consumers.

Let's assume that your group has decided to combat high food costs by starting a community garden to provide nutritious, low-cost vegetables for members and interested neighbors.

But before planting can begin, smaller goals must be reached.

Sample Organizing Tool — Launching a Community Project

Step-by-Step Approach to Launching a Community Garden

Step 1. Find land

Step 2. Get permission to use the land

If the land is city-owned
- meet with local officials
- obtain clearances
- file permits

If the land is privately owned
- locate the owner
- get written permission from the owner
- negotiate mutual benefits (your group will clear land and owner can partake of produce, for instance)

Step 3. Publicize your efforts—continually (See Publicity in this Section.)

Step 4. Decide who will use the land
- determine eligibility requirements
- determine number of plots needed
- determine size of each plot

Step 5. Assess local growing conditions
- determine what vegetables grow best in your area

Step 6. Obtain needed supplies (topsoil, fertilizer, seeds, tools)

If Donated
- find donors (local farmers, merchants)
- arrange for pick-up

If Purchased
- price materials
- raise needed funds
- arrange for pick-up

Step 7. Clear the land
- assign chores to participants
- rally help from nearby residents interested in sprucing up neighborhood

Step 8. Draw up timetable
- decide when soil preparation, planting, weeding and other gardening chores should be performed
- decide who will be responsible for upkeep (individually maintained or rotating assignments)

Step 9. Teach gardening techniques

Hold classes
- find space
- develop curriculum (utilize materials from your local agricultural cooperative extension service and other free sources)[1]
- find teachers (use above services if possible)
- determine any costs
- publicize

Provide easy-to-follow materials
- develop materials
- print or mimeograph instructions and helpful hints
- determine place of distribution

Step 10. Begin planting

[1] For more information on cooperative extension services, see Appendix I under the United States Department of Agriculture.

Note: For more information on community gardens, see Chapter 2 of Food Section, Growing and Processing Your Own Food, beginning on p. 47.

Chart 2

Surveys

Step-by-step problem solving also works when your group is providing a service to consumers. For example, many groups have had great success conducting and publishing surveys on the price, quality and availability of local goods and services.

By giving consumers information on what and where the best buys are, you draw attention to your group. After all, who isn't interested in cutting costs? And if consumers are interested in your efforts, usually the press is too. Useful surveys can also boost your membership roster. Moreover, consumers can take action with their dollars, forcing sellers to vie for customers by offering better priced or higher quality products and services than their competitors.

But again, before your group can bask in the glory that a successful survey can bring, careful planning is necessary.

Price/Quality Surveys Uncover Startling Practices within Communities

Wide Discrepancies

Price/quality surveys conducted by the nonprofit Washington Center for the Study of Services in Washington, D.C., have revealed:

- Prices ranging from $3 to $11 for the same prescription drug among neighborhood pharmacies;
- Bids ranging from $850 to $2,150 for the same plumbing job—with some of the lowest bids coming from firms rated tops on performance by customers and consistently given high marks by government inspectors;
- Premiums that are $200 lower at some auto insurance companies which rate among the best for speedy and adequate claim payments and are less likely to terminate policyholders arbitrarily than their higher-priced competitors;
- Prices ranging from $91 to $105 among neighborhood supermarkets for baskets filled with the same products.[1]

[1] Surveys conducted by the Washington Center for the Study of Services are also mentioned in Health Section, p. 328. (For more information on the Washington Center, see Resources at end of Basic Tools Section.)

Chart 3

Sample Organizing Tool — Providing a Service for Consumers

Step-by-Step Approach to Conducting Surveys

Step 1. Get expert advice

- Make contact with professionals—in a social science department of a local university, for example—who can help with designing questionnaires, pre-testing and analyzing results. (Not everyone knows how to collect and interpret numbers and, without that knowledge, your efforts could prove useless—and embarrassing.)

Step 2. Determine what you (and other consumers) want to know

Step 3. Identify sellers of targeted product or service

Step 4. Test questionnaire

- Assemble a group of your friends to answer the questionnaire to ensure that consumers will understand what you are asking.

Step 5. Collect data

- Call, write or visit sellers to get the information you need. Double check to make sure it's accurate.
- Supplement information from sellers or providers by checking public records (i.e., public health agencies, weights and measures and licensing authorities, state and local complaint handling agencies).[1]
- Get needed information from consumers through the questionnaire (mail it out, publish it in newsletters or newspapers or get answers by phone).

Step 6. Interpret data

- Get expert help (See Step 1).

Step 7. Make results readable

- Put survey results in a clear and understandable form so consumers will know what facts your efforts uncovered.
- Include an explanation of how findings were obtained—and interpreted.

Step 8. Distribute results

- Notify the press of your findings.
- Make results available to the public by placing them in newsletters of neighborhood and civic organizations, announcing them at community gatherings, distributing them at shopping centers and other public places or featuring them in your own publication.

[1] For more information on such groups as public health agencies and weights and measures and licensing authorities, write for the *Consumer Resource Handbook,* United States Office of Consumer Affairs (OCA), 621 Reporters Building, Washington, D.C. 20201. (For more information on OCA, see Resources at end of Basic Tools Section.)

Chart 4

Keeping Your Group Intact

While you're busy pursuing a project or conducting a survey, ongoing organization is important. Be sure to keep good records of membership, research, press coverage and other matters. For instance, the membership committee should be responsible for keeping index cards on each interested member. Cards should list essential information: name, address, home and work phone numbers, job experience, other group affiliations, hours available, committee preferences, special skills (such as accounting, art or writing) and types of tasks the person is willing—or unwilling—to perform.

Work should be assigned democratically and group members should remember that every worthwhile project contains drudgery and ecstasy—usually in unequal amounts. There should be enough of each to go around if everyone cooperates.

Committee and Full Meetings

As a general rule, small working groups which have specific tasks need to meet more often than the group as a whole. Since meetings are usually the glue that holds the organization together, have them as often as needed. But don't discourage attendance by meeting unnecessarily. Here are some pointers on having lively and productive meetings.

Do's

- Do have a prepared agenda and keep meetings orderly. That can be difficult. You might try *Roberts' Rules of Order* (available at most libraries). Common sense and fair play are also useful guides.

- Do call for reports from each committee. Make sure reports cover accomplishments, obstacles and activities and assignments to be completed by the next meeting.

- Do make concrete, democratic decisions.

- Do decide on the time and place for the next meeting. Set up a telephone chain (the first person on the list calls the next one and so on) in case members need to be contacted between scheduled meetings.

- Do keep the meeting moving. This often requires tact!

- Do try to have some kind of refreshments, even if your group is broke. Food soothes the human spirit!

- Do try to arrange for child care at the meeting site.

Don'ts

- Don't hog the agenda. Keep others involved. You might try rotating the chair to increase participation from all members.

- Don't think long-term all the time. Set small winnable goals or members may lose interest.

- Don't hold meetings during the day if most of your members work.

Fundraising

Fundraising is essential for any group that wishes to have an impact. Besides filling the cash box, it can bring new members into the organization. And new members eager to volunteer their time are as important as money.

Fundraising techniques are many, but success depends largely on your group's credibility. And good coverage by the press of your group's fundraising events and other activities can help build your credibility. (for ideas on attracting press coverage, see Publicity in this Section.)

Remember to show your appreciation. Let donors know how important their contribution is to the success of your organization. Acknowledge their gift in your newsletter, with honorary membership or other special recognition. Public thanks may encourage others to contribute.

First Step

The first step to fundraising is selecting a chairperson—and perhaps other officers—to coordinate all activities. It will help if the chairperson is well known and familiar with your community. Then you will want to target potential contributors, set your goals and plan your strategy.

Internal Fundraising

Dues and pledges—based on members' ability to pay so that those on tight budgets aren't barred from your organization—are the most obvious sources of revenue.

Individual Solicitations

Small contributions from residents are the lifeline of many local organizations. There are numerous ways to reach your neighbors. You might send out a newsletter with a convenient tear-off sheet for those interested in contributing to your efforts, or a brochure—perhaps inexpensively prepared by the art department of a local college—describing your group and its activities. You might mail them, leave them at community centers or distribute them door-to-door. And of course members can raise funds by extolling the virtues of their group to family and friends.

Don't Overlook Big Donors

Nearly all established national organizations receive 90 percent of their money from 10 percent of their contributors. And local groups can learn from their techniques. The first step is to identify potential donors. Their names are often chiseled on building plaques, particularly hospitals, or printed in concert hall and theatre program guides. Also look at membership lists of other groups such as museums and local public broadcasting stations.

Already Believers

These large contributors already believe in charitable donations. They only need to be convinced of the worthiness of your project. A representative of the fundraising committee should make an appointment for a personal visit. Your group's program should be presented openly and honestly. Don't try to tailor it to meet the preference of prospective donors. But you might solicit money for a particularly exciting group project. In fact, raising money for a specific project is often more effective than soliciting general operating funds. Like consumers, donors want to know what they are getting for their money.

After meeting with prospective donors you should send a follow-up letter thanking them for their contributions or, if none were received, for the chance to talk with them. Be sure that donors receive formal receipts for their tax records. If your group has incorporated as a nonprofit organization, donors can deduct their gifts on Federal and state income tax returns. (For more information, see Incorporating in this Section.)

Large contributors can encourage fellow business leaders or their colleagues who support your efforts to also contribute. And if these leaders are convinced of the validity of your mission, they might also agree to serve on your fundraising committee.

There are all kinds of ways to raise funds and everyone can participate.

Fundraising Events

There are many other ways of raising money. Not all are appropriate for every organization. Special events such as fairs and auctions, for example, are time consuming and should be undertaken only if you are confident of a substantial return. All groups, however, can learn from the techniques listed below.

Fundraising Events

Bake Sales

- Ask all your friends and organization members to bake something.
- Set up a table in a public area or at a public event that attracts lots of people. A large shopping center or a big event, such as a county fair, would be ideal. (Get permission for use of space from owner or appropriate official.)
- Have lots of cakes, pies and other large items, but don't forget small goodies—such as cookies and brownies—that buyers can munch while learning about your organization.
- Talk to buyers and let them know why you are raising money. Invite them to meetings.
- Have brochures on your organization available.
- Appoint a clean-up crew.

Pot Luck Dinners

- Choose a date and assign each volunteer a dish. Themes, such as an international dinner, a picnic or a vegetarian meal are fun.
- Find a large meeting room with tables, chairs and running water. A church or school makes a good choice.
- Before the dinner, lay out the buffet table.
- Set up a ticket table at the door.
- Charge whatever is appropriate for your community and group. (Many groups charge about $3 for adults and $1 for senior citizens and children.)
- Prepare a simple program consisting of a welcome and *short* talk about what your organization does.
- Have members circulate and talk with guests. Also have membership forms available.

Direct Mailings

- Obtain mailing lists from community, church and other groups.
- Keep fundraising letters brief and to the point—usually no more than one page.
- Don't expect to get rich quick. An exceptionally good return is $2 for every $1 spent.

Donation Parties

- Plan a theme such as a St. Patrick's Day corned beef and cabbage dinner, a May Day celebration or an afternoon tea.
- Ask members to bring refreshments.
- Set a minimum donation such as $5.
- Publicize the event throughout your organization and within the community by using posters and flyers.
- Have some form of entertainment if possible. This may include a musical group, an interesting speaker or a fashion show.
- Stage a brief presentation about your organization and have literature available for people to read and discuss.

Auctions

- Select and get permission to use a site; a church or school hall is a good bet.
- Contact *everyone* in your community for donations—florists, restaurants, car washes, bakeries, gift shops. Don't forget about individual donations such as ball game or concert tickets or a weekend at a private country cottage.
- Have fill-in-the-blank form letters for each donor to sign.
- Keep detailed records of donors and bidders and arrange how items will be picked up or redeemed. Have a special table for redemption.
- Number all items and make lists of auction goods available to those attending.
- Start the bidding below market value for the item—you'll clear money for your group and participants will get a good deal.
- Don't let the donor know the amount of the winning bid. Feelings can be hurt when a beloved item garners only $5.

Fairs

- Seek permission from local officials to use the grounds you have selected. Plan ahead for a rain date.
- Estimate the crowd you anticipate, the time of the event and plan a trash collection system.
- Plan the activities. These might include games, bake sales and refreshments, white elephant sales using donated articles such as old books and records.
- Have a large booth to display literature on your organization.
- Publicize the fair by distributing leaflets, posters, balloons or banners.
- Notify the local media and keep them informed.

Chart 5

Publicity

Your group needs to establish credibility in order to gain local attention and focus the eyes of the community on your particular project. Without effective publicity —and that includes everything from television to radio to newspapers to posters to word-of-mouth—you can almost count on disappointing coverage, membership, fundraising and support.

Newsletter

A newsletter can help build membership and raise funds. Moreover it can give your group a sense of identity and closeness as well as keep members, area organizations and residents informed about your issues and activities.

It doesn't take a journalist to write a newsletter. If your group includes a professional writer willing to organize the newsletter volunteers, so much the better. But amateurs, especially those with an interest in writing, can be very effective.

A Few Tips

Keep the newsletter simple. Remember it can get more sophisticated as you go along. Use bullets or short paragraphs and lots of headings. Also include names. People like to know what others in the organization are doing—and they like to see their own names in print.

Leave stacks of the newsletter at local stores, churches and schools with a convenient tear-off sheet for those interested in volunteering or donating. To cut costs, try locating a business or organization in your community willing to let you use a mimeograph machine.

Reliable Posters and Leaflets

Posters and leaflets are "tried and true" publicity methods. But remember, people don't read posters—they glance at them. So make yours eye-catching and to the point—and be sure they contain the who, what, why, where and when as well as a phone number for more information.

Display your posters and distribute your leaflets at community or university centers and shopping areas. Bulletin boards—especially where residents must wait for services such as community health centers and credit unions—are good targets for posters.

Other good ways to publicize your meetings or events include church bulletins, announcements at other local group meetings or through banners for a "Main Street" parade.

How to Attract Media Coverage

There's no better way to reach large numbers of residents than to attract coverage from the local media. The most obvious ways to bring your story to the attention of local newspapers and television and radio stations are through press releases and news conferences.

Others include staging a "media event" such as inviting the press the day you harvest your community garden, holding a press conference to release survey findings, having a fundraising auction or conducting a seminar at which local leaders will speak. Also, when items concerning your issue appear in the paper or when you feel the press has misconstrued an item concerning your group, you might want to write a letter to the editor. But be polite and tactful. Moreover, you might have some interesting ideas for feature stories concerning your group or issue that you can feed to the city editor. And you should take advantage of free space and air time in newspapers and on radio and television to announce your group's upcoming events. (See Charts 6, 7 and 8.)

Publicity Committee

Appoint a publicity coordinator at one of your first meetings and make sure volunteers are available to help plan, plan, plan. The publicity committee should be responsible for developing a list of press contacts, finding out the deadlines for newspapers and radio and television stations in your community, clipping and filing articles about your group or your issue and developing good working relationships with the press.

Dealing Professionally with the Media

There are some important points to remember when working with the press:

- Call on them for legitimate reasons. The purpose of the media is to report on events—not on movements. A dull or unwarranted press conference can make media coverage much more difficult to obtain in the future.

- Remember, newspapers and radio and television stations are not public relations agencies. A journalist's job is to be objective—they will be interested in both sides of the story.

- Understand that the press has editorial privilege. Anything you send them can be—and probably will be—shortened because of space restraints or, sometimes, expanded to include the viewpoints of others.

Get to Know the Media in Your Area

Learn about the media in your community. Morning and afternoon newspapers have different news deadlines as do radio and TV stations. Also city newspapers have different interests than do community or other papers.

Develop a Press List

Think big. Include the major newspapers and broadcast media. Also use the wire services, including Associated Press (AP), United Press International (UPI) as well as regional wire services. But don't forget church, community and local college papers; professional association and community group newsletters; regional newspapers or magazines; local "shoppers;" and specialty publications.

Good Mileage from Smaller Papers

Even though they don't have large readerships, smaller papers have many advantages. They serve a different audience—people who might not see your message in the daily papers or on TV. They're more concerned with local coverage than with regional or national news and will often devote more space to your story. They may print more "good news"—positive, non-controversial events concerning their readers. Readers often identify more closely with community media and may be more likely to take action such as volunteering or attending your meetings.

Media Advertising

Also don't dismiss the idea of using the media for paid advertisements. Many newspapers offer special rates based on the placement and size of your ad. And even radio messages—especially short ones at off-peak times—are often surprisingly inexpensive.

Even more important, the Federal Communications Commission (FCC) requires radio and television stations to set aside a certain amount of air time for messages from nonprofit groups—free of charge! You can't control when—or if—your message will be aired, but public service announcements (PSAs) can reach large audiences. Give it a try.

Helpful Hints on Working With the Press

The following charts should provide helpful hints on working with the media in your area.

Working With Newspapers

City News Department

- The city desk usually deals with news items of local interest—not human interest stories or publicity. News releases are central to their work.
- City editors are key. They decide if a story is newsworthy, assign reporters to cover events and decide what will be printed.
- Reporters with appropriate "beats" should also be contacted.
- News releases should go to the city editor or city desk.
- Five to seven days advance notice of an event is usually enough. Two days before the event, phone to see if a reporter will attend.
- Prepare and send press packet with credible news articles, newsletters, endorsements and historical background of your group. Delivering in person can be helpful.

Public Service Announcements (PSAs)

- Most papers offer a free service to announce public meetings, conferences, speakers, events, etc.
- Call central switchboard of paper to find out with whom you should talk.
- Call before you want to make an announcement to learn deadlines and contact person, etc.
- Announcements should be typed.
- PSAs should be short and to the point and should include the who, what, why, when, where and how of the event, plus a contact phone number.

Letters to the Editor

- They can cover a wide range of issues.
- Letters should respond or react to something previously printed in the paper.
- They should be addressed to the editor.
- Your group should call in advance to find out deadlines, length, format, etc.
- The usual maximum length is 200-300 words.
- They should be typed, signed and contain an address and home and work phone numbers.

Special Sections

- Most dailies have sections or columns dealing with lifestyles, senior citizens, women and neighborhood issues, food, etc.
- Contact columnist or section editor.
- Special sections are good for special "angle" or more coverage on an issue, rather than an event.

Adapted from "Organizers' Packet," published by the National Family Farm Coalition, 815 15th Street, N.W., Room 624, Washington, D.C. 20005.

Chart 6

Working With the Broadcast Media

Television Stations

News Programs

- TV news programs deal with news items of national, regional and local scope.
- They cover events that look unusual.
- News releases should go to news director and appropriate reporters.
- Be sure to maintain contact with sympathetic reporters.
- Be aware of other events on the same day. Remember that Mondays and Saturdays are often "news short" and that planning an event on either day could improve coverage.
- Coverage depends on competition for air time to a greater extent than is true for space in newspapers.

Radio Stations

News Programs

- Follow advice given for TV.
- They will accept news releases and will use them in broadcast whenever possible.
- Releases should go to news director.
- Some stations prefer hand delivery—never a bad idea when you have the time.

Television and Radio

Public Service Announcements (PSAs)

- Phone central switchboard to find out details regarding format of PSAs and procedures for using them.
- Check to see if stations prefer taped announcements.

Special Programs/Call-in Shows & Interviews

- A variety of radio and television programs deal with issues of local interest. They often use interviews and stories with local flavor.
- Talk shows will often do a program with an articulate spokesperson—either local or out-of-town.
- Contact the host about a month in advance. Send background information, including biographical data of experts and other visitors as well as materials about the issue.
- Choose an articulate group member with a good voice.
- Plan your group's agenda in advance and role play questions and answers until you are comfortable. Have brief but complete opening statement for introduction.
- Public and cable television stations are generally more approachable than are commercial stations.
- Public, alternative and campus radio stations are usually very approachable and more issue-conscious than are commercial stations.

Adapted from "Organizers' Packet," published by the National Family Farm Coalition, 815 15th Street, N.W., Room 624, Washington, D.C. 20005.

Chart 7

Press Conferences and Releases

Press Conferences

- Plan your press conference at least a week in advance.
- Locate the best place to hold it. If the conference is going to be held in a public place, make sure you have a permit. Make sure reporters have the address and know exactly where to find you.
- Time your press conference so it does not coincide with other major events. Know deadlines so that you get stories in that day's papers and evening news programs.
- Alert the media in advance. Call the wire services such as United Press International (UPI) and Associated Press (AP). Send releases to newspapers and television/radio stations which include time, date, place and a brief description of the event. Follow up with a phone call the day before the event. Make sure you talk to the right editor or reporter.
- Ask media representatives to sign an attendance sheet at a press conference so you can contact them in the future.
- Prepare a statement to be read at the conference and distribute it before the conference begins. TV reporters appreciate this since they can read through the statement and decide at what point they want to turn on their cameras. Also distribute a press release.
- Be prepared to answer questions.
- Have good visuals for the TV cameras.
- Follow up! After the press conference, hand deliver a copy of all your materials to each important media person who missed it.

Press Releases

Press releases are for short announcements that don't need much clarification. Think of a press release as a pyramid—the most important points at the top, less important details at the bottom.

- Mix facts with quotes.
- Have two contact persons listed at the top of the release for more information.
- Put the date and time of the release at the top. Use a catchy—but not misleading—title.
- Don't go into too much detail.
- Don't write more than two pages unless it's absolutely necessary.
- Always double space.
- The final paragraph of the release should describe the aims and activities of your organization.
- If possible, make photographs—preferably exciting action shots—available for reporters.
- If you have done a background information sheet on your issue, attach it to your press release.
- Attach other background materials which may be appropriate.

Adapted from "Organizers' Packet," published by the National Family Farm Coalition, 815 15th Street, N.W., Room 624, Washington, D.C. 20005.

Chart 8

Sample Press Release

Contact: Ms. Sunshine Ray
(503) 123-4567 (office)
(503) 765-4321 (home)
or
Mr. Bill Bisson
(503) 567-8910 (office)
(503) 109-8765 (home)

For Immediate Release:
June 20, 1980

SOLAR CORONA CONQUERORS PLAN TRIP TO SUN

A manned spaceflight to the sun—targeted for the turn of the century—will be the topic of a public meeting sponsored by the Solar Corona Conquerors, a local group which has helped win Federal authorization for and funding of the project.

"By the turn of the century, our energy needs will be tremendous and our natural resources will be greatly depleted," says Ms. Lunar Summers, the well known author of *Our Accessible Sun* and the featured speaker for the meeting. "Not only will man's physical presence on the sun boost our understanding of how the sun creates energy, but valuable knowledge should surface in the course of planning this trip which will better help us rein in the sun's free energy."

The meeting is scheduled for 1:00 p.m. at the Sun Center, 1000 Torchlight Drive in Glowville. Topics to be covered include the continuing research and private and government funding necessary to ensure the spacecraft launching by the turn of the century.

An impressive list of community leaders, including Chamber of Commerce President Mr. David Shapiro and First National Bank's Board Chairperson Ms. Linda Casey have supported the group's efforts to push the solar project.

The Solar Corona Conquerors is a nonprofit organization dedicated to promoting the application of solar technology through community workshops and other educational programs.

-30-

Logo or typed heading

Release date (immediate or specific time)

Contact names and phone numbers

Headline—brief and informative

Final paragraph describing organization

Use either "-30-" or "#" to mark end of release. When additional pages follow, use "(more)" at end of first page and begin next page with "Corona-Add 1."

Chart 9

Coalitions

A small number of committed individuals can often accomplish more than a large, disorganized or less committed group. But large numbers of individuals can be a powerhouse—when they are all committed to the same goal. So when you want to really push an issue, you might consider multiplying your group by forming a coalition.

Group of Groups

A coalition is a group of groups. Their overall goals are different but they share a common interest in a single issue or in achieving a particular goal. A group concerned with keeping freeways out of a city, for example, may form a coalition with a neighborhood preservation club which wants to protect historic townhouses threatened by a highway builder's bulldozer and with a group of small business leaders who will have to close their shops if a freeway is built. Even though the overall purposes of the various groups are different, they can form a successful coalition if they share the fundamental goal of blocking the construction of the freeway.

Mutual Need

Shared issues and compatible goals aside, nothing so fuels the desire for coalition building as mutual need. There are numerous citizen groups in any given area that are as underfunded and understaffed and as much in need of increased numbers and visibility as your own. Your strength is multiplied by your numbers.

But nothing is as important to a successful coalition as mutual benefit. So make sure the coalition goal and issue is defined and that each member group understands what the coalition can do for their individual overall goals.

How to Form a Coalition

The most obvious place to look for coalition members is with other groups you've worked closely with throughout your project. You simply propose that your organizations pull together to take on a single issue or problem. Keep the ball rolling by asking those interested groups to contact organizations they have worked with in the past. Single issue organizations—small groups organized around one issue such as junk food in schools, highway safety or children's advertising—are another source to consider when building a coalition. And rely on your files to remind you which groups have supported your issue. Other potential coalition members include church, consumer, senior citizen, environmental, educational, business or labor groups in your community.

Tips on Working Successfully With Other Groups

- Each group should have something to contribute such as political influence, strategy skills, valuable contacts or large memberships.

- Each group must have something it wants from the coalition. Self-interest is the great motivator for each group and those interests should be respected. If each member group doesn't get something from the coalition, they are likely to withdraw early, putting the coalition's success in jeopardy.

- Concentrate on the coalition issue. It isn't important for all groups to agree on every issue. In fact, it's a sure bet they won't. But that isn't why the coalition was formed.

- Coalition members should be flexible, open-minded and respect other group members.

- Specific tasks should be established for the coalition. How will decisions be made? Who is responsible for fundraising? Who will make public statements?

- All member groups should have equal responsibility for determining the coalition strategy. Single members should have the responsibility of coordinating, administering and keeping other coalition members well informed of new developments.

Incorporating

Sooner or later, most successful organizations begin to consider incorporation.

A corporation is simply a group of individuals authorized to act as a single person endowed with various rights and duties. Incorporation protects individual members from lawsuits prompted by actions of the group as a whole. Only the organization's assets are endangered by lawsuits charging such improprieties as broken agreements or failure to perform.

To Incorporate or Not

The answer to the following questions can lead your group to the right decision when considering incorporation:

1. What will your tax status be as a corporation and how can it help you? You may be eligible for the nonprofit, tax-exempt status provided by 501(c)(3) of the Internal Revenue Service (IRS) Code. With it, your group is not allowed to lobby, but it is entirely exempt from Federal income taxation and contributors can deduct their donations on their income tax returns. Moreover, your group can apply to the Post Office for special mailing rates. (Other limited tax exempt classifications are available for groups wishing to lobby. For more information, contact your local IRS office or the Secretary of State's office in your state capital.)

2. How large is your organization now and how long is it likely to be around? If your issue is controversial and far-reaching, chances are that your numbers will grow and you might do well to incorporate. Any legal problems are better handled as a corporation rather than as individuals. Also, the bylaws and officers that come with incorporation can provide needed structure to a large group.

But if your group is organized around one issue that will be decided in a set period of time, such as a zoning change or the building of a highway or a new park, you may not want to take the time or money to incorporate.

3. How much money does your group have? If your organization has a lot of money or plans to do a great deal of fundraising, incorporate as a nonprofit group. Tax-exempt status will stimulate donations. Also, large sums of money are often handled more professionally and responsibly through a corporate structure. Moreover, government and private grants are often easier to obtain once you incorporate.

4. Does your group need to build its credibilty? If your group needs credibility, incorporating might help. And it can entice respected community leaders to join your Board of Directors.

How to Incorporate

Incorporating is one of the few legal procedures that is truly simple and inexpensive—costing about $20 to $30 to file the necessary papers. You might shop around for a lawyer willing to volunteer time to help you out and process your incorporation papers free of charge.

If You Do It Yourself

Obtain a copy of your state's law pertaining to nonprofit corporations (which includes a sample copy of bylaws) by writing to the Secretary of State in your state capital. Easier yet, get a copy of the articles of incorporation and bylaws from another nonprofit organization in your community.

Your group will need to select incorporators (most states require three) who will also serve on the initial Board of Directors. Later you might expand your Board to include community leaders who can lend additional credibility to your organization.

If you have trouble filling out incorporation papers, contact the Secretary of State's office. Most have a staff member assigned to assist nonbusiness groups.

File the documents with the appropriate office—either the Secretary of State or Recorder of Deeds in your state. Don't worry about mistakes. They will be pointed out to you and you'll be given ample opportunity to correct them.

Federal Exemption

Application for Federal tax exemption is made on Internal Revenue Service Form 1023. In considering the application, the IRS looks at the purpose of your organization as spelled out in the bylaws and articles of incorporation as well as your proposed fundraising activities.

Remember, the IRS has regional offices around the country with toll-free information lines. And there are agents assigned to helping people cope with the tax laws, including citizen groups filing for tax-exempt status. Take advantage of this free help.

Go to it

This chapter should give you an idea of the type of basic organizing that should be done to get your group off to a good start. The Resource Section that follows will direct you to more in-depth material on organizing and raising funds.

Remember, local problems that may seem insurmountable now can be solved. Most of the successful groups in this book began just as you are beginning, with hope and commitment and little else. Much of what they have accomplished is truly miraculous; all of it inspiring. Read on.

Basic Tools Resources

The following resources contain descriptions of organizations and publications which can be of help to consumer groups across the country that wish to organize and launch community projects designed to combat high prices.

Of course, it is not possible to list every organization or publication in the country that might prove helpful to you and your group, but we believe those we do mention are representative of the various kinds of assistance available. Chances are you'll hear of many other useful resources as you become involved in your own community project.

Space limitations made it extremely difficult to choose among the many fine groups considered, and we sincerely hope we haven't offended the many deserving organizations and/or authors of useful publications that have not been included.

Organizations

Association of Community Organizations for Reform Now (ACORN)
628 Barrone Street
New Orleans, Louisiana 70113
(504) 528-1619
and
523 West 15th Street
Little Rock, Arkansas 72202
(501) 376-7151

Works for the advancement of low-to-moderate income people. Efforts encompass a variety of issues, including utility rates, tax policies and housing.

Campaign for Human Development (CHD)
United States Catholic Conference
1312 Massachusetts Avenue, N.W.
Washington, D.C. 20005
(202) 659-6650

An action-oriented education program sponsored by the Catholic Bishops of the United States to fund projects fighting poverty. Publishes annually, *CHD Report,* which presents CHD goals and programs. (Free.)

Center for Community Change
1000 Wisconsin Avenue, N.W.
Washington, D.C. 20007
(202) 338-3134

Provides technical assistance to community organizations on housing, manpower, economic development and other grassroots concerns. Publishes quarterly newsletter, *Federal Programs Monitor,* which updates community developments and analyzes pertinent Federal programs. ($15/year.)

Common Cause
2030 M Street, N.W.
Washington, D.C. 20036
(202) 833-1200

National nonpartisan public affairs lobbying organization concerned mainly with government reform and accountability.

Consumer Education Resource Network (CERN)
1555 Wilson Boulevard, Suite 600
Rosslyn, Virginia 22209
(703) 522-0870

National resource and service network for the consumer education field; serves as a repository of information and materials designed to meet the needs of consumer educators. CERN encourages and fosters networking among consumer education interests and provides access to human and material resources on a nationwide basis.

Consumer Federation of America (CFA)
1012 14th Street, N.W., Suite 901
Washington, D.C. 20005
(202) 737-3732

A federation of 225 national, state and local nonprofit groups that advocates consumer interests before Congress, the executive branch, regulatory agencies and the courts on food, energy, credit and banking and health issues. Publishes monthly newsletter, *CFA News.* ($24/year.)

Consumer Information Center
Pueblo, Colorado 81009

Distributes Federal consumer publications and works with and encourages other Federal agencies to develop consumer information. Publishes quarterly, *Consumer Information Catalog,* listing more than 200 selected Federal consumer publications on such topics as automobiles, health, energy, housing, food and health care. Also published in Spanish. (Free.)

National Association of Farmworker Organizations
1332 New York Avenue, N.W.
Washington, D.C. 20005
(202) 347-2407

National coalition of organizations advocating farmworker rights and concerns. Sponsors programs on energy crisis assistance, food, housing, health and education. Publishes monthly newsletter, *National Farmworker,* which covers a variety of topics concerning farmworker rights and welfare; available in English or Spanish. ($15/year.)

National Center for Appropriate Technology
P.O. Box 3838
Butte, Montana 59701
(406) 494-4577

Offers technical assistance and small grants to primarily low-income groups working with appropriate technology and self-help projects in areas such as food, housing, health and energy. Provides assistance to groups which demonstrate and develop technology that addresses problems of low-income people. Publishes monthly, *A.T. Times. (Free.)*

National Citizens Committee for Broadcasting
P.O. Box 12038
Washington, D.C. 20036
(202) 462-2520

An organization dealing with all aspects of broadcasting, including reform in commercial and public television. Participates in FCC rulemaking and acts as an information clearinghouse for consumer-related issues in broadcasting.

National Consumers League
1522 K Street, N.W., Suite 406
Washington, D.C. 20005
(202) 797-7600

The nation's oldest consumer organization; sponsors consumer education programs and lobbies for consumer rights in a variety of areas. Publishes bimonthly newsletter, *The Bulletin.* ($15/year to members.)

National Council of Senior Citizens
1511 K Street, N.W.
Washington, D.C. 20005
(202) 347-8800

Nationwide organization with membership of three million senior citizens from 3,500 clubs. Offers discount programs for insurance, drug prescriptions, travel, etc. Also promotes and testifies before Congress on bills concerning the elderly.

National Economic Development and Law Center
2150 Shattuck Avenue, Suite 300
Berkeley, California 94704
(415) 548-2600

Provides legal and technical assistance in the areas of business, housing, health and job development for low-income neighborhood and community economic development groups. Center also represents and assists these groups in dealing with state and local government agencies.

National Public Interest Research Group Clearinghouse
1329 E Street, N.W., Suite 1127
Washington, D.C. 20004
(202) 466-6390

Brings attention to many vital issues through state public interest research groups (PIRGs) by lobbying, researching and organizing. Inspired by Ralph Nader, PIRG projects range from energy to scholastic testing reform. Publishes bimonthly newsletter, *Of the People.* ($5/year to individuals, $12 to organizations.)

National Self-Help Clearinghouse
33 West 42nd Street
New York, New York 10036
(212) 840-7606

Acts as a data bank and referral service for self-help groups. Supports and conducts training programs in areas of mental health, parenting and care of the elderly. Publishes bimonthly newsletter, *Self-Help Reporter,* featuring articles on self-help mutual aid groups in the United States and abroad. (Free.)

National Self-Help Resource Center
2000 S Street, N.W.
Washington, D.C. 20009
(202) 338-5704

Provides information services including resource listings, access to funding and technical assistance for local citizen participation efforts. Publishes *Network Notes* every six weeks. (Free.) Also, *Community Resource Center: The Notebook,* which explains the Community Resource Center concept and how to implement it. 1976. ($5 to members, $8 to nonmembers.)

National Trust for Historic Preservation
1785 Massachusetts Avenue, N.W.
Washington, D.C. 20036
(202) 673-4000

A nonprofit, private group chartered by Congress which provides a range of published and technical assistance to preservation and conservation groups nationwide. Six regional offices with staff ready and able to provide general advice and guidance and lead nonprofit groups to other resources. Publishes bimonthly newsletter, *Conserve Neighborhoods,* which contains helpful tips for organizing and valuable resource information. (First year subscription free for nonprofit groups; $2.50 a year for others.) Also index to newsletter available. (First eight issues of newsletter plus index free to nonprofit groups; $3 for others.)

National Urban Coalition
1201 Connecticut Avenue, N.W.
Washington, D.C. 20036
(202) 331-2456

National organization which focuses on the survival and vitality of American cities. Local coalitions examine formulas for their communities. Informs the public on urban issues and national policy via quarterly magazine, *Network,* and monthly newsletter, *Work and Training News.* (Both free.)

Neighborhood Information Sharing Exchange
1725 K Street, N.W., Suite 1212
Washington, D.C. 20006
(202) 293-2813

Network of neighborhood groups which links individuals with appropriate organizations. Serves as a referral center and clearinghouse for information. Membership is free.

Public Citizen
1346 Connecticut Avenue, N.W.
Washington, D.C. 20036
(202) 293-9142

Promotes consumer interests in many areas such as marketing safe drugs and products, tax reform, congressional accountability and a consumer-oriented energy policy. Publishes quarterly, *Public Citizen* newspaper, which, among other things, probes the activities of related groups. (Free on a trial basis.)

Rural America
1346 Connecticut Avenue, N.W.
Washington, D.C. 20036
(202) 659-2800

Represents people in small towns and rural areas to help them with energy, housing and health problems. Publishes monthly newsletter, *Monitor* (free to members); monthly newspaper, *Rural America* ($10/year); and monthly newsletter, *RHA* (Rural Housing Alliance) *Reporter* (free to members).

United States Office of Consumer Affairs
621 Reporters Building
Washington, D.C. 20201
(202) 755-8810

Coordinates and advises other Federal agencies on issues of interest to consumers. Represents the interests of consumers in proceedings of Federal agencies and provides support to the Special Assistant to the President for Consumer Affairs. Also develops consumer information materials, assists other agencies in responding to consumer complaints and provides information to consumers about issues pending before other Federal agencies.

Volunteer: The National Center for Citizen Involvement
1214 16th Street, N.W.
Washington, D.C. 20036
(202) 467-5560

Stimulates and strengthens citizen volunteer involvement. Publishes quarterly, *Voluntary Action Leadership* ($9/year). Also two bimonthly newsletters: *Volunteering* (on advocacy) and *Newsline* (on program activities). (Both free on a trial basis.)

Washington Center for the Study of Services
1518 K Street, N.W., Fourth Floor
Washington, D.C. 20005
(202) 347-9612

Provides technical assistance to groups wishing to develop surveys of quality or price of local service establishments. Also specializes in developing, printing and distributing materials at low-cost to low-income consumers. Publishes quarterly, *Washington Consumers' Checkbook,* which contains evaluation of Washington, D.C. area service establishments such as auto repair shops, hospitals and food stores. ($16/year, discount for quantity orders.)

Worldwatch Institute
1776 Massachusetts Avenue, N.W., Suite 701
Washington, D.C. 20036
(202) 452-1999

Reports on global problems such as food, population and energy. Publishes research papers and books, including *Local Response to Global Problems: A Key to Meeting Basic Human Needs,* by Bruce Stokes, 1978. ($2, bulk quantities available at reduced rates.)

Youth Project
1555 Connecticut Avenue, N.W., Room 501
Washington, D.C. 20036
(202) 483-0030

Provides funding through regional offices for community organizing. Publishes *Annual Report* (free); and the *Grass Roots Fundraising Book* by Joan Flanagan, 1977. ($5.75 plus 50 cents handling.)

Publications

Anderson, Joanne Manning, ***For the People.*** Public Citizen, 1346 Connecticut Avenue, N.W., Washington, D.C. 20036. Second printing, April 1978. ($5.95.) Consumer action handbook that cites several action-oriented consumer projects from health care to food marketing practices to energy.

Bibliography of Fundraising and Philanthrophy. National Catholic Development Conference, 119 North Park Avenue, Rockefeller Center, New York, New York 10017. (1975, with 1976 supplement, $22.50.) An extensive listing of fundraising books, periodicals and materials for use by directors of fundraising activities.

A Bibliography for Neighborhood Leaders. National Trust for Historic Preservation, 1785 Massachusetts Avenue, N.W., Washington, D.C. 20036. 1980. (Single issues free; bulk orders, minimum of 40, 10 cents each.) Designed as a road map to basic information on subjects of interest to nonprofit neighborhood conservation and preservation groups. Contains resources as well as information on fundraising, zoning and neighborhood revitalization.

Consumer Reports. Consumers Union of the United States, Inc., 256 Washington Street, Mount Vernon, New York 10550. ($12/year, 11 issues.) Features test reports and ratings on appliances, automobiles, etc. and general buying guidance. Subscribers also receive annual ***Consumer Reports Buying Guide,*** a compilation of the previous year's ratings and reports ($3.50 to nonsubscribers).

Consumer's Resource Handbook. The White House Office of the Special Assistant for Consumer Affairs, Consumer Information Center, Dept. 635H, Pueblo, Colorado 81009. (Free.) This step-by-step what-to-do and where-to-go manual provides everything from how to write a complaint letter to complete listings of local, state and national groups and offices, their addresses, phone numbers, contact names, as well as what areas they work in to assist consumers with complaints.

A Directory of Rural Organizations. National Rural Center, 1828 L Street, N.W., Washington, D.C. 20036. 1977. (Free.) Comprehensive listing of major national organizations involved in rural affairs.

Federal Register. Superintendent of Documents, U.S. Government Printing Office, Washington, D.C. 20402. Daily. ($75/year or in local library.) Charts changes in rules and regulations applicable to all Federal agencies. Also, Federal agencies are required to publish in the *Federal Register* information about new Federal assistance programs and changes in existing programs—including cutoff and deadline dates; requirements; and how to apply.

Flanagan, Joan, ***Grass Roots Fundraising Book.*** National Office, The Youth Project, 1555 Connecticut Avenue, N.W., Room 501, Washington, D.C. 20036. 1977. ($5.75 plus 50 cents handling.) How-to information to help organizations move toward financial self-sufficiency. Includes a detailed analysis on choosing the most profitable fundraising event for your organization.

Funding Sources for Neighborhood Groups. Office of Neighborhoods, Voluntary Associations and Consumer Protection, Department of Housing and Urban Development, 451 Seventh Street, S.W., Washington, D.C. 20410. 1980. (Free.) Contains information on organizing, including such topics as fundraising and proposal writing. Large resource listings of Federal programs as well as churches, national foundations and other private groups which provide assistance. Also lists useful books, articles and periodicals.

The Grantsmanship Center News. The Grantsmanship Center, 1015 West Olympic Boulevard, Los Angeles, California 90015. ($15/year, six issues.) Reviews new books on obtaining grants and offers reprints of articles dealing with private and government grants.

How to Get Access to News Media. Metrocenter Y.M.C.A., 909 Fourth Avenue, Seattle, Washington 98104. 1978. ($2.11.) Details how community groups can use the news media effectively in publicizing important issues and events. Lists resources that provide more information. Written for citizens in Pierce, King, and Snohomish Counties (Washington), but applies to community groups elsewhere.

If You Want Air Time. National Association of Broadcasters, 1771 N Street, N.W., Washington, D.C. 20036. 1974. (Free.) How-to book for groups interested in radio and television advertising. Cites six sample public service announcements.

Just Economics. Just Economics, 1605 Connecticut Avenue, N.W., Washington, D.C. 20009. (Bimonthly, $12/year.) Provides practical how-to information on community organizing.

Kahn, Si, ***How People Get Power.*** McGraw-Hill Paperbacks, 1221 Avenue of the Americas, New York, New York 10020. 1979. ($2.95.) Gives a step-by-step progression of an organizer's techniques used in organizing communities.

Neighborhood Notebook. Neighborhood Development and Conservation Center, 525 N.W. 13th Street, Oklahoma City, Oklahoma 73103. 1978. ($2 plus 50 cents handling.) A self-help guide for community organizations wishing to improve their neighborhood environment. Contains how-to information on organizing, fundraising, publicity, etc.

Neighborhoods: A Self-Help Sampler. Office of Neighborhoods, Voluntary Associations and Consumer Protection, Department of Housing and Urban Development. 1980. ($5.50, order from U.S. Government Printing Office, Washington, D.C. 20402.) Tells the story of what people across the country have done to revitalize their communities. Describes projects in housing rehabilitation, economic development, energy conservation, arts and culture, social services and neighborhood improvement; includes sections on organizing, fundraising and neighborhood planning.

The Older Person's Handbook. Handbook-Mutual Aid Project, P.O. Box 136, Church Street Station, New York, New York 10046. 1979. (Individual requests from citizens 60 years of age or over, $1; others, $3; 10 or more copies, $2 each.) Contains ideas and how-to tips for organizing voluntary projects which assist older people in playing a major role in community life.

Periodicals of Public Interest Organizations: A Citizen's Guide. Commission for the Advancement of Public Interest Organizations, 1975 Connecticut Avenue, N.W., Washington, D.C. 20009. June 1979. ($4 for public interest groups, $5 for individuals, colleges and libraries, $15 for all others.) A comprehensive listing of periodicals dealing with citizen action in the areas of health, housing, taxes, agriculture and food policies, energy, community organization, telecommunications and appropriate technology.

Private Funding for Rural Programs. National Rural Center, 1828 L Street, N.W., Washington, D.C. 20036. 1978. (Free.) Identifies some of the major national, regional and local foundations that fund programs for rural people as well as other sources of private assistance.

Resource Guide for Rural Development. National Rural Center, 1828 L Street, N.W., Washington, D.C. 20036. 1978. (Free.) A guide for learning about financial and technical resources for rural development.

United States Government Manual, 1979/80. Superintendent of Documents, U.S. Government Printing Office, Washington, D.C. 20402. Revised May of each year. ($7.50/yearly.) Official handbook of the Federal government containing information on the activities, functions, organization and principal officials of Federal agencies. Contains Sources of Information section with addresses and telephone numbers for obtaining specifics on consumer activities, contracts and grants, employment, publications and films and many other areas of citizen interest.

The following publications are available from Gale Research Company, Book Tower, Detroit, Michigan 48226:

Consumer Sourcebook. 1978. ($58, ppd.) Two-volume sourcebook for consumer information. Tells where to go, who to see, write or telephone with consumer complaints. Updated yearly.

Directory of Directories. 1980. ($48, ppd.) Reference guide covering business and industrial directories, professional and scientific rosters and other lists covering public affairs, government, education and other broad areas. Updated yearly.

Encyclopedia of Associations. 1980. (Three-volume edition. $275, ppd.) Exhaustive encyclopedia of associations which dispenses information on almost every field of human activity. Valuable as a resource for background materials, statistics and hard-to-find information on activities of various organizations. Updated yearly.

Research Centers Directory. 1979. ($110, ppd.) Provides basic operating information concerning all university-related and other nonprofit research centers throughout the United States and Canada. Includes principal fields of research, etc. Updated yearly.

Trade Names Dictionary. 1979. (Two-volume set. $110, ppd.) Reference guide to consumer-oriented trade, brand and product names with addresses of manufacturers, importers, marketers and distributors. Updated yearly.

The following publications are available from Public Citizen, P.O. Box 19404, Washington, D.C. 20036:

Grubb, David and Zwick, David, *Fundraising in the Public Interest.* 1977. ($4.50.) A citizen's guide to direct mail fundraising and door-to-door canvassing for groups who are raising funds for their organizations.

Public Citizen Action Manual. 1973. (Free.) Provides information to promote effective citizen involvement in community, state and national consumer issues.

Ross, Donald K., *A Public Citizen's Action Manual.* 1977. ($5.95.) Cites consumer action projects that individuals can organize in their own community.

The following publications of the Washington Center for the Study of Services are available at no cost from the United States Office of Consumer Affairs, 621 Reporters Building, Washington, D.C. 20201:

Demonstration of Metropolitan Area Consumer Services Evaluation: Guide for Starting a Local Service Evaluation Magazine.. Final Report. 1975. How to conduct price/quality surveys on health, auto repair and other services and how to start a local magazine to disseminate the information.

Evaluating Consumer Services: A Guide for Assessing and Responding to Service Information Needs of Low-Income Consumers. 1978. Geared toward use by and for low-income individuals. Useful, low-cost methods of doing price/quality surveys of pharmacies, lenders, auto insurers, TV repair shops and distributing the information.

OPERATION BROTHERHOODS
MOBILE GROCERY STORE

Food

General Introduction

Consumers can make a difference in the price and quality of food. The groups profiled in this section paint vivid pictures of how to attack high food bills while maintaining healthy diets. It might not be easy, but their stories prove it can be done.

Unfortunately we are all being squeezed by the economics of growing, processing and distributing food. Grocery store food prices have to include packaging, handling, transporting and other marketing costs. And inflation is felt at every step along the way—from the farmer to the middleman to the distributor.

In this section we'll learn how consumers have successfully worked with the public and private sectors to fight food inflation. Their experiences show how rewarding it can be to hurdle high food costs and help themselves and others—especially the poor, the elderly and others on fixed incomes—maintain nutritious diets.

We'll see how small and large community groups have organized to bypass the conventional marketing system and purchase food at nearly wholesale prices. We'll take a look at gardening projects that bolster diets with inexpensive home-grown produce. And we'll see how some groups have reached out to help those most in need take advantage of Federal assistance programs. Everything from food co-ops to solar greenhouses to a successful effort to repeal state food taxes is included.

The groups profiled illustrate a variety of successful approaches to food problems. We hope that you'll be able to learn from their experiences and adapt the methods that best suit the particular needs of your area and organization. These groups welcome brief inquiries about their projects. But since most have limited resources, please enclose a self-addressed, stamped envelope when you contact them. Additional information on funding sources can be found in the Basic Tools and Resource Sections as well as in the Appendices.

As with other sections, we hope this one does more than provide you with case studies or a list of funding agencies. We hope it will inspire you.

NATIONS FIRST SENIOR CITIZENS CROCERY STORE

Finding Marketing Alternatives

Introduction

The increasing cost of food is forcing low- and middle-income families around the country to look for marketing and retailing alternatives. In this chapter we see how community groups are organizing to hurdle rising food prices.

The poor, of course, are especially hard hit. Low-income residents spend more than one-third of their income on food, but many still don't have enough to eat. And for inner-city residents, often the only food stores left after chains move out are corner groceries with high prices and limited selections. So creating low-cost alternatives is particularly important.

Fortunately, in many cities and states, residents are forming food cooperatives and buying clubs that offer large savings, usually in return for volunteer labor and minimal dues.

Here we examine four cooperative concepts: a food buying club whose members pre-order and purchase food from wholesalers; a storefront cooperative that grew out of a small food buying club; a full-scale co-op supermarket that tripled in size from its early storefront days; and a multi-state cooperative warehouse system that provides local co-ops with less-expensive food while creating new jobs.

We also look at other marketing alternatives that cut food costs. The success stories profiled include farmers' markets that save city consumers money while boosting small farmer profits; seasonal food fairs that offer low-cost produce fresh from farmers' trucks to thousands of consumers; and a food store run for and by senior citizens featuring lower cost groceries.

And we explore how some determined Arizona residents organized a food bank to salvage some of the billions of dollars in edible food wasted each year and channel it to those most in need.

As you'll see when reading about these groups, organizing to save on food costs takes some effort. But the popularity of these varied programs shows that many think they're worth doing.

Food Buying Clubs

Central Davenport Food Buying Club
c/o Sue Wallinger
1318 Brown
Davenport, Iowa 52804
(319) 322-2386

These days grocery shopping can bring on a bad case of "inflation shock." The impact of rising food costs is really felt at the checkout counter. By the time the cashier rings up the meat, vegetables and milk, it's hard to believe so much has been spent for so little.

Neighborhood organizations such as the Central Davenport Food Buying Club in Davenport, Iowa are tackling high grocery store prices by pooling their food needs and purchasing directly from wholesalers. By sharing the work normally done by distributors and retailers, eliminating most packaging costs and paying in advance, the 60 families belonging to the Davenport food club are saving as much as 30 percent on such items as fresh fruits and vegetables, meats, grains and beans.

"I would say we save 18 to 19 percent by being in the club," says Mary Thompson, whose four-member family was an early member of the Central Davenport food club. "We save up to 60 cents a pound on cheese, depending on the type, and on our low income, I use a lot of cheese—in casserole-type cooking."

Finding a Sponsor

In 1978, eager to hurdle rising food prices at already expensive small neighborhood stores, the Central Davenport organizers tackled the job of forming a food club. They knew they needed members, wholesalers and equipment.

The Central and Western Neighborhood Development Corporation, a nonprofit center dedicated to helping Davenport community groups, offered to sponsor the new project, providing such essentials as food scales, a deep freeze and an adding machine. More importantly the center would serve as the food club's base—a place to hold ordering meetings and package and distribute food to members bimonthly.

Research and Outreach

The center's staff began contacting existing clubs for helpful do's and don'ts of food club organizing and, along with the club organizers, launched a campaign to spark resident interest by calling on neighbors. And the center's newsletter carried word that residents could cut food costs by joining the club.

After arousing resident interest, a meeting was called and duties, such as locating willing wholesalers, were assigned.

Costs

Within three months and expenditures of only $30, the first food ordering meeting was held of the Central Davenport Food Buying Club. The club now spends about $70,000 a year on food, and members pay a yearly fee of $5 ($2 for elderly and low-income residents). A monthly mailing to members contains meeting dates, lists of available goods and prices and other pertinent information.

Membership Help Spells Success

Probably the most crucial key to success for a food club is the volunteer help of the members. Like most food clubs, the Central Davenport members share in the labor, including writing nutrition articles for the center's newsletter, publicizing the food club, bookkeeping, making the monthly orders to wholesalers and separating orders for member pick-up.

Food buying club members separate, weigh and package fresh produce.

"On food club day (every third Thursday), I'm over there from about nine in the morning to six at night," says Mary Thompson. "I do everything from calling suppliers to get prices to weighing produce and sacking the food. Being a member of the club is worth it. I've made so many new friends."

But according to organizer Sue Wallinger, not all members are as conscientious as Mary Thompson. The most difficult task, she says, can be impressing members that their own labor is essential to keep the club going.

"We have a hard time getting volunteers to work," she says. "Most folks just want to order their food, pay for it and pick it up. Many don't want to, or don't have time to, help out with labor."

Wallinger suggests that a successful food club needs at least three strong leaders to supervise ordering, bookkeeping and coordinating activities.

Hoping to Expand

As the club becomes more stable, Wallinger says, they are hoping to buy space and form a storefront co-op in the neighborhood, possibly with financial and technical help from the newly created National Consumer Cooperative Bank.**

Other Buying Clubs

A number of other buying clubs have also discovered ways to insure the success of their projects.

In Humphreys County, Mississippi the Humphreys County Union for Progress, a nonprofit community group, has opened its food buying club to low-income residents eligible for assistance under the Department of Agriculture's (USDA) Food Stamp Program.* The group helped the low-income families file permit forms for authorization to spend their food stamps at the Humphreys County Buying Club.

In 1971 the Riverdale Neighborhood House, a nonprofit community center in Bronx, New York, recruited high school drop-outs to mobilize community support for forming the Riverdale Neighborhood Food Co-op. Today that food club boasts a membership of 40.

And elsewhere in New York City, local buying clubs teamed up with the Broadway Local Food Co-op, the oldest co-op in the New York area, to enhance their buying power. Each club submits an order and picks up the food at a central headquarters. A 5 percent surcharge on all food products covers expenses and all labor is donated by members, who receive an estimated 35 percent discount on food purchases.

Groups Highlighted

Broadway Local Food Co-op
95 West 95th Street
New York, New York 10025
(212) 864-8165

Humphreys County Buying Club
Humphreys County Union for Progress
513 Hayden Street
Belzoni, Mississippi 39038
(601) 247-1170

Riverdale Neighborhood House
5521 Mosholu Avenue
Bronx, New York 10471
(212) KI9-8100

* State and/or local government agencies are frequently responsible for administration of Federal program funds. For further information, see Appendix I under appropriate Federal agency.

** For further information, see Appendix II under "National Consumer Cooperative Bank."

NOTE: For a complete listing of groups featured throughout this book, see Index.

Starting a Food Co-op
The Basic Steps

I. Plan a Strategy

1. Spark community interest in a food co-op.
2. Determine if sufficient community commitment exists.
3. Define co-op needs and determine goals.
4. Review different kinds of co-ops and various operating methods by contacting existing co-ops and researching subject.
5. Establish basic rules:
   - One member, one vote;
   - Open membership;
   - Profits revert to members or back into co-op;
   - Cooperation with other co-ops, whenever possible.

II. Hold the First Meeting

1. Marshal support and help from core group of interested friends, fellow workers, neighbors or classmates.
2. Publicize meeting by word of mouth, distributing flyers and posters and contacting organizations such as:
   - PTAs;
   - Churches, temples and synagogues;
   - YMCAs;
   - Local settlement houses;
   - Tenant groups;
   - Senior citizen groups.
3. Discuss at Meeting:
   - What types of food wanted;
   - Where it is available;
   - How to buy it;
   - How to distribute it;
   - How to pay for it;
   - What systems to use for running the co-op.
4. Inform the group that members are expected to exchange their labor for cheaper food.
5. Solicit volunteers to help with:
   - Researching sources of food supplies;
   - Recruiting more people to work;
   - Locating a distribution site;
   - Coordinating supplies and equipment.

III. Select the Food:

1. The Checklist System: Small groups compile a list of foods by looking through a variety of cookbooks and recipe files. The list is then distributed to each co-op member who checks off whether or not an item is wanted and in what quantities.
2. The Two-Week Menu Survey System: Each family records what they eat over a two-week period and compiles a list.
3. Using survey results, make a list of those foods most desired by members and eliminate others.

IV. Buying the Food:

1. Contact Food Distributors such as:
   - Wholesalers (found in the Yellow Pages under type of food sought);
   - Farmers;
   - Other food co-ops;
   - Food co-op federations.

V. Get Money into Circulation

1. Potluck: Each member pays a prearranged sum which designated shoppers use to purchase as much quality food as they can. Food is then distributed to members in equal shares. Drawbacks:
   - Some members may not be able to pay in advance;
   - Food tastes vary;
   - Members may not trust others to make food selections.
2. Preorder/Prepaid Credits: Members fill out order forms and pay in advance. A tabulator combines the orders and makes a master shopping list. The money and the master list then go to the shopper(s).
3. Preorder/Pay On Delivery: Members fill out order forms but do not pay until the food is delivered. Initially co-op members pay a deposit covering the cost of approximately one week's food order. Deposits are then used to purchase food.

VI. Distribute the Food:

1. Individual: Similar foods are placed on tables around the room and members, with order forms in hand, make rounds picking up their food.
2. Teams: Unpacking is done by a worker before members arrive to pick up their food. Different foods are placed at stations around the room and a person is assigned to each post. Another person takes a family's order form, fills it by going from station to station and attaches the order form to the filled bag(s).
3. Everybody works: Every time a member gets food, he/she performs a co-op task such as unpacking food or filling orders.

VII. Monitor Performance:

1. Establish a record keeping system.
2. Hold regular meetings to evaluate co-op performance and resolve problems.
3. Determine if co-op members are getting maximum savings.

VIII. Beware of Potential Pitfalls such as:

- Ignoring decline of enthusiasm among members;
- Overlooking the needed involvement of the right neighborhood leaders;
- Forgetting to factor operating expenses (travel costs, small equipment purchases, nominal rent fees and unexpected price increases) into the business;
- Opening a co-op without determining interest, enthusiasm and feasibility;
- Buying unwanted food;
- Being too ambitious;
- Extending too much credit;
- Giving one person all responsibilities;
- Making rules arbitrarily (be democratic).

Adapted with permission from "Co-op How To" by Paul Kaplan, Food Monitor, *No. 13, November/December 1979, pp. 24-27. Copyright 1979. Food Monitor Magazine, published by World Hunger Year, Inc., Box 1975, Garden City, New York 11530. (Entire issue is about co-ops and is available for $2 by writing Food Monitor Magazine.)*

Storefront Co-ops

East End Food Co-op
5472 Penn Avenue
Pittsburgh, Pennsylvania 15206
(412) 361-3598

In these days of rising food prices, a storefront food cooperative is a logical "next step" to a food buying club and offers a real alternative to conventional grocery stores.

When a food buying club's membership mushrooms, it's a sign of success. But a large food club membership makes distribution of bulk food orders difficult from cramped quarters such as home garages. To overcome this problem, successful food buying clubs often decide to locate rental space and form storefront co-ops. Storefront co-ops not only reach more residents; their presence can also prod nearby food chains to compete by lowering prices.

Successful co-ops depend most of all on the volunteer work of their members. One of the most inspiring is the East End Food Co-op, operating in a low-income, ethnically rich area of Pittsburgh, Pennsylvania. Today this group does over $250,000 worth of business each year, saving its 400 members an average of 25 percent on fruits, vegetables, packaged foods and some meat and dairy products.

Checking out at the storefront co–op

Randa Shannon, a nurse and mother of two, says she saves about 25 percent at East End Co-op. But that's not the only reason she shops there. "I suppose some people wouldn't enjoy East End because it's very unadorned, the walls are institutional gray and it's dimly lit," she says. "But there are also vats of peanut butter and honey and barrels of things. Instead of having nine million cereal packages with cartoons and athletes on it, there are little bags of oats and bran. It's like an old-time grocery."

And she adds, the workers are friendly. "If I don't know how to use a food item," she says, "I just ask and they give me recipes and nutritional information."

Origins

As with many other storefront food co-ops, East End grew out of a food buying club. In 1972 three neighbors on the East End decided they could save money by ordering in bulk. "We just refused to pay those supermarket prices, so we decided to start a food club," says one neighbor.

The word spread, other residents became interested, and by 1975 five clubs with over 30 members had surfaced. Those clubs decided to group together and find a permanent store space.

First Funding

But they needed money. In 1976, with support from the nonprofit East End Cooperative Ministeries (EECM), a coalition of 30 church groups, the East End Food Co-op received a $20,000 grant from the

Campaign for Human Development, the economic and social assistance arm of the Catholic Church, to start a federation of food clubs in Western Pennsylvania and to lease space and pay for needed equipment for the East End Co-op.[1]

The group then obtained two workers from ACTION's Volunteers in Service to America (VISTA) Program* to organize and operate all aspects of the co-op from ordering to cashiering. Private foundations kicked in money for a truck. And EECM pitched in a full-time co-op coordinator to provide technical assistance in getting the operation going. (Although not available in time to assist the East End group, co-ops may now qualify for technical and financial assistance from the newly created National Consumer Cooperative Bank.**)

Staff and Budget

Today, through hard work, the co-op is financially independent, doing about $5,000 worth of business a week. The three full-time and one part-time paid staff is bolstered by members who, except for those over age 65, either volunteer their labor at least two hours a month or pay 10 percent more for purchases.

Randa Shannon and her nine-year-old son contribute an hour a month each at the co-op. "Most of the jobs the kids can do," she says. "The last time we went, they had big 10-pound bags of nuts. You wash your hands, scoop the nuts out, and put them in little plastic bags and twist-tie and label them. The kids enjoy it and it's a good experience for them."

Co-op Federation

Since 1976 the co-op staff and members have also been successful at increasing the number of food co-ops in the Pennsylvania area by forming the Consumer Cooperatives of Pittsburgh (CCP), a federation of over 40 food co-ops serving thousands of members throughout western Pennsylvania and parts of West Virginia. Operating out of the same warehouse that serves as the East End co-op storefront, CCP's staff of three buys products from local farmers and packers and sells them to member co-ops who enjoy average savings of 25 percent over retail costs. Representatives from each co-op serve on the CCP Board of Directors which controls the federation's activities.

Weighing herbs and spices at the storefront co-op

Help for Others

The success of CCP and the East End Co-op prompted the formation of a nonprofit spin-off group to train others. The Alliance for Cooperative Education (ACE) offers how-to workshops and conferences for those interested in forming food co-ops in the area.

Other Co-ops

Another successful co-op organization is Weaver's Way in Philadelphia, Pennsylvania. The group's 17-member staff is bolstered by 22 volunteers and serves a membership of 1,650. Weaver's Way also publishes a valuable newsletter keeping members abreast of co-op activities and offering tips on nutrition.

Rural communities are also finding that storefront cooperatives reach more residents than buying clubs. The Natchitoches Area Action Association in Natchitoches, Louisiana, a Community Action Agency (CAA)* funded by the Community Services Administration's Community Action Program (CAP),* launched food co-ops in Cloutierville and Provencal, Louisiana when staffers found that low-income residents spend 43 percent of their income on food.

Groups Highlighted

Alliance for Cooperative Education
5472 Penn Avenue
Pittsburgh, Pennsylvania 15206
(412) 521-2099

Consumer Cooperatives of Pittsburgh
5474 Penn Avenue
Pittsburgh, Pennsylvania 15206
(412) 361-1521

Natchitoches Area Action Association
New Courthouse Building
P.O. Box 944
Natchitoches, Louisiana 71457
(318) 352-8085

Weaver's Way
559 Carpenter Lane
Philadelphia, Pennsylvania 19119
(215) 843-6945

Why Belong to a Co-op?

Reasons For and Against Given by 20 Co-op Members and 5 Former Members Representing 5 Washington D.C. Area Co-ops
(Percent giving each reason)

	Reason To Belong	Reason Not To Belong	Not a Factor or Can't Assess
Views of 20 Current Members			
Prices	95%	0%	5%
Quality of products	100%	0%	0%
Variety of product selection	60%	0%	40%
Convenience	40%	40%	20%
Surprise factor	65%	20%	15%
Sociability	75%	0%	25%
Feeling of doing good—self-satisfaction	50%	0%	50%
Satisfaction in beating supermarkets	55%	5%	40%
Avoidance of the supermarket shopping experience	45%	0%	55%
Importance to economy of having competition for supermarkets	50%	0%	50%

Adapted from WASHINGTON CONSUMERS' CHECKBOOK: FOOD, *p. 57, 1979, published by the Washington Center for the Study of Services, 1518 K Street, N.W., Fourth Floor, Washington, D.C. 20005.*

[1] For more information on the Campaign for Human Development, see Resources at end of Basic Tools Section.

* State and/or local government agencies are frequently responsible for administration of Federal program funds. For further information, see Appendix I under appropriate Federal agency.

** For further information, see Appendix II under "National Consumer Cooperative Bank."

NOTE: For a complete listing of groups featured throughout this book, see Index.

Supermarket Co-ops

New Haven Food Co-op
320 Whalley Avenue
New Haven, Connecticut 06511
(203) 777-9607

We've seen how neighborhood food co-ops—residents pooling their food orders and buying from wholesalers—can fight high grocery bills. Some neighborhood food buying clubs grow into storefront co-ops and, eventually, into full-scale supermarkets, effectively competing with major grocery chains by offering convenient hours, lower prices and the personal service of old-time corner markets.

"I used to have to go to a butcher for meat, a farmers' market for produce and pick up canned goods at a supermarket because one store didn't have the quality I wanted in everything I needed," says Ruth Douglas, who now does all her grocery shopping at the supermarket-size New Haven Food Cooperative in New Haven, Connecticut.

"But the best thing about shopping at the co-op," says Douglas, "is the money you don't have to spend! If there wasn't a co-op, I don't know what I'd do, because I've got three boys and they really like to eat." And she adds, "It's not the big grocery store 'business, business, business.' People take time out to talk to you if you need to know something."

Real Alternative To Chain Store Shopping

The New Haven Food Co-op started as a small food buying club in 1972. But with success came expansion and in 1979, the co-op purchased a large supermarket offering all the conveniences of major store chains—good location, convenient hours, a complete line of merchandise and a full-time staff. Today New Haven boasts 4,800 members who save an average of 12 percent—and much more on some items—by shopping at the co-op. Weekly sales average $80,000 and are expected to top $100,000 by June 1980. The group's history provides an example of how food buying clubs can grow and offer large numbers of residents lower food prices while creating jobs for their communities.

"New Haven Co-op is the best store in the whole world. I do all my shopping there," says Irma Coleman, the mother of two and a co-op member since 1972. Coleman, who spends about $40 a week on groceries, estimates she saves about $32 a month by shopping at New Haven. "And I save on transportation," she adds, "because I used to go all over to different places to find the sales. I don't think we could eat as well as we do if I didn't shop at the co-op."

New Haven Food Co-op

The supermarket-size New Haven Food Co-op

Origins

The New Haven Food Co-op began in 1972 as a Yale University student-based food buying club. The next year, eager to help community residents save on food bills, its leaders decided to rent a storefront in the predominantly black Hill section of the city.

Storefront

It was a good move. Within a year the storefront co-op's business grew from $800 to $5,000 a week. The one full-time staffer, who earned $75 a week, was assisted by co-op members, each of whom paid a $3 annual fee and volunteered to help in the store one hour a month. In return for their support, co-op members paid up to 15 percent less on food purchases than they would have paid at traditional supermarkets.

Moving Up

With business growing, the co-op leaders wanted to offer longer business hours and a greater variety of products as well as create jobs for residents. They knew a good location was essential to draw the customers needed to insure success of the expanded store. So, in 1974, with the storefront profits, the group took over a small abandoned chain store in a run-down commercial area of the Hill neighborhood. The larger store and increased profits made it possible to operate a butcher shop and stock a more complete line of goods, including natural foods and housewares. In 1978 sales topped $1 million and paid staff numbered 14.

Growth

In 1979, with increased sales and a desire to reach more residents and create still more jobs, the co-op decided to expand to a full-scale supermarket. The group located a 24,500-square-foot, recently-closed store in downtown New Haven—complete with fixtures and equipment and three times bigger than their previous location. Cheaper food could be offered to a larger number of residents and there would be more employment opportunities.

New Haven Food Co-op

Inside, the expanded co-op provides many choices.

The group secured a $96,000 interest-free loan from the Campaign for Human Development, the economic and social assistance arm of the Catholic Church, to help buy the new store.[1] (Although not in time to help the New Haven group, co-ops may now qualify for financial and technical assistance from the newly created National Consumer Cooperative Bank.**)

The expanded co-op employs area residents for 30 full-time and 12 part-time positions. All members—except those over 65—donate one hour of labor a month at the store. Nonmembers are welcome but a surcharge is tacked onto their purchases.

More Training

The switch to supermarket size hasn't been easy. "Up until now we haven't had the volume to allow for many apprentices, and we haven't had access to much supermarket training," says one staffer.

To hurdle management problems, the co-op has enlisted help from the New England Co-op Training Institute (NECTI), a technical assistance and training organization for co-ops in the region.[2]

Other Co-ops

Of course food co-ops vary greatly in service, size and style. The Puget Consumer Co-op in Seattle, Washington is another outstanding model of the natural growth possible in the food co-op structure. The group started in 1959 as a small food buying club working out of various members' garages. But the all-volunteer club outgrew its temporary headquarters and expanded into a storefront. By 1969 Puget Consumer Co-op boasted a membership of 650; six years later its roster had climbed to more than 3,400.

With success came good local publicity which helped spur membership growth while creating the need for further expansion. The co-op opened a supermarket in 1976—and a second one in 1978.

Today, with yearly sales of about $7 million, the Puget Consumer Co-op helps nearly 22,000 members save on food bills and provides jobs for almost 100 residents.

Bedford-Stuyvesant Supermarket

In the low-income Bedford-Stuyvesant neighborhood in Brooklyn, New York, the Bedford-Stuyvesant Restoration Corporation, eager to bring a quality supermarket into the area, linked up with a Northeast U.S. grocery chain, Pathmark Supermarkets, to establish a low-cost grocery store for residents. Today "Bed-Stuy" residents save on food costs as well as on car fare. Food stamps are welcome and "no frill" items are offered. Moreover, 160 jobs have been created, and the supermarket's success has attracted other businesses to the Bed-Stuy neighborhood.

Life Line Foods

Lifeline foods combine low price and good nutritive value. These foods are on sale Oct. 30 thru Nov. 5 and were selected by Co-op home economist Betsy Wood in cooperation with Co-op buyers.

Protein Foods

Chicken - Fryers, Fresh Southern, whole body........................ lb. **57¢**
Bake in oven 1 hr. 350° with soy, sherry, oil, ginger.

Refried Beans, Rosarita reg. 49¢........... lb. **43¢**
Heat, add cubed Jack Cheese for quick main dish. Serve with taco sauce.

Beef Franks, Hebrew National, Kosher, Trial size................ 3 oz. **29¢**
These do contain nitrites — as do most frankfurters.

Fruits & Vegetables

Cabbage, green.............................. lb. **15¢**
For lower calorie cole slaw dressing use 2 parts buttermilk, 1 part mayonnaise.

Carrots, fresh clip top.......................... lb. **15¢**
Rich in vitamin A but doesn't have many other nutrients.

Frozen Vegetables, Co-op corn, mixed vegetables, peas, peas & carrots, reg. 35-41¢.. 10 oz. **28¢**
For small portions bang box on counter to loosen. Wrap remainder carefully.

Milk & Cheese

Jack Cheese, Montco..................... lb. **1.79**
If you don't drink milk, cheese does supply calcium.

Low Fat Dry Milk, Milkman reg. 1.49... 4 qts. **1.09**
Read the label. Lower in fat than fresh "low fat" milk.

Breads & Cereals

Wheat germ, bulk reg. 74¢.................. lb. **65¢**
Add wheat germ to biscuit, pancake or cake mixes. 1-2 tablespoons per cup.

Co-op Special Formula Bread reg. 83¢...................................... 1½ lb. **59¢**
A white bread with extra dry milk, soy flour, wheat germ.

Also

Grapes, Red Emperor........................... lb. **59¢**
A nice dessert after a heavy meal.

1978 ad for Consumer Co-op of Berkeley's "lifeline foods" includes cooking and nutrition tips.

Berkeley Co-op

Another cooperative supermarket winner is the Consumer Co-op of Berkeley in Richmond, California, which began in 1938. The co-op discounts only widely-used foods with high nutrient values such as milk, certain meats and cereals. Members say that selective discounting helps low-income families reduce the amount they spend for nourishing food.

Groups Highlighted

Bedford Stuyvesant Restoration Corporation
Public Information Department
1368 Fulton Street
Brooklyn, New York 11216
(212) 636-7721

Consumer Cooperative of Berkeley, Inc.
4805 Central Avenue
Richmond, California 94804
(415) 526-0440

Pathmark Supermarket
c/o Supermarket General Corporation
Public Affairs Department
301 Blair Road
Woodbridge, New Jersey 07095
(201) 499-3000

Puget Consumer Cooperative
6504 90th Street, N.E,
Seattle, Washington 98115
(206) 525-1451

[1] For more information on the Campaign for Human Development, see Resources at end of Basic Tools Section.

[2] Trainers from the New England Co-op Training Institute (NECTI) have helped train the co-op's departmental store managers in areas such as marketing, displaying of products and general business principles. NECTI trainers have also developed a program for the training of store apprentices. (For more information on NECTI, see Resources at end of Food Section.)

* State and/or local government agencies are frequently responsible for administration of Federal program funds. For further information, see Appendix I under appropriate Federal agency.

** For further information see Appendix II under "National Consumer Cooperative Bank."

NOTE: For a complete listing of groups featured throughout this book, see Index.

Warehouse Co-ops

Tucson Cooperative Warehouse
1716 East Factory Avenue
Tucson, Arizona 85719
(602) 884-9951

As we have seen, neighborhood food buying clubs and storefront cooperatives have helped many of our country's residents battle skyrocketing food prices. In turn, some groups have formed to help food co-ops get high-quality, low-priced foods for their members.

One of the most successful groups is the nonprofit Tucson Cooperative Warehouse (TCW) in Arizona. Since 1973, the group, owned and managed by the co-ops it serves, has hurdled budget and other problems to build an annual business of $1.5 million. TCW trucks travel to wholesalers from Maine to Washington finding best-priced foods to stock the Tucson warehouse. Their bounty is distributed to 150 food buying clubs and 15 storefront co-ops in four Southwestern states, which save 30 to 50 percent over retail food prices.

Moreover, because staff is recruited from the TCW Co-op membership, most are willing to work for salaries which meet their needs but are below comparable wages—cutting warehouse operating costs.

Origins

It all began in 1973 when leaders of two co-ops and one food buying club in the Tucson/Phoneix area decided there had to be a way to save co-ops even more than the prevailing 25 percent on food. One group boasted a truck which traveled between Phoenix and Los Angeles for the best food buys. Another had a crackerjack bookkeeper. And the third had a stellar credit rating with distributors. So in December 1973, the three groups combined their resources and expertise to stretch their money saving capabilities and launch a warehouse operation to serve food buying clubs and storefront co-ops.

Growing Pains

But the tiny warehousing operation soon suffered growing pains. Within six months, member co-ops mushroomed to 75, cramping the tiny storage area and bogging down the bookkeeper who was inexperienced in large-scale financing. With the help of the *Thomas Grocery Register,* which contains a listing of national food wholesalers, additional suppliers were readily located, but they were based all over the country—from California to Wisconsin.[1] The situation called for more space, trucks and staff.

Workers store bulk food in the warehouse co-op.

Expansion

In May 1974 the member co-ops incorporated as the Tucson Cooperative Warehouse, a nonprofit, cooperatively owned and managed organization. Member co-ops were asked to advance TCW the estimated $50,000 to finance the expanded operation. (Although not available in time to help TCW, co-ops may now qualify for technical and financial assistance from the newly created National Consumer Cooperative Bank.**)

Additional staff was recruited from the co-op membership, and suppliers were persuaded to extend credit to the cooperative effort.

To absorb the $1,134 monthly rent for a larger 9,000-square-foot warehouse, a small fee was added to each co-op order. And three trucks were leased from a firm which agreed to help train the drivers.

To solve the bookkeeping problem, TCW sent an employee to the University of Arizona to earn a master's degree in business finance. In the meantime the slack was taken up by co-op members who were hired to handle purchasing, accounts receivable and other bookkeeping chores.

Staff

Today TCW has a staff of 20. Its co-op members serve 11,000 residents in New Mexico, Arizona, Utah and Colorado.

Helping Others

TCW's enterprise and hard work stimulated the creation of the Blue Sky Alliance in 1979, a private nonprofit organization composed of TCW members who provide technical assistance to hopeful co-ops and warehouses in the four-state area.

Other Groups

Major co-op warehouse programs are flourishing across the nation. The largest one, Intra-Community Cooperative (ICC) in Madison, Wisconsin does $5.5 million worth of business yearly, half of which is in cheese shipments. In fact, ICC has helped nine cheesemakers market their raw milk cheeses nationwide. In addition, ICC's "alternative trucking system" distributes goods to co-op members throughout the Midwest.

Distributing Alliance of the Northcountry Cooperatives (DANCe) based in Minneapolis, Minnesota distributes approximately $2 million annually of beans, flour, nuts, seeds and other dry products to co-ops in a five-state region. Its educational and technical assistance arm, the All Cooperating Assembly (ACA)—a federation of 150 food, housing, health and other cooperatives—helps potential customers who are trying to organize co-ops or buying clubs.[2]

In Seattle, Washington a direct wholesale marketing program, Bulk Commodities Exchange (BCE), links small-scale farmers with bulk purchasers including food co-ops, buying clubs, institutions, restaurants and individuals. BCE is co-sponsored by Pike Place Market—the local farmers' market—and the King County Office of Agriculture Cooperative Extension Service,* working in conjunction with the United States Department of Agriculture (USDA). BCE has a permanent location in the Pike Place Market and operates five days a week, seven months a year.

Groups Highlighted

All Cooperating Assembly
P.O. Box 6022
Minneapolis, Minnesota 55406
(612) 376-8357

Blue Sky Alliance
c/o New Mexico Federation of Cooperative Living
632A Aqua Fria
Santa Fe, New Mexico 87501
(505) 988-5977

Bulk Commodities Exchange
1432 Western Avenue
Seattle, Washington 98101
(206) 447-9516

Distributing Alliance of the Northcountry Cooperatives (DANCe)
510 Kasota Avenue, S.E.
Minneapolis, Minnesota 55414
(612) 378-9774

Intra-Community Cooperative
1335 Gilson Street
Madison, Wisconsin 53715
(608) 257-6633

[1] For more information on the *Thomas Grocery Register*, see Resources at end of Food Section.

[2] For more information on the All Cooperating Assembly (ACA), see Resources at end of Food Section.

* State and/or local government agencies are frequently responsible for administration of Federal program funds. For further information, see Appendix I under appropriate Federal agency.

**For further information, see Appendix II under "National Consumer Cooperative Bank."

NOTE: For a complete listing of groups featured throughout this book, see Index.

Farmers' Markets

Greenmarket
24 West 40th Street
New York, New York 10007
(212) 840-7355

Imagine being able to buy juicy sweet corn, plump aromatic peaches and other freshly picked fruits and vegetables straight from the farm—and at lower prices than in local supermarkets!

Thanks to farmers' markets, that's a dream come true. A popular alternative to grocery stores for thousands throughout the country, farmers' markets are offering consumers less expensive, fresher produce while enabling growers to earn more money for their products.

Farmers' markets had been popular for many years, but they began to fade in the late 1950s because of increased urbanization of farmland, stricter health codes and tough selling and site regulations. But today, with the price of food skyrocketing, there has been a dramatic and welcome comeback.

Greenmarket

New York City's Greenmarket has been especially successful since it was set up in July 1976. Now operating at eight locations, it handles $1 million a year in produce and serves as many as 30,000 New York City residents each week.

''It's wonderful,'' comments one Greenmarket shopper. ''We don't have to go to the country. It makes the neighborhood more of a neighborhood and it smells like the country! I feel like I'm in another time.''

Origins

The story of Greenmarket is an inspiring one of cooperation and dedication. It is the brainchild of Barry Benepe, a New York-born architect who had been a planner for the city and for New York's mostly rural Orange County. Farmland in the surrounding Hudson Valley had dwindled by nearly a third since 1950 making it necessary for about 85 percent of New York's food products to be shipped in from far away orchards and farms.

Helping Both Farmer and Consumer

Benepe envisioned that a farmers' market could blunt the loss of farmland by prodding growers to harvest more crops. By selling directly to consumers, the farmers could boost their incomes while selling their goods for less than grocery stores, which pass on long-distance shipping costs and overhead to the consumer. He also knew that city residents would welcome the chance to buy large leafy heads of crisp lettuce, eggs right from the henhouse and other fresh produce.

"You won't find cauliflower like this at the local grocer!" A justifiably proud farmer shows off the fruit of his toil.

First Funding

So Benepe and Robert Lewis, a concerned resident who worked for the New York State Department of Agriculture and Markets, began lobbying private foundations for support. In April 1976 an $800 grant from the America the Beautiful Fund provided the initial capital to launch their effort. Soon after, the Council on the Environment of New York City agreed to sponsor the program.[1] Benepe was named project director, and he and Lewis set out to find more money and willing farmers. A lot at 59th Street and Second Avenue, lodged between a high-density residential neighborhood and busy shopping district, was selected as the market site.

The big break in funding came in June of that same year when the J.M. Kaplan Fund and two other foundations pumped a total of $25,000 into Greenmarket.[2] A paid staff of five handled all the initial legwork—contacting state and city officials and county agents of local Cooperative Extension Services,* working in conjunction with the United States Department of Agriculture (USDA), inspecting farms to determine crop availability and timing, and getting the word out to farmers.

Overcoming Obstacles

But many obstacles had to be overcome. For example, to use the city-owned site, permits and approvals were needed from various city agencies.[3] Also, much time had to be spent developing community support. A small but vocal group of residents feared the market would create traffic congestion, an influx of ''undesirable'' people and a carnival-like atmosphere. Nevertheless, an ad hoc group, Friends of Greenmarket, knocked on doors and were able to capture strong support from East Side residents.

Media

A media blitz was especially important in launching the project. Repeated mailings to over 100 local and regional media outlets attracted news coverage from papers, TV and radio stations.

And at 7:00 a.m. on July 17, 1976, seven fruit, vegetable and plant growers from Long Island, New Jersey and upstate New York counties arrived at the 59th street lot. Their trucks and vans were stocked full of fresh-picked, vine-ripened tomatoes, long golden carrots, plump green beans and dozens of other wholesome hours-old products. An eager crowd waited for the growers to unload and display their produce under eight foot brightly colored umbrellas. The gates swung open at 8:00 a.m. and by early afternoon, nearly all the display crates were empty.

Expansion

Today Greenmarket has expanded to eight open-air locations, each operating one day a week. Sites close to transportation systems and high density residential and shopping areas are selected to cut down on traffic congestion and ensure the large clientele needed to make the venture profitable for farmers.

Greenmarket

A farmers' market shopper listens as a farmer tells how to judge corn.

Staff and Financing

In 1979 over half of Greenmarket's $75,000 operating budget came from farmers who paid $20 per space in rental fees each marketing day. The rest was covered by Foundation grants. Greenmarket estimates that their buyers save from 20 to 40 percent on their annual produce budget and farmers make from $100 to $1,200 per market day, more than double what they could get in wholesale outlets.

The four-member staff coordinates market activities and monitors the produce to ensure that only quality, locally grown goods are sold.

An added bonus is the community spirit and rapport between residents and farmers that the markets have fostered. The old fashioned country-like at-

Greenmarket

On a summer day, New York City residents flock to Greenmarket to buy fresh produce.

mosphere and robust vegetables and fruits delight many residents. And the farmers, appreciative of their eager clients, gladly give cooking advice and answer questions while weighing purchases on the hanging scales.

Lola Dalzelle, a 20-year resident of East Side, calls Greenmarket a "godsend to New York City," and not only because of the fresh vegetables. She says, "The elderly and other lonely, depressed citizens walk down to Greenmarket with shopping bags in hand, all spruced up, and with big smiles—it's a wonderful thing for them. It gives them something to do on Saturday." And she adds, "There's an excellent rapport between the people and those that come in with the trucks."

Other Markets

Many cities today are starting farmers' markets similar to Greenmarket. In Hartford, Connecticut the farmers' market was one of the first projects under the Hartford Food System.[4] And in Boston, the Massachusetts Department of Food and Agriculture has been very successful in working with community garden and nutrition groups to initiate successful farmers' markets in that area.

Groups Highlighted

FarmMarket
(Hartford Food System)
c/o Connecticut Public Interest Research Group (ConnPIRG)
30 High Street, Room 108
Hartford, Connecticut 06103
(203) 525-8312

Massachusetts Department of Food and Agriculture
Division of Agricultural Land Use
100 Cambridge Street
Boston, Massachusetts 02202
(617) 727-6633

Tips for Markets

Greenmarket organizers have learned a few lessons along the way that they want to share with others.

- Allow eight months to get farmer participation and to find a vacant lot or existing abandoned building for the site.
- Be sure the site is located close to other stores, local transportation and neighborhoods.
- Research which farmers grow what crops and their production rate. Contact your local Cooperative Extension Service,* working in cooperation with the United States Department of Agriculture (USDA) for names of producers. Time the farmers' entry into the market with their harvesting season.
- Personally visit participating farmers. Check produce quality and acreage to determine realistic crop yields.
- Frequently spot-check participating farmers' produce to ensure good quality.
- Plan on at least one paid full-time and several part-time staffers to administer the program, depending on the number of markets.

** State and/or local government agencies are frequently responsible for administration of Federal program funds. For further information, see Appendix I under the United States Department of Agriculture (USDA).*

[1] For more information on the Council on the Environment of New York City, see Resources at end of Food Section.

[2] The other two foundations contributing funds to Greenmarket were the Fund for the City of New York and the Vincent Astor Foundation.

[3] The City agencies whose approval was needed to launch Greenmarket included the Departments of Real Estate, Transportation, Traffic, Highways, Consumer Affairs, City Planning, Police and Economic Development.

[4] The Hartford Food System is also profiled in the Food Section, p. 86.

* State and/or local government agencies are frequently responsible for administration of Federal program funds. For further information, see Appendix I under appropriate Federal agency.

NOTE: For a complete listing of groups featured throughout this book, see Index.

Food Fairs

Agricultural Marketing Project
2606 Westwood Drive
Nashville, Tennessee 37204
(615) 297-4088
and
Alabama Agricultural Marketing Project
P.O. Box 435
Tuscaloosa, Alabama 35401
(205) 758-0343

How can consumers save on food and farmers still make decent profits? One way is for the groups to come together at food fairs, a concept rediscovered by students at Vanderbilt University in Nashville, Tennessee.

In 1979 efforts by the Nashville-based Agricultural Marketing Project (AMP) led to food fairs being held in 39 Tennessee and Alabama cities with over 1,000 farmers participating. Sales in 1979 more than doubled those of 1978, topping an estimated $1 million.

A typical AMP-sponsored food fair is held once a week on a church parking lot where from 15 to 25 farmers park their trucks, open their tailgates and sell fruits, vegetables, canned goods and other produce to about 3,000 eager customers who pay 15 to 75 cents less per item or pound than they would at retail stores. Only those who grow their own produce may participate.

Origins

In 1974 a group of Vanderbilt University students, concerned about pressing problems facing both consumers and farmers—the decline in the number of small farms in the South, the small profits being made by farmers, the decrease in consumer demand for fresh fruits and vegetables and the problem of ever-rising food prices—formed AMP, dedicated to bringing farmers and consumers closer together. Out of numerous meetings of that group with community residents came the idea for a food fair—an open-air bazaar—where farmers would sell directly to consumers.

First Project

AMP's goal was to learn enough about food fairs to spur the concept by providing technical assistance to interested consumers and farmers. So in the summer of 1975, with a $3,200 grant from Vanderbilt and the local office of the National Association of Farmworker Organizations (NAFO), a nonprofit advocacy group, AMP set up a series of demonstration food fairs in Nashville.[1] Strong and hearty support from farmers and consumers for the successful fairs showed that the idea could work.

Growth

Today both the food fair concept and AMP have grown. Soon after the Nashville demonstration fairs, area farmers formed the Farmers Association for Retail Marketing (F.A.R.M.). Now 20 financially self-sufficient F.A.R.M.s in six states are putting on food fairs with technical assistance from AMP.

AMP

A F.A.R.M. dinner meeting

Three Steps to Success

The demonstration fairs were beneficial in another way as well—they highlighted for AMP organizers the key elements of a successful food fair. Here's what they found:

- First, a publicity campaign should be launched to inform farmers and consumers about the food fair. Farmers are reached best through posters in seed stores, calls to local agricultural agencies and articles or ads in rural newspapers. Consumers learn of the fairs through posters, radio and television public service announcements, television talk shows and feature stories and ads in local newspapers.
- Second, AMP learned that farmers and consumers each need an organizer to work with them: one to show farmers how to wholesale their produce; another to make consumers aware of the nutritional and economical benefits of buying unpackaged, unprocessed food from the farmer.
- Third, AMP students learned that the organizers must research and comply with city and county health, zoning and licensing requirements before food fairs can legally open for business.

AMP

A local farmer sells his produce.

AMP

The food fair comes to town.

And AMP, with a staff of eight and a yearly budget of $130,000 raised from private foundations and church organizations, now operates in two states as an independent, nonprofit organization separate from Vanderbilt University. Every two months over 7,000 farmers and consumers receive AMP's newsletter, *Farm, Food and Land,* containing information on food fairs, local food issues, market prices and helpful garden and nutrition tips.

Other Food Fairs

Other areas in the United States also have direct farmer-to-consumer marketing outlets.

In Loveland, Ohio the nonprofit Rural Resources, Inc. has started a program similar to AMP's, offering technical assistance to farmers wishing to launch food fairs or tailgate markets.[2]

And in 1979 Pennsylvania's tailgate market boasted sales of $68 million. This farmer-to-consumer market was established by the Pennsylvania State Department of Agriculture working with the local Cooperative Extension Service,* in conjunction with the United States Department of Agriculture (USDA).[3]

Similarly, in West Virginia, the state Department of Agriculture working with the Cooperative Extension Service, owns and operates seven successful farmers' markets.[4]

Groups Highlighted

Pennsylvania Department of Agriculture
Bureau of Markets, Room 310
2301 North Cameron Street
Harrisburg, Pennsylvania 17120
(717) 787-4210

Rural Resources, Inc.
Rural Route 1, Box 11
Loveland, Ohio 45140
(no phone)

West Virginia Department of Agriculture
Produce Development Section
State Capitol Building
Charleston, West Virginia 25305
(304) 348-3708

[1] For more information on the National Association of Farmworker Organizations (NAFO), see Resources at end of Food Section.

[2] For more information on Rural Resources, Inc., see Resources at end of Food Section.

[3] For more information on the Pennsylvania Department of Agriculture, see Resources at end of Food Section.

[4] For more information on the West Virginia Department of Agriculture, see Resources at end of Food Section.

* State and/or local government agencies are frequently responsible for administration of Federal program funds. For further information, see Appendix I under appropriate Federal agency.

NOTE: For a complete listing of groups featured throughout this book, see Index.

Salvaging Food

St. Mary's Food Bank
816 South Central Avenue
Phoenix, Arizona 85004
(602) 253-3407
and
Second Harvest
1001 North Central
Phoenix, Arizona 85004
(602) 252-1777

How can we afford to waste perfectly good food when so many of our citizens are too poor to afford a decent diet? Clearly we can't. Yet the United States Department of Agriculture (USDA) reports that each year about 20 percent of all food produced in the United States is lost or wasted—enough to feed 49 million hungry people.

Fortunately for our country's poor, as well as our economy, food banks are springing up across the country to rein in food that farmers and food producers don't sell. They are successfully marshaling some of that edible but discarded food—valued at $31 billion a year—and providing nutritious meals to needy people while helping to eliminate waste.

Food Worth Saving

Each year food banks collect millions of pounds of edible food cast aside because of over production, dented cans, broken boxes or expired marketing dates and distribute them to charitable groups for use in their on-premises meal programs. Some banks also provide food boxes to help disaster victims through the first few harrowing days following a crisis.

Gleaning

Food for food banks is "gleaned" by people who move into the fields, canneries, orchards and packing houses to collect produce that is slightly bruised or has been plowed under and unused meats or day-old bakery goods that have been shoved aside. Food donors not only reduce waste but also can deduct as a charitable contribution the cost of the food from their taxable income.

Feeding the Hungry

The organization responsible for developing the food bank concept is St. Mary's Food Bank in Phoenix, Arizona. In 1978 St. Mary's channeled nearly two

Food Bank organizer unloads surplus food at St. Mary's warehouse.

million pounds of food from packing sheds, warehouses and bakeries to nearly 300 alcoholic rehabilitation houses, schools in poverty areas and other social service groups, each of which feeds from six to 1,000 hungry citizens on premises daily. And that same year St. Mary's Emergency Food Box Program provided about 48,000 emergency victims with nutritious food for three days. Moreover, their three-year-old training and technical assistance program, Second Harvest, has led to the formation of independent food banks around the country.

Praises for St. Mary's

Casa de Amigas, a Phoenix-based, private, nonprofit alcoholic rehabilitation center for women, has been using St. Mary's Food Bank for the last ten years. "They have been a great adjunct to our purchasing power," says Director Mabel Maremont. "We get so many things such as fresh fruits and fresh vegetables that we wouldn't be able to afford on our poverty-level budget. I can't say enough about St. Mary's."

Origins

The food bank concept was born in the minds of two Phoenix residents, Robert McCarty and John Van Hengel, who in the mid-1960s were running a dining room for the needy sponsored by the St. Vincent de Paul Society, a lay organization of the Catholic church. To get food for the facility, the men began asking farmers and other food producers to let them have crops left behind when harvesting, and under- or over-sized vegetables and other edible but unsaleable food. Soon they had more than they needed and began to share their bounty with other nonprofit charitable groups. Seeing the value of the concept, Van Hengel decided to organize a food bank.

Hard Work

Like other groups, St. Mary's had to use imagination and hard work to get started. Operating funds and a storehouse were needed as well as volunteers to run the program.

Van Hengel approached a friend and member of the clergy at St. Mary's Catholic church who persuaded the Franciscan Community to furnish a recently donated warehouse rent free. The church also loaned Van Hengel about $4,000 for operating expenses. And a dilapidated old truck was donated by a local organization.

Mutual Cooperation

Van Hengel turned to the Salvation Army and other charitable social service agencies for volunteers to help staff the bank and collect the food.

As news of St. Mary's Food Bank spread, citizens began clearing pantry shelves, and churches and other local groups held food drives to bolster the warehouse supply. Residents also reached into their pockets. By the end of the year, thanks to community contributions, the $4,000 loan was paid in full.

Budget and Staff

Residents continue to appreciate the bank's need for operating capital. St. Mary's annual budget of $128,000 comes from donations from citizens, businessmen, churches and local organizations. About $70,000 of those funds are used to supplement the cost of their Emergency Food Box Program. And all of the Food Bank's equipment—including eight trucks—has been donated by local groups and citizens.

Until 1979 there were no paid staff members. Now the 28-strong staff includes three paid from operating funds, nine sponsored by the Department of Labor's Comprehensive Employment and Training Act (CETA) Program* and 16 permanent and some 200 part-time community volunteers.

Spreading the Word

St. Mary's is now helping other communities across the country discover the mutual-help method of cutting waste while feeding the poor. Funded by a $160,000 Community Services Administration (CSA) Community Food and Nutrition Training and Technical Assistance grant,* St. Mary's Second Harvest program holds workshops and conferences for interested groups and aims to establish food banks in all metropolitan areas across the country. So far over 40 independent food banks have been established in 23 states through St. Mary's efforts.

Obstacle

A major problem facing all such groups are rigid food laws which restrict distribution of unsaleable but edible foods. The Arizona group handles this problem by signing disclaimers which free donors of responsibility. All the food that comes into St. Mary's is checked for quality and only about one-fifth of the two and one-half million pounds collected in 1978 was rejected. And some states, such as Washington, Oregon and California, have enacted "Good Samaritan" laws which limit the liability of farmers and food processors who donate to charitable organizations.

California Food Banks

Food banks and other gleaning groups are becoming increasingly visible and valuable parts of communities around the country.

California groups are especially active. The California Food Network operates like a grocery marketing system. It collects food from donors and sends it to some 200 food banks and coalitions which distribute the food to local social service agencies.

The Food Bank, Inc. of Santa Clara County, California, partially funded by the Santa Clara County Department of Social Services, has a "Brown Bag Program" which provides senior citizens with five or six pounds of food each week for a $2 annual membership fee. And in Sacramento the Senior Gleaners, a 1,700-strong group of retired volunteers, help fill idle time by picking their own produce from farmers' fields.

Banks Elsewhere

Other states have active groups too. In St. Louis, Missouri the Food Crisis Network, made up of 60 neighborhood food banks, provides food to more than 13,000 needy people each month.

And the Tri-County Community Council Food Bank in Portland, Oregon operates effectively without a warehouse. Last year they managed to divert over 700,000 pounds of salvageable food to some 80 government social service agencies and private, nonprofit groups. They have a small walk-in freezer and some short-term borrowed space, but mostly their two pickups remain on the road constantly picking up and immediately delivering donated food.

Similar gleaning groups are springing up in rural areas as well. The Washington, D.C.-based National Association of Farmworker Organizations (NAFO), a nonprofit group concerned with the civil and labor rights of migrant and seasonal farmworkers, has helped develop about a dozen rural food banks across the country in the last two years.[1]

Second Harvest Food Banks

Surplus bounty will be put to good use.

Groups Highlighted

California Food Network
942 Market Street
San Francisco, California 94102
(415) 421-8131

Food Bank, Inc. of Santa Clara County
312 Brocaw Road
Santa Clara, California 95050
(408) 249-9170

Food Crisis Network
1210 Locust Street
St. Louis, Missouri 63103
(314) 621-8840

National Association of Farmworker Organizations
1332 New York Avenue, N.W.
Washington, D.C. 20005
(202) 347-2407

Senior Gleaners
2718 G Street
Sacramento, California 95816
(916) 448-1727

Tri-County Community Council Food Bank
718 West Burnside Street
Portland, Oregon 97209
(503) 223-1030

[1] For more information on the National Association of Farmworker Organizations (NAFO), see Resources at end of Food Section.

* State and/or local government agencies are frequently responsible for administration of Federal program funds. For further information, see Appendix I under appropriate Federal agency.

NOTE: For a complete listing of groups featured throughout this book, see Index.

How to Organize a Food Bank

Starting a Food Bank is much the same as starting any business. Two questions must first be answered in the affirmative: Is there a need? and Will the community support it? Once answered, the following need to be considered: What food is available and where it is • What community agencies would like to cooperate and where they are • Who will do the work • Where the money will come from • What materials and equipment are necessary and where they can be found • What type and size of building is needed and where it should be located • What types and sizes of vehicles are needed.

The Basic Steps

I. Finding the Food

• University Extension Service: Contact to determine when and what crops are ready for harvest.

• Farmers: Determine if there has been over–production; what crops are scheduled to be plowed under; what happens to culls.

• Packing Houses: Determine what they are doing with culls and surplus purchases.

• Food Processors: Approach wholesale houses, food brokers and retail stores for food they would discard because of damaged cases, over–production, mislabelling, underweight, discontinued lines, expiring code dates, shrinkage, and so on.

After you have determined that surplus food is available and that there is support in the food industry you are ready for Step II.

II. Community Food Agencies

Write to every charitable institution in your community that is involved in feeding the needy. Solicit their support. Explain who you are and what your purpose is. Emphasize that you are a supportive agency whose only interest is in salvaging food and supporting efforts to get it to the people who need it. Make it clear that you will not be in competition with them. Remember:

• You are partners, not competitors! If XYZ Rescue Mission already has a good working relationship with Handy Grocery Store, back off. Remember, the goal is to eliminate food waste and get it to those in need. Where this is being done, do not muddy the water.

• Existing charities can help with extra hands too. When you are swamped or short–handed they may be able to provide extra trucks, drivers, necessary equipment or other things.

• You should have a volunteer on your staff with interest and/or experience in public relations.

III. Site — Materials — Equipment

• Housing: You will need a type of warehouse in the poverty section of your city. You should be thinking along the lines of five to eight thousand square feet. A loading dock is helpful but not necessary. The important thing is to get a building—almost anything to start. You may soon have to move to larger quarters. Try to have the building donated or lent. Perhaps the city owns a vacant building and will lease it for a nominal amount.

Consider the hours you want to be open. You may decide to be open one or two days a week or mornings only. Once your hours are set—and you are in operation—keep them! Regular hours are important.

• Vehicles: You will need to be able to pick up food and to distribute it. Any kind of truck will do for a start—just so long as it runs. Look for companies that are replacing some of their trucks.

• Storage: You will need a place to store perishables; the best solution is a used walk–in freezer. Contact all food outlets and appliance stores. Ask for volunteers in the refrigeration business who might be able to put an older unit into working order for you.

• Equipment: While you are at the grocer's begging for storage equipment, keep your eye open for other items such as: carts, shelving, counters, tables, pallet jacks, a standing scale and tubs for washing any items that need it.

IV. Seeking Community Help

• Legal Aid: Find a lawyer who will help you with incorporation (nonprofit, of course) for filing fees only. By this time you should have your proposal in concise form for distribution to interested people and the media.

An organization name is important. Avoid making it sound like a government agency. Keep it short. By all means identify with the community you are going to serve and what it is you will do.

• Outreach: Unless you are asking your mother for assistance, stay away from the telephone—at least for the initial contact. Eyeball–to–eyeball contact is slower, but much more effective.

Surround yourselves with people of like mind, with needed expertise, who can volunteer. Look for workers . . . not talkers.

Thank all whom you contact, all who give you support of any kind—whether it is food, time, money, equipment or even suggestions.

Keep a card file on all your contacts. Record name, address, what was given, when it was given and who is next in command in the organization, and whether or not you thanked them.

V. Money

You will need seed money to begin. Not everyone will donate a product or service. Three to five thousand dollars should be sufficient to get you going. This could be a grant or loan from sponsoring organizations, but you must think about a steady supply of necessary funds.

• Fees: Some food banks charge benefitting organizations a flat, per–month fee of a small amount, while others may charge on a cents–per–pound basis for food picked up or received.

• Solicitation: (Do not forget a solicitation permit, as it may be required in your community.) You can approach the community–at–large or employee clubs, the Community Chest, churches, foundations, community service organizations.

• Donations: Do not limit yourself to thinking only of food and food–related items. Remember the job to be done and what is needed: paper, auto mechanics, label makers, sign painters, carpenters, electricians, and so on. Because someone is in a field normally considered outside the area of food do not assume there is nothing to be offered. Lay your problems, goals and needs before all who will listen and let them decide if they can help and how they can help. Do not hesitate to ask anyone for anything. The worst response will be a "no" and you might get a positive one later on.

Above all, you have to keep telling your story over and over. People of your community will support you but they have to know about you, and they have to be reminded. Enthusiasm is contageous.

About the media: It is interested in news . . . Make it!

Reprinted with permission from St. Mary's Food Bank How-to Guide.

A Grocery Store for Seniors

Senior Citizens Grocery, Inc.
4707 North Lombard Street
Portland, Oregon 97203
(503) 285-4141

When North Portland's senior citizens asked a local grocery store chain owner to lower prices, he wouldn't budge. "It's not too practical an idea," he told them in February 1977. The matter might have ended there but, instead, storeowner John Piacentini then offered the senior citizens a grocery of their own.

Utterly surprised, they quickly accepted. The group spread the word to their elderly neighbors, drummed up volunteer help and, within four months, opened the doors of the nonprofit Portland, Oregon Senior Citizens Grocery, Inc. run exclusively for and by elderly residents.

Satisfied Shoppers

Today Senior Grocery boasts a membership of 7,000 and sales of $3,000 a week, saving elderly shoppers an average of 13 percent on food purchases.

"I've shopped there since the day it opened," says Mrs. Edwin Sworden who, along with her husband, is retired. "There's a good variety of different foods and everything they have is really quality stuff. The soup my husband likes is about 69 cents in other stores but I pay about 53 cents at Senior's."

Lucky Timing

Through a stroke of luck, the elderly group was in the right place at the right time on that February day. Piacentini had just heard a stirring speech by Oregon Governor Robert Straub about the heavy burden of rising food costs on elderly citizens, most of whom have fixed incomes. Moreover, Piacentini had no plans for the convenience store which he had just closed.

Without hesitation, Piacentini offered the group a rent-free storefront, equipment and $20,000 for merchandise to launch the grocery.

Planning the Store

In late February, the enthusiastic senior organizers called a public meeting for elderly residents to create a planning committee and draw up a list of things to do such as publicize the new store to area seniors, write bylaws for the soon-to-be nonprofit corporation and establish a Board of Directors.

Manager Wayne Henry displays Senior Grocery offerings on grand opening day.

Getting the Word Out

The elderly volunteers continued spreading the word about the new discount grocery for seniors. Piacentini helped by providing a media expert who designed and distributed brochures describing the market and who also created advertising skits which ran as free public service announcements on television.

A local lawyer volunteered to draw up the needed legal papers such as the nonprofit corporation application, a constitution and bylaws.

Readying the Store

The planning committee busily readied the store for the May opening—doing everything from scrubbing dusty shelves to ordering merchandise. Senior store manager Wayne Henry, a retired grocer, says a single supervisor is essential during these pre-opening stages.

"In this kind of operation, too many bosses can cause friction," he says, "and we didn't have time for that kind of foolishness."

The last but equally important step was to choose a three-member Board of Directors to govern and watch over the store's operations, decide what merchandise would best meet senior needs and set store policy. The Board set an annual membership fee of 50 cents and a minimum shopper age of 60. Elderly residents can shop at the store once before joining, and those who can't afford the fee get free memberships.

The Grand Opening

At the store's opening on May 11, 1977, Governor Straub declared, "This store is going to enhance the purchasing power of seniors." Not only was the Governor right but so was Piacentini who predicted the store would be brisk, lively, congenial and successful.

During the first six months of operation, Piacentini and other private donors kicked in funds to pay the store's utility and phone expenses. But by the end of the first year, with a membership of 6,000 and escalating sales, the seniors were able to pay for expenses out of the store's operating budget.

Elderly in Charge

Manager Henry and three other paid elderly employees are assisted by senior volunteers who order food, stock shelves and clean. The store is open seven days a week from 9 a.m. to 5 p.m. and offers fruits, vegetables, sundries, dry goods, a delicatessen and a range of foods for diabetics.

"It's a very delightful little store," says widow Lydia Clairmore who compares prices at other area stores. "They carry national brands and their prices are lower all around."

Clairmore, who grows lots of her own vegetables at home, gives Senior Grocery's produce her stamp of approval. "It's fresh and nice," she says, "and there are a lot of members who bring in some of their own surplus produce to sell or give away."

Minimizing Costs

The store minimizes operating costs and saves customers money because the rent is free, the staff is mostly volunteer and the stock is limited. Markups on the various goods average about 3 percent—well below that of most supermarkets which must pay large staffs, store rents and advertising and promotion costs.

Each week senior citizens from all over the city visit the store to see what it's like. Many become members.

Michigan Program

The success of the Portland store has been followed by other efforts nationwide. The Michigan Office of Services to the Aging (OSA) is developing several alternative food systems for seniors. So far eight food co-ops have been organized, one of which is building a greenhouse. This venture, like all cooperatives, may now qualify for financial and technical assistance from the newly created National Consumer Cooperative Bank.**

Group Highlighted

Office of Services to the Aging
State of Michigan
300 East Michigan, Corr Building
P.O. Box 30026
Lansing, Michigan 48909
(517) 373-8230

* State and/or local government agencies are frequently responsible for administration of Federal program funds. For further information, see Appendix I under appropriate Federal agency.

**For further information, see Appendix II under "National Consumer Cooperative Bank."

NOTE: For a complete listing of groups featured throughout this book, see Index.

Growing and Processing Your Own Food

General Introduction

Neighborhood gardening, canning, composting and solar greenhouse projects help revitalize communities while providing residents with economical and nutritious food. In this chapter we look at groups dedicated to helping people grow and preserve their own food.

If you garden now, or would like to, you're not alone. A 1979 Gallup survey conducted for Gardens For All, a national gardening clearinghouse, shows that 33 million American households—two million more than in 1978—grew some of their own food in home or community gardens. In fact, according to the survey gardening is more popular than 22 other activities, including fishing, golf, tennis, jogging and photography. The Gallup study estimates that the retail value of produce from U.S. "backyard gardeners" in 1979 was $13 billion, saving families an average of $367.

With such an explosion in gardening interest, it's worth seeing how different groups around the country are organizing community gardening and related projects.

The first three groups we'll examine promote community gardening programs that differ widely in sponsorship, number of participants and organization. One project is in a low-income neighborhood and features a resident-constructed windmill that provides water for the community garden. Another is a city-wide coalition of gardening groups and technical experts who help city residents find scarce land, top soil and water supplies to start neighborhood gardening projects. And a third shows how housing authorities and other city agencies are helping residents grow their own produce.

Other featured groups working to promote self-reliance and food cost savings include a massive composting project in the South Bronx, solar greenhouses in big cities and rural areas and a community cannery.

Finally, we look at a dynamic Vermont-based group that promotes gardening throughout the country and helps community groups organize garden projects. We'll also see how Federal agencies such as the United States Department of Agriculture (USDA) and Community Services Administration (CSA) are promoting home gardening through special programs.

Windpower for Gardens

39th Avenue Community Garden Windmill Project
Trust for Public Land
82 Second Street
San Francisco, California 94105
(415) 495-4014

When was the last time you saw a windmill in the heart of a city neighborhood? For residents of Fruitvale, a low-income Chicano community in Oakland, California, this has become a common sight. Poised between two high-rise apartment buildings and jutting 40 feet in the air, a Dempster Multi-Blade, Annu-oiled windmill contrasts with its surroundings like a Nebraska landscape next door to the Empire State Building. But its impact is more than just visual. It provides a reliable supply of water for the bountiful community garden below.

"Because the windmill is a rural type of thing," says Al Cruse, chairman of the 39th Avenue garden, "it fascinates a lot of people who've never seen one before. But on top of that is the idea of an alternative system—it means that we could survive if Oakland water were turned off."

And Cruse adds, the community garden does more than provide low-cost nutritious vegetables for his neighborhood. It brings residents together. "We have no serious problems," he says. "When one comes up, we all talk about it and solve it together. That's how things work."

Beginnings

Back in 1977, when community gardens were springing up on vacant land all over, residents from Fruitvale's 39th Avenue, spurred by community organizers, decided to launch a community garden of their own.

The Search for Land

Working with the Trust for Public Land (TPL), a non-profit organization based in San Francisco, Califor-

Young and old face a new planting season together.

nia and dedicated to conserving open-space lands for public use, the 39th Avenue group joined with other Fruitvale garden clubs to form a land trust, a nonprofit corporation which enables members to own or manage land in common.[1]

With help from TPL, the group found a 39th Avenue lot that was up for sale. But the land was appraised at $5,000—far too much for the Fruitvale families. TPL came to the rescue, helping the group negotiate with the landowner to sell for $500. The "bargain sale" enabled the landowner to deduct from income taxes the portion of the land that was "donated."[2]

Preparing the Garden

The residents of 39th Avenue then planned their garden, assigned plots and began clearing and cultivating the land. And in the spring of 1977 they planted a variety of vegetables in anxious anticipation of their first harvest.

But the drought that had been plaguing the West Coast for two years proved to be the worst in over 100 years—and hit its peak that summer.

Old Idea Rediscovered

With city water severely limited, the gardens were almost surely doomed. But some elderly Fruitvale residents remembered a waterpumping windmill that had stood some 50 years earlier. And one old-timer recalled digging a well and finding water just 15 feet below the ground.

At the same time, TPL was interested in exploring the use of windmills for urban water conservation. So the Fruitvale group and TPL got together to discuss the possibility of pumping water from an underground well with a windmill.

Demonstration Project

Windmills had not graced the Oakland countryside since the 1920s, but it was an exciting idea—a relatively low-cost method of bolstering scarce city water supplies. In 1977, after completing an encouraging feasibility study, TPL recommended construction of a Fruitvale windmill as a model urban water conservation project for the entire San Francisco Bay area. TPL and Aeropower, a local cooperative which has expertise in windmills and energy, agreed to provide technical assistance. In June of that year the National Center for Appropriate Technology (NCAT), a nonprofit technical assistance organization, kicked in $2,800 for equipment.[3]

Trust for Public Land

Organizer Al Cruse overlooks the fruits of the summer's labor.

Delays

Fruitvale residents busily began digging the well and laying the foundation for the windmill. Completion of the project was delayed because of the city's concerns about the structure's stability. But after lengthy testing, modifications were made and flyers went out hailing the "windmill raising" on Saturday, October 29, 1977. Residents gathered to watch and help hoist the 40-foot structure.

Today the windmill, like the one 50 years earlier, stands as a symbol of community spirit and neighborhood self-reliance. It also provides an important example of appropriate technology and serves as an educational tool for area residents.

Other Neighborhood-Based Gardens

Community gardening is proving to be an effective way to organize for change while serving as an educational tool and bolstering food production throughout the country.

Lebanon In Service To Each Neighbor (LISTEN) in Lebanon, New Hampshire is a nonprofit community organization which began in 1972 as a small neighborhood food buying club. LISTEN has campaigned for permanent community gardening sites enabling Lebanon residents to raise their own food and has been instrumental in providing seeds, plants, fertilizer and tools.

Special Populations

Various groups have assisted youth, the handicapped and prisoners in starting gardens.

In Cleveland, Ohio one of the country's most famous public school gardening programs has involved up to 20,000 pupils in youth gardens.

The Camphill Village in Copake, New York, a community for handicapped adults, offers horticultural therapy through gardening.

And in South Burlington, Vermont adult inmates at the Chittenden Community Correctional Center are involved in gardening at a nearby site. In a single day inmates have canned up to 1,000 pounds of surplus tomatoes and cucumbers in quart jars at the area cannery.[4]

Groups Highlighted

Camphill Village, U.S.A., Inc.
Copake, New York 12516
(518) 329-7924

Chittenden Community Correctional Center
7 Farrell Street
South Burlington, Vermont 05401
(802) 864-0344

Cleveland Board of Education
1380 East Sixth Street
Cleveland, Ohio 45202
(216) 696-2929

Lebanon in Service to Each Neighbor (LISTEN)
P.O. Box 469
60 Hanover Street
Lebanon, New Hampshire 03766
(603) 448-4553

Capsule: Starting a Community Garden

Find a site — preferably fairly level and fertile, accessible by car or bus and sizable enough to serve your group. Then find out if the owner will allow you to use it. Often private owners of vacant and overgrown lots will welcome the improved appearance and fertility that community gardeners can bring to their land. But be sure the land will be available long enough to make your efforts worthwhile.

Find a livewire food coordinator who is knowledgeable about gardening and has the enthusiasm and organizational ability to keep the project together. The coordinator will need a committee of volunteers to assist.

Look for a sponsor. Try churches, the local or county government, service clubs, the PTA or other area groups.

Plan in advance. Determine plot sizes, who will have access, whether tools and an onsite toolshed will be provided, how clearing and tilling will be done, what water supply will be used (the local fire department might cooperate by sharing a hydrant), whether the highway department will bring in its fall collection of swept-up leaves, etc.

Look into insurance. Community garden groups, once organized and sponsored, usually obtain insurance for protection against lawsuits resulting from injuries due to faults in the garden area (breaking a toe in a hole, for instance).

Determine rules. Let gardeners know they are expected to weed and harvest; decide on the consequences for those who neglect their plots; decide if printed information, classes or other teaching means should be provided for new gardeners.

Set a fee to cover costs for clearing and tilling, seeds (if provided), mail and phone expenses, radio or newspaper ads (if needed), etc. As much work as possible will be done by volunteers so expenses should not be excessive. And your sponsoring organization might pick up the costs of larger items such as tools and a toolshed.

Adapted from "Capsule: Starting a Community Garden," Gardens for All News, *Autumn 1979. Gardens for All, 180 Flynn Avenue, Burlington, Vermont 05401.*

[1] A land trust is a locally based corporation. It is an active, responsible alternative to private, individual ownership that allows local residents to make decisions about land use in the community.

[2] The Internal Revenue Service (IRS) code allows a tax deduction for land that is donated to charitable organizations, encouraging landowners to sell to charitable groups at below-market values.

[3] For more information on the National Center for Appropriate Technology (NCAT), see Resources at end of Food Section.

[4] The Chittenden Community Correctional Center gardening program is also mentioned in Food Section, p. 66.

* State and/or local government agencies are frequently responsible for administration of Federal program funds. For further information, see Appendix I under appropriate Federal agency.

NOTE: For a complete listing of groups featured throughout this book, see Index.

A Coalition of Gardeners

Boston Urban Gardeners
66 Hereford Street
Boston, Massachusetts 02115
(617) 267-4825

What can unite your neighborhood, cut down on food bills, and at the same time decrease the number of rubble-strewn lots which thwart the potential and charm of your city? Community gardens can do all three.

Boston Gardens

In some cities, residents are starting to organize to make the best use of vacant land through urban gardening. One of the most successful groups is Boston Urban Gardeners (BUG), a coalition of over 20 community groups and technical assistance people. Boston residents found that by joining together as a single force, such city problems as finding land, topsoil and adequate water could be hurdled. BUG has helped its 600 members and hundreds of other families grow a variety of nutritious fruits and vegetables, saving a family of four an average of $350 annually on grocery bills.

BUG

Tending the community garden

Promoting Unity

And residents have found that the gardens can also unite neighborhoods. In the middle of a 25-plot garden in Boston's ethnically rich South End stands a resident-built gazebo—a place for gatherings and

BUG

Young "farmers" watering the crops

cookouts and a symbol of the community spirit gardening has created. "BUG is a forum for teaching and bringing people together who would otherwise not have a thing to do with each other," says South End resident Raymond Almeida. "The Latino, Lebanese, Puerto Rican and middle-class folks have a common interest in community gardening."

Origins

It all began back in 1976 when the State Legislature passed a bill making unused state land available rent-free to community gardeners. Using this ammunition, a group of local community leaders began organizing residents and exposing them to the merits of gardening.

With the help of Judy Wagner, legislative assistant to Mel King, the state representative credited with spearheading the gardening bill, the group was able to capture eight state-owned lots.

The Problem

With loads of enthusiasm, they set out to find a plentiful supply of topsoil. Although they persuaded the Metro District Commission to donate tons of soil, it was 26 miles away and delivery costs were prohibitive.[1] There had to be a better, less costly way.

Call in the National Guard

Wagner suggested calling in the National Guard. Earlier the Guard had been involved with a rubble removal effort in the city, and Wagner suggested that the unprecedented activity had established community services as an acceptable alternative function of the Guard. The scheme worked, and that summer 24 National Guardsmen began hauling in and dumping 12 trucks filled with $20,000 worth of topsoil while community leaders and residents busily shoveled it onto the empty lots.

Structure

The group then set up a more formal organization to better coordinate activities. A steering committee was formed, tasks were assigned, and early in 1977 BUG was officially incorporated.

Today over 120 community garden lots—each with 20 to 400 individual plots—form the heart of BUG's activities. All city gardeners are welcome to attend weekly meetings to share information and help solve mutual problems. The staff holds workshops to teach gardeners ways to improve their gardening efficiency. The group also helps organize garden clubs, shows residents how to negotiate with the city for land and leads them to city wide gardening resources.

BUG

BUG educational exhibit at Boston Commons

Newsletter

Moreover, the staff puts out an informative bimonthly newsletter which includes coverage of BUG's activities and gardening tips. For a $1 yearly fee, members of BUG receive not only the newsletter but also a discount card honored at 15 Boston hardware and gardening stores.

Young gardener with an armful of priceless bounty

Staff and Funding

In 1978 BUG's $22,000 budget came mostly from state and local foundations and resident donations. Government agencies have also demonstrated their trust in BUG by contracting with them to write gardening manuals.[2] A board of 65 community residents, elected by BUG members, oversees the staff's activities and has final approval of all projects. Paid staff consists of the original co-directors, Judy Wagner and Charlotte Kahn, but BUG also receives assistance from a score of community volunteers and student interns.

Major Projects

In addition to encouraging community gardening, BUG is involved in everything from composting to conserving water.[3] The group promotes the planting of fruit trees and protective bushes, water conservation and gardening in public housing projects. And they are working with the Trust for Public Land, a national land conservation organization, to develop a large citywide land trust to be used for community gardening.[4]

BUG members remain determined to do all they can to spur the development and insure the good health of their gardens. In 1977 the group drew nationwide attention to a crop-killing problem caused by auto fumes and other urban pollution. After testing the soil from 900 gardens, the group discovered that these environmental hazards were causing a high lead content in the soil. BUG sent out newsletters warning gardeners about the problem and recommending effective treatment.

Andrew Brilliant

Clearing a cluttered lot for a community garden

[1] The Metro District Commission is a Massachusetts agency charged with providing sewage, water and other metropolitan services.

[2] Funding sources for Boston Urban Gardeners (BUG) include the Massachusetts Foundation for Humanities and Public Policy, other local foundations and Department of Housing and Urban Development's (HUD) Community Development Block Grant (CDBG) Program.* With a $5,000 contract from the National Center for Appropriate Technology (NCAT), a non-profit technical assistance group based in Butte, Montana, BUG wrote a handbook on heavy metals in soil, which is still available from the group. And last year BUG entered a contract with the Department of Health, Education and Welfare (HEW) to write a gardening guide.

[3] Composting is the process of turning decomposed vegetables, manure, other organic wastes and sometimes lime into a rich mixture (humus) used to fertilize and condition soil.

[4] The Trust for Public Land (TPL) is also profiled in Food Section, p. 48. (For more information on TPL, see Resources at end of Food Section.)

A land trust is a locally based, nonprofit corporation that enables a group of people to own or manage land in common. It is an active, responsible alternative to private, individual ownership that allows local residents to make decisions about land use in the community.

* State and/or local government agencies are frequently responsible for administration of Federal program funds. For further information, see Appendix I under appropriate Federal agency.

NOTE: For a complete listing of groups featured throughout this book, see Index.

Gardening in Housing Projects

Chicago Housing Authority Gardening Project
22 West Madison Street
Chicago, Illinois 60602
(312) 791-8592

Delores and Willis Bryant, residents of Trumbull Park Homes, a 443-unit low-income housing development in Chicago's far south end, have what many urban residents want: a garden of their own. They enjoy cultivating their 32- by 20-foot garden, but it's more than a hobby. Last year the seven-member family enjoyed tomatoes, eggplant and other vegetables while saving about $500 on their food bill. And with the fresh grown celery and peppers, Delores Bryant made enough celery seasoning and relish to last the winter.

Success Today

The Chicago Housing Authority (CHA), a city corporation charged with building and operating public housing projects for low-income families, isn't the kind of operation usually associated with gardening. But it is one of an increasing number of city agencies which have gotten into the act and are bolstering the urban gardening movement. Through CHA's anti-inflation Flower and Vegetable Garden Program, the Bryants and 6,000 other gardeners receive free seeds, fertilizer, water and technical assistance to grow flowers and vegetables. In 1978 CHA gardens produced 270 tons of produce valued at $250,000. Over 60 percent of the 1,500 individual and group plots sprout vegetables only, but the land is also used for flowers and herbs—adding color and beauty to the surroundings of CHA's 19 family and senior citizen housing developments.

"The garden program gives a lot of elderly people something to do and it helps set up the place real nice. Lawns are well kept and we have a lot of beautiful flower beds," says Willis Bryant. And he continues, "It draws people together. We sit around and discuss what we are growing and how it's turning out."

Origins

The program, which began in 1973, was inspired by the New York City Housing Authority's successful flower garden program. CHA's garden advocates viewed it as a way to help low-income residents com-

Chicago Housing Authority

Neighbors pitch in to beautify their community.

bat soaring food costs while enjoying fresh air and exercise and bolstering morale and community pride.

It took several months for the program to get off the ground. After CHA's executive director approved the idea, it was presented to the Central Advisory Council (CAC), a tenant advocacy group which includes representatives from the 19 housing developments. After approving the plan, CAC members and development managers submitted names of residents to serve on a 25-member steering committee to push the project and recruit interested gardeners.

Technical and consultant help was wooed from a variety of sources, including the county Cooperative Extension Service,* working with the University of Illinois in cooperation with the United States Department of Agriculture (USDA).[1]

Attracting Residents

Resident interest was aroused by announcements in CHA's monthly newsletter that all supplies and gardening costs would be picked up by the housing authority. CHA's home economist and outside consultants further spurred resident interest with slide shows of successful gardening projects around the country and how-to workshops held at development social rooms. And a media blitz by CHA's information department sparked 30 newspaper articles and TV spots featuring the gardening program.

Growth

Since launching the program, a half-million square feet or about 12 acres of land have been cultivated.

Chicago Housing Authority

Nurturing the common garden

CHA maintenance personnel prepare group plots for planting while individual gardeners are responsible for their own. And each housing development picks up the costs of supplies from its own budget.

The CHA's how-to manual and a special monthly newsletter containing timely garden tips are a source of encouragement to eager gardeners as are the demonstrations on food preservation conducted on development premises.

Youth Gardens

Since 1977 youngsters have been sporting "I'm a Whale of a Gardener" buttons—a testimony to CHA's commitment to its youthful residents. The buttons are given to participants in the Big Tomato Program, which enables 5- to 8-year-olds to grow tomatoes in their parents' or neighbors' plots and exhibit the fruits of their labor in annual competition. The 9- to 21-year-olds participating in the Buddy Gardening Program grow a variety of vegetables and flowers on their own plots. And in 1979, in honor of the International Year of the Child, CHA launched a program in which over 1,000 school children beautified their developments with marigolds, the friendship flower.

Festival and Awards

A highlight of the CHA gardening project is the annual Harvest Festival. Each housing development exhibits its bounty at the city's Civic Center Plaza in hopes of capturing a prize. Balloons and banners hailing "Gardens in the City" wave in the wind, and colorful tablecloths cover each display booth. The well-attended gala reflects the residents' enthusiasm for the gardening program.

Other City Agency Gardens

The New York City Housing Authority (NYCHA) began promoting gardening in 1963 with a flower garden program. In 1974 vegetable gardens were added. Since New York has less available land than Chicago, group rather than individual gardens are the rule. In 1979 the program boasted 1,215 group gardens with 8,000 participants.

A highlight of the program is the annual competition and awards ceremony attended by city officials and held on the steps of City Hall. The agency publishes a *Tenant Gardening Competition Manual*, which tells gardeners how to raise prize-winning plants.

In 1977 the Parks and Recreation Department in San Jose, California, prodded by community requests, won staff support from the Department of Labor's Comprehensive Employment and Training Act (CETA) Program* and funding from private industries to begin a public garden program. More than 500 families in 1979 were provided with garden plots averaging 600 square feet and yielding from $450 to $600 worth of produce.

And a garden program sponsored by the Parks and Recreation Department of the Municipalities of Anchorage in Alaska offers free garden plots to senior citizens and low-income families.

Groups Highlighted

Municipalities of Anchorage
Community Garden Program
Parks and Recreation Department
Sports Facilities
6-650 Anchorage, Alaska 99502
(907) 264-4476

New York City Housing Authority Tenant Gardening Program
250 Broadway
New York, New York 10007
(212) 433-4198

San Jose Parks and Recreation Department
151 West Mission Street, Room 203
San Jose, California 95110
(408) 277-4661

[1] Other groups offering the Chicago Housing Authority (CHA) technical help included the Chicago Horticulturists, a private, nonprofit group, and Morton Arboretum, a nonprofit, private group concerned with the cultivation of trees and shrubs. Virginia Beatty, a Chicago writer and urban horticulturist, also offered technical assistance.

* State and/or local government agencies are frequently responsible for administration of Federal program funds. For further information, see Appendix I under appropriate Federal agency.

NOTE: For a complete listing of groups featured throughout this book, see Index.

Compost for Gardens

Bronx Frontier Development Corporation
Compost Project
1080 Leggett Avenue
Bronx, New York 10474
(212) 542-4640

The South Bronx in New York has been portrayed as a grim wasteland of abandoned buildings, vacant lots and unsafe streets. But thanks to the Bronx Frontier Development Corporation (BFDC), it is changing for the better. This nonprofit organization, founded in 1976, is dedicated to the greening and revitalization of wasted South Bronx space.

Success Today

Beginning with a staff of two and only $1,000, BFDC now boasts 17 staffers and a budget topping $2 million. The group's efforts have led to the greening of hundreds of acres of devastated, non-productive land. The organization's composting project provides community groups—free of charge—with 50 tons of recycled waste a day to transform rubble-strewn land into gardens and parks. And BFDC is so successful that it now provides technical assistance on composting, nutrition and gardening to groups throughout New York City.

Beginnings

Before BFDC began, the concept of "greening" the South Bronx was considered all but impossible. But some of the community's residents thought otherwise and, after forming BFDC, they set out to convince the Mayor, the Commissioner of Sanitation, city planners, environmental commissioners and gardening experts.

They argued that revitalizing the area's vacant land would mean more jobs, improved nutrition, social benefits and a new sense of pride for South Bronx residents.

After a year their efforts began to pay off. First, the Mayor helped the group get 3.7 acres for gardening projects from the city's Department of Sanitation. Then the local congressman helped BFDC establish contacts with others around the country who were already working on greening their communities.

Grieg Cranna

View of BFDC's compost operation from the top of the windmill

Composting

Rich soil was scarce in the city, and BFDC leaders learned that it would cost about $10,000 to import enough good soil to cover even a small plot of land. So the group decided to tackle the problem by composting—making rich garden-growing humus out of decomposed vegetables, manure and other organic wastes.

The group sought help in developing a composting operation large enough to make an impact in the South Bronx from the Institute for Local Self-Reliance, a nonprofit consulting and technical assistance organization in Washington, D.C., and the Council on the Environment of New York City.[1] These organizations studied the possibility of launching a composting operation and then located experts to design it.

Funding

Private foundations and city and state sources kicked in over $100,000 to prepare the site, purchase equipment and hire personnel.[2]

Educational facility and the windmill at BFDC's compost site

Then BFDC members scouted around for vegetable wastes from local produce markets, trucking companies, landscapers and food processing centers, and arranged for pick-up and delivery of any offerings.

Great Demand

In October 1977 the composting operation began. Today residents continue to be enthusiastic. The demand for compost far exceeds supply because composting works. BFDC's compost has proven to be ideal for growing vegetables, shrubs and grass. As a result, during the project's first three years, hundreds of community gardens, parks and playgrounds have been developed.

Moreover, the construction of a windmill has made the composting operation energy self-sufficient.[3] The windmill, which is the first commercial application of wind power in the city, supplies all the electricity needed to run the site, including the compost turning machine. To construct the windmill, BFDC won an Energy Demonstration Grant* from the Community Services Administration's (CSA) Energy Office.

Bronx Frontier plans to begin marketing two-thirds of its compost in 1980, continuing to make the rest available to community groups.

Through its efforts the organization has earned the respect and confidence of the city. Under a $300,000 grant from the New York City Department of Sanitation, BFDC will launch a solid waste management program. Leaves and other solid wastes will be composted and may prove to be a partial solution to the city's ever increasing volume of waste.

Goal

Bronx Frontier continues to work toward its major goal—the greening of South Bronx. By giving hard-working community groups the material and the technical assistance to start new gardens, what was once thought impossible is becoming a reality.

Other Projects

While other composting projects do exist, few have reached the scale of Bronx Frontier's. The city of Bangor, Maine has converted an old, abandoned airport runway into a municipal composting site. The compost is given to citizens and nurseries for landscaping.

Group Highlighted

City of Bangor Compost Project
760 Main Street
Bangor, Maine 04401
(207) 942-2065

[1] The Institute for Local Self-Reliance is profiled in Energy Section, p. 184. For more information on the Council on the Environment of New York City, see Resources at end of Food Section.

[2] Funding to start the Bronx Frontier Compost Project came from the Rockefeller Brothers Foundation, the local Unitarian Church, the New York City Department of Sanitation and the State Department of Parks and Recreation.

[3] The Bronx Frontier windmill is also mentioned in Energy Section, p. 221.

* State and/or local government agencies are frequently responsible for administration of Federal program funds. For further information, see Appendix I under appropriate Federal agency.

NOTE: For a complete listing of groups featured throughout this book, see Index.

Urban Community Greenhouses

The Sun Project
Center for Neighborhood Technology
570 West Randolph Street
Chicago, Illinois 60606
(312) 454-0126

The old fable "Give a man a fish and he eats for a day; teach a man to fish and he eats for a lifetime" never had more meaning than for inner-city residents.

Now, thanks to the Center for Neighborhood Technology (CNT), a nonprofit technical assistance group based in Chicago, Illinois, people who live far from both sea and fertile ground are learning to build solar greenhouses to help them "eat for a lifetime."[1]

CNT Executive Director Scott Bernstein explains the problem of low-income, inner-city residents best: "Low-income people in general have been cut out of the system that allows them to provide for their own basic needs and leaves them with welfare as the sole alternative to starvation."

CNT's Sun Project aims to give inner-city residents a chance at self-reliance by helping seven low-income neighborhood groups build passive solar greenhouses.[2]

Multiple Benefits

This kind of innovation pays for itself in several ways. It provides higher quality fruits and vegetables, reduces illness by improving nutrition and allows people to be self-reliant. Moreover, it puts people to work, saves residents transportation costs to supermarkets, takes up little room and cuts heating bills.

But there's no such thing as a free lunch for Sun Project participants. Although greenhouse gardening instruction is free, produce isn't. Depending on the individual project, the greenhouse harvest may be exchanged for services rendered by resident volunteers, sold at urban farmers' markets or distributed to neighborhood feeding programs.

It all began in 1965 in the low-income, mostly black Garfield community of Chicago where major chain stores were closing and moving to the more profitable suburbs, thus limiting the quality and availability of affordable food in the area.

A local church coalition, the Christian Action Ministry (CAM), decided to do something to help.

Operation Brotherhood's greenhouse manager checks tomatoes.

CAM persuaded the Northwestern University Center for Urban Affairs to conduct a study of Chicago's inner-city health problems.[3] Financed by a $10,000 grant from the Illinois State Department of Education, the study revealed that too many inner-city residents were victims of poor nutrition and had few stores at which to shop for high-quality, affordable food. Moreover, the study recommended a resident involved solution to foster self-reliance.

Easing the Problem

With a small grant from a national business and the technical help of Northwestern, a specially designed 880-square-foot solar greenhouse was constructed in 1977 on the roof of CAM's building. Labor was provided by area senior volunteers who still act as its cooperative managers.

Solutions

Not only did the CAM greenhouse, which provides up to 6,500 pounds of produce during peak seasons, help ease food problems for the low-income residents, it also demonstrated how problems in energy, shelter, joblessness and greenhouse construction could be solved.

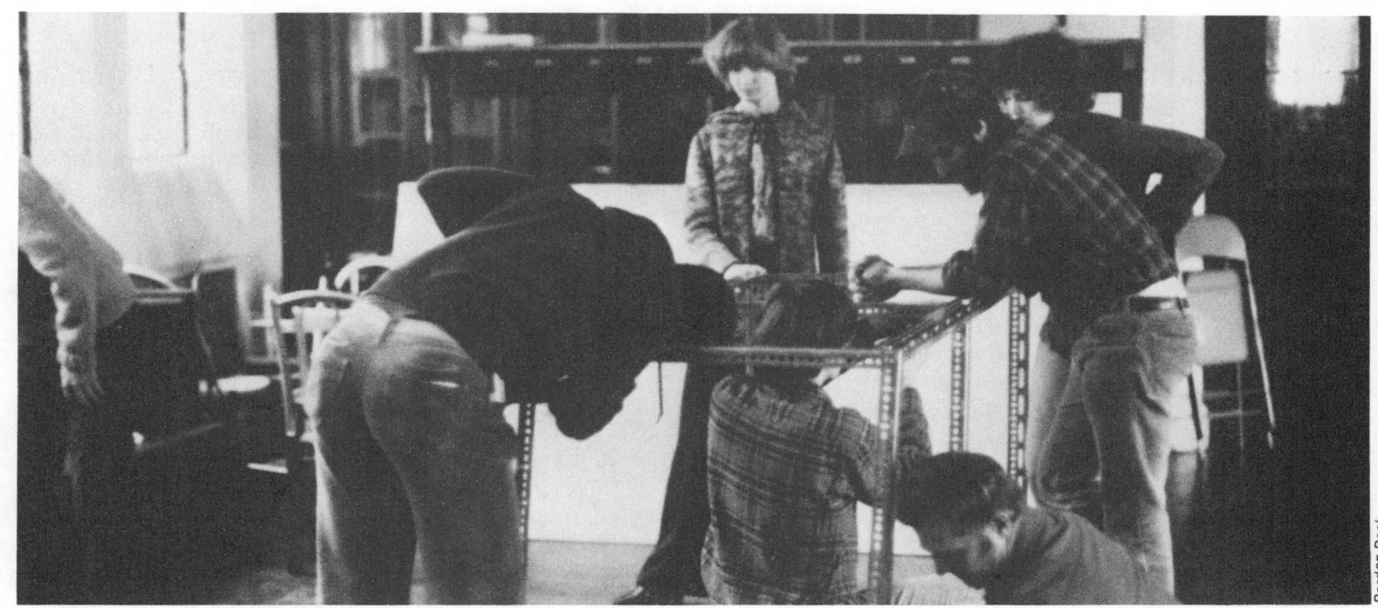

Learning by building at greenhouse workshop

Others Attracted to Greenhouses

Other neighborhood groups saw the many benefits of producing their own food and stormed Northwestern with requests to help build greenhouses in their areas. But lacking funds, the university could not fill the numerous requests for help. So several students who had provided technical assistance to the CAM project; their professors, who helped with special problems; and the Community Renewal Society (CRS), which provided seed money and organizational help, formed the Center for Neighborhood Technology in 1977.[4]

CNT's first action as a service group was to provide organizational and technical help to the many community and church groups wishing to build greenhouses of their own.

Budget and Staff

Today the neighborhood groups working with CNT on the Sun Project are building solar greenhouses and exposing other Chicago neighborhoods to the benefits of greenhouse production and self-reliance. Major funding comes from the Community Services Administration's Local Initiative (Section 221) Program* and from the National Center for Appropriate Technology (NCAT), a nonprofit technical assistance organization, as well as from many public trusts, private corporations and foundations.[5] Employment opportunities are provided by the Department of Labor's Comprehensive Employment and Training Act (CETA) Program* and ACTION's Volunteers in Service to America (VISTA) Program.*

Among the four completed greenhouses, more than 12,000 square feet of growing space are bringing tons of fresh produce directly to the tables of those most in need. According to Bernstein, "Every little bit that you start to produce within the community is a recapturing of the money that normally leaves the community. It's community power."

Individual Projects

Residents from each of the neighborhood groups form the Sun Project Governing Board and make all project decisions. In that way, residents are exercising their right to take care of themselves. Bernstein explains, "In order to make a project work, you must have a good organizational base, adequate resources and technical help, and interested people to make sure that the thing will be around long enough to make an impact."

Workers construct the frame of the Eighteenth Street Development Corporation's greenhouse.

Spin-Offs

There have been spin-offs from the Sun Project. CNT is helping other Chicago groups build their own greenhouses. For example, the nonprofit North River Commission is renovating an old tuberculosis sanatarium to provide 15,000 square feet of growing space at 40 to 50 percent less than it would cost to build a new greenhouse of that size. When completed it will be the largest solar greenhouse of its kind in the country.

And CNT is also providing technical assistance to communities across the nation interested in building solar greenhouses. They work closely with the newly created National Consumer Cooperative Bank, which provides technical assistance and financing to eligible cooperatives.**

Other Projects

Other cities with greenhouse projects underway include New York City, where the Eleventh Street Movement, a nonprofit neighborhood association, is completing a 525-square-foot greenhouse on top of a renovated building.[6]

Group Highlighted

Christian Action Ministry
5130 West Jackson
Chicago, Illinois 60644
(312) 626-3300

Eleventh Street Movement
519 East 11th Street
New York, New York 10009
(212) 982-1460

North River Commission
3440 West Lawrence
Chicago, Illinois 60625
(312) 463-5420

[1] Solar greenhouses are also profiled in Food Section, p. 62 and Energy Section, p. 235.

[2] For a definition of a passive solar energy system, use glossary in Energy Section, p. 275.

[3] The Northwestern University Center for Urban Affairs is a research center dedicated to working with community groups using academic resources to help improve the quality of urban life.

[4] The Community Renewal Society (CRS) is a well-established ecumenical metropolitan organization which provides assistance to low-income minority community development groups through a variety of social change programs.

[5] For more information on the National Center for Appropriate Technology (NCAT), see Resources at end of Food Section.

[6] The Eleventh Street Movement is also profiled in Energy Section, p. 219.

* State and/or local government agencies are frequently responsible for administration of Federal program funds. For further information, see Appendix I under appropriate Federal agency.

**For further information, see Appendix II under "National Consumer Cooperative Bank."

NOTE: For a complete listing of groups featured throughout this book, see Index.

Sun Project's Greenhouses

1. Christian Action Ministry:

- Coalition of local churches offering wide range of social programs.
- Greenhouse (880 square feet constructed in 1976) to provide nutritious food, reduce food costs and create jobs.
- Neighborhoods served: East and West Garfield Park, South Austin, North Lawndale (mostly black, low-income).

2. First Presbyterian Church:

- Neighborhood church offering community service programs in food distribution and outdoor gardening.
- Greenhouse (1,100 square feet to be completed in June, 1980) to produce food, facilitate the education of children and senior citizens and supply food for day care center.
- Neighborhood served: Woodlawn (black, low-income).

3. Eighteenth Street Development Corporation:[1]

- Housing rehabilitation and job training organization.
- Greenhouse (400 square feet completed) used to sell food, create jobs, train residents and provide auxiliary heat for center.

4. Jane Addams Center/Hull House:

- Settlement house offering wide range of social and educational programs.
- Greenhouse (250 square feet completed) designed to educate, create jobs for youth and bring senior citizens and teens together.
- Neighborhood served: Lakeview (multi-ethnic and wide income range).

5. Operation Brotherhood:[2]

- Senior Citizen organization offering wide range of food, social and educational services.
- Greenhouse (500 square feet completed) used to produce food for food co-op, create jobs, train residents and provide auxiliary heat for center.

6. Voice of the People and Chrysalis Learning Community:[3]

- Housing rehabilitation and management organization and alternative high school.
- Greenhouse (1,100 square feet, to be completed in June 1980) to be used for high school curriculum development in the fields of science, health, shop and job training; reduce energy costs; and develop marketing skills.
- Neighborhoods served: Uptown and Ravenswood (Appalachian, Native American, Latino, low-income).

[1] The Eighteenth Street Development Corporation is mentioned in Housing Section, p. 112.

[2] Operation Brotherhood is profiled in Food Section, p. 78.

[3] Voice of the People is profiled in Housing Section, p. 111.

Doug Fernandez

Roof work at Operation Brotherhood's greenhouse

Borden Beck

Workers move inside the Eighteenth Street Development Corporation greenhouse.

Borden Beck

The Jane Addams Center greenhouse takes shape.

Rural Community Greenhouses

Cheyenne Community Solar Greenhouse
c/o Laramie County Community Action Agency
1603 Central Avenue
Bell Building, Suite 400
Cheyenne, Wyoming 82001
(307) 635-9340

"April showers bring May flowers," the saying goes, but in the Rocky Mountain plains of Cheyenne, Wyoming, April and May bring heavy winter snowfalls—hardly a setting for celebrating the sun.

But on May 3, 1979, that's exactly what Cheyenne residents did. With 17 inches of snow outside, they celebrated the nationwide Sun Day by harvesting hundreds of pounds of fresh vegetables from the 5,000-square-foot Cheyenne Community Solar Greenhouse which was fought for and built by city residents and the nonprofit Laramie County Community Action Agency (CAA).[1]

Helping the Needy

The three-part community solar greenhouse can produce $75,000 worth of fresh vegetables a year, most of which are given to local groups to help feed the elderly, the handicapped and the poor.[2] And 24 surrounding community gardening plots are harvested by and provide nutritious summertime eating for low-income Cheyenne families.

Other Benefits

Some of the greenhouse benefits can't be measured in dollars and cents. For instance, greenhouse gardening provides therapy and work for residents. Seniors daily volunteer time and expertise, youth offenders work to pay off court fines and the area's handicapped get gardening training at the greenhouse.

Although Clara Marshall has never seen a greenhouse, she's an active volunteer. Marshall, who is blind, helps with transplanting and pruning chores.

And learning about gardening at the greenhouse has inspired Hettie Johnson, a 43-year-old low-income resident, to work for a new career. "I'm going to work hard at getting my degree in horticulture," she says. "I took a while to think about it and decided that's what I really want to do."

The model greenhouse gives thousands of visitors each year an opportunity to see that, as greenhouse Director Shane Smith puts it, "There's no magic to solar gardening."

Uphill Battle

These tremendous victories didn't come easily for Cheyenne's solar greenhouse gardeners. Experts told organizers that the project just wasn't feasible. Passive solar construction, which captures the sun's energy and spreads the heat with no mechanical devices, wouldn't heat the space adequately, they said, and plants wouldn't grow in the cold environment. Nowhere in the country was there a three-part solar greenhouse. And to create different climates in three sections to grow seasonal crops year-round was unthinkable. But these discouraging words only served to challenge the organizers.

Grant Award

In December 1976 Laramie County CAA won a $42,000 grant from the Community Services Administration's (CSA) Community Food and Nutrition Program* to construct a community solar greenhouse capable of providing a continued source of low-cost food for Cheyenne's poor. But getting the funding before finding the land became a case of putting the cart before the horse.

Staking the vegetables in the Cheyenne Solar greenhouse

The Land Search

For six months the search for a site dragged on. Meanwhile, spiraling inflation chipped away at the dollar value of the grant. Finally, in the early fall of 1977, a low-income Cheyenne couple who had heard of the project's plight donated two acres of land outside of town.

Community Support Saves Project

An incredible array of volunteers, most of whom had recently participated in the solar workshops conducted by Laramie County CAA, pitched in on the construction. But materials had risen so much in price during the land search that money ran out before the job was completed.

Once again community support rescued the embattled project. Residents had been turned on to the solar greenhouse idea by the workshops, newspaper articles and Laramie County CAA education programs and materials. So when cash ran short, sympathetic local merchants donated materials and extended credit. The Laramie County Commissioners kicked in $2,000 and even a local high school's welding class got into the act by building two wood-burning stoves to serve as back-up heating systems. With this help, volunteers, determined to beat the coming winter, busily completed the outside structure.[3]

Beating Winter

As winter approached, workers moved inside the greenhouse to ready the first section for the scheduled January 1978 planting. With 200 donated 55-gallon oil drums, the passive solar heating system was installed. The drums were filled with water, sealed and painted black to capture the sun's energy for 24-hour-a-day heating. The first crops were planted as planned. And one year after the bountiful Sun Day harvest, the other two sections were completed—with another CSA Community Food and Nutrition Program grant.

Three-Section Greenhouse

Two sections of the greenhouse are used to grow food which is distributed to senior volunteers and the area's senior citizen Meals-on-Wheels and feeding programs for the handicapped.[4]

Surplus produce is sold to the public in the third volunteer-operated commercial section, which includes a small store area. Houseplants, cut flowers and plant supplies are also sold, with all proceeds used to help cover greenhouse operating expenses.

The greenhouse also includes a composting system to fertilize the soil naturally.[5] And by the end of 1979, Shane Smith estimates that some crop yields doubled and others tripled because of increased expertise.

And on the Navajo Reservation

In Arizona on the Navajo Nation Reservation, resting in the Little Colorado River Canyon, stands a 16- by 52-foot community solar greenhouse built of native stone. The Cameron Chapter Farm Project, a non-profit group based in Phoenix, Arizona, sponsored the passive greenhouse to demonstrate to the people of the tribe that winter gardening is possible. The greenhouse was built with local resources and its bounty of tomatoes, radishes, green peppers and other produce will provide more balanced meals for the tribe's people than their predominantly squash and corn diet.

Different sectors of the Navajo Nation along with workers paid by the Department of Labor's Comprehensive Employment and Training Act (CETA) Program* are pooling their resources to insure that the greenhouse meets the needs of the tribe.

Group Highlighted

Cameron Chapter Farm Project
P.O. Box 85
Cameron, Arizona 86020
(602) 679-2219

[1] The Community Services Administration's (CSA) Community Action Program (CAP)* funds local Community Action Agencies (CAAs)* aimed at helping low-income residents with their food, housing, energy and other needs.

[2] Solar greenhouses are also profiled in Food Section, p. 58 and Energy Section, p. 235.

[3] Basic drawings of the Cheyenne Solar Greenhouse structure are available by writing to the Laramie County Community Action Agency, 1603 Central Avenue, Bell Building, Suite 400, Cheyenne, Wyoming 82001.

[4] The local Meals-On-Wheels Program* is administered by the Department of Health, Education and Welfare (HEW) under Title III of the Older Americans Act,* working in cooperation with the United States Department of Agriculture's (USDA) Food Distribution Program.*

[5] Composting is the process of turning decomposed vegetables, manure, other organic wastes and sometimes lime into a rich mixture (humus) used to fertilize and condition soil.

* State and/or local government agencies are frequently responsible for administration of Federal program funds. For further information, see Appendix I under appropriate Federal Agency.

NOTE: For a complete listing of groups featured throughout this book, see Index.

Community Canning

Community Self-Reliance, Inc.
16 Armory Street
Northampton, Massachusetts 01060
(413) 586-0543

Now that you've grown your food, you soon realize that you can't possibly eat it all before it spoils. How can families save harvest surplus and enjoy it long after the growing season? The choices come down to basically four: dry it, freeze it, store it in a root cellar or can it. Throughout the country, many individuals and groups are experiencing the joy and savings of canning.

Canning is the most economical and universally used method of food preservation, but it requires some specialized equipment and know-how.[1]

In 1977 the gardeners of Hampshire County in Northampton, Massachusetts formed Community Self-Reliance, Inc. (CSR), the state's first community canning center. In 1979, despite a temporary set-back due to funding and site problems, a larger cannery was opened, doubling the center's capacity to 20,000 pints of local produce a year. The new cannery was open 10 hours a day, seven days a week during the peak growing season, and over 900 residents canned their own food for an average fee of 12 cents per pint. The Center's low canning fees almost cover operating costs so CSR soon expects to be self-sustaining.

"For Thanksgiving dinner, I fed 17 people for $14.52," says one happy canner. "The big saving was in my pocketbook. And the fruits and vegies that I canned at the Community Canning Center were the talk of the meal."

Origins

It all began in November 1975. The members of Women in Agriculture, Food Policy and Land-Use Reform, an outgrowth of the Governor's Commission on the Status of Women, recognized a need to help Hampshire County residents reduce their dependence on expensive out-of-state food sources.

To solve this problem and to bring consumers and growers together in an economical and productive way, they decided to open a community cannery to promote existing community gardens, farmers' markets, roadside stands and pick-your-own orchards. The cannery would teach people how to preserve local produce for later use, thereby increasing self-reliance and providing low-cost nutritious food on a year-round basis.

The obvious first step was to raise funds; the second was to generate community support.

Funding

They succeeded in obtaining funds for staffing the cannery through the Department of Labor's Comprehensive Employment and Training Act (CETA) Program.* Necessary funding for the canning equipment came from various local and state sources.[2]

The space for the cannery was provided rent-free by the Hampshire County Commissioners. And with a lot of volunteer work, the canning operation began to take shape.

Community Support

In June 1977, to enlist community participation and support, a hiring committee was formed representing the area's minorities—the elderly, poor, Hispanics and disadvantaged youths. Seventeen workers paid by CETA were hired to operate the cannery. Technical assistance came from a national canning company and county agents of the Cooperative Extension Service,* working in conjunction with the United States Department of Agriculture (USDA).

Then the group launched a public relations campaign. They passed out flyers, held public meetings and started a promotional newsletter, *Digging In,* to stress the benefits of a canning operation—such as the additional jobs it creates for elderly and low-income Northampton residents. But large bilingual posters displayed in store windows and word-of-mouth advertising proved to be the best ways of spreading the word and attracting support.

Families Save

At the cannery, families learned food preservation skills and saved money—about 20 cents a pint over commercially canned items such as applesauce, tomatoes and tomato juice. Low-income families canned free, and the group arranged for those families to purchase local produce with food stamps.[3] By the end of the first growing season, 100 families canned over 4,000 containers at the center.

Processing fresh produce at the community cannery

Outreach

Things looked brighter, but staffers at CSR soon realized that a cannery alone wasn't enough to promote full use of local agriculture. So they developed outreach programs. CSR's Project Greenbean educates and familiarizes low-income residents with gardening, bulk ordering, pick-your-own harvesting and self-help canning. Free seeds help program participants get off to a good start. And the From Seed to Table Program directly involves consumers in every phase of food production and processing.

Other Projects

CSR has bolstered resident food self-reliance through a number of other programs as well. They have prepared educational food and nutrition materials for elementary schools, sponsored youth gardening programs in housing projects, established a direct farmer-to-consumer referral service and organized a series of workshops aimed at teaching residents the skills necessary for greater self-reliance.

Other Efforts

Since CSR began, seven more canneries have opened in Massachusetts. And in Barre, Vermont the Cherry Hill Co-op received funding from the Campaign for Human Development, the economic and social assistance arm of the Catholic Church, and workers from CETA to rehabilitate three old World War II food canneries. (Although not available in time to assist Cherry Hill, co-ops may now qualify for technical and financial assistance from the newly created National Consumer Cooperative Bank.**)

In Decatur, Georgia the Dekalb County Food Processing Center serves 25,000 people with its community cannery and meat processing facilities.

Groups Highlighted

Cherry Hill Co-op
MR #1
Barre, Vermont 05641
(802) 476-8738

Dekalb County Food Processing Center
c/o Georgia Cooperative Extension Service
101 Court Square
Decatur, Georgia 30030
(404) 294-7449

[1] Community and home-canning has become so widespread that in 1979 a National Conference on Food Preservation was held in New York. One result was the establishment of the National Clearinghouse on Food Preservation. (For more information on the National Clearinghouse on Food Preservation, see Northeast Task Force for Food and Farm Policy in Resources at end of Food Section.)

[2] Funding for the canning equipment came from the Campaign for Human Development, the economic and social assistance arm of the Catholic Church; the Massachusetts Society for Promoting Agriculture; the Highland Valley Elder Service Center, a local trust fund; and two private companies. (For more information on the Campaign for Human Development, see Resources at end of Basic Tools Section.)

[3] The Food Stamp Program* is administered by the United States Department of Agriculture (USDA).

* State and/or local government agencies are frequently responsible for administration of Federal program funds. For further information, see Appendix I under appropriate Federal agency.

**For further information, see Appendix II under "National Consumer Cooperative Bank."

NOTE: For a complete listing of groups featured throughout this book, see Index.

National Gardening Clearinghouse

Gardens For All
180 Flynn Avenue
Burlington, Vermont 05401
(802) 863-1308

Near a well-traveled road not far from the Chittenden Community Correctional Center in Burlington, Vermont lie three acres of land. At harvest time the beauty is so striking with tall golden corn and bushy tomato plants that many passersby pull over just for the view. But the garden has more than aesthetic value; it saves the state money while providing healthy therapy for some of the state institution's adult offenders.[1] Planted and cultivated by five inmates, the garden yields $15,000 worth of fresh produce per year to help feed the 150 prisoners. And inspired by the garden's success, the Chittenden inmates have built a 14- by 23-foot cellar at the prison to store surplus vegetables.

"It is definitely the most productive program I've ever seen," says George Africa, Chittenden's superintendent and a 10-year prison administration veteran. "It makes the workers feel more useful and, if you could measure self-esteem, that improves considerably. People stop regularly to see the garden and comment on how nicely it is cared for. There's no way you can buy that kind of ego-boosting exposure."

Clearinghouse

The innovative prison garden project was spurred and assisted by a group dedicated to providing everyone in the country with the opportunity and know-how to garden successfully. The Burlington, Vermont-based Gardens for All (GFA) is a national clearinghouse of A-to-Z gardening information. Its various publications are full of helpful hints on how-to, when-to and what-to plant. Their step-by-step *Guide to Community Garden Organization* is an easy and practical roadmap for organizing and building community garden projects.[2] And their Annual Survey of some 2,000 community gardens across the country provides insightful gardening trends for gardeners and the media as well as state and Federal legislators.

Highlights of the GFA/Gallup Poll 1979 Gardening Survey:

- Gardening is the eighth favorite leisure time activity in this country, falling behind such passive time-fillers as watching television and reading books, but ahead of sports like tennis and bowling.
- In 1979, 33 million American "backyard gardeners," or 42 percent of all families, produced $13 billion worth of food, saving an average of $367 on annual food bills.
- People plant gardens: first, to save money; second, to have fun; and third, for better tasting produce.

Origins

Gardens for All began in 1972 when B.H. "Tommy" Thompson, a retired restaurateur and long-time garden lover, launched a community garden project in Burlington. That year, with a small salary-paying donation from a private corporation, Thompson helped start 40 garden plots.

But he knew more should be done. So he began knocking on doors, commandeering rent-free land from churches, businesses and the government while sparking resident interest in gardening. By the end of 1973 the number of gardening plots in Burlington mushroomed to 540. Thompson's success drew unsolicited local and national media attention.

Phone calls began pouring in from communities across the country. Thompson and his small contingent of volunteers began furiously answering the inquiries. The group sent the callers detailed how-to material along with appeals for financial support.

GFA

Home grown turnips will make mighty fine eating.

Publication

In 1974, after discovering there was no national clearinghouse for gardening information, GFA began performing that much-needed function. Not until 1979, after launching a successful membership drive that drew 4,000, did they officially incorporate as the Gardens for All National Association for Gardening.

Staff and Budget

Today GFA's budget of $750,000 comes mainly from donations from business, industry and residents. Proceeds from its publications and membership fees also add to the group's income.[3]

A powerhouse for gardening know-how, GFA's 10-strong staff is called on by both government and private groups wishing to begin or learn about community gardens.

Reflecting the admiration the group has stirred in government leaders, GFA staffers have been asked to: share their gardening knowledge at state and Federal legislative hearings; hold workshops to teach Bureau of Reclamation personnel and neighborhood groups how to organize community gardens; and provide government officials with updates on gardening trends.

Strong Lobby

GFA staffers are experts when it comes to lobbying for more land and resources for gardeners. For example, in 1976 they helped persuade the General Services Administration (GSA), charged with controlling excess Federal land, to make unused land surrounding government buildings available to neighborhood gardening groups.[4]

And one of the most important issues the group is grappling with today is the lack of permanent gardening sites—government and other land legally placed in trust to be used only for gardening purposes. According to GFA, there were only 64 permanent sites nationwide in 1979. Most of our country's 10,000 community gardens are planted on borrowed government land. GFA is working with the Trust for Public Land, a private, nonprofit group with an impressive record for winning land trusts across the country, to lobby for many more permanent gardening sites.[5]

Judi Loomis, active in GFA since its early days, attributes the low permanent site figure to a lack of public awareness of the land shortage problem and the virtues of gardening. But GFA aims to change that as they continue to flood the media, legislators and gardeners with information.

Government-Sponsored Gardening Programs

The United States Department of Agriculture (USDA) and state and local governments share in the financial support and program direction of Cooperative Extension Service* gardening programs across the country. A variety of such programs exist nationwide. Here are a few examples:

Philadelphia, Pennsylvania is one of 16 cities involved in a Cooperative Extension Service Urban Gardening Demonstration Program.*[6] Working with the Governor's Anti-Inflation Garden Program and the Schuylkill Valley Nature Center, 3,500 inner-city families have been helped to grow, harvest and preserve their own produce. And in St. Louis, Missouri, another demonstration city, urban gardeners are provided with everything from free seeds to gardening lots and technical help. Assisting with the gardening effort are the city's Community Development Agency, Land Revitalization Authority and the Metropolitan St. Louis Human Development Corporation.[7]

And 15 states are reaping the benefits of the Cooperative Extension Service's Master Gardener Program.* For example, Oregon State University's Extension Service in Oregon City offers 60 hours of free classes in garden care and disease control for those individuals who have a blooming interest in becoming "master gardeners." Graduates then donate 80 hours to help backyard gardeners through workshops and a "Dial-an-Answer" service.

And the Community Services Administration (CSA) is increasing food for the poor through its Community Action Program (CAP)* which funds local Community Action Agencies (CAAs)* aimed at helping low-income residents with food, housing, energy and other needs. In an eight-county area of South Dakota, for instance, CAAs have helped launch 225 community gardens. Oklahoma's statewide program combines the efforts of 24 CAAs in 66 different counties to help an estimated 18,000 low-income families experience the joys and benefits of gardening.

And in Ithaca, New York the Tompkins County Economic Opportunity Corporation, a CAA, provides indoor and outdoor gardening for seniors at convenient areas throughout the city.[8] The seniors get exercise and gardening training while making friends and saving on food.

GFA

"This is fun!" A youngster happily picks beans from the family garden.

Groups Highlighted

Department of Economic and Community Affairs
Division of Human Development
5500 Northwestern Avenue
Oklahoma City, Oklahoma 73118
(405) 840-2811

Master Gardener Program
Oregon State University Extension Service
756 Warner-Milne Road
Oregon City, Oregon 97045
(503) 655-8631

Tompkins County Economic Opportunity Corporation
318 North Albany Street
Ithaca, New York 14850
(607) 273-8816

Urban Gardening Program
Pennsylvania State University Cooperative Extension Service
Broad and Grange Streets
Philadelphia, Pennsylvania 19141
(215) 224-1821

Urban Gardening Program
University of Missouri Extension Council
724 North Union Street
St. Louis, Missouri 63108
(314) 367-2585

Western South Dakota Community Action Agency, Inc.
1331 West Main Street
Rapid City, South Dakota 57701
(605) 348-1460

Gibby Edwards

New York City Youth Corps workers unload compost for a garden sponsored by USDA's Urban Gardening Program.

[1] The Chittenden Community Correctional Center gardening Program is also mentioned in Food Section, p.50.

[2] *Guide to Community Garden Organization* is available for $2 by writing postpaid to Gardens for All, 180 Flynn Avenue, Burlington, Vermont 05401.

[3] A one-year membership fee to the National Association for Gardening is $10.

[4] The General Services Administration's (GSA) Living Buildings Program* makes Federal buildings available to the public for art shows, meetings and other activities. An offshoot of that program, the Community Gardens Program,* makes land surrounding Federal buildings available for community gardeners.

[5] The Trust for Public Land (TPL) is also profiled in Food Section, p. 48. (For more information on TPL, see Resources at end of Food Section.)

[6] The sixteen cities participating in the United States Department of Agriculture's (USDA) Urban Gardening Demonstration Program* include Atlanta, Georgia; Baltimore, Maryland; Boston, Massachusetts; Chicago, Illinois; Cleveland, Ohio; Detroit, Michigan; Houston, Texas; Jacksonville, Florida; Los Angeles, California; Memphis, Tennessee; Milwaukee, Wisconsin; Newark, New Jersey; New Orleans, Louisiana; New York, New York; Philadelphia, Pennsylvania; St. Louis, Missouri.

[7] The St. Louis Human Development Corporation is a Community Action Agency (CAA)* funded by the Community Services Administration's (CSA) Community Action Program (CAP).*

[8] The Tompkins County Economic Opportunity Corporation is also mentioned in Food Section, p. 72.

* State and/or local government agencies are frequently responsible for administration of Federal program funds. For further information, see Appendix I under appropriate Federal agency.

NOTE: For a complete listing of groups featured throughout this book, see Index.

FOOD STAMPS
OPERATION
BROTHERHOOD'S
WEST CENTER
522-0433
Handicapped
522-0433

Providing Food And Better Nutrition for All

Introduction

As food prices rise, many people, especially the poor and the elderly, have a difficult time maintaining nutritious diets. They might not be able to afford the quality and variety of food that helps keep them healthy. And many don't know where to go for help in overcoming hunger and malnutrition.

In this chapter we look at citizen organizations that are fighting poor nutrition by giving people, regardless of income, a chance to eat well.

Fortunately, Food Stamp, School Breakfast and similar Federal programs enable people to eat better. But to take advantage of these worthy programs, people must know about and have access to them. That's where citizen action comes in.

In this chapter we see how community groups have used a variety of programs to improve nutrition for low-income citizens. We explore the country's first community-based food stamp distribution center which reaches those people who need it most; a unique lobbying campaign that led to the implementation of school breakfast programs in a number of Tennessee schools; and a senior citizens center that helps elderly residents maintain nutritious diets by providing meals, a mobile grocery, gardens and a greenhouse.

Finally, we show the value of political action in helping the hungry and the poor tackle high food costs. We examine a successful campaign in the state of Washington to repeal the food sales tax, which hits hardest at low-income families.

All these efforts mean that fewer people are going hungry—a worthwhile and rewarding goal.

Food Stamps

Food Stamp Program
Watts Labor Community Action Committee
11401 South Central Avenue
Los Angeles, California 90059
(213) 564-5901

The Federal government's Food Stamp Program,* administered by the United States Department of Agriculture (USDA), helps millions of eligible low-income families buy food they otherwise could not afford. Today over 16 million needy people receive food stamps—coupons that can be used like cash to buy food or garden seeds. Still, lack of public awareness about eligibility, as well as distribution problems, keep the program from reaching another 10 million who need help.

Sometimes government-designated food stamp centers can't reach all those eligible for program benefits. Centers may be located too far from poor neighborhoods and have limited business hours, they may lack the bi-lingual staff needed to communicate with residents who speak little English, or they may not have the resources to establish extensive outreach programs.

Some community-run issuing centers, however, have remedied these problems and, at the same time, stimulated local economic growth. Located within the communities they serve, these centers are contracted by state governments to issue food stamps.

The Success of Watts

The first, and one of the most successful such centers, is run by the Watts Labor Community Action Committee (WLCAC), a Community Action Agency (CAA).[1] Since 1969 WLCAC has issued food stamps to over 1,500 households monthly. This nonprofit group, based in a low-income area of Los Angeles, California, is now one of the largest anti-poverty organizations in the country. In 1978 they had an operating budget of nearly $11 million with 120 paid staffers. WLCAC owns and operates everything from a community gas station to a credit union to an employment training program.[2]

But one of their most important contributions is their food stamp program.

Beginnings

In 1967 a regional USDA administrator approached WLCAC about taking over the local food stamp program. Impressed by the organization's track record and sensitivity to community concerns, the administrator felt that the group would be more effective in reaching needy citizens than other local distributors. Some traditional food stamp outlets, such as banks, viewed issuing food stamps to community members as a disruption of business. Also, many eligible food stamp recipients, too embarrassed or proud to apply at traditional centers, found it easier to turn to community-run organizations for help.

The Challenge

WLCAC accepted the challenge and set out to meet the Federal and state requirements necessary to become an official issuing center.[3] With funding from foundations and local community organizations, they were able to hire an administrator and an accountant. In addition, five youths from the Neighborhood Youth Corps, WLCAC's youth employment group, assisted the two paid workers. These people later trained new employees as the food stamp program expanded.[4]

Spreading the Word

With the groundwork laid, WLCAC's next step was to spread the message that food stamps were available through a locally run organization and educate residents about eligibility requirements. The staff launched a media blitz. Public service announcements were aired on TV and radio, and flyers were handed out door-to-door by the youth workers. Word-of-mouth also contributed to the growth of the program.

The results have been gratifying. Participation in Watts after the center's first year mushroomed by 30 percent. And WLCAC now operates two more centers. In 1978 alone the group issued food stamps valued at over $20 million.

Outreach

Other communities have also sought to expand food stamp use through effective outreach campaigns. The Indiana Nutrition Campaign (INC) in Indianapolis, a private, nonprofit group, has a statewide food stamp outreach program which has successfully disseminated accurate food and nutrition information to Indiana residents.

And in Ithaca, New York a successful promotion campaign by the Tompkins County Economic Opportunity Corporation, a CAA, has boosted food stamp participation by using such methods as providing transportation for applicants, establishing a hotline and hiring a coordinator with funds from the state's Department of Social Services.[5]

Sample Six-Week Food Stamp Campaign

Week One: Getting Started
- Call initial meeting to explain campaign, plan dates and times of prescreening sessions, determine tasks to be done, etc.;
- Continue throughout the week to firm up committees and recruit volunteers through churches and other organizations;
- Begin arranging for public service announcements (PSAs) on local radio and television stations.

Week Two: Publicity
- Inform local food stamp office about the campaign;
- Hold press conference to announce campaign to local media;
- Announce pertinent information on PSAs and in church bulletins;
- Hold initial committee meetings;
- Continue recruiting and organizing volunteers to flood community with leaflets and conduct prescreening.

Week Three: Publicity and Education
- Display posters and distribute leaflets at stores, health centers, etc.;
- Begin speaking to community groups and arranging interviews for radio and television shows;
- Publish endorsements of campaign by prominent citizens in local newspapers.

Week Four: Training and Publicity
- Train prescreeners and make site arrangements;
- Continue to freshen television and radio ads;
- Bulk mail leaflets to residents, if possible;
- Assign volunteers to provide needed transportation and other services;
- Place flyers in banks, stores, post offices, etc.;
- Consider follow-up press conference.

Week Five: Prescreening
- Distribute more leaflets, particularly to grocers;
- Confirm prescreening arrangements;
- Arrange appointment with food stamp office for following week to certify new clients;
- Conduct heavy media campaign day before prescreening begins;
- Plan two full days of prescreening with late hours (such as 1–9 p.m.).

Week Six: Certification
- Remind clients the evening before of appointments with food stamp office and what to bring;
- Arrange needed transportation and child care;
- Accompany applicants and monitor certification, if needed;
- Follow up on problems;
- CELEBRATE! Throw a party to thank—and credit—volunteers.

Adapted from "A Six-Week Affair: Increasing Food Stamp Participation Awareness," CFNP (Community Food and Nutrition Program) REPORT No. 28, February 1, 1979, Community Nutrition Institute (CNI), 1146 19th Street, N.W., Washington, D.C. 20036. (Food stamp campaign developed by Pete Sessa and Kay Kosow.)

In Zanesville, Ohio the Muskingum Citizens for Nutrition (MCN), a nonprofit community group, found that a short-term and inexpensive food stamp outreach and publicity campaign can reach thousands of people. In less than six weeks MCN, operating on a shoestring budget of $100, organized a campaign that increased food stamp participation in the county by 1,200 people.

Peter Sessa, a legal services attorney who helped organize MCN's campaign, with long-distance help from Kay Kosow, an organizer for Utahans Against Hunger, has developed a manageable outreach campaign model that runs no longer than six weeks and can be adapted to fit local needs. (See Chart: "Sample Six-Week Food Stamp Campaign.")

Groups Highlighted

Indiana Nutrition Campaign, Inc.
38 North Pennsylvania Avenue, Suite 312
Indianapolis, Indiana 4204
(317) 634-4172

Muskingum County Citizens for Nutrition
333 Market Street
Zanesville, Ohio 43701
(614) 454-0161
(Program was short-term; no longer exists)

Tompkins County Economic Opportunity Corporation
318 North Albany Street
Ithaca, New York 14850
(607) 273-8816

[1] The Community Services Administration's (CSA) Community Action Program (CAP)* funds local Community Action Agencies (CAAs)* aimed at helping low-income residents with their food, housing, energy and other needs.

[2] The Watts Labor Community Action Committee (WLCAC) is also mentioned in Housing Section, p. 102.

[3] All food stamp issuers must be bonded and insured to cover possible loss. The amount of insurance needed is determined by the number of stamps likely to be in the issuer's inventory at any particular time. They must also meet security requirements which vary from state to state and include standards for physical facilities, alarm systems and safekeeping for coupons.

[4] There are several potential sources of funding other than private loans which may help organizations obtain the initial capital needed to start an issuing center: Community Services Administration's Community Action and Community Food and Nutrition Programs* are examples. Cooperatives may be eligible for financial and technical assistance from the newly created National Consumer Cooperative Bank.**

[5] The Tompkins County Economic Opportunity Corporation is also mentioned in Food Section, p. 68.

* State and/or local government agencies are frequently responsible for administration of Federal program funds. For further information, see Appendix I under appropriate Federal agency.

** For further information see Appendix II under "National Consumer Cooperative Bank."

NOTE: For a complete listing of groups featured throughout this book, see Index.

How to Determine Food Stamp Eligibility

To qualify for food stamps, a household's "net income," after approved deductions, must fall below the Federal poverty guidelines. For the period July 1979–July 1980, the net income for a four-member household was $596 per month.

How to Figure Net Income Using the New Deductions

Under the new food stamp procedures, there are three deductions:

A deduction of 20 percent of earned income for working households;

A standard $75 deduction for all households;

And a $90 maximum deduction for actual dependent care and excess shelter costs.

A case example of a four-member household:

The family's gross monthly income includes:

$200 in wages (earned income)
$210 in public assistance
$410 total GROSS income

Their monthly expenses include:

$ 40 in child care
70 in heat and utilities
120 in rent

USDA

USDA

To determine net monthly income

1. Subtract 20 percent deduction from earned income:

   $200 × .20 = $ 40
   $200 − 40 = $160

2. Add all other income:

   $160 + 210 = $370

3. Subtract the $75 standard deduction:

   $370 − 75 = $295

4. Subtract child care costs:

   $295 − 40 = $255 adjusted income

5. Determine balance available for excess shelter costs ($90 limit on combined dependent care and excess shelter deduction minus amount deducted for child care):

   $ 90 limit
   − 40 child care deduction
   $ 50 balance available

6. Determine whether household qualifies for excess shelter deduction (are shelter costs more than half of adjusted income?):

   $255 adjusted income
   ÷ 2 divided by two
   $128 (approximately)

   $ 70 heat and utilities
   + 120 rent
   $190 total shelter cost

7. Shelter cost is more than half of adjusted income. Therefore, determine amount of excess shelter cost:

   $190 total shelter cost
   − 128 half of adjusted income
   $ 62 excess shelter cost

Excess shelter cost ($62) is more than balance available after child care deduction was taken ($50). Therefore, no more than $50 can be deducted for excess shelter costs.

8. Determine net monthly income:

   $255 adjusted income
   − 50 shelter deduction
   $205 NET monthly income

To determine eligibility, see if household's net income is below income eligibility limits:

income limit for 4-person household: $596
household's net income: $205

To determine household's monthly benefits, subtract 30 percent of household's net income from the maximum allowed in food stamps for a four-person household ($209).[1]

$205 net income
× .30
$ 62

$209 maximum allowed
− 62
$147 food stamp allotment

[1] *Maximum food stamp allotments differ for various size households. USDA bases maximum amounts on a number of low-cost food items necessary for a balanced diet; i.e., the least amount of money a family could spend to get a nutritious, adequate diet.*

NOTE: Special medical and shelter deductions are available to households with elderly or disabled people.

Chart materials provided by Food and Nutrition Service (FNS), United States Department of Agriculture (USDA).

School Breakfast Campaigns

School Breakfast Program Campaign
MANNA
1502 Edgehill Avenue
Nashville, Tennessee 37212
(615) 242-3663

A few years ago, the kids were restless at Cavert, a school for children with behavioral disorders in Nashville, Tennessee. Too many of the 170 students, it seemed, weren't getting a proper breakfast at home. And even though a Federal program—inspired by studies directly linking nutrition to learning ability—would provide full funding of public school breakfasts, Nashville's School Board had turned down its own Blue Ribbon Panel's recommendation that the program be implemented immediately in the city.[1]

Two Cavert teachers were convinced that the students' hyperactivity and inability to concentrate were magnified by their poor eating habits. So in 1976 they turned to MANNA, a local anti-hunger coalition, for help.

This largely volunteer group encouraged Cavert's principal, teachers and parents to help them research the issue. Within four months Nashville's School Board reversed itself. The program at Cavert soon spread to other Nashville schools. And by 1979 over 4,000 first through ninth graders in 39 of the city's public schools began their day with a nutritious school breakfast.

Martha Monroe, principal of Cavert School, has seen the change in her students firsthand: "Some of the children spend an hour-and-a-half on the school bus in the morning. That means leaving home at 6:30 a.m.—a time when nobody is in the mood to eat anything. So they are hungry when they get to school," she says. "Since the breakfast program, they are less restless, less hyperactive and it's made teaching a pleasure again."

Origins

MANNA began in 1975 as an all-volunteer community organization concerned with a range of hunger and food-related problems. Inspired by a series of city-sponsored national and international hunger seminars, Janet Christiansen, now executive director of MANNA, and several other concerned citizens launched a Hunger Watch Task Force aimed at boosting community concern about local, national and international hunger problems.

Students enjoy a hearty breakfast before starting the day.

Initial Funding

In the fall of 1975 MANNA incorporated, and in 1976 five local religious organizations pumped in $3,000 to hire a part-time coordinator for MANNA's activities. Among its impressive list of accomplishments, MANNA's effort to bring school breakfast programs to Nashville's children most aptly demonstrates the group's perseverance and hard work.

MANNA's Plan to Help Cavert

In response to Cavert teachers, MANNA set out to uncover why the breakfast program hadn't been started. They quickly rallied the support of the school's principal, teachers and parent leaders who formed a breakfast committee to push for the program. But when the committee set out to prove a school breakfast program was workable and needed, they were overcome by resistance.

Board Objections

School Board officials feared the program would cause bus and class scheduling headaches and boost administrative and labor costs. Moreover, they argued, the responsibility of providing breakfast rests with parents. And, they said, the majority of the public opposed the idea.

Rebuttal and Fact-Finding

Realizing that the support and involvement of parents and students was critical to their success, MANNA helped the committee gather ammunition. They sent out flyers to parents, made door-to-door visits and spoke at parent-teacher meetings. Other cities in the country are reaping the benefits of this program, the parents were told, why shouldn't we? The response was overwhelming.

Board Approval

Their tireless efforts paid off in the spring of 1977. After much negotiation, the Board approved Cavert's breakfast program.

The successful pilot project, which serves cold and hot breakfasts to 98 percent of Cavert's students, paved the way for similar programs in 27 Nashville public schools in the fall of that same year. MANNA is now helping 67 other counties in Tennessee start school breakfast programs.

Budget and Staff

In 1979 MANNA's operating budget of $31,000 was donated primarily by members, churches and community organizations. In addition, MANNA, as a sponsoring agent, channels about $200,000 yearly from the United States Department of Agriculture's (USDA) Child Care Food Program* to over 70 area Federal and private day care centers to ensure that thousands of mostly poor preschool children receive nutritious meals. Moreover, a grant from the Community Services Administration's (CSA) Community Food and Nutrition Program* pays the salaries of three regional coordinators, allowing the group to function statewide. And a grant from the United Methodist Church supports MANNA's food education program in Tennessee schools and communities.

With a staff of 40 and scores of volunteers, MANNA continues to play a leading role in awakening many in Tennessee to hunger and food-related problems.[2] It is the forerunner in bringing about a host of reforms and is credited with bringing a variety of food programs into Tennessee.[3]

Other Programs

Groups in other states have also tackled the problem of hungry students. In Alabama a group of cooperatives, church groups and local organizations formed the Alabama Coalition Against Hunger (ACAH) to encourage state and local agencies to request a share of the $20 million the Federal government provides annually for school breakfast programs. In one year alone, the coalition was instrumental in starting 138 new programs with 17,000 children participating.

And in Murrysville, Pennsylvania the Franklin Regional School Board and the school system's food services director took the initiative for implementing a school breakfast program. There, the main obstacle was parental pride. School officials sent press releases to local newspapers which reached 80 percent of the area's taxpayers. Many parents became supportive of the breakfast program after reading that lack of time and desire to eat—not parental neglect—were considered the reasons children came to school with empty stomachs.

Based in Norfolk, Virginia, the Southeastern Tidewater Opportunity Project (STOP) has formed an alliance of church, consumer and community groups which serves as a regional catalyst for increasing access to food and nutrition programs and advocacy and service efforts throughout Virginia.

In Kansas City, Kansas, PRAXIS, a nonprofit corporation, is involved in nutrition and education issues and provides training and technical assistance for hunger and food-related projects to community groups in Iowa, Kansas, Missouri and Nebraska.

Incorporated in 1975, its five-member Board of Directors includes clergy, educators and other professionals—all concerned with community development and nutrition. PRAXIS is credited with launching a food cooperative network in Kansas City and has received praise for its strong commitment and service to community food stamp outreach campaigns and the promotion of food and nutrition programs.

Groups Highlighted

Alabama Coalition Against Hunger
P.O. Box 409
Auburn, Alabama 36830
(205) 821-8336

Franklin Regional School Food Service
3220 School Road
Murrysville, Pennsylvania 15668
(412) 325-1977

PRAXIS
1620 South 37th Street
Kansas City, Kansas 66106
(913) 236-8336

Southeastern Tidewater Opportunity Project
415 St. Paul's Boulevard
Norfolk, Virginia 23510
(804) 627-3541

[1] In 1966 Congress amended the National School Lunch Act to include a School Breakfast Program,* which is administered by the United States Department of Agriculture (USDA). Under that program, low-income children are entitled to eat free while others pay according to their parents' income.

[2] MANNA's staff includes workers from ACTION's Volunteers in Service to America (VISTA) Program* and Title V of the Older Americans Act,* administered by the Department of Labor (DOL).

[3] Other MANNA efforts include a food stamp outreach campaign aimed at finding and assisting low-income families eligible for the United States Department of Agriculture's (USDA) Food Stamp Program* and a campaign to reach Nashville's low-income elderly who are eligible for the local Meals-On-Wheels Program.* That Program is administered by the Department of Health, Education and Welfare (HEW) under Title III of the Older Americans Act,* working in cooperation with the United States Department of Agriculture's (USDA) Food Distribution Program.*

* State and/or local government agencies are frequently responsible for administration of Federal program funds. For further information, see Appendix I under appropriate Federal agency.

NOTE: For a complete listing of groups featured throughout this book, see Index.

Help for the Elderly

Operation Brotherhood
3745 West Ogden Avenue
Chicago, Illinois 60623
(312) 522-0433

The high cost of food makes growing old even more difficult. Many of our country's elderly face particular obstacles in maintaining healthy diets. Those on fixed incomes are forced to limit the quantity and quality of their meals as inflation pushes up food prices. Others, at least partially immobilized by age and poor health, find it hard to get out and shop.

Seniors Get Assistance

A number of dedicated groups across the country have organized to help their elderly neighbors fight inflation and loneliness while improving nutrition. One of the most successful of these is Operation Brotherhood in Chicago. Each week 3,000 senior residents in the low-income, predominantly black Lawndale community are served by Operation Brotherhood's mobile grocery and other food programs. And the elderly find companionship and fun at Operation Brotherhood's community center, a converted factory complete with food store, recreation and dining rooms and food storage facilities. Moreover, many of the group's part-time paid staff and volunteers are senior Lawndale residents.

"Without Brotherhood I would be sitting in the house and I'd never get out," says 72-year-old Katherine Lindsley. "I don't have anybody—just friends. Before Brotherhood, there was nobody to take me anywhere." Lindsley, who calls herself an "old bachelor girl," was paralyzed by a stroke in 1952. Operation Brotherhood does her grocery shopping, provides her with household help and makes her life a lot less lonely. "They are so nice to everybody," she says. "They come pick me up and carry me over to the center to have dinner. A lot of people—all colors—go there. I love it."

Origins

Operation Brotherhood is the brainchild of Belle Whaley who, as a community coordinator for the Greater Lawndale Conservation Commission, saw first-hand the plight of Lawndale's elderly residents.[1] In 1970 she persuaded the Little Brothers of the Poor, a private, nonprofit group, to sponsor and let her run a small-scale kitchen and food delivery service for the older citizens of Lawndale. That operation reached about 300 elderly residents a week, but Whaley knew many more needed help. So in 1975 she broke away from Little Brothers of the

Checking out at Operation Brotherhood's food co-op

Poor to form Operation Brotherhood, an independent organization with expanded services.

Going it Alone

Through word of mouth, Whaley's operation gained the respect of the community, and she was able to woo $100,000 from Catholic Charities and private sources to shore up the meal programs and begin implementing plans for new services. With $33,000 from the Department of Labor's Comprehensive Employment and Training Act (CETA) Program,* 14 part-time workers were hired and trained to do difficult housekeeping chores for elderly residents. And a food cooperative was launched with $15,000 from Title III of the Older Americans Act,* administered by the Department of Health, Education and Welfare (HEW).[2]

Staff and Budget

Today Operation Brotherhood's budget of $500,000 comes from a variety of Federal, state and local agencies as well as donations from businesses, churches and industries.[3] The $12-a-year membership fee also helps defray costs. Lawndale residents and representatives from business, industry and community organizations make up the membership which elects the 37-strong Board of Directors charged with overseeing and approving Operation Brotherhood's programs.

A staff of 40 full-time and 12 part-time employees is bolstered by CETA workers and a score of community volunteers—many of them elderly. "One of the strengths of our organization," says Whaley, "is the older people who come in and share their wisdom and experience with us."

Food Resources

Operation Brotherhood gets the food it needs to run its programs in a variety of ways. Workers frequent wholesale markets, farmers' fields and the Greater Chicago Food Depository to find quality food at prices about one-fourth less than retail.[4] For the group's free food programs, flour and other staples are available from the United States Department of Agriculture's (USDA) Food and Nutrition Service.*

Tomatoes, beans and other vegetables are cultivated by volunteers on a minifarm—an acre of land donated by an Operation Brotherhood Board member. And two years ago, the Center for Neighborhood Technology (CNT), a nonprofit technical assistance organization, kicked in $9,000 to build a 360-foot greenhouse on the center's rooftop which yields between 1,200 and 1,800 pounds of fresh produce each year.[5]

Experienced hands cook meals for Operation Brotherhood's elderly.

Food Store and Roving Van

The food they gather is used for a number of Operation Brotherhood's programs. For example, the co-op food store offers elderly citizens a full range of grocery items as well as first aid and household needs at a scant 5 percent above wholesale prices. And the fully-stocked mobile grocery—staffed by a manager, nine cashiers and distribution aides—frequents seven low-income housing developments each week to serve those unable to shop at the center. A large corporation provided $5,000 to buy the food to launch the mobile grocery, and the specially built two-ton truck was donated by Chicago's Department of Human Services.

Dining Room

In the center's dining room, several cooks and four waitresses serve breakfast and lunch to about 200 elderly citizens each day. Diners pay what they can afford and get a greater variety of often more nutritious meals than they could prepare at home—and they gain the fellowship of being with people. Moreover, Operation Brotherhood workers prepare and send out about 20 meals a day to ailing residents.[6]

Elderly residents temporarily pinched for funds can also get help from Operation Brotherhood. Each month about 48 emergency food packages, valued at $14.50 each and filled with a week's supply of meat, produce and dairy products, are delivered to cashless residents by volunteers from the Jaycees.

Elderly citizens enjoy a meal in Operation Brotherhood's dining room.

Other Services

But more than just feeding goes on at Operation Brotherhood. The group offers counseling and referral services for those elderly citizens in need of housing or welfare. And Chicago's St. Luke's

Preparing mobile grocery store for the day's journey

Hospital provides two nurses who treat ailing residents at the center and in their homes.

Transportation is also provided. Drivers and a fleet of three minibuses and two cars stand ready to fetch those residents who need rides to the doctor, church, stores or the center.

Readying an item for sale at Operation Brotherhood's "good-as-new" shop

At the center, the elderly enjoy the camaraderie of their neighbors—talking, playing cards or watching television in the recreation area. Arts and crafts courses and physical fitness activities are also available.

Other Programs

Programs similar to Operation Brotherhood's have been established around the country. In 1975 two housewives from California's Bay Area started the Food Advisory Service (FAS), a food distribution center for senior citizens. Based in Brisbane, California, more than 7,000 elderly shoppers in seven northern California counties and Honolulu save 30 to 50 percent on fresh fruits, vegetables, meat and poultry at "minimarkets" set up in community halls and meeting centers.

In 1979 the Jefferson County Seniors' Resource Center, based in Lakewood, Colorado, provided a full range of services to about 12,000 senior citizens—reducing the unpleasantness of searching for help with such vital needs as health care, housing repair, food stamps and preparing income taxes. Free door-to-door transportation is provided for senior citizens who can't afford taxis for shopping, medical and personal needs. And every day senior citizens in an eight-county region get nutritious meals at one of 32 sites, paying whatever they can afford.

Groups Highlighted

Food Advisory Service
185 Valley Drive
Brisbane, California 94005
(415) 467-1343

•

Jefferson County Seniors' Resource Center
1651-C Kendall Street
Lakewood, Colorado 80214
(303) 238-8151

[1] The greater Lawndale Conservation Commission is a private, nonprofit organization whose goals are to conserve and rebuild the Lawndale community.

[2] Although not available in time to assist Operation Brotherhood, co-ops may now qualify for technical and financial assistance from the newly created National Consumer Cooperative Bank.**

[3] Operation Brotherhood is funded by a Community Services Administration's (CSA) Community Food and Nutrition Training and Technical Assistance Grant,* the Illinois Department on Aging, the Mayor's Office for Senior Citizens and the Handicapped and the city's Department of Human Services.

[4] The Greater Chicago Food Depository is a food bank similar to that of St. Mary's Food Bank, which is profiled in Food Section, p. 40.

[5] The Center for Neighborhood Technology's (CNT) community greenhouse projects are profiled in Food Section, p. 58. (For more information on CNT, see Resources at end of Food Section)

[6] Operation Brotherhood's Meals-On-Wheels Program* is administered by the Department of Health, Education and Welfare (HEW) under Title III of the Older Americans Act,* working in cooperation with the United States Department of Agriculture's (USDA) Food Distribution Program.*

* State and/or local government agencies are frequently responsible for administration of Federal program funds. For further information, see Appendix I under appropriate Federal agency.

**For further information, see Appendix II under "National Consumer Cooperative Bank."

NOTE: For a complete listing of groups featured throughout this book, see Index.

Elimination of Sales Tax on Food

Repeal of Sales Tax on Food in Washington State
Hunger Action Center
2524 16th Avenue, South
Seattle, Washington 98144
(206) 324-5730

Among the many penalties of being poor, some groups feel perhaps the cruelest is food taxation. They argue that a food sales tax adds to the already great burden shared by low- and fixed-income families who spend more of their income for food than others.

According to the Bureau of Labor Statistics, families who make between $5,000 and $6,000 yearly spend 22 percent of their income for food while those with incomes of more than $25,000 spend 7 percent. So for the family earning $25,000 or more, food taxes take a smaller percentage of their income than for the family earning only $6,000.

Today 30 states tax groceries through a general or specific food sales tax.[1] But it used to be 31—until some concerned Washington citizens set out to change the law. Despite opposition from the media and many community, business and political leaders, a broad-based citizens' coalition of over 50 organizations took their case to the people and won. They worked to get the issue on the ballot, and in 1977 proudly cheered as voters repealed the food tax law.

Origins

It all began with The Hunger Action Center, a non-profit corporation devoted to the development of new ways to tackle Washington's food and hunger problems. In the summer of 1974 members of the group began lobbying the state legislature to wipe out the food sales tax law. They argued that a family of four could buy an additional two and one-half weeks of groceries annually if they didn't have to pay food taxes.

But legislators were cool to conventional lobbying attempts, countering that repealing the food sales tax would cost the state $313 million annually in revenues and the resulting decline in social services would hit hardest at the poor. Hunger Action certainly didn't want to cut services to the poor, so the group offered counter proposals such as adopting a more progressive income tax structure, which would call for upper-income individuals to pay a higher tax rate.[2]

Organizing for Change

But their arguments fell on deaf ears. So the determined group formed a coalition of more than 50 senior citizen, consumer, child welfare and self-help groups. Nutritionists, political and media experts also joined the forces. In the spring of 1976, dubbing themselves the "Coalition Opposing Sales Tax on Food" (COSTOF), they waged a new battle.

With $20,000 primarily from Hunger Action, COSTOF's first step was to get 120,000 voter signatures on a petition calling for the question to be put on the 1977 election ballot.[3] Without these signatures, the issue could not be brought to a popular vote.

Selecting Repeal

By rallying around the moral issue—should people be taxed for one of the most important necessities of survival—COSTOF was able to gain the support of liberals and conservatives as well as attract media attention. Thousands of brochures were printed and distributed by COSTOF volunteers and public meetings were held to explain the issue. COSTOF argued that:

- Low-income families are hit harder than any other group by food taxes;
- Senior citizens on fixed incomes cannot afford higher food prices than necessary;
- Food prices are climbing faster than many other costs; and
- Food—a basic necessity of life—should not be taxed.

COSTOF supplemented their speeches, workshops and public forums with radio and television advertising, door-to-door visits, bumperstickers, posters and yardsigns. As a result of their active campaign, they delivered 175,000 signatures—45,000 more than needed—months before the deadline for the November 1977 election.

Food Taxes Hard to Swallow

When the ballots were counted, the residents of Washington had repealed the tax by a vote of 475,000 to 400,000. Since the food tax repeal, effective since July of 1978, low-income consumers spend approximately $142 less on their annual food bills. Moreover, opponents' fears have not been realized. And because the state has experienced a growth in population as well as rapid business reinvestment, state revenues have risen by 5 percent. These factors have led the state to lower the general sales tax by one-tenth of one percent.

Other State Initiatives

Food tax initiatives are underway in other states as well.[4] In Mississippi, after an unsuccessful attempt to get the entire food tax repealed, citizens began working to exempt low-income residents who participate in the Department of Agriculture's (USDA) Food Stamp Program.* They are hoping that the exemption will be put into effect over a two-year period to ease the anticipated burden on state revenues.

Group Highlighted

Mississippi Legal Services Coalition
P.O. Box 22887
Jackson, Mississippi 39205
(601) 944-0765

Food Sales Tax Burden in Washington State

Low-income family budget $5,000

40% of a low-income budget is used for food.
2.2% of a low-income budget is eaten away by the sales tax on food.

2.2% Tax

40% Food Costs

Moderate-low income budget $10,365

26% of a moderate income budget is used for food.
1.4% is swallowed-up by the sales tax on food.

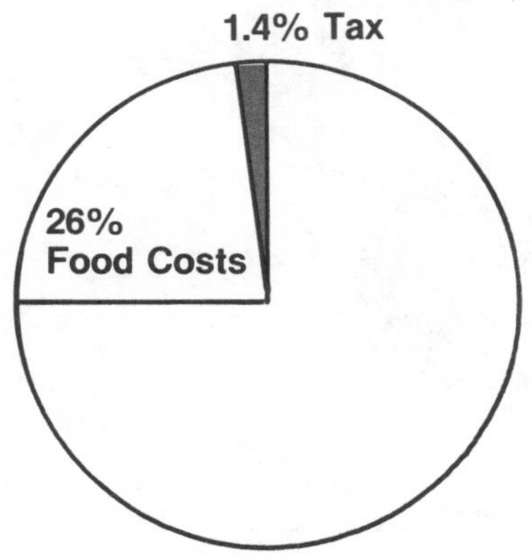

Higher-income budget $22,100

18% of a higher budget is used for food.
0.9% goes for the sales tax on food.

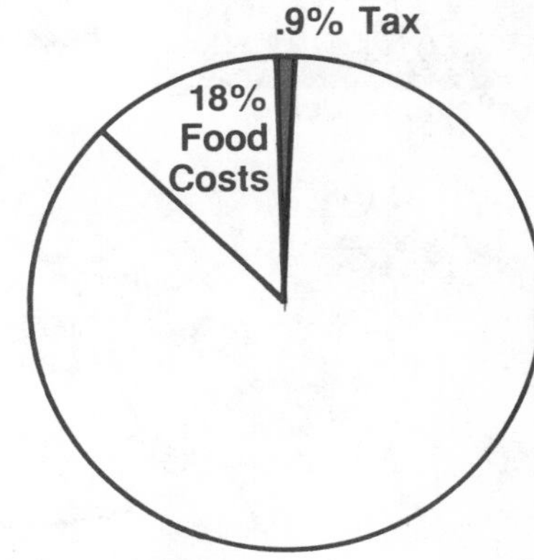

Adapted from "Food Taxes are Hard to Swallow," 1977, from Hunger Action Center.

[1] Those states which exempt food from taxation are: California, Connecticut, Florida, Indiana, Iowa, Kentucky, Louisiana, Maine, Maryland, Michigan, Minnesota, New Jersey, New York, North Dakota, Ohio, Pennsylvania, Rhode Island, Texas, Wisconsin, and Washington. (The District of Columbia also exempts food from taxation.) In addition, seven states offset food taxes by providing a tax credit. They are Colorado, Hawaii, Idaho, Massachusetts, Nebraska, New Mexico and Vermont.

[2] The Hunger Action Center discussed three other ways to replace the lost revenue: 1) increasing the general sales tax by 1 percent; 2) extending the sales tax to include non-essential professional services; and 3) closing business loopholes by 10 percent each year.

[3] Other organizations that could not give money to the Coalition Opposing Sales Tax on Food (COSTOF) contributed an equivalent of $40,000 in staff and labor, office space, equipment, supplies and expertise.

[4] Other states attempting to lessen the burden on the poor by promoting food tax repeals are Utah and Illinois.

* State and/or local government agencies are frequently responsible for administration of Federal program funds. For further information, see Appendix I under appropriate Federal agency.

NOTE: For a complete listing of groups featured throughout this book, see Index.

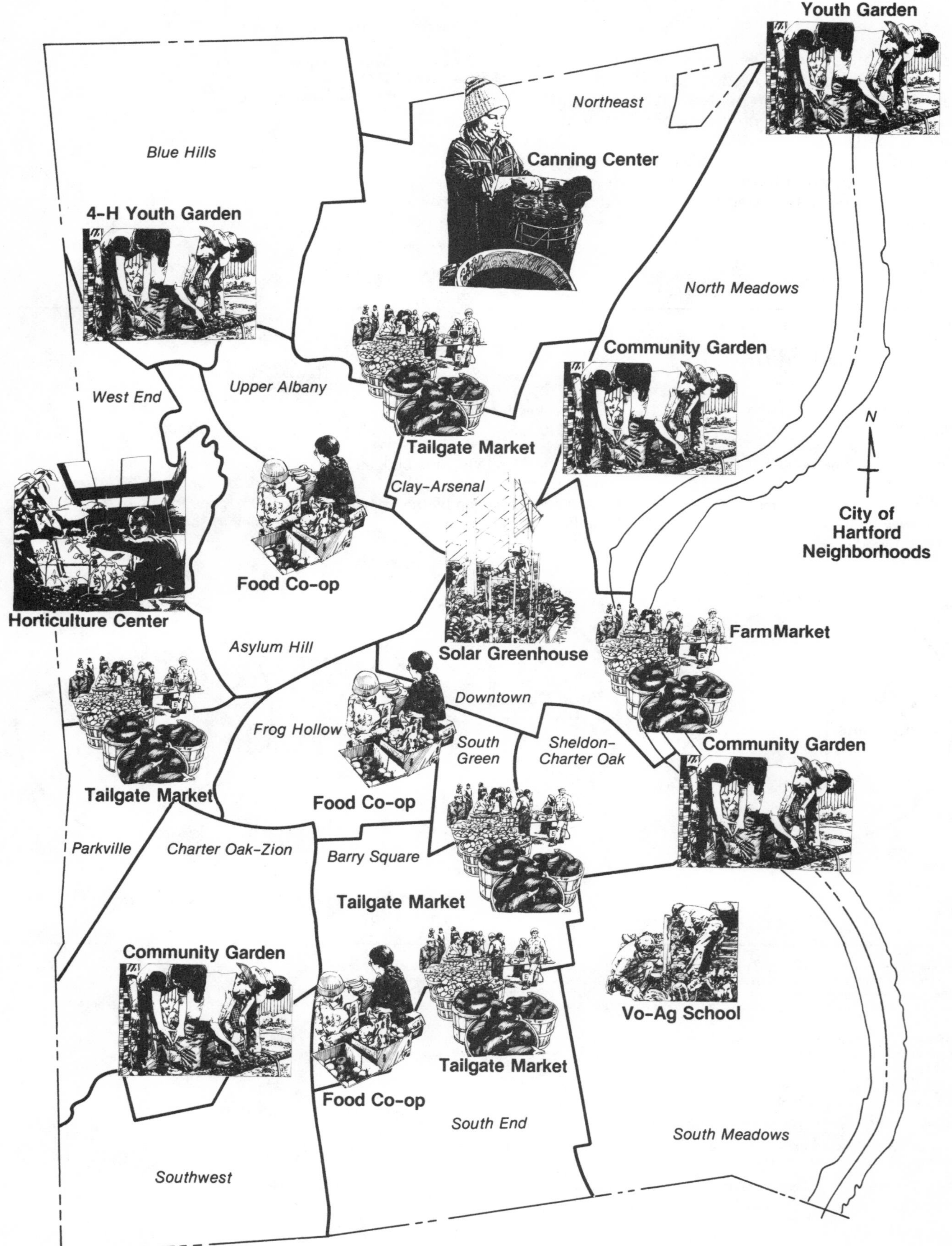
Youth Garden
Northeast
Blue Hills
Canning Center
4-H Youth Garden
North Meadows
Community Garden
West End
Upper Albany
Tailgate Market
N
Clay-Arsenal
City of
Hartford
Neighborhoods
Food Co-op
Horticulture Center
FarmMarket
Asylum Hill
Solar Greenhouse
Downtown
Frog Hollow
South
Green
Sheldon-
Charter Oak
Community Garden
Tailgate Market
Food Co-op
Parkville
Charter Oak-Zion
Barry Square
Tailgate Market
Community Garden
Vo-Ag School
Tailgate Market
Food Co-op
South End
South Meadows
Southwest

Fighting Food Inflation—The Comprehensive Approach

Introduction

In earlier chapters we've talked about such projects as farmers' markets, solar greenhouses, food co-ops, community gardens and canneries. The Hartford, Connecticut experience, profiled in this chapter, shows that it is indeed possible to put it all together in a comprehensive approach.

There, a coalition of citizens groups is fighting inflation on several fronts by tackling marketing, production and nutrition problems. And the resources of many different organizations in the city, both government and private, are being directed toward the goal of cutting residents' food bills.

A City Puts It All Together

The Hartford Food System
c/o Community Renewal Team
3580 Main Street
Hartford, Connecticut 06120
(203) 278-9950—Ext. 352

Although this nation is the best fed in the world, soaring food costs are causing many of our people to go hungry. But in Hartford, Connecticut the comprehensive Hartford Food System (HFS) is helping thousands of low- and middle-income families eat better, save an average of $500 a year on grocery bills and boost self-reliance by providing tools and by showing them how to grow, process and distribute their own food.[1]

By marshaling community resources, the Hartford System is giving residents access to food buying cooperatives and farmers' markets—all leading to self-reliance and better family nutrition.

Daniel Kelman

Bringing the farm to the city

Organization

HFS, a nonprofit corporation, is comprised of local foundations, research groups, community organizations, neighborhood development centers, city agencies and youth clubs. By mid-1980 the Hartford System aims to bolster four targeted inner-city neighborhoods—home to two-thirds of Hartford's population—with cost-saving food co-ops, community and youth gardens and farmers' markets.[2] Seedlings for the neighborhood gardens will come from a central solar greenhouse. And residents in each area will have access to a community cannery where they will learn food processing skills while canning their own produce.

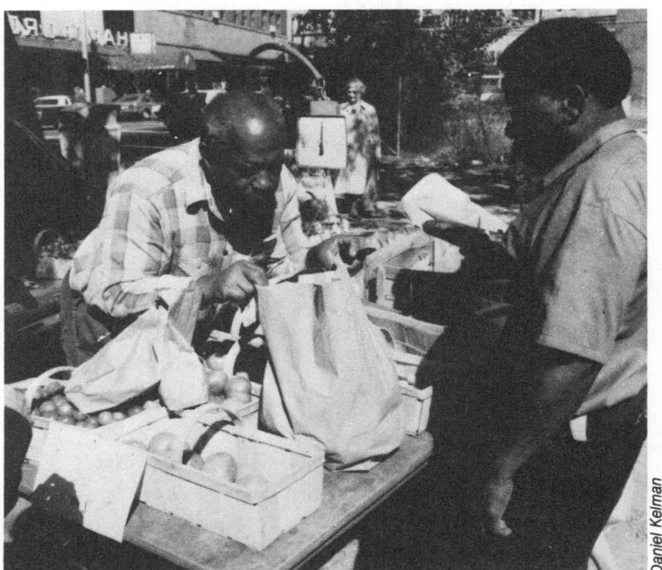

Daniel Kelman

Checking out at the downtown farmers' market

Goals

The goal of the Hartford Food System is to provide the technical tools necessary for each neighborhood to develop and control its own food system. And by including neighborhood representatives on its Board of Directors, all areas have direct input into the decisions affecting them.

Origins

The dynamic Hartford group began in the summer of 1977, when neighborhood residents and representatives from local and state advocacy groups met to explore solutions to the food problems of Hartford's mostly low- and moderate-income inner-city families. As a result of the meeting, the city commissioned the Public Resource Center, a Washington, D.C.-based research group, to conduct a study and outline a comprehensive solution to

Careful young planters begin their first garden.

reduce food costs for Hartford residents through increased self-reliance. That study laid the groundwork for the cooperative effort which was officially established as the Hartford Food System.

Outreach

To spread the word, the group talked to block clubs, tenant associations, senior centers and church organizations about the benefits of self-reliance.

And through a large but inexpensive promotion campaign which included displaying posters and distributing flyers and banners, they rallied resident support for the idea. In addition, they held news conferences, mailed out press releases and arranged radio and television public service announcements to promote consumer self-reliance.

Current Programs and Plans

Since the Food System was launched in the summer of 1978, several successful citywide programs have been established.

• **Farmers' Market**—Coordinated by the Connecticut Public Interest Research Group (ConnPIRG), the farmers' market enjoyed immediate success. Kip Bergstrom, one of the market's organizers, spoke to a local reporter about the first hectic market day. "We had nine farmers here and half of them had sold all their vegetables by noon." The 1979 farmers' market was equally successful and was four times larger than the previous year. That summer a survey conducted by workers from ACTION's Volunteers In Service to America (VISTA) Program* revealed that farmers' market shoppers paid an average 24 percent less than they would at supermarkets.

Daniel Kelman

Farmers' market shopper holds fresh golden prize.

• **Agriculture School**—The area vocational agriculture school, coordinated by the Hartford School Board, was also launched in 1978. The school provides practical training in all phases of food production and processing. And construction has begun on an agriculture vocational training wing at one of the area high schools—the first urban agriculture technical school in the country.

• **Community Gardens**—The community and youth gardening programs, started in 1979, involve 1,500 gardeners and are sponsored by the local Knox Park Foundation and the 4-H Youth Program* of the county Cooperative Extension Service,* working in conjunction with the United States Department of Agriculture (USDA).

• **Solar Greenhouses**—Two centralized passive solar greenhouses are under construction and scheduled for completion in the summer of 1980.[3] Eventually, with the addition of several more greenhouses, year-round gardening will be available for residents in each targeted neighborhood.

• **Cannery**—Nearly complete is the community cannery where residents will can their own produce and save 40 percent over commercially processed goods. The facility has the capacity to can 12,000 quarts in a growing season.

Funding

Full implementation of Hartford's programs is expected to cost approximately $250,000 (excluding the agriculture school).

The System has received funding for the varied programs from many sources. Among them are grants from the Hartford Foundation for Public Giving and the Whitney Foundation as well as assistance from the Department of Energy's (DOE) Appropriate Technology Small Grants Program* and the Department of Housing and Urban Development's Community Development Block Grant (CDBG) Program.* And ACTION has shown its support by channeling VISTA workers to help operate the programs.

Looking Ahead

Hartford plans to push forward with other innovations for the community. In the initial stages is a

Seattle Department of Community Development

Outside the food distribution warehouse in Seattle, Washington

food plant capable of producing, processing and storing food for a community-wide feeding program for seniors. Plans are also underway for creation of cooperative warehouses that will more closely link farmers and consumers.

Other Citywide Efforts

Another citywide program which is helping residents garden is the P-Patch Program in Seattle, Washington, named after Rainie Picardo who provided the first plot of land. Begun as a small elementary school program aimed at teaching children to grow vegetables, the P-Patch concept of community gardening has spread throughout the city and now includes nearly 1,000 plots, a composting program and, because of mild Washington winters, a winter program which includes a gardening workshop.[4]

And to further bolster resident food self-reliance, Seattle has set up the Neighborhood Technology Coalition (NTC), which consists of 16 neighborhood groups, to coordinate and monitor programs including community greenhouses, a food distribution warehouse, educational workshops and a processing center.[5]

Group Highlighted

Neighborhood Technology Coalition
c/o Metro Center YMCA
909 Fourth Avenue
Seattle, Washington 98104
(206) 447-3625

[1] The Hartford Food System (HFS) is also mentioned in Food Section, p. 37.

[2] A possible funding source for Hartford's food co-ops is the newly created National Consumer Cooperative Bank.**

[3] For a definition of a passive solar energy system, use glossary in Energy Section, p. 275.

[4] Composting is the process of turning decomposed vegetables, manure, other organic wastes and sometimes lime into a rich mixture (compost) used to fertilize and condition soil.

[5] For more information on the Neighborhood Technology Coalition (NTC), see Resources at end of Food Section.

* State and/or local government agencies are frequently responsible for administration of Federal program funds. For further information, see Appendix I under appropriate Federal agency.

**For further information, see Appendix II under "National Consumer Cooperative Bank."

NOTE: For a complete listing of groups featured throughout this book, see Index.

Food Resources

The following resources contain descriptions of organizations and publications which can be of help to consumer groups across the country that wish to organize and launch community projects designed to combat high prices.

Those organizations offering assistance in a variety of areas are listed under "General" and are followed by a list of publications under the same heading. Other organizations and publications that provide help in specific areas are listed under corresponding chapter title headings.

Of course, it is not possible to list every organization and publication in the country that might prove helpful to you and your group, but we believe those we do mention are representative of the various kinds of assistance available. Chances are you'll hear of many other useful resources as you become involved in your own community project.

Space limitations made it extremely difficult to choose among the many fine groups considered, and we sincerely hope we haven't offended the many deserving organizations and/or authors of useful publications that have not been included.

General Food

Organizations

Agricultural Marketing Project
2606 Westwood Drive
Nashville, Tennessee 37204
(615) 297-4088

Provides technical assistance to help organize food fairs, farmers' markets and nutrition education programs. Works with farmers on appropriate technology. Publishes bimonthly newsletter, *Farm, Food and Land.* ($3/year.)

Center for Neighborhood Technology
570 West Randolph Street
Chicago, Illinois 60606
(312) 454-0126

Provides technical assistance in energy, urban agriculture, solar greenhouses, waste recycling and training. Publishes bimonthly, *The Neighborhood Works,* which discusses alternative technology in neighborhood development. ($25/year.)

Conference on Alternative State and Local Policies Agriculture Project
2000 Florida Avenue, N.W.
Washington, D.C. 20009
(202) 387-6030

Provides information and concrete models to public officials and community activists. Organizes conferences and workshops in the area of innovative farm, land and food policies. Offers technical assistance to individuals and organizations forming state-wide agriculture and food policy coalitions. Serves as a clearinghouse on alternative legislation. Publishes bimonthly newsletter, *Ways and Means.* ($10/year.)

Council on the Environment of New York City
51 Chambers Street, Room 228
New York, New York 10007
(212) 566-0990

Provides information on urban gardens,open-space development, neighborhood parks, farmers' markets and composting. Publishes bimonthly newsletter, *Environmental Bulletin.* (Free.)

Domestic Technology Institute
Box 2043
Evergreen, Colorado 90439
(303) 674-1597

Conducts workshops on rural solar greenhouse design/construction, community energy technology, small-scale food production, nutrition and food preservation.

Earthwork
3410 19th Street
San Francisco, California 94110
(415) 626-1266

Clearinghouse for information on farm, food and land issues. Also concerned with direct marketing and food co-ops. Publications list available on request.

Food Policy Center
538 Seventh Street, S.E.
Washington, D.C. 20003
(202) 547-7070

Dedicated to eliminating world hunger and malnutrition. Monitors food policy and development legislation. Through research and public education, seeks the formulation of a coherent food policy designed to end hunger. Publishes monthly, *Food Policy Center News Views.* (Free.)

Hartford Food Systems, Inc.
c/o Community Renewal Team of Greater Hartford
3580 Main Street
Hartford, Connecticut 06120
(203) 278-9950

Cooperative network of self-help food programs designed to provide an opportunity for residents to participate directly in the production, distribution and consumption of high quality food at a lower cost.

Institute for Local Self-Reliance
1717 18th Street, N.W.
Washington, D.C. 20009
(202) 232-4108

Offers technical assistance on community gardens, neighborhood parks, waste recycling, community-based economic development projects, etc. Publishes bimonthly newsletter, *Self-Reliance,* ($8/year to individuals, $15 to institutions.)

National Association of Farmworker Organizations
1332 New York Avenue, N.W.
Washington, D.C. 20005
(202) 347-2407

National coalition of community-based, farmworker-governed organizations. Works in support of civil and labor rights for migrant and seasonal farmworkers and provides training and technical assistance for programs that serve them. Assists in organizing emergency food programs for rural areas; provides technical assistance for nutrition education. Publishes bimonthly newsletter, *National Farmworker.* ($15/year.)

National Center for Appropriate Technology
P.O. Box 3838
Butte, Montana 59701
(406) 494-4577

Offers technical assistance and small grants to primarily low-income groups working with appropriate technology and self-help projects in areas such as food, housing and energy. Provides assistance to groups which demonstrate and develop technology that addresses problems of low-income people. Publishes monthly, *A.T. Times.* (Free.)

Neighborhood Technology Coalition
c/o Metro Center YMCA
909 Fourth Avenue
Seattle, Washington 98104
(206) 447-3625

Develops and supports programs for neighborhood groups aiming to reduce food costs through alternative food projects. Works to secure Federal community development funding for such efforts.

Tennessee Valley Authority
Small Farm Management Program
Division of Agricultural Development
Muscle Shoals, Alabama 35660
(205) 386-2601

Provides grants and technical assistance in direct marketing, alternative energy projects, greenhouse construction and use, etc. Conducts research and development programs in forestry, fish and game services and economic development.

Publications

Agriculture in the City—El Mirasol Education Farm. Community Environmental Council, 924 Anacapa Street, Suite B4, Santa Barbara, California 93101. 1976. ($2.50.) Provides a summary of the operation of the El Mirasol Urban Farm. Includes tips on urban organic farming.

Belden, Joe; Edwards, Gibby; Guyer, Cynthia; and Webb, Lee. ***New Directions in Farm, Land and Food Policies.*** Conference on Alternative State and Local Policies, 2000 Florida Avenue, N.W., Washington, D.C. 20009. 1980. ($9.95.) Focuses on state and local farm, land and food issues. Provides analysis of such issues and lists many additional resources.

Food Monitor. Food Monitor, Inc., P.O. Box 1975, Garden City, New York 11530. Bimonthly magazine. ($15/year.) Presents articles on the family farm, agricultural policy, nutrition, rural development and food-aid programs. Lists other publications that may be of interest.

The Integral Urban House: Self-Reliant Living in the City. Farallones Institute, 1516 Fifth Street, Berkeley, California 94710. 1979. ($14.50.) Serves as a resource guide for the city dweller who wants to develop an economic self-sustaining lifestyle.

New Roots. Northeast Appropriate Technology Network, Inc., P.O. Box 548, Greenfield, Massachusetts 01301. Bimonthly. ($8/year to individuals, $12 to institutions.) Covers the movement toward self-reliance. Encourages local control of food, housing and social needs.

New York Self-Help Handbook. Citizens Committee for New York, Inc., 3 West 29th Street, Sixth Floor, New York, New York 10001. 1978. ($6.10.) Contains information on more than 100 neighborhood self-help projects in New York. Subject areas include food, housing, health care, energy, neighborhood preservation, etc. Applicable to groups outside of New York City.

Rain: The Journal of Appropriate Technology. Rain Magazine, 2270 N.W. Irving, Portland, Oregon 97210. Ten issues per year. ($15.) Provides information to individuals who are seeking ways to make their communities and regions economically self-reliant.

Rainbook: Resources for Appropriate Technology. Schocker Books, 200 Madison Avenue, New York, New York 10016. 1977. ($7.95 paperback, $15 hardcover.) Resource book that provides options and choices through appropriate technology in the areas of food, energy, economics and health.

Smith, Frank, ***Food in the City.*** Public Resource Center, 1747 Connecticut Avenue, N.W., Washington, D.C. 20009. 1977. ($3.) Report of the Urban Food Conference held in Washington, D.C. in 1977. Papers focus on roles of alternative food systems in meeting the urban food crisis, nutrition and food quality in urban areas, organizing a low- and middle-income food co-op and gardening in the city.

Washington Consumers' Checkbook: Food. Washington Center for the Study of Services, Fourth Floor, 1518 K Street, N.W., Washington, D.C. 20005. 1979. ($4.95.) Dedicated to helping Washington area consumers find high quality, reasonably priced services. Suggests many cost-saving tactics for trimming the food bill.

Finding Marketing Alternatives

Organizations

Agricultural Teams
Farm to Market Project
436 Alameda Avenue
Youngstown, Ohio 44505
(216) 746-8551

Project on direct marketing alternatives for low-income and minority farmers and consumers. Publishes annually, *Annual Report and Description of Services.* (Free.)

All Cooperating Assembly
P.O. Box 6022
Minneapolis, Minnesota 55406
(612) 376-8357

Regional clearinghouse of education, information and resources for food cooperatives, collectives and buying clubs. Assists with new co-ops and helps to improve existing ones. Publishes monthly magazine, *Scoop.* ($5/year to individuals, $10 to institutions.)

Boston Farmers' Markets
Division of Land Use
Massachusetts Department of Food and Agriculture
100 Cambridge Street
Boston, Massachusetts 02202
(617) 727-6633

Provides technical assistance to community groups working on farmers' markets and urban agriculture projects. Publishes *Report on Boston Farmers' Markets . . . Stalk Exchange.* (Free.)

Cooperative League of USA
1828 L Street, N.W.
Washington, D.C. 20036
(202) 872-0550

Trade association of producer and consumer cooperatives. Maintains extensive publications list. Publishes monthly newsletter, *In League.* ($5/year to members.)

Greenmarket
24 West 40th Street
New York, New York 10018
(212) 840-7355

Provides technical assistance, contacts and resources on farmers' markets and direct marketing alternatives. Assists with farmland preservation and land-use planning. Publishes monthly newsletter, *Greenmarket News.* ($4/year.)

National Family Farm Coalition
918 F Street, N.W., Second Floor
Washington, D.C. 20004
(202) 638-6848

Coordinates information and public education on the Family Farm Development Act introduced in Congress in 1980. Strives to improve family farm income and to protect and conserve soil. Publishes *Periodic Membership Update* and *Legislative Alert.* (Free to members.)

New England Co-op Training Institute
Food Co-op Training Center
384 Whalley Avenue, Room 226
New Haven, Connecticut 06511
(203) 776-0451

Provides speakers, workshops and technical assistance for food co-ops, as well as training for Board members and staff. Supplies resource material and general information on all aspects of cooperatives and the food industry. Major work is regional (New England), but will lend assistance to others.

New School for Democratic Management
589 Howard Street
San Francisco, California 94105
(415) 543-7973

Provides basic business instruction for small organizations (food co-ops, housing co-ops, senior citizens' organizations, community development centers, etc.). Numerous publications available.

North American Students of Cooperation
Box 7293
Ann Arbor, Michigan 48107
(313) 663-0889

Provides education, publications and technical services to members and the public. Offers workshops for Boards of Directors of cooperatives nationwide. Publishes bimonthly, *Co-op Magazine.* ($8.67/year to individuals, $10.50 to institutions.)

Pennsylvania Department of Agriculture
2301 North Cameron Street
Harrisburg, Pennsylvania 17110
(717) 787-4737

Responsible for inspection of food products and accuracy of weights and measures. Provides technical assistance on direct marketing to farmers and farm product companies.

Rural Resources, Inc.
Rural Route 1, Box 11
Loveland, Ohio 45140
(no phone)

Serves as an educational forum for rural communities on matters such as food resources and farm/land issues. Provides lectures and consultation on rural and food issues.

Second Harvest Food Banks
1001 North Central, Suite 303
Phoenix, Arizona 85004
(602) 252-1777

National food gleaning network which provides on-going training, technical assistance and workshops in establishing food banks. Coordinates distribution of national manufacturers' surplus food. Publishes quarterly newsletter, *Thought for Food.* (Free.)

Strongforce
2121 Decatur Place, N.W.
Washington, D.C. 20008
(202) 234-6883

Provides various publications and workshops on community/worker controlled businesses such as food co-ops and buying clubs.

West Virginia Department of Agriculture
State Capitol
Charleston, West Virginia 25305
(304) 348-2201

Provides technical assistance on direct marketing and information on best food buys. Publishes quarterly newsletter, *Consumer Newsletter.* (Free.)

Publications

Alternative Marketing Systems. Rural America, Inc., 1346 Connecticut Avenue, N.W., Washington, D.C. 20036. 1977. (65 cents.) Gives brief description of several ways to by-pass the middleman in the marketing of farm products. Includes lengthy resource listing.

Co-op Stores and Buying Clubs. Publications Department, Community Services Administration, Office of Public Affairs, 1200 19th Street, N.W., Washington, D.C. 20506. 1972. (Free.) Emphasizes the preliminary process of deciding what type of co-op structure will be most beneficial to an organization or group.

Cotterill, Ronald; Freshwater, David; and Houseman, David. ***More Effective Direct Marketing: A Proposal to Establish an Inner-City Farmer-Consumer Warehouse in Detroit, Michigan.*** Agricultural Economics Department, Michigan State University, East Lansing, Michigan 48824. 1977. (Staff paper #77-101, free.) Has application for groups elsewhere.

"Emergency Food," ***Food Monitor,*** Department 1, P.O. Box 1975, Garden City, New York 11530. Issue 11, 1979. ($1/copy.) Cites several working examples of community food programs and explains how to establish similar programs.

A Food Co-op and Buying Club Organization Kit. Nutritional Development Services, Archdiocese of Philadelphia, 222 North 17th Street, Philadelphia, Pennsylvania 19103. 1978. ($1.50.) A basic step-by-step guide to organizing a food club. Includes a resource listing.

Food Co-op Directory. Cooperative Directory Association, P.O. Box 4218, Albuquerque, New Mexico 87196. ($5 to individuals; $10 to commercial, libraries and professionals.) Tracks the co-op movement by updating and printing lists of federations, warehouses and regional contacts as well as a list of newsletters and other directories.

How-to Manual on Emergency Food Banks. Northeast Task Force, 99 Washington Avenue, Room 1111, Albany, New York 12210. 1980. (Free.) Step-by-step guide for operating a community food bank. Provides information on facilities needed, how to get help from organizations and how to conduct food drives.

Organizer's Guide for Setting Up an Open Air Farmers' Market. Food Resource Developer, Executive Office of Communities and Development, 10 Tremont Street, Boston, Massachusetts 02108. 1980. ($1.) Step-by-step guide including information on organizing, task descriptions and resource listing.

Pike Place Market News. Pike Place Merchants Association, 1900 Pike Place, Seattle, Washington 98101. Monthly. ($5/year.) Contains information relevant to the market community in the Seattle area. Includes profiles of people involved with and current issues affecting the market. Has application for groups wanting to learn about farmers' markets.

Ronco, William, *Food Co-ops: An Alternative to Shopping in Supermarkets.* Beacon Press, 25 Beacon Street, Boston, Massachusetts 02108. 1974. ($3.95.) Relates experiences of people in cooperatives and emphasizes human resources.

Stern, Gloria, *How to Start Your Own Food Co-op.* Walker and Company, 720 Fifth Avenue, New York, New York 10019. 1974. ($4.95.) Probes the concept of starting a food co-op to save money.

Thomas Grocery Register. Circulation Director, Thomas Grocery Register, 110 Plaza, New York, New York 10001. Revised yearly. ($69/year.) Large three-volume catalog providing information on food and grocery items categorized by Products and Services, Brand Names and Sales and Distribution. Lists suppliers of items within each category.

Vellela, Tony, *Food Co-ops for Small Groups.* Workman Publishing Company, 1 West 39th Street, New York, New York 10008. 1975. ($2.95.) Describes how a group can start and operate a food co-op.

NOTE: Also see Food Resources under "General."

Growing and Processing Your Own Food

Organizations

Boston Urban Gardeners (BUG)
300 Massachusetts Avenue
Boston, Massachusetts 02115
(617) 267-4825

Coalition of neighborhood community organizations and urban agriculture enthusiasts. Provides technical assistance and organizes workshops. Publishes newsletter, *BUG.* (5 or 6 issues/ year, $1.)

California Office of Appropriate Technology
1530 10th Street
Sacramento, California 95814
(916) 322-8901

Assists and advises organizations in the development and implementation of less costly and less energy-intensive technologies and programs. Areas include waste recycling and conversion, food supply and land use, building design and energy and water conservation. Publishes bimonthly, *Grants Newsletter.* (Free.)

Gardens for All
180 Flynn Avenue
Burlington, Vermont 05401
(802) 863-1308

National clearinghouse of gardening information to assist all who want to garden. Lobbies for more land and resources for gardeners. Publishes materials of interest to gardeners. Also, quarterly newspaper, *Gardens for All News.* ($10/year.)

Northeast Task Force for Food and Farm Policy
99 Washington Avenue, Room 1111
Albany, New York 12210
(518) 455-5203

Provides information on canning and preserving and sponsors various food conferences. Its subcommittee, the National Clearinghouse on Food Preservation, provides information on food processing procedures and potential funding sources.

Solar Sustenance Team
Route 1, Box 107AA
Santa Fe, New Mexico 87501
(505) 455-7550

Involved with the design and construction of solar greenhouses. Provides workshops to train people to lead solar greenhouse workshops. Numerous publications available. Offers a 35mm slide/ audio tape presentation, *The Solar Greenhouse,* which features such topics as design, construction and horticulture. 1978. ($90.)

Trust for Public Land
82 Second Street
San Francisco, California 94106
(415) 495-4015)

Provides information, training, technical assistance and financing for community ownership of land. Assists in a variety of open space projects, community gardens, parks, etc. Publications include *Citizen's Action Manual: A Guide to Recycling Vacant Property in Your Neighborhood.* 1979. (Free.)

Publications

Community Gardening: A Handbook. Brooklyn Botanic Garden, 1000 Washington Avenue, Brooklyn, New York 11225. 1979. ($2.55.) Manual on how to start and operate a community garden. Chapters contributed by 27 experienced gardeners giving case histories from all over the United States, as well as observations on why some programs have succeeded and others have not.

A Complete Course in Canning. Canning Trade, Inc., 2619 Maryland Avenue, Baltimore, Maryland 21218. 1975. (Two-volume set $45; special price to students, $15 per volume.) Textbook for students on food technology, food plant management, etc. Complete coverage of canning along with detailed information on the processing of more than 200 canned products.

Guide to Community Garden Organization. Gardens for All, 180 Flynn Avenue, Burlington, Vermont 05401. 1977. ($2.) Provides tips on gardening and a step-by-step guide for organizing and building community garden projects.

The Integral Urban House: Self-Reliant Living in the City. Farallones Institute, 1516 Fifth Street, Berkeley, California 94710. 1979. ($14.50.) Applies the concept of the ecosystem to the urban dwelling. Develops an appropriate technology around all systems linked together within a dwelling, such as food cultivation, energy use and waste disposal.

Life Begins . . . The Day You Start a Garden. Gardens for All, 180 Flynn Avenue, Burlington, Vermont 05401. 1979. (Free.) Describes the Gardens for All organization and the benefits and advantages derived from gardening.

Organic Gardening and Farming Magazine. Organic Gardening, 33 East Minor Street, Emmaus, Pennsylvania 18049. Monthly. ($9/year.) Provides information on vegetable gardening year-round, plus tips for planning and planting. Covers other food-related topics such as cooking, nutrition, etc.

NOTE: Also see Food Resources under "General."

Providing Food and Better Nutrition for All

Organizations

Center for Science in the Public Interest
1755 S Street, N.W.
Washington, D.C. 20009
(202) 332-9110

Involved in research and education activities which focus on nutrition, food programs and the food industry. Publishes monthly, *Nutrition Action,* which carries articles on nutrition, food policy and family farmers. ($10/year.)

Children's Foundation
1420 New York Avenue, N.W., Suite 800
Washington, D.C. 20005
(202) 347-3300

Works in support of poor children and their families in the struggle against hunger in the United States. Strives to achieve fully responsive food assistance programs at the national, state and local levels. Reviews and analyzes Federal food assistance programs and assists community groups working to improve or establish programs. Numerous publications available.

Community Nutrition Institute (CNI)
1146 19th Street, N.W.
Washington, D.C. 20006
(202) 833-1730

Works on food and nutrition issues such as hunger, nutrition research, food programs, labeling and other marketing issues. Publishes *CNI Weekly Report,* which monitors food policy and program development from a consumer viewpoint. ($25/year.)

Food Research Action Center
2011 Eye Street, N.W.
Washington, D.C. 20006
(202) 452-8250

Public interest law firm which works in support of low-income people and communities to end hunger and malnutrition. List of publications available at no charge.

Publications

Eating Better at School: An Organizer's Guide. Sponsored by the Center for Science in the Public Interest, 1755 S Street, N.W., Washington, D.C. 20009 and The Children's Foundation, 1420 New York Avenue, N.W., Washington, D.C. 20005. 1980. ($2, multiple copies available.) Guide for organizing campaigns for the improvement of school food. Includes steps in launching a successful campaign, success stories, health facts, discussion of food issues, school lunch information, contacts and other guidance.

Katz, Deborah and Goodwin, Mary, *Food: Where Nutrition, Politics and Culture Meet.* Center for Science in the Public Interest, 1755 S Street, N.W., Washington, D.C. 20009. 1976. ($4.50.) Serves as a resource and activity guide for teachers in high schools and colleges.

Simko, Margaret D. and Babich, Kathleen S., *Home Delivered Meals: A Selected Annotated Bibliography.* Department of Health, Education and Welfare, Administration on Aging, Washington, D.C. 20201. 1974. (Publication No. OHD 74-20195, free.) Selected bibliography presenting comprehensive coverage of information on the subject of meals for the homebound.

Wieloszynski, Roberta B., *Toward a Rational Policy on Nutrition and Food in America.* Syracuse Consumer Affairs Office, 442 City Hall, Syracuse, New York 13203. 1976. (Free.) Booklet provides recommendations for improving the diet of Americans.

The following publications are available from the Food Research and Action Center, 2011 Eye Street, N.W., Washington, D.C. 20006:

Guide to the Food Stamp Program. 1979. ($1.) Question-and-answer format explaining the program in simple terms.

Guide to the National School Lunch and Breakfast Programs. 1978. ($1.) Describes these two programs, outlines methods of organizing a school breakfast campaign and probes ways of improving meal quality.

Profile of the Federal Food Programs. 1979. (One copy free; multiple copies 30 cents each.) Outlines the seven major government food programs.

NOTE: Also see Food Resources under "General."

Cape and
Islands Tenant
Council Wants
Decent Year-R
Housing for All

Housing

General Introduction

Everyone needs housing but with interest rates and apartment rents skyrocketing, many of us have trouble affording it.

In the past 10 years new home prices have jumped by more than 127 percent and apartment rents have nearly doubled. These increases make it harder for all of us to buy or rent and properly maintain homes. It also means that good housing in decent neighborhoods is hard to come by for those who need it the most such as the poor and the elderly. All too often they lack decent, safe and sanitary housing and are forced to live in deteriorating neighborhoods without the services, safety or conveniences the rest of us take for granted.

Housing costs are more than just rent checks to a landlord or mortgage payments to a bank. There are also the costs of utilities, furniture, insurance, repairs and dozens of other expenses. As inflation pushes these costs upward, it becomes more difficult to keep our homes in good shape.

But housing inflation also affects our communities. If houses and apartments aren't kept up, neighborhoods become unattractive and seedy—perhaps even dangerous. Vacant buildings become more than symbols of decay. The neighborhood deterioration is real and directly affects the value of our own homes.

But neighborhood groups around the country, often starting with little more than desire and determination, are fighting high housing costs. In many cases they are joining with government and private agencies to find ways to get adequate, affordable housing for their communities.

The Housing Section's seven chapters are filled with ideas that you and your neighbors can use to tackle rising housing costs. Some of our profiled groups have helped low-income citizens find—and maintain—decent housing at prices they can afford. Others have successfully fought discriminatory practices that hit at neighborhood stability and character or have tackled community decay by fighting for—and winning—a fair share of public services and funds. Still others have brought credit and jobs to their communities.

We hope you will be able to learn from their experiences and adapt the methods that best suit the particular needs of your area and organization.

These groups welcome brief inquiries about their projects. But since most have only limited resources, please enclose a self-addressed, stamped envelope when you contact them. Additional information on funding sources can be found in the Basic Tools and Resource Sections and the Appendices.

These groups have shown that the high cost of housing can be overcome. We hope their stories will inspire you.

Chapter 1

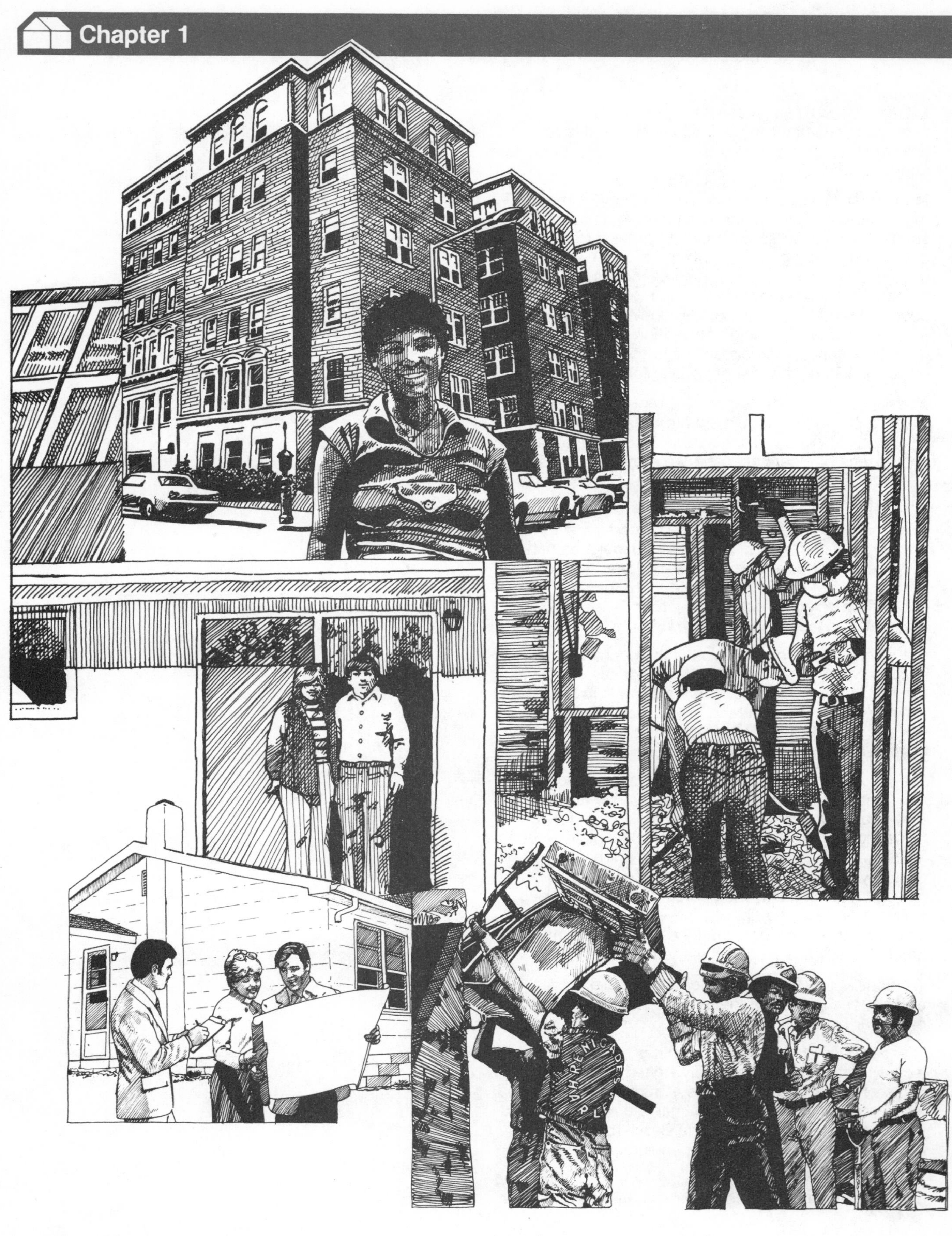

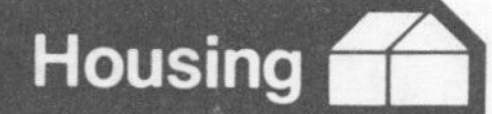

Building Together: How to Get Housing You Can Afford

Introduction

Owning a home is part of the American dream. But for many families it is becoming another casualty of inflation. In 1979 average new home prices hovered at $75,000 — beyond the reach of most Americans. But community groups around the nation are finding innovative ways to build low-cost houses and apartments. This chapter will give residents of both rural and urban areas helpful ideas and tips on building affordable housing for themselves and their neighbors.

Our featured groups have taken a close look at the factors behind skyrocketing building and renovation costs. And they have mapped ingenious strategies to get around the three basic culprits: land, building costs and interest rates. By working with government and private agencies, many community groups have found ways to cut some or all of these costs.

For example, some groups have reduced the cost of traditional building practices by finding volunteer help or training workers paid for through government job programs. Others ask the future owners or renters to contribute labor.

These organizations have also found ways to buy land at less than full value. One technique is locating a benevolent owner who will give land away or sell at a fraction of the market value and write all or the major portion off as a tax deduction.

In addition, there's a surprising variety of reduced interest loan programs available for community groups in low-income areas. You'll see how other organizations have effectively used these long-term loan repayment plans.

Organizations pass on these savings to area residents, with the biggest benefits often going to low-income families. So for the first time in their lives many poor people are able to obtain adequate housing at reasonable prices.

Each of the community groups in this chapter has created a special kind of success story. By learning from what they've done, we hope other groups will have the opportunity to achieve something important for their neighbors.

Building New Houses— Even If You Aren't Rich

Kentucky Mountain Housing Development Corporation
P.O. Box 431
Manchester, Kentucky 40962
(606) 598-5128

December is always a cruel month in the Appalachian Mountains of Clay County, Kentucky. But in 1974 the holiday season became something special for 60-year-old Cleo Hobbs, a miner's widow with eight children to raise. Less than two weeks before Christmas, she moved into a new three-bedroom home that costs her only $54 a month to own.

"That was the best Christmas I ever had," she recalls, her sharp country twang as clear as her memories. "Right when I was signing the papers, I said, 'well, I got all the Christmas I wanted;' they could tell from the smile on my face. So I'll just live here till death parts. I don't think I could better myself a bit."

The Pride of Ownership

Cleo Hobbs was one of the first people in her area to move into a new house built by the nonprofit Kentucky Mountain Housing Development Corporation (KMHDC), based in Manchester. And thanks to the tireless efforts of the group and its executive director, Dwayne Yost, she won't be the last.

Since the group was launched in 1973, KMHDC has helped nearly 170 Clay and Jackson County families with average annual incomes of under $5,000 to purchase affordable new homes. In addition, thanks to the group, almost 500 low-income residents are taking pride in their newly restored homes.

Moreover, by obtaining needed funds from government agencies, church groups and local businesses, KMHDC has boosted the local economy by sprucing up area housing and hiring formerly unemployed residents to do the building and renovating.

In 1979 KMHDC's budget topped $847,000. And its 51 paid staffers and roster of 300 to 500 volunteers have made an impact on their mostly coal mining neighbors.

Mrs. Hobbs' Old House

Cleo Hobbs will never forget what it was like living in Clay County before KMHDC came along. "It was just a house, kind of like a box and it was an old house when we moved in it," she recalls. "When it'd start to rainin', it took every pan and pot in the house to catch the water. When we heard it thunder, we had to get runnin' for our pans and pots. I sure had a hard time."

It seems that many people have a hard time in Clay and Jackson Counties, but KMHDC is working to help them.

Origins

It all started when Yost, a Church of the Brethren minister, had something close to a vision: the poor people in Clay and Jackson Counties should have a chance to live in decent housing.

Yost had come to Appalachia on a special assignment in 1960, but he stayed on to work with the local people and area institutions. In 1972 he asked his church to let him work full time to get good housing for the people in southern Kentucky. And it was his intimate knowledge of Appalachia's resources, combined with his effective organizing skills, that helped make his housing goals a reality.

Fundraising

In the beginning Yost used all his ingenuity to get what he needed for his housing construction program. For administrative and personnel costs, he wooed money from church organizations and the Community Services Administration's (CSA) Community Economic Development Program.* To buy the land and housing materials, he received funds primarily from his own Church of the Brethren. A coalition of church groups donated the tools that were used, plus a van.

And when it came to building or renovating houses, Yost found alternatives to traditionally high-priced building practices.

Labor Costs

Here's how they saved money: Yost served as construction foreman for the first house, supervising five formerly unemployed residents who were paid under the Department of Labor's Comprehensive Employment and Training Act (CETA) Program.* The workers were referred from a nearby Community Action Agency (CAA), the Daniel Boone Development Council.[1] Today CETA workers, plus one foreman paid by the Kentucky Mountain firm, continue to do most of the hard work of building new houses.

For home renovation and minor repairs, the new firm initially used volunteers from the United Methodist Appalachian Service Project and other church groups. Volunteer work has always played a vital role in all KMHDC housing programs.

Currently renovation and repairs are done primarily by 51 paid resident employees. Some are paid by the Human Economic Appalachian Development Corporation (HEAD), a nonprofit coalition of 19 organizations dedicated to promoting economic development, which Yost also helped start. Other paid workers are drawn from the CETA program.

Organization

Kentucky Mountain Housing is run by a Board of Directors composed of Protestant and Catholic clergy, social agency members and local residents (some of whom own the houses which the corporation has built). The housing firm is supported by the United Methodist Church and other religious groups and has received funds and assistance from Federal and local government agencies.[2] In addition, the group received funding from the Housing Assistance Council.[3]

Low-Cost Houses

The innovation and hard work of the KMHDC has paid off for the people of Appalachia. Because of the group's low construction expenses, the houses can be sold to low-income residents at or below building costs, depending on what each family can afford. The houses cost less than $16,000—almost half the price of comparable housing in the area.

Affordable Monthly Payments

But the real savings for KMHDC-assisted families are reflected in the monthly payments they make on their repair loans or home mortgages. To purchase new KMHDC homes, the low-income families are eligible for low-cost, long-term loans from the United States Department of Agriculture's Low-to-Moderate Income Housing Loans (Section 502) Program,* administered by the Farmers Home Administration (FmHA). And families whose homes are renovated get help from FmHA's Very-Low-Income Housing Repair Loans and Grants (Section 504) Program.*

So while KMHDC homeowners pay an average mortgage of $60 a month, owners of similar housing in the area might be paying over $200 a month.

New Spirit

But more than new houses have been added to the Appalachian landscape because of the hard work of Dwayne Yost and those who joined him. There's a new spirit there too—a sense of pride, of accomplishment, of pulling together. And there are tangible economic benefits. Area businesses have new

Future homeowners inspect plans for the finishing touches to their new KMHDC home.

Shingling the roof of a new KMHDC house

orders to fill, formerly unemployed workers are now holding jobs and, most of all, families in Appalachia have decent homes.

Other Cost-Cutting Groups

The success of Kentucky Mountain Housing in building new homes is matched by other rural and urban groups. Several organizations—such as Homes in Partnership, Inc., in Apopka, Florida, and St. Landry Low-Income Housing in Palmetto, Louisiana—have gone one step further by getting the people who are going to live in the houses personally involved in building them. In addition, other groups—such as the Northeastern Connecticut Community Development Corporation in Danielson, Connecticut; Macon Programs for Progress in Franklin, North Carolina; and Rural California Housing Corporation in Sacramento, California—encourage would-be homeowners to form work crews and help each other build their homes.

Perhaps one of the most unusual methods of providing new houses originated in the Watts section of Los Angeles, California. There, the Watts Labor Community Action Committee (WLCAC), a CAA, discovered that city-owned houses in another section of town were slated to be torn down to make way for a proposed highway project.[4] Eyeing several houses in good condition, the group's leaders brainstormed for a while and concluded: Why not move the houses to Watts?

That's how they invented a program called "Operation Move-On." WLCAC buys good housing from the city at minimal prices and moves it intact on flatbed trucks to Watts. The houses or apartments are then placed on vacant land which WLCAC has acquired under a special loan program.[5] And after some fixing up by WLCAC, the housing is ready to be occupied by low-income families.

So from Appalachia to Watts, groups who want to build houses for their people are finding ways to get the job done. And despite inflation, they are showing how hard work and a few good ideas can lead to solving some critical housing problems.

Groups Highlighted

Homes in Partnership, Inc.
8 East Fifth Street
Apopka, Florida 32702
(305) 886-2451

Macon Programs for Progress
P.O. Box 688
38½ East Main Street
Franklin, North Carolina 28734
(704) 524-4471

Northeastern Connecticut Community
Development Corporation
P.O. Box 156
Danielson, Connecticut 06239
(203) 774-7020

Rural California Housing Corporation
2007 O Street
Sacramento, California 95814
(916) 442-4731

St. Landry Low-Income Housing
P.O. Box 82
Palmetto, Louisiana 71358
(318) 623-5815

Watts Labor Community Action Committee
11401 South Central Avenue
Los Angeles, California 90059
(213) 564-5901

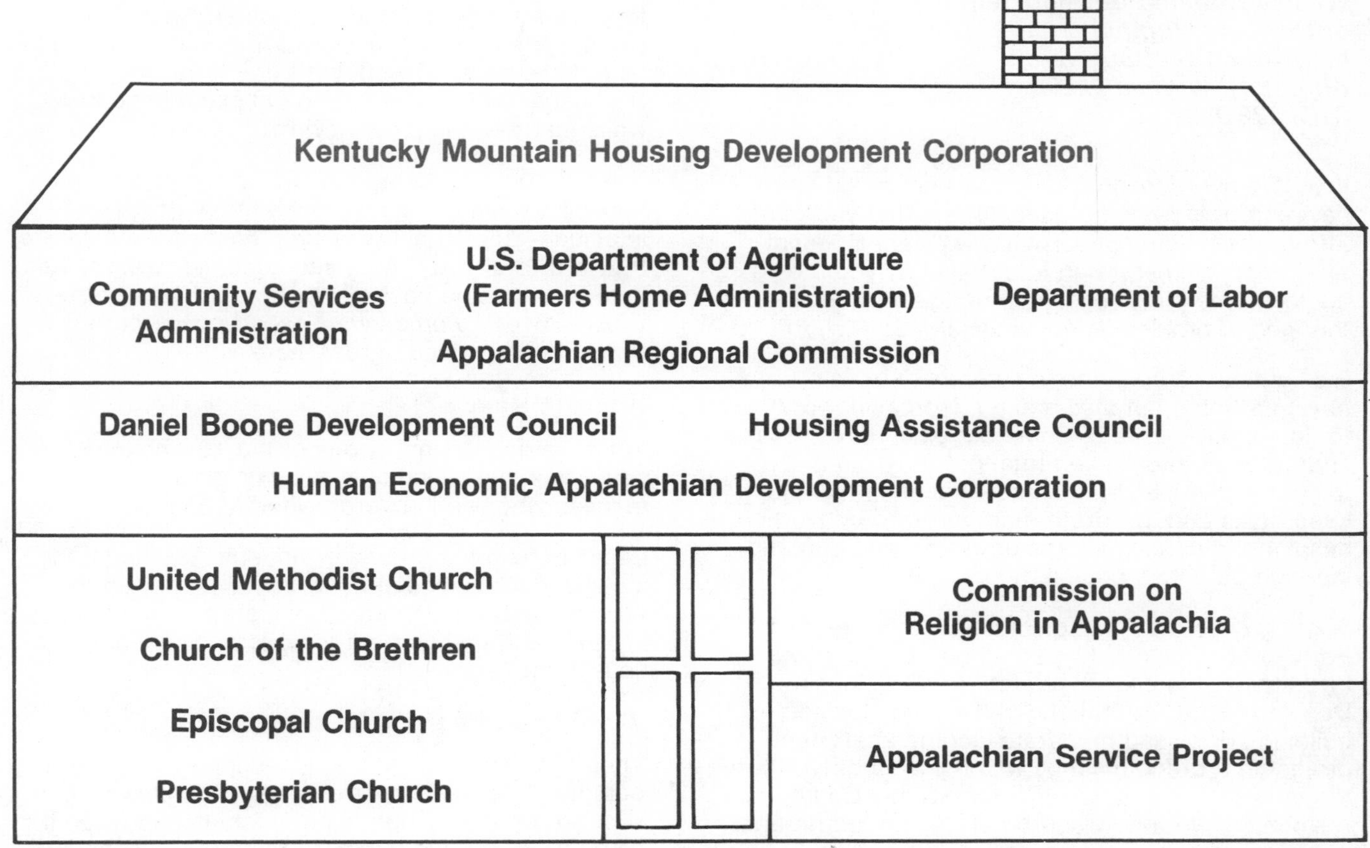

The foundation of a nonprofit house is set through the cooperation and support of several church, government and private groups.

Adapted from Grapevine, *Vol. 10 No. 2, August 1978, Joint Strategy and Action Committee, Inc. (JSAC), 475 Riverside Drive, Room 1700A, New York, New York 10027. Single reprints available by sending 10 cents plus a self-addressed, stamped envelope to JSAC.*

[1] The Community Services Administration's (CSA) Community Action Program (CAP)* funds local Community Action Agencies (CAAs)* aimed at helping low-income residents with their food, housing, energy and other needs.

[2] Other church groups which support Kentucky Mountain Housing Development Corporation (KMHDC) include the Church of the Brethren, the Presbyterian Church, the Episcopal Church, the Appalachian Service Project and the Commission on Religion in Appalachia. Government agencies helping KMHDC include the statewide Kentucky Housing Corporation, a nonprofit group which sells bonds to provide financing to help groups with construction projects; and the Appalachian Regional Commission, a Federal-state government agency concerned with the economic, physical and social development of the 13-state Appalachian region.

[3] The Housing Assistance Council is a nonprofit, national rural housing technical assistance group. (For more information on the Housing Assistance Council, see Resources at end of Housing Section.)

[4] The Watts Labor Community Action Committee (WLCAC) is profiled in Food Section, p. 72.

[5] In 1971 the Watts Labor Community Action Committee (WLCAC) received a $2 million grant from the United Auto Workers (UAW), a labor union, which allowed them to purchase land in the Watts area from various realtors. Purchasing the land at that time allowed WLCAC to avoid escalating real estate prices and, at the same time, provided the group with collateral for loans and other capital assets.

* State and/or local government agencies are frequently responsible for administration of Federal program funds. For further information, see Appendix I under appropriate Federal agency.

NOTE: For a complete listing of groups featured throughout this book, see Index.

Building Low-Cost Apartments

Wesley Housing Development Corporation
of Northern Virginia
4701 Arlington Boulevard
Arlington, Virginia 22203
(703) 522-9432

If you've ever looked for an apartment, you know how hard it is to find a suitable one that you can afford. Often you'll be shown one disappointment after another, then listen in disbelief as you are quoted some mind-boggling rent figure. Unfortunately this kind of problem is not unusual.

Rising housing costs not only prevent people from buying a home but also make it increasingly difficult to find a place to rent. Some big cities have severe shortages of affordable rental property. To make things worse, many landlords—claiming high upkeep costs and low-profit margins—are converting buildings to condominiums or co-ops and demanding high purchase prices.

Some groups are finding solutions to the rent crisis. For example, with only a small out-of-pocket cash investment, the church-related Wesley Housing Development Corporation (WHDC) has finished building a low- and moderate-income apartment project in a predominantly wealthy area of Northern Virginia. As a result, low-income Fairfax County residents have a new source of decent apartments.

Wesley apartment building takes shape

Nancy Spenser, a mother of one, appreciates the two-bedroom, $245-a-month Wesley townhouse that she recently occupied. "It's really nice. I've gotten to know my neighbors and it's quiet. If you call and say something's wrong, they come right away and fix it," she says. "I wouldn't trade it for anything. My husband takes me by the old place once in a while just to remind me how much we have now."

The "old place" rented for $230 a month and was "pretty raunchy," Spenser says. "If was roach-infested—so bad that when you opened the cabinets, they'd dive at you." And, she adds, her washer and dryer were in the basement where "it was pretty scary. Several women were raped down there; I mean I always lived in fear there."

Housing Need

While Fairfax County is one of the 10 wealthiest counties in the nation, it is also home for many poorer families who live in overcrowded accommodations.

Eager to help the area's low-income residents, the local United Methodist congregations formed the Wesley Housing Development Corporation (WHDC) in 1974, and then set out to build a low-income housing project.

Winning Community Support

Their first objective was to win support from the community's wealthier residents. "It's easy to get support for a housing project such as this when it's going to be located somewhere else, but nobody wants it in his or her community," explains Virginia Peters, the group's executive director. "We knew that developing decent housing was only a part of the problem; we had to gain community acceptance for subsidized housing."

Of key importance in building support was Wesley's strategy of keeping anxious residents informed as plans progressed and responding adequately to their concerns. For example, many upper-middle-class residents worried that the new housing complex would overcrowd neighborhood recreational facilities, so nine of the 20 acres which had been donated to the project were turned over to the Fairfax County Park Authority for a public park. Additionally, a community center was included in the project's design.

Raising Funds

A big problem was raising funds to build the 128-unit apartment complex. Their first step, because of tax advantages, was to create a new nonprofit corporation, Strawbridge Square, Inc. (SSI), controlled by the Wesley Housing Develop-

In Indianola, Mississippi Delta Housing Development Corporation workers panel apartment building.

ment Corporation. In turn, the Strawbridge firm formed a business partnership with the National Corporation for Housing Partnerships (NCHP), enabling the group to obtain the $600,000 needed to start construction.[1] A $3.6 million insured mortgage loan financed the remaining building costs. The loan came from the Department of Housing and Urban Development's (HUD) Tandem Programs,* administered by the Government National Mortgage Association (GNMA—commonly called Ginnie Mae). And the Wesley housing organization spent a few thousand dollars for filing fees and other administrative expenses.

Tenants

Realizing that a key to the project's success is finding reliable, trustworthy tenants, SSI is fully involved in screening and selecting families. Screening procedures include assessing family needs, income and ability to maintain the property. Representatives of SSI are present at all interviews with prospective tenants and must approve each family.

Income Range

Eligible families range from those with two members and incomes under $7,000 to those with six members and incomes not over $21,950. All of the occupants receive rent subsidies from HUD's Lower-Income Rental Assistance (Section 8) Program,* which insures that lower-income families pay no more than 25 percent of their incomes for their housing expenses.

Other Groups

The Wesley group's apartment project is not unique. Other groups around the country have managed to raise the funds needed to build low-income apartments. They include the Town of Bolton Development Corporation of Bolton, Mississippi; Delta Housing Development Corporation in Indianola, Mississippi; Impact Seven in Turtle Lake, Wisconsin; and The Woodlawn Organization in Chicago, Illinois.[2]

Groups Highlighted

Delta Housing Development Corporation
Box 847
Indianola, Mississippi 38751
(601) 887-4852

Impact Seven
Route 2, Box 8
Turtle Lake, Wisconsin 54889
(715) 986-4460

Town of Bolton Development Corporation
P.O. Box 10
Bolton, Mississippi 39041
(601) 866-2221

The Woodlawn Organization
1180 East 63rd Street
Chicago, Illinois 60637
(312) 288-5840

[1] The National Corporation for Housing Partnerships (NCHP) was chartered by Congress in 1968. The Corporation, privately run and operated for profit, funds the development of low- and moderate-income housing projects. Funds for NCHP come from individuals in the 50 percent plus tax bracket who are looking for tax shelters. So far these wealthy individuals have invested $131 million in the corporation and, in turn, have been able to write off their contributions as tax deductions. (For more information on NCHP, see Resources at end of Housing Section.)

[2] The Woodlawn Organization is also mentioned in Housing Section, p. 112. Impact Seven is also mentioned in Housing Section, p. 159.

* State and/or local government agencies are frequently responsible for administration of Federal program funds. For further information, see Appendix I under appropriate Federal agency.

NOTE: For a complete listing of groups featured throughout this book, see Index.

Providing Homes For The Elderly

Improved Dwellings for Altoona
P.O. Box 705
Altoona, Pennsylvania 16603
(814) 944-9466

The decline in railroads which followed World War II devastated the economy of the once-booming railroad town of Altoona, Pennsylvania. By the 1960s, due to railroad layoffs, the city's population had dropped from 80,000 to 60,000.

Hardest hit by the depressed economy were Altoona's less mobile elderly who were left behind to provide their own services while younger residents sought jobs in other cities. In no area were the aged more incapacitated than in the maintenance of their homes and apartments.

''My landlord, he didn't take care of anything. The heating was bad. The plumbing was terrible. Everything was just going down, down, down,'' remembers Dorothy Pratt, a widow of 70 and daughter of a railroad blacksmith.

To solve the problem, the town's ministers and other citizens launched a program to build and rent low-cost apartments to seniors. At first they didn't have much to work with except seed money from churches and synagogues in the Altoona area. In 1968, they incorporated and gave themselves an official name, Improved Dwellings for Altoona (IDA). But no one really knew anything about housing programs or building plans or funding applications.

Learning Experience

So they set out to learn. They learned about ways they could use their corporation status to get funds and about the range of assistance programs offered by the Department of Housing and Urban Development (HUD).

In 1971 they planned a 125-unit seniors building and broke ground in the downtown area two years later. By 1974 the first senior citizens moved into the IDA Tower. Designed for their safety and enjoyment, the building is complete with community rooms, stores and other facilities and is considered to be a city landmark.

The Tower building replaced an eyesore. ''Oh, it was awful. You'd be half afraid,'' Pratt says, her fragile voice describing the neighborhood's pre-Tower days. ''Well, nobody would walk down there at night—all closed up, dilapidated buildings. When they tore that block all out of there, it was a godsend.''

Pratt, an early resident of the Tower building, adds that things have changed: ''We have a drug store in the building and my doctor's not far away. It's all so

The community room is one of many facilities available to IDA Tower residents.

handy. It's wonderful."

How did they do it? Here's a sampling of methods IDA members used to realize their goals.

Building and Financing

With the seed money they purchased city-owned urban renewal land originally left by developers unwilling to build in the depressed downtown area. The group also used HUD's Rental and Cooperative Housing Assistance for Lower-Income Families (Section 236) Program,* which subsidizes mortgage interest rates on low-income housing and thereby reduces monthly rents.

Other funding came from the Appalachian Regional Community Development Corporation, a nonprofit housing assistance agency, and the Pennsylvania Department of Community Affairs.

Tenants' Costs

IDA manages the Tower building. Apartments range from $165 a month for efficiencies to $186 for one-bedroom units. And the low-income senior residents are eligible for subsidy programs.[1]

More Housing for Seniors

IDA did not stop with the Tower building. Even before it was completed, the group began a second project for older citizens. Blair Tower, a 100-unit complex was occupied in November 1978. The funding for the $3 million building came from HUD's Direct Loans for Housing for the Elderly or Handicapped (Section 202) Program,* which provides funding to nonprofit organizations to build and manage housing for seniors and handicapped citizens. The IDA group is now rehabilitating single-family homes and is sharing its expertise with other groups.[2]

Other Groups

Other groups around the country have also shown persistence in building housing for the elderly. St. Nicholas Neighborhood Preservation and Housing Rehabilitation Corporation in Brooklyn, New York and the Detroit Shoreway Organization in Cleveland, Ohio are two examples.

Groups Highlighted

Detroit Shoreway Organization
6516 Detroit Avenue, Room 242
Cleveland, Ohio 44102
(216) 961-4242

St. Nicholas Neighborhood Preservation and Housing Rehabilitation Corporation
1129 Catherine Street
Brooklyn, New York 11211
(212) 388-4726

[1] Programs which have provided help to Altoona's senior citizens include the Department of Housing and Urban Development's (HUD) Lower-Income Rental Assistance (Section 8) Program,* and Title III of the Older Americans Act,* administered by the Department of Health, Education and Welfare (HEW).

[2] Additional funding for Improved Dwellings for Altoona's (IDA) rehabilitation project came from the City of Altoona and the Pennsylvania State Housing Finance Agency.

* State and/or local government agencies are frequently responsible for administration of Federal program funds. For further information, see Appendix I under appropriate Federal agency.

NOTE: For a complete listing of groups featured throughout this book, see Index.

Turning Empty Houses Into Homes

Renew, Inc.
1016 West Washington Street
South Bend, Indiana 46625
(219) 287-3371

It's hard enough for most people to buy a home, but it's rougher still for low-income families. Many can't afford big down payments or renovation costs and haven't established the credit ratings necessary to qualify for bank loans. Meanwhile old houses in their areas might be standing empty and unused.

Renew, Inc., a nonprofit, citywide group in South Bend, Indiana, is bringing dilapidated, empty houses back to life while helping low-income residents experience the pride of good credit ratings and home ownership. Renew buys and renovates vacant houses and sells them to low-income residents unable to qualify for bank or mortgage company loans. But first they teach their clients how to budget, build up savings and establish good credit ratings, as well as how to make minor home repairs, conserve energy and even garden.

Success Today

Since 1972, 50 families whose annual incomes average $8,000 have purchased homes from Renew

Workers don't miss a thing when rehabilitating a Renew home.

at affordable payments of as little as $130 a month. As a result of Renew's comprehensive housing program that includes continuing financial counseling, the default rate of Renew homeowners over the years has been a remarkably low 2 percent.

George and Blanca Garcia, both former migrant farmers, see their Renew-sponsored home as a symbol of their new life. "When you're in the fields," Blanca says, "you never have a home—just going from place to place." But in 1976 both Blanca and her husband left the fields to finish high school. "My dream was to complete my education, and I wanted a good home," Blanca recalls. And with the help of Renew, they've learned that dreams can still come true.

The Garcias had been paying $150 a month for a damp, cold basement apartment where the utilities averaged an incredible $280 per month. With one bedroom and three children, Blanca recalls, "It was so bad that we felt like we were getting back to where we started."

In December 1978 the Garcias moved into their four-bedroom, two-story Renew home, paying rent of $120 and utilities of about $100 a month—with an option to buy. "I liked it the first time I saw it," Blanca remembers gratefully.

Improving the City's Appearance

In the process of helping low-income residents, Renew is sprucing up economically deprived areas of the city. With ownership, explains Renew Director Sister Dorothy Ann, "A family will take better care of their property, and that will increase the value of the homes in the neighborhood and stimulate other people in the area to do the same thing."

Origins

The organization started simply enough in 1972 when several people approached Father Ken Maley, a local parish priest, for help in buying houses. Father Maley raised $1,000 from parish members for a down payment on an old house. He then borrowed the money needed to buy and renovate it. Inspired by Father Maley's efforts, other parishes and neighborhood groups began purchasing and renovating vacant houses for resale to residents who otherwise could not afford them. Together they formed Renew, Inc.

Funding

Over the years the group has received financial assistance from such diverse agencies as the Campaign for Human Development, the economic and social assistance arm of the Catholic Church; the South Bend Department of Human Resources and Economic Development; the South Bend Bureau of Housing; and Federal agencies.[1]

The success of the group is due in large part to the personal relationship Renew staffers establish with the families they help and their ability to put together a range of funding sources.

Screening

Key to Renew's program is the thorough applicant screening which weeds out those unwilling to ac-

A Renew renovated home

cept home ownership responsibility and encourages those who are willing. Renew's four-strong staff checks income and credit ratings and visits families to determine if they can afford and are willing to buy, manage and maintain a home. If the family doesn't make the grade at first, Renew will work with those willing to learn.

The screening process includes enrollment in home education classes where applicants learn about budgeting, housing repairs, taxes, loans and other subjects vital to home management and ownership. A token $15 fee is charged for the 20 classes which last six months.

During the six months, Renew monitors the family to ensure standards of fiscal responsibility, stable employment and a determination and willingness to maintain their present property.

Finding and Fixing Houses

Once the classes are completed and families have demonstrated their commitment to responsible home ownership, Renew helps them select a house. Usually Renew buys run-down homes that average $9,000 in price. Then local contractors, volunteers, trainees from the Department of Labor's Comprehensive Employment and Training Act (CETA) Program* and, if possible, family members begin renovating. Renovation averages $4,000 and is usually funded by the Department of Housing and Urban Development's Community Development Block Grant (CDBG) Program.*

Land Contracts Lead to Good Credit

Initially most Renew families can't qualify for loans from traditional lending institutions, so they rent homes from Renew for a time to prove credit worthiness, and then buy the home under a land contract which is similar to buying a washing machine on the installment plan. A $100 down payment is required and as long as monthly payments are made, the home belongs to the family. By the time the five-year contract is up, the family has established a sufficient credit record and switches over to a credit union or bank for longer-term mortgage loans.[2]

For instance, the Garcias rented from Renew for over a year and, after they proved their commitment to home ownership, Renew offered them a land contract on their home in February 1980.

Follow-up

Renew's concern for the families doesn't stop after they move into their homes. Follow-up visits are made and counseling and other assistance is offered if families face financial problems.

Renew's program clearly works because of the care and intelligence applied at every stage of the operation.

Other Groups

Groups in other cities are also buying and rehabilitating vacant houses and selling them to low-income families at prices substantially below market value.

Take a look at Community Training Dynamics, Inc. and Ronan Neighborhood Associates, two nonprofit groups in Boston, Massachusetts. Active in the city's Department of Housing and Urban Development-sponsored Multifamily Homesteading Technical Assistance Project,* they provide much-needed services to the city and assistance to potential homesteaders.[3]

Groups Highlighted

Community Training Dynamics, Inc.
10 Fairway Street
Boston, Massachusetts 02126
(617) 298-0825

Ronan Neighborhood Associates
252A Bowdoin Street
Boston, Massachusetts 02120
(no phone)

[1] For more information on the Campaign for Human Development, see Resources at end of Basic Tools Section.

[2] For more information on credit unions, see Housing Section, p. 162.

[3] Families become "homesteaders" by purchasing from the city abandoned property for a token sum. Repairs must be made on a dwelling so that it meets the minimum city housing code standards. The city makes funds for rehabilitation available in the form of low-interest loans which the homesteaders pay back after all rehabilitation is complete and the deeds have been turned over to them.

*State and/or local government agencies are frequently responsible for administration of Federal program funds. For further information, see Appendix I under appropriate Federal agency.

NOTE: For a cross-reference of groups featured throughout this book, see Index.

Saving Apartments and Communities

Voice of the People
4927 North Kenmore Avenue
Chicago, Illinois 60640
(312) 769-2442

Some parts of Chicago's Uptown neighborhood look like a bombed-out ghost town. Abandoned apartment buildings stand scarred and damaged by vandals, junkies and arsonists. Other areas have been leveled by institutions, such as universities or hospitals, seeking to expand their facilities. Rubble cluttered vacant lots await future construction. Other buildings will soon be demolished, and gleaming new institutional facilities will replace the homes of tenants who once lived there.

Fighting Neighborhood Decay

But Uptown's low-income residents are being helped, and the cycle of neighborhood decay is slowly being broken by a nonprofit group aptly called Voice of the People. They are buying apartment buildings from absentee landlords, fixing them up and renting them to low-income residents. Since 1972 Voice has entered into agreements with the city to renovate four buildings and has purchased and renovated three others which now house 21 families. It is a painstaking effort, but it allows longtime residents to remain in the area and is an important contribution to the neighborhood's preservation.

Helping Low-Income Families

Janice Shepard, the mother of 13 and the wife and daughter of coal miners, moved to Chicago 14 years ago from Logan County, West Virginia and was an early Voice recipient. Her husband, a victim of the dreaded black lung disease that plagues coal miners, was forced to stop work. He had to quit, Shepard says, "because of his lungs—they were gettin' real bad. He can only walk about a half block 'fore he can hardly breathe."

Voice children get into the act by marching for decent housing at the International Parade.

Teamwork makes finishing the ceiling a lot easier.

The $180-a-month rent the Shepards paid for a four-room house strained their small budget. Thanks to Voice, now the Shepards pay $60 a month rent and have more space. And Janice Shepard will never forget the first time she saw her new apartment seven years ago.

"Its walls were just white as snow, floors with bright, shiny tiles—just a beautiful thing," says Shepard, who is now active in organizing maintenance crews for her building. "I couldn't believe my eyes. I'd never seen nothin' like this. I figured that I'd always be livin' in coal camp housing."

Fighting Institution Takeover

Voice has helped blunt institutional expansion in the Uptown area, says Barbara Beck, development coordinator for the Voice staff. "Our buildings are right in their path," she says. "And they know we won't sell. Voice efforts are proving to be pivotal to the rest of the block. We can see, for the first time, that dollars are starting to go into other privately owned apartment buildings nearby."

Cycle of Decay

But Voice is just beginning to break the cycle of decay which has been at work since the 1960s. Rising costs make it harder for landlords to maintain buildings and force them to raise rents. In turn, rising rents force many tenants to leave and landlords begin operating their buildings at a loss. Owner abandonment frequently results. When utilities are cut off due to lack of payment, the remaining tenants soon must give up too.

The empty buildings fall prey to arsonists and vandals. The blight spreads. Real estate values tumble. Meanwhile, institutions begin buying up nearby properties, and a once-thriving residential neighborhood is ruined.

Group Origins

In 1968 several Uptown church and civic groups decided to fight the cycle of decay that was plaguing their neighborhood. They formed Voice of the People to protest building abandonment and institutional expansion in the Uptown area.

But mere protest wasn't enough. The decay continued. Then in 1972 a concerned owner, rather than abandon his 34-unit rooming house, donated it to Voice. Voice members didn't know the first thing about renovating old buildings, but they learned soon enough.

First Project Funding

Voice put together money and manpower from different sources. A Chicago bank lent them $40,000 for construction costs and several Chicago foundations also granted funds. Several neighborhood architects and construction firms assisted in teaching repair skills to workers who were provided by ACTION's Volunteers In Service to America (VISTA) Program.* Within a year, the old rooming house was turned into six large apartments, each with five rooms.

Cutting Costs

To keep building maintenance up and rents down, Voice encourages tenants to organize and manage their buildings. Voice also teaches tenants to make minor repairs and shows them how to further cut costs by conserving on fuel and electricity.

Tenants also get help from the Department of Housing and Urban Development's (HUD) Lower-Income Rental Assistance (Section 8) Program,* which ensures that low-income families pay no more than 25 percent of their income for housing. As a result, rent is much lower than for comparable apartments in the area.

A patchwork of sources provide Voice with operating funds. Rent payments are pumped into building maintenance. Foundation grants and bank loans supply necessary renovation materials. The Department of Labor's Comprehensive Employment and Training Act (CETA) Program,* provides manpower for repairs. And working capital is supplied through the neighborhood-owned and operated Community Development Credit Union (CDCU).[1]

Changing Neighborhood

The group's hard work is paying off. An increasing number of low-income residents have affordable, decent apartments. But now Voice faces a new challenge. Common to many inner-city areas, urban displacement is creeping into Uptown. As suburban middle- and upper-income residents rediscover the convenience and charm of the city, apartment rents are climbing beyond the reach of long-time, low-income residents. But Voice plans to face this situation head-on by boosting its efforts to help long-time residents remain in Uptown.

Other Groups

Other Chicago neighborhood groups have shown that they can provide decent, low-cost apartments for their neighbors. These groups include Eighteenth Street Development Corporation, Community Housing Education Corporation of Chicago, South Austin Realty Association, and The Woodlawn Organization (TWO).[2]

New York groups that are also successful in this area include the Brooklyn-based Southside United Housing Development Fund Corporation and the South Bronx Community Housing Corporation.[3]

Thom Clark

Tenants and owners learn skills at Voice home repair workshops.

Groups Highlighted

Community Housing Education Corporation of Chicago
2753 West Armitage
Chicago, Illinois 60647
(312) 235-2144

Eighteenth Street Development Corporation
1900 South Carpenter Street
Chicago, Illinois 60608
(312) 733-2287

South Austin Realty Association
5082 West Jackson Street
Chicago, Illinois 60644
(312) 378-3755

South Bronx Community Housing Corporation
391 East 149th Street, Room 520
Bronx, New York 10455
(212) 292-0800

Southside United Housing Development Fund Corporation
238 South Second Street
Brooklyn, New York 11211
(212) 387-3600

The Woodlawn Organization
1180 East 63rd Street
Chicago, Illinois 60637
(312) 288-5840

[1] Community Development Credit Unions (CDCUs) are profiled in Housing Section, p. 162.

[2] The Community Housing Education Corporation of Chicago is also mentioned in Housing Section, p. 131. The Woodlawn Organization (TWO) is also mentioned in Housing Section, p. 105.

[3] The Southside United Housing Development Fund Corporation is profiled in Housing Section, p. 129.

* State and/or local government agencies are frequently responsible for administration of Federal program funds. For further information, see Appendix I under appropriate Federal agency.

NOTE: For a complete listing of groups featured throughout this book, see Index.

Sweat Equity Pays Off

Renegades Housing Movement
251 East 119th Street
New York, New York 10035
(212) 534-5971

They were once the "Renegades of Harlem," a tough street gang swaggering through the East Harlem ghetto. They walked tall in their nail-studded jackets, flaunting knives and looking for trouble. It was their turf, and it seemed that they almost owned it.

But then something happened. East Harlem, the traditional heart of New York City's 900,000-strong Hispanic community, was becoming something of a ghost town and there was little left to fight over. Their neighborhood had deteriorated. Houses were being abandoned, vandalized and burned. Stores were closing and everyone who could was leaving.

So in 1972 East Harlem street gangs gathered for a "Third World Meeting" to solve their common problems. The outcome marked the beginning of a new era for the Renegades. It was time to fight new battles.

Early Projects

It started with playgrounds in 1973. One of their leaders heard about a New York City program that provided tools and equipment to neighborhood groups willing to clean up vacant lots and turn them into mini-parks or playgrounds.

Finding empty spaces in East Harlem was no problem. There were plenty of sites where abandoned tenements had been demolished or burned. The Renegades picked two lots on East 118th Street. They turned one into a children's playground and the other into an outdoor basketball court. When the playgrounds opened, the gang felt a pride they hadn't experienced before.

Moving on to other projects, the Renegades next organized a blood donor drive for New York City hospitals and conducted a voter registration campaign. But their most ambitious project still lay ahead.

Rehabilitation Site

On the corner of 119th Street and Second Avenue stood a large, abandoned skeleton of what had been a tenement house. With families fleeing the area because of lack of decent housing, the Renegades saw an opportunity to do something for themselves and the neighborhood they loved. So in 1974 they incorporated as the Renegades Housing Movement.

Funding

They didn't have much other than a willingness to work hard. But with the knowledge that the city would soon take over the building, and the help of a $20,000 interest-free loan from the Consumer Farmers Foundation (CFF), the Renegades started making repairs.[1]

"For two years we worked on the building without pay to demonstrate to the city, on those merits alone, that we were serious," recalls Executive Director Eulogio Cedeño. "The loan made it possible for us to demonstrate to the city that we meant business."

Their determination paid off. In 1974 city officials, impressed by the gang's accomplishments, agreed to sell the building to the Renegades for $1,000 and grant them a $350,000 rehabilitation loan.[2]

Renovation Begins

Renovation was far from easy. On a typical day, 15 or more gang members worked as carpenters, masons, plumbers, electricians or bricklayers—doing everything it takes to gut an old structure and rebuild it into 21 modern apartments. A member of the group had several years of construction experience and acted as the teacher-foreman. And the Urban Homesteading Assistance Board (UHAB), a nonprofit technical assistance agency, served as consultant to the group.[3]

Renegade members begin the hard work of renovation by gutting the building.

One worker recalls, "I was heavy into the drug thing and heard about the work from one of my brothers. So I figured, why not give it a try. No pay, but at least I would be doing something besides drugs. But now I got a skill. I know how to do a job."

Sweat Equity

At first the Renegades worked without pay. But soon they needed money for expenses and equipment. So they renegotiated the loan with the city and arranged for minimum salaries for those most in need.

They called the difference between normal construction wages and the pittance they were paid "sweat equity," which refers to the value of the sweat and labor the workers put into the building. Housing built with sweat equity creates more than savings for those who buy or rent—it fosters a sense of neighborhood pride that is almost as tangible and real as the dollars saved.

Cooperative

When renovation of the East 119th Street building was completed in 1975, the Renegades turned it over to the cooperative housing corporation they had organized.[4] The co-op included several gang members, their families and other neighborhood residents in need of decent housing who now jointly own and operate the building. The average $140 monthly payments would have been twice as steep if the building had been renovated in a conventional manner. (Although not available in time to assist the Renegades, co-ops may now qualify for technical and financial assistance from the newly created National Consumer Cooperative Bank.**)

New Image

The Renegades still walk tall, leaving their mark on East Harlem. But now they earn respect in a different way. Two more buildings have been acquired, renovated and turned into cooperatives. They have gone from a street gang to a housing development organization—an odyssey that has done more than change their lives and the lives of their neighbors. It has also made their turf a place truly worth fighting for.

Other Groups

The sweat equity approach to renovation is still fairly new, but it is having some success in New York City. One pioneer has been Inter-Faith Adopt-a-Building, which has completed the renovation of two tenements on Manhattan's Lower East Side.[5] Another New York City group taking the rehabilitation approach is the Brooklyn-based Oceanhill-Brownsville Tenants Association.

Demonstration Programs

The Department of Housing and Urban Development (HUD) is impressed with the sweat equity idea and has supported Multifamily Sweat Equity Homesteading Demonstrations in New York City neighborhoods.[6] As a result of the demonstration, but still in its early stages, the HUD-sponsored Multifamily Homesteading Technical Assistance Project* has introduced sweat equity urban homesteading into other cities including Chicago, Illinois; Cleveland, Ohio; Boston and Springfield, Massachusetts; Hartford, Connecticut; and Oakland, California.

Groups Highlighted

Inter-Faith Adopt-a-Building
605 East Ninth Street
New York, New York 10009
(212) 677-8700

Oceanhill-Brownsville Tenants Association
319 Rockway Avenue
Brooklyn, New York 11212
(212) 346-1588

[1] The Consumer Farmers Foundation (CFF) is a nonprofit endowment fund which encourages the development of cooperative homeownership among low-income individuals. It provides no-interest loans, primarily in the New York City area.

[2] The rehabilitation loan came from the city Housing Development Administration which, today, is the Housing Preservation and Development Administration.

[3] For more information on the Urban Homesteading Assistance Board (UHAB), see Resources at end of Housing Section.

[4] For more information on housing cooperatives, see chart in Housing Section, p. 119.

[5] Inter-Faith Adopt-a-Building is also mentioned in Energy Section, p. 220.

[6] Families become "urban homesteaders" by purchasing abandoned property from the city for a token sum. Repairs must be made on the dwelling so that it meets the minimum city housing code standards. The city makes funds for rehabilitation available in the form of low-interest loans which the homesteaders pay back after all rehabilitation is complete and the deeds have been turned over to them.

* State and/or local government agencies are frequently responsible for administration of Federal program funds. For further information, see Appendix I under appropriate Federal agency.

**For further information, see Appendix II under "National Consumer Cooperative Bank."

NOTE: For a complete listing of groups featured throughout this book, see Index.

Converting Your Apartment To A Co-op

Jubilee Housing, Inc.
1750 Columbia Road, N.W.
Washington, D.C. 20009
(202) 332-4020

At first glance it seems like a great idea: let tenants own their apartments by converting buildings to cooperatives or condominiums. All sorts of wonderful changes will take place if renters become owners, some say. The new owners will take better care of their apartments; become more involved in the community; and because services are paid for out of their own pockets, owners will cut down on the use of utilities.

To be sure, cooperatives and condominiums are on the upswing as Americans seek answers to spiraling rent and housing costs. Cooperatives are owned and managed jointly by the tenants who buy shares in the building and have the right to sell their interest should they wish to move. In the case of condominiums, tenants own their apartments and pay monthly fees to a management group for "common ground" maintenance.

But tenant groups pushing to convert their buildings into cooperatives or condominiums often face obstacles. For instance, it is difficult for tenants to all agree on the conversion. Some fear that the high cost of renovation and repair will more than offset the benefits of ownership. Also, financing is difficult to obtain when so many parties are involved. And tenants often lack confidence in their ability to manage a large cooperative apartment building.

One Group's Success

In 1973 Jubilee Housing, Inc., a nonprofit, mostly volunteer group in Washington, D.C., acquired and renovated two deteriorated but fully occupied apartment houses—without displacing anyone. The renters helped plan and now assist in operating a wide range of service programs such as a health clinic and a children's recreation center. After some coaching in management skills from Jubilee workers, the refurbished apartments are now being managed by the tenants. And residents will become official owners in 1980 when the buildings are converted into cooperatives.

When paid help is needed, Jubilee recruits tenants, a policy which has given Rosa Hatfield a new sense of self-worth. "Before I was a mother on welfare," says the full-time manager of one of the buildings, the 60-unit Ritz, "I never imagined that I could ever do anything like this. It was scary at first, but I'm getting to know the ropes."

The Problem

It all began in the early 1970s when a group of parishioners belonging to the ecumenical Church of the Savior studied the housing problems of low-income people in the nation's capital. They found that two-thirds of Washington's residents rented housing and that one-third of those lived on less than $5,000 per year. To make matters worse, much of the housing was substandard, and utility and maintenance costs as well as rents were rising constantly. So in 1973, to help low-income residents combat the problem, they formed Jubilee Housing, Inc.

Jubilee chose to tackle the once posh Adams Morgan area. Although Adams Morgan had its share of old apartment buildings with low-income residents, the ethnically mixed area was blessed with a unique vitality that stems from its strong community spirit.

To launch Jubilee, a prominent developer and member of the church bought two badly run-down buildings having a total of 90 apartments and promised to sell them to Jubilee when they raised the needed funds. Although the buildings were called the "Ritz" and the "Mozart," whatever elegance they once knew had long since faded.

Jubilee took over management immediately. To cut down on the high cost of renovation, Jubilee decided to refurbish the buildings themselves. A broad-based group of volunteers from area churches and other organizations began cleaning up, repairing and painting the buildings. Needed materials such as doors, paint and even a roof were donated, and contributions from individuals and foundations were scraped together as necessary during the two years of renovation. To avoid dislocating families, residents temporarily moved into other apartments in the buildings while their units were being redone.

Overcoming Tenant Reluctance

As reconstruction work proceeded, thought was given to converting the buildings into cooperatives. But tenants balked at the idea initially. "The overriding problem was distrust," recalls John W. Branner, president of Jubilee. "We were just another outfit coming in, trying to suggest something new. They were so used to absentee landlords who let the place get in really unfit shape—but who were always there to collect the rent and that's it. It's an old, old story."

Resident manager Rosa Hatfield outside the Ritz

The tenants also questioned their ability to manage the buildings, Branner adds. "These are the poorest of the poor," he says. "Many of these people have never been in a position to provide leadership."

Daily interaction between Jubilee volunteers and the tenants paid off. In 1977 the Jubilee Institute was formed to teach residents how to manage and maintain their buildings. It was funded by local foundations and staffed by two part-time directors and a score of volunteers.

Buying the Buildings

But the crucial step to conversion still remained. Jubilee needed $606,000 to purchase the buildings as well as funds to renovate the deteriorated electrical, heating and other systems. In 1978, with the help of the Lilly Foundation and many private donations, Jubilee took over ownership. (Although not available in time to assist Jubilee, co-ops may now qualify for technical and financial assistance from the newly created National Consumer Cooperative Bank.**) To help with renovation expenses and to acquire other buildings, they received a $1.6 million Innovative Grant* from the Department of Housing and Urban Development's (HUD) Office of Community Planning and Development.

In 1979, six years after Jubilee began managing the Ritz and Mozart, the tenants, working in committees, took over. "There's a lot of leadership among these people," Branner says of the management transition. Seeing that leadership surface, he adds, "is the satisfying part of Jubilee's work."

Taking Over

The Ritz and the Mozart are now worthy of their names. Ownership will soon be transferred to the tenants with Jubilee's staff continuing to assist when needed. Down payments to purchase apartments will be kept to a minimum. And to keep the buildings available for those on low incomes, moving tenants will sell their share in the buildings back to the cooperative.

More Co-ops Planned

Jubilee has already done more. It now owns and manages five buildings in the Adams Morgan area—all slated for tenant cooperative ownership. The secret of the organization's success is simple: hard work. Hundreds of people donated over 50,000 hours of labor—not to mention untold hours organizing, fundraising and teaching tenants management techniques.

Other Groups

This co-op conversion approach to housing is spreading around the country. Groups using the renovation and conversion method include Jubilee Housing, Inc. in Louisville, Kentucky; Concerned Citizens of Butchers Hill, Inc. in Baltimore, Maryland; and the Settlement Housing Fund, Inc. in New York City.

In many college communities high rents and apartment shortages have led to the formation of student housing cooperatives. Two examples are the Madison Community Cooperative in Madison, Wisconsin, and the Inter-Cooperative Council at the University of Michigan, Ann Arbor, Michigan.

Condominium Conversion

Middle- and higher-income residents are also turning to conversion as a way of avoiding displacement. In Washington, D.C. a 1978 law requires landlords who are selling to give tenants first option to buy their buildings. And more and more tenants are doing just that. This method of conversion gives tenants the power to go cooperative or turn condominium.

For example, many of the middle-income residents of the 88-unit Swathmore complex in the District's Foggy Bottom area opted for the condominium route and will soon own their apartments. A one-bedroom unit will cost Swathmore residents about $45,000 while nonresidents will pay in the neighborhood of $60,000. A professional management firm will be hired to run the building, and resident owners will pay a monthly fee to cover building maintenance, ground care and other operating costs.

In 1978, when Swathmore tenants learned that the owner intended to sell, over half decided to form a corporation and buy the building. Interested tenants kicked in $1,500 to $2,500 each for the $90,000 deposit needed to purchase the $1.8 million building. In addition, the tenants put down payments on their individual units.

The Swathmore conversion won't displace elderly residents who choose not to buy their units. "Under any other situation, they would be forced to leave," says Despina Caneles, president of the Swathmore Tenant Association. But the association was able to find investors willing to buy the units and rent them back to the elderly residents at affordable prices. The investors are attracted by the tax shelter. They are able to write off on their income taxes the difference between market value and actual rent charged.

New Trend Predicted

The tenant conversion taking place in Washington, D.C. "is just the tip of the iceberg countrywide," says consultant John Iwaniec, who has represented Swathmore tenants and other conversion groups. The Advanced Mortgage Corporation, the nation's third largest mortgage banker based in Detroit, Michigan, estimates that nationwide condominium and cooperative conversions more than tripled between 1977 and 1979—from 45,000 to 145,000.

Tips for Converting

Iwaniec recommends that tenants interested in purchasing their buildings first find legal and real estate counsel. After drawing up a contract to purchase the building, the search for financing begins. For many people this is new and confusing ground.

"Most tenants aren't familiar with how to get multimillions in financing," Iwaniec says. And he adds, the time element makes it even harder for low-income tenants who must often go through the lengthy process of applying for Federal funds.

For those D.C. tenants unable to afford consultants, two District of Columbia organizations offer free services. The Metropolitan Washington Planning and Housing Association helps low-income tenants organize, raise funds, determine conversion costs and find Federal subsidies.

The other group, Ministries United to Support Community Life Endeavors (MUSCLE), helps tenants organize to purchase their building and also aids low-income residents who are displaced.

Groups Highlighted

Concerned Citizens of Butchers Hill
2027 East Baltimore Street
Baltimore, Maryland 21231
(301) 276-8827

Inter-Cooperative Council at the University of Michigan
Michigan Union, Room 4002, Box 66
Ann Arbor, Michigan 48109
(313) 662-4414

Jubilee Housing, Inc. of Kentucky
125 West Burnett Avenue
Louisville, Kentucky 40208
(502) 637-4086

Madison Community Cooperative
254 West Gilman Street
Madison, Wisconsin 53707
(608) 251-2667

Metropolitan Washington Planning and Housing Association
1225 K Street, N.W.
Washington, D.C. 20005
(202) 737-3700

Ministries United to Support Community Life Endeavors
680 Eye Street, S.W.
Washington, D.C. 20024
(202) 554-1675

Settlement Housing Fund, Inc.
1780 Broadway, Suite 600
New York, New York 10019
(212) 265-6530

Swathmore Tenants Association
1010 25th Street, N.W.
Washington, D.C. 20037
(no phone)

* State and/or local government agencies are frequently responsible for administration of Federal program funds. For further information, see Appendix I under appropriate Federal agency.

**For further information, see Appendix II under "National Consumer Cooperative Bank."

NOTE: For a complete listing of groups featured throughout this book, see Index.

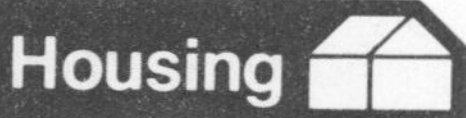

Differences Between Cooperatives and Condominiums

QUESTIONS	COOPERATIVE	CONDOMINIUM
Who owns the common areas of the building such as hallways, roof, elevators, land?	The corporation, with all shares owned by the cooperative tenants.	Residents belong to an owners' association and own common areas jointly.
Who owns the individual units?	The same corporation which owns the land and building. The members of the co-op rent their units from the corporation usually under long-term "proprietary" leases.	Each occupant owns his/her unit. He/she gets a deed similar to a deed on a private home.
Who manages the property?	The cooperative corporation. Since the tenants own the corporation, they control and are responsible for managing the building themselves or for hiring a management firm.	The owners' association often hires a professional management firm. But each owner is fully responsible for the management and upkeep of his/her own unit.
Who has a vote?	Each member has one vote.	Generally each owner has a vote in proportion to the value of his/her unit relative to the total value of all units.
Do unit occupants have to pay rent?	Yes. But it is usually called a "carrying charge." Occupants share operation and maintenance costs of the building apart from upkeep of their own unit. This carrying charge has to be large enough to include a portion of the real estate taxes and mortgage payments on the entire building.	No. There is a monthly charge for building maintenance and services which benefit all occupants. Mortgage payments and taxes are paid separately.
Can the owner borrow to acquire the unit?	Yes. Also the Federal Home Loan Bank Board now permits all lenders to accept shares in the co-op corporation as security. In addition, the Department of Housing and Urban Development (HUD) will provide mortgage insurance to permit an individual to acquire equity in an existing, insured co-op.	Yes. The unit owner can obtain a separate mortgage loan, just like a homeowner.
Are there any restrictions on selling the unit?	Usually. The co-op member must get the corporation's approval before selling the shares. The buyer will then sign a new proprietary lease.	Usually not. The unit owner may sell the apartment like any homeowner.
Who pays the real estate taxes?	The corporation.	Each unit is separately assessed and the owner pays the taxes directly.
What are the tax benefits?	The co-op member may deduct from personal income on their income tax returns the portion of the carrying charge used to pay the taxes on the building and mortgage interest on loans used to buy shares in the building.	Owners may deduct the taxes and mortgage interest on their units from their personal income on income tax returns.

Adapted from U.S. Department of Housing and Urban Development Fact Sheet, *"HUD-FHA Comparison of Cooperative and Condominium Housing," 1976, Office of the Assistant Secretary for Housing, Washington, D.C. 20140.*

Repairing, Maintaining and Managing Housing

Introduction

Inflation never leaves us alone. Even if we're lucky enough to find affordable apartments or houses, upkeep costs are often beyond our incomes.

As with building new homes, several factors drive up home repair and renovation costs including labor, materials and the interest on borrowed money.

As inflation takes its toll, low-income residents especially have a difficult time keeping their homes in shape. This worries community groups as much as it does individual families, because the entire neighborhood is affected by deteriorated buildings. Shabby residential areas make real estate values plummet, and neighborhood character and stability are damaged if landlords or homeowners can't afford to take care of their dwellings.

In the long run neighborhood decay can mean a loss of available housing and displacement of long-time residents. This happens when unkept houses are demolished because it's cheaper to tear them down than fix them up.

Fortunately, community groups across the country are finding ways to help low-income families pay for home repairs. In this chapter we'll look at programs that subsidize repairs, encourage and show neighbors how to help each other fix their homes and provide tools and materials for self-helpers.

We'll also learn about special repair programs for the elderly and the handicapped and efforts by local groups to fix up apartments when landlords won't. Equally important, we'll look at home repair financing available for low-income residents. Energy-saving repairs, however, are examined in the Energy Section.

Low-Cost Home Repairs

Eastside Community Investments, Inc.
3228 East 10th Street
Indianapolis, Indiana 46201
(317) 633-7303

"Not only is there no God," Woody Allen once said, "but try getting a plumber on weekends."

Regardless of the theological implications of his statement, Allen has singled out one of the major dilemmas facing homeowners. Skilled mechanics and handy workers are both expensive and hard to find. We might know what repairs our homes need, but all too often we put them off because of the expense. Then things go too far and our homes—and possibly our neighborhoods—begin to show signs of serious decline.

Murphy's Law—if something can go wrong, it will—seems to apply specifically to parts of a house. Different parts wear out at different speeds, but sooner or later they all need fixing. Parts that are exposed to the weather, such as exterior walls, gutters and downspouts, are the most vulnerable—and they affect the appearance of the neighborhood most.

Neighborhood Gets New Look

Eastside Community Investments, Inc. (ECI), a nonprofit community group in the predominantly low-income Near Eastside area of Indianapolis, Indiana, has tackled high repair costs by designing and managing an innovative repair program that is subsidized by the city.[1] The spruced-up homes have improved the appearance of the neighborhood as well as inspired nonparticipating residents to fix up their houses. But the program wouldn't have succeeded without active participation by the mostly long-time homeowners.

The program's impact was "startling," recalls ECI project coordinator John Eaglesfield. "There was a multiplier effect. For every house we repaired, there was at least one other house nearby where the exterior was fixed-up by an owner who didn't participate in our program."

Beginnings

The "Paint-Up, Fix-Up Program" began in 1978. ECI staffers knew that the best way to beef up the area was to encourage homeownership and attract private capital and public resources into the area. But their efforts had been frustrated by the run-down appearance of many of the houses.

Dressing up a weathered home

Eastside Community Investments, Inc.

After rallying resident support, ECI approached the city government for a Department of Housing and Urban Development Community Development Block Grant (CDBG)* for neighborhood repairs and revitalization.[2]

Early Funding

An area with 2,500 homes was targeted by the residents for the program. And in 1978 ECI received a $62,000 CDBG grant to be used for home improvements over a six-month period.

At the end of the six months, 46 homes boasted improvements such as exterior painting and repair and replacement of gutters and downspouts.

The Program

All homeowners in the targeted area were eligible to participate—but only 80 applied, partially because many residents were reluctant to accept government subsidies. The grant money was paid to low-income homeowners for all repairs.[3] And families with higher incomes were eligible for rebates of 25 percent of repair costs. Rebates averaged $250.

To help the participants, ECI compiled a list of reputable contractors, but homeowners were free to select their own. And many chose to do repair work themselves.

Higher Rebates for Continued Program

The successful program has been renewed for another year and, to encourage more residents to participate, rebates have been boosted to 40 percent.

Eastside Community Investments, Inc.

A participant in the Paint-up Fix-up Program busy at work

But, warns coordinator Eaglesfield, "This kind of program may not be successful in every neighborhood. What you need is basically a stable area, with a high percentage of resident homeowners. These criteria were followed in selecting our target area, and it's working extremely well."

Other Programs

Other repair programs have been launched by Allies for a Better Community (ABC) in Chicago, Illinois, and by the Monmouth County Board of Social Services in Freehold, New Jersey. Both efforts have been funded in part by HUD's CDBG Program.

Groups Highlighted

Allies for a Better Community
1233 North Ashland Avenue
Chicago, Illinois 60622
(312) 252-7140

Monmouth County Board of Social Services
P.O. Box 3000
Freehold, New Jersey 07728
(201) 431-6028

[1] Eastside Community Investments, Inc. (ECI) is a Community Development Corporation (CDC)* which receives funds from the Community Services Administration's (CSA) Special Impact Program,* administered by the Office of Economic Development (OED).

[2] The Department of Housing and Urban Development's (HUD) Community Development Block Grant (CDBG) Program* funds are targeted at mostly low-income areas and channeled through city governments.

[3] When setting eligibility standards for housing assistance, the Department of Housing and Urban Development (HUD) takes several factors into consideration, including the number of wage earners and dependents in a family and total family income.

* State and/or local government agencies are frequently responsible for administration of Federal program funds. For further information, see Appendix I under appropriate Federal agency.

NOTE: For a complete listing of groups featured throughout this book, see Index.

Self-Help Home Repairs

Brothers Redevelopment, Inc.
2519 West 11th Avenue
Denver, Colorado 80204
(303) 573-5107

The do-it-yourself approach to home repairs has some obvious appeal, but we all know how hard it can be to do it right. Often we don't have the skills, know-how or money for needed tools or equipment. At that point, many of us just give up and call in a high-priced specialist.

But community groups are showing that you don't have to throw in the towel (or wrench) that easily. One way to solve these problems is for neighbors to pool their skills, time and resources and help each other keep their homes in good repair. One group demonstrating this kind of cooperation is Brothers Redevelopment, Inc. (BRI) in Denver, Colorado.

BRI Success

Thanks to Brothers, over 700 repair and renovation projects have been completed in deteriorating inner-city neighborhoods at savings of as much as $2,150 to the low-income residents whose incomes average $5,000 per year. Since BRI began in 1973, assisted families have saved an estimated $2 million on home repairs.

Self-Help

Mutual self-help is the core of BRI. The group coordinates home repairs and supervises volunteers. Those who reap the benefits then pitch in on the next project.

"Brothers had some volunteers paint my house on the outside and they did a beautiful job," recalls one participant. "They didn't ask me to pay but they called me up to make tortillas and green chili. But that's not enough. I think I still owe them."

When they can afford it, residents purchase materials and help repair their own homes. Others return the favor by working on other projects. Since 1973 over 450 Denver residents have given life to Brothers' repair program through their involvement.

Origins

The group was founded in response to a housing crisis throughout Colorado. Outraged by poor housing conditions in some low-income Denver neighborhoods, Don Schierling and Joe Giron, two community organizers, joined forces with clergyman Richard Magnus to do something about the problem. Their goal: to repair and fix up substandard houses.

Early Funds and Staff

Brothers Redevelopment started with a single church volunteer who had carpentry, plumbing and electrical skills. The Mennonite and Lutheran Churches kicked in enough money to pay for a qualified construction supervisor and, equally important, a fundraiser. Publicity and word-of-mouth attracted more volunteers as well as homeowners who needed help with repairs.

Since the program began in 1973, 80 percent of those receiving home repair assistance have offered to help on other projects, providing BRI with a steady pool of volunteers.

A Brothers' worker installs insulation.

Elderly and Handicapped

Many of the elderly and disabled find ways other than physical labor to repay those who help repair their homes. Fifty-nine-year-old Angelica Ruiz expresses her appreciation this way, "Tom did the painting and you ought to see it. We put storm windows and storm doors on, and Ernie fixed the yard. We fixed everything. I made a lot of food for them when they worked here and we also gave them a big wheelbarrow."

Staff and Budget

Brothers now has a staff of 21 and an annual budget of over $1 million. Funding comes from a variety of government and private agencies, including the Department of Housing and Urban Development's Community Development Block Grant (CDBG) Program* and the Denver Housing Authority.[1]

Long-Range Goal

The organization sees as its long-range goal nothing less than the revitalization of Denver's older, deteriorating low-income neighborhoods. To this end, they've expanded their operation to include major rehabilitation of vacant or dilapidated buildings—and even the building of new houses. They also help with some city programs, including an emergency maintenance program for welfare families and a low-interest renovation loan program.

Other Groups

Another kind of self-help approach is provided by a group that teaches "all-thumbs" tenants how to do their own repairs. The helpless "I-hate-repairs" attitude might be a frivolous luxury for the rich, but it is downright costly for the poor.

So Housing Conservation Coordinators, Inc. (HCC) is showing residents in low-income New York City neighborhoods how to do major repairs. HCC offers repair courses to tenants, using actual buildings in need of repair as classrooms. The multiplier effect is at work since the students are also trained to set up classes in their own neighborhoods.[2]

City governments have also joined the self-help efforts. One example is the Department of City Development in Milwaukee, Wisconsin, which provides guidance to low-income homeowners on how to get repairs done properly at a minimum cost.

Old-fashioned altruism often plays an important part in home repairs. For example, the Lake Braddock Good Neighbor Club in Burke, Virginia maintains a "skills bank" of residents who are willing to help others in the community free of charge. If no one with the skill is available and professional-level work is needed, the club has a list of qualified persons and firms willing to do the work at a reduced fee. Club members also agree to lend their own tools and equipment to other members.

Groups Highlighted

City of Milwaukee, Department of City Development
734 North Ninth Street
Milwaukee, Wisconsin 53233
(414) 278-2671

Housing Conservation Coordinators, Inc.
777 10th Avenue
New York, New York 10019
(212) 541-5996

Lake Braddock Good Neighbor Club
c/o Ms. Judy Anderson
9509 Ashbourn Drive
Burke, Virginia 22015
(703) 978-0631

[1] Additional funding for Brothers Redevelopment, Inc. (BRI) comes from the Colorado Housing and Finance Authority, the United Bank of Colorado, various savings and loan associations and local foundations.

[2] Housing Conservation Coordinators, Inc. (HCC) is also profiled in Energy Section, p. 193.

* State and/or local government agencies are frequently responsible for administration of Federal program funds. For further information, see Appendix I under appropriate Federal agency.

NOTE: For a complete listing of groups featured throughout this book, see Index.

Home Repairs For The Elderly

Maintenance Central for Seniors, Inc.
3750 Woodward Avenue
Detroit, Michigan 48201
(313) 832-2134

The self-help approach to home repairs doesn't work very well for our nation's elderly. Often limited by their age, fragile physical condition and fixed or low income, there is little they can do as their homes gradually deteriorate. Usually they cannot do repair work themselves, nor can they afford to hire others to do it for them.

When Harriette Hunter, a 29-year-old mother of one, moved into the low-income Cass Corridor section of central Detroit, she couldn't tolerate watching elderly residents give up eating to pay for furnace repairs.

Senior workers impart their expertise to the younger set.

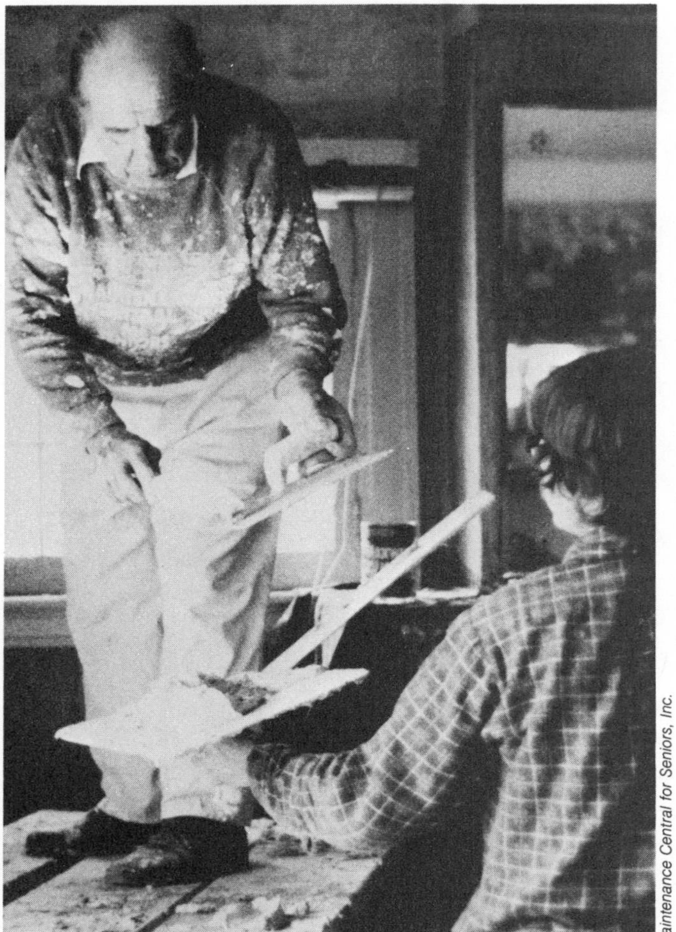

Maintenance Central for Seniors, Inc.

Maintenance Central for Seniors, Inc.

Surveying the problem before plotting action

So in 1975 she became a self-appointed community organizer. With her baby on her back, she called on elderly neighbors. Her husband could do some repairs, she told them. And, in return, she would like their expertise and help on other jobs around the neighborhood.

Initial Funding

She soon learned of Title III of the Older Americans Act,* administered by the Department of Health, Education and Welfare (HEW). Under the Act, she would be eligible for a demonstration grant to help start a senior citizens maintenance organization. But in order to qualify for the assistance necessary, she first had to raise 15 percent in matching funds.

Like other fledgling organizations, she approached large corporations, banks and foundations. But her idea was too new and didn't have a track record. So Hunter hit the neighborhood bars—not to drown her sorrows, but to tell the locals about a program for their own people. Within 10 days she came up with $1,500—enough to convince the National Bank of Detroit that residents believed in the effort. A month later their group received a $49,000 grant, and Maintenance Central for Seniors was formally established. Today the organization has a staff of about 50 and an annual budget of nearly $3 million.

Maintenance Central for Seniors, Inc.

Building a covered porch

It started small. Originally two full-time workers were employed and some part-time and volunteer help was utilized. The work was targeted for only one section of the city.

Hunter soon realized that her workers were not skilled enough for the major repairs many of the homes needed. So they lobbied the city for more money. They ended up getting funds from the Department of Housing and Urban Development's Community Development Block Grant (CDBG) Program* to hire and train a five-person repair staff, each with a specialty in a major area of home maintenance. The city also helped by having its personnel make site inspections and undertake more extensive renovation projects whenever needed.

Tapping Seniors' Talent

The group's decision to use retired workers whenever possible has benefited practically everyone. Some senior citizens with years of construction and maintenance experience enjoy the opportunity to help other retired people—while getting paid for it. They're paid $10,000 to $15,000 a year, and if older workers are unable to put in a full work schedule, part-time hours are set up. Senior craftsmen also conduct classes for younger persons. The age range of Maintenance Central workers is 18 to 87.

"Many of these older craftsmen have unbelievable talents that would have been lost," Hunter notes. "They know these older houses much better than those younger folks, because they built these kinds of houses in their younger days."

Mr. Welsh's Downspouts

That kind of experience paid off when Maintenance Central repaired an old house that was part of a historical landmark preservation district. A retired handyman's skills ended up saving them thousands of dollars. Here's how it happened:

An old house needed downspouts, but tough city regulations governing historical districts demanded that the original material—a hard-to-find copper—be used. The group finally found an out-of-town manufacturer who would sell the copper downspouts for $5,000—an impossible sum. Then 61-year-old Charlie Welsh, who had been a tinsmith in his younger days, came to the rescue.

"Get me some copper sheets," Welsh said, "and I'll make you a set of downspouts that will do the job." With $150 worth of copper, the downspouts—replicas of the originals—were added.

Program Growth

In 1975 the group averaged 105 repair jobs a month. That figure skyrocketed to 600 per month in 1979. And Hunter announces proudly, "The cost per unit has not risen a single cent in that period, not even with massive inflation."

Moreover, Maintenance Central is now active all over Detroit, and a portion of its budget is used to train other groups across the country.

Today Maintenance Central is primarily funded by the Department of Housing and Urban Development's CDBG Program as well as by various businesses, foundations and even the local Law Enforcement Agency. The group also supplements its income with a popular easy-to-read repair manual. Using simple pictures, large print, diagrams and step-by-step instructions, it shows how to perform the most necessary and common kinds of house repairs, illustrating exactly what tools and materials are needed.

Maintenance Central for Seniors, Inc.

Maintenance Central worker builds fence

Other Efforts

Helping older persons maintain and repair their homes isn't just confined to Detroit. For example, a similar effort is provided by Catholic Social Services, Inc. in Atlanta, Georgia.

Group Highlighted

Catholic Social Services, Inc.
756 West Peachtree Street, N.W.
Atlanta, Georgia 30308
(404) 881-6571

* State and/or local government agencies are frequently responsible for administration of Federal program funds. For further information, see Appendix I under appropriate Federal agency.

NOTE: For a complete listing of groups featured throughout this book, see Index.

Managing Apartments

Southside United Housing Development Fund Corporation
238 South Second Street
Brooklyn, New York 11211
(212) 387-3600

Those who own their houses or apartments have little idea of the terror and misery that can plague tenants in buildings owned by landlords who don't care or lack the money to maintain them. Perhaps trash litters the hallways, the plumbing doesn't work or neglect has invited vandalism causing frightened tenants to barricade themselves behind locked doors.

The embattled tenants can scream on the phone, threaten lawsuits or refuse to pay rents—but the owner might simply ignore them.

Despite housing laws already on the books and legal commissions which attempt to settle landlord/tenant disputes, the hard reality is that renters all too often have a difficult time forcing landlords to take care of their buildings.

One of many New York City groups that have hurdled this problem by taking over mangement of neglected and abandoned buildings is the Southside United Housing Development Fund Corporation (nicknamed "Los Sures" for Southside) in Brooklyn's low-income, largely Hispanic Williamsburg community.[1] The nonprofit organization, along with 20 other New York City neighborhood groups, manages almost 6,000 apartment units which they help tenants fix up and eventually sell to tenant cooperatives or other neighborhood groups.[2] These groups help blunt the decline of neighborhoods like Williamsburg and insure a supply of decent, low-cost housing for those residents who need it the most.

One Salvaged Building

For 40 years, Bill Bisshyn has lived in a Williamsburg building which, a couple of years ago, was abandoned by the landlord and taken over by the city. He well remembers what life was like before Los Sures helped the tenants organize a cooperative and assisted them in renovating and managing their building.

"The plumbing was very bad," he recalls. "Virtually all the pipes were rusted out—walls were detached from the ceiling and would fall down, window frames were rotted out."

Now the five-story 29-unit building boasts new plumbing, plaster, heaters and windows and should be completely renovated by March 1980. At that time the city will turn the deed over to the tenant cooperative.

Los Sures

A Los Sures building

Los Sures' Success

Los Sures manages eight once neglected or abandoned buildings under a special city program and 11 others owned by absentee landlords with whom they have contracts. Moreover, the group has purchased 60 run-down apartments and expects to buy 300 more by June 1980. Once these buildings are renovated, they are slated to be sold to tenant cooperatives or neighborhood groups, providing low-income housing for area residents.

And with funds from the Department of Housing and Urban Development's (HUD) Community Development Block Grant (CDBG) Program,* the group provides technical assistance to tenants in managing and operating their own buildings.

In 1979 Los Sures had a paid staff of 195 which included workers from the Department of Labor's Comprehensive Employment and Training Act (CETA) Program.* Its budget of $4.8 million came primarily from various HUD Programs.[3]

Beginnings

Los Sures began in 1972 when Fathers Brian Karvelis and Augustin Ruiz, along with community organizers Louis Olmedo and Manuel Ayala, decided to fight neighborhood decay in Williamsburg's southside. The foursome set out to save the old run-down apartment buildings and, more importantly, help their occupants.

The group persuaded local banks and foundations to donate money, and with resident volunteers, a small staff was formed.

Organizing Tenants

Los Sures staffers began organizing tenants of neglected buildings, boosting their interest in demanding needed services—and giving them hope. The plan was simple enough. First, Los Sures would try to bargain with the landlord on behalf of the tenants. If the landlord couldn't be found or refused to talk, Los Sures would then take over management of the building, withholding rent from the landlord and using it for needed repairs.[4]

"In essence, when the landlord wasn't getting an income, that was the final straw and he completely abandoned the property," explains Doug Moritz, Los Sures' executive director. "We were saying that we were gutsy enough to confront any legal body with our plan. And as long as we could give them a responsible accounting of the rent money that we collected, people were willing to listen."

Receivership Program

But the rent money just wasn't enough to cover the major repairs that many of the buildings needed. It was at that point that Los Sures took a close look at the advantages offered by the city's "receivership" program.

Under state law, the receivership program authorizes city governments to become administrators of landlord neglected apartment buildings that are "dangerous to the life, safety or health of the residents." As administrator, the city is the authorized landlord, responsible for rent collection and maintenance.

The old Williamsburg buildings that the group was assisting fit the "dangerous" test, and in 1973 Los Sures asked the city's Housing and Development Administration to take them into receivership—but with a different twist. The neighborhood group wanted to take over management responsibilities. So marked the beginning of what is now known as New York City's Community Management Program.

Tenant management meeting

Gut renovation—putting in the floor

Others Show Faith in Los Sures

In January 1977 Los Sures put its skills to good use when it was asked to manage a newly built 534-unit, low-income apartment project sponsored by a church group. The apartment complex was built with funds from HUD's Rental and Cooperative Housing Assistance for Lower-Income Families (Section 236) Program,* as well as with a state construction program subsidy.

Mr. Moritz sums it up this way: "You can manifest your own destiny. Sounds lofty but if people can be convinced that they, individually, can make a difference, it will happen. The initiative has to be in the neighborhood."

Other Groups

Community organizations outside of New York City are also helping tenants manage apartment buildings. Among them are two Chicago, Illinois groups, the Kenwood-Oakland Community Organization and the Community Housing Education Corporation of Chicago.[5]

Working at a Los Sures building

Groups Highlighted

Community Housing Education Corporation of Chicago
2753 West Armitage Avenue
Chicago, Illinois 60647
(312) 235-2144

Kenwood-Oakland Community Organization
4618 South Lake Park
Chicago, Illinois 60653
(312) 548-7500

[1] Southside United Housing Development Fund Corporation is also mentioned in Housing Section, p. 112.

[2] Housing cooperatives are owned and managed jointly by the tenants who buy shares in the building and have the right to sell their interest should they wish to move. (For more information on housing cooperatives, see chart in Housing Section, p. 119.)

[3] Los Sures' main sources of funding include the Department of Housing and Urban Development's (HUD) Rehabilitation Loan (Section 312); and Lower-Income Rental Assistance (Section 8) Programs.*

[4] It is recommended that money collected during rent strikes be held by the city as authorized under local "escrow" ordinances or landlord/tenant legislation. Escrow accounts are opened through the city treasurer and are used as "bargaining chips" to force landlords to upgrade properties. In most escrow accounts, funds can be released only for direct payment of building repairs. If, in the specified time period, buildings do not meet city code standards, the landlord has breached the contract of habitability which is standard in most rental agreements, and the escrow funds are returned to the tenants who are free to seek alternative housing. The latest legal decisions involving escrow cases are cited in the *American Law Report,* 3rd edition, Volume 40, page 810.

[5] The Community Housing Education Corporation of Chicago is also mentioned in Housing Section, p. 112.

* State and/or local government agencies are frequently responsible for administration of Federal program funds. For further information, see Appendix I under appropriate Federal agency.

NOTE: For a complete listing of groups featured throughout this book, see Index.

Financing Home Repairs

Neighborhood Housing Services, Inc.
809 Middle Street
Pittsburgh, Pennsylvania 15212
(412) 321-2909

Let's say you've decided to fix up your home. Where do you get the money? Go to a bank, you might say.

Unfortunately, for people in low-income areas or those with bad credit ratings, it's not that easy. Usually they can't borrow the money. And their homes, their neighborhoods and, ultimately, their cities are the losers.

Neighborhood housing service organizations, now active in over 75 communities around the country, are striving to change all that. By effectively using the model developed 12 years ago by the resident-inspired Neighborhood Housing Services, Inc. (NHS) of Pittsburgh, Pennsylvania, community residents are getting help in locating funding and contractors to purchase and repair homes.

Pittsburgh's Success

During 1978 alone, the Pittsburgh group helped 427 families start home repairs and oversaw the completion of 377 others—at an estimated total cost of $6.5 million. On all repair projects, NHS offers a range of technical services including securing contractors and phase-by-phase inspection of work. And that's just the beginning. Over the years NHS has assisted residents in obtaining more than 1,000 loans, averaging $6,500 each. About $1.5 million in loans have come from the group's high risk fund, which offers loans at reasonable rates to residents who are unable to qualify at traditional lending institutions.

The NHS high-risk fund improved life for Isabel Mike and her family. "My house was coming apart. The front porch was falling down; pipes weren't covered in the bathroom and froze; the whole thing needed major plumbing and brick work, and banks turned their backs on us," Mrs. Mike recalls. With an NHS long-term loan, the Mikes were able to have the repairs made. And the $69 monthly payments fit their modest budget.

Housing renovations help spruce up neighborhood.

Organization

It takes a well-run organization to supervise so many activities, and Pittsburgh's Neighborhood Housing Services certainly meets the test. It has a full-time staff of 25 and its annual operating budget of about $550,000 comes mostly from the Department of Housing and Urban Development's Community Development Block Grant (CDBG) Program.* NHS receives fees for providing technical assistance to other housing groups and also receives contributions from local lending institutions.

Origins

This high-powered organization started simply enough. In 1967 residents of Pittsburgh's Central North Side found it was becoming difficult to obtain money for home purchases and repairs. The area, with a racial mix of about 60 percent white and 40 percent black, was aging and many of the homes needed work. But lending institutions were reluctant to lend money to the low- and middle-income residents, and even the city seemed to be slipping in providing services to the area.

To turn things around, local leaders launched a remarkably well-organized effort involving private lending institutions, the city government and the residents themselves. Only if everyone worked together, they said, could the decline of the Central North Side be halted.

Working Together

NHS Executive Director David McCall attributes the group's success to their persistence in convincing lenders and city officials that, with help, Central North Side residents could boost the area's image, save it from decay, and thereby benefit the entire city. "We just wouldn't give up," he says.

Two local bankers who were concerned about the lack of reinvestment in the city generally, and in Central North Side specifically, were of great help. "They had so much clout in the lending community," notes McCall, "their endorsement paid off."

After much debate and several joint meetings, agreements were reached which led to the establishment of the basic NHS model.

The Model

- First, the local banking institutions agreed to consider applications for home purchase loans strictly on their merits and vowed not to reject any applicant who met normal requirements for credit worthiness.

- Second, the city agreed to retain and improve public services and to target the Central North Side area for street and facility repairs and maintenance. Additionally, the city committed itself to regular inspections for violations of city codes and promised to make its own loan programs available to neighborhood residents.

- Third, the residents created the wide-ranging Neighborhood Housing Services organization.

First Funds

Once NHS was established in 1968, funding was needed to set up the high-risk loan fund and pay for a staff. Although most of their initial $750,000 funding came from Pittsburgh's Hillman and Scaife Foundations, local banks and businesses also made donations. Now over 20 lending institutions make annual contributions for NHS activities.

Staff Role

The NHS staff has a broad range of responsibilities. Among other activities, the staff balances residents' needs with their incomes, counsels them on buying and repairing homes, refers them to appropriate lending institutions and helps them negotiate loans. NHS also provides technical assistance such as locating reputable contractors.

Concept Spreads

In 1974, six years after NHS Pittsburgh was incorporated, the Federal government formed a task force to promote the NHS concept in other communities around the country. The task force has since evolved into the Neighborhood Reinvestment Corporation (NRC), a Federally-funded public corporation which in 1979 provided technical assistance to 97 neighborhoods in 79 cities.[1]

New Directions

Since 1968 NHS Pittsburgh has expanded its activities to include other neighborhoods. And recently the city government gave the group a vote of confidence by enlisting its help in monitoring a citywide program which provides poor and elderly citizens with low-interest repair loans. Moreover, NHS has set up a for-profit subsidiary corporation, Home Improvement Specialties (HIS), which offers competitive prices for home repair services.

[1] For more information on the Neighborhood Reinvestment Corporation (NRC), see Resources at end of Housing Section.

* State and/or local government agencies are frequently responsible for administration of Federal program funds. For further information, see Appendix I under appropriate Federal agency.

NOTE: For a complete listing of groups featured throughout this book, see Index.

Chapter 3

Helping People Find a Place to Live

Introduction

Finding an affordable apartment or house to rent or buy can be difficult, especially for low-income families. Looking through the want ads often isn't enough. In fact, reading all about those $400 per month apartments and expensive houses can be an exercise in self-torture.

As higher-income "urban pioneers" rediscover the inner city, many low-income, often long-time residents are forced out by the subsequent increased rents and property values. And they have a particularly hard time finding decent, affordable housing.

In this chapter we'll look at what neighborhood groups are doing to fight displacement by helping residents keep their homes or find new ones in the same area. We'll also examine how some groups are providing neighbors with financial counseling and helping to stabilize their communities by matching renters and landlords. All these activities serve family needs and help preserve a neighborhood's character.

The lessons these groups have learned can help your neighborhood organization as well.

Fighting Urban Displacement

St. Ambrose Housing Aid Center
321 East 25th Street
Baltimore, Maryland 21218
(301) 235-5770

In many cities, once undesirable inner-city neighborhoods are being rediscovered by professionals and turned into "hot" property areas. Lured by the elegance of old houses and the nearness to city jobs, these new residents are changing the structure and character of the neighborhoods in which they settle—and boosting property values.

In their wake, however, they have created problems for poorer families, many of whom are long-time residents. Landlords are often anxious to sell to the newcomers and real estate speculators for financial gain. And local residents, who can't afford the higher rents and increased property taxes, are forced to search for new neighborhoods, often settling for sub-standard housing.

The St. Ambrose Housing Aid Center in Baltimore, Maryland, is hurdling urban displacement. Since 1972 it has helped over 1,100 low- and middle-income families find and purchase affordable houses and remain in their neighborhoods. And they don't wait for residents to come to them. They reach out to those in danger of being displaced by counseling and nursing them through what can be a complicated and difficult venture: the process of becoming homeowners.

One Neighborhood's Experience

In the last two years St. Ambrose has helped 70 residents in one neighborhood alone. In 1977 Baltimore's 450-family strong Harwood area was mostly black and low-income. But middle-class whites, attracted by its proximity to Johns Hopkins University, began moving in. To curb displacement, the group spread the word that St. Ambrose could help residents buy their houses.

"It didn't look like we were ever going to have anything to call our own," recalls Pauline Mason, a Harwood resident who had house shopped for several years before hearing about St. Ambrose from a friend. "By the time the banks finished going down the line with the down payment and everything, we just couldn't get it together."

The Masons and their three children began renting a three-bedroom, one-bath home which St. Ambrose had purchased for $9,000. To help the family eventually take over ownership, St. Ambrose began setting aside part of the $130 monthly rent for the down payment. With $4,000 from the Department of Housing and Urban Development's Community Development Block Grant (CDBG) Program* and $1,000 from their own budget, St. Ambrose made essential repairs—new plumbing, a new kitchen ceiling, new paint.[1]

Seven months later the group helped the Masons find a local bank willing to lend them $10,000 to buy the house—a price below the market value but within reach of the Masons' budget. And with their monthly payments increasing by only $15, the Masons now are enjoying the privilege of homeownership.

Origins and First Funding

It all began in 1968 when Father George W. Bur and a local real estate agent, Vincent Quayle, began studying housing conditions in Baltimore. They found that low- and middle-income residents living in blighted areas were finding it difficult to get bank loans. Realtors seemed unwilling to help them, and many of the residents didn't know how to buy a house.

So in 1971 Quayle and his partner set up a prepurchasing counseling service for those who had been shut out of the housing market. Baltimore's Associated Catholic Charities and the State Housing Commission each kicked in $6,000, and in June 1972 St. Ambrose Housing Aid Center began

Baltimore residents learn how to become homeowners at St. Ambrose Housing Aid Center.

matching residents with houses and financing. That first year 50 of the 150 families counseled bought homes.

Staff and Budget

In 1979 St. Ambrose had a paid staff of 16. Its $250,000 annual operating budget came primarily from Associated Catholic Charities, but it also received CDBG funds. St. Ambrose buys mostly run-down, small houses which they fix up and sell to low- and middle-income residents. Their staff includes four contractors who make the needed repairs. St. Ambrose then helps clients find affordable financing. Their generous funding allows them to absorb some renovation costs to keep selling prices within clients' reach. Almost one-third of their clients are single-parent women who earn $6,000 to $12,000 a year. In two-parent families, incomes average between $10,000 and $18,000.

House Fund

Thanks to an anonymous donor who has pumped $100,000 into a house-buying fund over the last five years, St. Ambrose is able to keep 50 homes in stock for renovation and sale. Also five local banks have shown confidence in the group by boosting the fund with lines of credit. The fund provides St. Ambrose with the cash to compete with speculators for bargain homes which have been repossessed or are being sold for back taxes.

Moreover, in 1974 the group opened its own brokerage company, Charm Realty. The firm's only agent earns her modest salary through commissions and helps those residents with limited funds who are shunned by other realtors. In addition, Charm provides St. Ambrose with access to complete listings of available Baltimore housing.

Reputation Spreads

The determination to fit the costs of a house neatly into their clients' budgets has paid off. Only one of the 1,100 families obtaining mortgage money with St. Ambrose help has ever defaulted. That impressive record has spurred once hesistant local banks to open their lending windows to St. Ambrose referrals. And for those who have trouble meeting expenses and mortgage payments, St. Ambrose has been named a counseling agency under the Department of Housing and Urban Development's (HUD) Neighborhood Housing Counseling Program.* The group offers counseling to all Baltimore homeowners.

The media has been helpful in promoting St. Ambrose's good reputation. A staff member produces skits on home buying and home care which are aired on Baltimore's three major television channels as public service announcements.

Promoting Neighborhood Stability

In addition to St. Ambrose, other groups have been successful with encouraging homeownership while minimizing displacement and ensuring a stable neighborhood. One of these is Stop Wasting Abandoned Property (SWAP) in Providence, Rhode Island, which tracks down the owners of vacant houses and arranges sales to families willing to buy and fix up houses at moderate costs.

Even lending institutions are getting into the act. In Los Angeles, California, for example, the Home Loan Counseling Center, financed by 32 savings and loan associations, operates two neighborhood store-front offices. At no charge, the group offers pre-ownership counseling and helps low- and moderate-income residents of the Los Angeles metropolitan area obtain mortgage financing.

Groups Highlighted

Home Loan Counseling Center
2207 North Broadway
Los Angeles, California 90031
(213) 224-8011

Stop Wasting Abandoned Property
439 Pine Street
Providence, Rhode Island 02907
(401) 272-0526

[1] For more costly renovations, St. Ambrose arranges low-interest loans for residents through the Maryland Housing Rehabilitation Program.

* State and/or local government agencies are frequently responsible for administration of Federal program funds. For further information, see Appendix I under appropriate Federal agency.

NOTE: For a complete listing of groups featured throughout this book, see Index.

Matching Landlords and Tenants

Flatbush Development Corporation
1418 Cortelyou Road
Brooklyn, New York 11226
(212) 469-8990

If fixing up two people for a date is hard, try matching would-be tenants with prospective landlords.

Some local housing groups are finding this real estate version of "the dating game" a valuable tool in preserving the ethnic character and stability of a neighborhood. For the landlord it means vacant apartments are filled by responsible, stable tenants. For the tenants it means, at long last, a suitable place to live and raise a family. And for the community, it can mean a broadening of cultural experiences.

The Problem

Landlord/tenant match-ups can prevent illegal and discriminatory tactics such as "blockbusting" and "racial steering." Realtors engaging in blockbusting create fear and tension among white residents by telling them that property values are likely to fall because minorities will soon be moving into the area. Frightened by this faulty logic, some homeowners sell below market value. And the blockbusting realtors resell the homes to minorities at or above market value, making a handsome profit on the transaction. The presence of the new minority families gives the realtors added fuel for continued blockbusting tactics.

Racial steering further compounds the problem. By intentionally steering white families to one neighborhood and minorities to another, real estate agents and apartment managers who engage in the practice are determining the ethnic makeup of a community.

Changing the Pattern

That's what was happening in the ethnically rich North Flatbush community of Brooklyn, New York. But in 1975, eager to stop the growing checkerboard pattern of segregation that was plaguing their three-square-mile 100,000-strong neighborhood, some residents decided to face blockbusting and racial steering head-on. They formed the Flatbush Development Corporation (FDC) and set out to spruce up their community and, more importantly, ensure that people of different incomes and ethnic backgrounds could continue to take pride in their neighborhood while living side by side.

Apartment building in Flatbush attracts prospective tenants.

With the aid and cooperation of the New York City Human Rights Commission's Neighborhood Stability and Fair Housing Enforcement Unit, FDC launched an apartment referral service to promote ethnic diversity and resident stability and short-circuit the segregation plan being forced on their community. Since then FDC has placed 234 landlords and tenants according to family income and housing needs—regardless of race.

A young Panamanian woman who resides in North Flatbush has seen the change in her neighborhood since FDC was formed. "We all keep ourselves together," she says. "It's up to each person to take an active interest in working together. That's definitely more important to a good community than the color of people's skin."

Striking Back at Segregation

FDC leaders interviewed landlords and managers to involve those willing to help revitalize Flatbush into an integrated community.

About 50 percent of Flatbush apartment buildings were deteriorating. The Human Rights Commission helped the group's efforts to spruce up the area by exercising its authority and ordering landlords and owners to bring buildings into city health and safety code compliance or face legal proceedings.

Meanwhile, FDC fought the problem by helping renters organize tenant associations to work closely with the Commission in monitoring building violations and repairs.

Also the city Human Rights Commission conducted investigations and issued complaints against landlords and realtors suspected of blockbusting and racial steering.

In addition, a $30,000 two-year grant from the Ford Foundation and $10,000 raised by community members helped staff FDC and paid for promotional materials. The group set up a neighborhood storefront office to provide counseling and help tenants find decent, suitable housing.

Tenant and Landlord Screening

FDC staffers interview families interested in moving to Flatbush—in their homes, whenever possible. Staffers make credit checks and assess housing needs and budgets before matching families with suitable landlords. Once placed, FDC maintains contact with their tenant and landlord clients, the vast majority of whom report they are pleased with FDC's matchmaking. To ensure proper maintenance and services, inspections of buildings continue as well.

Selling Flatbush

With increasing economic and residential stability, FDC started promoting the benefits and housing opportunities in Flatbush to other Brooklyn residents. They drew attention to their community through a promotion campaign, publishing an area newspaper, conducting open-house tours and holding neighborhood fairs, all of which are still ongoing.

FDC credits its success to effectively rallying Flatbush residents around the positive aspects of integration. Citizen pride is a central theme in their promotion campaign and word-of-mouth advertising has proven to be most effective.

And FDC continues to make important progress in realizing the dream of a stable, integrated community as owners and renters actively use its services. As one lifetime Flatbush resident put it, "We have people—that's what makes it good."

Other Groups

Other successful groups providing housing referral services are the Ouachita Multi-Purpose Community Action Program, a Community Action Agency (CAA)* in rural Ouachita Parish, Louisiana and the Oak Park Housing Center in Oak Park, Illinois.[1]

Groups Highlighted

Oak Park Housing Center
1041 South Boulevard
Oak Park, Illinois 60302
(312) 848-7150

Ouachita Multi-Purpose Community Action Program
920 Louberta Street
Monroe, Louisiana 71201
(318) 322-7151

[1] The Community Services Administration's Community Action Program (CAP)* funds local Community Action Agencies (CAAs)* aimed at helping low-income residents with their food, housing, energy and other needs.

* State and/or local government agencies are frequently responsible for administration of Federal program funds. For further information, see Appendix I under appropriate Federal agency.

NOTE: For a complete listing of groups featured throughout this book, see Index.

Chapter 4

Standing Up for Homeowner and Tenant Rights

Introduction

As the cost of decent housing soars, many renters and homeowners feel as though they are being dropped off the edge of a cliff. Often actions taken by private industry and government have the effect of adding to housing costs and limiting the ability of residents to find affordable and decent homes.

But community groups across the country are beginning to raise their voices and wield their influence in the housing marketplace. For example, some local governments have enacted rent control laws to prevent landlords from significantly increasing rents during times of housing shortages. But this short-term solution also can have the long-term effect of stimulating condominium conversion which can displace many tenants. So community groups are increasingly turning to rent control commissions that strive for a fair balance between renters and legitimate needs of owners.

Community groups are also taking on banks and insurance companies that refuse to make loans or provide fire insurance in certain "high risk" areas, a discriminatory practice known as "redlining."

In these and other housing areas, citizens are starting to assert their rights. This chapter will give you an idea of what you can do to protect yours.

Protecting Homeowners Against Discrimination

South Brooklyn Against Investment Discrimination
591 Third Street
Brooklyn, New York 11215
(212) 875-0835

Often the most difficult task of buying a home or making repairs is figuring out how to raise the needed money. Financing problems often take on an added burden for residents in certain minority or low-income areas who face discrimination in obtaining loans for home repairs, home purchases or even fire insurance.

Some lending institutions and insurance companies set policies that keep residents in "high risk areas" from getting loans or coverage in spite of laws prohibiting such discrimination. The phrase "redlining" comes from the apparent practice of taking a city map, drawing a red line around certain neighborhoods and saying to those residents, in essence, "We can't help you."

But through community education and vigorous enforcement of Federal laws, citizens can stabilize their community by insuring the availability in their area of home purchase and repair financing.

Origins

In January 1977 eight residents in the ethnically mixed, primarily middle-income area of Park Slope in Brooklyn, New York decided to fight redlining. They saw that local banks were not lending money to people who wanted to buy or improve homes in their neighborhood. The mile-long area is replete with brownstone row houses and four-to-eight family dwellings but area banks were refusing loans for multifamily houses.

So Herb Steiner, a machine shop operator and an eight-year Park Slope resident, along with seven others, formed South Brooklyn Against Investment Discrimination (AID). They challenged the apparent discrimination practices of banks and insurance companies—and they won.

South Brooklyn Against Investment Discrimination

Residents "redline" a Park Slope bank

Key to Success

Their success is due to several factors. They boned up on Federal laws that protect residents against illegal lending and insurance practices, and then set out to insure these laws were being enforced. Once they set their goals, they gathered the needed facts, rallied community support and, with their findings, approached the banks and insurance companies. In brief, they fought fair, hard and never quit.

Strategy

The group's first target was Park Slope banks. They did the research needed to prove that redlining was actually occurring. By using the Home Mortgage Disclosure Act of 1975, a Federal law requiring lending institutions to open loan records for public in-

South Brooklyn Against Investment Discrimination

Organizer Herb Steiner explains AID's campaign against Park Slope banks to local reporter.

spection, they discovered that few Park Slope loans were being made. With this evidence in hand, AID moved into the second stage.

Organizing for Change

In order to force lending institutions to change, AID took the newly discovered facts to the community. "Once we hit the street," Steiner recalls, "it only took a month to get 1,500 people to sign a petition pledging to withdraw their money from the vaults of the worst offenders if lending policies didn't change."

AID leaders also met with officials of banks which they suspected of discriminating against Park Slope residents. The petition tactic was somewhat successful. A few banks publicly announced that Park Slope property owners, or prospective ones, would be welcome customers.

But some banks still refused to change or admit to any possible wrongdoing. So AID moved to step three.

More Ammunition

AID learned in 1978 that a large bank, with over $1.4 billion in deposits and two offices in Park Slope, was applying to the Federal Deposit Insurance Corporation (FDIC) for permission to open a new branch office in Manhattan. AID petitioned the FDIC to deny the request because of the bank's extremely poor lending record in Park Slope. They argued that during 1977 the bank made $4 million in mortgage loans in New York City—few of which benefited Park Slope residents—and $200 million in other investments.

AID took action based on the new Federal Community Reinvestment Act of 1977. That law requires that, before approving new branch requests, the FDIC and other Federal financial regulatory agencies must examine the lending policies and records of regulated institutions to ensure they are meeting local community credit needs—especially in low- and moderate-income neighborhoods.

New Lending Policies Announced

The FDIC denied the bank's request. Meanwhile, the bank announced a new set of lending terms, making mortgage and home repair money more accessible for those living in both single and multifamily dwellings. In fact, the bank's loans in all of New York City increased dramatically—from $4 million in 1977 to $32 million in 1978. And in December 1979 a new branch office application by the bank was pending before the FDIC.

The group's research shows that the impact of AID and similar groups on the New York banking industry has been extensive since 1976. Private lending institutions have boosted mortgage loan approvals to 60 percent on one- and two-family Park Slope dwellings—a vast improvement over the former 33 percent record. In addition, loan approvals on multifamily Park Slope homes increased from less than 17 percent to 30 percent during the same period.

Obtaining Insurance for Homeowners

In 1978, after learning that many large insurance companies were not writing policies on Park Slope homes, AID launched another highly visible and successful campaign.

Their organizing efforts—which included circulating 5,000 flyers, taking their case to community residents and lobbying the insurance companies—attracted newspaper coverage. And within three months, several insurance companies agreed to relax their guidelines. The companies guaranteed to inspect all applicants' homes regardless of locality and to assign more independent agents to serve Park Slope residents.

Organization and Funding

AID welcomes to their executive board anyone willing to put in the time. In 1978 they received funding under the Department of Labor's Comprehensive Employment and Training Act (CETA) Program* to hire a professional staffer to coordinate activities and conduct research. And the group's $100-a-month budget for printing, stamps and other expenses comes from private contributions.

Other Efforts

Several groups are successfully attacking redlining in their communities. Among them are the Chicago Metropolitan Area Housing Alliance in Illinois; Massachusetts Fair Share in Boston, Massachusetts; Fillmore-Leroy Area Residents, Inc. in Buffalo, New York; and the Illinois Public Action Council in Chicago.[1]

Groups Highlighted

Chicago Metropolitan Area Housing Alliance
1123 West Washington Boulevard
Chicago, Illinois 60607
(312) 243-5850

Fillmore-Leroy Area Residents, Inc.
307 Leroy Avenue
Buffalo, New York 14214
(716) 838-6740

Illinois Public Action Council
59 East Van Buren Street
Chicago, Illinois 60605
(312) 427-6262

Massachusetts Fair Share
304 Boylston Street
Boston, Massachusetts 02116
(617) 266-7505

[1] Fillmore-Leroy Area Residents is also mentioned in Housing Section, p. 155.

* State and/or local government agencies are frequently responsible for administration of Federal program funds. For further information, see Appendix I under appropriate Federal agency.

NOTE: For a complete listing of groups featured throughout this book, see Index.

Protecting Tenant Rights

Hartford Fair Rent Commission
250 Main Street
Hartford, Connecticut 06103
(203) 566-6024

Recently in Hartford, Connecticut, a low-income widow with two children was faced with a whopping 25 percent rent increase on her two-bedroom apartment. She was already spending over one-third of her income on housing and the increase would devastate her small budget.

But with escalating fuel, maintenance and other operating costs, the landlord was losing money. And because Hartford has no rent control laws which forbid or place ceilings on rent hikes, the landlord felt justified in asking for a higher monthly payment.

The widow, unable to meet the increase, might have been forced to settle for substandard housing elsewhere. But instead she turned to the Hartford Fair Rent Commission, the city's alternative to rent control. Charged with settling rent disputes, the Commission acts on about 100 cases a year, attempting to balance tenant and landlord interests. After studying the finances of the landlord and the widow and surveying comparable housing costs in the area, the Commission ruled in favor of both parties—allowing the landlord to boost rent enough to make a small profit and leading the widow to a Federal rent subsidy program for low-income families.

Rent Control

A city fair rent commission is an alternative to rent control laws which are often controversial. Many tenants favor rent control because of the protection against rent hikes which hit at their pocketbooks and home security.

Not surprisingly, however, many landlords strongly oppose rent control, arguing that it serves as a subsidy for tenants at a time when the landlord can't raise rents to cover operating expenses. Moreover, some landlords and other housing experts blame rent control for a host of housing ills such as building neglect and abandonment which occur when owners lose money on their apartments.

Fair Rent Commission Not for Everyone

A fair rent commission is one answer to the problem, but it doesn't necessarily work for all cities, cautions William Gardiner, administrator of Hartford's Commission.

"The case load for a city the size of Los Angeles or New York would be an administrative nightmare," he says. "But in a town like Hartford, one can only speculate on how high rents might have risen in the absence of the Commission."

Origins

The Hartford Fair Rent Commission was created in 1970 following passage of state legislation authorizing Connecticut communities to establish fair rent commissions and providing guidelines and standards.

Launching a fair rent commission was especially important to Hartford's inner-city residents, 80 percent of whom live in rental housing. But getting the Commission off the ground and functioning took tough organizing and active legal advice from a local public interest law firm. Nearly two years elapsed after the passage of enabling legislation before the Hartford Commission heard its first case.

"The minute we heard of the state legislation," remembers local activist lawyer Sydney Schulman, "we went around to community groups and met to decide what we wanted to see in the local ordinance."

After rallying community interest, the group lobbied the city to include in the ordinance such provisions as forbidding landlords to harass complaint-filing tenants and ensuring a fair representation of tenants on the Commission. After six months of negotiating, the City Council approved the local ordinance establishing the Rent Commission.

Getting the Commission in Operation

"At that point we naively thought our work was done," Schulman says. "But the most difficult thing was to get the local ordinance operating and operating properly. It took another five months for the mayor to get around to appointing Commission members. And once appointed, the Commission had no staff, no money, no procedures and was simply not operative."

Tired of delays and determined to show their persistence, Hartford tenants took a creative step to get the complaint process churning. They drew up and circulated complaint forms to tenants. And on Christmas Eve, 1971—a beautiful night with a soft snow falling—they delivered over 100 complaints to the Fair Rent Commission Chairman's doorstep.

"That's what worked," Schulman recalls with a slight grin.

Staff and Budget

The nine Commission members, appointed by the mayor and approved by the City Council, must include at least three landlords and three tenants. In 1979 the Commission had a staff of four and city funding of $65,000.

The staff does the research necessary for Commission hearings. They conduct surveys to determine fair market values of comparable apartments, instruct city inspectors to check apartment buildings for possible health and safety code violations and obtain financial statements from landlords and tenants.

Balance Both Sides

After hearings, Commission members make a final decision. If they rule in favor of the landlord, the city Housing Department helps low-income tenants find state housing assistance or help from such Federal programs as the Department of Housing and Urban Development's (HUD) Lower-Income Rental Assistance (Section 8) Program.* If the Commission decides that increases are unfair, those landlords refusing to lower rents are fined.

Other Groups

Other groups around the country have adopted various statutes protecting tenants. Some areas that have adopted rent control laws include Washington, D.C.; Miami, Florida; and Cambridge, Massachusetts. And city lobby groups, such as the Metropolitan Council on Housing in New York City and the New York State Tenant and Neighborhood Council, have formed to promote tenant protection laws.

Twenty-six states and the District of Columbia have enacted legislation requiring landlords to keep buildings in good repair. In those states without legislation, groups such as the Indiana Housing Coalition are actively lobbying for passage of responsible laws.

Fighting Back

And in swank resort towns, some low-income year-round residents are fighting seasonal rent hikes and displacement caused by summer vacationers. Residents of Cape Cod, Massachusetts and the off-shore islands have formed the Cape Cod and Islands Tenants Council to demand year-round leases from property owners.

Groups Highlighted

Cape Cod and Islands Tenants Council
Box 195
Hyannis, Massachusetts 02601
(617) 775-1070

Indiana Housing Coalition
P.O. Box 44329
Indianapolis, Indiana 46244
(no phone)

Metropolitan Council on Housing
24 West 30th Street
New York, New York 10001
(212) 725-4800

New York State Tenant and Neighborhood Council
198 Broadway, Room 1100
New York, New York 10038
(212) 964-7200

* State and/or local government agencies are frequently responsible for administration of Federal program funds. For further information, see Appendix I under appropriate Federal agency.

NOTE: For a complete listing of groups featured throughout this book, see Index.

The Hartford Fair Rent Commission
A Model Study

What it is:

- A city agency with an administrative staff.
- A nine-member Commission — including at least three tenants and three landlords — appointed by the Mayor and confirmed by the City Council for three-year terms.
- A group that receives complaints from area tenants who believe their rent hikes to be excessive, harsh and unconscionable.

What it can do:

- Schedule hearings for landlords and tenants.
- Decide that rent increases are fair or unfair based on hearings and other information from staff.
- Reduce rent hikes to an amount considered fair based on the facts presented.
- Order tenants to escrow rent with the Commission until landlords correct city health and safety code violations.
- Issue orders which become effective on the first date rent is due after a hearing.
- Take legal action to enforce its orders.
- Provide interpreter services when necessary.

What it considers in determining fair rent:

- The rents charged for comparable apartments in the city.
- The sanitary conditions of the apartments.
- The number of kitchens, sinks, bathtubs, showers and toilets.
- The services, furniture and equipment supplied by landlords.
- The number and size of bedrooms.
- The repairs necessary to make apartments reasonably livable.
- The landlords' compliance with city health and safety codes and ordinances.
- The landlords' taxes, overhead and operating expenses.
- The tenants' income and availability of other housing.
- The availability of utilities.
- The damage to properties by tenants other than ordinary wear and tear.

What it can't do:

- Help tenants who don't file written complaints.
- Accept complaints when written leases are in effect. (Violations of written leases are matters for the courts to handle.)

What landlords can do:

- Petition for new hearings when there are significant changes in circumstances such as increased operating costs, capital improvements or boosted services.

What tenants and landlords can do:

- Obtain help from attorneys or others.
- Appeal to the Court of Common Pleas if dissatisfied with the Commission's decision.

Adapted from a Hartford Fair Rent Commission brochure.

Getting Help for Housing and Community Development

Introduction

Housing costs in a given community are directly affected by the deterioration of any single neighborhood. Decay in some communities boosts housing costs in better maintained areas and restricts housing choices for everyone.

One of the best ways neighborhood groups can preserve their area is to make sure their communities get a fair share of government services, from police protection to playgrounds—all of which contribute to a neighborhood's character.

In this chapter we'll explore how one citywide organization has worked to get better services and public improvements in low-income neighborhoods. We'll also see how informal block associations can be transformed into powerhouses that revive their communities. In addition, we'll examine how some dynamic neighborhood groups are providing technical assistance to local government officials while ensuring that Federal and state funds are pumped into their communities.

Strengthening Block Associations

Chicago Mini-Zone Program
Fifth City Human Development Project
410 South Trumbull Street
Chicago, Illinois 60624
(312) 722-3444

Block associations—small groups of residents working together to upgrade their neighborhoods—can greatly help local governments improve city life. Traditionally block clubs have performed many good deeds such as helping new arrivals, organizing clean-ups and winning improved government services. They are usually informal organizations, generating virtually all of their funds from the donations of members.

Recognizing these inexpensive and ready-made resources, some city governments are beginning to make full use of block clubs. Showing the way are cities like Chicago, Illinois. There, in 1977, city officials developed a "Mini-Zone" Program aimed at bolstering efforts by block associations to spruce up their neighborhoods.

Administered by the city's Department of Human Services and funded by the Department of Housing and Urban Development's Community Development Block Grant (CDBG) Program,* the Mini-Zone Program strives to bring housing in low-income areas up to city code standards and teach residents how to economically improve their own homes.

The government-citizen partnership has led to housing rehabilitation, community gardens and resident pride in their communities. At the heart of the activity is the neighborhood block club, sponsored by the community organization.

One Success Story

The success of one community association, the Fifth City Human Development Project, operating in the low-income, predominantly black section of East Garfield on Chicago's West Side, shows how well the Mini-Zone Program can work. Fifth City, active for the past 15 years in a 40-block area of East Garfield, enjoys private and government funding and sponsors an array of housing, education and other programs to help area residents. Fifth City's Mini-Zone Program, which began in 1977, has prompted the creation of five neighborhood block clubs, each covering a one or two block area.

One of Fifth City's greatest successes is the 3500 Van Buren Block Club. Lee Haley, a resident of Van Buren Street since 1963, speaks of the change: "I would say, I think anyone familiar with the block before the Block Club started operating can see the improvement. Some have put sod in front of their homes. And trees, nice flowers and quite a few lights have been installed."

"It wasn't so presentable before," he continues, "I have to admit that. But we cleaned up the whole thing—the garbage, the sidewalks, the streets and the alleys. The vacant lots were bad—abandoned cars and all different kinds of debris. Most of them we cleared away and we put in garden lots."

Here's how the Mini-Zone Program works:

Criteria

A community organization applies to the city for Mini-Zone status.[1] The area under consideration must be eligible for CDBG funds and the community group must agree to sponsor and help form at least one block club. Moreover, a majority of the residents in the targeted area must be willing to join and participate in the activities of the club.

Chicago residents clean up their neighborhood.

Benefits

Once approved, each sponsoring organization is eligible to receive up to $30,000. The money is used to hire a city-approved and trained professional to serve as liaison between block club members and the city. That person's responsibilities include leading residents to other government and private funding sources for help in improving their homes and neighborhoods .

The Mini-Zone Program offers city-sponsored workshops to teach residents how to make minor home repairs. And a technician, such as a plumber or electrician, can be hired to hold how-to workshops for more difficult repairs. Since it was established about $500,000 of the city's CDBG dollars have been pumped into the program, with 11 community organizations actively participating.

Achievements of Van Buren Block Club

Fifth City's Van Buren Block Club members began their spruce-up campaign by preparing a land-use map of their area and deciding what changes they wanted. Club members then set to work. First, they planted 25 trees donated by their area's political ward. Then, working with the city-trained staffer, the Club members persuaded the city to contribute most of the funds needed to repair sidewalks, picking up about one-fourth of the expense themselves.

A new pride was in the air. More changes took place as each Saturday became clean-up day. Squads of volunteers, armed with brooms, shovels and trash cans swept the streets and vacant lots.

Enthusiasm Spreads

The Mini-Zone Program has the added effect of stimulating the birth of new block organizations and also serves as an inspiration to existing club members to do more.

For example, nine families in the 3500 Van Buren Club—encouraged by the neighborhood's new look—have asked for help in financing major home repairs. In addition to CDBG funding, assistance is available from HUD's Rehabilitation Loan (Section 312) Program* and the Department of Energy's (DOE) Weatherization Assistance Program.* An additional boost to eager families comes from the city's Neighborhood Rehabilitation Services, which receives funds from the Department of Labor's Comprehensive Employment and Training Act (CETA) Program* to hire and train workers to repair homes that do not meet city code requirements.

Expansion

Block clubs like 3500 Van Buren are spreading to nearby streets. Other neighbors see their achievements and, with the help of Fifth City, they too are learning how to organize their own block associations. With the $20,000 in Mini-Zone funds targeted for Fifth City in 1980, the group hopes to organize five more block clubs.

Moreover, the city government has been so impressed with the work of Fifth City's block clubs that it is providing CDBG funds and CETA workers to help area residents launch a maintenance corps to insure that local improvements are kept up.

The Fifth City group expects the block club concept to spread around the country. The Chicago model, they believe, can also work for other areas.

Other Improvement Efforts

Some citizen groups are organizing to improve the appearance of their cities. For instance, in Iowa City, Iowa Project GREEN (Grow to Reach Environmental Excellence Now), a nonprofit, loosely structured group of local residents, contributed $200,000 in planting materials, volunteer labor and other services to Iowa City between 1968 and 1979. Working with the city and county governments and local schools, hundreds of Project GREEN volunteers have spruced up the city by planting trees along major streets, beautifying unused downtown lots with mini-parks and other landscaping projects. Funds are raised from Project GREEN's annual plant sale as well as from donations by individuals, local groups and businesses.

Project GREEN
Civic Center
410 East Washington Street
Iowa City, Iowa 52240
(319) 354-1800

[1] Groups applying for Mini-Zone status must be nonprofit and licensed to do business within the State of Illinois. The Department of Housing and Urban Development's (HUD) Community Development Block Grant (CDBG) Program* funds are limited to city-designated Community Development areas, which are mostly low-income neighborhoods with much low-grade housing.

* State and/or local government agencies are frequently responsible for administration of Federal program funds. For further information, see Appendix I under appropriate Federal agency.

NOTE: For a complete listing of groups featured throughout this book, see Index.

Developing Your Neighborhood

Jeff-Vander-Lou, Inc.
2754 Bacon Street
St. Louis, Missouri 63106
(314) 534-3530

There's nothing quite as heartening as seeing how much community organizations can do to spruce up their neighborhoods while helping residents cope with rising inflation by creating jobs and boosting the area's economy.

One remarkable St. Louis organization, Jeff-Vander-Lou, Inc. (JVL), has been a whirlwind of activity since 1966 in the predominantly black, low-income Jeff-Vander-Lou section of the city.

Accomplishments

Their members' achievements are as varied as the people they serve. They have built and renovated $15 million worth of housing, brought in low-cost medical care and wooed a shoe factory to their community. In addition, they have opened two day care centers and have helped unemployed youth and the elderly.

Communities help themselves by launching programs such as day care centers.

The changes in the 500-square-block area have led to reduced crime and increased income, rising property values and higher employment for the 40,000 residents.

Jeff-Vander-Lou resident Walter Short recalls his community in 1966: "Eighty percent of the houses were declared by the city unfit for human habitation, and the area had the highest crime rate in the city." Now, according to Short, "The area has a reduced crime rate and a lot of families are moving in—buildings have been repaired and new ones are being built."[1]

Staff and Budget

JVL is a nonprofit organization. Residents elect the Board of Directors and have input in policy decisions. In 1979 its $230,000 "core staff" budget covered the salaries of an eight-strong administrative staff, office expenses and the planning and developing of new projects. And each completed project operates with its own budget. In total, JVL employs 40 people, about 90 percent of whom live in the area. Moreover, it has developed a network of volunteers from churches, schools and the business community.

Most of JVL's funding comes from private sources—foundations, churches and other groups. But they use every subsidy they can find to fund housing projects and help residents spruce up their homes. They also receive assistance from the National Corporation for Housing Partnerships (NCHP) and from several Federal programs.[2]

In addition, all profits JVL receives from managing its own properties are pumped back into the organization to use for other projects.

Origins

The group was started by an upholstery shop owner, a Canadian Mennonite minister, a retired school teacher and a minister from the Urban League. Seeking to turn around a community that had fallen on hard times, these few determined people set out to attack the urban blight which had stricken the Jeff-Vander-Lou area.

Organizing efforts began in 1965 when the group rallied community opposition to a $79 million bond issue for a project that had been termed "neighborhood development." The project, however, was a proposed cross-town highway and group leaders insisted that it would divide the JVL community and cause the displacement of many area residents. They began visiting and phoning their neighbors. Word spread and residents began making posters, picketing and lobbying against the issue. Even though both St. Louis newspapers had endorsed the bond issue and local officials strongly favored it, the measure was defeated.

With that victory buoying resident interest and awakening city officials to the new Jeff-Vander-Lou force, the community organization incorporated in 1966.

Target Area

JVL next turned to housing development. The first target for rehabilitation was a 15-block section in the heart of Jeff-Vander-Lou. Seventy-five percent of the housing was substandard and 13 people—mostly absentee landlords—controlled all of the dwellings.

The group began renovating a two-family house at a cost of about $18,000 using private donations, a bank loan, and a lot of volunteer help. By 1979 that section had been 90 percent rehabilitated and many of the residents now own their homes. And JVL continues to tackle the problem of housing its area residents. Work is currently underway to construct and rehabilitate an additional 300 units.

A JVL worker on the job

Basic Principles

In doing all this building, whether with nonprofit or limited profit developers, JVL has insisted on two basic principles: first, that JVL, as a community group, decides what kind of housing is developed and for whom; and second, that housing and other programs in the area be planned to attract people of varying income levels into the JVL neighborhood.

Other Impressive Accomplishments:

- *1968:* Several physicians organized a joint medical facility. JVL renovated a building for their use, bringing low-cost health care to the community for the first time. Since then, a Department of Health, Education and Welfare (HEW) public health facility has moved into the area and the joint medical building has been converted to housing for the elderly.

- *1969:* JVL persuaded Brown Group, Inc. to build a shoe factory in the area, creating jobs for 450 residents.

- *1973:* JVL opened a child care center in one of its apartment houses. Two years later another was added.

- *1974:* JVL opened a Senior Citizens Center, providing meals, recreation and counseling to the elderly.

- *1977:* JVL opened an educational center in conjunction with the city's public school system to train high school students in communications techniques.

Track Record

Jeff-Vander-Lou has been able to grow because its track record inspires lender confidence. A year after it renovated its first building, the Mennonite Church provided interest-free loans, grants and skilled craftsmen to help JVL launch larger scale projects. In addition, from 1967 to 1973 the Arrowhead Foundation, established by a successful St. Louis businessman, contributed $1 million in interest-free loans and grants, allowing the group to hire staff and start new projects.

The new pride and determination in the Jeff-Vander-Lou area are visible on the street in several ways. And many of their achievements are a testament to JVL's lobbying effectiveness with the local government. Of course the neighborhood is hardly prosperous yet, but on virtually every level life clearly is better for the residents.

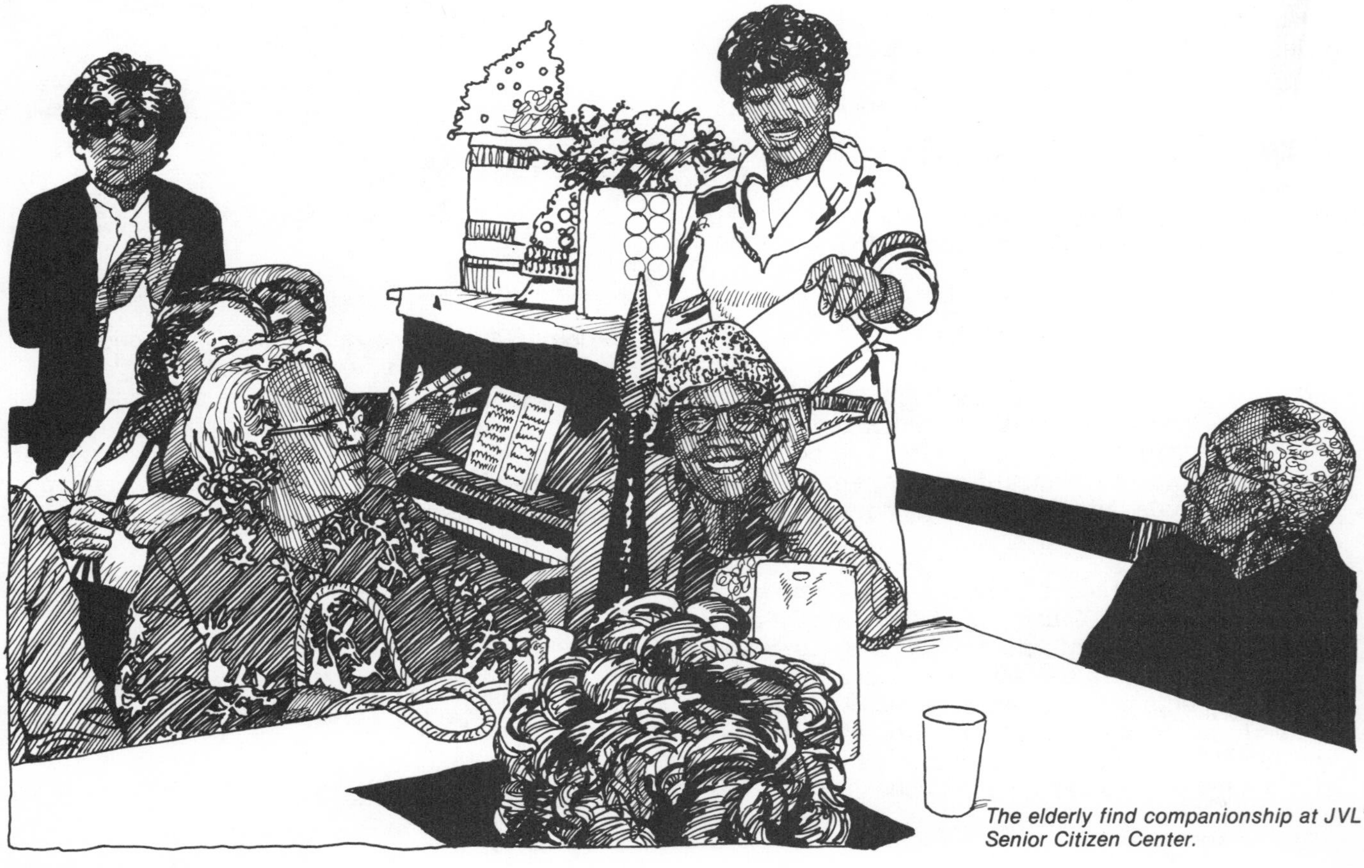

The elderly find companionship at JVL's Senior Citizen Center.

A renovated JVL building shows its original elegance.

Other Neighborhood Projects

Other groups around the country are also successfully developing their neighborhoods. One good example is Fillmore-Leroy Area Residents, Inc. (FLARE) in Buffalo, New York.[3]

Group Highlighted

Fillmore-Leroy Area Residents, Inc.
307 Leroy Avenue
Buffalo, New York 14214
(716) 838-6740

[1] According to a St. Louis Police Department report, in 1969 the crime rate in the Jeff-Vander-Lou area was almost double that of the overall city rate. By 1977, the crime rate in Jeff-Vander-Lou fell by 33 percent while the city rate declined by only 7 percent.

[2] For more information on the National Corporation for Housing Partnerships (NCHP), see Resources at end of Housing Section.

Department of Housing and Urban Development (HUD) assistance used by Jeff-Vander-Lou (JVL) includes the Community Development Block Grant (CDBG); the Neighborhood Development; Direct Loans for Housing for the Elderly or Handicapped (Section 202); Homeownership Assistance for Low- and Moderate-Income Families (Section 235); Multifamily Rental Housing for Low- and Moderate-Income Families (Section 236) Programs.* In addition, the group receives funding from Title III of the Older Americans Act* and Title XX of the Social Security Act,* both of which are administered by the Department of Health, Education and Welfare (HEW).

[3] Fillmore-Leroy Area Residents, Inc. is also mentioned in Housing Section, p. 144.

* State and/or local government agencies are frequently responsible for administration of Federal program funds. For further information, see Appendix I under appropriate Federal agency.

NOTE: For a complete listing of groups featured throughout this book, see Index.

Getting Your Share

Communities Organized for Public Service
122 East Durango
San Antonio, Texas 78204
(515) 222-2367

Is your community getting its fair share of government services? If not, you might organize a neighborhood group to work for the services your community needs.

One such group, Communities Organized for Public Service (COPS), has become a powerful force in San Antonio, Texas. It has helped change the makeup of city government and reorder the city's spending priorities—resulting in major improvements for poor sections of town.

COPS has given once neglected residents in San Antonio's low-income neighborhoods a voice in city government and has made believers out of skeptics. "When COPS began, even our own neighborhood leaders—priests, business people—didn't believe we could change the system," says Aldolfo Pena, a COPS community leader from the predominantly Mexican American Far West Side. "Now they have seen results." He points to the $2 million drainage project being constructed in his neighborhood. "That's something I haven't seen in my area in 45 years."

In the last few years the group has won about $150 million worth of public projects for low-income areas such as street repavement, classroom renovation and much needed drainage systems. Those improvements, in turn, have helped blunt inflation for the entire city by pumping into the housing market more homes in well-maintained neighborhoods.

COPS' strength is more impressive because it makes no political endorsements and its officers must resign should they decide to run for elected offices. Moreover, COPS' $100,000 annual budget is raised entirely from membership dues and advertisement sales in its yearly publication.

Origins

As with other success stories we've looked at, the group started as the long-shot effort of a few determined individuals. One of them was Ernie Cortez, a young West Side Mexican American who had become increasingly angry at the city's neglect of Hispanic and other poor neighborhoods. Cortez and Father Edmundo Rodriquez, a West Side priest who shares Cortez' concern for San Antonio's poor, began masterplanning a new community organization. Its goal: to get improvements for the poor Hispanic, black and ethnic white areas of San Antonio.

First Funding

To get off the ground, Father Rodriquez put together a sponsoring committee representing four church denominations. The church groups also kicked in most of the $80,000 for the first year's operating budget to pay Cortez' salary, office expenses and training sessions for community leaders.

Organizing

With the backing of the ecumenical sponsoring committee, Cortez met with parish priests and other church leaders in low-income areas—listening to their problems and stirring their interest in fighting for improvements. Interest mushroomed with other community leaders helping to rally support. During the first six months of 1974 Cortez met with over 1,000 neighborhood leaders.

As neighborhoods organized, training sessions were conducted to teach leaders how to rally resident support and work for change. By the summer of 1974 a temporary steering committee of the newly recruited neighborhood leaders was formed and COPS was officially born.

First Battle

Their first big issue was perfect for rallying support: the need for storm drainage.

Heavy rains cause major flooding problems in San Antonio, particularly in the low-income southwest and southeast areas where runoff from the well-developed and paved North Side settles. The water can sit for days, ruining cars and homes and preventing children from going to school.

In 1970 San Antonio voters approved a bond issue for storm drainage projects, but the city used the money for other things. People were upset. COPS community leaders set to work drumming up resident interest and researching the problem. Armed with facts and figures, they went to city hall. The Public Works Department turned them away and the city manager refused to meet with them. So the group of 500 leaders organized a public meeting—complete with press and television cameras—to confront the city officials and draw attention to the misused funds. At the meeting residents received a commitment from the city manager and Council members to place another bond issue before the citizens of San Antonio. In November it was approved.

COPS members gather for a city hall meeting.

Changing the System

Another sign of COPS influence came in 1975 when it went after a system that was depriving minorities of representation. All 11 members of the City Council were elected at large by the voters of the entire city. Even though San Antonio is 52 percent Mexican American, Anglos dominated the Council.

The Mexican American Legal Defense and Education Fund (MALDEF) filed a suit in Federal court charging that the system was undemocratic under the Voting Rights Act because one section of town could outvote another. The U.S. Attorney General agreed with MALDEF and directed the city to change the system. MALDEF worked closely with the Mayor's office to develop a new election charter which had to be approved by San Antonio voters. Crucial to its passage were COPS' efforts to drum up minority support by educating eligible citizens unfamiliar with registration and voting procedures and persuading them to exercise their voting rights at the polls. The revised charter passed by a narrow margin, and in 1977 five City Council members were elected from predominantly minority districts.

That victory gave minorities a voice in city government for the first time. "Now, we have our own Council member," says COPS community leader Pena. "And we can go pound on his desk and if he's not responsive we can kick him out. And he knows it."

Beating Projects

Lobbying for civic improvements has also meant COPS' unflinching resolve to defeat projects which they view as wasteful or harmful. For example, in 1975 when the city proposed to spend $1.6 million for a new school administration building, the COPS machinery took charge. The School Board was persuaded to use the funds instead to improve classrooms, primarily in the low-income South and West Sides.

Community Impact

The organization's activities have also had an impact on the spirit of life in San Antonio's poor neighborhoods. COPS community leader Pena speaks of the change. "The people that belong to our parish (the heart of many local COPS groups) have a certain pride. They feel now that they belong someplace, that what they say is important and that they can help themselves."

Similar Efforts

Other groups have had achievements similar to COPS. Successful groups include the Buckeye-Woodland Community Congress in Southeast Cleveland, Ohio; the Cherry Hill Coalition in the Central District of Seattle, Washington; and the Citizens for Community Improvements of Waterloo in Iowa.

Groups Highlighted

Buckeye-Woodland Community Congress
10613 Lamontier Avenue
Cleveland, Ohio 44104
(216) 368-1070

Cherry Hill Coalition
810 18th Avenue
Seattle, Washington 98122
(206) 324-0980

Citizens for Community Improvements of Waterloo
P.O. Box 875
Waterloo, Iowa 50704
(319) 232-8268

NOTE: For a complete listing of groups featured throughout this book, see Index.

Helping Local Governments Get Housing Funds

Rural Housing Improvements, Inc.
218 Central Street
Winchendon, Massachusetts 01475
(617) 297-1376

Rural governments can be at a disadvantage when tackling housing problems, especially if local officials don't know how to go about getting needed financial assistance. The greater proportion of our nation's poor live in small towns, which have more than their share of substandard housing. And even though state and Federal low-income housing assistance programs are available, many small town officials lack the staff and expertise to bring those resources into their communities.

Providing Expertise

One group working to overcome this problem is Rural Housing Improvements, Inc. (RHI) in Winchendon, Massachusetts. The nonprofit organization has become a major developer of low-income housing in northcentral Massachusetts and is helping public and private, nonprofit agencies get housing programs for their areas. Through its efforts, $6 to $10 million a year in state and Federal housing funds are channeled to 75 small communities.

Helping Towns

For instance, several years ago the town of Leominster had only one subsidized family housing project. Yet many of its 35,000 residents held low-paying jobs in the city's plastics industry. As rents rose with inflation, poorer residents unable to pay the higher costs were forced out of apartment complexes. Despite the great need, the Leominster Housing Authority lacked the staff to apply for and administer state and Federal rent subsidy programs. So they turned to RHI for help.

Today, because of RHI's assistance, 96 Leominster families receive rent subsidies from the Department of Housing and Urban Development's Lower-Income Rental Assistance (Section 8) Program* and 40 more are slated for aid next year. Moreover, in 1978 RHI helped Leominster get rental subsidies from the State Department of Community Affairs, enabling 21 low-income families to move to decent housing at rents they can afford.

Origins

It all began in 1968 when community leaders from seven small towns in northcentral Massachusetts joined forces to compete for awards from the Office of Economic Opportunity (OEO).[1] OEO was testing the ingenuity of Community Action Agencies (CAAs)* nationwide by offering grants for the most innovative community service idea.[2] Spearheaded by workers at the Montachusett Opportunity Council, a

An RHI-assisted housing project

rural CAA, the leaders surveyed small towns and found that housing was the most serious problem. Additionally, many of the local officials in rural areas served on a part-time basis and lacked the education or time to gain access to government housing resources, while others were intimidated by the Federal bureaucracy.

Only 6 percent of Massachusetts' state and Federal housing funds were channeled to rural areas which contained 15 percent of its population and an even larger percentage of the state's substandard housing. It was clear that Massachusetts towns weren't getting their fair share of government funds.

The group's proposal to create an agency to help rural families, housing authorities, community organizations and other nonprofit groups obtain Federal and state housing resources was a winner, and the $140,000 OEO grant opened RHI's doors.

Staff and Budget

In 1979 RHI had a staff of 67. Its $1.1 million annual operating budget came primarily from the Community Services Administration (CSA), the United States Department of Agriculture's Farmers Home Administration (FmHA), the Department of Housing and Urban Development (HUD), the Department of Labor (DOL) and the Massachusetts Department of Community Affairs.[3]

Activities

RHI's activities are varied. The group has helped more than 700 families obtain mortgage loans and over 1,200 low-income families acquire rent subsidies from both Federal and state programs. In addition, RHI administers $2.6 million in housing subsidy payments to landlords in 75 communities.

The organization shows CAAs and other rural groups how to bring low-income new and rehabilitated housing and rental assistance programs into their communities. They help clients prepare necessary proposals and applications, supervise construction and develop and implement management of the new housing and social services programs for area residents.

Moreover, the group has helped funnel over $600,000 from HUD's Community Development Block Grant (CDBG) Program* into several small towns in north-central Massachusetts. For example, the town of Greenfield received a $200,000 CDBG grant to rehabilitate a dilapidated neighborhood. And the town of Orange was able to open an elderly meals center and other community facilities as a result of CDBG grants they obtained with RHI's assistance.

Other Groups

Other groups are lending their assistance to local governments and, thus, helping low- and middle-income people obtain affordable housing. One such group is Impact Seven, Inc. of Turtle Lake, Wisconsin, which operates in a rural, six-county area.[4]

In upstate New York, the importance of getting funding expertise was realized by three primarily rural counties. Their legislative bodies created the Regional Housing Council of Southern Tier, Inc. based in Elmira, New York, to provide expert planning and program administration for the towns and county governments in the area.

Groups Highlighted

Impact Seven, Inc.
Route 2, Box 8
Turtle Lake, Wisconsin 54889
(715) 986-4460

Regional Housing Council of Southern Tier, Inc.
307 East Church Street
Room 101
Elmira, New York 14901
(607) 734-5266

[1] The Office of Economic Opportunity (OEO), an antipoverty agency, was replaced by the Community Services Administration (CSA) in 1975.

[2] The Community Services Administration's (CSA) Community Action Program (CAP)* funds local Community Action Agencies (CAAs)* aimed at helping low-income residents with their food, housing, energy and other needs.

[3] Rural Housing Improvements' (RHI) major funding sources include Community Services Administration's (CSA) Office of Community Action's Local Initiative Program;* United States Department of Agriculture's (USDA) Farmers Home Administration's Rural Self-Help Housing Technical Assistance (Section 523) and Technical and Supervisory Assistance (Section 525) Programs;* Department of Housing and Urban Development's (HUD) Neighborhood Housing Counseling, Lower-Income Rental Assistance (Section 8), and Community Development Block Grant (CDBG) Programs;* and the Department of Labor's Comprehensive Employment and Training Act (CETA) Program.* It also utilizes Massachusett's Chapter 707 Rehabilitation Program, one of few state-funded rental assistance programs which guarantee landlords fair market prices on low-income properties if they are fixed up to meet housing code requirements.

[4] Impact Seven, Inc. is a nonprofit Community Development Corporation (CDC)* which receives funds from the Community Services Administration's (CSA) Special Impact Program* administered by the Office of Economic Development (OED). Impact Seven, Inc. is also mentioned in Housing Section, p. 105.

* State and/or local government agencies are frequently responsible for administration of Federal program funds. For further information, see Appendix I under appropriate Federal agency.

NOTE: For a complete listing of groups featured throughout this book, see Index.

Chapter 6

HOSPITALITY
COMMUNITY
FEDERAL CREDIT
UNION
JOIN OUR
CHRISTMAS CLUB
NOW

Providing Housing, Jobs and Credit

Introduction

Anyone seeking to upgrade a community should know that without jobs or access to credit, a neighborhood can't thrive.

If neighborhood businesses can't get needed or borrowed money, they will close down or decline. Lack of credit also makes it difficult for owners and landlords to maintain housing. And the community's downturn will be hastened if residents can't find work.

These credit and job failures feed on each other and when the signs of decay are evident on every street and in every home, it's too late to place blame.

In this chapter we look closely at two communities that are preventing economic collapse. Both programs receive some government assistance but they are marked by determined self-help. One of our featured groups brought much needed credit into their neighborhood by establishing a resident-owned and managed community development credit union. The other launched a program to train delinquent youths and unemployed adults in valuable housing repair skills — pumping jobs into the neighborhood while renovating abandoned houses.

These community organizations show yet again the importance of group innovation and determination in shaping our country's future.

Organizing Credit Unions

South Minneapolis Community
Federal Credit Union
916 East 28th Street
Minneapolis, Minnesota 55407
(612) 871-2325

Most of us face money crises from time to time—too many bills and too little cash. But the crisis worsens when financial institutions turn down loan requests from residents living in low-income "high risk" areas. Desperate for help, these residents might turn to costly finance companies and pay up to 33 percent in annual interest rates.

Two years ago, residents living in the low-income ethnically diverse south side of Minneapolis, Minnesota, were confronted with this situation. The illegal practice of redlining and other discriminating practices were rampant.[1] Many residents had been in the clutches of finance companies for more than 20 years and were plagued with poor credit ratings, bankruptcies and a host of other ills which surface when borrowed cash comes at a premium. Lack of financing and high interest rates were causing area small businesses to fold and housing to deteriorate at a rapid rate.

Taking Control

The residents of South Minneapolis, however, were determined to do something about their plight. They decided to stop relying on traditional financial institutions and depend instead on themselves. The result was the formation of a Community Development Credit Union (CDCU), a neighborhood owned and operated financial and educational institution dedicated to boosting a community's economy by making money available for the needs of residents and area businesses.[2]

"The credit union is something everybody I know had hoped and dreamed of for years," wrote Elizabeth Thurber in the South Minneapolis Community Federal Credit Union's annual report. "As a woman and a single parent, it's very important to me that I can borrow without feeling clumsy or awkward—without feeling like I'm begging."

Community Credit Union

In less than two years of operation, the South Minneapolis Community Federal Credit Union has grown from 45 members with about $225 in deposits to a full service financial institution boasting 850 members and $389,000 in assets.

Since it is member-owned, the residents of South Minneapolis decide how their money is used. About 10 percent of all loans at the credit union are made to local small businesses. In turn, the local businesses help stabilize South Minneapolis by pumping the money back into the community and creating jobs for residents.

"I feel a sense of satisfaction knowing that my money is being used in my own community," says Judy Cooper, a South Minneapolis resident and employee of the South Minneapolis CDCU. "The credit union is really meeting a basic need that residents have—we're doing it, not just dreaming about it or yakking all the time about it."

Origins

It all began in the fall of 1976 when three South Minneapolis residents attended a credit union conference sponsored by the National Center for Urban Ethnic Affairs (NCUEA), a nonprofit organization dedicated to helping city neighborhood groups stem urban blight and revitalize urban communities.[3] Inspired by the idea of organizing a community-owned financial institution, they obtained funds from Southside Community Enterprises, Inc., a local, nonprofit community development corporation, to hire a part-time credit union organizer. And NCUEA provided technical assistance.[4] "Without the constant help and support of NCUEA," comments credit union organizer Steve Schamback, "the South Minneapolis Credit Union would have been nothing more than a pipe dream."

Overwhelming Support

Within a short time the Southside Community Credit Union Sponsoring Club was created. To rally community support, a newsletter heralding the group's progress was sent to residents. Local newpaper articles prodded interest even more and, in less than one year, the club had 300 members, each pledging $3 to $5 toward the goal of establishing a credit union.

The group also received $1,600 from private sources to train area residents in credit union management. And local churches, foundations and an insurance company pledged a total of $60,000 in deposits to the soon-to-be-chartered credit union. (Although not available in time to assist South Minneapolis, credit unions may now be eligible for technical assistance from the newly created National Consumer Cooperative Bank.**)

Becoming Official

On November 29, 1977 the group filed for a Federal credit union charter.[5] With residents from diverse sectors of the community serving on the Board of Directors, South Minneapolis citizens were assured that their concerns would be priorities when policy decisions were made. In fact, those concerns would become the framework for operating the Credit Union.

Staff and Service

The Credit Union opened on March 8, 1978 with a full-time worker from the Department of Labor's Comprehensive Employment and Training Act (CETA) Program* and two temporary employees paid with a $5,000 foundation grant. At first, services were limited to deposits and withdrawals. But after winning another $15,000 foundation grant and receiving over $50,000 in deposits from nonmembers, the Credit Union began making loans. By August 1978 the Credit Union had moved to a permanent location and boasted a membership of over 420 with $150,000 in assets.

New Help for Community-Based Credit Unions

The more than 500 community-based Federally or state-chartered credit unions should get a boost from the recently passed legislation creating the Community Development Credit Union Initiative.* The limited demonstration project, jointly administered by the Community Services Administration (CSA) and the National Credit Union Administration (NCUA), aims to strengthen community-based credit unions by providing technical assistance in neighborhood revitalization.[6]

Other Credit Unions

Community groups across the nation are finding fresh solutions to traditional lending problems by creating Community Development Credit Unions. For example, in San Juan, Texas, the Amigos Unidos CDCU has helped migrant farmworkers solve transportation problems with loan policies aimed at meeting the special needs of migrants. A major portion of Amigos Unidos' loans are targeted at residents who are purchasing vehicles to transport workers to and from their jobs.

And La Casa Credit Union in Springfield, Massachusetts became the major force in sprucing up the Brightwood neighborhood by earmarking most loans for home purchases and repairs.

Groups Highlighted

Amigos Unidos Federal Credit Union
P.O. Box 114
San Juan, Texas 78589
(512) 787-6081

La Casa Credit Union
384 Plainfield Street
Springfield, Massachusetts 01107
(413) 734-8287

[1] Redlining is a term applied when banking and insurance companies refuse to lend money or write fire insurance on dwellings because of their location. It is as if these institutions took a map of a city and drew a red line around certain neighborhoods saying "No loans or insurance in these high risk areas."

[2] A credit union is a voluntary association of members sharing a common bond, existing to encourage thrift and to make low-cost loans among member owners through higher dividend rates on savings accounts and lower interest rates on loans. And the member owners make all decisions about how their money is used. A Community Development Credit Union (CDCU) goes one step further by working to coordinate economic development in the community by simultaneously serving as a financial, neighborhood and learning institution.

[3] For more information on the National Center for Urban Ethnic Affairs (NCUEA), see Resources at end of Housing Section.

[4] The National Center for Urban Ethnic Affairs (NCUEA) received a grant from the Department of Commerce's (DOC) Economic Development Administration (EDA) to provide technical assistance and training to the South Minneapolis group as well as to other Community Development Credit Unions (CDCUs) around the country.

[5] A state or Federal credit union charter spells out rights and responsibilities of the specific credit union. A Federal charter is filed through the National Credit Union Administration (NCUA) which is responsible for regulating the 13,000 existing Federally chartered credit unions. There are approximately 10,000 state-chartered credit unions. Because laws vary from state to state, credit union charters and the responsibilities differ.

[6] For more information on the National Credit Union Administration (NCUA), see Resources at end of Housing Section.

* State and/or local government agencies are frequently responsible for administration of Federal program funds. For further information, see Appendix I under appropriate Federal agency.

**For further information see Appendix II under "National Consumer Cooperative Bank."

NOTE: For a complete listing of groups featured throughout this book, see Index.

Steps to Organizing a Community Development Credit Union (CDCU)

1. **Form a sponsoring committee which:**
   - is responsible for coordinating the organizing effort;
   - is composed of interested people, dedicated to the idea of forming a CDCU.
2. **Look for seed money and support from community groups and others by:**
   - calling on local churches, businesses, industries and established community organizations for volunteers and possible sponsorship;
   - discussing possible grants and subsidies.
3. **Organize people in the neighborhood by asking volunteers and/or paid organizers to:**
   - hold block meetings and gather information;
   - generate enthusiasm for a CDCU among residents.
4. **Check resources available by:**
   - contacting other agencies and CDCUs familiar with organizational problems of credit unions;
   - contacting sources, such as the National Credit Union Administration (NCUA), the National Federation of Community Development Credit Unions (NFCDCU) and the National Consumer Cooperative Bank,** which will provide technical assistance and help on organizational problems.[1]
5. **Hold a public meeting and discuss:**
   - the purpose of a CDCU and how it operates;
   - the reasons one is needed;
   - the rights and responsibilities of credit union members;
   - the field of membership;
   - the roles of volunteer work in CDCU creation.
6. **Take a survey of the community to:**
   - determine the extent of community interest;
   - determine whether the CDCU can make it through the difficult early stages.
7. **Hold a second public meeting to:**
   - review the information obtained from the survey;
   - elicit volunteer help;
   - inform residents what services the CDCU will provide to members.
8. **Prepare for the NCUA review of chartership by:**
   - working closely with a group experienced with the necessary charter procedure.
9. **Hold the charter organizational meeting at which:**
   - all subscribers attend and sign the charter document;
   - a Board of Directors, credit committee and supervisory committee are selected;
   - the CDCU is named.
10. **Hold the first Board Meeting at which:**
    - all executive officers, chair people and secretaries are elected;
    - a bank in which funds will be deposited is selected;
    - the monetary and interest rates as well as policy decisions are made.
11. **Obtain a Charter by:**
    - completing all needed reports and materials;
    - reviewing and submitting charter materials promptly to the regional office of NCUA or state supervisory agent for state-chartered credit unions.
12. **Acquire funds and staff to begin operations by:**
    - applying for grants;
    - using volunteer staff or obtaining slots from the Department of Labor's Comprehensive Employment and Training Act (CETA) Program.*
13. **Obtain nonmember deposits to provide capital for loans.**
14. **Prepare to open an office by:**
    - developing goals and objectives;
    - training a staff;
    - ordering supplies.
15. **Open an office no later than 60 days after charter approval.**

[1]For more information on the National Credit Union Administration (NCUA) and the National Federation of Community Development Credit Unions (NFCDCU), see Resources at end of Housing Section.

*** State and/or local government agencies are frequently responsible for administration of Federal program funds. For further information, see Appendix I under Department of Labor.**

**** For further information, see Appendix II under "National Consumer Cooperative Bank."**

Adapted from Community Development Credit Unions, *1979, published by The National Center for Urban Ethnic Affairs, 1521 16th Street, N.W., Washington, D.C. 20026.*

Providing Housing and Jobs

Operation Fresh Start
2322 Atwood Avenue
Madison, Wisconsin 53704
(608) 244-4721

A special kind of housing rehabilitation is going on in Madison, Wisconsin: juvenile law offenders are learning valuable job skills while renovating houses. In one stroke, low-income residents get newly restored homes and potential hard-core criminals become productive citizens.

The housing industry is tailor made for these reform opportunities because it is labor-intensive. Labor accounts for about 50 percent of the total cost of a new home, and even more for home rehabilitation and repair.

Neighborhood organizations can save a good deal on labor costs by including job training programs in their housing plans. Moreover, the added jobs help pump up a community's economy by cutting welfare and unemployment rolls and boosting the revenues of local businesses.

Repeat Offenders

Jack Osteraas, a youth counselor for the Dane County Juvenile Detention Department and a former Madison policeman, wanted to do more than add new jobs to his community. He wanted to help the area's juvenile delinquents rebuild their lives. And housing renovation seemed just the vehicle to halt what he calls the "revolving door syndrome." Over and over again he witnessed the cycle at work. A youth offender is arrested, placed on probation and turned back into the streets—only to commit another crime. Then the whole brutalizing process begins again. After a few arrests, the city has another hardened and angry criminal on its hands.

The Plan

If he could buy an old, dilapidated house and train juvenile delinquents to fix it up, Osteraas thought, they might go straight. Their newfound skills might give them a sense of self-worth, enable them to land a permanent job and give them a fresh start on life. And on top of all that, he'd have a house to sell to a needy family.

First Funding

Osteraas soon sold others on his idea for the non-profit Operation Fresh Start (OFS). In 1971 the Department of Justice's Law Enforcement Assistance Administration (LEAA), United Way and several local foundations contributed funds to back his renovation project.[1] With enough money to pay the salaries of a director, the enrollees and a supervisor-foreman, Osteraas borrowed the additional $19,500 needed to buy his first dilapidated house and materials to renovate it.

Operation Fresh Start

Pouring the basement of an OFS house

First Crew

Eight 15- to 17-year-olds were among the first recommended for the program by social workers and parole officers at the Dane County Department of Social Services and the Division of Corrections. Seven of the youths were under court supervision, but living at home. Osteraas hired a former teacher who was a self-taught cabin builder and cabinetmaker as supervisor-foreman. The men went to work. In less than a year's time their first home was restored and sold to a low-income family.[2]

Napolean Elvord was 16 when he became a carpenter trainee on that project. He had been warned by juvenile authorities to clean up his act. "I was on my way to real trouble," he recalls. "I had dropped out of school. I was fighting—I did a lot of fighting. And I had left home quite a bit."

In 1979 at the age of 25 Elvord had a high school education and was a carpentry journeyman for a Madison construction company. He credits Operation Fresh Start with redirecting his life. "It taught me how to deal with people, how to face responsibility, that sort of thing," Elvord says. "It made me feel more useful—like I had a chance."

Operation Fresh Start

Women help pour concrete for an Operation Fresh Start project.

Budget and Staff

Today Operation Fresh Start has a staff of 18 and an operating budget of $525,000, most of which comes from a variety of Federal and state sources.[3] Since its birth OFS has renovated about 25 homes and has helped numerous nonprofit organizations with their building needs. For instance, they recently

Operation Fresh Start

The hard work will pay off handsomely for everyone.

completed a ramp to make a community center accessible to the handicapped.

Most of the restored homes are sold at a slight loss, but when a profit is made it is pumped back into OFS for future projects.

Others Attracted to Program Benefits

OFS' solid reputation has attracted others to its program. Now adult law offenders and women in Dane County who want non-traditional careers are clamoring to take part. About one-third of the trainees are women, many of whom later find careers in the construction field. One group of women, for example, has set up their own home repair contracting company.

About 75 percent of the trainees attend basic education classes at Madison Area Technical School.[4] Moreover, they receive individual counseling and job hunting assistance from criminology and sociology students at the University of Wisconsin.

The success of OFS is reflected in its statistics. Eighty-five percent of those who complete the training program get permanent jobs or return to school, becoming useful citizens with valuable skills.

Other Groups

This welcomed combination of job training and housing renovation is also being pursued by such groups as Exodus, Inc. in Atlanta, Georgia. There, with funds from the Comprehensive Employment and Training Act (CETA) Program,* administered by the Department of Labor, unemployed disadvantaged youths are taught valuable skills while renovating and landscaping low-cost housing developments.

Housing renovation programs can also provide jobs for rural residents, as shown by the Federation of Southern Cooperatives (FSC), a nonprofit group in Epes, Alabama.[5] Working in a rural area plagued with a majority of substandard houses, FSC formed a cooperative home rehabilitation program with the assistance of the United States Department of Agriculture's Low- to Moderate-Income Housing Loans (Section 502) Program,* administered by the Farmers Home Administration (FmHA). It provides homeowners with long-term, low-interest loans to finance the cost of materials. And unemployed area residents are hired with CETA funds and taught construction and renovation skills, thus repairing houses at one-third of the usual costs.

Groups Highlighted

Exodus, Inc.
355 Georgia Avenue, S.E.
Altanta, Georgia 30312
(404) 622-1056

Federation of Southern Cooperatives
P.O. Box 95
Epes, Alabama 34560
(205) 652-9676

[1] Operation Fresh Start (OFS) received funds from the Department of Justice's (DOJ) Law Enforcement Assistance Administration (LEAA) which are channeled through the Wisconsin Criminal Justice Department. The program under which funds were received is no longer in existence. Neighborhood groups may now get assistance from LEAA's Office of Juvenile Justice and Delinquency Prevention,* which provides funding for service groups and organizations with innovative programs aimed at employing youth.

[2] Operation Fresh Start (OFS) homes are sold to those qualifying for the Department of Housing and Urban Development's (HUD) Homeownership Assistance for Low- and Moderate-Income Families (Section 235) Program.*

[3] Operation Fresh Start's (OFS) funding sources include the Wisconsin State Department of Community Directions; the Department of Housing and Urban Development's (HUD) Community Development Block Grant (CDBG) Program;* and the Department of Labor's (DOL) Comprehensive Employment and Training Act (CETA) Program.*

[4] Operation Fresh Start's (OFS) education classes at Madison Area Technical School are funded by the school and the Department of Labor's (DOL) Comprehensive Employment and Training Act (CETA) Program.*

[5] The Federation of Southern Cooperatives (FSC) and other co-ops may now qualify for technical and financial assistance from the newly created National Consumer Cooperative Bank.**

* State and/or local government agencies are frequently responsible for administration of Federal program funds. For further information, see Appendix I under appropriate Federal agency.

**For further information, see Appendix II under "National Consumer Cooperative Bank."

NOTE: For a complete listing of groups featured throughout this book, see Index.

Fighting Housing Inflation on All Fronts

Introduction

Inflation affects neighborhoods on several fronts. High food, medical care and energy costs eat away at community stability. Other threats might come from "urban renewal" programs, highway projects or a number of other city plans which are proposed under the name of progress but can displace low-income residents and spoil a community's character.

Some housing groups begin by organizing around a single issue, then gradually expand the scope of their efforts, tackling several problems at once.

In this chapter we focus on a community group that did just that. It was transformed from an opponent of an urban renewal program into a comprehensive community organization dedicated to revitalizing its ethnically rich neighborhood. Their story provides lessons for all of us.

From Protesters to Builders— One Group's Growth

Inquilinos Boricuas en Accion
Puerto Rican Tenants in Action
405 Shawmut Avenue
Boston, Massachusetts 02118
(617) 262-5274

Can you fight City Hall and win?

Of course you can, if the success story of an Hispanic community group in Boston, Massachusetts is any guide. Not only that, but the organization went on to work as partners with the city government to revive their neighborhood. With Federal and city backing, the group has built and rehabilitated hundreds of apartments.

Inquilinos Boricuas en Accion (IBA) or "Puerto Rican Tenants in Action," has lived up to its name since it started in the late 1960s.

Success Today

Through its efforts 625 families in Boston's South End have been placed in sound low-cost housing. And they've done this without displacing residents or changing the traditional Spanish Colonial and New England architectural styles of the old neighborhood. IBA's rehabilitation and building activities have eliminated community eyesores and have created badly needed jobs in the economically depressed area.

Cindy Simon, a social worker for the Massachusetts Department of Welfare, has lived in the South End for four years. She hates to think what would have happened to many of its residents if IBA had not been there to help them fight the housing inflation that was displacing them. "Low- and moderate-income people here would be very much in trouble," she says, "and many, mainly Hispanics, would be living in substandard housing."

Origins

It all began as a reaction to plans developed by the Boston Redevelopment Authority (BRA), which emphasized large scale clearance and new construction in the largely Puerto Rican low-income South End neighborhood. The area appeared ripe for revitalization with its attractive old row houses and closeness to downtown.

Inquilenos Boricuas en Accion

A park inside IBA's Plaza Betances

Protest

But most of the 23,000 residents who lived there didn't want "revitalization." They feared it would boost property values and force them out of their neighborhood.

Their utmost concern centered on the plan for the redevelopment of a 20-acre tract in the heart of the barrio. Residents referred to the area as "Villa Victoria," but on the maps of the urban planners it was simply called "Parcel 19."

Although the city's plans included rehabilitating and building new rental units, recreational facilities and a multiservice center, there were no provisions for low-income housing. Moreover, BRA hadn't consulted with the residents about its redevelopment plans.

Campaign

To avert what they considered a potential disaster, a group of Villa Victoria leaders, spurred by the community's Episcopal church, launched a door-to-door organizing campaign against the project. Their rallying cry was "We shall not be moved from Parcel 19!"

It took them little time to obtain community support. "When you tell people they could be kicked out of their apartments, they get upset," explains Jorges Fernandez, IBA's executive director. So in 1968, 500 residents formed an "Emergency Tenants Council," which later became IBA.

First Funding

The Episcopal Church contributed money to pay a small staff to organize and build a strong coalition to lobby on the community's behalf. Although the Puerto Rican community had little clout or credibility

with city officials, the power of their increasing numbers soon drew city attention. And in 1969 they began negotiating with BRA, explaining resident concerns and needs. As a result the community members became the planners, developers and managers of Parcel 19.

The mostly undereducated residents lacked the expertise to plan and develop their area, but concerned lawyers and architects from other parts of the city agreed to work on a contingency basis at reduced fees. And in late 1969 IBA's staff got an additional boost when ACTION's Volunteers in Service To America (VISTA)* workers came aboard.

Goals

Early on, through its resident-elected Board, IBA set objectives. They called for affordable housing for low-income families and the elderly without displacing residents, plus cultural and social facilities for use by the entire South End community. Underlying their goals was a commitment to have community residents decide what projects would be developed.

Inquilinos Boricuas en Accion

A playlot in Plaza Betances

Staff and Budget

Today with a staff of 70 and a budget of $1.3 million, IBA has come a long way toward realizing its goals. Most of its budget comes from private donations and a variety of government housing programs.[1] In addition, funds from the State Legislature and a modest yearly grant from the National Foundation on the Arts and Humanities' Expansion Arts Program* allows IBA to bring cultural classes and presentations to South End residents and train mostly high school students in television production and other media skills.

Inquilenos Boricuas en Accion

IBA's housing complex

Using the Department of Housing and Urban Development's (HUD) Community Development Block Grant (CDBG) Program,* IBA buys city-owned land at bargain prices. Then construction and rehabilitation begin.

IBA's Achievements

- Rehabilitated 108 apartments in previously vacant or deteriorated structures;
- Effectively lobbied for and now manages a 136-unit public housing project which has community meeting rooms and recreational facilities;
- Built a 19-story, 201-unit apartment house complete with health and other services for elderly and disabled residents of varied racial and ethnic backgrounds;
- Completed 181 units of a large apartment and townhouse complex which will ultimately house over 300 low- and moderate-income families;
- Created a housing management firm whose 30-member staff manages IBA's rental units and ensures that they are well maintained.

Community Plaza

Perhaps IBA's most exciting project is "Plaza Betances," named after a Puerto Rican hero. The plaza boasts islands of trees, small water fountains and recreational areas that beckon residents to watch cultural presentations, play ball or just relax. In the brick building across the street, IBA offers South Enders day care and laundry facilities as well as family counseling services. The plaza has become the physical and symbolic center of the redeveloping community.

Women's musical group entertains at the annual Betances Festival.

By doing so much, the group has surely enriched the lives of all those who live in the South End, while giving new pride to Boston's 50,000-strong Hispanic community.

Other Groups

Other groups have undergone evolutions similar to the one in Boston. In Pittsburgh, Pennsylvania, for example, the Manchester Citizens Corporation began as a "Project Area Committee" in an urban renewal area.[2] After years of trying to convey neighborhood views on urban redevelopment, the group now administers $500,000 of Pittsburgh's Urban Redevelopment Authority funds. They maintain and manage over 100 properties for the 4,000-strong community in lower Pittsburgh and have a direct say in policy decisions concerning their area.

Group Highlighted

Manchester Citizens Corporation
1120 Pennsylvania Avenue
Pittsburgh, Pennsylvania 15233
(412) 323-1743

[1] Funding for Inquilinos Boricuas en Accion's (IBA) projects include Department of Housing and Urban Development's (HUD) Rental and Cooperative Housing Assistance for Lower-Income Families (Section 236), Lower-Income Rental Assistance (Section 8), Low-Income Public Housing "Turnkey," Homeownership Assistance for Low- and Moderate-Income Families (Section 221) and Multifamily Rental Housing for Low- and Moderate-Income Families (Section 221) Programs.*

[2] Project Area Committees were designated under the Department of Housing and Urban Development's (HUD) former Urban Renewal Program and designed to give residents a voice in their community's development. There is now no formal designation for such groups but funding is available from HUD's Community Development Block Grant (CDBG) Program,* which is channeled through city governments.

* State and/or local government agencies are frequently responsible for administration of Federal program funds. For further information, see Appendix I under appropriate Federal agency.

NOTE: For a complete listing of groups features throughout this book, see Index.

Housing Resources

The following resources contain descriptions of organizations and publications which can be of help to consumer groups across the country that wish to organize and launch community projects designed to combat high prices.

Those organizations offering assistance in a variety of areas are listed under "General" and are followed by a list of publications under the same heading. Other organizations and publications that provide help in specific areas are listed under corresponding chapter title headings.

Of course, it is not possible to list every organization and publication in the country that might prove helpful to you and your group, but we believe those we do mention are representative of the various kinds of assistance available. Chances are you'll hear of many other useful resources as you become involved in your own community project.

Space limitations made it extremely difficult to choose among the many fine groups considered, and we sincerely hope we haven't offended the many deserving organizations and/or authors of useful publications that have not been included.

General Housing Organizations

Alternative Economics, Inc.
P.O. Box 29146
Washington, D.C. 20017
(202) 832-5200

Provides technical assistance in financial aspects of neighborhood economic development; also provides training to community credit unions. Published 46-page pamphlet, *Community Development Credit Unions, Economics for Neighborhoods.* 1977. ($3.)

Association of Neighborhood Housing Developers, Inc.
115 East 23rd Street
New York, New York 10010
(212) 674-7610

Provides technical assistance and information on housing and community development activities to organizations in the New York City area. Publishes *City Limits,* containing information on housing and general community issues which is applicable to groups outside of New York City. (10 issues/year, $6.)

Carolina Action
305 East Chapel Hill Street
Durham, North Carolina 27702
(919) 687-6076

Assists individuals and local organizations in housing and community development. Publishes monthly newsletter, *Action Power,* which probes organization activities and community development issues. ($15/year.)

Center for Community Change
1000 Wisconsin Avenue, N.W.
Washington, D.C. 20007
(202) 338-6310

Provides technical assistance to neighborhood and community organizations in rehabilitation and other housing and community development projects; also involved in disinvestment and neighborhood preservation activities. Publishes quarterly newsletter, *Federal Programs Monitor,* which includes tracking of Federally funded housing programs. ($15/year.)

Community Design Centers
Community Design Center Directors' Association
380 Main Street
East Orange, New Jersey 07018
(201) 678-9720

Provides planning, architectural and other technical assistance to nonprofit neighborhood and community organizations for housing and local development projects, particularly in depressed/disadvantaged communities. There are presently 64 Community Design Centers located in 33 states. To contact the one nearest you, write or phone the Community Design Center Directors' Association.

Community Economics, Inc.
6529 Telegraph Avenue
Oakland, California 94609
(415) 653-6555

Provides technical and managerial assistance to neighborhood and community organizations working in rehabilitation and cooperative conversion activities. Publishes quarterly newsletter, *Public Works,* which updates community housing and land trust issues. ($5/year.)

Institute for Local Self-Reliance
1717 18th Street, N.W.
Washington, D.C. 20009
(202) 232-4108

Provides information and technical assistance to local groups on community-based housing and development projects. Publishes bimonthly newsletter, *Self-Reliance,* which updates community housing issues. ($8/year.)

National Association of Neighborhoods (NAN)
1612 20th Street, N.W.
Washington, D.C. 20009
(202) 332-7766

Works in support of neighborhood organizations by promoting local government decentralization and responsiveness to neighborhood-based development activities; also involved with displacement issues. Publishes monthly newsletter for members, *NAN Bulletin,* which contains neighborhood development information and describes NAN involvement in housing development activities across the country. ($10/year to individuals, $25 to institutions.)

National Center for Appropriate Technology
P.O. Box 3838
Butte, Montana 59701
(406) 723-6533

Information clearinghouse on alternative technology projects, including innovative technologies applicable to housing development. Provides grants for research and small demonstration projects.

National Center for Urban Ethnic Affairs
1521 16th Street, N.W.
Washington, D.C. 20026
(202) 232-3600

Provides information and assistance to neighborhood and community groups. Especially concerned with community development credit unions. Publishes monthly newsletter concerning Center activities. (Free.)

National Council of Senior Citizens
1511 K Street, N.W.
Washington, D.C. 20005
(202) 347-8880

Develops, sponsors and manages housing for low-income senior citizens. Provides information for groups on how to develop, sponsor and manage senior citizen housing.

National Economic Development and Law Center
2150 Shattuck Avenue, Suite 300
Berkeley, California 94704
(415) 548-2600

Provides legal support and technical services to community development corporations and offers legal services programs in the field of economic development.

National Endowment for the Arts
Architecture and Environmental Arts Program
2401 E Street, N.W.
Washington, D.C. 20506
(202) 634-4276

Administers "Livable Cities Program" which provides grants to local government and nonprofit organizations for architectural, environmental and other projects designed to improve the quality of life in inner-city neighborhoods.

National Rural Center
1828 L Street, N.W.
Washington, D.C. 20036
(202) 331-0258

Develops and advocates housing policy alternatives relating to rural needs by conducting demonstration programs, using the results of existing research, evaluating Federal programs and pursuing basic research. Monitors the writing of national legislation and program regulations. Provides information services and publications, including monthly, *Rural Community Development Newsletter.* (Free.)

Neighborhood Information Sharing Exchange
1725 K Street, N.W.
Washington, D.C. 20006
(202) 293-2813

Network of organizations involved in neighborhood development and housing rehabilitation. Serves as referral center and clearinghouse. Funded by the Office of Neighborhood Development, Department of Housing and Urban Development.

Rural America, Inc.
1346 Connecticut Avenue, N.W.
Washington, D.C. 20005
(202) 659-2800

Represents rural interests by providing information and technical assistance on rural housing and other programs. Assists groups in identifying funding sources for housing rehabilitation. Publishes many publications, including monthly newspaper, *Rural America* ($10/year); and monthly newsletter, *RHA* (Rural Housing Alliance) *Reporter* (free to members).

Shelterforce Collective
380 Main Street
East Orange, New Jersey 07018
(201) 678-6778

Provides technical assistance to nonprofit housing and community development groups. Serves as information clearinghouse. Publishes quarterly newsletter, *Shelterforce,* which contains tenant organization information and analyses of housing programs and issues. ($5 for six issues.)

Publications

Community Development Digest. Community Development Publications, 399 National Press Building, Washington, D.C. 20045. Biweekly newsletter. ($117/year.) Federal, state and local happenings in housing and community development. Each issue has a reference section listing where to obtain copies of Congressional bills, reports on Federal agency actions and regulations, etc.

FNMA Neighborhood Directory. Federal National Mortgage Association, 3900 Wisconsin Avenue, N.W., Washington, D.C. 20016. Looseleaf, regularly updated. Quarterly. ($10/year.) Compendium of government and private housing and community development programs.

Housing and Development Reporter. Bureau of National Affairs, 1231 25th Street, N.W., Washington, D.C. 20037. Biweekly. ($350/year.) Bibliography of housing and community development activities. Covers all national and most state and local activities. Also provides complete updated review of challenges to Federal laws and regulations related to housing.

Housing Resource Manual. Pratt Institute Center for Community and Environmental Development, 275 Washington Avenue, Brooklyn, New York 11205. 1979. ($5.) Source of information on housing and community development programs. Lists and describes resources to assist neighborhood and community groups with self-help projects. Primarily focuses on New York City, but should be useful to housing groups elsewhere.

Journal of Housing. National Association of Housing and Redevelopment Officials, 2600 Virginia Avenue, N.W., Washington, D.C. 20037. Monthly magazine. ($33/year.) Covers all aspects of housing, including recent developments in the national public sector. Frequent reports on locally based housing projects.

New York Self-Help Handbook. Citizens Committee for New York City, Inc., 3 West 29th Street, New York, New York 10001. 1978. ($4.95.) Step-by-step manual for organizing and carrying out neighborhood self-help projects in housing and other areas. Information included is also applicable to groups outside New York City.

People Building Neighborhoods. Superintendent of Documents, U.S. Government Printing Office, Washington, D.C. 20402. 1979. (Publication No. 052-003-00616-2, $7.50.) Final Report to the President. A study by the National Commission on Neighborhoods (a presidential advisory group no longer in existence). Features case studies of neighborhood reinvestment and decline.

Self-Help Housing Handbook. Rural America, Inc., 1346 Connecticut Avenue, N.W., Washington, D.C. 20005. 1976. ($12.50.) Provides comprehensive view of self-help housing, from program planning to follow-up with participating families. Contains a guide to Farmers Home Administration regulations. A 27-page addendum updates the book through 1979.

Source Catalog: Communities, Housing. Swallow Press, Inc., 1139 South Wabash Avenue, Chicago, Illinois 60605. 1972. ($10.) Provides tips for organizing tenant associations. Covers broad range of housing issues, both rural and urban.

The following publications are available at no charge from the Department of Housing and Urban Development (HUD), Publication Service Center, Room B-237, 451 Seventh Street, S.W., Washington, D.C. 20410:

Bibliography of Publications. 1979. Comprehensive listing of publications available through HUD, with prices (if any) and information for ordering.

Programs of HUD. 1978. Summarizes Federal housing and community development programs administered by the Department of Housing and Urban Development. Also lists HUD Area Offices.

Building Together: How to Get Housing You Can Afford

Organizations

Chicago Rehab Network
343 South Dearborn Street, Suite 1508
Chicago, Illinois 60604
(312) 427-2630

Organization of Chicago neighborhood groups engaged in housing rehabilitation. Provides information and resource referrals to nonprofit rehabilitation organizations. Publishes monthly, *Chicago Rehab Newsletter,* which updates organization activities and discusses general housing issues. (Free.)

Cooperative League of the USA
1828 L Street, N.W., Suite 1100
Washington, D.C. 20036
(202) 872-0550

National federation of cooperatives. Provides training materials to member organizations, schools, civic groups. Publishes biweekly, *Cooperative News Service,* which reports on all aspects of cooperatives. ($60/year.)

Cooperative Services, Inc.
7404 Woodward Avenue
Detroit, Michigan 48202
(313) 874-4000

Provides management services to multifamily housing cooperatives. Publishes quarterly newsletter, *The Cooperator,* containing information concerning current and planned housing projects. (Free to members.)

Housing Assistance Council
1828 L Street, N.W., Suite 606
Washington, D.C. 20036
(202) 872-8640

Offers technical assistance to groups in the development of low-income housing for nonprofit and public organizations. Works exclusively with rural housing. Provides a predevelopment loan fund for groups to secure options on land, preliminary architectural and engineering fees, etc.

National Association of Housing Cooperatives
1012 14th Street, N.W., Suite 805
Washington, D.C. 20005
(202) 628-6242

Serves as principal national clearinghouse of information and technical assistance to housing cooperatives. More than 50 publications available.

National Corporation for Housing Partnerships (NCHP)
1133 15th Street, N.W.
Washington, D.C. 20005
(202) 857-5700

Private corporation chartered by Congress in 1968 which provides funds for the development of low- and moderate-income housing projects through partnership with developers, builders and community organizations. NCHP funds come from individuals who are looking for tax shelters and can write off their contributions as tax deductions.

North American Students of Cooperation
Box 7293
Ann Arbor, Michigan 48107
(313) 663-0889

Provides educational and technical services. Conducts workshops for directors of cooperatives. Produces many publications on the operation and management of student cooperatives. Publishes bimonthly magazine, *CO-OP.* ($8.67/year.)

Pratt Institute Center for Community and Environmental Design
275 Washington Avenue
Brooklyn, New York 11205
(212) 636-3486

Provides design assistance for homesteading groups and promotes community ownership of housing, utilizing community development funds.

Urban Homesteading Assistance Board
1047 Amsterdam Avenue
New York, New York 10025
(212) 749-0602

Provides technical assistance for city- and tenant-owned housing and rehabilitation projects. Conducted a study resulting in the first Federally supported demonstration of sweat-equity multifamily homesteading. Assists the Association of Neighborhood Housing Developers, Inc. (see Resources, General Housing, Organizations) in the publication of the magazine, *City Limits.* Also publishes quarterly, *Multi-family Urban Homesteading Newsletter.* (Free.)

Publications

Challenge. Department of Housing and Urban Development, Publications Service Center, 451 Seventh Street, S.W., Washington, D.C. 20410. Volume 10, Number 5, May 1979. ($1.40.) Describes some of urban homesteading's variations, and explores various techniques and resources local urban homesteading agencies use as part of their programs.

Directory of Localities with Community Development Block Grant (CDBG) Property Rehabilitation Financing Activities. Department of Housing and Urban Development, Publication Service Center, 451 Seventh Street, S.W., Washington, D.C. 20410. 1979. (Free.) Lists names, addresses and telephone numbers of 1,443 local government agencies that have budgeted CDBG funds for rehabilitation financing activities.

"From Plow to Pliers—Urban Homesteading in America," ***Fordham Urban Law Journal,*** Vol. 2, page 273, Winter 1974. (Try your local library.) Comparative analysis of various urban homesteading statutes.

Hughes, James W. and Bleakly, Kenneth D., ***Urban Homesteading.*** Center for Urban Policy Research, Rutgers University, New Brunswick, New Jersey 08903. 1976. ($15.) An analysis of homesteading in Wilmington, Delaware; Baltimore, Maryland; and Philadelphia, Pennsylvania. Contains a comprehensive bibliography.

Myer, Joseph A., ***Urban Homesteading: An Annotated Bibliography.*** Vance Bibliographies, P.O. Box 229, Monticello, ''linois 61856. 1976. ($2.) Comprehensive bibliography concerning urban homesteading. Write for information on availability.

The following publications are available from the National Association of Housing Cooperatives, 1012 14th Street, N.W., Suite 805, Washington, D.C. 20005.

Cooperative Housing—A Consumer Guide. 1977. (25 cents.) Pamphlet describing advantages of housing cooperatives as well as principles and recommended operating procedures.

Cooperative Housing—A Handbook for Effective Organizations. Midwest Association of Housing Cooperatives and Organization for Applied Science in Society. 1977. ($15.) Oriented toward Federal Housing Administration insured groups. Deals with all aspects of managing a housing co-op, including selection of members, responsibilities of the Co-op Board, preparation and monitoring of the budget, maintenance and evaluation of management.

The following publications of the National Association of Housing and Redevelopment Officials, 2600 Virginia Avenue, N.W., Washington, D.C. 20037, may be helpful to neighborhood and community organizations interested in housing rehabilitation:

Financing Techniques for Local Rehabilitation Programs. 1976. ($9.)

Making Local Rehabilitation Work: Public/Private Relationships. 1978. ($9.)

Rehabilitation Guidelines for Small Agencies (including supplement). 1977. ($15.50.)

Rehabilitation Operational Guide and Training Manual. 1971. ($5.)

NOTE: Also see Housing Resources under "General."

Repairing, Maintaining and Managing Housing

Organizations

National Association of Housing and Redevelopment Officials
1600 Virginia Avenue, N.W.
Washington, D.C. 20006
(202) 333-2020

Involved in research activities and local government initiatives. Publishes a number of publications on various aspects of housing rehabilitation. Also publishes monthly, *Journal of Housing.* ($33/year.)

National Center for Housing Management
1133 15th Street, N.W.
Washington, D.C. 20005
(202) 872-1717

Provides technical assistance and training in managing multifamily housing.

Neighborhood Reinvestment Corporation
1700 G Street, N.W., Fifth Floor
Washington, D.C. 20052
(202) 377-6815

Conducts programs designed to stimulate development of local, public, private and resident partnerships committed to stemming neighborhood decline. Creates local Neighborhood Housing Services Programs. Provides technical assistance, comprehensive rehabilitation and financial services as well as modest demonstration grants to selected programs.

Urban Institute
2100 M Street, N.W.
Washington, D.C. 20037
(202) 223-1950

Conducts research activities in many aspects of neighborhood preservation. Publishes quarterly newsletter, *Urban Institute Policy Research Report,* which reports on Institute's activities. (Free.)

Publications

American Preservation. 620 East Sixth, Little Rock, Arkansas 72202. Bimonthly magazine. ($15/year.) Devoted to neighborhood preservation and related issues.

Neighborhood Preservation: A Catalog of Local Programs. Department of Housing and Urban Development, Publication Service Center, 451 Seventh Street, S.W., Washington, D.C. 20410. 1975. (Free.) Describes 100 locally initiated neighborhood preservation programs.

NOTE: Also see Housing Resources under "General."

Helping People Find a Place to Live and Standing Up for Homeowner and Tenant Rights

Organizations

Metropolitan Washington Planning and Housing Association
1225 K Street, N.W.
Washington, D.C. 20005
(202) 737-3700

Provides technical assistance to neighborhood groups on reinvestment issues and strategies. Monthly newsletter, *The Advocate,* updates reinvestment activities. (Free to members.)

National Committee Against Discrimination in Housing
1425 H Street, N.W.
Washington, D.C. 20005
(202) 783-8150

Works with fair housing advocacy and community development groups to ensure rights of minorities and poor persons to decent housing of their choice. Offers legal and technical assistance, field services and research and public information programs. Publishes two newsletters: *The Flash,* which is published periodically to report on important news in the housing field ($2 for 15 issues); and bimonthly, *Trends in Housing,* which updates organization activities ($5/year).

National Training and Information Center
1123 West Washington Boulevard.
Chicago, Illinois 60607
(312) 243-3035

Provides information, training and technical assistance on neighborhood organizing and reinvestment strategies. Publishes *Disclosure Newsletter.* (9 issues/year, $10.)

National Urban Coalition
1201 Connecticut Avenue, N.W.
Washington, D.C. 20036
(202) 331-2456

Has conducted a national displacement study. Publishes two newsletters, *Washington Update* (5 issues/year) and *Policy Watch* (monthly), which update urban policy legislation and programs. (Both free.)

Publications

Fair Mortgage Lending: A Handbook for Community Groups. Center for National Policy Review, Catholic University School of Law, Washington, D.C. 20064. 1978. (Free.) Manual for neighborhood groups combatting mortgage redlining and disinvestment practices.

How to Research Your Local Bank (or Savings and Loan Institution). Institute for Local Self-Reliance, 1717 18th Street, N.W., Washington, D.C. 20009. 1976. ($12.) Guide to using the National Mortgage Disclosure Act as a tool to combat neighborhood redlining.

Levy, Paul R., ***Queen Village: The Eclipse of Community.*** Institute For the Study of Civic Values, 401 North Broad Street, Philadelphia, Pennsylvania 19108. 1978. ($3.50.) Detailed look into the consequences of the dislocation of low- and moderate-income persons in an urban community by upper-income individuals. Also addresses the impact of urban highway construction.

Neighborhood Reinvestments: A Citizen Compendium for Programs and Strategies. National Center for Urban Ethnic Affairs, 1521 16th Street, N.W., Washington, D.C. 20036. 1977. ($4.) Handbook of initiatives for neighborhood reinvestment by public, private and community sectors.

Pass the Buck . . . Back! National Training and Information Center, 1123 West Washington Boulevard, Chicago, Illinois 60607. 1979. ($5.) Information on how to use the Federal Community Reinvestment Act to secure improved access to mortgage credit in neighborhoods.

Super Tenant. Holt, Rinehart and Winston, New York, New York 10017. 1978. ($4.95.) While written primarily for New York City residents, this book contains valuable information and advice for all residential tenants.

Tenant Law Handbook. New Jersey Tenant Organization, P.O. Box 1142, Fort Lee, New Jersey 07024. 1978. ($3.) Non-technical explanation of basic tenants' rights and how to enforce them.

Why Tenant Organizations? Department of Housing and Urban Development, Publication Service Center, 451 Seventh Street, S.W., Washington, D.C. 20410. 1976. (Free.) Explains purpose of tenant organizations and how to operate them. Available in Spanish or English.

NOTE: Also see Housing Resources under "General."

Getting Help for Housing and Community Development Organizations

Center for Community Economic Development (CCED)
639 Massachusetts Avenue
Cambridge, Massachusetts 02139
(617) 547-9695

Publishes reports, case studies and other materials on neighborhood-based economic development activities; assists economic development organizations. Publishes quarterly, *CCED Newsletter.* (Free.)

Center for Economic Studies
457 Kingsley Avenue
Palo Alto, California 94301
(415) 328-1039

Involved in research and policy studies on alternative economic enterprises. Serves as information clearinghouse.

Center for Neighborhood Technology
570 West Randolph Street
Chicago, Illinois 60606
(312) 454-0126

Provides technical assistance in community development and neighborhood revitalization, as well as in issues related to energy, urban agriculture, etc. Publishes bimonthly, *The Neighborhood Works,* which probes alternative technology in neighborhood development. ($25/year.)

National Congress for Community Economic Development
1828 L Street, N.W., Suite 401
Washington, D.C. 20036
(202) 659-8411

National association of Community Development Corporations. Publishes bimonthly newsletter, *Interchange,* which updates organization activities and community issues. ($12/year.)

National Rural Center
1828 L Street, N.W.
Washington, D.C. 20036
(202) 331-0258

Seeks to ensure that national legislation and program regulations are in the best interest of rural housing and community development needs. Conducts demonstration programs as a means of developing rural policy alternatives. Publications include monthly, *Rural Community Development Newsletter.* (Free.)

Strongforce
212 Decatur Place, N.W.
Washington, D.C. 20008
(202) 234-6883

Serves as information clearinghouse and provides technical assistance to worker- and community-controlled enterprises involved in community development activities.

Publications

Citizen Involvement in Community Development: An Opportunity and a Challenge. Center for Community Change, 1000 Wisconsin Avenue, N.W., Washington, D.C. 20007. 1978. ($2.) Explains the Community Development Block Grant Program and supports citizen involvement in this and other community development programs.

Community Development Digest. Community Development Publications, 399 National Press Building, Washington, D.C. 20045. Biweekly newsletter. ($117/year.) Probes Federal, state and local happenings in housing and community development. Each issue has a reference section on where to obtain copies of Congressional bills and committee reports, reports of Federal agency actions, regulations, and government and private publications.

Mercer, Florence, *Getting Started: Funds For Community Based Economic Development.* Center for Community Economic Development, 639 Massachusetts Avenue, Suite 316, Cambridge, Massachusetts 02139. 1978. ($1.50.) Suggests ways in which community groups might raise funds.

Neighborhood Reinvestments: A Citizen Compendium for Programs and Strategies. National Center for Urban Ethnic Affairs, 1521 16th Street, N.W., Washington, D.C. 20036. 1977. ($4.) Handbook of initiatives for neighborhood reinvestment by public, private and community sectors.

Stone, Margaret J. and Brown, Barbara L., *Community Development Block Grants: A Strategy For Neighborhood Groups.* National Economic Development and Law Center, 2150 Shattuck Avenue, Berkeley, California 94704. 1978. ($7.50.) Explains the Community Development Block Grant and Urban Development Action Grant Programs. Suggests ways of researching block grants and getting proposals approved. Includes a copy of the Housing and Community Development Act of 1977.

NOTE: Also see Housing Resources under "General."

Providing Housing, Jobs and Credit

Organizations

Community Development Credit Union Institute
National Center For Urban Ethnic Affairs
1521 16th Street, N.W.
Washington, D.C. 20036
(202) 232-3600

Provides training, technical assistance and information to Community Development Credit Unions (CDCUs) nationwide. Pamphlet outlining steps to take in organizing a CDCU. (Free.)

National Credit Union Administration
1776 G Street, N.W.
Washington, D.C. 20456
(202) 357-1000

Federal government agency regulating credit unions.

National Federation of Community Development Credit Unions
16 Court Street, Room 3301
Brooklyn, New York 11201
(212) 643-1580

National association with membership comprised of credit unions located in low-income communities.

New School for Democratic Management
589 Howard Street
San Francisco, California 94105
(415) 543-7873

Offers courses and workshops in financial management, marketing and accounting, with emphasis on community development. Has several regional offices and administers educational programs in a number of cities.

Publications

An Analysis of Community Development Credit Unions, 1971–1976. National Federation of Community Development Credit Unions, 16 Court Street, Room 3301, Brooklyn, New York 11201. ($5.) Contains general information about community development credit unions.

Community Development Credit Unions. National Economic Development Law Project, 2150 Shattuck Avenue, Berkeley, California 94704. 1979. (Free.) Manual designed to assist those wishing to start a Community Development Credit Union.

NOTE: Also see Housing Resources under "General."

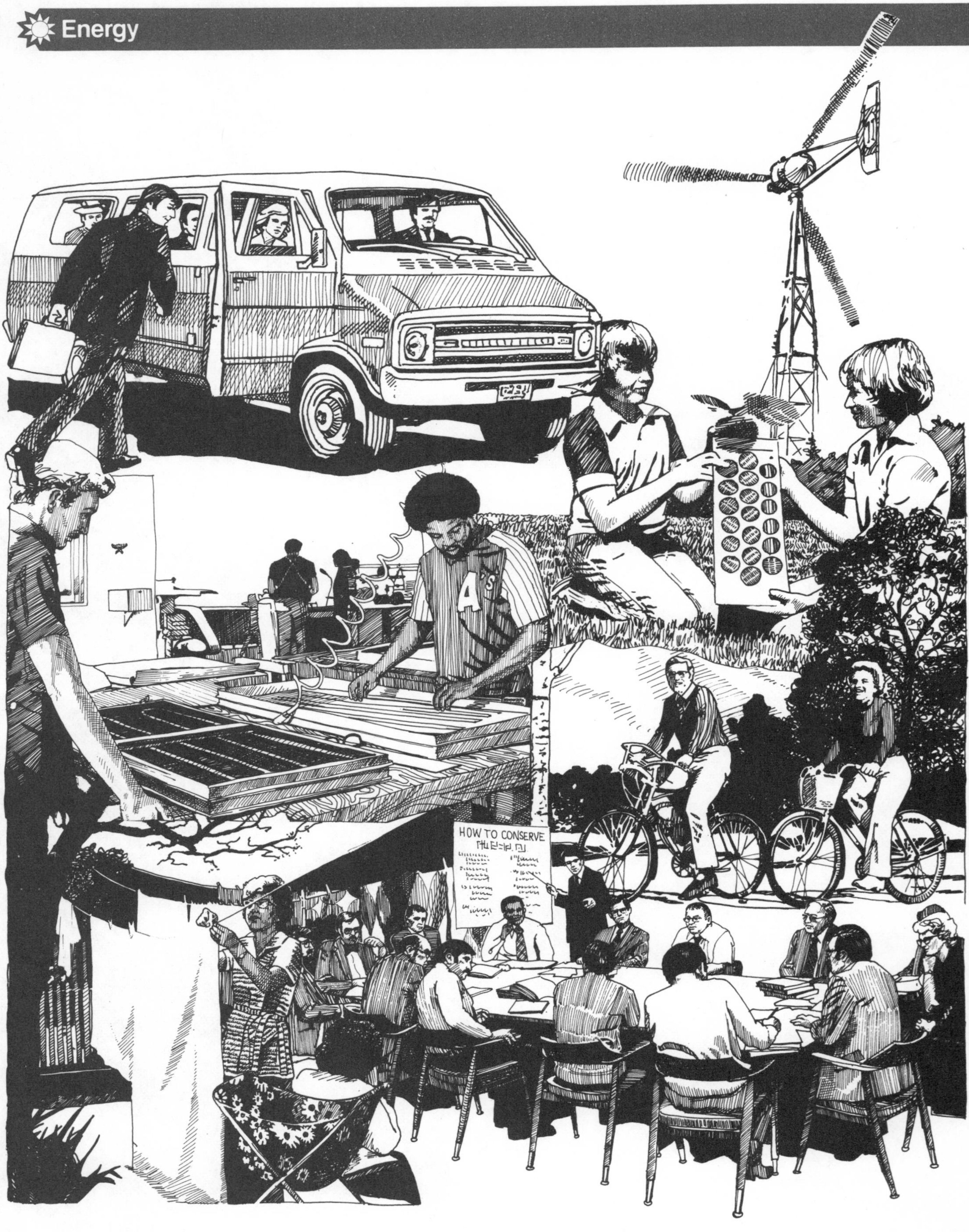

HOW TO CONSERVE

Energy

General Introduction

You don't need a book to tell you that energy prices are skyrocketing. The evidence is everywhere. We spend more money each year to drive our cars, heat and cool our homes, power our appliances and warm our tap water.

It was the 1973 energy crisis that led to huge price increases and made Americans painfully aware that the era of cheap energy was over. From 1973 to 1978 energy was the leading culprit of inflation—jumping in price by a whopping 96.2 percent. And rising energy costs have a dramatic effect on the price of nearly everything we buy.

What's worse is that those who can least afford it suffer the most from energy inflation. The wealthiest of our population spend about 4 percent of their income on energy while the poor spend 25 percent or more.

But groups across the country are fighting back. That's the bright side of the picture and that's what this chapter is all about. Federal, local and state governments, neighborhood organizations and private groups are promoting money-saving energy conservation measures through innovative and creative programs.

Here's a peek at what you'll learn:

(1) How private and public groups are helping residents cut energy bills through inexpensive conservation programs.

(2) How rural and urban community groups are tackling high energy prices by harnessing the power of the sun and wind.

(3) How schools and community organizations are paving the way to a more energy-efficient future by teaching students and other residents about alternative and renewable energy resources.

(4) How private and public groups are helping residents save energy and transportation costs through ridesharing and other programs.

(5) How consumers are making their voices heard in the debate over electric utility reform and how national and local groups are helping consumers organize campaigns calling for fairer rates.

We hope the two brief glossaries included in this section will be helpful. Definitions of a broad range of energy terms begin on page 275. And a glossary of terms relevant to utilities can be found on page 274.

Our featured groups welcome brief inquiries about their projects. But since most have limited resources, please enclose a self-addressed, stamped envelope when you contact them. Additional information on funding sources can be found in the Basic Tools and Resource Sections and in the Appendices.

We hope the projects in this chapter will inspire you to develop similar programs in your community.

Conserving Energy

Introduction

Individuals can do a lot to conserve energy. We all have a self-interest in keeping lights off, thermostats down and in weatherizing our homes. These conservation efforts save families hundreds of dollars yearly in energy costs.

But sometimes individuals need help in conserving. Fortunately, a growing number of private and public groups have launched conservation programs so even more residents are reached and energy savings are magnified.

In this chapter we look at innovative conservation programs that help homeowners and renters in city and rural areas cut high energy costs.

Here are some highlights:

- An energy audit program that saves residents money while pumping jobs into the low-income community;
- A Federal program that offers free home weatherization to low-income citizens;
- An innovative program sponsored by a major utility that reduces weatherization costs for homeowners regardless of income;
- A determined city that has dramatically reduced energy costs through new building codes and efficient transportation planning;
- A recycling program that creates new jobs and cuts energy-intensive waste disposal costs for the city.

Encouraging conservation at the local level is an effective way to hurdle rising energy costs. Good ideas spread naturally as residents tell their neighbors about the money they've saved through conservation.

We hope this chapter will give you some ideas for your community.

Energy Audits

Anacostia Energy Alliance
c/o Institute for Local Self-Reliance
1717 18th Street, N.W.
Washington, D.C. 20009
(202) 889-7932

Wouldn't you like to slash your heating and cooling bill by a third —or even more? An invaluable tool for trimming utility bills is a home energy audit conducted by a specialist who shows you how to fight energy leaks.

Energy auditors, knowledgeable about building construction, heating, air conditioning, insulation and thermostat control, can save homeowners $300 or more yearly by pointing out sources of energy loss like uninsulated attics, poor caulking, lack of storm windows and other energy eaters.

Yet many families—often skeptical of recommendations by large utility companies—don't take advantage of the free energy audits offered by them.[1]

Some community groups, such as the Institute for Local Self-Reliance in Washington, D.C., a nonprofit consulting and technical assistance organization, have hurdled this problem by forming neighborhood energy audit centers.[2]

Energy Center Helps Community

The Institute's Anacostia Energy Alliance (AEA), based in the low-income, mostly black Anacostia section of the District, does more than offer free audits to residents. It educates the community through energy workshops and creates jobs for the area by hiring and training residents as energy auditors.

Moreover, AEA serves as an information center for other Washington, D.C. groups interested in launching energy audit centers and workshops in their neighborhoods.

Success Today

AEA's energy audit program began in April 1979 and, by the end of the year, trained Anacostia residents had visited 225 single-family homes and 100 apartments, saving families who followed recommendations about 30 percent on energy bills. In addition, AEA had wooed 500 residents to workshops, further bolstering energy conservation awareness.

Joseph Jones, a 23-year-old energy auditor, was unemployed when he heard of the Anacostia training program through the local job placement center. Now Jones has learned valuable skills and has a profession which he calls fulfilling. "It's nice," he says, "just helping people to save a little money. And a lot of people are grateful for the information we give them."

Program Beginnings

Early in 1979 Institute leaders targeted Uniontown, an especially economically deprived area of Anacostia, for the energy auditing program. To spark resident interest, Institute workers knocked on doors, posted notices around the area and encouraged community leaders to lend support. They quickly won approval from the Anacostia Neighborhood Advisory Commission (NAC), one of 36 D.C. community groups responsible for setting neighborhood policy and advising the mayor and the City Council.

A real boon to the program came in February with the hiring of Jim Nutall, a well-known and respected community leader and former Anacostia NAC commissioner who helped generate community support, proving that residents are willing to listen to people they know and trust.

First Funding

That same month the United Planning Organization (UPO), a Community Action Agency (CAA)* funded by the Community Services Administration's Community Action Program (CAP),* contributed $17,000 for training expenses and auditing supplies.

Training positions were advertised at the D.C. Department of Labor's Job Bank office in Anacostia and ten area residents were selected for the $4 per hour positions. Trainees spent two weeks learning building construction, heating, ventilation, weatherization techniques and local energy issues. They also learned about Federal and local assistance programs so they could lead low-income residents to help in financing needed alterations.

Audits Begin

In April, armed with their new knowledge and guided by Nutall and Program Director David Cawley, auditing crews began inspecting homes. Ever mindful of their neighbor's low budgets, the auditors stress low-cost energy savers such as adjusting thermostats, cleaning boilers and weatherstripping doors.

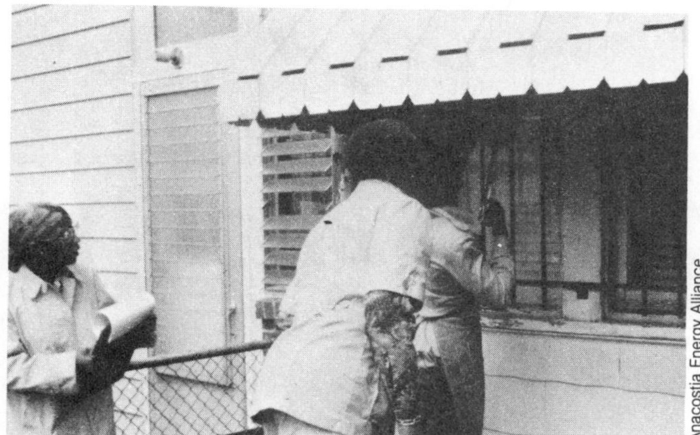

Anacostia Energy Alliance

Checking windows for leaks

With the UPO grant, 100 residents received audits. And during the summer, the D.C. Department of Housing and Community Development showed faith in the group by pumping in $33,000 for additional audits.

Anacostia Energy Alliance

Anacostia energy auditor notes energy waster.

The Institute estimates that initially each audit cost about $170. But the trainees learned quickly and expenses declined. By the end of the year auditing costs fell to $50 per household. "Our auditors today know what they're looking for," Cawley explains. "They can take rapid measurements and inspections."

Workshops

With satisfied homeowners spreading the word, interest in the Institute's energy-saving workshops has mushroomed. Participants learn how to read utility meters and select good insulation materials. They also learn about solar energy design and theory.

And the Institute's demonstration solar project, funded by the Department of Housing and Urban Development's Community Development Block Grant (CDBG) Program,* also prods residents to attend. After each workshop one lucky participant receives a free energy-efficient solar water heating system—built and installed by the students. By the end of 1979 six such systems graced Anacostia homes.

Other Groups

The Anacostia program is just one example of neighborhood energy audit programs. Several years ago a group of Minneapolis, Minnesota residents formed Common Ground, an audit program aimed at bolstering energy-saving awareness in a four-block residential area. Funded by the Minnesota Office of Energy, the group encourages residents to monitor electric, gas and water usage; weatherize; clean boilers; and think about energy alternatives.

In New York City the Energy Task Force (ETF), a nonprofit technical assistance group, with funds from the Department of Labor's Comprehensive Employment and Training Act (CETA) Program,* holds twelve-week training courses, giving low-income neighborhood groups actual experience in measuring heat loss, installing energy-saving devices and maintaining efficient boilers.[3]

And the League of Women Voters in Northfield, Minnesota organized block parties to demonstrate simple energy-saving procedures.

Rhode Islanders Saving Energy (RISE), a statewide, nonprofit corporation based in Providence and funded by the state and nine utilities, was launched in

1977. By 1979 RISE "house doctors" had conducted free audits for 5,000 homeowners and unsolicited public demand for the program had made advertising unnecessary. More than 60 percent of the participants followed audit recommendations, installing in their homes an average of $1,200 worth of energy-savers.

Anacostia Energy Alliance

Taking a break from building "Trombe wall"—a passive solar heating system—at the Anacostia energy audit office.

Groups Highlighted

Common Ground
c/o Mary Kumpula
2929 Bloomington Avenue, South
Minneapolis, Minnesota 55407
(No Phone)

Energy Task Force
156 Fifth Avenue
New York, New York 10010
(212) 675-1920

League of Women Voters
c/o Rhonda May Kriss
306 East Sixth Street
Northfield, Minnesota 55057
(507) 645-6914

Rhode Islanders Saving Energy
334 Westminster Mall
Providence, Rhode Island 02903
(401) 272-1040

[1] The Residential Conservation Service Program,* established under the 1978 National Energy Conservation Policy Act (NECPA) and administered by the Department of Energy (DOE), mandates utility companies to offer energy audits and, if requested, provide customers with installation financing for suggested alterations.

[2] For more information on the Institute for Local Self-Reliance, see Resources at end of Energy Section.

[3] The Energy Task Force (ETF) is also profiled in Energy Section, p. 219. (For more information on ETF, see Resources at end of Energy Section.

* State and/or local government agencies are frequently responsible for administration of Federal program funds. For further information, see Appendix I under appropriate Federal agency.

Note: For a complete listing of groups featured throughout this book, see Index.

Low-Income Weatherization

Pennsylvania Department of Community Affairs
Bureau of Community Energy
P.O. Box 156
Harrisburg, Pennsylvania 17120
(717) 783-2576

The soaring fuel costs which followed the 1973 energy crisis forced most of us to realize the dollar and cent value of weatherizing our homes by adding insulation, storm windows and other energy-saving devices.

But many low-income Americans already spend as much as 50 percent of their income on heating bills. They don't have the money to weatherize even though their need to reduce energy bills is great. According to the Department of Energy (DOE), the average cost of weatherizing a home ranges from $470 to $950 and, in some regions of the country, the figure tops $1,000.

Low-Income Weatherization Program

Fortunately, there is help available for low-income residents through a free Federal weatherization assistance program authorized under the Energy Conservation and Production Act* of 1976. The program, formerly run by the Community Services Administration (CSA), is now administered by DOE. Weatherization money is funneled to states, and the program is carried out on the local level by a network of more than 1,000 local, nonprofit action agencies across the country. These agencies aim to help low-income residents—particularly the elderly and handicapped—with housing, energy, food and health needs. In 1980 DOE budgeted $199 million for the weatherization program.

One State's Success

Pennsylvania has enjoyed a good track record in implementing the weatherization program. Between 1976 and 1979, 53,000 homes were weatherized. "With fuel savings averaging 25 percent per completed house, more than 30,000 barrels of oil have been conserved by Pennsylvania's low-income families," says Carolyn Boardman, director of the Harrisburg-based Pennsylvania Department of Community Affairs (DCA), charged with establishing state guidelines for the program and funneling weatherization money to local, nonprofit action agencies. Boardman adds that total savings to residents in fuel bills have topped $5 million.

By January 1980 some 1,500 homeowners were being helped by more than 50 nonprofit groups such as the Redevelopment Authority of Allegheny County based in Pittsburgh, the Beaver-Butler Area Agency on Aging in New Brighton as well as by Community Action Agencies (CAAs)* across the state.[1]

How the Weatherization Programs Work

For instance, the Commission of Economic Opportunities (CEO) of Luzerne County, a CAA based in Wilkes-Barre, weatherized more than 3,600 homes since April 1975, saving residents an average of 25 percent on fuel bills. The Luzerne County CEO weatherization program is similar to the programs of all participating Pennsylvania nonprofit action agencies. It is advertised through word-of-mouth, newspaper articles or public service announcements on local radio and television stations.

"People meet in pool rooms, bars, wherever—the word gets out," says Mike Fedor, Luzerne County CEO weatherization project director. Area residents submit applications to the Luzerne County CEO. Guidelines on who qualifies are spelled out by DOE.

Eligibility Requirements

"The Commission substantiates the family's income (to ensure they qualify) and further checks to make sure they own their home," Fedor says. "Checks are made on deeds of ownership at the courthouse."

Low-income renters also get help from the weatherization program. But owners must first agree not to raise the rent or terminate the lease for 18 months after weatherization, which allows renters to save enough on energy bills to cover the cost of the work.

Once approved, the Luzerne County CEO proceeds with plans to weatherize. "We call the applicant to make an appointment to visit his home," Fedor explains. "Once we get there, we measure the home and determine its condition and what needs to be done."

According to Fedor, storm windows are custom made, holes in the building's structure are plugged, exterior doors are weatherstripped and cellulose insulation is blown into the attic.

Pennsylvania Department of Community Affairs

Insulation saves plenty on energy bills.

Pennsylvania Department of Community Affairs

Installing storm windows also helps.

Pennsylvania Department of Community Affairs

Caulking windows prevents energy loss.

Pennsylvania Department of Community Affairs

Blowing insulation into the attic

Satisfied Residents

A Luzerne County CEO study of homes weatherized in the winter of 1976-77 showed that residents of oil heated homes saved an average of 18.4 percent yearly in fuel bills and those with gas heated homes saved about 20.3 percent.

Frances Smith of Loyalville, which is near Wilkes-Barre, had her home weatherized just over a year ago. "We just love it. It's so much warmer now and we don't have to use so much heat," she says, adding that they used at least two tons less coal last year than the year before. "We saved over $100 on our heating bills last winter."

Changing Administering Agencies

DOE assumed full responsibility for the weatherization program from CSA in 1979. Differences in DOE and CSA regulations governing how weatherization funds are spent have caused some difficulties for states and participating local agencies. But DOE is now streamlining and simplifying the regulations to help resolve these problems.

Inflation Pushes Up Costs

The maximum amount allowed under current law to weatherize a home is $800. And some argue that with the ever-rising cost of weatherization, that figure is too low to do the job right. Several bills are now before Congress to raise the ceiling to $1,600.

According to Pennsylvania DCA Director Carolyn Boardman, the average cost of materials for weatherizing a Pennsylvania home rose from $175 in 1977 to $250 in 1979. And Boardman expects that figure to climb rapidly, reaching approximately $400 in 1980. Moreover, administrative costs and other items such as transporting weatherization materials and purchasing and maintaining needed trucks and tools are also rising. According to Rollie Clifton, manager of the weatherization program for DOE's regional office in Philadelphia, the total average cost of weatherizing a Pennsylvania home is expected to reach $800 or $900 in 1980.

But in some areas these costs will rise even more. "Experience indicates that in some locales where there is extremely poor housing, the average cost of weatherizing a home could well exceed $1,000," Clifton explains. This will be especially true in colder areas where homes require more extensive work such as roof and exterior wall repairs.

Another feature of the weatherization program—adding passive solar greenhouses to homes.

Pennsylvania Department of Community Affairs

Training Workers

DOE's weatherization program has been almost totally dependent on the Department of Labor's Comprehensive Employment and Training Act (CETA) Program,* which has supplied funds to train workers. With CETA funding reduced, DOE has allowed waivers—and soon expects to simplify the process for obtaining them—which permit the use of labor other than CETA workers. But in the process, some DOE funds targeted for purchasing materials will have to be used to hire and train workers. Some groups are dealing with the problem by obtaining additional money from local organizations and churches to keep their programs operating at full capacity.

In spite of the problems, the weatherization program is helping those most in need save money and stay warmer. And it is conserving scarce energy for our country. A study by DOE's Oak Ridge National Laboratory estimates that almost two million barrels of oil will be saved each year due to the 640,000 homes weatherized as of January 1980 through the Federal program.

Group Highlighted

Commission on Economic Opportunities
of Luzerne County
211-213 South Main Street
Wilkes-Barre, Pennsylvania 18701
(717) 825-8571

Department of Energy's Weatherization Program

Provides funds to install insulation, storm windows, caulking and weatherstripping and to make minor furnace repairs in homes occupied by families which meet established income guidelines.

History

- In 1973 Federal weatherization efforts began on an emergency basis after the oil embargo.
- In 1975 a formal program was established under the Community Services Administration (CSA).
- In 1976 Congress directed the Federal Energy Administration (FEA), now the Department of Energy (DOE), to set up a weatherization grant program aimed at low-income families.
- In 1977 and 1978 the DOE program was to run parallel to and supplement the CSA program.
- In 1979 DOE assumed sole Federal responsibility for weatherization of low-income housing.
- In 1980 DOE's weatherization program was funded for $199 million.

Appropriated Funds by Fiscal Year

($ in millions)

	1975	1976	1977	1978	1979	1980
CSA	16.5	27.5	110	65	0	0
DOE	0	0	27.5	65	199	199

Homes Weatherized

CSA	400,000	1975 through September 1979
DOE	240,000	August 1977 through December 1979
Total	640,000	Through December 1979

Program Criteria

Families within 125 percent of the poverty level set by the Office of Management and Budget (OMB) are eligible for weatherization assistance. The Federal poverty income level was $8,375 in 1979 for a non-farm family of four. For a farm family of four that same year, the poverty income level was $7,125.

How It Works

- Grants are made by DOE to states which, in turn, fund more than 1,000 local nonprofit action agencies which select the homes to be weatherized and complete the work.[1]
- Funds are provided for materials, administration, program support, training and technical assistance
- Labor for the weatherization work has been provided mainly by the Department of Labor's Comprehensive Employment and Training Act (CETA) Program.*
- Labor other than CETA can be hired under DOE waivers.

[1] DOE's low-income weatherization funds are channeled to one of various state departments. For the name of the nonprofit agency in your area that administers the low-income weatherization program, contact your regional Department of Energy office. (A complete listing of DOE regional offices as well as a map to help you locate the one closest to your area can be found in Appendix I under Department of Energy.

* State and/or local government agencies are frequently responsible for administration of Federal programs funds. For further information, see Appendix I under the Department of Labor.

Adapted from a DOE information sheet.

[1] The Community Services Administration's (CSA) Community Action Program (CAP)* funds local Community Action Agencies (CAAs)* aimed at helping low-income residents with their food, housing, energy and other needs.

* State and/or local government agencies are frequently responsible for administration of Federal program funds. For further information, see Appendix I under appropriate Federal agency.

Note: For a complete listing of groups featured throughout this book, see Index.

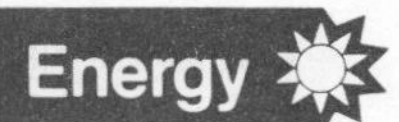

Weatherization Financing

Pacific Power and Light Company
920 South West Sixth Avenue
Portland, Oregon 97204
(503) 243-1122

When a large utility company starts giving customers free insulation and storm windows, some consumers might greet the offer with skepticism. But the program run by Pacific Power and Light Company (PP&L) does exactly what it appears to do: saves the utility and its customers money.

In January 1979 the Portland-based electric utility started promoting a weatherization program for customers in its Oregon, Washington, Montana and Idaho service area. By the end of the year 4,000 homes boasted an average of $1,300 worth of insulation, storm windows and other energy savers—all paid for by PP&L. And the alterations reduce customers' electricity use—and bills—by an average of 20 percent annually.

Satisfied Customers

PP&L spent about $1,000 weatherizing Mrs. Kenneth Bryan's three-bedroom home in Portland, Oregon. With added insulation, including storm doors and windows and weatherstripped exterior doors, the Bryans are staying warmer while using less energy. "I can set my thermostat at 64 degrees. Last year it had to be 72 for us to be comfortable," boasts Mrs. Bryan. And she adds gratefully, "The PP&L auditor spent a lot of time with us answering questions. It was like he was really concerned about our house."

Since the program began the company has been flooded with over 16,000 inquiries from eager customers. And PP&L, hoping to reach another 100,000 homes within five years, has hired 60 additional employees.

The Conservation Story

As energy use continued to escalate, company officials realized that excess and wasteful use of electricity simply wasn't profitable. Customers were already burdened with high electric bills, and building costly generating plants to expand PP&L's capacity would boost rates even more.

The answer seemed clear: the best way to control rate increases is through conservation. So in 1978, anxious to forestall spending several million dollars on new generating plants, officials planned the weatherization program. Although the company estimates it will cost about $1 million if all eligible homeowners participate, they are confident it's worth it.

How the Program Works

All of PP&L's 585,000 customers are eligible for free energy audits, which pinpoint heat and air conditioning leaks. And auditors recommend countermeasures such as installing storm doors and weatherstripping, PP&L audit crews immediately insulate free of charge electric water heaters that stand in unheated areas. This energy saver costs the company about $25 in materials.

And for 100,000 eligible customers—single dwelling and duplex homeowners—PP&L does even more. The company pays for labor and materials to plug energy leaks by wrapping heat ducts, weatherstripping doors and making other alterations based on energy audit findings.

Independent contractors bid for the weatherization jobs and must provide warranties for materials and workmanship. And to further ensure quality, PP&L inspects all work.

The only catch to this weatherization freebie is that customers must pay the company back, without interest, if and when the house is sold or transferred.

"Financially the program is a very good one," says Mrs. Rodney Crawford of Portland, whose three-bedroom Cape Cod style home has PP&L-installed insulation under the floors. "There's no interest so, regardless of when we sell, we will still only have to pay PP&L $400."

Everyone Saves

C. P. Davenport, PP&L's vice president for rate and regulatory affairs, explains that even nonparticipating customers benefit from the program. It keeps electricity rates down by conserving energy and stalling the need for new generating plants. And PP&L has not ruled out the possibility of expanding the program to nonowner customers in the future.

All in all, the weatherization and audit program run by PP&L seems almost too good to be true. Everybody wins. The customer takes no risks while saving money and energy. The nonparticipating customer suffers fewer rate hikes in the coming years. And the company saves capital expenditures and gains a better public image.

This kind of progressive thinking makes widespread conservation seem a reality.

Another Utility-Sponsored Program

The municipally owned Seattle City Light in Seattle, Washington offers homeowners free audits and gives a discount on ceiling and floor insulation. The costs are added to participants' electric bills in 36 monthly installments at an annual interest rate of 6 percent.

Other Conservation Efforts

In 1979 two unusual partners, the Maine Audubon Society, a nonprofit environmental organization based in Falmouth, and the state's largest commercial bank, Casco Bank and Trust Company based in Portland, launched a progressive Energy Conservation Program independent of government financing.

The bank offers customers reduced interest loans for energy-saving home alterations and new depositors are presented with free conservation hardware such as low-flow shower heads. Also, free lectures held statewide offer Maine residents tips on inexpensive ways to conserve energy. Moreover, an energy conservation catalog, funded by the bank and written by Maine Audubon, informs customers about energy-saving ideas—some of which qualify for Federal tax credits.[1] The program aims to promote energy conservation statewide and to spur banks in other states to start similar programs.

Groups Highlighted

Casco Bank and Trust Company
1 Monument Square
Portland, Maine 04101
(207) 774-8221

Maine Audubon Society
Gilsland Farm
118 Old Route 1
Falmouth, Maine 04105
(207) 781-2330

Seattle City Light
1015 Third Avenue
Seattle, Washington 98104
(206) 625-3738

[1] For a free copy of the Maine Audubon Society's *Buyers Guide to Home Energy Savings,* write to the Casco Bank and Trust Company, 1 Monument Square, Portland, Maine 04101.

Note: For a complete listing of groups featured throughout this book, see Index.

Apartment Boiler Repair

Housing Conservation Coordinators, Inc.
777 10th Avenue
New York, New York 10019
(212) 541-5996

If you live in an apartment, you might feel left out of the weatherization craze and other energy-saving programs spurred by the energy crisis. That's because most conservation programs are aimed at property owners. Lack of knowledge or money to hire experts to show them ways to save energy throughout an apartment building often discourages conservation efforts by apartment owners and managers.

The nonprofit Housing Conservation Coordinators, Inc. (HCC), based in the Clinton neighborhood of Manhattan, New York, is tackling this problem by conducting training courses on boiler and burner maintenance and repair—a conservation method especially well suited for apartment buildings heated by boiler systems.[1] Energy experts estimate that as much as 25 percent of a building's heating fuel is wasted during winter months because of poorly maintained or inefficient boilers and burners.

Course Wins Praise

Since 1975 over 500 residents, representatives of community groups and apartment building superintendents from all over the city have taken the HCC course. Testifying to its success, HCC boasts a waiting list of about 150. Because many students know what it's like to live in a drafty, old apartment building, they have deep, personal reasons for taking the course.

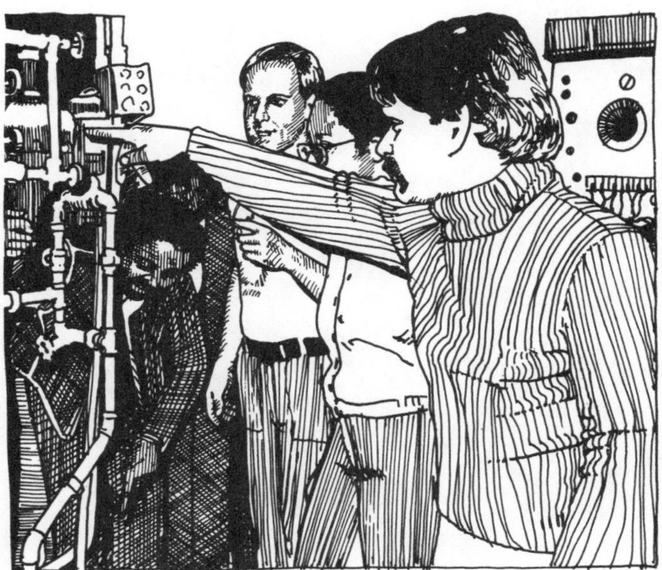

HCC training courses teach the nuts and bolts of boiler maintenance repair.

"It has helped me to help the other tenants and that makes me feel great," says Courtney Reid, an HCC graduate and maintenance supervisor of a tenant-managed Clinton apartment building. Prior to taking the HCC course, Reid knew nothing about boilers and was even a little afraid of them. Now she says, "I'm less likely to be ripped off by repairmen and salesmen who assume I don't know what I'm doing because I'm a woman."

Beginnings

In New York City and other areas rising costs are prompting many private landlords to cut back on services, including boiler maintenance. And as operating costs continue to escalate, the number of city-owned buildings taken from landlords in tax foreclosures is rising significantly. For example, in 1978 the city owned 9,500 buildings with a total of 35,000 apartments. In some of these owner-abandoned dwellings, residents who often lack maintenance training collect money from other tenants to pay for parts and attempt to make boiler repairs themselves. The results of their well-intentioned efforts can be very disappointing.

Realizing the problem, HCC began its training course aimed at using layman's terms to reach a broad audience. Boiler systems operate like this: The oil burner heats the water-filled boiler, producing steam heat somewhat the way a stove burner heats a tea kettle. An inefficient system can send air as hot as 800°F up the chimney—a terrible waste of heat.

Tips on Starting Maintenance Course

Richard Marans, executive director of HCC, recalling problems in launching the course, offers two essential tips for other groups wishing to do the same:

- Think small. Staff salaries and equipment may be expensive.

- Because locating course instructors might be the hardest and most crucial step, contact local fuel suppliers for assistance in recruiting. And be careful to select technical experts with the ability to transfer their knowledge to laypersons.

Course Length and Costs

Today HCC offers four 11-week courses a year with about 30 students per course. Each course costs HCC about $2,000, some of which is paid by the $15-per-student tuition fees. The rest is donated by local banks, corporations, foundations and religious groups.

Training

Students first receive practical experience working on burners and boilers in the HCC training room or in a tenant-managed building in the Clinton area.

Course participants learn how to clean and vacuum boilers and burners, change oil filters and make repairs. They also learn how to install such energy savers as insulation and weatherstripping throughout the building. After the practical experience, lectures follow to reinforce their new knowledge.

Job Development

The course also gives students skills that make them valuable employees to apartment building owners. About 30 graduates now manage apartment buildings and another 50 or more have secured jobs as building superintendents.

Other Groups

In 1979 the Institute for Human Development, a private, nonprofit organization in Philadelphia, Pennsylvania dedicated to developing employment for inner-city residents, started a boiler mechanic training program. Funds for expenses and trainee salaries came from the Community Services Administration's (CSA) Emergency Energy Conservation Services Program,* the Department of Labor's Comprehensive Employment and Training Act (CETA) Program* and the Department of Housing and Urban Development's Community Development Block Grant (CDBG) Program.*

So far 83 low-income residents have learned to install thermostats and flue dampers and maintain, repair and rebuild existing burners. The Institute hires many of the graduates to man its 24-hour emergency repair service which is available to low-income residents. Other graduates have been hired by major oil companies.

Group Highlighted

Institute for Human Development
718 West Norris Street
Philadelphia, Pennsylvania 19122
(215) 763-0742

[1] Housing Conservation Coordinators, Inc. (HCC) is also mentioned in Housing Section, p. 125.

* State and/or local government agencies are frequently responsible for administration of Federal program funds. For further information, see Appendix I under appropriate Federal agency.

Note: For a complete listing of groups featured throughout this book, see Index.

Putting Garbage to Good Use

Seattle Recycling, Inc.
5718 Empire Way South
Seattle, Washington 98118
(206) 723-2051

Americans pay a staggering $4.5 billion annually—and untold time and energy—for sanitation trucks, employees, landfills and dumps to collect and dispose of our garbage. But those costs can be cut by boosting public interest in separating and selling reusable trash. About half of all garbage—glass, aluminum, newsprint, bottles and other reusables—can be recycled by manufacturers and industries. And they can then be turned into new products less expensively and using less energy than with raw materials.

Paying for Trash

By putting a price tag on trash, recycling businesses across the country are beginning to prosper while prodding residents to build trash-separating habits which benefit themselves, their communities and local governments. For instance, the for-profit Seattle Recycling, Inc. (SRI) in Washington is making a significant contribution to the city by reducing garbage and decreasing the need for costly landfills. Recycling-conscious residents earn an average of $10 to $15 per SRI pick up, getting as much as two cents a pound for newspapers, 26 cents a pound for aluminum cans and from 35 to 50 cents for a case of beer bottles.

Moreover, SRI has helped about 100 church, school and other nonprofit community groups raise funds by encouraging them to launch reusable garbage drives. Not only are the groups paid for the recyclables they collect from residents, but they also get a 10 percent bonus for their organizations. Since SRI began in 1976 over $100,000 has been paid to community groups.

Origins and First Funding

It all started in 1975 when two environmentally minded enterprising young men, Don Kneass and Jim McMahon, set up a toll-free, statewide Recycling Information Hotline to give Washington residents information on recycling reusable garbage.[1] After one year the successful hotline was taken over by the State Department of Ecology.

Convinced that Seattle needed another recycling operation, Kneass and McMahon formed Seattle Recycling, Inc. They wooed $14,500 from private investors and kicked in $2,500 of their own money to launch their business in a low-income Seattle neighborhood.

Rocky Times

They had little trouble finding buyers for the reusables. Paper mills were eager to save lumber and pulping expenses by buying old newspapers to produce paper goods, and large aluminum companies like Kaiser were anxious to purchase cans to shred for their products.

The men soon learned that this was not enough to ensure success. They knew they had to attract a large volume of customers to get the quantity of reusable materials needed to put SRI in the black.

Capturing Public Interest

So in the summer of 1977, determined to build a strong business, the men launched a public awareness campaign. They advertised in local newspapers, held workshops and met with school assemblies and other groups to push the recycling concept. Within a year SRI's sales to manufacturers totaled $61,000, allowing Kneass and McMahon to draw a small salary for the first time and hire a part-time helper. That year SRI collected 75 tons of aluminum cans, 427 tons of newspapers and dozens of other items such as corrugated cardboard. They paid out almost $42,000 to area residents.

In 1979 SRI collected about 1,800 tons of newspapers and 264 tons of aluminum cans, boosting their sales to $500,000 while paying out almost $200,000 to conserving citizens.

Moreover, they have provided jobs in the low-income area in which their operation is based by hiring most of their 18-strong staff from that community.

City Demonstrates Support

In April 1978 the city tipped its hat to SRI by enlisting them as partners in a $185,000 pilot project aimed at saving city trash removal costs while increasing resident awareness about the value of reusable wastes. The city-administered program, Separate Our Recyclables from Trash (SORT), offers lower garbage collection rates to about 5,000 families in 20 targeted neighborhoods who are willing to separate glass, tin and other reusables from their trash. Eligible families pay a per-trash-can rate for garbage collection, and the city pays SRI to collect and market the reusable materials—and to continue its recycling education program. SRI estimates the city will get about $40,000 from the sale of the reusables to manufacturers and save an untold amount in waste removal costs.[2]

Drop Stations

SRI continues its efforts to make Seattle's residents responsive to recycling. In May 1978 the group installed a mobile recycling drop station 25 miles from its headquarters. On designated days residents can get on-the-spot cash for reusables. The success of that station led to two additional mobile stations, and eight more strategically placed sites across the city are planned by March 1980.

Other Groups

SRI is just one of the many excellent recycling programs across the country. The Community Environmental Council in Santa Barbara, California, which operates similarly to SRI, is another.

The town of New Paltz, New York uses workers from the Department of Labor's Comprehensive Employment and Training Act (CETA) Program* to oversee its recycling project. Ecocycle of Boulder, Colorado collects 340 tons of reusable garbage a month and pays $35,000 a year to community groups. And ENCORE in Berkeley, California—a self-sufficient bottle washing business started by the Berkeley Ecology Center in 1975 with a $25,000 grant from Alameda County's general revenue funds—now employs eight full-time people and pays $3,000 to $4,000 a month to recycling-conscious residents.

Start a Recycling Drive

1. Form a committee of those interested in recycling and train volunteers to work at the center.
2. Find a location with access for trucks to pick up collected refuse (for example, a vacant lot rather than a basement). Obtain permission to use the site.
3. Locate containers for collected materials. (Ask companies that recycle the materials.)
4. Notify local merchants and residents about the program. Let them know what materials to collect and how to prepare them (tie newspaper stacks, rinse and flatten cans, etc.).
5. Annouce the location of the recycling center and dates and times that materials will be accepted by posting notices throughout the neighborhood and placing ads in local newsletters and community papers.

Adapted from the New York Self Help Hand Book, *Citizens Committee for New York City, Inc., 3 West 29th Street, Sixth Floor, New York, New York 10001.*

Groups Highlighted

Community Environmental Council
924 Anacapa Street, Suite B-4
Santa Barbara, California 93101
(805) 962-2210

Ecocycle
P.O. Box 4193
Boulder, Colorado 80306
(303) 444-6634

ENCORE
2701 College Avenue
Berkeley, California 94705
(415) 849-2525

Town of New Paltz
P.O. Box 550
New Paltz, New York 12561
(914) 255-0100

[1] The toll-free, statewide Recycling Information Hotline was funded with a $50,000 grant from the State Department of Ecology.

[2] A city-conducted study is underway to determine how much recycling operations save Seattle in garbage collection and landfill building costs.

* State and/or local government agencies are frequently responsible for administration of Federal program funds. For further information, see Appendix I under appropriate Federal agency.

Note: For a complete listing of groups featured throughout this book, see Index.

One City's Answer to the Energy Crisis

City of Davis
226 F Street
Davis, California 95616
(916) 756-3740

Individually we can do a lot to save energy such as insulating homes, keeping thermostats down and turning off unneeded lights. But imagine the energy savings if an entire city were determined to cut energy use.

The college town of Davis, California, which lies in the Sacramento Valley not far from the state's capital, stands as a model for other American cities eager to rein in energy use. Its 42,000 residents and responsive local officials have called for energy conservation in every facet of life. They have passed tough energy-saving building codes for new and old homes and supported a range of other conservation programs from increasing the use of bicycles and clotheslines to developing economic public transportation.

The results have paid off. Nationwide between 1973 and 1978 individual use of electricity rose by 11.2 percent and natural gas use dropped by 8.5 percent. During that same period Davis residents cut their electricity consumption by a whopping 18 percent and used 37 percent less natural gas. And by 1990, as existing energy-saving measures take

Bicycling saves gasoline, keeps the air clean and it's fun!

firmer hold and others are implemented, city officials hope heating and cooling demands will plummet by 50 percent.

Revising City Plans

Even before the 1973 oil crisis shocked our country, energy conservation was an important issue tc Davis residents. In 1971 officials decided to revise the city's long-term development goals. Anxious for resident input and support, a study was launched. Questionnaires were sent to citizens asking about energy use and concerns. The 1974 report on the study was clear: an overwhelming number of residents cared about and were willing to support energy conservation programs.

Moreover, the report cited cars as well as heating and cooling as the greatest energy culprits in town, accounting for 75 percent of all energy use. So transportation and building construction became focal points of the city's new development plans.

Citizens Vote for Energy Savings

Four individuals at the University of California at Davis took on the job of researching and creating a new building code which would reflect the city's findings. By 1975 Davis residents reinforced their commitment to conservation by passing a building ordinance which makes new homes twice as energy efficient. The code requires increased insulation, limited window areas to conserve energy loss and light colored roofs to reflect summer heat. Also, homes must be built on an angle which allows easy conversion to solar heat. The average cost of adding these energy-saving features to new homes is about $300. But city officials think the investment makes good business sense.

Davis resident utilizes the sun's drying power.

Other Energy Saving Programs

The 1976 building ordinance was the first in a series of resident-supported conservation programs in Davis. Since then:

• Gas-guzzlers have been traded in for an energy-efficient fleet of compact city vehicles. And second-hand, diesel-powered, double-decker buses now provide public transportation.

• A citywide recycling service offers residents curb-side pick up of bottles, aluminum cans and other reusable wastes.

• Davis now boasts more bicycles than cars. Twenty-four miles of bicycle lanes and paths grace the city and every major street is now safe for cyclists. Bicycle and pedestrian overcrossings span once dangerous intersections and undercrossings are provided at railroad tracks.

• Zoning regulations were changed to allow more businesses operated from homes, thus cutting transportation use.

• With funds from the Innovative Grants Program,* administered by the Department of Housing and Urban Development's (HUD) Office of Policy Development and Research, the city built a demonstration passive solar single-family house and three solar duplexes which serve as models for developers and builders.

• Since 1978 new residential dwellings must be equipped with solar-heated plumbing.

• And an ordinance, effective in January 1980, requires all homes at the time of resale to have adequate ceiling insulation, shower water restrictors, weatherstripping of exterior doors and heater insulation jackets. The city's utility company offers residents financing, and the city is considering establishing a $25,000 loan fund to further assist with needed alterations.

Davis' comprehensive energy planning shows how energy problems can be solved when citizens and city officials work together.

Other Groups

Many cities around the country, jolted by the energy crisis of recent years, are beginning to implement energy-saving programs.

In Wichita, Kansas, for example, an energy policy study involving government officials, citizen groups and business representatives led in 1979 to a countywide plan to cut energy waste by promoting such programs as home weatherization and usable waste recycling. Already the city's Energy Commission is responsible for the weatherization of 150 Wichita homes.

Group Highlighted

City of Wichita
Energy Commission
City Hall
455 North Main
Wichita, Kansas 67202
(316) 265-4193

* State and/or local government agencies are frequently responsible for administration of Federal program funds. For further information, see Appendix I under appropriate Federal agency.

Note: For a complete listing of groups featured throughout this book, see Index.

Chapter 2

Using Renewable Sources of Energy

Introduction

The hard fact is that our country has a limited supply of oil, natural gas and coal. We know we have to look elsewhere for our energy needs. One good alternative is to capture the free energy of the sun and the wind.

The Federal government, through tax incentives, research and grants, is promoting renewable energy sources. But government alone cannot reach solar utopia. In many cases the hard work and ingenuity of community groups, both with government assistance and on their own, have developed exciting cost-saving devices using renewable energy sources.

In this chapter we review a variety of innovative and creative energy projects from California to New York, all of which aim to decrease fuel bills and energy dependence by using sun and windpower.

We profile a group in California that has helped its low-income community with solar energy projects and some rugged individuals in rural Colorado who have taught their neighbors to build energy-saving solar devices.

Equally important is the economic impact solar energy can have on a community. We look at how an Arizona Indian reservation was transformed by an exciting solar training and manufacturing project. We also look at a program in Memphis that makes hot water solar heating systems available to all homeowners—even the poorest of the poor.

We glimpse at one rural farm organization that has built a gasahol still to cut gasoline costs and another that taught residents to build solar home and farm heating devices.

Finally, we review a dynamic group in New York that has converted a gutted tenement into an energy-efficient apartment cooperative using solar and windpower.

These exciting programs show how much can be done to conserve energy and that the solar future is happening today.

Neighborhood Solar Systems

San Bernardino West Side
Community Development Corporation
1736 West Highland Avenue
San Bernardino, California 92411
(714) 887-2546

Starting your own neighborhood utility to fight high energy costs may seem a bit farfetched, but supplementing your energy supply and reducing energy bills with a neighborhood solar heating system isn't.

On the West Side of San Bernardino, California a block of ten homes is heated by a centralized sun-powered energy system, giving a much needed dose of energy independence to the low-income, mostly black and Chicano neighborhood.

One of the owners of the solar heated houses, Arlene Nolin, has noticed real savings. "Before moving," the mother of six says, "I used to pay around $37 a month on my gas bills. Now I pay $12 in the winter and only $7 in the summer. I've grown to like living here more and more."

Lower Food Bills Too

Owners save an average of 25 to 40 percent on space heat and hot water bills. In addition, a solar greenhouse—located beneath the energy system—provides nutritious produce, cutting residents' food costs. Even more heartening, West Side residents were trained to build the solar system and greenhouse, learning valuable job skills.

The system—one of the few multi-home solar heating units in the country—is the creation of the San Bernardino West Side Community Development Corporation (CDC), a nonprofit group dedicated to teaching residents valuable job skills while rehabilitating the economically deprived area. From 1973 to 1979 West Side CDC staffers trained over 650 residents in such skills as carpentry, plumbing and painting as well as solar construction. And 75 percent of the trainees have landed jobs with nearby California corporations.

Origins

West Side CDC was the inspiration of Valerie Pope-Ludlam and other women active in the San Bernardino Welfare Rights Organization, a nonprofit group dedicated to helping low-income residents. In the late 1960s, determined to help get the community back on its feet, Pope-Ludlam organized residents to lobby local, state and Federal offices to draw attention to West Side problems.

Her efforts paid off. In 1968 the group won a small grant from the Office of Economic Opportunity (OEO) to rehabilitate run-down and abandoned housing in West Side's Delman Heights and California Gardens neighborhoods.[1] California Gardens, with West Side CDC's help, is now rehabilitated.

Expansion

In 1973, after being awarded a $19,250 administrative grant from OEO, Pope-Ludlam's group launched their rehabilitation and resident job training program.

Turning to Solar

In 1977, recognizing the great job potential in the new solar industry, the West Side CDC decided to install a central solar heating system in a block of ten vacant houses which needed extensive repairs.

Funding for the $85,000 system and greenhouse came from the Department of Housing and Urban Development (HUD), the Community Services Administration (CSA) and the California State Energy Commission (CSEC).[2]

The Department of Labor's Comprehensive Employment and Training Act (CETA) Program* provided money to hire five community craftsmen who trained 25 local residents in weatherization and carpentry skills, and the Veterans Administration (VA) kicked in $3,500 to help rehabilitate the homes. And West Side CDC staffers helped interested residents obtain funding from local financial institutions to purchase the VA-owned houses.

Capturing the Sun

The trainees began rehabilitating and weatherizing the houses. To capture the sun's energy, trainees constructed 72 solar collectors, arranged in elevated rows along the utility right-of-way which runs behind the homes. A four-ton, 5,000-gallon tank with a storage capacity to heat all ten homes for four sunless days was placed beneath an adjacent park. By the end of the year the homes were ready for their new owners.

Staff and Budget

In the meantime West Side CDC continues other efforts at sprucing up the community and training residents. In 1979 its funding was nearly $3 million and about half of its 200-strong staff were CETA workers. Funding for their various projects came from a number of county, state and Federal sources. ''We looked long and hard,'' Pope-Ludlam said, ''to find different agencies that had funding for all our needs.''

Bread Box Collector

Since installing the neighborhood solar heating system West Side CDC has started other solar energy projects. In late 1977, with $42,000 from the CSEC, staffers developed a ''bread box collector,'' a simple device to attract the sun's energy which is used to heat water for bathing and cooking. Bread boxes have been installed in 20 West Side public housing projects bringing low-cost hot water to about 100 residents. A low-income minority construction crew, paid by CETA, insulated and weatherstripped the duplexes and installed the solar collectors.

Certified Solar Vocational School

In 1979 West Side CDC opened its Energy Technology Center which is certified as a solar vocational school by the State Office of Education. Seventy-eight of West Side's 150 trainees are enrolled in the school with CETA funding. Students learn how to construct and design the bread box and other solar collectors.

Solar trainees can produce four solar collectors a day. And the group hopes to open a solar collector manufacturing business by October 1980.

Other Groups

Other low-income community groups are looking at energy conservation alternatives as a way to upgrade their neighborhoods and provide employment for residents. In Maui County, Hawaii, Maui Economic Opportunity (MEO), Inc., a Community Action

Students at West Side CDC's solar vocational school learn valuable construction skills.

Spray painting a solar hot water heater

Agency (CAA),* and three other CAAs in the state have provided free solar hot water heating systems to over 6,200 low-income residents statewide.[3]

Because Hawaii has no local fuel, stocks must be imported, making electricity cost about 80 percent more than on the United States mainland. In 1975, eager to help residents cut energy costs, MEO began manufacturing and installing the solar panels which cost about $900 each.

In the spring of 1978 the Solar Project, sponsored by the Community Action Program of Lancaster County, Inc., a CAA in Lancaster, Pennsylvania, launched a small-scale solar weatherization program funded by CSA's Emergency Energy Conservation Services Program.* About 20 residents, paid by CETA, were trained to build and install solar water heaters. By the end of 1979, 40 homes were equipped with the solar heating systems, saving residents an average of 20 to 25 percent yearly on energy bills. The Center also offers tips on energy conservation to all low-income county residents—renters and homeowners.

Solar Home Building

Another group, the Shelter Institute in Bath, Maine, is teaching solar home building and design courses to interested individuals from all over the world.[4] Courses stress engineering and physics concepts as well as the effects of sun and weather on home design. In addition to home designing, Institute students learn how to weatherize and add solar greenhouses to old homes.

Groups Highlighted

Community Action Program
of Lancaster County, Inc.
Solar Project
630 Rockland Street
Lancaster, Pennsylvania 17602
(717) 299-7301

Maui Economic Opportunity, Inc.
189 Kaahumann Avenue
Kahului, Maui, Hawaii 96732
(808) 871-9591

Shelter Institute
38 Center Street
Bath, Maine 04530
(207) 442-7938

[1] The Office of Economic Opportunity (OEO), an antipoverty agency, was replaced by the Community Services Administration (CSA) in 1975.

[2] Funding for the solar energy system and greenhouse came from the Department of Housing and Urban Development's (HUD) Cycle II Residential Solar Research and Demonstration Grant Series* and Community Services Administration's (CSA) Emergency Energy Conservation Services Program.*

[3] The Community Services Administration's (CSA) Community Action Program (CAP)* funds local Community Action Agencies (CAAs)* aimed at helping low-income residents with their food, housing, energy and other needs.

[4] For more information on the Shelter Institute, see Resources at end of Energy Section.

* State and/or local government agencies are frequently responsible for administration of Federal program funds. For further information, see Appendix I under appropriate Federal agency.

Note: For a complete listing of groups featured throughout this book, see Index.

Country Style Solar Energy

San Luis Valley Solar Energy Association, Inc.
512 Ross Street
Alamosa, Colorado 81101
(303) 589-2233
and
People's Alternative Energy Services, Inc.
Route 1, Box 3A
San Luis, Colorado 81152
(303) 672-3602

Residents in the vast, sparsely populated San Luis Valley in southcentral Colorado are building their own energy systems and saving hundreds of dollars yearly on home and farm heating bills.

Fuel savings are especially important to the mostly Hispanic families in the six-county area, almost half of whom earn less than $5,000 a year. Over 20 percent of the 42,000 San Luis Valley residents are dependent on agriculture for their livelihood—difficult at best in an area with long, harsh winters and one of the shortest growing seasons in the country.

The Solar Message

Two nonprofit resident-inspired organizations, the San Luis Valley Solar Energy Association, Inc. in Alamosa and People's Alternative Energy Services, Inc. in San Luis, are devoted to spreading the good solar word across the Valley. These ingenious citizens have built more than 400 solar systems—collectors, greenhouses, water heaters and crop dryers—all of which capture the free energy of the sun and save as much as 50 percent on utility bills.

"The experience in the San Luis Valley has shown that community-based efforts can bring about energy awareness and action which Federal and state programs have not been able to accomplish," says architect Akira Kawanabe, former president of San Luis Valley Solar Energy Association.

Origins

The creation of the Association was spearheaded in 1976 by a San Luis Valley couple, Bob and Julie Dunsmore, who were well aware of the sun's energy potential. Eager to see if others were interested in learning about it, they advertised a meeting for solar enthusiasts through public service announcements on radio. More than 60 residents from the Valley showed up that night, a Board of Directors was formed and the San Luis Valley Solar Energy Association, Inc. was born.

Bill North, a construction supervisor, attended that meeting. North and his father-in-law, while toying with ways to keep water pipes from freezing, had created a simple vertical wall solar collector to harness the sun's energy and save as much as 50 percent on heating bills. The North passive solar collector cost about $100 to build, using scrap material such as plywood, metal and plastic sheets, and took about five months to design. The low-cost design brought solar power within the reach of Valley residents. By the end of 1979 over 350 Valley homes were being heated—at least partially—with "North" collectors.

San Luis Valley Solar Energy Association, Inc.

A row of North solar collectors provides low-cost heat for a San Luis Valley home.

Kawanabe estimates that North collectors save as much as 50 percent on fuel bills and can be built at home with recycled materials for about one-fifth the cost of commercial solar units—or about $300 for a two-bedroom, single-story home. And smaller units, which cost about $100 for the same size home, save up to one-third yearly on fuel bills.

During the Association's early years North generously wrote specifications for the collector which the group mimeographed and sold for $1. More than 4,000 plans were mailed around the country and overseas. The group is currently putting together a larger, more detailed packet.[1]

Holding Workshops

In 1976 Association members began conducting how-to workshops throughout the Valley to promote solar power. They enlisted from New Mexico the help of Bill Yanda, a nationally recognized expert in the field of solar greenhouse design.[2] Reimbursed only for his mileage, Yanda held a workshop to teach residents to build their own solar greenhouses.

And with Bill North's help many residents began building onto their homes solar greenhouses with rock floors to absorb the energy harnessed by the North collector. As the rocks cool in the evening the heat radiates throughout the greenhouse and into the attached home.

Funding

After the first few years of making it on their own, the 300-member Association received Federal help. In 1978 the Federal Energy Administration (FEA) awarded the Association $4,500 under the Energy Conservation and Production Act* for a part-time staff position.[3]

In 1979 the nonprofit National Center for Appropriate Technology (NCAT), based in Chicago, Illinois, awarded the group a grant of over $6,500 to hire additional staff and start a newsletter.[4]

Other Energy Efforts in San Luis Valley

While the Association was establishing itself, individual efforts at solar construction were underway throughout the Valley. For instance, Arnie and Marie Valdez of Costilla County began by building their own energy self-sufficient solar adobe house and are now codirectors of People's Alternative Energy Services, Inc.

Maria Valdez explains that their initial interest in solar design "just stemmed from our own needs. We lived in a small, cold house and wanted to improve it."

So in 1973 the couple obtained a loan from the United States Department of Agriculture's Farmers Home Administration (FmHA) enabling them to install a solar collector to heat their home, a solar hot water unit and a solar greenhouse.[5]

"The house functions like a giant thermos," says Maria Valdez. Heavy shutters are closed at night and the collected energy radiates throughout the house. And during the day the shutters are thrown open to let in the sun's warmth.

People's Alternative Energy Services

In 1977, in cooperation with the San Luis Valley Solar Energy Association, Arnie and Marie Valdez began conducting workshops to teach residents solar design. By the end of 1979 their workshops had resulted in the construction of 30 solar crop dryers, 25 solar collectors, 20 solar hot water heaters and 19 home and community solar greenhouses.

In 1978, because of their work in this field and interest in their community, the Valdez' received a $7,820 grant from the Caroline Foundation, a private, nonprofit group, to establish the People's Alternative Energy Services (PAES) aimed at encouraging low-income families to become self-reliant through solar energy.

"We promoted 'do-it-yourself' projects—or if the residents were very poor, we'd give them a grant incentive," Maria says.

That same year PAES received a $4,850 grant from the private New York-based Arca Foundation. The money enabled the group to dispense small self-help grants, publish blueprints for solar food dryers and water heaters, and write a soon-to-be-published book which emphasizes wind and water power and is geared to rural residents.

"We should all push the self-reliance philosophy," Maria Valdez says. "If we had waited for big technology to bring solar energy to our area, we wouldn't have it—we needed something appropriate for *our* community."

[1] "The New North Collector" packet is available for $2.20 by writing to the San Luis Valley Solar Energy Association, Inc., 512 Ross Street, Alamosa, Colorado 81101.

[2] Bill Yanda and the Solar Sustenance Team's solar greenhouse workshops are profiled in Energy Section, p. 235.

[3] The Federal Energy Administration (FEA) was replaced by the Department of Energy (DOE) in 1977. DOE now administers the Energy Conservation and Production Act.*

[4] For further information on the National Center for Appropriate Technology (NCAT), see Resources at end of Energy Section.

[5] Arnie and Marie Valdez received a loan from the United States Department of Agriculture's (USDA) Farmers Home Administration's (FmHA) Low-to-Moderate Income Housing Loans (Section 502) Program.*

* State and/or local government agencies are frequently responsible for administration of Federal program funds. For further information, see Appendix I under appropriate Federal agency.

Note: For a complete listing of groups featured throughout this book, see Index.

Solar Energy Creates Jobs

Little Singer Community School
Birdsprings, Navaho Nation
Star Route, Box 239
Winslow, Arizona 86047
(602) 774-7444

For the Navajo Indians the sun has always had special meaning. It has been worshipped for centuries as the provider of abundant harvests and the one certainty in a life fraught with hardship. And once again the sun has proven its worth to 20th century Indians of the Navajo Nation, which spans the entire northeast corner of Arizona.

Solar energy has brought a sense of community spirit and an improved standard of living to the 1,200 residents of Birdsprings, a community nestled in the midst of the barren, remote Navajo Nation, almost devoid of electricity and other traditional energy sources.

But thanks to a vision shared by the community medicine man, area leaders and a concerned nuclear physicist, energy scarcity has been overcome. Birdsprings now boasts a sun-heated, wind-powered elementary school which enables Navajo children to learn at home instead of traveling hundreds of miles to government boarding schools.

Beth Kachinhongva, who attends senior high school in Phoenix, knows all to well the loneliness boarding school can bring. "When I was younger, I used to cry all the time. I missed out on a lot of things—like family outings on weekends," she says wistfully.

Success Today

The success of the energy self-sufficient Little Singer Community School spurred the creation of the Birdsprings Solar Corporation, the first non-government, Navajo-owned and operated solar business in the country. And with help from the Indian Development District of Arizona, Inc. (IDDA), a nonprofit corporation founded and directed by Arizona Indian tribes, "The Arizona Solar Savages" was formed.[1]

The Solar Savages, comprising men and women from nine tribes, were trained in solar design and have installed more than 40 solar hot water systems free of charge in the homes of low-income and elderly Indian residents throughout Arizona.[2] Using the "Shandiin" (ray of sunlight) solar panel model that was developed during the school's construction and manufactured by the Birdsprings Solar Corporation, the solar system provides 80 percent of hot water needs, saving tribal families an average of $336 yearly in fuel costs for heating water.

Pipes for passive heating system at Little Singer School

Equally important, the solar projects have created jobs for the community which has been long plagued with high unemployment. In 1977 there were no local jobs in Birdsprings; most residents were welfare recipients.

"It's a real success story," says one Department of Energy (DOE) official commenting on the school and other solar projects at Birdsprings. "The approach to training and business opportunities is very interesting and is something we would like to see continued and expanded."

Solar panels are lowered into the Grand Canyon terrain on the Navajo Indian Reservation.

The Dream

In 1968, shortly after coming to Birdsprings to write a book, Tom Ryan, a nuclear physicist with a passion for solar energy, met medicine man Little Singer. They forged a deep friendship and soon shared a dream that would change the lives of hundreds of Navajo Indians: building a school in the Birdsprings community.

The isolated reservation communities are too small to have their own schools so Indian youngsters are sent away for education to central boarding schools operated by the Department of Interior's Bureau of Indian Affairs (BIA).[3]

For years Little Singer had conducted tribal ceremonies—praying that someone with the technical expertise and compassion for the lonely plight of the village elders would help Birdsprings' children come home. Tom Ryan was his answer.

Ryan convinced Little Singer that the school had to be energy self-sufficient. The closest power line was miles away and bringing in needed electricity or fuel would make the school too expensive to build—and operate. But Birdsprings had plenty of sunshine and plenty of wind.

The money needed to make the dream a reality was a long time coming. For years Birdsprings residents raised funds through bake and quilt sales.

Ground is Broken

Little Singer died in 1971 and Ryan moved back to San Francisco to teach engineering, but he didn't give up the dream. He fired his students with enthusiasm over the solar system he had designed for the Birdsprings school. And in 1976, after obtaining grants from the Packard Foundation, the Save the Children Federation and other private donations, 23 students journeyed to Birdsprings, surveyed the site and dug deep pits for the solar storage units. After that it was up to the determined community residents.

That same year the school organizers won a $68,000 grant from the Community Services Administration's

(CSA) Emergency Energy Conservation Services Program* to buy needed materials for the solar system.

In a borrowed workshop, Birdsprings residents busily constructed solar panels to harness the sun's energy. But the construction of the school was slow and painstaking. Community workers laid the foundation by hand and had nearly completed half of all construction before an electric generator was hooked up so motorized tools could be used.

Dream Comes True

In 1978 Little Singer Community School won a $113,000 grant from the Department of Health, Education and Welfare's (HEW) Office of Indian Education to operate the school.[4]

And in October 1979 the Little Singer Community School, equipped to handle as many as 44 students, opened its doors to Birdsprings' 23 elementary school youngsters.

Growth

The dedication and spirit of the Indian residents who built the school has far from faded. Because of the highly successful solar panel design used on the school, residents formed the Birdsprings Solar Corporation. The company produces solar panels and other parts for solar hot water and space heating units and provides equipment and training to Navajo Nation residents.

And Solar Savages, the Birdsprings Solar Corporation and the nonprofit Cameron Chapter Farm Project, a group based on the Navajo reservation, marshaled their technical expertise and launched the Shandiin Institute in late 1979.[5] Funded by DOE, Shandiin Institute is a clearinghouse of solar engineering information for Arizona Indians and is dedicated to promoting the use of cost-saving solar units.[6]

One Indian official with the Indian Development District of Arizona sums up Birdsprings' energy future this way: "Solar energy fits in with our heritage. We've been using the sun for hundreds of years and it has almost unlimited potential."

Groups Highlighted

Birdsprings Solar Corporation
Birdsprings, Navaho Nation
Star Route, Box 239
Winslow, Arizona 86047
(602) 774-7444

Indian Development District
of Arizona, Inc.
1777 West Camelback Road, Suite A-108
Phoenix, Arizona 85015
(602) 248-0184

Shandiin Institute
Route 3, Box 35
Flagstaff, Arizona 86011
(602) 526-4258

[1] The Indian Development District of Arizona (IDDA) is a nonprofit corporation founded and operated by Arizona Indian tribes and dedicated to promoting community self-reliance. IDDA's programs include technical assistance to tribal governments, agricultural projects, senior citizen and summer youth employment programs, construction training for reservation residents and community planning and health care.

[2] A $250,000 grant for training the Arizona Solar Savages came from the former Solar Utilization/Economic Development and Employment (SUEDE) Program, jointly administered by the Department of Energy (DOE), the Department of Labor (DOL) and the Community Services Administration (CSA).

[3] The Department of Interior's (DOI) Bureau of Indian Affairs (BIA) is responsible for encouraging and training Native Americans to manage their own affairs and to mobilize public and private assistance in achieving these goals. The Bureau assists in creating and managing educational systems for the benefit of Native Americans.

[4] The Department of Health, Education and Welfare's (HEW) Office of Indian Education granted $113,000 to the Little Singer Community School under Part A, Indian Controlled Schools Non-Local Education Agency (Non-LEA) Program.*

[5] The Cameron Chapter Farm Project is also mentioned in Food Section, p. 63.

[6] The Shandiin Institute is funded by a $300,000 grant from the Department of Energy's (DOE) Training, Information and Education Branch of the Office of Solar Applications for Buildings.*

* State and/or local government agencies are frequently responsible for administration of Federal program funds. For further information, see Appendix I under appropriate Federal agency.

Note: For a complete listing of groups featured throughout this book, see Index.

Citywide Solar

South Memphis Development Corporation
Solar Resource Center
219 Madison Avenue
Memphis, Tennessee 38103
(901) 521-1031
and
Tennessee Valley Authority
c/o Solar Memphis
240 Chestnut Street, Tower II
Chattanooga, Tennessee 37401
(615) 755-6851

As energy costs soar, it's becoming more and more obvious that cheap fuel has gone the way of high-button shoes. And it's a pretty sure bet that we face even higher priced energy in the years ahead.

But Solar Memphis, a project in Tennessee, has helped area homeowners cut high heating costs now and in the future by making them an offer that's hard to refuse: an affordable water heating system that captures the free energy of the sun and cuts utility bills, conserves fuel and boosts home values.

Solar System Affordable By All

The solar system—which provides 60 to 70 percent of a family's hot water needs—is available for all Memphis homeowners and is affordable to the poorest of the poor. Solar Memphis offers 20-year loans, which include maintenance contracts, at incredibly low annual interest rates of 3.37 percent and monthly payments of $13. And the solar system becomes more economical as the years go by. Regardless of how much electricity costs rise, Solar Memphis homeowners will still pay $13 a month for most of their hot water needs.

Since May 1978 the nonprofit group has installed 2,400 systems in over 400 homes in Memphis and surrounding Shelby County.

"The one thing I've noticed is that the water gets hot—I think a lot hotter than with electricity," says Jo Ann Day, a recent Solar Memphis recipient who considers the heating system remarkable. "I wouldn't believe it except I know they disconnected the other system and *something's* heating that water!"

Wink Dickey

Hoisting solar panels for the rooftop hot water system

Joint Effort

The credit for this innovative program goes to the cooperative efforts of a nationally known solar energy architect and consultant; the South Memphis Development Corporation (SMDC), a nonprofit minority-operated group dedicated to community development; the Tennessee Valley Authority (TVA), a government-owned corporation; and the municipal utility company.[1]

Boosting Local Economy

Solar Memphis has made a significant impact on the economy of downtown Memphis where residents, many of whom are minorities, are plagued with high unemployment. The systems are installed by a company especially created for the project by SMDC and parts are purchased from area businesses. Local minority contractors and unemployed youths are hired and trained to install the solar systems. The success of Solar Memphis has led project leaders to plan expansion of the project across the western Tennessee Valley, a 41-county area with a population of more than two million.

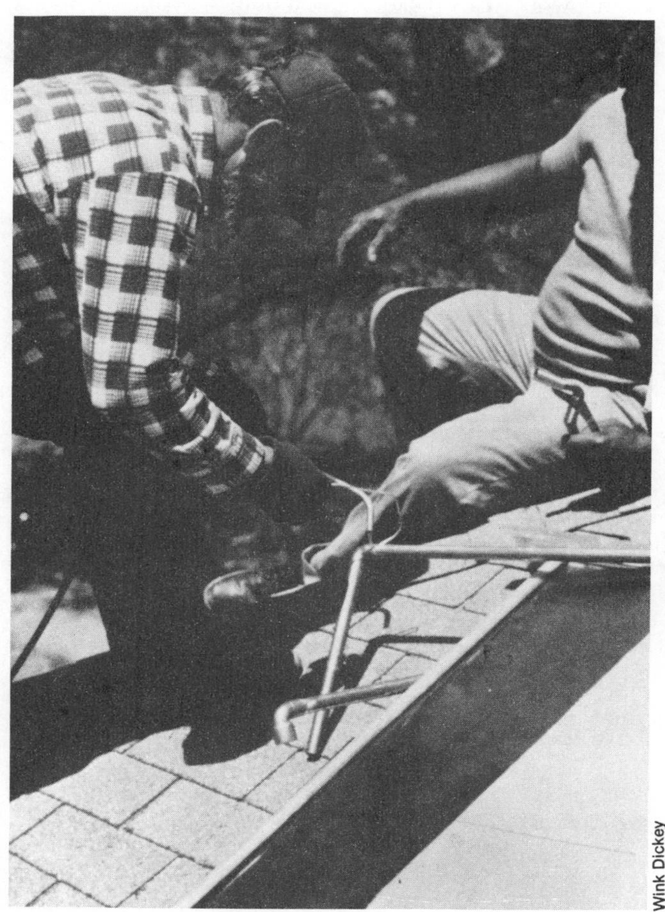
Wink Dickey

Connecting the solar hot water system

Origins

In 1978 Travis Price and others in his consulting firm, Sun Harvester, Inc., began promoting the solar hot water heating project for Tennessee Valley residents. To launch the project Price knew that a lot of money and the cooperation of many would be needed. Also, if the project was to be successful, he realized the solar hot water heaters must be affordable to all residents—regardless of income.

Price approached TVA with his plan. TVA, charged with producing power for the entire Tennessee Valley, would save money in the long run, Price argued, because the project would boost usage of the sun's natural energy and reduce power demand in the area. David Freeman, a newly appointed TVA Director, agreed with Price and both set out to convince the Board to give the project a chance.

The next step was to find a responsible organization willing to manage the project. Based on their sound reputation and commitment to community development, the South Memphis Development Corporation was chosen.

TVA agreed to place $3 million in a trust fund which SMDC would use to buy parts for the solar heaters, hire contractors and train unemployed youths to install the systems. SMDC helped develop a manufacturing company to make the solar devices. And the local utility handled customer billing, returning the payments for the solar system to SMDC to use for project expenses.

Overcoming the Quality Barrier

Price, local minority leaders and TVA jointly determined that a top quality system could be built with solar components from a number of companies in the area. The design of the system promised quality and the flexibility needed to operate in a variety of homes.

To ensure that quality control would continue throughout the program, TVA held three-day training courses for contractors. The contractors learned solar theory, installation and inspection techniques. After installation TVA advisors checked each system and the city inspected them for code compliance.

Moving Along

In March 1978 the solar hot water heating project was launched with "Memphis 10," a demonstration program which provided 10 residents with free systems to show the public that solar hot water is an inexpensive and viable energy alternative for the homeowner. With the success of that program came "Memphis 1,000" which since has evolved into Solar Memphis.

Success Tips

Here are a few keys to the success of the Solar Memphis program:

- Organizers who are willing and able to marshal needed funding and the support of local leaders, solar enthusiasts and residents for the project;
- Technical expertise among organizers which enables them to convince skeptics that solar energy —and the program—can work;
- Adequate start-up funds;
- Involvement of the local utility and a local nonprofit group which understands area conditions and needs so the program is rooted in the targeted city or town;
- A training program for unemployed residents and the development of an industry that will provide permanent jobs long after the specific project ends;
- A financing program which enables all homeowners, regardless of income, to take advantage of the program.

Other Groups

The use of solar energy is limited only by the sun's ability to produce it. In other words solar energy is here to stay. And groups across the country are beginning to recognize and use this free energy source.

For instance, in Santa Clara, California, where backyard swimming pools are almost as common as kitchen sinks,the city-owned utility company offers a solar heating system for pools which saves owners 20 to 30 percent yearly on heating bills. Customers pay for the $300 system and its maintenance in monthly installments which are added to utility bills.

Wink Dickey

Preparing to harness the sun's energy

Solar Memphis' Financing Plans

Homeowners can make equal monthly payments on the loan for up to 20 years.

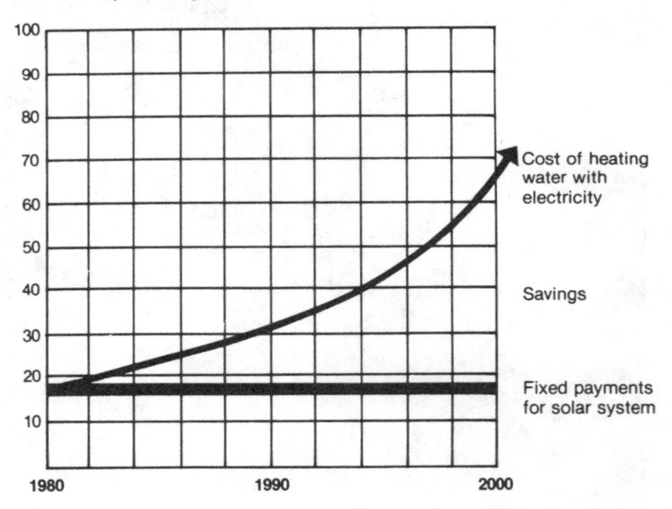

Group Highlighted

City of Santa Clara
Santa Clara Water, Sewer and Solar Division
1500 Washington Avenue
Santa Clara, California 95050
(408) 984-3183

[1] The Tennessee Valley Authority (TVA) conducts a comprehensive resource development program in the Tennessee Valley region. TVA's activities include flood control, electric power production, recreation improvement and other areas of resource development. (For more information on TVA, see Resources at end of Energy Section.)

Note: For a complete listing of groups featured throughout this book, see Index.

Homegrown Gasahol

Southwest Alabama Farmers Cooperative Association
Highway 80 West
Selma, Alabama 36701
(205) 872-6227

A group of small farmers, eager to beat skyrocketing fuel prices, are using their fathers' and grandfathers' moonshining methods to produce an energy alternative that may in time make them energy self-sufficient. The alternative is gasahol, a blend of 90 percent gasoline and 10 percent farm-made alcohol which yields the same mileage as unleaded gasoline and offers an ever renewable energy source.

Seeking ways to save money isn't new to the Selma-based Southwest Alabama Farmers Cooperative Association (SWAFCA), an agricultural co-op of some 1,000 black, small farmers in a 10-county area.[1] They had banded together in 1967 to cut costs by bulk buying and sharing a marketing system which meant better prices for produce and hogs. In the late 1960s membership had mushroomed to over 2,500 but as spiraling feed, fuel and other costs forced many to give up their land, membership plummeted. However, recent years have seen a resurgence in membership, and the co-op has expanded to include custom services in liming, fertilizing and harvesting.

Experimental Distillery

The idea of gasahol isn't new either. SWAFCA members knew it was being used elsewhere in the country, and they had all heard stories of moonshiners adding a little homemade alcohol to their tanks when they were running low on gas. So producing alcohol for fuel was a natural response to the energy crisis and a natural outgrowth of their earlier activities.

As a result, in 1976 a small group of co-op members decided to build an experimental distillery modeled after a simple moonshiner's still and made from parts scavanged from local junk yards.

Building A Working Distillery

That effort paved the way in 1978 to a bigger, more sophisticated still. Having obtained a license from the Internal Revenue Service's Bureau of Alcohol, Tobacco and Firearms (BATF), which guards against illegal use of alcohol in manufacturing whisky, SWAFCA members began looking for funds. With help from the Federation of Southern Cooperatives, a nonprofit technical assistance group for over 100 rural co-ops and credit unions in 10 southern states, the group won a $326,000 grant from the Department of Commerce's Minority Business Development Agency (MBDA), and about two dozen co-op members began volunteering time to the project.[2]

Although the grants helped to defray the costs of building the distillery, SWAFCA's biggest savings was realized by scrounging for materials and doing the work themselves. For instance, even a used distillation unit, which separates water from alcohol, would have cost $80,000 but the co-op built its own with scraps for just $7,000.

Completed Plant

Completed in 1978, the distillery produces up to 500 gallons of alcohol every week. The alcohol is mixed with gasoline on SWAFCA's Selma grounds and is distributed to members who pay only for the gasoline—saving 10 percent on every tankful.

Ultimately SWAFCA would like to produce enough alcohol to sell to nonmembers but that would require more funding for a bigger plant.

The alcohol is made basically the same way as the oldtime moonshine. Ground corn, enzymes and yeast are cooked in water over a wood fire to produce mash. The liquid is then separated and distilled into ethyl alcohol or ethanol. The water is recycled into the cooker for the next batch and the corn residue is fed to livestock.

Potential of Gasahol

SWAFCA and other groups see enormous potential in the production of gasahol because ethanol can be made from almost anything: waste paper, wood pulp, fruits, sugar cane, soybeans and even household garbage. One Minnesota scientist-turned-farmer, Lance Crombie, says five acres of sugar beets could be turned into a year's supply of alcohol for a small- to medium-sized farm. In addition, gasahol production could put thousands of idle acres of farmland back into use.

Increasing Self-Reliance

SWAFCA would like to begin producing methane, an alternative heating source made from livestock manure and other decomposed organic matter. Using methane as the heating gas for alcohol production would create a complete cycle of renewable energy sources and make the co-op more energy self-sufficient: growing corn to make alcohol, feeding the corn residue to farm animals, using the manure to

Conventional Process for Production of Fuel-Grade Ethanol from Sugars or Starch.

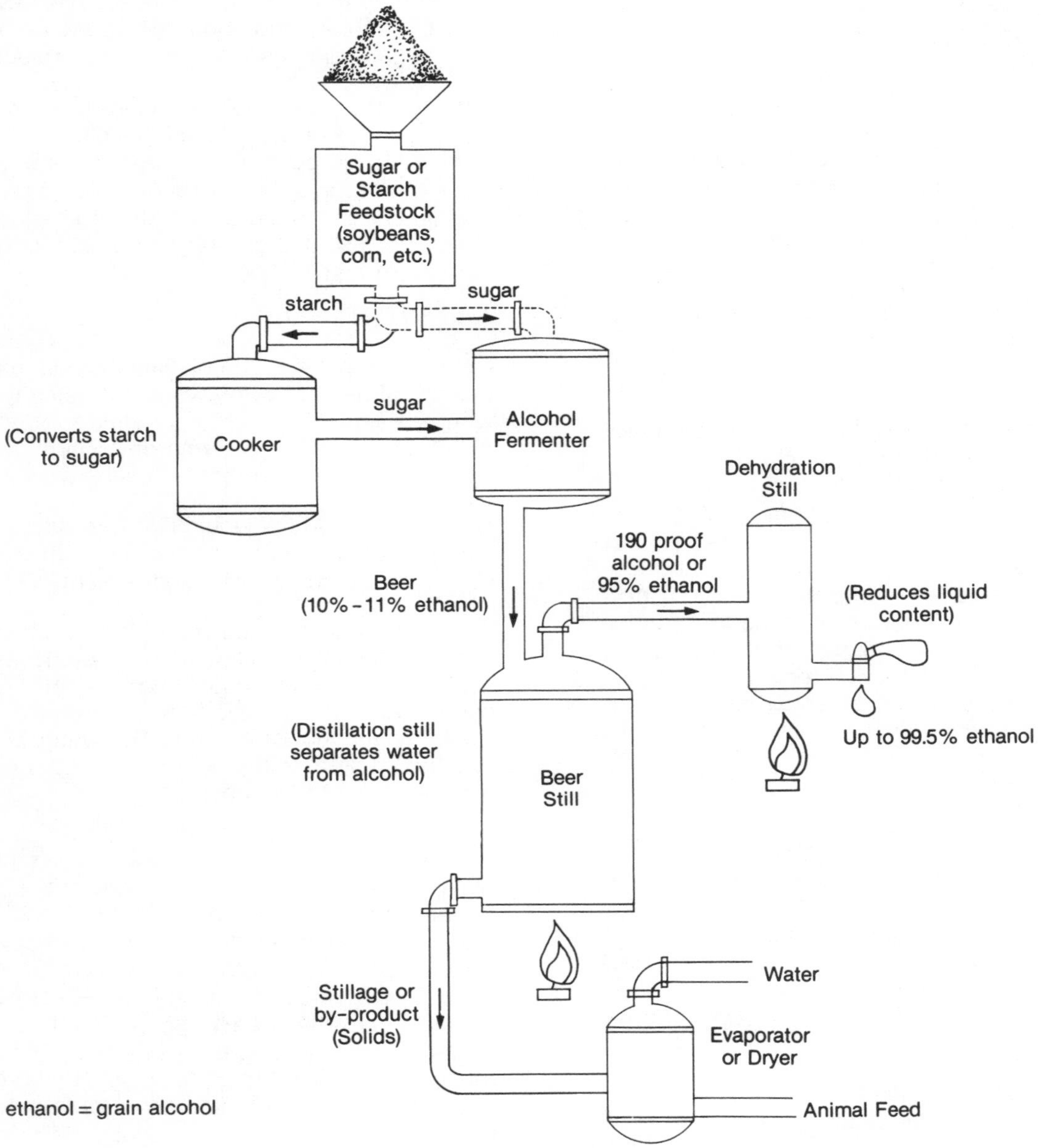

A combination of 10 percent ethanol and 90 percent gasoline makes gasahol.

Adapted with assistance from the Department of Energy from For Today: For Tomorrow, *a demonstration publication from the Department of Chemical Engineering and Applied Chemistry, Columbia University, sponsored by the Office of Technology Commercialization, Office of Minority Business Development Agency, Department of Commerce.*

make methane, and the methane to cook the alcohol.

Gasahol Gains Support

So far gasahol is mainly being produced in small quantities for farm use but support is growing for larger scale production. The fuel has been endorsed by President Carter and a number of Congressional leaders. Congress, in fact, passed a law in 1978 exempting the fuel from the four-cents-per-gallon Federal gasoline tax and the Environmental Protection Agency (EPA) has since given the go-ahead to authorized service stations to sell gasahol.

Other States Push Gasahol

Several states are actively promoting gasahol. For example, in the Midwestern Plains states, where corn is abundant, over 500 filling stations do a brisk gasahol business. Stations in Indiana sell 250 thousand gallons of gasahol every month, and Colorado plans to construct five alcohol plants to produce 50 million gallons a year by 1981.

Success at SWAFCA has convinced co-op President Albert Turner that gasahol is here to stay. "The facts are," he says, "that 50 percent of the fuel coming into this country is coming from unfriendly nations. And we're running out. So new fuel sources have to be the alternative. For us poor, small farmers, gasahol is that alternative."

[1] Although not available in time to help the Southwest Alabama Farmers Cooperative Association (SWAFCA), co-ops may now qualify for technical and financial assistance from the newly created National Consumer Cooperative Bank.**

[2] The Federation of Southern Cooperatives is also mentioned in Housing Section, p.167.

The $326,000 grant from the Department of Commerce's (DOC) Minority Business Development Agency (MBDA), formerly the Office of Minority Business Enterprise, came from the Experiment and Demonstration Program which is no longer in existence.

** For further information, see Appendix II under "National Consumer Cooperative Bank."

Note: For a complete listing of groups featured throughout this book, see Index.

Small Farm Alternatives

Small Farm Energy Project
P.O. Box 736
Hartington, Nebraska 68739
(402) 254-6893
and
Center for Rural Affairs
P.O. Box 405
Walthill, Nebraska 68067
(402) 846-5428

Rising energy costs hit farmers both as producers and consumers. They need energy to heat their homes and drive their cars as well as to plant, harvest and market the farm products that provide their incomes.

Small farm owners, often on tight budgets, are particularly squeezed as energy-related production costs rise along with fuel prices. For instance, between 1970 and 1975, some fertilizers rose in price by a whopping 147 percent and fuel prices have also skyrocketed.

But by building solar devices to warm their homes and operate their grain dryers and wind-powered generators which provide electricity for machinery, 24 low-income farmers in central Nebraska have saved hundreds of dollars a year in utility costs.

Success Today

From 1977 to 1980 the Small Farm Energy Project, based in Hartington and sponsored by the nonprofit Center for Rural Affairs, coordinated the Project and spurred alternative energy participation by staging solar design workshops for area farmers.[1] Experts provided technical assistance but all construction was done by the farmers.

Each participating farmer had to build two alternative energy devices for the farm or home during the course of the Project. A total of 137 energy innovations resulted.

The Small Farm Energy Project picked up an average of 50 percent on construction costs. After two years participating farmers had paid an average of $500 a year to build energy-savers and were enjoying a savings of about $700 yearly in fuel and electricity bills.

And by the time the Project ended in February 1980 it had won the respect of once skeptical agricultural experts at the University of Nebraska and state energy experts. Moreover, ACTION showed confidence in the group by awarding a $122,500 National Demonstration Grant, funded under its Special Volunteer Program,* to replicate the Project elsewhere in Nebraska as well as in Minnesota, South Dakota and Iowa.

Small Farm Energy Project

A big project—solar paneling a dairy barn

One Happy Experience

"We got a lot more out of the Energy Project than I expected," says Rick Pinkelman of Hartington, an early Project participant. For $10 Pinkelman built a solar window box collector which harnesses the sun's energy and helps heat his home. After installing the collector, Pinkelman says, he didn't use his oil furnace until temperatures dropped to 40°F.

Small Farm Energy Project

Smaller solar systems help lower home heating bills.

Since then Pinkelman has installed a larger collector which he estimates saves more than $600 yearly on heating bills.

And Pinkelman's success spurred a dozen neighboring farmers to join the Project and build solar window box collectors for their homes.

Origins

The Walthill-based Center for Rural Affairs faced obstacles when it decided to launch the Project in October 1976. Opposition was raised by experts at the University of Nebraska and the Nebraska State Energy Office who feared the Project would duplicate their own energy efforts in the area. Center leaders countered that a focus on small farms would be unique and that the Project would spur the use of widespread alternative energy systems by local farmers.

Funding

After five months the group convinced the State Energy Office to channel to them a $400,000 grant from the Community Services Administration's (CSA) Emergency Energy Conservation Services Program* for the three-year Project, which paid for technical assistance, staff, publications and construction costs. Initially the Project had one part-time and two full-time staffers, but as it grew four employees worked full time.

Farmers Encouraged to Build Their Own

Project staffers set out to get farmers involved in the Project. Since staffers were from the area they didn't have to overcome suspicions that outsiders might have faced. They talked to the farmers about the long-time, money-saving benefits of alternative energy and the help available for construction costs.

Participating farmers report favorable and varied experiences with their energy projects. For instance, Earl Fish of Belden, Nebraska began harnessing the sun's rays for his 6,000-bushel grain dryer in 1977. Fish spent two months and less than $500 building the solar grain dryer with lumberyard materials. The device saves $100 a year in fuel costs. It would have been twice as expensive to build but the Project picked up 50 percent of construction costs.

Solar dryers take longer to reduce grain moisture than traditional propane gas dryers and aren't as suitable for large farms. But for Earl Fish the savings are real and immediate.

Three other farmer participants chose to build vertical wall "North" collectors, inexpensive devices developed by Bill North of the San Luis Valley Solar Energy Association in southern Colorado, to heat their homes.[2]

Small Farm Energy Project

A window box solar collector

Hindsight

Project leaders admit they made a few mistakes in setting up the program. A basic understanding of the principles of solar technology is needed and they overestimated the participants' knowledge. Coupled with some skepticism and seasonal demands on farmers' time, that lack of knowledge caused a nine month delay between funding and completion of the first project. Also, they didn't expect the deluge of requests for information and materials that poured in as word of the Project spread. The Project had neither sufficient staff nor financial resources to handle the requests.

Methane—A Viable Alternative

Other farm groups around the country are showing just how much can be done with alternative energy sources. One of the most promising developments is the creation of methane or bio-gas. Methane is produced by the decaying action of organic wastes combined with certain bacteria. The process, which occurs in airtight containers called digestors, produces a substance similar to natural gas. The current annual production of five billion cubic feet is enough to supply 40,000 homes with gas for a year.

Ecotope Group, a nonprofit research and consulting organization based in Seattle, Washington, designed and operates a 50,000-gallon digestor that provides enough bio-gas to power a steam boiler at the State Honor Dairy Farm in Monroe.[3] Funding came from a $214,000 grant from the Fuels from Biomass Program,* administered by the Department of Energy (DOE), and a state grant of $125,000 to demonstrate the use of digestors on medium- and large-sized dairy farms. The digestor produces 8,000 cubic feet of methane a day from the manure of 180 dairy cows.

There's also a nationwide methane experiment underway by the New Life Farm based in Drury, Missouri.[4] The nonprofit group's 40-acre farm serves as a conservation center for farmers, individuals and communities. New Life Farm's Rural Gasification Project (RGP), funded by CSA's Emergency Energy Conservation Services Program,* is building about a dozen digestors on farms across the United States to determine the feasibility of cutting high energy costs with low-cost, owner-built bio-gas systems.

Crop Dryers

The East River Electric Power Cooperative in Madison, South Dakota is experimenting with solar grain dryers. In cooperation with the South Dakota State University, they built dryers for about $300 a unit out of used material from an offset printing plant. The solar grain dryer saves an estimated $125 a year in fuel costs.

Groups Highlighted

East River Electric Power Cooperative
Locker Drawer E
Madison, South Dakota 57042
(605) 256-4536

Ecotope Group
2332 East Madison Avenue
Seattle, Washington 98112
(206) 322-3753

Rural Gasification Project
New Life Farm
Drury, Missouri 65638
(417) 261-2553

[1] For more information on the Center for Rural Affairs, see Resources at end of Energy Section.

[2] The San Luis Valley Energy Association and the North collector are profiled in Energy Section, p. 205.

[3] For more information on Ecotope Group, see Resources at end of Energy Section.

[4] For more information on the New Life Farm, see Resources at end of Energy Section

* State and/or local government agencies are frequently responsible for administration of Federal program funds. For further information, see Appendix I under appropriate Federal agency.

Note: For a complete listing of groups featured throughout this book, see Index.

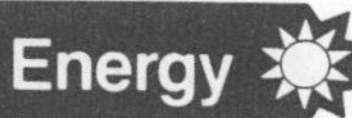

Windpower

Eleventh Street Movement
519 East 11th Street
New York, New York 10009
(212) 982-1460
and
Energy Task Force
156 Fifth Avenue
New York, New York 10010
(212) 675-1920

November 13, 1976 was a particularly cold and windy day for a press conference staged on the roof of an 11-apartment cooperative tenement owned by 22 mostly Puerto Rican residents of New York City's impoverished Lower East Side.[1] The main attraction: the unveiling of the first urban windmill in the United States.

The windmill's small two-kilowatt generator provides about one-third of the lighting in the building's halls and other common areas, saving the co-op owners as much as $200 a year in electric bills. Even more unique, when excess electricity is generated by the windmill on windy days, it flows into Consolidated Edison's (Con Ed) grid. And New York's Public Service Commission has ruled that the giant public utility must pay the co-op for the excess electricity.

The windmill's unveiling wasn't the first time the press corps had climbed the five flights of stairs to the tenement's sooty roof. Nearly a year before they had been summoned to view America's first urban active solar water heating system.

Model of Energy Independence

The windmill and solar heating systems are proud symbols of energy independence for the resident-owners of 519 East 11th Street. In 1973, starting with an abandoned, burned-out shell of a building, 519's co-op residents—with the help of some concerned solar and windpower experts—sweated and toiled to rehabilitate and thoroughly weatherize the gutted structure. Their efforts led to big energy savings and the creation of two nationally respected nonprofit groups: the Eleventh Street Movement and the Energy Task Force (ETF).[2]

Gibby Edwards

The 11th Street windmill becomes part of the New York City skyline.

Success Today

A combination of high quality insulation, energy conservation and the active solar water heating system provided 70 percent of the building's heating requirements in 1979. "Our utility bill for the building in 1976 was $2,500," says Michael Freedberg, former director of the Eleventh Street Movement. "A normal utility bill for that size building would have been around $7,500."

Origins

The 519 Housing Co-op began in 1973 when Freedberg and Roberto (Rabbit) Nazario, director of Inter-Faith Adopt-a-Building, a nonprofit group dedicated to restoring the impoverished Lower East Side area, began organizing unemployed residents to buy and renovate the abandoned building.[3]

Once organized, the group had no money for the hefty down payment needed for a loan to buy and restore the dwelling. But a revolutionary city program called "sweat equity" came to the rescue. Sweat equity allows low-income residents to use their labor as a down payment on city loans to buy and renovate deteriorated dwellings.[4] "Sweat equity produces housing for low-income people at half the cost of conventional methods," Freedberg says. As a result residents become co-op owners in the renovated building at payments they can afford.

In 1974, with backing of Inter-Faith Adopt-a-Building and the nonprofit Urban Homesteading Assistance Board (UHAB), the 11th Street co-op won a $177,000 sweat equity loan from the city.[5] And the prospective tenants began the hard work of renovation. (Although not available in time to assist the group, co-ops may now qualify for technical and financial assistance from the newly created National Consumer Cooperative Bank.**)

Installing Solar Savers

Meanwhile, at a UHAB meeting Freedberg met Travis Price, a solar architect from New Mexico who had learned of New York's sweat equity program and realized its potential for cutting solar installation costs for poor residents.

The two got together at 519 in the spring of 1974 and Price was given the green light to apply for funds and design a solar system for the building.

Funding

In October of that year Price began teaching the co-op members how to weatherize the building by installing storm windows and insulating exterior walls. A $43,000 grant from the Community Services Administration's (CSA) Emergency Energy Conservation Services Program* paid for solar hardware, insulation and technical consultants.

Meanwhile, Price and several young architectural students formed the Energy Task Force, a nonprofit technical assistance group which, for three months during the cold 1975 winter, worked with co-op members in building the solar heating system.

Gibby Edwards

Eleventh Street windmill stands in the forefront of Con Ed's facilities.

"There we were up on the roof Saturday nights working by droplight, the wind whistling through our beards, our fingers freezing off as we fitted the pipes," Price recalls. By March 1976 the solar water heating system was complete and the co-op owners moved in.

The Windmill

But the work still wasn't over. During the building's reconstruction, the 11th Street group had tangled with Con Ed over a $1,000 electric bill. The dispute led Price to an alternative energy conference in New York where Ted Finch, a recent college graduate with a major in wind energy, lectured. Price asked Finch to take a look at 519 and offer suggestions. On the day of Finch's visit, Con Ed pulled the plug on 519, cutting off the building's electricity and causing the solar collectors to overheat.

Finch reacted instantly. Determined to minimize the co-op's dependence on the large utility company, in October 1976 he acquired a $4,000 secondhand, 2,000-watt windmill that measured 14 feet in diameter. And with another small CSA grant from the Emergency Energy Conservation Services Program, construction and installation of the windmill was completed.

Hoisting the Windmill

ETF and 11th Street co-op members prepared for the windmill by constructing a concrete base and reinforcing the roof to hold the structure tightly in place. Scaffold material was borrowed from the Cathedral of St. John the Divine, a local Episcopal church, to hoist the windmill onto the roof. And a rugged pully system was attached to the side of the building.

Mustering all the know-how and ingenuity they could, a group of about 40 neighborhood residents managed to hoist the two 20-foot windmill sections to the top of the five-story building, as Freedberg recalls, "with a lot of luck, sweat and muscle power."

Once the windmill was in place, the group used wire to secure it to the reinforced sections of the roof.

ETF

Hoisting the windmill

Bronx Windmill

Solar systems and weatherization techniques have spread much more rapidly than windmills on New York's Lower East Side. But the small demonstration windmill on 11th Street led to another impressive project in the Hunts Point section of the South Bronx. The 64-foot structure is the first commercial windmill of its size in New York. The windmill—constructed with ETF's technical assistance—is part of an innovative plan dreamed up by the Bronx Frontier Development Corporation (BFDC), a nonprofit community group, to "green over" some of the beleaguered borough's worst rubbled areas.[6] The windmill provides low-cost electricity for the nonprofit group's composting operation which occupies four acres near the Hunts Point sewage treatment plant.

Other Groups

Near Allentown, Pennsylvania the Energy Development Corporation's Dorney Park windmill, christened in May 1979 by Miss USA with the traditional bottle of champagne, is providing nearly 20 percent of the electricity needs of the amusement park.

A less glamorous but highly effective use of windpower is the system designed and installed by WTG Energy Systems, Inc., a Buffalo, New York company specializing in the development of wind turbine generators. In 1977 the prototype windmill was constructed on the island of Cuttyhunk off New Bedford, Massachusetts and today provides nearly 75 percent of the winter residents' electric needs. WTG Energy Systems is currently negotiating with the island's utility company to combine their power sources.

Groups Highlighted

Bronx Frontier Development Corporation
1080 Leggett Avenue
Bronx, New York 10474
(212) 542-4640

Energy Development Corporation
3830 Dorney Park Road
Allentown, Pennsylvania 18104
(215) 395-3724

WTG Energy Systems, Inc.
251 Elm Street
Buffalo, New York 14203
(716) 856-1620

[1] For more information on housing cooperatives, see chart in Housing Section, p. 119.

[2] The Eleventh Street Movement is also mentioned in Food Section, p. 60.

[3] Inter-Faith Adopt-a-Building is also mentioned in Housing Section, p. 115.

[4] Sweat Equity is the difference between the normal labor cost of building rehabilitation and the small amount paid renovators. Sweat equity means the value of the sweat and labor put into the building by the people who built or renovated it.

[5] For more information on the Urban Homesteading Assistance Board (UHAB), see Resources at end of Housing Section.

Families become "urban homesteaders" by purchasing from the city an abandoned property for a token sum. Repairs must be made on the dwelling so that it meets the minimum city housing code standards. The city makes funds for rehabilitation available in the form of low-interest loans which the homesteaders pay back after all the rehabilitation is complete and the deeds have been turned over to them.

[6] The Bronx Frontier Development Corporation (BFDC) is profiled in Food Section, p. 56.

* State and/or local government agencies are frequently responsible for administration of Federal program funds. For further information, see Appendix I under appropriate Federal agency.

** For further information, see Appendix II under "National Consumer Cooperative Bank."

NOTE: For a complete listing of groups featured throughout this book, see Index.

Chapter 3

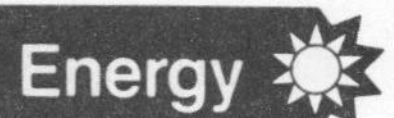

Educating the Public on Energy

Introduction

With limited fuel resources and soaring prices, energy education is becoming more and more important. Although the issues often seem complex, a practical knowledge of alternative and renewable energy sources is vital to all of us.

Groups around the country are finding ways to make energy an interesting and lively subject. In this chapter we look at some creative education programs that make citizens aware of energy choices while helping them cut fuel costs.

We glance at a comprehensive program in Ocean County, New Jersey that uses everything from puppets for kindergarteners to solar construction projects for high schoolers to spark interest in energy. And two high school teachers in Seat Pleasant, Maryland taught students to build and install a solar collector that provides heat for their prefabricated school building.

We also look at two community programs that dramatize alternative energy in unforgettable ways. One is a traveling solar carnival that leaves behind newly inspired solar advocates as well as good cheer. The other is a unique self-contained model home in Berkeley, California that demonstrates how much urban residents can do to become energy self-sufficient.

Finally we describe a special kind of education program—one that multiplies its solar efforts by teaching others to teach. The New Mexico-based Solar Sustenance Team has trained residents from every corner of the country to conduct solar greenhouse workshops for their neighbors. Hundreds of solar greenhouses dot our nation's countryside because of these workshops.

All of these education projects offer practical, sure-fire ways to interest residents in learning about energy alternatives. You can set up exciting education programs in your community as well. The following groups provide some good hints on how to start.

Teaching Kids About Energy

Ocean County Youth Energy Conservation Corps
127 Hooper Avenue
Toms River, New Jersey 08753
(201) 244-2121—Ext. 3250

When puppet Solar Sal told kindergarteners in Toms River, New Jersey to save energy, one youngster became so enthusiastic that he insisted his family eat by candlelight for three evenings.

And more than 100 juniors and seniors at the Ocean County Vocational and Technical School—part of Toms River's public school system—built an energy-efficient house boasting a passive solar design and heavy insulation which was sold at public auction for $17,000. The $5,000 profit is slated for the students' next project: an energy-efficient counseling center and library.

Success Today

These activities and others reflect the success of a Toms River-based group dedicated to promoting energy education in Ocean County's 33 municipalities. The Ocean County Youth Energy Conservation Corps aims to bolster student and teacher knowledge about energy alternatives and conservation while awakening youngsters to energy employment opportunities.

The Corps' free resources include an energy library with films and brochures, energy fairs, symposiums and speakers who sometime assume the role of cartoon characters or use puppets to enliven their messages.

How-to-Teach Packages

Since 1976 over 700 kindergarten through high school teachers have made learning fun with the Corps' how-to-teach energy packages which are geared to specific age levels. In fact, requests are pouring in from all over the country for information on the packages which contain hundreds of ideas for classroom discussions, field trips, games and easy blueprints for a range of energy-saving devices—from pretty energy-saving windowblinds to makeshift solar hot dog cookers to solar heaters.

"The teaching materials are easy to incorporate in the classroom and make the students aware of energy conservation," says Virginia Blinn, a teacher at Ella Clarke Elementary School in Lakewood who uses film strips and other Corps materials to teach her fourth graders.

Children learn about the sun's power through a solar collector.

Origins

The Corps was launched in 1976 by the Ocean County Energy Council, a citizens advisory group to the County's governing body, the Board of Freeholders. The best way to raise resident consciousness about energy conservation, Council staffers thought, was to start with the youth whose enthusiasm would spread from classrooms to homes to the community at large.

Council members and several interested Ocean County teachers and students began pushing the idea, winning support from state and county educators.

Budget and Staff

Soon after, the Council passed a resolution creating the Corps. Council staff member Sally T. Burt, an early supporter, was named coordinator. The group won a $10,000 Federal Energy Administration (FEA) grant enabling them to buy cameras and other equipment to stock the library and assemble how-to-teach packages.[1]

The Corps' annual budget, an unbelievably low $850, is used to buy promotional materials and comes from the county-funded Council's budget. The Council pays for two Corps employees and the Department of Labor's Comprehensive Employment and Training Act (CETA) Program* provides an additional worker.

Involving Teachers, Students and Others

The Youth Corps' low budget and small staff are greatly enhanced by a large contingent of volunteers. From 1976 to 1979 over 300 students and teachers donated time to speak at school assemblies and classrooms, plan symposiums, film and produce an energy slide show and perform other duties.

For example, in 1979 Blinn and her team teacher busied their 60 students with a "trash to treasure" recycling project which was later incorporated in the Corps' how-to-teach packages. The students made over 50 items from reusable trash, including napkin rings from cardboard and hanging flower pots from margarine and whipped cream tubs. And at the Corps' one-day statewide energy fair in Toms River, a crowd of about 1,000 battled a rainy day to eye the treasures and other student-made exhibits such as solar panels, energy-saving shades, a gasahol still and a solar oven.

The private sector helps too. For instance, in 1978 an owner of a solar-powered restaurant volunteered to speak at the Corps' solar symposium. Students, plumbers and other technicians learned how to plan, apply for grants and construct a solar building.

"We're showing our young people that energy conservation is not just a matter of saving Mom and Dad money," coordinator Burt says, "but the (alternative energy field) offers career opportunities right here in Ocean County."

Other Groups

In Staples, Minnesota the Regional Energy Information Center, developed by 30 school teachers, provides practical how-to-teach energy packages for use in a variety of elementary and secondary classrooms in a six-county area.[2]

In home economics classes, for example, students logged their families' transportation for one week and compared energy costs with alternatives like carpooling and bus riding.

And in a computer math course students surveyed the community's energy usage and worked out a computer program to measure heat loss. Then at the group's energy fair, a student-operated computer pinpointed areas of heat loss in residents' homes, prompting many to caulk, weatherstrip and add insulation.

In addition, at the Center the public is treated to displays ranging from woodburning stoves to solar-powered hot dog cookers and a wealth of alternative energy literature.

Every day the Energy Management Center in Port Richey, Florida offers students from nearby school districts an Outdoor Education Center with demonstrations of energy alternatives.

Groups Highlighted

Energy Management Center
P.O. Box 190
Port Richey, Florida 33568
(813) 848-4870

Regional Energy Information Center
Staples, Minnesota 56479
(201) 894-2430—Ext. 146

[1] In 1977 the Federal Energy Administration (FEA) was replaced by the Department of Energy (DOE).

[2] The Regional Energy Information Center was initially funded by Title IV of the Elementary and Secondary Education Act (ESEA),* which is administered by the Department of Health, Education and Welfare (HEW). The Center is now funded by the Minnesota Energy Agency and the Staples Vocational Technical Institute.

* State and/or local government agencies are frequently responsible for administration of Federal program funds. For further information, see Appendix I under appropriate Federal agency.

Note: For a complete listing of groups featured throughout this book, see Index.

Solar Power: Learning By Building

Central Senior High School
200 Cabin Branch Road
Seat Pleasant, Maryland 20027
(301) 336-8200

In the winter of 1976 some students and teachers at Central Senior High School in Prince George's County, Maryland learned about the energy crisis the hard way. Due to overcrowding, many classes were held in temporary, prefabricated propane-heated buildings which were shut down because of fuel shortages.

Learning From Crisis

But a couple of enterprising Central High teachers decided to turn the energy crisis into a learning experience for students. Jerry Silver, a science teacher, and math instructor Kurt Johnson created a project for math, science, drafting and other students to design, construct and install a simple solar collector to provide heat and slash the amount of propane fuel needed.

"Probably the strongest message that students receive from their school about energy is the example set by the school itself," Silver and Johnson wrote in a 1977 *Today's Education* article. "The types of energy choices made by an educational institution influence students' perceptions of what is appropriate use of energy."[1]

Developing Plans

In class 20 students and the two teachers discussed and evaluated ideas and agreed on a design to capture the sun's energy—an efficient but simple solar heating system for their classroom. The 8-by-24 foot collector is made from six plywood boxes—or panels—painted black inside to absorb the sun's rays and filled with aluminum cans to collect the heat. Fiberglass covers the box to keep in the heat. The panels are connected, creating a long single solar collector which faces the sun. Air is circulated through ducts by two blowers, one pumping solar-heated air into the room and the other pulling the room's cool air into the collector for heating.

Getting Started—A Joint Effort

The teachers persuaded the local utility to donate lumber. School maintenance personnel and a local electrician and sheet metal worker offered their expertise. The Board of Education kicked in $800 for other materials such as paint, nails, insulation and fans.

Jerry Silver

Central Senior High students attach the solar heating system to the schoolhouse.

With resources in hand the students tackled the project. Drafting students drew up plans for the collector. Others gathered, cleaned and painted 1,200 aluminum cans and calculated room dimensions and volume to determine energy needs.

Building and Installing

With materials ready and two textbooks for reference, the crew of students, teachers and technical helpers began work one March weekend. By the end of the day three of the collector panels were completed and within a few weeks all six were finished. By May the solar collector was operational.

Valued at $2,000 the solar heating system, which is controlled by an automatic thermostat, costs about $10.40 a year to operate. On winter days the collector's temperature reaches between 140°F and 180°F. So even on cloudy days when the sun's rays are harder to capture, heat from the collector is capable of boosting room temperatures from 5 to 30 degrees above those outside.

Second Solar Project

In 1978 Central High students tackled another project —a solar heating system for the William S. Schmidt Environmental Education Center in Orme, Maryland. Funding again came from the Board of Education. And because the Center is so well insulated, the system provides nearly all heating needs on clear days. "The projects gave us a chance to interact with students in a new context and provided a vehicle for students to tie in what they were doing in other classes," Johnson and Silver wrote in the *Today's Education* article. "For example, students in woodworking classes used their skills in building the first collector. It also gave us many opportunities to present concepts that are part of our regular math and science curriculum."

And Silver has a tip for other teachers planning a similar project. "You should involve as many different teachers and program areas as possible," he suggests.

Other Schools

The Utah Technical College in Salt Lake City is among the many schools which have added solar energy to their curriculum. The state-funded school has included the building of passive solar devices as part of construction courses and will soon add the new discipline to bricklaying and electrical contracting courses. Each year students build four homes. In the 1978-79 school year two of the houses were built with passive solar heating systems.

Another approach to energy education is a program in McConnellsburg, Pennsylvania sponsored by the Fulton County Cooperative Extension Service,* working in conjunction with the United States Department of Agriculture (USDA).

Responding to a great number of requests for educational energy programs, the Extension Service organized a countywide Appropriate Technology Club for youth with chapters in vocational and agricultural classes of county high schools.

Groups Highlighted

Fulton County Cooperative
Extension Service
Pennsylvania State University
Courthouse Annex
McConnellsburg, Pennsylvania 17233
(717) 485-4111

Utah Technical College
4600 South Redwood Road
Salt Lake City, Utah 84107
(801) 967-4111

[1] Silver, Jerry and Johnson, Kurt, "Our School-Made Solar Project," *Today's Education* (September, October 1977), p. 62.

* State and/or local government agencies are frequently responsible for administration of Federal program funds. For further information, see Appendix I under appropriate Federal agency.

Note: For a complete listing of groups featured throughout this book, see Index.

Traveling Energy Show

New Western Energy Show
226 Power Block
Helena, Montana 59601
(406) 443-7272
and
Alternative Energy Resources Organization
424 Stapleton Building
Billings, Montana 59101
(406) 259-1958

"Step right up ladies and gentlemen. The show is ab-soo-lutely free," says Homer C. Breeze, emphasizing his carnival jargon with flicks of his rainbow suspenders. "Don't miss the exciting opportunity to get your membership to the Friends of the Wind Society. You, too, can have all the free wind you need for the rest of your life. Come on in folks. The show is about to begin."

The animated Homer C. Breeze uses the make-believe organization to lure a fair-going crowd to the trailer-turned-stage. Once there he regales his audience in common sense language about the benefits and methods of harnessing the wind as an alternative source of energy.

Novel Approach

The idea of getting the public interested in alternative energy resources in a circus-like atmosphere with high spirited dancing, singing and joke telling is the brainchild of the Billings, Montana-based Alternative Energy Resources Organization (AERO), a private, nonprofit group dedicated to bolstering the use of alternative energy resources.

Since 1976 AERO's New Western Energy Show (NWES) has delighted over 100,000 people in parks, fairs and on schoolgrounds in five midwestern and western states. In addition to short, dramatic presentations, the theatre is used for light-hearted energy skits. NWES fairs also boast energy displays with technicians eager to conduct tours and answer questions, a library and bookstore, slide show and solar construction workshops. And with their increasing popularity, requests for tour stops are coming in from all over the country.

New Western Energy Show

Skits are an interesting way to spread the conservation word.

Origins

The idea of a roving energy fair was conceived by AERO staffers who realized that people need first-hand experience to understand alternative energy technologies. In 1974, when AERO was born, staffers gave slide shows and talks and published fact sheets and monthly newsletters—useful and worthwhile work but hardly anything that mesmerized audiences. So in 1975 a series of construction workshops was launched at which participants actually built such devices as wind generators and solar ovens.

New Western Energy Show

Energy fairs teach communities about alternative energy sources and conservation.

New Western Energy Show

Playing while learning about the importance of energy conservation

First Funding

Those successful workshops in 1976 paved the way to the road shows. The $30,000 needed for salaries and the brightly painted trucks and trailer carrying the group's sun logo came from Montana's Renewable Energy Resources Grants Program.[1] Grey Jacobs, an Indiana designer and AERO friend, was hired to design the show's trailer which converts into a stage for the group's presentations. That summer a staff of 14 toured 13 Montana towns to the delight of 10,000 fair-goers.

Staff and Budget

Today the NWES fair reaches beyond Montana to towns in California, Washington and Oregon. In 1979 their $100,000 budget came mainly from state and Federal sources, sales and rental fees from their scripts and films and private donations.[2] Some community groups also kicked in money to help defray expenses.

The staff, which swells to 20 from 5 during touring season, actively enlists the help of local energy enthusiasts interested in bringing the fair to their communities. Local groups seek permission for fair sites and, along with NWES staffers, flood the local media with news releases, wangle public service announcements from TV and radio stations and arrange guest appearances for NWES personnel on local talk shows.

The Show Goes On

When the show hits town the exhibits and displays of windmills, solar ovens, small turbines and other alternative energy devices are set in place. For the next two to 10 days local residents are treated to demonstrations and performances.

Local residents are also encouraged to participate in the shows. Last year, with a grant from the Community Services Administration's (CSA) Emergency Energy Conservation Services Program,* the group performed on the Northern Cheyenne and Crow Indian reservations where children and other members of the audience played active roles in the NWES production.

Energy Center

Following a successful tour in 1977, NWES was established as a year-round energy center focusing on school programs in the winter and carnival touring in the summer. Based in Helena, Montana, the NWES office boasts a resource center and library. Their programs have expanded to include adult education classes and how-to workshops.

During its winter tours the show has traveled to 50 schools across Montana intriguing students with easy-to-understand energy information and conducting in-school workshops where students and teachers build alternative energy devices. The group also teaches CSA staffers and local teachers how to hold energy education programs for their personnel and students.

AERO's Initiative/Enthusiasm Continues

AERO is developing other ways to encourage localities to launch their own energy education projects. In 1978, with funds from the Department of Labor's Comprehensive Employment and Training Act (CETA) Program,* organizers in eight cities were trained to spearhead energy education programs. Through AERO training sessions, the organizers learn to hold workshops, organize energy fairs and get media attention. Local groups donate office space and money for telephones.

Other Fairs

Energy exhibits and demonstrations are taking root across the country. In May of 1979 an Appropriate Community Technology Fair (ACT '79) was held on the Mall in Washington, D.C. depicting completely self-contained community energy demonstrations, including alternative technologies such as windmill and solar projects. Exhibitors, speakers and entertainers from throughout the Mid-Atlantic region shared their skills, ideas and talents in promoting the concept of self-sufficiency. Act '79 was sponsored by the National Park Service and the D.C. Cooperative Extension Service,* working in cooperation with the United States Department of Agriculture (USDA), and a host of government agencies and nonprofit organizations.

AERO

Preparing a booth for the energy fair

And in Manhattan, Kansas the Community Development Department, working with Kansas State University and community residents, put on a local energy fair featuring demonstration exhibits, training and education programs and an information exchange. Fair participants learned through real projects how to lower local energy costs while increasing public awareness of local options for energy conservation.

Groups Highlighted

ACT '79
c/o National Park Service
Department of the Interior
Washington, D.C. 20240
(202) 343-1100

Community Development Department
City of Manhattan
P.O. Box 748
Manhattan, Kansas 66502
(913) 537-0056

[1] The money to launch the traveling fair came from Montana's Renewable Energy Resources Grants Program, dubbed Bill 86, which provides grants for innovative alternative energy research and development projects with revenues received from coal severance taxes levied on coal stripminers.

[2] The New Western Energy Show (NWES) received funding from Alberta Gas Truck Line, Montana-Dakota Utilities and the Wyoming Energy Conservation Office.

* State and/or local government agencies are frequently responsible for administration of Federal program funds. For further information, see Appendix I under appropriate Federal agency.

Note: For a complete listing of groups featured throughout this book, see Index.

A Model of Self-Reliance

Integral Urban House
Farallones Institute
1516 Fifth Street
Berkeley, California 94710
(415) 525-1150

The early morning sun casts its spell on the two-story white wood home that stands proudly as a model of self-sufficiency. Rabbits and chickens lazily rise to greet the new day. A windmill spins gracefully sending air bubbles to the fishpond below where trout and bluegill surface here and there. And bees leave the nearby hive to make their morning call to the plants in the lush green garden.

Sound like a rolling Kansas farm? Actually this house stands in the middle of a long, narrow city lot in Berkeley, California. It houses the office of its creator, the Farallones Institute, and serves as an energy-efficient urban demonstration home for solar advocates and alternative energy enthusiasts as well as a research and education center. The many people who tour it daily are delighted by these incredible features:

- Solar energy warms the house, heats the water, fires the oven and makes the greenhouse garden grow.

- The windmill filters fresh air to the fishpond to keep the water free of bacteria.

- Chickens and rabbits, raised in coops in the backyard and fed with wastes and produce from the house gardens, provide part of the well-balanced, home-grown diet for the human dwellers.

- Bees pollinate the crops and provide mouth-watering honey.

Pat Goudvis

Visitors at the Integral Urban House

• All wastes are reused. A recycling system on the grounds converts nonliquid wastes biologically into compost used to condition the backyard soil. And liquid wastes from toilets, sinks and showers are recycled providing high-nutrient irrigation for the backyard gardens.

Origins

The Integral Urban House is the brainchild of a group of San Francisco Bay area architects, engineers and biologists who wanted to combine their talents to create a self-sustaining dwelling which relies on nature to operate and power nonpolluting sanitary systems. The group included University of California at Berkeley instructor Jim Van der Ryan, who later became California State Architect, and biology professors Bill and Helga Olkowski.

Gordon Ashby and Bill Wells

A cross section of the Integral Urban House

Since the 1950s the Olkowskis had been experimenting in their home with ways to reduce waste of precious resources and dependence on city water and other systems—techniques that would be utilized, improved upon and eventually make the Olkowskis' dream a reality.

In 1973 the group formed Farallones Institute and began recruiting students to help launch the project.

First Funding

The group secured $110,000 from private foundations and institutes for labor and materials to rehabilitate the run-down urban house and fit it with solar energy and nonpolluting sanitation and other systems. In October 1974 the house was opened to the public. For the thousands of people who have visited since then, it provides a popular and persuasive tour.

Staff and Budget

Today the Institute receives funding from membership dues, tour fees and its publications, which include a voluminous and spellbinding book containing everything you want to know about building and maintaining a self-sustaining, energy-efficient urban house.[1] Until all systems were functional the monthly expense of operating the house was $2,000. But by the end of 1979 electricity, gas and water bills for the seven-bedroom house averaged an incredibly low $30 a month.

Teaching Others

The Institute's educational programs mean more than just showing off the exciting demonstration house.

They also include public classes and practical construction workshops on solar energy systems, gar-

Holly Kaufman

Students visit and learn at the Integral Urban House.

dening and other subjects related to urban self-reliance. In fact, the only things passive about these people are their solar collectors. Since the winter of 1979 the Institute's free courses at Vista Community College have attracted between 40 and 80 people at each class. Also students at nearby colleges can earn credit while interning at the house.

Building on a Dream

In 1975 the Farallones Institute took the self-reliant living system concept to the country and in 1978 opened the Integral Rural House on a large farm in California.

And in January 1980 Institute staff began working with a group in a low-income residential area of Berkeley to develop ideas for an Integral Urban Neighborhood. Institute leaders believe that conversion of an entire neighborhood will reduce costs since materials can be bulk ordered. In addition, conversion will bring residents together in sharing the common bond of their land.

Other Projects

Another energy education demonstration project is the nonprofit Glover's Mill Energy Center in Randolph, New York. Visitors to the Center are treated to demonstrations on energy conservation and alternative energy sources at a grist mill which serves as the group's information center. The Green Thumb Program of the local Community Action Agency (CAA)* and the Department of Labor's Comprehensive Employment and Training Act (CETA) Program* provide funding for staff.[2]

Group Highlighted

Glover's Mill Energy Center
RD 2, Box 202
Randolph, New York 14772
(716) 358-3306

[1] Farallones Institute has a membership of 1,000 who pay fees upward from $10 per year. The group's publication, *The Integral Urban House: Self-Reliant Living in the City,* is available for $14.50 prepaid by writing to The Integral Urban House, Farallones Institute, 1516 Fifth Street, Berkeley, California 94710.

[2] The Community Services Administration's (CSA) Community Action Program (CAP)* funds local Community Action Agencies (CAAs)* aimed at helping low-income residents with their food, housing, energy and other needs.

* State and/or local government agencies are frequently responsible for administration of Federal program funds. For further information, see Appendix I under appropriate Federal agency.

Note: For a complete listing of groups featured throughout this book, see Index.

Training Solar Organizers

Solar Sustenance Team
P.O. Box 733
El Rito, New Mexico 87530
(505) 471-1535

Bill and Susan Yanda teach people to build solar greenhouses in much the same way as our forefathers built barns. Their students may be strangers on Friday, but by the time the structure is completed on Sunday they are bound in fast friendship, sharing the pride and hard work of long-ago townspeople who helped their neighbors raise barns.

The Yandas and other members of the Solar Sustenance Team, now based in El Rito, New Mexico, know that a well-constructed solar greenhouse attached to the side of a house which best captures the sun's energy not only provides low-cost nutritious fruits and vegetables but also cuts home heating costs.[1]

Promoting the Sun's Energy

From 1974 to 1976 the Yandas swept through towns from Maine to Washington teaching residents how to build and maintain solar greenhouses. In 1978 they enlarged their staff and beckoned interested solar greenhouse promoters from around the country to tiny Ghost Ranch, New Mexico, giving them the know-how to conduct workshops for their own neighbors. Over 150 solar greenhouses across the country now stand as proud symbols of the success of those workshops.

One workshop member from Cheyenne, Wyoming was already an expert horticulturist when he came to Ghost Ranch. "Although I didn't get much new information in the area of horticulture, I learned a tremendous amount about solar greenhouse construction and such things as community organizing, thermal design and use of the media," says Shane

Solar greenhouse workshop participants are almost finished.

Smith, director of the Cheyenne Community Solar Greenhouse.[2] "In order to be effective in a particular community, you really need to have a good knowledge of the whole scope (of solar technology)."

Beginnings

In 1974, eager to bolster interest in solar greenhouses, the Yandas formed the Solar Sustenance Project, holding three-day workshops around the country to show residents how to construct and maintain solar greenhouses. After leaving each community an average of 10 solar greenhouses were built thanks to the efforts of the citizens-turned-experts. But as word spread the Yandas were unable to handle the demand for workshops from other communities.

Teach Others to Teach

The solution was clear: bring together people from around the country and teach them how to conduct workshops in their own neighborhoods.

So in 1976 the Yandas sought help from the New Mexico Solar Energy Association, a nonprofit solar energy advocacy group.[3] That effort brought gardening and construction expert Leslie Davis to the new Solar Sustenance Team along with environmental attorney Bill Lazar and Dennis Kensil who marshaled needed materials. And with the addition of Maureen Meade, a graphics artist, and consulting engineer Greg Shenstone, the Team was complete.

Funding

In 1978 the group won a $63,000 grant from the Department of Energy's (DOE) Energy Extension Service* to hold two training seminars to teach people from around the country how to conduct local workshops. Except for travel, the grant covered the participants' expenses for the three-day seminars.

Workshop Participants

The Team sent over 100 announcements describing the solar greenhouse training program and inviting applications from local DOE Energy Extension Services, local nonprofit Community Action Agencies (CAAs) * and other community groups across the country.[4]

Three- to four-member groups from 25 communities representing every section of the country were chosen to come to Ghost Ranch to participate in the seminars.

Workshop Pattern

The Ghost Ranch workshops followed a pattern developed over several years by the Yandas.

Here are how-to tips which participants took back to their communities:

- First, publicize and enlist the help of local organizers to spread the word about the workshops;

- Locate residents or community groups who are eager to add greenhouses to homes or buildings, are willing to pay for materials and agree to attend the workshop to learn how to use and maintain the structure;

- Open the workshop with a slide show covering gardening, solar greenhouse design and construction as well as zoning and legal problems;

- For the next two days, let participants put the theory into practice by building a solar greenhouse averaging 8-by-16 feet onto a home or community building.

By the end of the third evening, the greenhouse adorns the building and the occupants have learned how to use and care for it.

Each Ghost Ranch seminar group left with a complete guide of the principles, organization, coordination and implementation of solar greenhouse workshops.

And the Solar Sustenance Team continued to support their trainees by traveling to assist the new organizers in their first local workshops.

Workshops Prove Successful

The success of the workshops is capsulized in the Team's final report to DOE, which revealed that 22 of the 25 teams returned to their communities to conduct workshops, exposing nearly 5,000 people in 20 states to solar building design.

Pioneers Accept New Offer—Others Continue Effort

Recently Bill and Susan Yanda accepted a one-year contract to manage the Passive Solar Retrofit Program for the Tennessee Valley Authority, a Federally owned corporation charged with resource development in the Tennessee Valley area.[5] But the Team continues to spread the greenhouse gospel under the direction of Leslie Davis.

Looking back at the Ghost Ranch seminars, Davis offers two tips for hopeful workshop organizers: hold the seminars in the spring to take advantage of better weather; and if possible make them longer so more construction of solar devices can be included.

Other Groups

Many other groups are conducting solar greenhouse construction workshops, including Domestic Technology Institute in Evergreen, Colorado, which specializes in rural design; Total Environmental Action in Harrisville, New Hampshire; Portland Sun in Portland, Oregon; and Lehigh Valley Manpower Consortium in Easton, Pennsylvania.[6]

Groups Highlighted

Domestic Technology Institute
P.O. Box 2043
Evergreen, Colorado 80439
(303) 674-1597

Lehigh Valley Manpower Consortium
Project Easton, Inc.
633 Ferry Street
Easton, Pennsylvania 18042
(215) 258-4361

Portland Sun
628 Southeast Mill Street
Portland, Oregon 97214
(503) 239-7470

Total Environmental Action
Church Hill
Harrisville, New Hampshire 03450
(603) 827-3374

[1] Solar greenhouses are also profiled in Food Section, pp. 58 and 62.

[2] The Cheyenne Community Solar Greenhouse is profiled in Food Section, p. 62.

[3] For more information on the New Mexico Solar Energy Association, see Resources at end of Energy Section.

[4] The Community Services Administration's (CSA) Community Action Program (CAP)* funds local Community Action Agencies (CAAs)* aimed at helping low-income residents with their food, housing, energy and other needs.

[5] The Tennessee Valley Authority (TVA) is profiled in Energy Section, p. 210. (For more information on TVA, see Resources at end of Energy Section.)

[6] For more information on Domestic Technology Institute, see Resources at end of Energy Section.

* State and/or local government agencies are frequently responsible for administration of Federal program funds. For further information, see Appendix I under appropriate Federal agency.

Note: For a complete listing of groups featured throughout this book, see Index.

Chapter 4

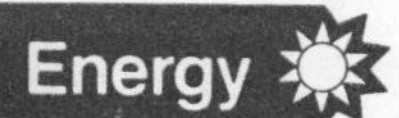

Providing Alternative Transportation

Introduction

America's love affair with the automobile is reluctantly changing. Our society was built on the assumption of limitless mobility and cheap, plentiful fuel. But today we face a harsh reality.

As citizens dole out more and more money for gasoline and pay the high social costs of traffic congestion and pollution, the nation has begun to look for transportation alternatives.

For most Americans, the automobile is still the first travel choice. But the need for greater independence and conservation has prompted innovative responses from citizens throughout the country.

This chapter explores several promising alternatives inspired by citizen groups, businesses, local governments and cooperatives.

Well-maintained cars use less gas than those in ill-repair. Our first profile highlights a resident-owned auto cooperative that ensures quality service at reasonable rates and offers consumers do-it-yourself maintenance and repair classes.

We'll also look at ridesharing programs run by private companies, local governments and citizen groups. And we feature a low-cost bus service that operates in 90 Missouri counties and provides the elderly with transportation to medical appointments and gives them a chance to visit friends in neighboring towns.

We conclude the chapter with profiles showing how walking and biking can be fun and save money. For example, we feature North Carolina's ambitious bicycle office and the impact it has had on the state.

The groups in this chapter illustrate what you and your neighbors can do to cut transportation costs.

Auto Co-ops

Cooperative Auto, Inc.
2232 South Industrial Highway
Ann Arbor, Michigan 48104
(313) 769-0220

Poorly maintained cars are big energy wasters. A car in need of tuning, for instance, uses as much as 9 percent more gasoline than one that is well-tuned. And such things as under-inflated tires also eat up fuel. With nearly 134 million motorists in this country, the energy waste from poorly maintained cars is staggering.

But no one needs to be reminded of the increasing costs of maintaining an automobile these days. Americans spend over $50 billion a year for auto repair and maintenance, according to the National Highway Traffic Safety Administration (NHTSA). Even more disheartening, about $20 billion of that astonishing figure is due to improper diagnosis and unnecessary or poor repairs.

No wonder auto repairs consistently top the hit parade list of consumer complaints!

Preventing Rip-Offs

Some community groups are tackling the problem of car repair rip-offs by forming automobile cooperatives—public corporations which are owned and managed by the residents who use their services.

Staffed by professional auto mechanics, Cooperative Auto, Inc. of Ann Arbor, Michigan offers residents a range of honest, reliable and efficient auto repair and maintenance services as well as consumer classes and workshops that teach auto upkeep. Today Co-op Auto welcomes nonmember customers and boasts a membership of 1,800 residents. The Co-op's expert mechanics repair about 12,000 cars a year at prices comparable to or lower than other repair shops in the area.

"I trust Co-op Auto; I don't feel intimidated," says Beryl Schulman, a Co-op member and customer for four years. "You can feel the commitment and their willingness to explain things. And if something is wrong I can get it checked out quickly."

Co-op member Ann Antell, a social studies teacher at a local high school, agrees with Schulman. "They check things you don't ask them to check," she says. "The estimates have always been accurate within a couple of dollars—and sometimes even lower."

Cooperative Auto, Inc.

Woman learns about her car from a Co-op mechanic.

Bumpy Beginning

Co-op Auto began in 1972 when several community leaders decided to face high car repair costs head-on. They drew up a proposal detailing the Co-op's service plan, which would be limited to preventive maintenance such as changing oil and checking tire pressure and fluid levels. They presented the plan to other business and civic groups. In addition, they placed ads in the local media to attract others who believed the need existed for such an operation.

About 150 people were intrigued enough to pay an annual $200 service fee which covered all preventive maintenance costs. But in less than a year the venture failed, partly because of the Co-op's limited clientele. The Co-op's structure also penalized those with few auto needs who paid the same amount as those whose cars needed more attention.

Experienced Worker Brings Success

The guiding light behind Co-op Auto's transition to a successful business is general manager David Friedrichs who had prior cooperative experience and restructured the operation. He asked the original members to join together in an open auto cooperative which would welcome nonmembers and provide residents with a full range of services. The response was an overwhelming "yes."

Friedrichs also launched a campaign to bolster the Co-op's membership. "We did door-to-door canvassing," he recalls, "but mostly we increased our membership through word-of-mouth advertising."

By 1976 Co-op Auto was financially solvent enough—with membership fees of $100 per household in addition to fees from repairs, towing services and consumer courses—for the group to purchase the building that houses the repair cooperative.

Helping Others

To help other groups form auto cooperatives, Friedrichs submitted a proposal and won a contract from the Department of Transportation's (DOT) National Highway Traffic Safety Administration to write a how-to manual. The manual should be available by early summer 1980 through the National Technical Information Service (NTIS).[1]

Services to Members

Co-op members elect the Board of Directors and receive discount rates for all services—repairs, towing, maintenance, parts and supplies. All profits from the business are pumped back into the Co-op.

And members get cut rates on Co-op Auto's U-Do-It clinics, where consumers repair their cars under the supervision of an expert mechanic, as well as other educational courses that boost understanding of motor vehicle functioning, auto repair and maintenance.

Moreover, the Members Value Club offers shareholders discount coupons for area car washes, doughnut shops and other merchants and free door-to-door bus service when their cars are being serviced.

Budget and Staff

Key to the group's success, Friedrichs points out, are the Co-op's ten expert, committed and experienced mechanics. And 14 other staffers handle parts, towing and administrative matters.

Co-op members learn the fundamentals of auto mechanics while repairing their own cars.

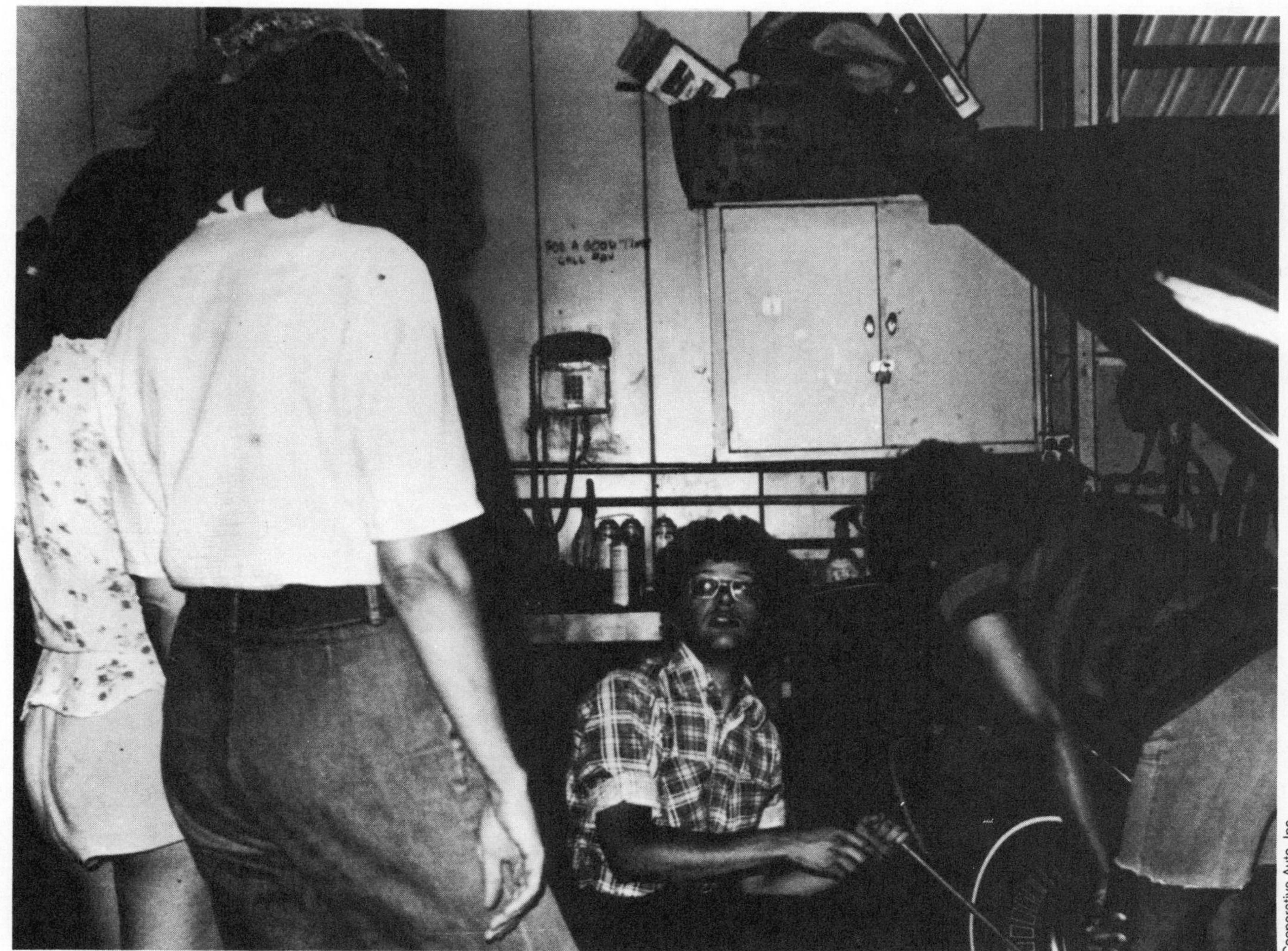

Cooperative Auto, Inc.

Co-op Auto's budget has grown from less than $100,000 in its first year of operation to $700,000 in 1979. With that kind of success, Co-op members are now considering launching another consumer auto care center in Ann Arbor.[2]

Choosing a Mechanic

"Choosing a competent mechanic has got to be the hardest part of getting your car repaired properly," says Auto Co-op's manager David Friedrichs. "Knowing your mechanic is very important, but also important is understanding how your car operates."

If an auto co-op isn't available in your community, Friedrichs has these suggestions for choosing a mechanic to service your car:

- Check the mechanic's credentials, certification and reputation;
- Talk to others who have used the mechanic's services, especially those who have the same kind of car as you do;
- Visit the mechanic in question to establish good rapport and communication;
- Read your automobile driver's manual and get to know your car.

Rockland County Co-op

Cooperative auto shops are catching on around the country. Another successful group is the consumer-owned Cooperative Garage of Rockland County, Inc. in West Nyack, New York. The Co-op requires a one-time membership fee of $50 and offers expert auto repair and consumer education classes as well as use of the group's garage facilities, equipment and mechanics for self-help car repairs.

Group Highlighted

Cooperative Garage of
Rockland County, Inc.
14 Bobby Lane
West Nyack, New York 10994
(914) 358-9452

[1] The how-to manual for organizing auto co-ops may be obtained by writing the National Technical Information Service (NTIS), Department of Commerce, 5285 Port Royal Road, Springfield, Virginia 22161, and asking for the publication entitled *Cooperative Auto Services.* (The fee for the publication has not yet been determined.)

[2] In launching a new auto care center, Cooperative Auto, Inc. may be able to qualify for technical and/or financial assistance from the newly created National Consumer Cooperative Bank.**

** For further information, see Appendix II under "National Consumer Cooperative Bank."

Note: For a complete listing of groups featured throughout this book, see Index.

Community Ridesharing

Action Now, Inc.
Action Now Vanpool Program
Village West Center Mall
1015 West Chestnut Street
Louisville, Kentucky 40203
(502) 584-1823
and
Atlantic Richfield Company
515 South Flower Street
Los Angeles, California 90071
(213) 486-2090

It's nice to leave the driving to someone else—especially when commuting to work. Ridesharing eases city traffic congestion and pollution and also helps eliminate frazzled nerves that result from zig-zagging through rush hour traffic jams.

Ridesharing is a simple concept—commuters who live and work near each other share driving and, usually, expenses. But it can be a real hassle to find people who just happen to be going the same way. However, governments, business leaders, corporations and community groups across the country, eager to conserve energy and help residents cope with rising gasoline prices, are sponsoring programs to link ridesharers. And their efforts are adding up to big savings.

City Program

In Louisville, Kentucky, for instance, efforts by civic and business leaders have led to special highway lanes for poolers and buses and a ridematching service for Louisville residents.

The vanpool program, managed by Action Now, Inc., a nonprofit group formed by business leaders to help solve community problems, and sponsored by the Louisville Chamber of Commerce, provides commuting for 240 Louisville residents who pay about $30 a month for a 20-mile round trip.

By the end of 1979, after persuading area auto dealers to give van discounts and banks to provide no-down-payment van loans, Action Now had enticed 20 residents into becoming vanpool owner-drivers.

One Pool's Savings

"My people are happy," says Ben Ferrell, driver of Louisville's Shepherdsville vanpool. "They know what they're saving in wear and tear on their own cars."

Ferrell's vanpool saved over 5,600 gallons of gas in 1979. In terms of dollars and cents, that means big bucks. In 1979 his vanpool gasoline costs were $996. The passengers of the eight cars his van replaced, Ferrell says, would have paid a whopping $5,549 for gas!

Linda Parrish, one of Ferrell's riders, had this comment, "Not only am I more relaxed when I get to work, but I put 4,000 miles a year on my car now as opposed to 12,000 miles before."

How It Began

The Louisville ridesharing campaign began when the Kentucky State Department of Transportation asked the Louisville Chamber of Commerce to promote the idea with brochures and radio and television advertising spots. And in January 1978 the Chamber asked Action Now, whose good reputation was firmly established in the community, to manage the program.

Action Now and Chamber Work Together

The Chamber of Commerce surveys area businesses to find interested ridesharers, feeding names into a computer to match addresses, work destinations and hours.

Using the computer list, Action Now matches riders and drivers. Drivers must adhere to guidelines, including keeping vans in good repair, adhering to safe driving practices, submitting monthly mileage and gasoline reports and using vans primarily for pooling. And Action Now helps drivers arrange insurance coverage and suggests fares that will meet van payment and transportation costs.

Funding and Staff

In 1979 Action Now's budget for vanpooling and other activities was about $50,000. And two part-time retired businessmen and one full-time Action Now staffer were paid by the Department of Transportation's (DOT) Federal Highway Administration's Federal Aid to Urban Systems Program.*

Testifying to its success, Action Now has been asked to administer a $200,000 Federal Highway Administration National Ridesharing Demonstration Program.* The funds will be used to purchase additional vans and further promote ridesharing.

Corporate Ridesharing

Corporations, recognizing that ridesharing eases employee absenteeism, enhances worker morale and decreases the need for expensive parking lots, are also promoting pooling programs.

In many large cities, carpoolers share special commuter lanes with buses—and breeze by rush hour traffic.

Having company makes the trip to work more pleasant and less expensive.

The Atlantic Richfield Company (ARCO), based in Los Angeles, California, began in 1973 by picking up a portion of the tab for those employees using city buses and by offering poolers free parking.

"In view of the congestion, limited parking and air pollution in the Los Angeles area," says Steve Giovanisci, manager of ARCO's Public Relations Operations, "we felt we had an obligation to use our corporate resources to benefit our community as well as our employees."

In 1974, with the help of other public and private agencies, ARCO formed Commuter Computer, Inc., a nonprofit ridematching service which offers companies and individuals in a five-county area alternative modes of transportation—such as carpools, commuter buses and taxi pools.[1]

Funded primarily by the California Department of Transportation (CALTRAN) and county agencies, Commuter Computer match-ups save ridesharers an estimated two million gallons of gasoline a year and $4 million in commuting costs.

And in 1976, with the backing of area banks which provide financing for vans, the support of many private companies and the managerial expertise of ARCO, an offshoot of Commuter Computer was launched. Commuter Vanpools, Inc. serves 1,000 commuters daily with 120 vans which save over 190,000 gallons of gas yearly. And the two computer programs reduce automobile pollutants in the Los Angeles area by an impressive 2.9 million pounds a year.

As a Commuter Vanpool driver, ARCO employee Russell Turner's 48-mile round-trip commute costs him nothing. "It saves me a lot of money, and it's good to talk to people during the ride," he says.

The Action Now and ARCO programs are just two examples of how public and private groups in rural and urban areas around the country are bolstering ridesharing.

Other Company Efforts

The 3M Company, based in St. Paul, Minnesota, initiated the first United States corporate vanpool program in March 1973. By July 1979, 130 vans served 1,450 employees of five 3M plants in three states. Vanpoolers pay about $1.60 a day for an average 50 mile round-trip, and officials estimate the program has saved 3M $2.5 million by blunting the need for parking lots during a time when employment rose by 23 percent.

Since July 1975 the Prudential Insurance Company of America, based in Newark, New Jersey, has purchased 208 vans for a vanpool program that offers employees "reverse commuting" from the city to suburban offices.

Corporations on the Move

And in 1972 when Erving Paper Mills moved its plant from Erving, Massachusetts to Brattleboro, Vermont, about half of their 300 employees were forced to commute from homes near the old facility. So the following year the company started a vanpool program that operates during three work shifts.

Similarly, in 1975 when Nabisco moved its facilities from New York City to East Hanover, New Jersey, the company launched a ridesharing program for its 1,000 employees that includes charter buses, company automobiles and 13 leased vans which make daily round trips of between 20 and 120 miles.

Other Cooperative Efforts

In 1979 the Knoxville Commuter Pool (KCP) in Knoxville, Tennessee—a cooperative ridesharing effort by the city, 400 area businesses and private and public vanpooling groups—matched 25,000 commuters who saved $9 million in car expenses while conserving four million gallons of gas.

An offshoot of KCP, the nonprofit Knox Area Vanpooler Association (KAVA), boasts a membership of over 70 vanpooling groups who exchange helpful cost-saving hints and other ridesharing information.

The North Dakota State Highway Department operates a vanpool program for rural residents who must travel an average of 60 miles to and from work. The program offers companies and interested drivers interest-free loans for up to 75 percent of van purchases. So far 36 vans have been purchased, saving 360,000 gallons of gas annually.

And since 1975 Carpool Boise in Ada County, Idaho has offered such services as area parking lots where ridesharers can meet and, since 1977, a van leasing program for local employers.

The Personal Mobility Committee, Inc. (PMC) in Salt Lake City, Utah is promoting ridesharing through family, church and other groups. "By using groups which are already at home with one another," explains PMC's Dan McLaughlin, "we hope to make ridesharing a community activity to save energy, money and clean up our air."

Groups Highlighted

Ada County Highway District
Ridesharing Office
318 East 37th Street
Boise, Idaho 83704
(208) 345-7665

Erving Paper Mills
Vernon Road
Brattleboro, Vermont 05301
(802) 257-0511

Knoxville Commuter Pool
South Stadium Hall
University of Tennessee
Knoxville, Tennessee 37916
(615) 637-7433

Nabisco, Inc.
East Hanover, New Jersey 07936
(201) 884-0500

North Dakota State Vanpool Program
Transportation Services
State Highway Department
Capitol Grounds
Bismarck, North Dakota 58505
(701) 224-2512

Personal Mobility Committee, Inc.
347 South 400 East
Salt Lake City, Utah 84111
(No Phone)

Prudential Insurance Company of America
745 Broad Street
Newark, New Jersey 07102
(201) 623-8000

3M Company
Central Engineering
Building 422E
St. Paul, Minnesota 55101
(612) 733-1110

Annual Costs (Per Person) of Commuting to Work — in 1979 Dollars
Driving Alone and Ridesharing

Cost Category:
Operating = costs for gasoline, oil, tires, repairs and maintenance.[1]
Owning = costs for insurance, depreciation, finance charges, taxes and license fees.

One-Way Commute (miles)	Vehicle Type	Cost Category	Drive Alone	Ridesharing Options: Shared-Driving Carpool[2] 2-person	Shared-Driving Carpool[2] 4-person	Shared-Riding Carpool[3] 2-person	Shared-Riding Carpool[3] 4-person	Vanpool 8-person	Vanpool 12-person
10	Subcompact (Pinto Chevette, etc.)	Operating	$ 412	$ 206	$ 103	$ 206	$ 103	$ 82	$ 54
		Owning	314	192	114	157	79	372	248
		Total	726	398	217	363	182	454	302
	Standard (LTD, Caprice, etc.)	Operating	620	310	155	310	155		
		Owning	442	272	161	221	111		
		Total	1062	582	316	531	266		
20	Subcompact	Operating	823	412	206	412	206	163	109
		Owning	439	306	192	220	110	372	248
		Total	1262	718	398	632	316	535	357
	Standard	Operating	1240	620	310	620	310		
		Owning	617	433	272	309	155		
		Total	1857	1053	582	929	465		
40	Subcompact	Operating	1646	823	412	823	412	327	218
		Owning	548	427	306	274	137	372	248
		Total	2194	1250	718	1097	549	699	466
	Standard	Operating	2480	1240	620	1240	620		
		Owning	771	604	433	386	193		
		Total	3251	1844	1053	1626	813		

[1] Gasoline costs based on $1 per gallon.

[2] Shared-Driving: Poolers take turns using their cars and must carry car insurance that covers driving to and from work. Each pooler gets a 10 percent insurance discount because of reduced work mileage.

[3] Shared-Riding: One person's car is used. Insurance is based on distance being driven to and from work and must be provided for only the pool car. Car costs are shared equally by poolers.

Reprinted from "Rideshare and Save — A Cost Comparison," Federal Highway Administration, U.S. Department of Transportation, 1979. Copies available free by writing Consumer Information Center, Pueblo, Colorado 81009.

[1] For more information on Commuter Computer, Inc., see Resources at end of Energy Section.

* State and/or local government agencies are frequently responsible for administration of Federal program funds. For further information, see Appendix I under appropriate Federal agency.

Note: For a complete listing of groups featured throughout this book, see Index.

Transportation for the Elderly and Handicapped

Older Adults Transportation Service, Inc.
601 Business Loop
70 West Parkade Plaza, Lower Level
Columbia, Missouri 65201
(314) 443-4516

The elderly and the handicapped are perhaps hardest hit by escalating transportation costs. Often they are unable to get to public transportation, can't afford high priced taxis and are dependent on family or neighbors to go shopping, visit friends or see their doctors. And in rural areas—where public transportation is scarce and distances are longer—they are restricted even more.

"After my husband died in 1971, I sold the car. Driving made me nervous and I didn't know how to take care of it," recalls senior citizen Alma Hodges of Bloomfield, Missouri. Still, she adds, she was luckier than others. "Some of my folks live here and would take time from work to take me where I just *had* to go. But I sure hated asking because it worked a hardship on them."

The state of Missouri is showing the nation how much can be done to help people like Alma Hodges. Each month 115 buses and vans belonging to the Older Adults Tranportation Service (OATS), based in Columbia, provide door-to-door transportation to over 100,000 senior and handicapped residents of 800 communities in 88 Missouri counties. Services include transportation to doctors' offices, food shopping centers and even to friends' homes. And OATS riders pay only what they can afford.

OATS began in 1971 when Quinnie Benton, a 70-year-old St. Joseph resident, and other members of the Cooperative Transportation Service, a nonprofit community group in Calloway County, decided to help their elderly neighbors become more mobile and independent.

The group convinced the Missouri Office of Aging to kick in $30,000, and with three county-loaned buses and an all-volunteer staff, the service was launched in Calloway County. OATS quickly expanded to other counties and in 1973 was incorporated as a nonprofit group.

Staff and Funding

In 1979 most of OATS' almost $2 million budget came from Title XX of the Social Security Act* and Title III of the Older Americans Act,* both administered by the Department of Health, Education and Welfare (HEW); and from the Urban Mass Transportation Act,* administered by the Department of Transportation (DOT). A small portion of their funding came from rider fares and fundraising efforts.

The staff of 192 drivers and 50 administrators includes workers from the Department of Labor's Comprehensive Employment and Training Act (CETA) Program.* But the core of 500 volunteers across the state—many of them riders—form the backbone of OATS. They laboriously schedule routes and arrange rides in their communities, plan OATS outings and raise funds through potluck dinners, quilt sales and a host of other activities.

OATS

OATS bus drivers and managers stand ready to serve the elderly and handicapped.

How OATS Works

Each van seats 12 people who have different destinations, so getting everyone where they need to go on time takes a lot of coordination. Here's how it's done: After using the OATS system once, riders receive a monthly schedule of the day-to-day destinations of OATS vans. When riders need transportation they call their local OATS contact to schedule a place on the driver pick-up list.

For example, after checking the monthly OATS schedule to see when "doctor day" vans are available, Alma Hodges makes a doctor's appointment. To arrange for a ride she calls her community OATS worker. The OATS driver accompanies her into the office to find out when she should be picked up and often coordinates the date of her next appointment to prearrange the next ride.

OATS Wheel Club

To keep up with OATS activities riders can become members of the OATS Wheel Club. For a small yearly fee, they receive a monthly newsletter and are eligible for low-cost OATS tours such as trips to St. Louis for Cardinals games.

Easing Loneliness

OATS enriches the lives of the elderly and handicapped by freeing them from dependence on neighbors and friends and the headaches and expense of maintaining and operating a car. Even more important, riders experience a sense of comraderie when riding in the vans.

OATS

Ninety-seven year old Anna Cromwell on a tour in St. Louis gets help from OATS driver Arline Holper.

"It's a convenient pleasure to have the OATS Bluebird No. 40 come," wrote Marie Sagler of Mendon in a letter to OATS. "We (the riders) feel that we are part of one big family and realize how much this means to so many that travel by OATS."

Other Cities Offer Special Services

Cities across the country are supplementing their transit systems with special services for the elderly and handicapped. For example, in San Antonio, Texas the city-operated VIA TRANS service has cut local transportation costs in half for elderly and disabled residents. The program is funded by proceeds from a one-half cent local sales tax and utilizes city vans for those who can't use buses.

And in Ann Arbor, Michigan the Transportation Authority's Dial-A-Ride, funded by city property tax revenues, provides low-cost, door-to-door transportation service for the elderly and handicapped.

Groups Highlighted

Dial-A-Ride
(DART-UPTRAN)
Michigan Department of Transportation
P.O. Box 30050
Lansing, Michigan 48909
(517) 374-9183

VIA TRANS
P.O. Box 12489
San Antonio, Texas 78212
(512) 227-5371

* State and/or local government agencies are frequently responsible for administration of Federal program funds. For further information, see Appendix I under appropriate Federal agency.

Note: For a complete listing of groups featured throughout this book, see Index.

Bike Programs

North Carolina Bicycle Program
State Department of Transportation
Raleigh, North Carolina 27611
(919) 733-2804

Bicycles aren't just for fun anymore. People all over the country are realizing that the basic two-wheeler is an efficient, inexpensive and non-polluting way to travel to and from work, errands and recreation sites.

In an unusual state government bicycle program, North Carolina has improved highways and byways for bicyclists while educating riders and motorists about each others' needs and stepping up enforcement of bike safety rules.

A recent survey shows that there are over two million cyclists in North Carolina—half the population of the state. Aided by a mild climate that encourages nearly year-round cycling, the North Carolina project has attracted cyclists from all over the country. But that's not all—touring cyclists come from as far away as Holland to enjoy the North Carolina roads.

Origins

All this came about thanks to the perseverance of one state employee. Bicycle enthusiast Curtis Yates, a planner in the Department of Administration's Office of State Planning, began lobbying for a state bicycle program in 1973. An expert on issues such as rural transportation, Yates was keenly aware of a growing interest in bicycling among North Carolineans. So he drafted a report highlighting the need to include bicycles in overall state transportation planning and suggesting legislation to create a state bicycle program.

Yates' ideas intrigued State Senator McNeill Smith, a bicycle commuter himself, who introduced legislation creating a state program. And the influential Institute of Traffic Engineers, a professional research and information organization, lent support to the legislation because of the large number of citizen inquiries they had received about bicycling.

State Bicycle Office Launched

The bill passed in 1974. Soon the Office of Bicycle Programs was established within the North Carolina Department of Transportation and Yates was asked to take charge.

His first task was to produce a handbook for traffic engineers explaining how to make provisions for cyclists in road planning such as promoting paved shoulders, wider outside lanes and drainage grates designed to avoid catching bike wheels.

Funding and Staff

The state pays for three staffers and printing facilities. And since it opened five years ago, the office has received approximately $500,000 under Section 402 of the Highway Safety Act,* jointly administered by the Department of Transportation's National Highway Traffic Safety Administration (NHTSA) and Federal Highway Administration (FHA).

Staffers educate the public about bicycling and advise law officers on how to enforce bicycle and traffic safety. They encourage cycling by promoting bike rodeos, setting up display booths at shopping centers, conducting bicycle education programs in schools and placing public service announcements on radio and television.

They have published a myriad of educational pamphlets on safety, touring and other subjects of interest to cyclists. And their Bicycle Information Service, which is open to the public, offers maps of state bikeways and boasts an extensive file of relevant bicycling subjects. Moreover, the staff helps local groups start bike clubs and plan activities from bike-a-thons to bike trips.

Involving Citizens

An important key to the program's success is the seven-member citizens advisory committee, which was created by the legislature in 1976 and now includes a teacher, a recreation director and other residents from all parts of the state.

"Citizens now have a genuine voice in transportation planning and, frankly, they can advocate pro-bicycle measures that we, as bureaucrats, can't," Yates explains.

Last year, to protect bicycling interests, the committee developed a comprehensive set of policies which were adopted word-for-word by the governing body of the State Department of Transportation.

"In North Carolina bicycles are now an integral part of the system," says an understandably proud Yates. "Now when policymakers start thinking of road planning and design, bicyclists' needs must be considered."

Other Cities Promote Bikes

With 100 million Americans now owning bikes, it's no surprise that cyclists in other areas of the country are organizing and promoting bicycle use.

In New York City Bicycle Commuters of New York is spreading the word through street fairs, "bicycle pit stops"—which reward bike commuters with free lemonade—and a publicity campaign. According to the group, the benefits of cycling are numerous. A bicycle costs an average of $75 per year to operate for commuting purposes versus $1,150 to $2,000 per year for a car. In addition, many believe that bicycle commuters enjoy lower medical costs because of regular exercise. In fact, some insurance companies across the country give bicyclists discounts on life insurance policies.

Group Highlighted

Bicycle Commuters of New York
5 Beekman Street
Room 404
New York, New York 10038
(212) 732-8552

* State and/or local government agencies are frequently responsible for administration of Federal program funds. For further information, see Appendix I under appropriate Federal agency.

Note: For a complete listing of groups featured throughout this book, see Index.

Walking

The Walking Association
4113 Lee Highway
Arlington, Virginia 22207
(703) 527-5374

When you're out of gas and the pumps are closed, your bus breaks down or your train is late, your airline is on strike or you're waiting for your ship to come in, it's time to take a walk. Just point your feet toward the Walking Association in Arlington, Virginia.

As all-out champions of the most reliable and ancient form of transportation, The Walking Association is all about the pleasures of seeing a silent bloom sparkling in the sunlight, talking to your neighbors and enjoying the serenity of a stream along your path.

"Another nice thing about walking is that you can do it long after you're too old for wildly strenuous exercise like gymnastics. It's something that all ages can take part in," says Warren Young of Arlington, a 68-year-old Association member.

Energy Savings

But the Walking Association members and founder Dr. Robert Sleight are not just dreamers whose major goal is to stroll down the sunny side of the street.

"The potential impact on energy conservation is just staggering," Dr. Sleight says. "Twenty-five percent of our car trips take us less than one mile and more than one-third take us less than two." His research findings indicate that "if Americans walked to all trips that were less than a mile, we could save the country 3,300,000 gallons of gasoline per day, and the trip would only take 15 minutes."[1]

And Warren Young adds, "With the ridiculous amount being charged for gas, you might as well get some good exercise, some fresh air and save fuel too!"

Membership and Funding

The small association, which has a total membership of 100 and chapters in 22 states, actively promotes foot power and watches over pedestrian rights through educational campaigns and organized efforts to lobby institutions which ultimately determine how safe it is to stroll along a busy street.

Established in 1976, the Association is manned by the spare time efforts of Sleight, a behavioral scientist, and other volunteers. The $12 annual dues ($60 for industry and businesses) pays for publishing and distributing the Walking Association Newsletter and other materials.

Hoofing It

Association members' dedication to foot travel has led to serious research on such topics as the best surfaces for walking paths, the width necessary for safe strolls on major streets and crosswalk design and traffic signaling to ensure safe crossings for elderly and handicapped walkers.

From Federal agencies in Washington, D.C. to local traffic engineers and shopping mall planners, Association members have put their best feet forward to get research results to those whose decisions directly affect how enjoyable and safe walking will be.

For instance, members have lobbied the Department of Transportation (DOT) and state highway

authorities—with energy-saving facts in hand—for the installation of walkways alongside the shoulder of existing highways to encourage citizens to take short trips by foot rather than by car.

''Walkways could be installed with minimal effort along some existing highways,'' says Sleight, who walks at least two miles a day. ''These could be inexpensively installed right alongside the roadway, on the road's shoulder, and wouldn't encroach on anyone's private property or cause any personal disruption.''

Pedestrian Alert

And the group has launched letter writing campaigns—organized and promoted through the newsletter—to the Department of Housing and Urban Development (HUD) calling for strict pedestrian considerations in urban planning and neighborhood rehabilitation projects.

Young adds that the Walking Association's very existence helps keep pedestrians on the minds of government policymakers. ''The one very important thing,'' he says, ''is the fact that there is a Walking Association. It tends to promote publicity (in area newspapers) on walking. With publicity we have found that the county pays more attention to its care of paths and such, keeping them in good shape.''

Newsletter and Other Information

The Association's newsletter contains tips for organizing local projects such as trash pick-up jaunts, elementary school safety campaigns and historical walking tours. It reports on new books for walkers, improved walking facilities and timely research findings that members can use in their local campaigns.

The group offers other materials to the public as well—including how to form community walking clubs and walking guides for particular areas. And they help and encourage interested residents to stand on their own feet with such information as how to choose the best walking shoes and the number of calories a relaxing, energy-saving stroll will consume.

[1] Dr. Sleight's conservation findings are based on the assumption that people walk at a speed averaging four miles per hour, the average car gets 15 miles per gallon of gas, and 50 million miles per day are traveled in trips of less than one mile.

Note: For a complete listing of groups featured throughout this book, see Index.

Fighting Energy Inflation: The Comprehensive Approach

Introduction

This chapter shows how much one organization can do to help low-income residents hurdle soaring energy costs.

The project described provides poorer residents with free home weatherization, help with fuel bills, a low-cost transportation service and other programs. Moreover, the group launched an unusual woodburning stove company that offers residents old-fashioned and reliable energy alternatives at affordable prices.

Multi-Faceted Energy Program

Southeastern Vermont Community Action
P.O. Box 396
Bellows Falls, Vermont 05101
(802) 463-9951
and
Green Mountain Stove Works
Box 107 Westminister Station
Bellows Falls, Vermont 05158
(802) 463-9951

During cold New England winters, home heat has all but become a luxury for low-income residents as the price of oil continues to soar. But one organization, dedicated to helping the poor, has turned the clock back to yesteryear and reinstituted the woodburning stove which cooks food, creates a cozy atmosphere and heats a house at about half the cost of oil. And they are helping low-income residents cope with rising fuel costs in other ways as well.

Comprehensive Energy Program Pays Off

Southeastern Vermont Community Action (SEVCA) in Bellows Falls, Vermont is showing how much can be done to combat energy inflation. SEVCA, established in 1965, was one of the first of 900 nonprofit Community Action Agencies (CAAs)* in the country.[1]

SEVCA staffers have launched some unique energy programs that stand as models for other public and private groups across the country. For instance, through its efforts a private business was launched which manufactures woodburning stoves, some of which are sold at reduced costs to low-income families.

Transportation For Low-Income and Elderly

SEVCA also helped start a public transportation project with funds from the Department of Transportation's (DOT) Rural and Small Urban Public Transportation Assistance Program.*[2] The transportation project offers elderly and low-income residents free or reduced-fare rides to neighboring towns. Since June 1978 two vans have traveled over 40,000 miles providing transportation to 14 localities surrounding Brattleboro, the area's largest city.

Weatherization and Conservation

Like other CAAs, SEVCA offers poor families free home weatherization and helps them finance fuel bills. In addition, the agency runs a hot water conservation program for low-income families who pay $15 for the service and save an average of $60 a year on utility bills.

The program employs nine youths, paid with funds from the Department of Labor's Comprehensive Employment and Training Act (CETA) Program,* who are trained to insulate water heaters and hot water pipes and install water-saving devices on faucets and showerheads.

Blowing insulation into a rural home

Assistance to Wood Co-op

Moreover, SEVCA provided a $500 grant to purchase the first chainsaw needed to launch a wood cooperative in Vermont's West River Valley.[3] Twenty-five families pay about $35 per cord of wood versus the $90 open market rate. Members contract with local loggers for treetops and other unused wood which they gather, measure, cut to size and distribute. But perhaps SEVCA's most unusual effort was launching the woodburning stove company.

Origins

The woodburning stove program was a SEVCA project initially and the brainchild of David LaHue, a Vermont resident. LaHue approached SEVCA with the idea of helping low-income residents save on utility bills by building energy-efficient woodburning stoves with obsolete propane tanks. There was a large scrap supply of 60-pound tanks because national suppliers of propane gas had switched to larger storage tanks. SEVCA took the bait and granted LaHue $900 for welding torches and stove development. Local businesses donated space and work began.

Setting Up The Stove Works

The newly developed stove was tested and proved to be a safe and effective home heating device. The New England Regional Commission,* a Federal-state government agency under the Department of Commerce, kicked in $45,000 for equipment and production costs and CETA funds were used to hire and train residents in welding and machine shop skills. In 1975 the SEVCA Stove Works was born.[4]

Good Publicity Means Trouble

Initially the "tank" stoves were given away or sold at discount prices to low-income residents.

But success nearly doomed the woodburning stove venture. An October 1975 article in the *Country Journal,* a New England regional publication, hailed SEVCA's endeavor and rated their woodburning stove the most efficient on the market. Spurred by the article, higher-income residents began clamoring to buy the SEVCA stove. And by 1977 SEVCA was selling the stoves at full price to higher-income residents and pumping the profits back into the stove venture to expand the program.

Just as business was booming, problems set in. The Community Services Administration (CSA), the anti-poverty agency that funds CAAs, had strict rules against profit-making ventures. SEVCA lost its CETA and other funding because the stoves were generating profits. It looked as though the stove works might be out of business.

Changed Guidelines Come To Rescue

But in the fall of 1978, thanks to new CSA guidelines, SEVCA won a $172,500 grant from CSA's Emergency Energy Conservation Services Program* to launch a new, independent and profit-making stove manufacturing company. The new guidelines required SEVCA to purchase 51 percent or controling interest in the company and to use all profits and proceeds to promote the economic development of the region.

With production ready to go, management help on board and the books in order, Green Mountain Stove Works, Inc. opened on January 1, 1979.

Green Mountain sells stoves at cost to area CAAs which give them to needy families. The company also sells stoves at a discount to nonprofit groups in nearby Boston. And in 1980 the company plans to introduce a low-cost, energy-efficient coalburning stove made of recycled materials.

All of these projects—from water conservation to stove manufacturing—show just how much one group can do to ease the burden of high energy costs for low-income residents.

[1] The Community Services Administration's (CSA) Community Action Program (CAP)* funds local Community Action Agencies (CAAs)* aimed at helping low-income residents with their food, housing, energy and other needs.

[2] The Department of Transportation's (DOT) Rural and Small Urban Public Transportation Assistance Program* is administered jointly by the Federal Highway Administration and Urban Mass Transit Authority.

[3] The West River Valley wood co-op is now independent of SEVCA. (Co-ops may now be eligible for financial and technical assistance from the newly created National Consumer Cooperative Bank.**)

[4] The New England Regional Commission is concerned with the economic, physical and social development of the six-state New England region.

* State and/or local government agencies are frequently responsible for administration of Federal program funds. For further information, see Appendix I under appropriate Federal agency.

** For further information, see Appendix II under "National Consumer Cooperative Bank."

Note: For a complete listing of groups featured throughout this book, see Index.

Chapter 6

HOW TO CONSERVE
E.+G.P.:
STOP THE RATE INCREASE
Women's Action
You and Me
VS
PG and E
EG&P

Reforming Electric Utilities

Introduction

Electric utility rates have jumped by over 76 percent since 1973. Unfortunately, consumers who are unhappy with rates or service can't shop around for a better deal because utility companies are granted government-regulated, regional monopolies.

But consumer groups across the country are learning how to make their voices heard. They know that changes in utility policies can mean savings of hundreds of dollars yearly on their electric bills, and they are attacking what they consider to be a host of unfair and wasteful practices which company spokesmen argue are necessary in order to maintain good financial standing.

Although some of the issues discussed in this chapter are also relevant to gas, heating oil and other utilities, consumers have been most active in seeking reforms in electric company practices. So with the exception of the issue of terminating service, which especially affects gas companies, we limit our discussion to electric utilities.

We begin this chapter with an overview of ratemaking and the regulatory process, and we look at how existing state utility consumer offices, a new Federal law and a special grant program can help consumers influence this process.

Also discussed in this chapter are five of the most controversial utility policy issues:

(1) How some utility companies automatically pass along fuel costs to consumers through fuel adjustment clauses—and ways in which state commissions can better monitor this practice.

(2) How energy waste is encouraged when rates are reduced for big users—and how small customers are fighting this policy.

(3) How an accounting device, Construction Work in Progress (CWIP), allows utilities to charge customers for power plants under construction. Consumers argue that CWIP makes them pay rates based on plants that are not yet providing them with service. And in states such as Oregon, they've passed laws banning it.

(4) How consumer groups in Georgia and other states have won regulatory changes that protect customers from cold weather shutoffs while requiring gradual repayment of overdue bills.

(5) How in Connecticut and other states citizen groups have convinced public utility commissions to turn down requests for rate increases to finance construction of what they believe to be unneeded power plants.

A list of groups which have had success in winning reforms or that can offer technical assistance is also provided. Additional helpful information can be found in the Resources under Utility Reform at the end of the Energy Section. And a glossary of helpful terms follows the utility chapter.

Ratemaking and the Regulatory Process (An Overview)

If you don't know the rules, you can't win the game. That's why it's important to know how utilities are regulated, how rates are set and how citizens can participate in the process.

With the arrival of a new decade, there is increasing debate about America's energy future and the role of utility companies in controlling and pricing the world's dwindling supplies. It isn't surprising that the public has become concerned about electric utilities. After all, electricity is a basic necessity of life in the United States.

No Competition

Because there are no competing electric utilities, one must subscribe to the local company—at whatever price it charges—or go without. To prevent duplication of costly generating plants, transmission lines and distribution services, utility companies have been granted monopoly franchises to provide electricity for their areas. Over 75 percent of these franchises have gone to private companies known as investor-owned utilities (IOUs). The rest are governmentally or cooperatively owned.

Regulatory Process

In the words of one utility executive, "What the government giveth, the government taketh away." In exchange for franchise rights, IOUs are subject to government regulations that seek to ensure that utilities efficiently provide reliable and safe services at fair and nondiscriminatory rates.

To oversee this, most states have established statewide regulatory agencies, usually known as Public Utility Commissions (PUCs), to govern rates and standards of service. Commissioners are generally appointed by the governor and must be approved by the state legislature, although in a few states they are elected.

These commissions aim to avoid problems commonly associated with monopolies—unjustifiably high prices, poor service and no choice—but some consumer groups argue they are too often "rubber stamps," accepting almost anything the utilities say they need.

Rate Setting

When establishing rates, commissions determine:

- The company's costs such as salaries, fuel, maintenance and taxes (operating expenses);
- The company's investment in power generating plants, distribution and transmission facilities, and other items needed to provide electric service (rate base); and
- The amount of interest stockholders should earn on their investment in the utility (rate of return).

Based on this information, the commission determines the amount of money the utility can collect from its customers (overall revenue requirement). Finally, the commission decides what portion of its revenue requirement the utility will collect from each of its customer classes—residential, commercial and industrial (rate structure).

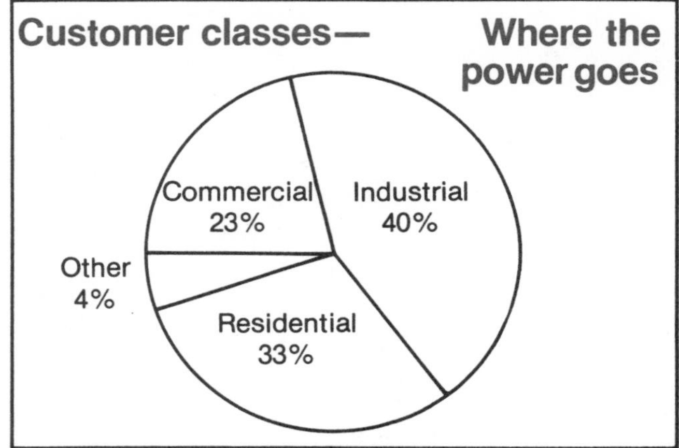

A rate hike results when customer fees fall short of the utility's predetermined overall revenue requirement or when that requirement increases.

Inequality Among Users

However, all users are not treated equally. Whether one class should pay a greater share of the utility's overall requirement than another is the subject of increasing debate. There is also considerable question over what operating expenses should be included and which plants and transmission lines should be built. There are no easy answers to these questions. Different rate-setting standards are applied by each regulatory commission—and the experts rarely agree.

Rate Hikes

Commissions must hold public hearings on utility applications for rate hikes. At the hearings, the utility presents testimony to support its application, and consumers who have requested permission to "intervene" present testimony opposing the rate increase. Both the utility and intervenors can cross-examine the witnesses who have presented testimony. In reaching a final decision, the commission is supposed to balance the best interests of the company and its customers.

Consumer Participation

In recent years consumer groups have had help from the Department of Energy (DOE) in presenting their point of view before utility commissions. Section 205 of the Energy Conservation and Production Act,* administered by DOE, provides grants to states to set up state agencies responsible for representing consumer interests in utility regulatory proceedings. Although these vary, the three most commonly charged with this responsibility are the Attorney General's office, the State Department of Consumer Protection and the utility consumer advocate's office.[1]

And the 1978 Public Utility Regulatory Policies Act (PURPA),* part of the National Energy Act (NEA) which is also administered by DOE, urges utility commissions to consider consumers when setting rates and regulatory standards. Also under PURPA, in some cases, consumers can recover the costs of their participation.

To further bolster citizen participation, the Washington, D.C.-based Environmental Action Foundation (EAF) has created a clearinghouse for utility consumers across the country.[2] EAF helps citizens participate in regulatory hearings by providing resource material and technical expertise.

Standards

Thanks to PURPA, public utility commissions must *consider* adopting certain innovative ratemaking and regulatory standards. The ratemaking standards are:

(1) **Cost of Service.** Rates charged by an electric utility to each customer should reflect the costs of providing service to that group. In other words, residential users should not subsidize industrial users or vice versa.

(2) **Declining Block Rates.** The rates charged for a unit of electricity (kilowatt hour) may not decline as usage increases unless the utility can prove that the cost of providing electricity does decrease with greater usage.

(3) **Time-of-Day Rates.** Except where it is proven not to be cost effective, rates should reflect the cost of providing electricity at different times of the day. There are times of the day when consumers demand more electricity. The times of greatest demand are called peak periods (mornings and late afternoons) and the times of less demand are called non-peak periods (nights). It is more expensive to provide electricity during peak periods when all generating plants are running than during non-peak periods when only some are in service.

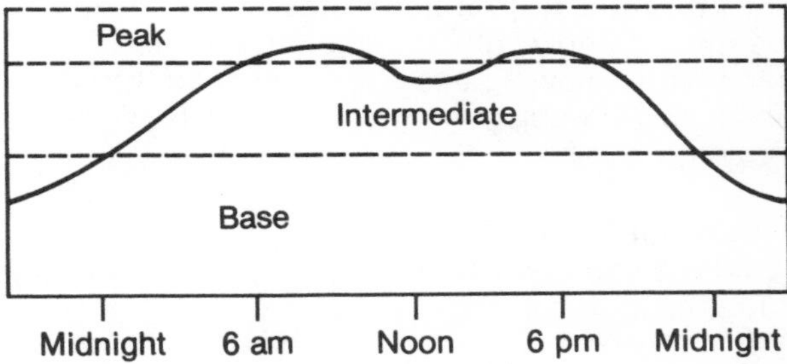

(4) **Seasonal Rates.** Rates should reflect the costs of providing service during different seasons of the year, which vary from region to region.

(5) **Interruptible Rates.** Electric utilities should offer lower rates to commercial and industrial customers willing to have service turned off periodically. By turning off some large users during peak hours the utility saves money.

(6) **Load Management Techniques.** All customers should be offered the money-saving option of allowing the utility to cut off certain services which are not needed during peak hours, by prearranged agreement.

The five regulatory standards which PURPA requires the public utility commissions to *consider* are:

(1) **Master Metering.** The use of a single meter in new multi-unit buildings should be prohibited or restricted. Instead, each apartment or office should have its own meter. When occupants control their own meters they are more likely to cut energy use.

(2) **Automatic Adjustment Clauses.** Electric utilities must comply with specific commission guidelines before allowing costs to be passed through to consumers via adjustment clauses such as fuel adjustment clauses.

(3) **Information to Consumers.** Electric utilities should provide consumers with information on rate structures.

(4) **Procedures for Termination.** Electric utilities should adopt and follow fair practices before terminating service.

(5) **Advertising.** Promotional or political advertising costs should not be passed on to customers.

Another very important ingredient of PURPA requires each regulatory authority to hold a hearing to determine whether "lifeline"—lower-than-cost rates for the electricity needed for essential residential services—should be adopted.

For further information on rate setting and the regulatory process as well as where to get financial assistance for citizen participation, see Resources under "Utility Reform" at the end of the Energy Section.

Be a knowledgeable consumer . . . doing your homework pays off.

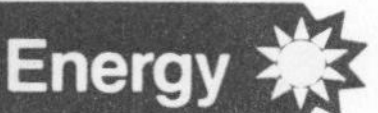

A. Fuel Adjustment Clauses

Before state commissions set rates, they allow the public to look closely at most of the expenses that utility companies are claiming. But amazingly most commissions limit public scrutiny of one of the biggest expenses: fuel.

Utilities are generally allowed to automatically pass increasing fuel costs directly to consumers through "fuel adjustment clauses." These charges appear as separate items on most utility bills. And with fuel prices soaring, many consumers argue that this automatic "pass through" blunts incentives for utilities to shop around for the cheapest fuel. Utilities argue that they must recover increases in fuel prices immediately to remain financially sound.

Consumers are starting to conduct their own investigations, and in states such as Illinois consumer groups have won laws which reform the automatic pass-through by calling for tougher auditing of utilities' expenses and requiring that customers be refunded for overcharges.

The Issue

Electricity is generated by converting one form of energy—primarily coal, falling water, oil, gas or uranium—into another.

The fuel used in the conversion to electricity is the greatest cost incurred in providing utility service, amounting to between one-fourth and one-half of the utility's total expenses.

Dealing With Fuel Price Instability

In recent years as a result of wide fluctuations in fuel costs and concern over the financial stability of electric utilities, most utility commissions have allowed a "fuel adjustment clause" (FAC), which in theory allows increases and decreases in fuel costs to be passed on to consumers. The charge is either automatic or is permitted after hearings, depending on the state. The adjustment is not a rate surcharge; rather, it is intended to recover changes in the utility's increase in fuel costs.

FACs are not new. They have been used during periods of fuel price instability since World War I. The clauses are now being used as a result of the 1973 oil embargo which led to sharp increases in oil, coal and uranium prices.

Utilities Argue Automatic FACs Necessary

Electric utilities argue that since they have little or no control over the price of the fuel they must purchase, automatic FACs are necessary to maintain financial stability. Moreover, since the automatic clauses reflect fuel price changes quickly, utilities contend that consumers receive immediate rate reductions when prices decline. Finally, utilities point to the fact that rapid recovery of outlays for fuel reduces a company's financing and regulatory expenses which would have to be passed on to consumers.

JUDD EDISON COMPANY
GENERAL OFFICE
1001 SMITH STREET
ALEXANDRIA, VIRGINIA 22310

Summary of Charges

Billing Period From	Billing Period To	Meter Readings Previous	Meter Readings Present	Kilowatthours or 100 Cu. Ft.	Type of Service or Charge	Amount
DEC 5 77	JAN 5 78	08720	11450	2730	ELECTRIC-SCHEDULE 5	143 78
		$.002980 PER KWH			FUEL ADJUSTMENT *	8 14
					TOTAL CHARGES	151 92
					UTILITY TAX	12 15
					TOTAL CURRENT AMOUNT	164 07
					BALANCE FROM PREVIOUS BILL	
					ACCOUNT BALANCE	164 07

This bill covers 31 days
Average Cost per Day for Service Used $ 4.90

SERVICE ADDRESS
WHITE CO
836 AMES RD
SPRINGFIELD VA 22151

A typical electric bill—where to find fuel adjustment "pass through"

Consumers Counter

Consumers counter that automatic fuel adjustment clauses remove incentives for utilities to purchase fuel at the lowest available cost. They add that automatic FACs also remove incentives for utilities to burn the least expensive fuel that they have in stock or to purchase the cheapest electricity from other utilities when needed. (Utilities are also often allowed to pass on to consumers through FACs the cost of purchasing electricity from other companies.) Finally, some utilities own fuel-producing companies such as coal mines, and consumers allege that intercompany transfers can be made at inflated costs which are passed on to the consumer.

Regulatory Commissions Favor Clause

Some utility regulatory commissions favor automatic FACs because they reduce commission workload, minimize utility requests for rate hikes and contribute to the financial stability of the industry.

Winning Concessions

But due to consumer complaints, utility abuses and unsatisfactory oversight, legislatures and utility commissions have made changes in automatic fuel adjustment clauses. Many states now require periodic utility company audits and hearings to reconcile fuel costs. Some commissions have now encouraged utilities to shop for the best priced fuel by limiting the amount of fuel increases and other costs, such as transportation, that can be automatically passed through to consumers.

Need for Citizen Participation

While these changes have reduced the abuse potential, automatic fuel adjustment clauses still have an important effect on utility rates. Consumers are continuing to seek improvements in the way FACs operate and question the need for their continued use—particularly once fuel prices have stabilized.

Active Groups

Consumer groups have been active in fuel adjustment clause issues in many states and a partial listing is provided below. Contact these organizations directly to learn how you can become involved:

Arkansas Consumer Research
Utility Staff
1852 Cross Street
Little Rock, Arkansas 72206
(501) 374-2394

Labor Coalition on Public Utilities
204 South Ashland Boulevard
Chicago, Illinois 60607
(312) 738-4233

Massachusetts Fair Share
304 Boylston Street
Boston, Massachusetts 02116
(617) 266-7505

Missouri Citizen Action
393 North Euclid Avenue, Suite 203
St. Louis, Missouri 63108
(314) 361-0777

Toward Utility Rate Normalization
693 Mission Street, Eighth Floor
San Francisco, California 94105
(415) 543-1576

B. Lifeline

Consumer groups around the country are focusing on what they consider to be rate discrimination by electric utility companies. Traditionally, utilities have charged a lower rate for additional kilowatt hours as usage increases. Under these "declining block" rates, residential consumers often pay twice as much per unit of electricity as do large industrial customers. The justification for declining block rates has been that it is cheaper to provide large quantities of electricity to one user than to supply the same amount to a number of users.

Consumer groups argue that these rates not only discriminate against residential users but also encourage industry to waste rather than conserve energy.

In response to this issue citizens in some states have won "lifeline" rates, which give residential users special low rates for the minimum amount of energy needed for life's essentials. In September 1975, after over a year of lobbying, petitions and demonstrations by California citizen groups, the state legislature passed a lifeline measure. It was the first such law in the country and has reduced residential electric bills by millions of dollars.

These reforms can be especially helpful to low-income customers. But utility spokesmen argue that lifeline rates cost their companies too much and threaten their financial stability.

The Issue

After a regulatory commission determines how much revenue an electric utility needs to remain financially sound, rates are set for each class of customer—residential, commercial and industrial. Traditionally, those classes using the greatest amount of electricity are charged less for each additional unit of electricity they consume.

Cost per Unit Increases

During the 1970s soaring energy prices, greater electricity demand and other factors resulted in a dramatic reversal of the declining cost theory. In many instances, additional units of electricity have become *more* expensive to produce, and the result has been a steep and unending increase in electric utility rates. Many utility commissions, however, continue to adhere to the declining cost theory when determining rate structure, thereby rewarding those customers who use more. Several other commissions continue to set rates for all customers equally, regardless of consumption levels.

Rewards for Conservation

Consumers have proposed alternatives to declining block rates which, they argue, will reward conservation efforts. For example, lifeline, particularly important for low- and fixed-income customers, offers all residential customers reduced rates for *minimum* quantities of electricity. (See Chart 1.) The rate increases for units consumed over the minimum. And under an "inverted rate structure," the per-kilowatt charge increases with greater usage. (See Chart 2.)

Controversy

Traditionally, utilities and regulatory authorities have opposed these reforms on the grounds that utility rates should be set according to the cost of the service provided. They contend that setting some rates below production costs or charging more for additional units subsidizes certain customers at the expense of others and is discriminatory.

While utilities have shown greater sensitivity in recent years to the problems of low- and fixed-income customers, some argue that rate reforms amount to social ratemaking. Instead, they argue, the problems of poorer residents should be solved through governmental subsidy programs such as energy stamps or changes in the tax structure.

Consumers Strike Responsive Chord

Nonetheless, consumer pressure has led some utility commissions to eliminate declining block rates and a few to adopt some form of lifeline or an inverted rate structure. Other commissions, while refusing to adopt specific lifeline rates, have limited residential customer rate hikes in other ways. Also, some state legislatures have enacted lifeline statutes or other rate structure reforms.

Hearings Mandated

The Public Utility Regulatory Policies Act (PURPA) requires commissions and large cooperative utilities (utilities which are customer-owned rather than privately owned) to review rate standards and adopt reforms where appropriate. In addition, each regulatory authority must hold hearings to consider a lifeline rate for residential consumers. PURPA authorizes the commission to adopt lifeline rates even though they don't reflect production costs associated with residential service. Many consumer groups are monitoring commissions to learn when those hearings will be held so they can plan their participation.

Chart 1

The **Lifeline Rate Structure** limits prices for *minimum* power usage.

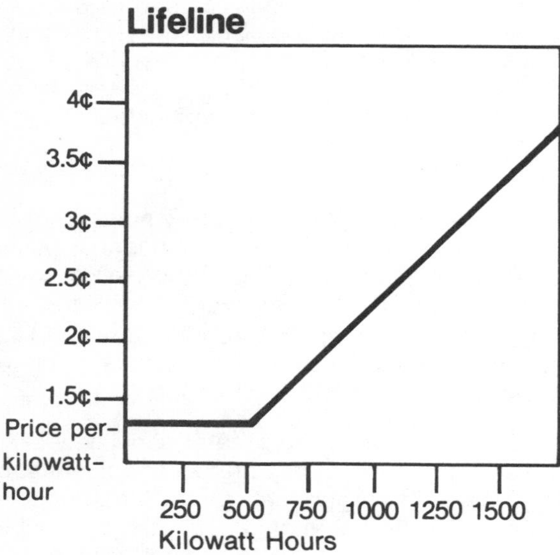

Chart 2

The **Inverted Rate Structure** encourages conservation by charging more per-kilowatt unit as usage increases.

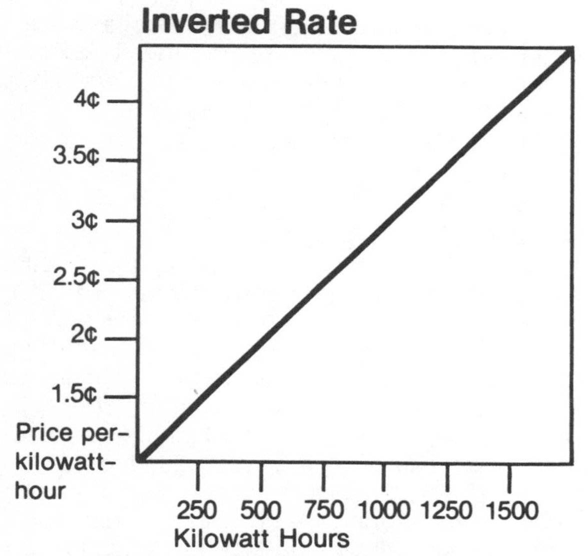

Active Groups

A listing of some consumer organizations that have been active in lifeline issues is provided below. Contact these organizations for information on how you can become involved:

Citizen's Action League
814 Mission Street
San Francisco, California 94103
(415) 543-4101

The Illinois Public Action Council
59 East Van Buren Street
Chicago, Illinois 60605
(312) 427-6262

New Jersey Federation of Senior Citizens
20 East Hanover Street
Trenton, New Jersey 08608
(609) 394-0001

South Dakota ACORN
611 South Second Avenue
Sioux Falls, South Dakota 57104
(605) 332-2328

Wyoming Energy Advocacy Coalition
1603 Central Avenue
Cheyenne, Wyoming 82001
(307) 635-9426

C. Construction Work in Progress

"We won't pay for electricity before we use it!"

That's the message voters in states such as Oregon and New Hampshire are sending to utility companies. These consumers are opposed to Construction Work in Progress (CWIP), an accounting device which allows utilities to charge consumers rates based on a utility's investment in power plants still under construction and not yet producing electricity.

CWIP can have a significant impact on our pocketbooks. The Federal Energy Regulatory Commission (FERC), the agency charged with regulating wholesale electric rates, has estimated that CWIP boosts utility rates by at least 11 percent—or $5 billion nationwide. Consumer groups consider CWIP rates especially unfair to senior citizens who might never receive the benefits of the new plant which may not begin to generate power for a number of years.

The utilities argue they need CWIP to finance construction to meet future energy needs. Consumers argue that CWIP makes them unwilling investors in company expansion plans and that conservation methods and more efficient use of current excess capacity would make much new construction unnecessary. They further argue that it is the role of a utility's stockholders and other investors—not consumers—to provide money to finance new construction.

In 1977 a coalition of Oregon consumer groups launched a drive to put the CWIP issue on the ballot. Over the years, anti-CWIP forces argued, Oregon utility customers had been forced to pay almost $45 million for new power plants under construction. In November 1979 the anti-CWIP measure was approved by 68.7 percent of the voters.

And in New Hampshire, after citizen groups successfully convinced the state legislature to outlaw CWIP, the governor vetoed the legislation. So the consumer groups made CWIP an election year issue. They helped elect an anti-CWIP governor who, along with the state legislature, supported the legislation. In May 1979 an anti-CWIP statute was enacted in New Hampshire.

The Issue

Inflation, the need to build facilities to meet future electricity demands, extended construction periods and rising interest rates have caused enormous increases in utility plant construction costs.

Consumers have always borne the cost of constructing electrical generating plants and equipment. But *when* these costs should be passed on to consumers is the subject of much controversy.

Traditionally, utilities could not include construction costs in rates until a facility was completed. Instead, a utility borrowed construction money and after the facility was operating—sometimes several years later—total construction costs, including financing charges, were included in the utility rate base.

But in recent years, utility companies have pushed to have CWIP automatically included in rate bases. They argue that CWIP helps avoid huge financing costs and in the long run reduces customer rates.

Consumers in some states have opposed the inclusion of CWIP in utility rate bases. They argue that it is unfair to charge customers for plants which will not provide service for many years.

Moreover, they contend, CWIP forces consumers to invest in utilities without receiving dividends or stockholders' voting privileges. They also argue that CWIP encourages utilities to build unnecessary generating plants and reduces incentives for utilities to operate efficiently or to pursue effective conservation programs.

CWIP Approved in Special Cases

FERC currently permits utilities to include CWIP in their rate bases for pollution control equipment and conversions of existing power plants from oil to coal. Additionally, utilities that can demonstrate severe financial hardship may be authorized to include some current construction costs in their rate bases. Practices vary widely among state utility commissions, and those that permit CWIP usually limit it to the last year or so of construction or allow only a percentage of construction costs to be included.

Active Groups

CWIP can represent millions of dollars in potential rate increases to customers. For information on how you can get involved, contact the consumer organizations listed below:

Granite State Alliance
83 Hanover Street
Manchester, New Hampshire 03101
(603) 627-4439

Oregonians for Utility Reform
P.O. Box 12763
Salem, Oregon 97309
(503) 370-8115

Utility Consumers Council of Missouri
393 North Euclid, Suite 203
St. Louis, Missouri 63108
(314) 361-5725

Vermont Public Interest Research Group
Vermont PIRG
26 State Street
Montpelier, Vermont 05602
(802) 223-5221

D. Termination of Utility Service

Would you rather eat or have heat?

That cruel choice faces many poor families each month when their utility bills arrive. If they don't pay their gas or electricity bills, they can face the prospect of almost immediate shutoffs.

As one consumer activist told the Georgia utility commission during a cold spell, ''Heat, electricity and telephones are a matter of life and death, particularly in the kind of weather we're having.''

Thanks to the determined efforts of consumer groups, the Georgia commission has forbidden utility companies to disconnect residential service between November 15 and March 15 if customers agree to pay back bills in monthly installments during non-winter months.

An increasing number of public utility commissions have issued regulations sharply limiting shutoffs, especially during colder months. At the same time, these regulations recognize the legitimate need of utilities to collect overdue bills from customers.

Although utility companies have expressed fear that customers would abuse liberal shutoff policies, some utility commissions report that those fears are unfounded.

Another way to avoid shutoffs, of course, is to pay your bills on time. To help low-income residents, a number of Federal and state programs assist qualifying consumers to pay fuel bills as well as reduce energy needs with weatherization programs.[3]

The Issue

Rising utility rates and reductions in purchasing power due to inflation have forced an increasing number of consumers to face utility cutoffs. The problem is most severe for those on low- and fixed-

Consumers learn more about how utility companies operate from Georgia Action worker.

Georgia Action

incomes and the elderly, who often live in drafty, substandard housing and are unable to control energy usage.

Cutoff Procedures

In the past several years consumers have urged state utility commissions to revise standards governing utility termination. Instances of customers freezing to death after termination of service have focused national attention on this issue.

Traditionally, utilities were permitted to shut off service with little advance notice to the customer. Procedures to protest the pending cutoff rarely existed and customers faced heavy late charges on outstanding bills as well as fees to prevent termination or to reconnect service. Utilities enjoyed wide discretion in deciding which customers to cut off and in many cases did not treat all customers equally. Finally, and most importantly, service cutoffs frequently occurred because customers could not afford to pay outstanding bills and many utilities were reluctant to extend credit.

Consumer Pleas Effect Change

Beginning in 1974, at the urging of consumer organizations, some utility commissions began revising standards for cutoffs. Many of these revisions establish uniform termination procedures and entitle customers to hearings and reviews before service is cut off.

Some states have required utilities to offer reasonable payment plans to customers instead of terminating service and to give customers the option of easing high winter costs by paying estimated annual utility bills over a 12-month period. In other states, commissions have forbidden utilities to terminate service when medical emergencies could result and have encouraged companies to get acquainted with public assistance programs so they can lead customers to help.

Other commissions have banned cutoffs during winter months or when temperatures fall below certain levels. And some require utility employees to personally contact customers before terminating service and to leave notices on the premises if no one is home.

Utilities' Defense

Utility companies counter that some customers have no intention of paying outstanding bills and that pre-termination hearings and other procedures invite customers to take advantage of the company. As a result, they argue, the vast majority of customers who pay utility bills promptly are required to subsidize a small number of uncooperative customers.

New Law Adopted

Even though some abuse the system, the Public Utility Regulatory Policies Act (PURPA) requires state regulatory commissions and large cooperative utilities to *consider* adopting cutoff procedures which specify:

(1) Service cannot be terminated without giving consumers reasonable prior notice (including information about rights and remedies and an opportunity to dispute the reasons for cutoff); and

(2) Service cannot be terminated during any period when it would be especially dangerous to the health of a utility consumer as determined by the state regulatory authority or nonregulated utility, and the consumer establishes that he or she is unable to pay for service or is able to pay but only in installments.

The Act also specifies that termination procedures should take into account the need to include reasonable provisions for elderly and handicapped consumers.

Although several commissions have made substantial progress in consumer rights regarding service cutoffs, consumers in many states continue to monitor commission proceedings to let their concerns be known.

EAF/Art for People

Active Groups

More information on successful developments on termination of service and how you can get involved can be obtained from the following organizations:

Citizen Labor Energy Coalition
600 West Fullerton Avenue
Chicago, Illinois 60614
(312) 975-3680

Coalition for Consumer Justice
622 Charles Street
Providence, Rhode Island 02904
(401) 521-1300

Colorado ACORN
1144 Cherokee Road
Denver, Colorado 80218
(303) 831-1094

Georgia Action
P.O. Box 7803
Atlanta, Georgia 30357
(404) 873-2223

E. Utility Expansion

Many consumers believe that utility bills are high enough and they shouldn't have to pay for unneeded new power plant construction. Some utility spokesmen insist, however, that big rate hikes are needed to build new plants which are necessary if future energy demands are to be met.

Opponents of new plant construction counter that utilities have sufficient excess capacity to meet future demands and that increased conservation efforts can reduce electrical use, making additional power plants unnecessary.

Search for Alternatives

Because of the work of citizen and other groups as well as some enlightened utilities, the search for alternatives to new construction is becoming increasingly attractive to some of the more cost-conscious utility commissions. For instance, public utility commissions in Connecticut and other states are viewing new plant construction with skepticism. The Connecticut commission turned down a utility's request for a $900 million rate increase to pay for the construction of five power plants. Instead the commission granted a $22.6 million increase for the construction of one plant but directed the company to cancel plans for the others.

The Issue

Electric utility companies are responsible for providing adequate, safe and reliable service to their customers. Part of that responsibility is to estimate future electricity use and construct generating plants and install transmission lines to meet the increasing demand. How many to construct, however, is a complicated question. Often these decisions must be made far in advance because, due to such things as regulatory procedures and construction time, it takes many years to complete a new plant.

Estimating Demand

Errors in this crystal ball forecasting can lead to excess capacity or insufficient reserves to meet customer needs. Either result can be very costly for consumers. It is generally accepted that a utility should have enough electrical capacity to meet its average peak demand (the time of day when the greatest amount of electricity is used) and still have 20 percent in reserve. Reserve capacity allows utilities to shut down some plants for maintenance and still meet needs as they arise. But underestimating demand can make it necessary for a utility to purchase higher priced electricity from other utilities. And overestimates can result in excess capacity which means consumers pay for unnecessary generators.

Citizen groups learn how to conserve energy —and help avoid the construction of costly generating plants.

Sharp reductions in electricity demand resulting from the 1973 oil crisis, inflation, increased rates and customer conservation have caused excess capacity in many utility systems throughout the country. At the same time, utilities have spent hundreds of millions of dollars on plants that have been deferred and on construction which has been halted. While certain construction costs might be necessary to meet new demand or save energy by converting oil and gas plants to coal, consumers are working to make sure that construction programs are absolutely necessary before construction begins.

Alternatives

There are alternatives to large scale utility expansion. Utility rate structure reforms which charge rates on today's cost of providing service can show consumers that excessive usage is not in their best interest. Load management programs, which alter peak-hour usage, together with rate reform can more evenly distribute energy demand—saving utilities and consumers money.[4]

Conservation, however, is the best way to ensure that energy will be available for future needs. Weatherization and mandatory utility conservation programs, appliance efficiency standards and other efforts can significantly reduce demand and delay costly construction.[5]

Consumers are carefully examining the construction plans of utilities to determine if there are less costly ways to meet future energy needs.

Active Groups

To find out how you can become involved, contact the following consumer organizations for further information:

Citizens for a Better Environment
59 East Van Buren Street, Suite 1600
Chicago, Illinois 60605
(312) 939-1984

Citizens United for Responsive Energy
3500 Kingman Boulevard
Des Moines, Iowa 50311
(515) 277-0253

Connecticut Citizen Action Group
P.O. Box G
Hartford, Connecticut 06106
(203) 527-7191

Light Brigade
810 18th Avenue
Seattle, Washington 98122
(206) 329-9764

Solar Oregon Lobby
720 Northeast Ainsworth Street
Portland, Oregon 97211
(503) 284-9320

Wisconsin's Environmental Decade
114 East Mifflin Street, Third Floor
Madison, Wisconsin 53703
(608) 251-7020

[1] To find out what office in your area represents the public interest, contact your state Public Utility Commission (PUC) or Governor's office.

[2] For more information on the Environmental Action Foundation (EAF), see Resources at end of Energy Section.

[3] A Federal weatherization program is profiled in Energy Section, p. 187.

[4] For a discussion of ratemaking and the regulatory process, see chapter "Overview" beginning on p. 260.

[5] A utility-sponsored conservation program is profiled in Energy Section, p. 191.

* State and/or local government agencies are frequently responsible for administration of Federal program funds. For further information, see Appendix I under appropriate Federal agency.

NOTE: For a complete listing of groups featured throughout this book, see Index.

Utility Glossary

Automatic Fuel Adjustment Clause: A rate provision which allows a utility to quickly pass through to consumers changes in fuel costs. Usually, a utility uses a fuel adjustment clause to recover the difference between a pre-established fuel price and the price actually paid for fuel used to generate electricity during a billing period.

Base Load: The basic demand for electricity from a utility system that will always be present during the period of lowest electricity usage.

Base-Load Plant: A generating plant that is designed to run nonstop and is intended to meet the basic demand on the system—the base load. Base-load plants are usually the most efficient facilities and operate on the least expensive fuel.

Construction Work in Progress (CWIP): An accounting device that allows utilities to base rates on the costs, including the stock dividends, of construction projects underway.

Declining Block Rate: A rate design that charges less per additional kilowatt hour as usage increases.

Demand: The amount of electricity required by the customers of a utility at any given time.

Federal Energy Regulatory Commission (FERC): The Federal agency that has jurisdiction over wholesale and interstate power sales. FERC is the Federal counterpart of the state public utility commissions (PUCs) but does not have jurisdiction to set rates charged to consumers. Rather, FERC sets only those rates one utility charges another.

Inverted Rate: A rate design that charges more per additional kilowatt hour as usage increases.

Lifeline Rate: A set low-cost rate charged to all residential consumers for the minimum amount of electricity needed to meet life's necessities.

Load Management: The techniques used to shift the demand for electricity from peak to off-peak periods. By flattening the peaks in a system, a utility can avoid the need to put more expensive generating units into service and/or build new facilities. (See "Non-Peak Period" and "Peak Period.")

Non-Peak Period: Those times during the day, usually late evening and early morning hours, when customers demand the least electricity and costs of producing electricity are lowest.

Operating Expenses: The day-to-day expenses of operating a utility such as wages, rent, taxes and employee benefits.

Overall Revenue Requirement: The total cash requirement of a utility is determined by multiplying the amount of money a utility has invested in its business (rate base) by the amount of profit a utility is permitted to earn (rate of return) and then adding that figure to the utility's operating expenses. The regulatory commission applies the overall revenue requirement when determining what the cost of a kilowatt hour of electricity will be for each class of customer (rate structure).

Peak Period: Those times when electricity is in the greatest demand. The greater the peak, the more generating units a utility must put into service. Units used to meet peak demand must be turned on and off quickly, since peak demand is not constant. They are generally oil-fired rather than coal-fired, since oil-fired units heat faster. Because oil is more expensive and less plentiful than coal, peaking units are more expensive to operate than base-load units, and it is therefore more expensive to generate electricity at peak than non-peak times.

Public Utility Regulatory Policies Act (PURPA): An Act administered by the Department of Energy (DOE) which establishes service and rate standards that must be considered by large utilities and state commissions. The Act also provides for expense reimbursement to consumers who participate at hearings concerning these standards if: the state commission adopts the positions consumers advocate in the hearings; consumers have no other way to fund such participation; and the state provides no other way for consumer interests to be represented in the hearings.

Rate Base: The amount of money a company has invested in its utility business. It consists of some measure of the value of the company's land, generating plants, transmission lines, buildings, and other equipment required to produce and sell electricity.

Rate of Return: The amount of profit a utility is permitted to earn.

Rate Structure: The schedule of charges for each class of utility customer which is designed to produce the company's overall revenue requirement.

State Public Utility Commission (PUC): Each state has its own name for the body that regulates utility rates. The purpose of the regulatory commission is to set the rates charged to consumers. Also, the commissions typically have jurisdiction over service quality and cutoffs.

Time-of-Day Rates: A rate based on the cost of providing electricity at different times of the day. For example, it is usually more expensive for utilities to generate electricity at midday, when demand peaks. Therefore, electricity used during that time would be more expensive than electricity used in the middle of the night. These rates are sometimes called "peak load prices" because the rates vary as demand for electricity increases to a peak and then decreases.

Energy Glossary

Absorber: A generally black painted matte surface in a solar collector used to absorb the sun's rays.

Active Solar Energy System: Any solar system that needs mechanical power, such as fans, pumps and blowers, to operate.

Adobe: A sun-dried, unburned brick of earthen clay used in constructing houses and buildings.

Alternative Energy Resources: Sources of power derived from the wind, sun and water rather than from "conventional" sources such as oil, coal and natural gas.

Appropriate Technology: Solving technological problems by building, maintaining and operating relatively small, inexpensive systems which are protective of human health, use renewable sources of energy, encourage human-scale operations and do not need high energy concentrations.

Auxiliary Heat: The heat that a conventional heating system provides to supplement a solar heating system during periods of cloudiness or intense cold.

Biomass Energy: A composition of living material (usually plants) and organic wastes used to produce heat, fuel or electricity.

Breadbox Collector: A simple solar device used to heat water for bathing and cooking.

Caulking: A putty-like material used to fill cracks around windows and doors to make an airtight seal.

Composting: The process of turning decomposed vegetables, manure and other organic material into a rich mixture (humus) used to fertilize and condition the soil.

Cover Plate: A sheet of glass or transparent plastic placed above the absorber to help prevent heat loss in a solar collector (commonly referred to as one type of glazing material).

Flat Plate Collector: A plane surface solar collector in which direct or indirect sunlight is converted into heat without the aid of reflecting surfaces.

Gasahol: A liquid fuel mixture of 90 percent gasoline and 10 percent alcohol. The alcohol is made from organic wastes or grains.

Glazing: A covering of transparent or translucent material (glass or plastic) which admits light and acts as a heat trap. (The result is referred to as the greenhouse effect.)

Hybrid Solar Energy System: A solar system which uses some mechanical device, such as a fan, to move collected heat into the space which is to be heated.

Insulation: Any material or system which prevents heat or cooling loss.

Heat Storage: A device that absorbs collected heat and stores it for use at night or during rainy or cloudy days.

Nonrenewable Resources: Sources of energy in limited or finite supply such as uranium, coal, oil and natural gas.

Passive Solar Energy System: A solar system designed and situated to capture and distribute the sun's energy without mechanical help. An example would be a building with large windows on the south side to allow greatest penetration of the sun's rays.

Photovoltaics: Thin wafer-like cells which directly convert sunlight into electricity.

Organic Matter: Living matter (such as plants) and its wastes (such as dead leaves, banana peels or manure).

R Factor: A unit of thermal resistence used to compare materials such as insulation. The higher the R factor (between one and 50), the greater the material's capacity to insulate.

Recycling: The process of reusing natural or manmade substances such as glass, water, aluminum or paper.

Renewable Resources: Sources of power in unlimited supply such as wind, water and sun.

Retrofitting: Installing a solar system in a building which was not designed or built to include that type of system.

Solar Collector: A device used to collect the sun's rays, which are then converted into energy (also referred to as a solar panel). Collectors range from simple window units to complex mechanical devices.

Solar Crop Dryer: A crop dryer that uses a passive or active solar system to dry grains.

Solar Greenhouse: A building in which vegetables, plants and fruits are grown. The building is covered with glass or plastic to allow the sun to penetrate and provide needed heat. A passive or active solar greenhouse attached to a house or building can also provide heat for the adjoining structure.

Solar Hot Water Unit: A solar collector that captures the sun's energy to heat water.

Solar Oven: A cooking device that uses metallic wings to reflect sunlight through a double glass cover into an insulated and blackened box. If the oven is pointed toward the sun during midday hours, temperatures can reach 350–400°F—adequate for most baking.

Solar Panel: See Solar Collector.

Solar Window Box Collector: A device made from a wooden box, black-painted plywood and a glass top and designed to capture the sun's rays. The collector fits into a window and usually provides heat for only one room.

Synfuels: The industrial conversion of minerals (such as coal and oil shale) into gaseous or liquid fuels.

Vertical Wall Solar Collector (North Collector): One type of passive solar collector built with scrap materials (such as plywood, metal and plastic) and usually attached to the south wall of a building. This unit generally provides only daytime heat and has no storage capacity.

Weatherization: An all encompassing term which refers to the process of making a structure as resistant to the elements as possible through such methods as weatherstripping, caulking or installing storm windows.

Weatherstripping: Strips of thin metal or other material placed around windows and doors to prevent air and moisture from entering a structure.

Windpower: Energy derived from the wind and used to generate electricity or operate machinery.

Woodburning Stove: A heavy metal stove which burns wood for heating and cooking.

Energy Resources

The following resources contain descriptions of organizations and publications which can be of help to consumer groups across the country that wish to organize and launch community projects designed to combat high prices.

Those organizations offering assistance in a variety of areas are listed under "General" and are followed by a list of publications under the same heading. Other organizations and publications that provide help in specific areas are listed under corresponding chapter title headings.

Of course, it is not possible to list every organization and publication in the country that might prove helpful to you and your group, but we believe those we do mention are representative of the various kinds of assistance available. Chances are you'll hear of many other useful resources as you become involved in your own community project.

Space limitations made it extremely difficult to choose among the many fine groups considered, and we sincerely hope we haven't offended the many deserving organizations and/or authors of useful publications that have not been included.

General Energy

Organizations

Cascadian Regional Library
1 West Fifth Street
Box 1492
Eugene, Oregon 97440
(503) 485-0366

Information network on energy and environmental issues. Publishes *Cascade, Journal of the Northwest,* which updates energy issues and policy planning in the Northwest. (10 issues/year, $10.)

Center for Community Economic Development
639 Massachusetts Avenue
Cambridge, Massachusetts 02139
(617) 547-9695

Assists with energy-related demonstration and economic development projects. Publishes reports, case studies and other materials.

Center for Neighborhood Technology
570 West Randolph Street
Chicago, Illinois 60606
(312) 454-0126

Provides technical assistance in energy, urban agriculture, solar greenhouses, waste recycling and training. Publishes bimonthly magazine, *The Neighborhood Works,* which discusses alternative technology in neighborhood development. ($25/year.)

Citizen/Labor Energy Coalition
600 West Fullerton Street
Chicago, Illinois 60614
(312) 975-3680

National grassroots coalition of labor, community and public interest groups advocating the consumer's interest on a variety of energy issues. Responsible for national and regional campaigns concerned with utility reform, ways to lower energy prices, equitable distribution of gas and oil supplies to low-income and elderly residents and antitrust issues. Has six regional offices. Produces legislative and educational reports/studies on energy issues. Serves as clearinghouse.

Conference on Alternative State and Local Policies Energy Project
2000 Florida Avenue, N.W., Fourth Floor
Washington, D.C. 20009
(202) 387-6030

Network of local public officials, public policy analysts and community leaders. Focuses primarily on state and local legislation to create jobs through alternative energy sources and energy conservation. Bimonthly newsletter, *Ways and Means,* focuses on innovative state and local policies, including energy issues. ($10/year.)

The Conservation Foundation
1717 Massachusetts Avenue, N.W.
Washington, D.C. 20036
(202) 797-4300

Involved in numerous issues (land use, water quality, energy conservation, etc.) to encourage proper management of earth's resources. Sponsors conferences, films, speakers and consultant services and produces conservation publications. Publishes monthly newsletter, *Conservation Foundation Letter,* which updates organization activities. ($10/year.)

Consumer Energy Council of America
1990 M Street, N.W., Suite 620
Washington, D.C. 20036
(202) 659-0404

Broad-based coalition of consumer, labor, farm, public policy, rural electric cooperatives and urban and senior citizen organizations advocating the consumer's interest in national energy policy through research and lobby efforts.

Energy Action Committee
1523 L Street, N.W., Suite 302
Washington, D.C. 20005
(202) 737-6220

A nonprofit public interest organization which monitors government and industry activities in the energy field.

Environmentalists for Full Employment
1536 16th Street, N.W.
Washington, D.C. 20036
(202) 347-5590

Provides research and publications on the employment impact of national energy and environmental policies.

Environmental Law Institute
1346 Connecticut Avenue, N.W., Suite 600
Washington, D.C. 20036
(202) 452-9600

Does research and conducts educational programs on institutional and legal issues affecting the environment.

Environmental Policy Center
317 Pennsylvania Avenue, S.E.
Washington, D.C. 20003
(202) 547-6500

Works to promote energy conservation, renewable energy resources, diverse decentralized energy production systems and to reform nuclear licensing procedures, Federal radiation standards and waste disposal policies. Specializes in representing broad-based citizen coalitions before Congress and the Executive Branch.

Friends of the Earth
124 Spear Street
San Francisco, California 94105
(415) 495-4770

National public interest group advocating environmental safety through lobbying, litigation, public education and other means. Focuses on such issues as fossil fuels, stripmining, clean air and soft energy issues. Publishes monthly magazine, *Not Man Apart,* which covers a wide range of energy and environmental issues. ($15/year.)

Institute for Local Self-Reliance
1717 18th Street, N.W.
Washington, D.C. 20009
(202) 232-4108

Offers research, demonstration and consulting services on technical feasibility of community self-reliance in high density living areas. Publishes bimonthly newsletter, *Self Reliance,* which covers energy and other issues. ($8/year.)

National Association of Farmworker Organizations
1332 New York Avenue, N.W.
Washington, D.C. 20005
(202) 347-2407

National coalition of organizations advocating farmworker rights and concerns. Sponsors programs on energy crisis assistance, housing and education. Publishes monthly newsletter, *National Farmworker,* which covers a variety of topics concerning farmworker rights and welfare; available in English or Spanish. ($15/year.)

National Center for Appropriate Technology
P.O. Box 3838
Butte, Montana 59701
(406) 494-4577

Offers technical assistance, scientific and technological research, small grants and information to primarily low-income groups working with appropriate technology and self-help projects in areas such as food, housing and energy. Publishes monthly, *AT Times.* ($10/year to individuals, free to organizations working with and for the poor.)

Natural Resources Defense Council
1725 Eye Street N.W., Suite 600
Washington, D.C. 20006
(202) 223-8210

Involved with research and litigation in water and air quality, land use and energy issues. Publishes quarterly newsletter, *Amicus,* which updates activities and covers a variety of energy topics. (Free.)

Northern Plains Resources Council
Room 419 Stapleton Building
Billings, Montana 59101
(406) 248-1154

Citizen agricultural group concerned with conservation, renewable resources, energy efficiency and land owners' rights. Involved with research, education and advocacy on energy and mineral development issues. Membership ($15/year) includes subscription to monthly magazine, *The Plains Truth,* which covers energy and other issues.

Office of Appropriate Technology
1530 10th Street
Sacramento, California 95814
(916) 445-1803

Agency of the California state government; promotes appropriate technology by providing workshops, seminars, information referrals and responses to public inquiries. Publishes bimonthly, *The Grants Newsletter,* which lists funding resources and grants for appropriate technology. (Free.)

Public Resource Center
1747 Connecticut Avenue, N.W.
Washington, D.C. 20009
(202) 483-7040

Concerned with research and education on alternative energy, health, appropriate technology and environmental policy. Publishes newsletter, *The Elements,* covering alternative energy and resource issues. (9 issues/year, $15.)

Rural America
1346 Connecticut Avenue, N.W.
Washington, D.C. 20036
(202) 659-2800

Represents people in small towns and rural areas to help them with energy, housing and health problems. Publishes monthly newsletter, *Monitor* (free to members); monthly newspaper, *Rural America* ($10/year); and monthly newsletter, *RHA* (Rural Housing Alliance) *Reporter* (free to members).

Scientists' Institute for Public Information (SIPI)
355 Lexington Avenue
New York, New York 10017
(212) 661-9110

Researches a broad range of energy issues. Reports on completed research are disseminated to the public and policymakers in an effort to contribute to the development of a sound national energy policy. Membership ($25/year) includes monthly, *Environment,* and bimonthly newsletter, *SIPIscope,* which covers a variety of current energy issues.

Sierra Club
330 Pennsylvania Avenue, S.E.
Washington, D.C. 20003
(202) 547-1141

Lobbies on issues such as forestry, wilderness, water quality, energy, offshore energy development, urban recreation, toxic substances and hazardous waste. Newsletter, *National News Report,* covers legislation dealing with energy issues. ($12/year; published every week Congress is in session, approximately 45 times a year.)

Tennessee Valley Authority
400 Commerce Avenue
Knoxville, Tennessee 37902
(615) 632-3257

Government-owned corporation that conducts programs of resource development for the advancement of economic growth in the Tennessee Valley region. In cooperation with other agencies, conducts research and development programs in energy conservation and management, forestry, watershed protection and economic development of Tennessee Valley tributary areas through citizen associations. Supplies power for local municipal cooperative electric systems serving seven states.

Urban Environment Conference
1302 18th Street, N.W.
Washington, D.C. 20036
(202) 466-6040

Coalition of lobbying organizations. Sponsors conferences and publications on issues relevant to urban environmental health and safety.

Publications

Boasberg, Tersh and Feldesman, James L., ***Coping With the Energy Crisis.*** Consumer Energy Council of America, 1990 M Street, N.W., Suite 620, Washington, D.C. 20036. 1974. (Free.) Provides detailed information on Federal energy regulations, especially those relating to heating fuels. Geared to community groups and voluntary organizations, with primary focus on the impact of the energy shortage on the poor.

Energy Efficient Planning: An Annotated Bibliography. American Planning Association, 1313 East 60th Street, Chicago, Illinois 60637. 1976. ($5.) Comprehensive listing of books and reports dealing with energy efficiency; includes prices and other order information.

Energy and Rural People and Agriculture. Rural America, 1346 Connecticut Avenue, N.W., Washington, D.C. 20036. 1975. (75 cents.) Describes how and why rural people have become dependent upon the petrochemical industry. Suggests means of making better use of existing energy sources and ways of developing alternatives.

New Roots. P.O. Box 548, 1 Osgood Street, Greenfield, Massachusetts 01301. Published bimonthly ($8/year to individuals, $12 to institutions.) Covers the movement toward self-reliance in the Northeast. Includes broad range of topics such as energy, waste recycling, food cooperatives, etc.

Rainbook: Resources for Appropriate Technology. Schocker Books, 200 Madison Avenue, New York, New York 10016. 1977. ($7.95 paperback, $15 hardcover.) Compendium of resources giving options and choices through appropriate technology. Covers energy, food, housing, and health.

Rain: The Journal of Appropriate Technology. Rain Magazine, 2270 Northwest Irving, Portland, Oregon 97210. Ten issues per year. ($15.) Geared to individuals and groups wishing to make their communities self-reliant. Covers many topics in addition to energy; e.g., housing, food.

Conserving Energy and Using Renewable Sources of Energy

Organizations

Alternative Energy Resources Organization (AERO)
435 Stapleton Building
Billings, Montana 59101
(406) 259-1958

Provides education on energy conservation and renewable energy resources. Offers workshops, tips on local organizing, demonstrations and programs for school curricula. Bimonthly newsletter, *AERO Sun-Times,* updates energy conservation issues. ($12/year.)

Arizona Community Action Association
2721 North Central Avenue, Suite 707
Phoenix, Arizona 85004
(602) 252-6067

Involved with interests of low-income consumers. Works with Community Action Agencies on solar construction and other energy alternatives. Sponsors demonstration projects, speakers and workshops. Offers studies, consultant services and publications on energy issues. Publishes monthly newsletter, *Call to Action,* which probes a wide range of energy topics. (Free.)

Center for Renewable Resources
1001 Connecticut Avenue, N.W.
Washington, D.C. 20036
(202) 466-6880

Conducts policy research, provides consumer information and offers technical assistance to those interested in renewable energy resources. Maintains a large variety of resources on energy education in the areas of conservation and renewable resources. Publishes monthly newsletter, *Sun Times,* which contains information on solar energy issues and related topics. ($15/year.)

Center for Rural Affairs
Small Farm Energy Project
P.O. Box 736
Hartington, Nebraska 68739
(402) 254-6893

Conducts research on energy alternatives for small farmers. Offers publications, farm tours, slide presentations and workshops. Publishes bimonthly, *The Small Farm Energy Project Newsletter,* which updates organization activities. (Free.)

Citizens' Energy Project
1413 K Street, N.W., Eighth Floor
Washington, D.C. 20005
(202) 387-7998

Serves as information clearinghouse for Mid-Atlantic states on conservation, solar and other appropriate technologies. Provides networking, speakers, reports and publications.

Community Action Research of Iowa, Inc.
P.O. Box 1232
Ames, Iowa 50010
(515) 292-4758

Does research on energy alternatives for the Midwest. Involved with litigation, legislation, research. Advises citizen groups. Publishes bimonthly newsletter, *New Criteria,* which reports on appropriate technology issues. ($8.50/year.)

Consumer Action Now, Inc. (C.A.N.)
355 Lexington Avenue
New York, New York 10017
(212) 682-8915

Advocates energy conservation and promotes the use of clean, renewable energy resources. Carries out an active program of public education to focus national attention on the practicality of solar energy. Produces information packages and several publications, including quarterly newsletter, *C.A.N. Report.* (Free to members.)

Ecotope Group
2332 East Madison
Seattle, Washington 98112
(206) 322-3753

Involved in application of appropriate technology, bioconversion, solar design and research. Provides networking, library demonstration projects, workshops and training services, feasibility studies, consultant services and publications. Publishes quarterly newsletter (jointly with the Pacific Northwest Solar Energy Association), *Sunstrokes.* ($15/year.)

Energy Design Team
30 Mystic Street
Charlestown, Massachusetts 02129
(617) 242-0162

Engineers and architects involved in energy efficient design and construction. Provides energy audits, cost/benefit analyses, consultant services, workshops and design studies on conservation and low-cost alternative technologies.

Energy Task Force
156 Fifth Avenue
New York, New York 10010
(212) 675-1920

Involved with energy conservation, solar and wind energy for low-income residents of New York. Provides consulting services, demonstration projects, workshops, training and publications.

Environmental Action of Colorado
P.O. Box 545
La Veta, Colorado 81055
(303) 742-3221

Publishes energy materials including *EARS* (Environmental Action Reprint Service), a solar and nuclear energy information catalog. (Free.)

Farallones Institute
1516 Fifth Street
Berkeley, California 94710
(415) 525-1150

Public education and research organization demonstrating feasibility of alternative energy and self-sufficiency. Sponsors educational programs, demonstration projects and tours. Provides an outreach consultant service on alternative energy design and construction. Publishes an *Annual Report* containing a comprehensive review of the Institute's activities. ($3.)

Max-Pot, The Center for Maximum Potential Building Systems
8604 Farm to Market Road 969
Austin, Texas 78724
(512) 928-4786

Works with passive and active solar systems. Focus is on small scale energy systems which require little expertise to build. Provides publications, lectures, workshops, exhibits and consultation services.

National Solar Heating and Cooling Information Center
P.O. Box 1607
Rockville, Maryland 20850
(800) 523-2929 (Toll-free)

Information center designed to promote the practical feasibility of solar energy and to encourage solar energy systems for homes and commercial buildings. Clearinghouse for those seeking speakers, exhibits and other solar energy services.

New Alchemy Institute
P.O. Box 47
Woods Hole, Massachusetts 02543
(617) 563-2665

Nonprofit research institute working on solar energy, aquaculture and gardening. Provides workshops, demonstration projects and publications. Open to the public for tours between May and September of each year. Publishes quarterly, *New Alchemy Newsletter.* (Free to members.)

New Life Farm, Inc.
Drury, Missouri 65638
(417) 261-2553

Educational and research group which furthers individual and community self-reliance through regionally based food production and efficient, low cost, renewable energy technology. Conducts research on methane digestion, alternative waste disposal, solar energy, etc.

New Mexico Solar Energy Association
P.O. Box 2004
Santa Fe, New Mexico 87501
(505) 983-2861

Dedicated to furthering solar energy and related topics. Provides solar design and construction services, technical assistance, public speakers, educational programs and other services on solar energy. Membership ($15/year) includes subscription to monthly magazine, *Southwest Bulletin.*

Shelter Institute
38 Center Street
Bath, Maine 04530
(207) 442-7938

Conducts three-week course for people interested in learning to build their own homes utilizing passive solar principles. Carries large line of energy-saving devices and books; list available free of charge.

Solar Energy Institute of America
1110 Sixth Street, N.W.
Washington, D.C. 20001
(202) 667-6611

Information source for architects, engineers, contractors, manufacturers, etc. Provides literature, audiovisual presentations, speakers and other services. Monthly newsletter, *Solar Life,* updates topics in solar energy. ($15/year.)

Solar Energy Research Institute
1617 Cole Boulevard
Golden, Colorado 80401
(303) 231-1190

Created by an Act of Congress in 1974 to provide leadership for the nation's solar energy program. Performs research and development in solar energy technology as part of national energy planning. Seeks to foster the widespread use of solar energy hardware. Assists the Federal government in formulating energy strategy and policy. Publishes monthly newsletter, *In Review*, which reports on the Institute's activities. (Free.)

SUN-REP
3110 Maple Drive, Suite 412
Atlanta, Georgia 30305
(404) 261-1764

Engaged in renewable energy projects in the South for individuals, state and local organizations. Bimonthly, *SUN-REP News*, probes appropriate technology topics and solar energy issues. (Free.)

Total Environmental Action, Inc.
Church Hill
Harrisville, New Hampshire 03450
(603) 827-3374

Offers engineering, design and consulting, research and education services on energy conservation as well as solar, wind and other energy alternatives. Offers workshops, training programs and many publications.

The Department of Energy has set up four regional information centers to disseminate information on solar energy. Newsletters available at no cost.

Mid-America Solar Energy Center (MASEC)
8140 26th Avenue, South
Bloomington, Minnesota 55420
(612) 853-0400

Newsletter: *MASEC News*

Northeast Solar Energy Center
7 Memorial Drive
Cambridge, Massachusetts 02142
(617) 661-3500

Newsletter: *The Update*

Southern Solar Energy Center (SSEC)
61 Primeter Park
Atlanta, Georgia 30341
(404) 458-8765

Newsletter: *SSEC News*

Western Sun
Pioneer Park Building
715 Southwest Morrison
Portland, Oregon 97204
(503) 241-1222

No newsletter

Publications

Alternative Sources of Energy Magazine. Alternative Sources of Energy, Inc., 107 South Central Avenue, Milaca, Minnesota 56353. Bimonthly. ($15/year to individuals, $20 to institutions.) Articles emphasize the exploration and innovative use of renewable energy sources. Columns written by experts and innovators in alternative energy fields.

Bio Times. International Biomass Institute, 1522 K Street, N.W., Suite 600, Washington, D.C. 20005. Bimonthly. ($10/year to individuals, $25 to institutions.) Features articles and updates on energy systems from biomass and other renewable energy resources. Explores agricultural practices which minimize adverse environmental consequences.

Citizen Energy Directory. Citizens Energy Project, 1413 K Street, N.W., Washington, D.C. 20005. 1980. ($10.) Contains 600 profiles of various solar energy organizations and businesses which can answer consumers' questions about solar energy.

Compendium of Federal Programs Related to Community Energy Conservation. Department of Housing and Urban Development, Publications Service Center, Room B–258, 451 Seventh Street, S.W., Washington, D.C. 20410. 1979. (Free.) Listing of Federal resources available to community groups wishing to conserve energy in various projects such as neighborhood development and revitalization, consumer protection and appropriate technology. Designed to introduce leaders of community groups to basic energy conservation techniques.

Federal Conservation and Renewable Energy Resource Directory. Department of Energy, Office of Consumer Affairs, Washington, D.C. 20545. 1980. (Free.) Provides information to consumer groups related to conservation and renewable energy. Offers a brief description of programs within the Department of Energy.

Grier, Eunice S., ***Colder . . . Darker: The Energy Crisis and Low-Income Americans.*** Community Services Administration, 1200 19th Street, N.W., Room 571, Washington, D.C. 20506. 1977. (Free.) Detailed study of the impact of the energy crisis on low-income citizens and the implications for future policy and programs of the Federal government. Covers energy use by low-income persons in their homes and in their personal travel.

Hayes, Denis, ***Rays of Hope: Transition to a Post-Petroleum World.*** W. W. Norton Company, 500 Fifth Avenue, New York, New York 10036. 1977. ($3.95.) Examines potential energy sources from historical and global perspectives. Discusses energy commitment for food production, transportation, housing and economic growth. Emphasizes a switch from fossil fuels to renewable resources (solar, wind, water and biomass).

The Integral Urban House: Self-Reliant Living in the City. Farallones Institute, 1516 Fifth Street, Berkeley, California 94710. 1979. ($14.50.) Provides detailed information on the application of appropriate technology in urban dwellings. Uses the Integral Urban House in Berkeley, California as a model, but stresses the fact that basic principles may be applied in any location. Many sketches, drawings, tables and charts as well as background information.

The Low-Cost Solar Collector. San Luis Valley Solar Energy Association, 512 Ross, Alamosa, Colorado 81101. 1979. ($2.30.) Booklet which provides details of designing, building and using a "north collector" (vertical forced-air solar collector). Includes complete information on installation, insulation required, etc.

NCRT Bulletin. National Center for Resource Technology, 1211 Connecticut Avenue, N.W., Washington, D.C. 20036. Quarterly journal. ($8/year to individuals, $12 to institutions.) Probes various aspects of resource recovery for professionals and laypeople. Articles include topics on recoverable materials, appropriate technology, operating facilities and resource recovery planning.

No Heat, No Rent: An Urban Solar & Energy Conservation Manual. Energy Task Force, 156 Fifth Avenue, New York, New York 10009. 1977. (Free.) Guide to developing, installing and maintaining a tenant-owned solar hot water system for tenement buildings. Also serves as an introduction to energy conservation techniques for use in such buildings.

Outlook. Governors State University, Park Forest South, Illinois 60466. Monthly magazine. ($10/year.) Updates activities in appropriate technology, alternative energy sources and community planning and policy. Contains information on employment openings, grants and programs in alternative energy. Also includes a calendar of events across the country (workshops, conventions, conferences) concerned with alternative energy topics.

"The Power to Change." Third Eye Films, 12 Arrow Street, Cambridge, Massachusetts 02138. 1980. (May be rented for $40 plus $5 shipping or purchased for $425.) A 38 minute, 16 mm color film. Introduces basic concepts of appropriate technology. Demonstrates alternatives to traditional patterns of production, distribution and energy use. Focuses on existing working projects around the United States including urban composting, rural solar energy and wind-powered automobiles.

Reaching Up, Reaching Out: A Guide to Organizing Local Solar Events. Solar Energy Research Institute, 1617 Cole Boulevard, Golden, Colorado 80401. 1979. Sponsored by the Department of Energy and available for purchase only from the Superintendent of Documents, U.S. Government Printing Office, Washington D.C. 20402. (Document number 061-000-00345-2, $8.50.) Presents 15 case studies of successful solar and energy conservation activities, including organizing information and a resource listing.

Solar Age. Solar Age Magazine, Church Hill, Harrisville, New Hampshire 03450. Monthly. ($20/year.) Official publication of the International Solar Energy Society. Covers a wide variety of topics on solar energy.

Solar Energy Books. National Solar Energy Education Campaign, 10762 Tucker Street, Beltsville, Maryland 20705. 1977. ($4.50.) Catalog of books on solar energy and related subjects with brief descriptions. Books are listed by type (general, engineering, policy, etc.).

"Solar Energy—The Great Adventure." Department of Energy Film Library, Technical Information Center, P.O. Box 62, Oakridge, Tennessee 37830. 1978. (May be rented free or purchased for $178.75.) A 27½ minute, 16 mm award winning, color, sound film. Features a cross section of innovative urban and rural groups who developed their own solar energy systems.

Solar Engineering Magazine. Circulation Fulfillment Services, 26 Court Street, Brooklyn, New York 11201. Monthly. (Free to members; others, $20/year or $2.50 an issue.) Official trade magazine of the Solar Energy Industries Association. Updates applications of solar energy systems and solar products. Includes government and professional association activities as they relate to solar and energy conservation.

Solar Heating and Cooling. Gordon Publications, P.O. Box 2126-R, Morristown, New Jersey 07960. Monthly industry news tabloid. ($15/year.) Deals with solar energy and alternative energy resource issues.

The Solar Survey. National Center for Appropriate Technology, P.O. Box 3838, Butte, Montana 59701. 1979. (First copy, free, 75 cents for each additional copy.) A composite of solar design projects. Includes description, contact person, follow-up comments and location of about 25 projects.

Stobauch, Robert and Yergin, Daniel (eds.), ***Energy Future: Report of the Energy Project at the Harvard Business School,*** Random House, Inc., New York, New York 10022. 1979. ($12.95.) By employing the business approach to the issue of energy, the report provides indepth study of both the history and future of various types of conventional and alternative energy. Makes recommendations on a future course of action which encompasses a combination of massive conservation and use of solar energy. Indepth resources and well-documented findings.

Sun Up Energy News Digest. J. Harrington and Associates, 55888 Yucca Trail, P.O. Drawer S, Yucca Valley, California 92284. Monthly newsletter. ($6.50/year.) Probes solar and alternative energy activities.

Windmill Power For City People. Energy Task Force, 156 Fifth Avenue, New York, New York 10010. 1977. (Free.) Complete documentation of the first urban wind energy system. Detailed report on the design and installation of an electricity generating windmill on a tenement building in New York City.

Wind Power Digest. 109 East Lexington, Elkhart, Indiana 46514. Quarterly. ($8/year.) Deals with issues concerning wind and other alternative energy resources.

NOTE: Also see Energy Resources under "General."

Educating the Public on Energy

Organizations

Cornerstones
54 Cumberland Street
Brunswick, Maine 04011
(207) 729-0540

Prepares comprehensive solar education curriculum for vocational technology and adult education programs. Conducts workshops and courses in passive solar design and construction, retrofitting and solar greenhouse design. Published a two-volume energy curriculum, *Solar Concepts,* 1979, ($13). Also, two textbooks: *From the Ground Up,* 1976, ($7.95); and *From the Walls In,* 1979, ($9.95).

Domestic Technology Institute
Box 2043
Evergreen, Colorado 80439
(303) 674-1597

Conducts workshops on rural solar greenhouse design/construction, community energy technology, small scale food production, nutrition and food preservation.

Maine Audubon Society
118 U.S. Route 1
Falmouth, Maine 04105
(207) 781-2330

Active in energy curriculum design. Prepares science and energy packets for secondary and vocational high schools. Publishes monthly newsletter, *Maine Audubon News,* which covers a wide range of environmental issues. ($25/year.)

National Science Teacher Association
1742 Connecticut Avenue, N.W.
Washington, D.C. 20009
(202) 265-4150

Prepared a series of 19 fact sheets on alternative energy technology for use in elementary and secondary school science classes. Fact sheets and other energy-related publications are available from the Department of Energy, Technical Information Center, P.O. Box 62, Oak Ridge, Tennessee 37830. (Free.)

Solar Sustenance Team
Route 1, Box 107 AA
Santa Fe, New Mexico 87501
(505) 471-1535

Involved with the design and construction of solar greenhouses. Offers training to others on how to conduct solar greenhouse workshops. Publishes many materials.

Publications

Morris, David and Friend, Gil, ***Kilowatt Counter.*** Institute for Local Self-Reliance, 1717 18th Street, N.W., Washington, D.C. 20009. 1975. ($2.) Consumer guide to energy concepts, quantities and uses. Explains how consumers can calculate energy usage and solve related problems. Includes formulas, conversion tables, sample problems, etc.

Norton, Thomas, ***Solar Energy Experiments for High School and College Students.*** Rodale Press, Emmaus, Pennsylvania 18049. 1977. ($5.95.) Compilation of experiments designed to acquaint students with solar energy measurement, collection and use. Designed to help students gain an appreciation of problems and possibilities associated with solar energy.

Terry, Mark and Witt, Paul, ***Energy and Order: A High School Teaching Sequence.*** Friends of the Earth, 124 Spear Street, San Francisco, California 14105. 1976. ($3.) Teachers' guide for junior and senior high school courses on energy and its relationship to social issues. Includes classroom experiments and projects designed to encourage students' awareness of energy's importance.

The following publications are available from the Center for Renewable Resources, 1001 Connecticut Avenue, N.W., Fifth Floor, Washington, D.C. 20036:

Solar Energy Education Bibliography for Elementary, Secondary and College Students. 1979. ($2.90.) Reference guide to hundreds of solar publications and audiovisual materials selected for their value and adaptability in classrooms and workshops.

Solar Energy Education Packet for Elementary and Secondary Students. 1979. ($4.35.) Selection of solar activities, reading lessons and background materials about all forms of renewable resources (sun, wind, water, biomass). Over 25 simple solar projects for students. Includes bibliography.

NOTE: Also see Energy Resources under "General."

Providing Alternative Transportation

Organizations

Bikecentennial
P.O. Box 8303
Missoula, Montana 59807
(406) 721-1776

Membership organization providing a wide range of services to touring cyclists. Established the Trans America Bicycle Trail in 1976. Publishes bimonthly, *Bike-Report,* for members, plus other materials such as trail directories, bicycling tips, etc.

Commuter Computer
3440 Wilshire Boulevard, Suite 610
Los Angeles, California 90010
(213) 380-7433

Promotes ridesharing and carpooling; uses a computer to match drivers and riders. Assists larger companies in implementing ridesharing programs for their employees.

Commuter Connection
3020 Bridgeway Boulevard, Suite 106
Sausalito, California 94965
(415) 332-8333

Operates flexible ridesharing program (drivers and riders show "passports" which identify them as participants and signal their destinations). Provides advice and technical assistance to others wishing to start such a program.

National Association of Vanpool Operators
610 Ivystone Lane
Cinnaminson, New Jersey 08077
(609) 786-1414

Membership organization of about 300 vanpool operators. Lobbies to influence issues such as legal and insurance matters affecting vanpools. Bimonthly newsletter, *VAN.* (Free to members.)

National Rural Center
1828 L Street, N.W.
Washington, D.C. 20036
(202) 331-0258

Develops and advocates transportation policy alternatives relating to rural areas by conducting research and demonstration programs. Evaluates Federal programs and monitors national legislation and program regulations. Provides information services and publications, including the monthly, *Rural Public Transportation Newsletter.* (Free.)

The Walking Association
4113 Lee Highway
Arlington, Virginia 22207
(703) 527-5374

Promotes walking for health and energy saving. Lobbies for recognition of walkers' rights, pedestrian safety. Publishes at least four issues a year, *Walking Association Newsletter.* (Free to members, $8.50/year to nonmembers.)

Publications

Consumer Problems with Auto Repair. Consumer Information Center, Department 505H, Pueblo, Colorado 81009. 1978. (Free.) Gives tips on how to prevent automobile repair rip-offs. Prepared by the Department of Transportation.

Washington Consumers' Checkbook: Cars. Washington Center for the Study of Services, 1910 K Street, N.W., Suite 201, Washington, D.C. 20006. 1976. ($4.95.) Comprehensive guide to auto services in the metropolitan Washington, D.C. area. Serves as good example for others wishing to publish such a guide to auto repair prices, customer ratings, etc., in their communities.

The following publications are available from Rural America, 1346 Connecticut Avenue, N.W., Washington, D.C. 20036:

Mobility in Rural America. 1975. ($1.) Outlines need for adequate transportation system in rural areas. Probes some Federal experiments in rural transportation.

Rural Public Transportation. 1977. (30 cents.) Probes transportation problems of rural people. Suggests measures that could bring relief in addition to Federal efforts.

Rural Transportation. 1979. ($2.) Contains a proposal for solving rural transportation problems. Includes policy framework for a "rural transportation administration."

The following publications are available free from the Department of Transportation, Office of Public Affairs, Room 9421, 400 Seventh Street, S.W., Washington, D.C. 20590:

Community Ridesharing: A Leadership Role. 1979. Pamphlet designed to introduce community leaders and elected officials to the idea of ridesharing and where to go to get help in starting a program.

How Ridesharing Can Help Your Company. 1979. How-to manual for businesses seeking to start a ridesharing program for employees.

Ridesharing: An Easy Way to Save Gas and Money. 1979. Pamphlet for the individual who wants the facts on ridesharing and information on how to start a ridesharing program.

NOTE: Also see Energy Resources under "General."

Reforming Electric Utilities

Organizations

Association of Community Organizations for Reform Now (ACORN)
532 West 15th Street
Little Rock, Arkansas 72202
(501) 376-7151

Grassroots membership organization of low- and moderate-income people, with chapters in many states. Concerned with helping people deal with issues such as utility rates, housing costs, etc.

Environmental Action Foundation
Utilities Project
1346 Connecticut Avenue, N.W.
Washington, D.C. 20036
(202) 659-1130

Provides information and technical assistance on a broad range of utility issues. Funded by the Department of Energy's Office of Consumer Affairs to assist consumer groups that wish to be involved in state regulatory commission proceedings as mandated by the Public Utilities Regulatory Policy Act. Publishes monthly newsletter, *The Power Line,* designed to keep citizens abreast of current utility issues around the country. ($15/year for individuals, $25 for organizations.)

National Consumer Law Center
Energy Project
11 Beacon Street
Boston, Massachusetts 02108
(617) 523-8010

Represents the legal interests of low-income energy consumers. Provides legal, technical and policy advice as well as education and training to those advocating reforms benefiting low-income consumers. Publishes periodic bulletins to keep utility groups informed of new developments in utility policy.

National Rural Electric Cooperative Association
1800 Massachusetts Avenue, N.W.
Washington, D.C. 20036
(202) 857-9500

National association representing rural electric cooperatives. Publishes monthly magazine, *Rural Electrification,* which covers activities of rural electric cooperatives. ($9/year.)

Publications

The following publications are available from the Environmental Action Foundation, Utility Clearinghouse, 724 Dupont Circle Building, Washington, D.C. 20036:

How to Challenge Your Local Electric Utility. 1974. ($3.50.) Basic guide for citizens. Explains how utility rates are set, how utilities operate and ways citizens can challenge rate hikes, expansion plans, rate structures, etc.

Jerebek, Sandra, *A Citizen's Guide to the Fuel Adjustment Clause.* 1975. ($2.50; $15 for profit-making businesses.) A thorough examination of the abuses of the clause, formulas for restructuring it to prevent overcharges and strategies to limit its use.

The Power Line. Monthly newsletter. ($15/year; $7.50 lifeline subscription available to senior citizens and low-income persons; $50.00 for profit-making businesses; $25.00 institutional rate.) Designed to keep citizens abreast of current utility issues around the country. Reports on such topics as rate structure reform, rate increases and growth projections.

Ratepayer's Guide to PURPA. 1979. (Free.) Explains the Public Regulatory Policies Act (PURPA) and what it means for those concerned with rate structures, fuel adjustment clause abuses, etc. Suggests ways to obtain funding for involvement in the regulatory process.

The Rate Watchers Guide: How to Shape Up Your Utility Rate Structure. 1980. ($4.95.) An all purpose handbook for citizens seeking utility reform. Explains how utility rates are designed, lifelines, peak load, pricing, etc. Strategic advice to rate reform organizers.

NOTE: Also see Energy Resources under "General."

HEALTH CARE
IS
NO
LAUGHING
MATTER
HEALTH CARE
IS
NO
LAUGHING
MATTER
Cape Cod
Nursing
Home Council
We want
Access
SAVE
OUR
HOME
SAVE
OUR
HOME
SAVE
OUR
HOME
SAVE
Nutrition

Health

General Introduction

In the last 15 years medical costs have increased by 400 percent. In 1979 alone, the cost of health care for Americans totalled a staggering $200 billion.

Yet for a number of reasons, consumers have avoided efforts to blunt rising medical costs by tackling the health care system. For one reason, the cost of health care is often hidden. Most medical bills are paid by private or government insurers so many consumers don't feel the pinch of rising costs even though we all pay for them through higher medical insurance rates.

Also, until recently most local health planning organizations were funded—and controlled—by medical professionals rather than by medical users. Moreover, competition, which helps keep prices down and quality of service up, has been thwarted in the health field. For example, the stigma attached to advertising of fees by doctors has eased only recently.

Of course our traditional health care system does offer excellent care to millions of Americans. But it also has some drawbacks which help fuel escalating medical costs. These include an emphasis on curing illnesses rather than preventing them; a lack of citizen knowledge about self-care or health issues; and too little citizen participation in community health planning.

But thanks to the hard work of local groups across the country and the passage of a Federal law placing consumers squarely in the center of community health planning, things are beginning to change.

The efforts of the groups highlighted in this chapter prove that, by getting involved, consumers can have a major impact on the cost and quality of the health care they receive. We feature groups that have established pace-setting clinics and dynamic health education programs and have found scores of ways to bring health power and affordable medical services to their neighbors and communities.

All the groups in this section are inspiring reminders of how we can improve health care in our own communities. We hope you'll be able to learn from their experiences and utilize those methods that best suit the particular needs of your area and organization. But since most have limited resources, please enclose a self-addressed, stamped envelope when you contact them. Additional information on funding sources can be found in the Basic Tools and Resources Sections as well as in the Appendices.

As with other sections, we hope this does more than provide you with case studies. We hope these success stories of consumers effectively tackling high health care costs will inspire you to become involved.

Providing Alternative Health Care

Introduction

For many citizens, finding needed health services poses special problems. They might live in rural areas that lack medical facilities. They might need more attention and understanding than a quick visit to an overworked doctor can provide or they might not be able to afford medical treatment because of rising fees.

To combat these and other problems, an increasing number of enterprising groups are finding ways to bring lower cost alternative medical care to their neighbors.

In this chapter we review some exciting health care alternatives that complement the services of private doctors or big hospitals by treating citizens who are sometimes overlooked. The alternative health care outlets which we examine vary in size and reach different audiences, but they all fill a vacuum. One sure sign that their services are needed is the terrific community effort responsible for their creation.

We'll start by looking at one of the most successful prepaid health plans or Health Maintenance Organizations (HMOs) in the country.

Next we'll focus on a group that places special emphasis on those neglected by traditional medicine. We describe a free health clinic for financially strapped residents who are without private insurance and can't qualify for government medical assistance programs.

We then turn our attention to an economically depressed rural area of South Carolina where a group of determined citizens successfully tackled environmental and health problems and improved life for their neighbors. Their efforts brought nine medical centers and a host of new water and sewage systems to the area.

And we'll see how retirees in a semi-rural Florida area, weary of traveling miles for their health needs, built their own medical center.

Finally, we'll explain how some groups are focusing on the "wholistic" approach to medical care. It treats not only the symptoms but also the emotional problems that can lead to illness.

The success stories we feature in this chapter illustrate how consumers working together can successfully bring needed medical services to their communities. Launching these alternative health care programs required hard work, but the residents who have benefited from them know the efforts were well worth it.

Health Maintenance Organizations

Group Health Cooperative of Puget Sound
200 15th Avenue East
Seattle, Washington 98112
(206) 326-6262

During the last six months of 1979, Helen McManus, a 40-year resident of Seattle, Washington, experienced her share of bad luck. A victim of broken bones and a stroke, she was hospitalized three times for a total of 100 days. But there is a bright side to the picture. "I came away with no bills," she says. "Now that really means something!"

Some 275,000 residents of the Puget Sound area can tell you how McManus managed to leave the hospital without owing a hefty bill. They are all members of Group Health Cooperative of Puget Sound (GHC), one of the oldest of some 200 Health Maintenance Organizations (HMOs) in the country that offer consumers lower-cost, comprehensive health care for prepaid fees.

Her monthly GHC payment, which was $50 in 1979, entitles McManus to choose a family practitioner from among 289 GHC doctors and to use the services of 11 community medical clinics and two hospitals. Group Health Cooperative's full service includes lab tests, surgery, ambulance service and unlimited doctor visits.

"Relatives and friends recommended the prepaid program," says McManus, who joined Group Health Cooperative six years ago at age 64. "And it's right for me because I never know what's going to happen. With Group Health, I know where to go and what to do."

Not for Everybody

HMOs do have some drawbacks however. Members are limited to those physicians associated with the HMO. And unlike GHC, some HMO members aren't allowed to select their HMO physician. Moreover, when members travel outside the service area of most HMOs, only emergencies such as car accidents or heart attacks are covered under the plan.

Success Today

Nevertheless the prepaid health plan is catching on across the country as residents look for low-cost

A wide range of medical care is available at an HMO medical center.

health alternatives. And Group Health Cooperative, established in 1947, is one of the most successful and one of few that is cooperatively owned and governed by its members. In 1979 it boasted a $100 million budget and 3,500 nurses and other personnel who bolstered the core of doctors. But for the health consumer, GHC's success might best be measured in savings. A University of Washington study shows that GHC provides members with comprehensive health care and costs about one-third less than other health plans offering similar coverage.

Architect Charles Bergmann and his family joined Group Health Cooperative soon after he moved to Seattle in 1968. "We had one child and another was on the way," he explains. "I had looked into insurance plans and, for a family, GHC made a lot more sense."

In 1979 his six-member family received medical care for about $119 a month. And Bergmann adds, "There aren't the fantastic exclusions other medical plans have. I know what I pay a month and I feel really good about the quality of medical care they offer."

Members Have a Say

Most HMOs are created and operated by doctors, other health professionals or private companies. But the Group Health Cooperative Board is comprised of and elected by consumer members. And according to Dr. William A. MacColl, a retired pediatrician and a GHC founder, cooperative ownership is a big plus because consumers have a direct say in the quality of their health care and in what new services are established.

"Consumer control is what makes GHC unique among Health Maintenance Organizations," says MacColl, who is now an active member of the co-op. "The cooperative is by no means a perfect organization but people who care can have an impact here."

Origins

The group was born out of a marriage between a fledgling cooperative group looking for medical care and a struggling physicians' practice looking for patients.

In 1945 a large group of consumers began promoting the idea of cutting high fee-for-service medical costs by forming a cooperative to provide Seattle residents with prepaid health care.[1] The group sold the idea to 400 Seattle families who pledged $100 each to the effort.

In the meantime, a local doctor-owned medical clinic, which had offered health care for a set fee since 1931, was floundering. The clinic, which served local defense industries and included a hospital, had flourished during World War II. But after the war, business slowed down and by 1946 the clinic was losing money.

Groups Merge

The two groups met at a public forum on community health needs. After a few meetings and months of discussion the consumers and the doctors reached an agreement. The consumers bought the clinic and the doctors agreed to work on salary for the health cooperative. GHC opened on January 1, 1947 with a hospital, a clinic and a staff of 16 doctors.

Disapproval of Medical Staff

But the local medical society, which had long disapproved of physicians working for salaries instead of fee-for-services-rendered, barred Group Health Cooperative physicians from membership in the society and positions on hospital staffs. In 1950, after years of fruitless negotiation with the society, GHC took the issue to court. And in 1951 the State Supreme Court ordered the medical society to lift its ban.

Another Obstacle Overcome

Also, several years of confrontations over personnel matters between the Board of Trustees—composed of elected consumer members—and the medical staff were finally resolved in 1954 with the formation of the Joint Conference Committee, which comprises equal numbers of Board members and medical staff. The Committee is charged with handling matters such as salaries, personnel decisions and consumer complaints.

Help for Low-Income Families

Under a contract with the Washington Department of Social and Health Services, the Group Health Cooperative provides comprehensive health care to low-income families. And with funds from the Department of Health, Education and Welfare's (HEW) Public Health Service, GHC provides transportation for rural, low-income residents as well as full health care coverage including counseling and educational services.[2]

Growth of HMOs

HMOs were given a shot in the arm with passage of the 1973 Health Maintenance Organization Act which authorizes Federal grants and loans for HMOs.[3] The Act also specifies that companies with over 25 employees located in communities with Federally approved HMOs must offer employees the insurance option of an HMO membership. Before the Act there were about 50 HMOs in the country. By 1979 more than 200 HMOs served eight million consumers in 37 states.

Other Groups

The Kaiser-Permanente Medical Care Program, with central offices located in Oakland, California, is the world's largest privately sponsored prepaid health care system. The program serves more than 3.5 million voluntarily enrolled members in California, Colorado, Hawaii, Ohio, Oregon and Washington. Launched in 1945, the prepaid plan served 25,000 Kaiser industrial employees and their families by the end of the first year. Kaiser-Permanente's success has spurred the interest of other corporations in creating and supporting HMOs.

And the Twin Cities of Minneapolis-St. Paul, Minnesota boasts seven HMOs. Four are serving employees of major area companies: 3M, Honeywell, General Mills and Control Data. The HMOs are competing with each other as well as with commercial insurers to provide area consumers with the best service at the lowest prices. Between 1972 and 1979 the number of HMO members in the area climbed from 2 to 12 percent of the area's 1.9 million population.

The other HMOs in the Twin Cities area are the MedCenter Health Plan; the Group Health Plan, the largest in the area; SHARE Clinic; and the Physician's Health Plan of Greater Minneapolis, made up of 1,400 doctors who conduct HMO practices in their private offices.

Groups Highlighted

Control Data Corporation
P.O. Box O-HQNO6U
Minneapolis, Minnesota 55440
(612) 853-3694

General Mills Corporation
Employee Benefits Department
9220 Wayzata Boulevard
Minneapolis, Minnesota 55441
(612) 540-3677

Group Health Plan, Inc.
2500 Como Avenue
St. Paul, Minnesota 55108
(612) 641-3100

Honeywell, Inc.
Honeywell Plaza
Mail Station MN12-6245
Minneapolis, Minnesota 55408
(612) 870-6220

Kaiser-Permanente Medical Care Program
1 Kaiser Plaza
Oakland, California 94612
(415) 271-2604

MedCenter Health Plan
4951 Excelsior Boulevard
St. Louis Park, Minnesota 55416
(612) 927-3185

Physicians Health Plan of Greater Minneapolis
500 National City Bank Building
510 Marquette Avenue
Minneapolis, Minnesota 55402
(612) 340-7800

SHARE Clinic
555 Simpson Street
St. Paul, Minnesota 55104
(612) 645-0171

3M Company
Group Insurance Department
Building 244-2E
3M Center
St. Paul, Minnesota 55144
(612) 736-1151

[1] Although not available in time to assist Group Health Cooperative of Puget Sound, co-ops may now qualify for technical and/or financial assistance from the newly created National Consumer Cooperative Bank.**

[2] Group Health Cooperative (GHC) received funding for the rural health program from the Department of Health, Education and Welfare's (HEW) Public Health Service's Community Health Services Group Health Buy-in Program which has been replaced by the Community Health Centers Program,* administered by the Bureau of Community Health Services.

[3] The 1973 Health Maintenance Organization Act* is administered by the Department of Health, Education and Welfare's (HEW) Public Health Service, Office of Health Maintenance Organizations (HMOs).

*State and/or local government agencies are frequently responsible for administration of Federal program funds. For further information, see Appendix I under appropriate Federal agency.

**For further information, see Appendix II under "National Consumer Cooperative Bank."

Note: For a complete listing of groups featured throughout this book, see Index.

What is an HMO?

A Health Maintenance Organization (HMO) is a health care plan that offers voluntarily enrolled members comprehensive, coordinated medical services — including hospitalization — for a set monthly or yearly fee.

Types of HMOs

Group
Members receive health care at clinics and hospitals at one or more central locations by a group of physicians *under contract*—at fixed rates—with the HMO. Group practice HMOs are the most popular type.

Staff
Members receive health care from doctors *employed by* the HMO. (Similar to the group practice model.)

Individual Practice Association (IPA)
Members receive health care at the offices of community doctors who retain their own practices. Doctors receive fees for treating HMO patients from the IPA.

Advantages of Group and Staff Model Practices

1. One-stop health care in most cases.
2. Better coordination of care.
3. Better follow-up and preventive care.

Advantages of IPA

1. More conveniently located doctors.
2. Wider choice of physicians.

Is an HMO for You?

HMO's are not for everybody.

- Many HMOs offer only those specialty services provided by, or arranged through, HMO physicians so consumers with unusual conditions are often reluctant to leave their personal doctors. (For instance, a consumer who has been seeing an opthamologist [eye doctor] that specializes in retina detachments might fear the HMO would not have such a specialist.)
- Most HMOs provide full or partial coverage for only *genuine* emergencies, such as heart attacks or car accidents, when members are visiting outside the service area.
- Most HMOs do not provide complete dental care for adults although some plans include checkups and referrals for children.
- Most HMOs provide some mental health services but the type and amount of care varies.
- Many HMOs have limited prescription drug coverage.

An HMO may be for you if you answer "yes" to any of the following questions.

1. Are your out-of-pocket health care expenses getting out of hand?
2. Do you hesitate to seek medical attention because of the deductibles or uncovered expenses in your traditional insurance plan?
3. Do you find that the health care you receive from several physicians could be better coordinated?
4. Could your follow-up health care be improved?
5. Would you like health education on a chronic ailment or advice about your general physical fitness?
6. Do you have difficulty finding the proper physicians to treat your health problems?

Typical HMO Health Care Coverage Includes but is Not Limited to:

- preventive care for adults and children and periodic checkups
- routine immunizations and boosters
- diagnosis and treatment of illness or injury
- specialist care when referred by HMO doctor
- eye examinations
- allergy testing and treatment
- contraceptives, sterilizations, maternity care
- surgical services on an inpatient or outpatient basis
- anesthesia
- laboratory, X-ray and other diagnostic tests including electrocardiograms, etc.
- medicines as provided and prescribed by HMO doctors
- mental health (i.e., at GHC Puget Sound, 10 visits per calendar year)
- physical therapy services when ordered by HMO physician
- respiratory and occupational therapy as needed
- home health care when ordered by HMO physician
- hospital care when ordered by HMO physician
- ambulance
- kidney dialysis when ordered by HMO physician (may have cost limit)
- alcoholism outpatient treatment

Some Things Not Covered

- artificial limbs and other devices not for specific treatment of disease
- contact lenses or eyeglasses
- cost of care or treatment for disease, sickness or injury resulting from occupations or on-the-job accidents that are covered by employer insurance
- dental care
- dietary supplements such as vitamins
- drug addiction treatment other than alcohol
- mental health drugs such as tranquilizers
- noncritical nursing home or institutional care
- psychiatric hospitalization
- surgery primarily for cosmetic purposes
- eye exercises
- hearing aids

Adapted from A Primer on HMOs, *prepared for Carnegie Press in cooperation with the American Institute of Professional Education by Robert Doran Associates, 1979. (Reprints of pamphlet available for 50 cents each and special rates for bulk orders by writing Carnegie Press, Health Care Division, Hillcrest Avenue, Madison, New Jersey 07940.)*

Primary Care Centers (Urban)

Green Bay Area Free Clinic
P.O. Box 2526
338 South Chestnut Avenue
Green Bay, Wisconsin 54303
(414) 437-9773

Good doctors and hospitals are often out of reach for those who fall between the cracks in our medical care system. Many Americans don't make enough money to pay for medical care and can't afford private health insurance. Their jobs don't provide free health benefits and their incomes are too high to qualify for government insurance plans.

The Green Bay Area Free Clinic in Green Bay, Wisconsin had these residents in mind in July 1971 when it opened on the second floor of a run-down drug abuse center. By 1979 the free clinic was serving over 10,000 residents who were financially unable to pay for medical care and weren't covered by government or private insurers. Now a Green Bay fixture, the Clinic plays to a standing-room-only crowd in an attractive, renovated house and to the applause of the Green Bay community.

For Florence Lambert the Clinic was literally a lifesaver. "I don't know what I'd have done if the Clinic hadn't been around. Since I'm only 61, I can't get Medicare and we make too much money for me to get Medicaid," she says.[1] "But my blood pressure requires me to be on constant medication to stay alive. I cannot be without it."

Praise For the Clinic

By January 1980 the Clinic enjoyed the support of 84 volunteer doctors and a score of other medical experts who offer free or discounted services to Clinic referrals. A 1977 survey found that the Clinic had earned the acceptance and gratitude of the community and of once skeptical physicians.

And the Clinic has won its share of honors. The area newspaper praised the group for its serious commitment to the working poor in and around Green Bay. And in 1979 the Wisconsin Medical Society cited the Clinic and its doctors for exemplary service to the community.

It is said that the greatest compliment is imitation. By the end of 1979 Clinic Administrator Richard Dresang was advising doctors and organizers from five states who were interested in starting free clinics in their own areas.

How It Began

In 1968, anxious to help those without health insurance, Linda Pratsch, a social services student at the University of Wisconsin/Green Bay, launched a door-to-door survey of residents. Armed with results proving a need for a clinic, she and John Randall, a young internist, began marshaling support from city doctors, dentists, nurses and other medical experts. They offered medical professionals an efficient well-run clinic with assurances that the clinic would fill a genuine need in the area.

Green Bay Area Free Clinic doctors provide examinations, testing and counseling for residents of all ages.

Community Backing

For financial support they lobbied area businesses and religious groups. "Two hundred dollars means 40 people get medical care they wouldn't otherwise get," they told potential contributors. Their premise that "medical bills are everybody's bills" and the no-frills health care budget were winners. And after three years of hard work, the backing of a handful of volunteer doctors and donations totaling $5,000 from businesses and religious groups, the Clinic was opened in space donated by the drug abuse center.

Growth

In 1979 the Green Bay Area Free Clinic's budget of $37,000 came primarily from private industry, churches and area social organizations. The Clinic's paid staff of three includes an administrator, a secretary/receptionist and a patient-advocate coordinator.

Staffers pride themselves on detecting early warning signs of illness. And five days a week volunteer nurse practitioners help ward off those illnesses by teaching patients about self-care and proper nutrition.

Two days a week volunteer doctors are available for those needing medical treament. And the patient-advocate coordinator and five volunteers also help patients find jobs, schools and housing.

Area Doctors Lend Support

The Clinic's effectiveness is bolstered by a network of area medical services that are available to patients. Some 84 physicians with varied specialties and over a dozen dentists treat the Clinic's referrals either free or at affordable fees. Patients with emotional problems, for example, are referred to supporting psychiatrists and psychologists. Laboratory services and X-rays are provided at no cost by three area hospitals. And 16 pharmacies offer Clinic patients free or discounted prescription drugs.

James Habeck has been a Green Bay Area Free Clinic patient for over three years. "The hard question to answer," he says, "is what I would have done without the Clinic. I probably would have gone as long as I could because I didn't have the money. Now I stop by every two weeks or so to get my blood pressure taken and I take better care of myself."

Other Clinics

East of the River Health Center, a nonprofit comprehensive medical clinic serving low-income residents in Southeast Washington, D.C., was launched in 1976 with funds from the Community Health Centers Program,* administered by the Department of Health, Education and Welfare's (HEW) Bureau of Community Health Services. Twelve Center doctors, seven of whom are full-time, help about 600 patients a month with health concerns ranging from immunization shots to heart disease.

The Country Doctor Community Clinic in Seattle, Washington was started after organizers noted a lack of primary care in their urban area. Established in 1971 with private donations, the Clinic now has a budget of $324,000 yearly and provides comprehensive low-cost medical services to approximately 1,000 patients a month.

Groups Highlighted

Country Doctor Community Clinic
402 15th Avenue East
Seattle, Washington 98112
(206) 322-6698

East of the River Health Center
5929 East Capitol Street, S.E.
Washington, D.C. 20019
(202) 582-7700

[1] The Medicaid and Medicare Programs* are administered by the Health Care Financing Administration of the Department of Health, Education and Welfare (HEW). Medicaid, through grants to individual states, provides medical services to the needy. Medicare provides basic health benefits to elderly residents on social security.

*State and/or local government agencies are frequently responsible for administration of Federal program funds. For further information, see Appendix I under appropriate Federal agency.

Note: For a complete listing of groups featured throughout this book, see Index.

Primary Care Centers (Rural)

Beaufort-Jasper Comprehensive Health Services, Inc.
P.O. Box 357
Ridgeland, South Carolina 29936
(803) 726-8171

Practicing preventive health care means more than telling people to exercise and eat properly. For the residents of rural Beaufort and Jasper Counties in South Carolina, it has meant an improved standard of living and a substantial easing of the deplorable conditions that once made the area one of the country's unhealthiest.

In 1970 the area lacked adequate health, water and sanitation facilities, causing massive health problems for residents. Located midway between Charleston, South Carolina and Savannah, Georgia, the counties' 125 miles encompass the lowlands along the Atlantic Ocean coastline. While the region is picturesque, the rural landscape is dotted with substandard housing and 80 percent of the counties' 72,000 residents have annual incomes of less than $6,000.

To the Rescue

But by 1979 life was better for many residents. Thanks to a decade of hard work by the Beaufort-Jasper Comprehensive Health Services, Inc., a private, nonprofit community development corporation, five health clinics now provide 26,000 citizens with much needed low-cost medical care; 500 run-down homes have been repaired; and new sewage and water systems are serving over 5,000 families.

Residents are provided door-to-door transportation to the clinics by 22 vans and station wagons. And two mobile units travel to area schools offering health care services to adolescents.

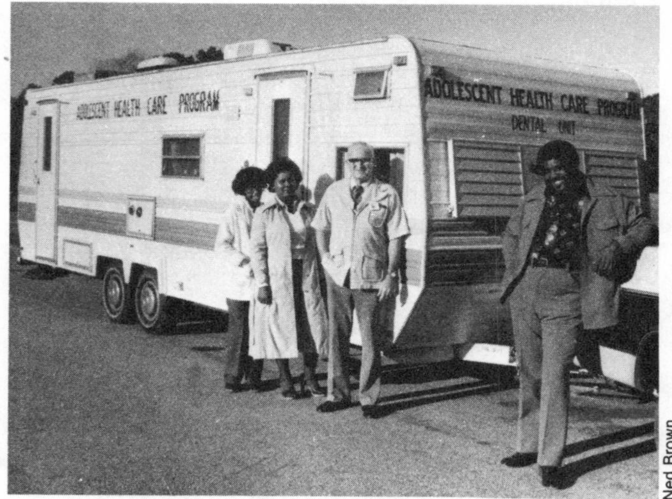

Ned Brown

Beaufort-Jasper mobile clinics bring medical and dental care services to rural residents.

Environment and Health Go Hand in Hand

Early on, the group linked environmental conditions with health problems, and working from the Health Services Center in Ridgeland, South Carolina they started a project aimed to combat both. Reflecting the project's success, the area's infant mortality rate—which in 1970 was one of the country's highest—had dropped from 62 to 16 deaths per 1,000 births by 1979.

"The project has done tremendous things for the community healthwise and that's what it's all about," says Hattie Murray of Ridgeland, a member of the Health Services Advisory Council and former chairperson of the Board. "When the clinic started, they didn't just give out medicine; they checked the residences to see if something there caused the problem," she adds, explaining that wells and pumps which provided water for most homes were not deep enough to tap pure water.

Sensitivity to the Poor

One reason for the group's success has been its sensitivity to the pride of the people it serves; self-help is stressed. Low-income families are charged $1 for most health services at the clinics and pay according to income for others. "Low-income residents share a rural tradition of pride in self-sufficiency, looking for the least help required to overcome their problems, not the most," notes a former Office of Economic Opportunity (OEO) official who helped the group obtain funding.[1]

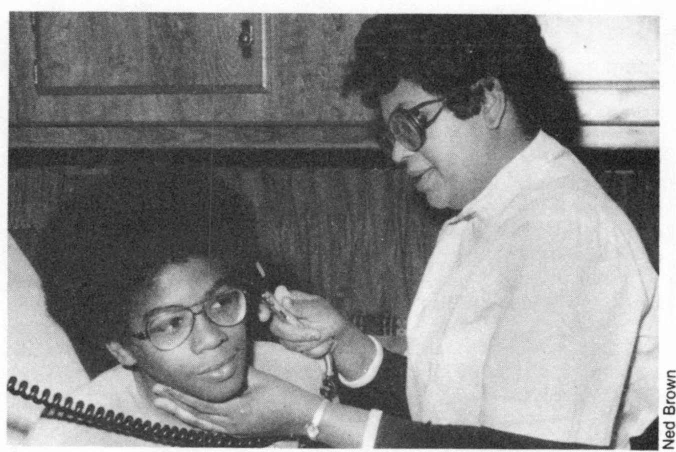

Low-income families receive needed health care checkups at fees they can afford.

Origins

It all began in 1970 when a group of concerned citizens—including families of children with intestinal parasites, housewives, teachers, salespeople and employees of the district health office—decided they would face area health problems head-on and formed the Beaufort-Jasper Comprehensive Health Services, Inc. Their first task was to conduct a study to determine the severity of the area's problems.

Survey Yields Shocking Information

The survey results were startling. The area had one of the country's highest infant mortality rates and half of the mothers surveyed were between 15 and 19 years old and had received little prenatal care or nutrition information. Also, more than 80 percent of the area's children under twelve were infested with worms.

The group's recommendations were merely requests for the necessities most of us take for granted such as safe drinking water, improved sewage systems, adequate housing, electricity and transportation.

Armed with hard facts the group approached local and state health officials and congressional representatives to generate support for their cause. And in 1971 OEO pumped in $754,000 to launch a comprehensive health program. A project director and core staff of 12, including two physicians, were hired. By February 1971 the project was underway.

Tackling Poor Water and Sewage Systems

The first item of business was to improve the water and sanitation systems which were causing so many of the problems. The Beaufort-Jasper Water Authority developed and planned the new systems with funds from the National Demonstration Water Project Program* of the Environmental Protection Agency (EPA). Local firms were enlisted to do the work. And low-income families paid an average of only $5.50 a month for the improved systems, thanks to the Low-to-Moderate Income Housing Loans (Section 502) Program* of the United States Department of Agriculture's (USDA) Farmers Home Administration.

Other Sources of Funding

Funds for staff and supplies for the health clinics came from OEO and the Economic Development Administration's (EDA) Public Works Grants Program,* which is administered by the Department of Commerce (DOC). Other funds came from state and county governments. Moreover, the group has won funds from the Community Health Centers Program* of the Department of Health, Education and Welfare's (HEW) Bureau of Community Health Services.

Budget and Staff

In 1979 Beaufort-Jasper Health Service's budget was $4 million and their paid staff of 175 included 10 doctors. In addition to Federal sources, the group received funding from the United Way, a non-profit charitable organization, the Presbyterian Church Task Force on World Hunger and private foundations.

The Beaufort-Jasper Comprehensive Health Services has been a godsend for one elderly Possum Hills resident. "Before the Center, when I was sick, I'd just stay sick," she recalls. "But the health clinic has been a big help to a lotta people—its changed my life for the better."

Other Rural Groups

Health clinics are providing much needed medical care for rural residents in other areas across the country as well. For instance, in 1979 the Florida-based Hendry-Glades County Health Services, Inc., which provides low-cost medical and dental care, served 30,000 migrant workers and other residents in a three-county area.

The Lee County Cooperative Clinic in Marianna, Arkansas, established in 1970 by local citizens, is providing health care for area residents. The nonprofit clinic is partly funded by local churches and receives additional money from such events as community fish fries.[2]

The nonprofit Delmarva Rural Ministries in Dover, Delaware provides health services for thousands of migrant farmworkers who travel to the largely rural Delaware-Maryland-Virginia Peninsula to become laborers during the April through November planting season. Rural Ministries' nurses, some of whom are provided by ACTION's Volunteers in Service To America (VISTA) Program,* visit migrant camps to screen for disease, provide health education, register workers and make needed appointments at one of the group's six strategically located medical clinics. Transportation to the clinics is also provided.

And based in Nampa, Idaho, the nonprofit Community Health Clinics, Inc. has facilities in three towns which serve 35,000 rural residents each year.

Rural Health Care Clearinghouse

A good source of information for those interested in rural health care is the Highlander Center in New Market, Tennessee, a residential education center and training facility for labor unions, local community leaders and low-income citizens wishing to work in or learn about rural community clinics.[3]

Groups Highlighted

Community Health Clinics, Inc.
1503 Third Street North
Nampa, Idaho 83651
(208) 466-7869

Delmarva Rural Ministries
Blue Hen Mall
Dover, Delaware 11901
(302) 678-2000

Hendry-Glades County Health Services, Inc.
P.O. Box 278
133 Bridge Street
LaBelle, Florida 33935
(813) 675-0313

Highlander Center
Route 3, Box 370
New Market, Tennessee 37820
(615) 933-3443

Lee County Cooperative Clinic
530 West Atkins Boulevard
Marianna, Arkansas 72360
(501) 295-5225

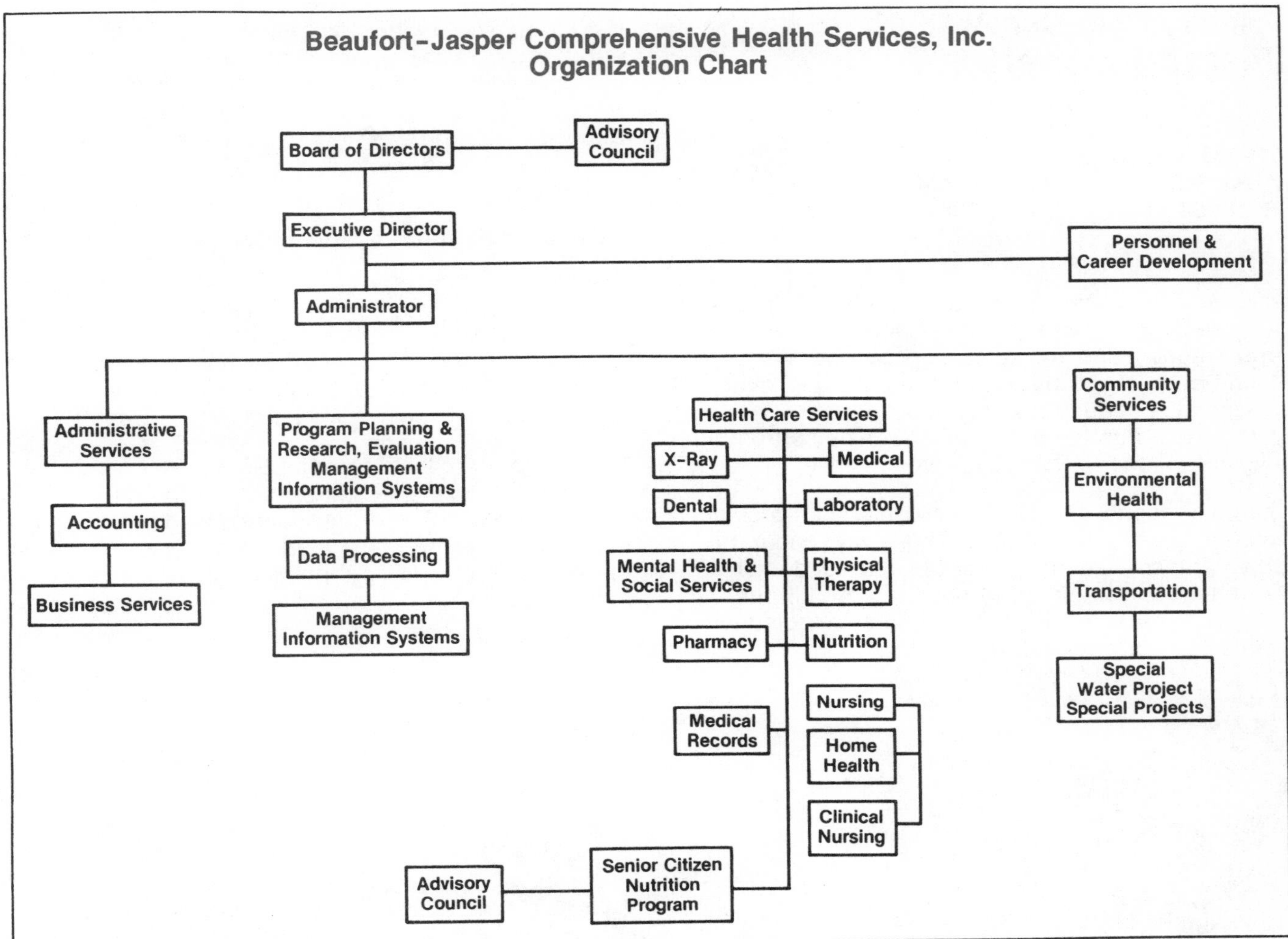

[1] The Office of Economic Opportunity (OEO), an antipoverty agency, was replaced by the Community Services Administration (CSA) in 1975.

[2] Although not available in time to assist the Lee County Cooperative Clinic, co-ops may now qualify for technical and/or financial assistance from the newly created National Consumer Cooperative Bank.**

[3] For more information on the Highlander Center, see Resources at end of Health Section.

*State and/or local government agencies are frequently responsible for administration of Federal program funds. For further information, see Appendix I under appropriate Federal agency.

**For further information, see Appendix II under "National Consumer Cooperative Bank."

Note: For a complete listing of groups featured throughout this book, see Index.

Primary Care Centers (Retirement Area)

Mid-County Medical Center, Inc.
8190 Okeechobee Boulevard
West Palm Beach, Florida 33411
(305) 684-1119

Palm Beach County, Florida boasts a heavily populated eastern seaboard but the inland areas are largely agricultural and sparsely populated. West Palm Beach stretches 50 miles and its splendid isolation is a natural attraction for retirees. "We live 25 minutes from the beach and 10 minutes from the alligators," one resident says with a smile.

But until recently the semi-rural area had a problem when it came to health care. Those who had cars drove at least half an hour to the nearest doctor. For others it was a day long bus trip. And if often took up to three weeks to schedule an appointment with a busy city doctor.

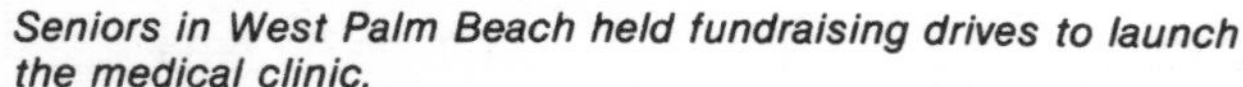

Seniors in West Palm Beach held fundraising drives to launch the medical clinic.

But in April 1979, after four years of community effort, West Palm Beach senior citizens became owners and managers of the modern one-story Mid-County Medical Center, Inc. on Okeechobee Boulevard. By the end of the year more than 5,000 patients had used the facility, which serves 40,000 residents.

Retired Residents Provide Expertise

The successful drive to build the medical center was due in large part to the talents of many retired residents who, as organizers, overcame initial skepticism by some community leaders that nonmedical residents were not capable of operating a clinic. They also helped plan, build and fund the Center.

The chairman of the Center's 36-member Board of Directors, for example, is Hy Ruchlis, an original founder and a retired author. Sitting with him on the Board are a retired Federal administrative judge, an ex-labor union leader, a former health educator and an insurance broker.

Senior citizen volunteers man vans that bring elderly rural residents to health clinic.

And the Center now enjoys the community's support. "Any community can start a medical clinic if everybody is interested in the same goal," says Administrator Byron Arbeit. "Mainly the Center is succeeding because the public is on our side."

Complete Care

At the Center five full-time salaried doctors treat patients from 8 a.m. to 5 p.m. five days a week and are available for telephone consultations at other times. Moreover, part-time specialists, from ophthalmologists to psychiatrists, are on staff for one or two days a week and are paid per session. And those patients who need treatment by a specialist not available at the Center are referred to appropriate physicians.

Patients qualifying for Medicare* or Medicaid,* the Federal medical programs for the elderly and low-income respectively, are accepted.[1] And those who don't qualify but have limited resources are offered treatment at discount prices.

And the Center offers more than conventional medical care. For example, retired pharmacists advise patients how to use medications and nutritionists provide diet counseling. Also, free courses on diabetes, heart disease and other illnesses that plague the elderly are offered so patients can actively participate in their own health care. Through these programs the Center hopes to emphasize health education and preventive medicine.

The Center's health care program also reaches out to residents in nearby communities. A van, operated by senior citizen volunteers, links patients in rural outlying areas with the Center.

Home Health Care Program

And the Center offers those residents unable to get to the clinic for treatment an alternative to expensive nursing homes or hospitals. The home health care service is staffed by residents who are trained by eight nurse instructors to help the homebound with their medication, baths and other needs and determine when more extensive medical treatment is needed. By January 1980, 400 home health aides had been trained in the Center's program, which is funded by the Department of Labor's Comprehensive Employment and Training Act (CETA) Program.*

Launching the Clinic

The Center's organizers began in 1975 by soliciting funds and volunteers, mostly from retirement communities in a 50-square-mile area. A key to their success was establishing close relationships with public health officials and political leaders who helped bolster community interest and find funding for the Center.

The Palm Beach County government donated $150,000 worth of equipment and the group raised $400,000 from individuals and businesses. In 1978 they won $460,000 from the Department of Health, Education and Welfare's (HEW) Health Underserved Rural Areas (HURA) Program* to construct the Center on donated land.

Members Make Management Decisions

The Center is owned by its 4,000 members who pay $10 annually to have a voice in its operations. Other donors who give between $100 and $5,000 become life members or major benefactors.

Now that the members are immersed in the practical operation of a medical center, new challenges arise daily. For example, the money-saving home health care service is not covered by Medicare so Mid-County members are working with state officials to change the regulations to include such services.

The experience of the Mid-County Medical Center is yet another example of what citizens working together can do for their community.

[1] The Medicare and Medicaid Programs* are administered by the Health Care Financing Administration of the Department of Health, Education and Welfare (HEW). Medicare provides basic health benefits to elderly residents on social security. Medicaid, through grants to individual states, provides medical services to the needy.

* State and/or local government agencies are frequently responsible for administration of Federal program funds. For further information, see Appendix I under appropriate Federal agency.

Note: For a complete listing of groups features throughout this book, see Index.

Wholistic Care

The Wholistic Health Center of Hinsdale, Inc.
137 South Garfield Street
Hinsdale, Illinois 60521
(312) 323-1920

"Four out of five times, I'd find out what was wrong with one of my patients sooner if I started by examining the patient's home life, his job and his bank account instead of his heart, his digestive system and his kidneys." When a Mayo Clinic doctor wrote those words nearly 40 years ago, many of his colleagues thought he was crazy or kidding. Today it's a widely accepted fact that emotions affect physical health and can be the direct cause of such ailments as headaches, backaches, allergies, insomnia and obesity.

Even though most Americans are still treated only for physical ailments by their medical doctors, the "wholistic" approach to health care—which advocates healing the body as well as the mind and spirit—is growing in popularity. Promoters of wholistic health care aim to cut medical costs by stressing preventive medicine and teaching patients how to cope with stress in life.

Treating the Whole Body

Since 1973 the Wholistic Health Center of Hinsdale, Inc., a nonprofit health facility occupying nine donated rooms in a local Illinois church, has been bridging the gap between emotional problems and body ills. The Center's medical team examines up to 30 patients a day, treating symptoms as well as reviewing health histories, lifestyles and habits to determine the causes of ill-health. Moreover, the physician, who is affiliated with a local hospital, along with a counselor, nurse and trained volunteers teach patients how to alleviate illness by coping with stress, exercising and eating proper foods.

"The reasons people come to us are not too different from those that send them to other doctors' offices and hospitals," says Director of Center Development John Riedel. "Our doctor makes the diagnosis and treats the symptoms, but in this setting we're looking for—and usually find—the nonbiological causes and problems as well."

Success Today

The group's dedication to wholistic health has spurred it to open 13 additional centers around the country.[1] And the group has formed Wholistic Health Centers, Inc. (WHC), which provides technical assistance and is devoted to educating hospitals and physicians around the country about the wholistic concept.[2]

Origins

Dr. Granger Westberg, a Lutheran clergyman with a background in psychology, was the inspiration behind the Wholistic Health Center idea. Believing that a community with numerous health problems and a shortage of physicians was the best testing ground for wholistic care, he established his first volunteer, church-based clinic which still operates in a low-income neighborhood of Springfield, Ohio.

A Challenge

But in 1972, while giving a lecture at Howard University Medical School in Washington, D.C., a medical student suggested that Westberg launch a center in an upper-income area to test "whether people who can afford health care will actually choose to see a doctor who deals with the human dimensions of illness." In 1973 to answer that question, Westberg decided to establish a center in Hinsdale, an old, well-established, upper-income suburban community west of Chicago.

Winning Community Support

To promote his preventive medicine concept Westberg began holding seminars on the wholistic concept, inviting area health professionals and local leaders. From these contacts a voluntary Board of Directors was chosen and community volunteers were recruited to help build public support, plan the design of the Center and handle administrative matters such as budget and financing.

Westberg won start-up capital from the W. K. Kellogg Foundation which has also provided funds to help the group launch new centers around the country and to defray operating costs of WHC.

The Center and Staff

The Hinsdale Center contains a reception and business area, doctor's office, two examining rooms, counselor's office and a conference room.

A full-time paid staff of four includes a physician, nurse, counselor and secretary. And a roster of 24 staff-trained, part-time volunteers help with clerical duties and assist patients by engaging them in relaxing conversations, answering questions and serving coffee.

"Volunteers are viewed as our most important asset," Westberg says, "and their skills and caring never cease to amaze us. Some volunteers are still here after eight years."

The Wholistic Health Center of Hinsdale, Inc.

Wholistic Center medical team meets with patient at the Health Planning Conference, the heart of the Wholistic approach.

Health Planning Conference

New patients fill out questionnaires before meeting with the medical team. The patients are asked to provide information on recent traumatic events such as deaths of loved ones, new jobs, illnesses or injuries and marriages or divorces.

The health planning conference, the most important aspect of the wholistic approach, follows. Patients team up with the clinic doctor, nurse and counselor to discuss their physical symptoms, feelings and future goals. Afterwards, patients are examined.

"It's a nice place to go," says Julia Beckman, who lives five miles west of Hinsdale and brings her family to the Center. Mrs. Beckman learned of the Center at her Unitarian Church where Westberg gave a series of seminars on wholistic health care. "Everyone is on the same wavelength," she says, "sympathetic and willing to talk."

The Wholistic Health Center of Hinsdale, Inc.

A wholistic physician lectures residents at an education seminar at the Center.

Educational

In addition to its clinic, the Center offers a selection of educational programs for $50. Patients may choose among a variety of activities, including swimming, exercises and seminars on aging, marriage and divorce.

Fees and Staff

When the Center opened in 1973 office visits cost $10. In 1979 the fee was $15 and the health planning conference, which runs about one-half hour, cost $25. And with additional fees from counseling, examinations and educational courses, the Center has become self-supporting.

Other Groups

The Wellness Associates, a private, nonprofit educational organization in Mill Valley, California, began in 1975. Its staff of three consultants counsels individuals and groups eager to learn about the importance of keeping mind, body and spirit healthy. They conduct seminars and workshops for businesses and industries throughout the country interested in maintaining and promoting employees' mental well-being.[3]

And in 1977 the Swedish Medical Center in Englewood, Colorado launched the nonprofit Swedish Wellness Center to promote physical, mental and spiritual health in the community. The group offers courses which explore such matters as personal values and stress management. In addition, the group helps area schools develop similar programs for kindergarten though college students as well as for local businesses and community groups.

Chart 1

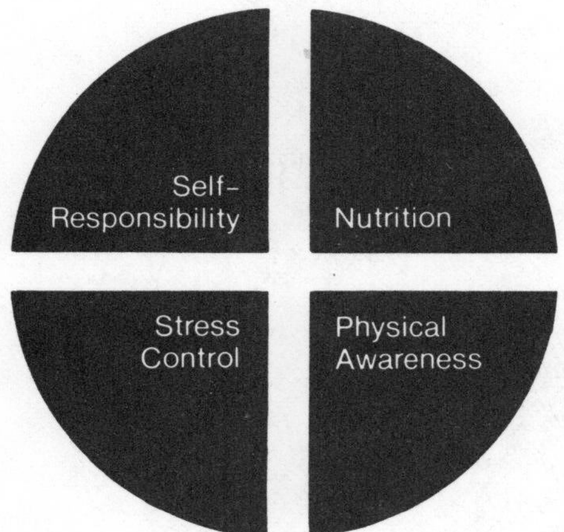

The four basic dimensions of wellness
Wellness Resource Center

Chart 2

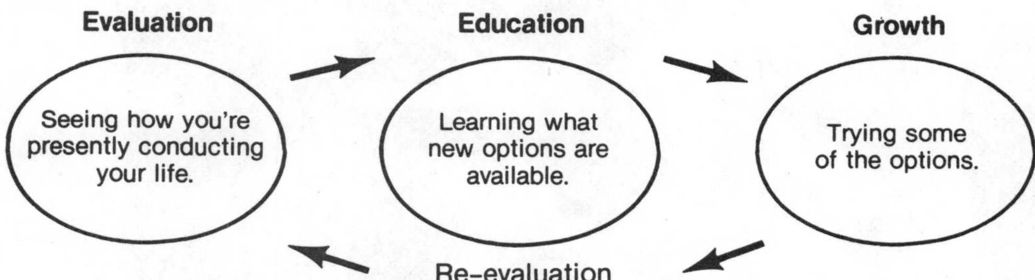

For each dimension of wellness, three phases (evaluation, education and growth) are developed at the Wellness Resource Center.

Groups Highlighted

Swedish Wellness Center
3444 South Emerson Street
Englewood, Colorado 80110
(303) 789-6940

Wellness Associates
42 Miller Avenue
Mill Valley, California 94941
(415) 383-3806

We would suggest that consumers check with their physician or other health care provider if they have questions about the value of a particular wholistic program. The term "wholistic health care" is often used to encompass therapies beyond those described above, some of which have not yet been proven safe and effective.

[1] Eight of the 13 additional wholistic centers are located in the Chicago, Illinois area. The others are in Cleveland, Ohio; Richmond, Indiana; Boulder, Colorado; Minneapolis, Minnesota and Washington, D.C.

[2] For more information on Wholistic Health Centers, Inc. (WHC), see Resources at end of Health Section.

[3] For more information on Wellness Associates, see Resources at end of Health Section.

Note: For a complete listing of groups featured throughout this book, see Index.

MENTAL HEALTH CENTER

Identifying Specialized Health Services

Introduction

Community groups and other organizations around the country are finding low-cost ways to help residents who have special health needs.

The needs of pregnant women, the mentally ill, the elderly and the dying are being addressed by alternative low-cost health programs that often can't be found in modern hospitals or institutions. Also, consumer health cooperatives are being formed to blunt the cost of special services such as eye care.

We begin this chapter by looking at a childbearing center in New York that provides low-cost prenatal and maternal care for mothers-to-be. And to the delight of patients, the center encourages the entire family to participate in mother's pregnancy and witness the miracle of baby's birth.

Also, the mentally and emotionally ill now have alternatives to expensive institutions. We feature a community mental health clinic in Missouri that offers outpatient treatment so disturbed residents can find peace of mind while living at home and continuing to work.

And elderly residents in San Francisco who need daily medical attention but aren't ready for expensive nursing homes are finding help and companionship at a Chinatown day health care clinic and recreation center.

Another group that is being singled out for special care is the terminally ill. Hospices across the country are offering dying patients and their families an alternative to high-cost and often lonely hospital treatment. We feature a group in Connecticut that pioneered the hospice movement in this country and has helped hundreds of dying patients and their families face death more comfortably—and at home.

Specialized health cooperatives are also growing in popularity. We look at a determined Detroit consumer-owned eye care cooperative that overcame early obstacles and now serves 100,000 members a year.

All these groups provide valuable insight on how determined community groups can help their neighbors by creating special health services. We hope their stories will give you some good ideas for your area.

Alternative Maternal Care

The Childbearing Center
48 East 92nd Street
New York, New York 10028
(212) 369-7300

With the surge of interest in getting back to basics, many families are eager to participate fully in the birth of children and are turning away from traditional hospital maternity care. Today there are about 45 childbearing centers around the country which offer homelike atmospheres, substantial savings on delivery costs and the bonus of involving the entire family in the baby's arrival.

Ten-year-old Frankie Perez attended classes at the Childbearing Center in New York City when his mother, Maria, was pregnant. "I learned how the baby forms and what happens if the baby is overdue and things like that," he says. And he'll never forget when baby brother Daniel was born. "I was so surprised to see the baby—seeing him coming out of my mother and seeing him cry," he excitedly recalls. "I cried I was so happy."

Not for Everyone

Family-centered deliveries in facilities other than hospitals may be objectionable to some, but for an increasing number of families childbearing centers are a long awaited alternative to traditional maternal care.

"When my son was born, I cut the umbilical cord and I held him when he was less than an hour old," says Harold McDougall, a law professor at Rutgers University whose wife Diane gave birth at the Childbearing Center. "Now," he says, "there are certain kinds of fears I won't have again. I'm concerned when he falls down and hurts himself but I remember that I've seen him born, which is a stressful event, and he is fine."

Welcoming the Whole Family

Frankie Perez' brother and the McDougall's son are two of the 575 babies delivered at the nonprofit Childbearing Center since it opened in October 1975. The Center welcomes women expecting normal births and their families and offers full maternity care, including natural childbirth, education classes and prenatal and postnatal checkups. And Center families—or their health insurers—save as much as $600 to $900 per delivery over hospital costs.

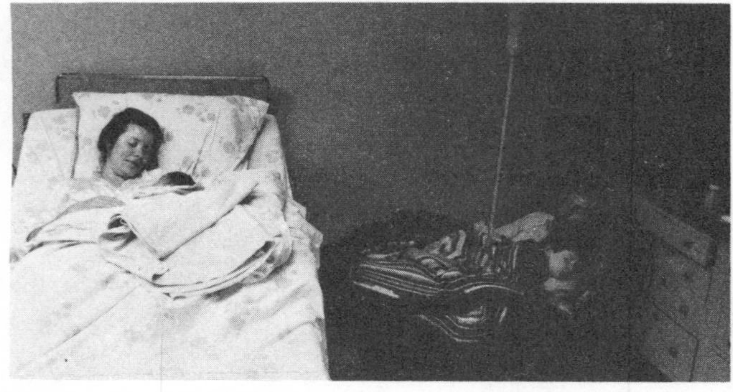

Mariette Allen

Mother proudly admires new baby while father and son rest following their exciting experience.

Patients are cared for by a team of nine nurse-midwives and educators, two consulting pediatricians, three consulting obstetricians and other support personnel.

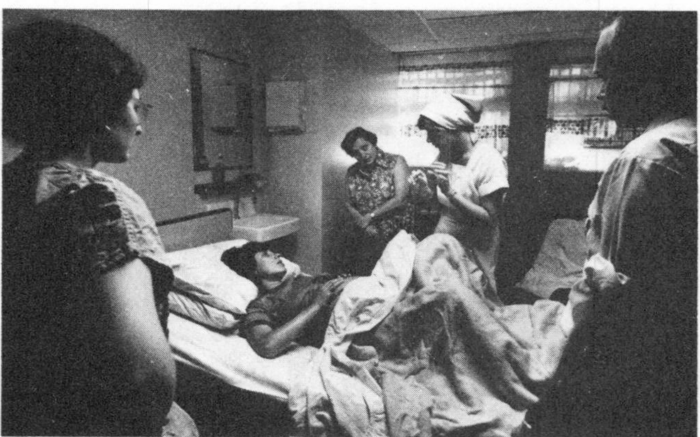

Ed Lettav

Loved ones stand ready to assist as nurse-midwife reviews the birth process with mother.

Medication Not Routine—But Available

Fewer than five percent of the Center's mothers are given medication during delivery, having learned and practiced both exercises to strengthen muscles used in delivery and breathing techniques that, with father's coaching, distract them from concentrating on labor pains. But medication is available and administered upon request.

"We reject the notion that there is a test involved and somehow if the mother has medication, she has failed," explains Public Relations Officer Martin Kelly. "The most important thing is that the mother and father have the kind of birth experience they both want."

Gil Roschuni

Team work—husbands help wives learn breathing techniques and practice exercises to prepare for childbirth.

Families return home 12 hours following birth. Within 24 hours and again three days later, visits are made by a public health nurse from a visiting nurse service.

Prepared For Emergencies

Arrangements with nearby hospitals have been made by the Clinic in case unforeseen difficulties arise. About 18 percent of the Center's patients have to transfer to a hospital during labor. But says Kelly, the hospital arrangements have forestalled critical problems. "There have been none of the feared emergencies," he says, "and there have been no infant deaths at the Center since its inception."

Origins

The Childbearing Center opened in 1975 after more than two years of careful preparation by New York's Maternity Center Association (MCA), a 62-year-old nonprofit organization dedicated to improving maternity care.[1]

Initially area obstetricians/gynecologists, heads of major teaching hospitals and the city health department resisted the Childbearing Center's nontraditional approach to pregnancy and birth. But relying on the excellent reputation they had built over the years, MCA leaders marshaled help from their many community contacts to win support from the medical establishment and city officials.

The group raised about $100,000 from individual contributions for start-up necessities and won additional funds from a private foundation.

Center's Focus

Focusing on childbirth education and the need for personalized health services, MCA designed the Center as a demonstration project to test whether safe, satisfying and economical out-of-hospital care by nurse-midwives could meet the needs of families opting for the "prepared childbirth" experience.[2]

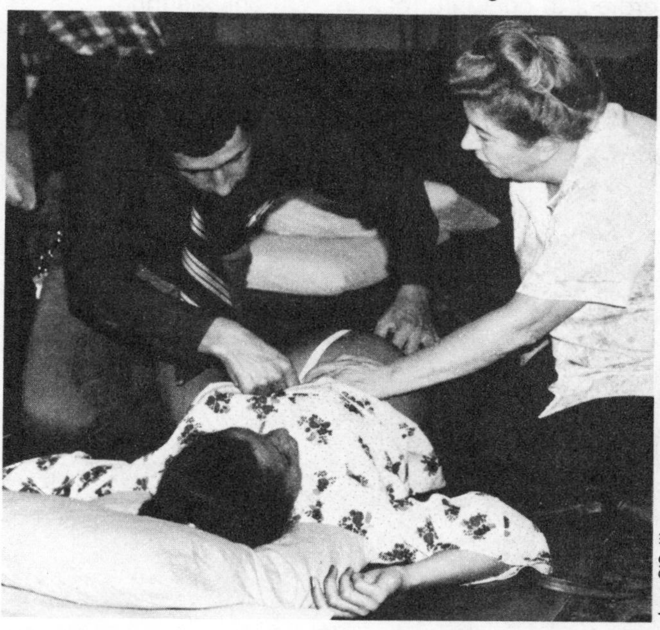
Jane O'Sullivan

Measuring baby—instructor teaches husband how to measure baby's growth.

Budget and Fees

The Childbearing Center's 1979 budget was about $310,000, according to Kelly. Patient fees now cover the majority of Center expenses and contributions by MCA members and individuals help defray the cost of education programs and publications. And with an anticipated 325 births in 1980, the Center is expected to become totally self-supporting.

The Center's maternity program of prenatal to postnatal care, including classes on nutrition and childbirth, costs $1,000. "The typical cost for having a baby in New York—depending on the physician's fee and other expenses—is $1,500 to $2,200," says Kelly, and can often climb as high as $3,000.

Assistance to Others

MCA and the Center also offer technical assistance to groups wishing to start clinics in their own areas. And MCA has 23 publications as well as visual aids and charts for sale to the public.

Moreover, MCA has launched a one-year research project to pool information from childbearing centers across the country in order to document the safety of the concept. Results will be available to the public when all data is collected and analyzed.

Another Birthing Center

Another exciting childbirth center is the Booth Maternity Center in Philadelphia, Pennsylvania. In a Salvation Army maternity hospital a small team of 12 nurse-midwives, educators and obstetricians provide care to women of all backgrounds.

The Booth Center was launched in 1971 by a childbirth educator with the help of the Salvation Army and MCA. In addition to the nurse-midwives and obstetricians, 30 nursing personnel help with patient checkups and deliveries. In 1979, 1,300 babies were delivered at the 16-bed clinic.

Group Highlighted

Booth Maternity Center
6051 Overbrook Avneue
Philadelphia, Pennsylvania 19131
(215) 878-7800

[1] For more information on the Maternity Center Association (MCA), see Resources at end of Health Section.

[2] In prepared or natural childbirth, expectant parents become involved with the psychological as well as physical aspects of pregnancy, birth and the post-partum period. Among other things, they prepare both emotionally and physically for labor and delivery and learn about proper nutrition and infant care.

Note: For a complete listing of groups featured throughout this book, see Index.

Mental Health Care Clinics

Community Mental Health Center South
769 Tudor Road
Lee's Summit, Missouri 64063
(816) 966-0900

By the age of 23 a man from Lee's Summit, Missouri had attempted suicide several times. His family moved around a great deal during his father's military career and the young man had faced numerous adjustment problems. When he entered a large and sophisticated high school at 17, his emotional problems became severe.

"I was very upset," he explains. "I had trouble sleeping and was nervous and shaky. I didn't have any friends and finally dropped out of school. I thought I was a failure."

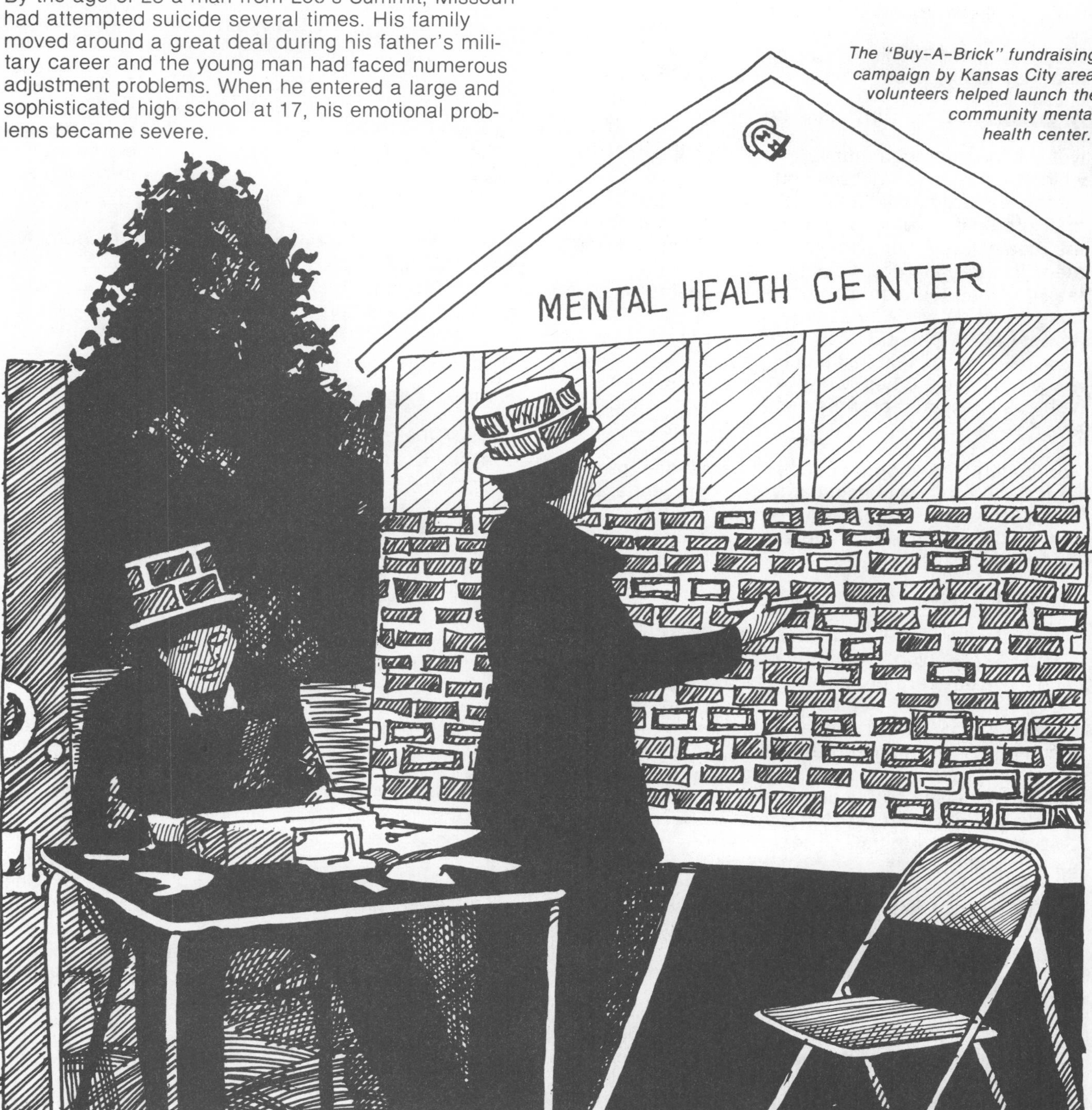

The "Buy-A-Brick" fundraising campaign by Kansas City area volunteers helped launch the community mental health center.

But two years ago, after moving to Lee's Summit, a suburb of Kansas City, his family discovered the Community Mental Health Center South (CMHCS), a nonprofit, low-cost facility dedicated to helping mentally and emotionally disturbed residents deal with their problems while remaining in their homes, schools and jobs. The Center gave the young man, who is now working and attending a local community college, a new lease on life.

"They gave me training to get out of my depression and they really stuck with me," he says gratefully.

Alternative to Institutional Care

Not too long ago community mental health centers, which treat mental illnesses and depression and help alcoholics, drug addicts and child abusers conquer their problems, were few and far between. Many in the medical community believed that effective treatment required lengthy stays in expensive, long-term facilities, and the emotionally disturbed were often considered outcasts by society. In 1955 some 77 percent of all mental health care was provided by expensive residential institutions, and it's likely many who needed help went without because of high costs, social pressures and fear of being locked away.

Fortunately, the stigma attached to emotional problems has lessened considerably in recent years. By 1975, 70 percent of those suffering emotional distress were treated as outpatients by local mental health facilities like CMHCS.

Success Today

Since it began in 1974 CMHCS has helped over 10,000 people with a well-rounded, inexpensive mental health care program. Its wide range of services include psychological testing and evaluation, individual and family counseling, group therapy, community mental health education, 24-hour call-in emergency service and personal growth training. The Center also helps elderly shut-ins cope with loneliness and other problems. And staffers in the 14-bed inpatient unit stand ready to treat more seriously ill patients.

And in 1979 CMHCS's four satellite clinics throughout the Kansas City area served a total of about 1,200 residents per month.

Center Fees

The Center welcomes residents of all ages and incomes. Fees are charged according to patients' ability to pay. Private physicians in the area charge as much as $50 to $65 an hour while the Center's average fee is $12.

The Center's effectiveness has been bolstered recently by a newly formed speakers bureau, manned by patients who volunteer to educate the community about the Center and mental health problems. Their efforts are increasing community acceptance of outpatient mental health care, helping to dissolve myths about emotional illness and giving hope to others who are hesitant to seek help.

Origin

The Mental Health Center was the inspiration of a group of ministers, school counselors, nurses and citizens who were concerned about the lack of mental health care facilities in their area. In November 1966 they gathered in a church basement to discuss how they might bring mental health resources to Kansas City area residents.

"We pooled our energy to find out what resources were available," recalls CMHCS Executive Director Shirley Fearon. "We dug out information on where the funding was and we called on agencies like the United Way and the State Department of Mental Health" for advice and support.

Helping Youth in Trouble

In 1967 the group formed the South Eastern Jackson County Mental Health Association. The group began with a counseling program to help delinquent youths redirect their lives. Members donated $5 each to help defray costs. Soon after they won $10,000 from the Missouri Criminal Justice System to start the counseling service in a local church, manned by volunteers and supported and assisted by staff from a state mental hospital, a child guidance clinic and a family service agency. The counseling service proved successful—serving 1,500 residents by 1974.

Funding and Staffing the Community Mental Health Center

Meanwhile plans for a community mental health center continued. Troops of volunteeers set out to win public support and funding. They got publicity through such events as entering parades and sponsoring school contests for the best posters depicting what mental health resources could do for the community. And they held fundraising drives at shopping centers, sent mass mailings to residents and lobbied area industries for support. Donations for the building were accumulated from residents and businesses through the gimmick of selling bricks. "Contributors would be able to say they 'owned' a brick of the Clinic," says Fearon.

Between 1966 and 1968, 60 volunteers raised $150,000. The Department of Health, Education and Welfare's Alcohol, Drug Abuse and Mental Health Administration (ADAMHA) kicked in $250,000 for construction and salaries. And in 1974, CMHCS opened with a full-time staff of 36 and an annual budget of $350,000.[1]

Helping the Elderly

In 1979 the Center's annual budget had grown to $1.6 million and the staff to 82.

But volunteers continue to be the backbone of the Center. Volunteers, supervised by the Center's nurses, provide companionship to elderly shut-ins and help with minor home repairs, grocery shopping, meal preparation and transportation. To help seniors cope with loneliness, isolation, poor health and poverty, professional counseling is provided at the Center.

Helping Children and Parents

Since 48 percent of the population in the Center's service area is under the age of 21, special attention is given to the emotional problems of children and their parents. Psychological testing and evaluation, counseling, group therapy and drug and alcohol educational programs are offered to troubled youths and their parents.

Parenting skills are taught to child abusers and how-to-care-for-newborn classes are conducted for new parents by CMHCS personnel in area hospitals.

Other Groups

Other community health centers helping troubled residents include the nonprofit Bexar County Mental Health/Mental Retardation Center in San Antonio, Texas. Five all-volunteer advisory committees, comprised of 51 percent consumers and 49 percent health professionals, help the Center's nine-member Board of Directors determine policy for their various programs. The Center's mental health, mental retardation and alcohol and drug abuse programs, which serve residents of all ages and income levels, helped 14,000 individuals in 1979.

Since 1970 the nonprofit Aroostock Mental Health Center in Fort Fairfield, Maine, one of the state's eight community mental health centers, has served 90,000 residents. It provides follow-up care to patients discharged from local mental health facilities; helps clients build skills in order to function in work, home and social situations; and conducts community education courses through workshops and a speaker's bureau.

And the Prairie View Mental Health Center in Newton, Kansas has a private psychiatric hospital, which offers 70,000 residents in a three-county area comprehensive mental health services in a therapeutic environment. Patients live in two-bedroom, homelike settings. There are no locked doors and both staff and patients wear everyday clothes. Hospital facilities include workshops and a gymnasium and other recreation areas.

Groups Highlighted

Aroostock Mental Health Center
P.O. Box 492
Fort Fairfield, Maine 04742
(207) 472-3511

Bexar County Mental Health/Mental Retardation Center
Central Administration Office
434 South Main Avenue, Suite 400
San Antonio, Texas 78204
(512) 225-4011

Prairie View Mental Health Center
P.O. Box 467
Newton, Kansas 67114
(316) 283-2400

[1] The Community Mental Health Center South (CMHCS) received funds from the Department of Health, Education and Welfare's (HEW) Alcohol, Drug Abuse and Mental Health Administration's (ADAMHA) Mental Health Formula Grant Program;* the Community Mental Health Center Grant Applications Program;* and matching construction funds for their building from the Community Mental Health Center Construction Grant Program, which is no longer in existence.

*State and/or local government agencies are frequently responsible for administration of Federal program funds. For further information, see Appendix I under appropriate Federal agency.

Note: For a complete listing of groups featured throughout this book, see Index.

Care For The Elderly

On Lok Senior Health Services
1490 Mason Street
San Francisco, California 94133
(415) 989-2578

In July 1979 Joe Dare, a 72-year-old resident of San Francisco's Chinatown, was hospitalized for a heart ailment. After being released he faced eviction from the tiny room which had been his home for 43 years.

Knowing that Dare needed some therapy and assistance but clearly wasn't ready for a nursing home, his doctor led him to the nonprofit On Lok Senior Health Services, an area senior citizen center.

On Lok's staff helped Dare find housing and gave him a new lease on life. Each day On Lok provides Dare with transportation to the center where he eats meals and receives therapy under the watchful eye of a professional health team.

"Before On Lok, I cannot walk, cannot eat, but now I getting stronger every day," Dare says gratefully.

For many elderly citizens who need help but don't need the expensive round-the-clock medical care offered by nursing homes, adult day care centers of-

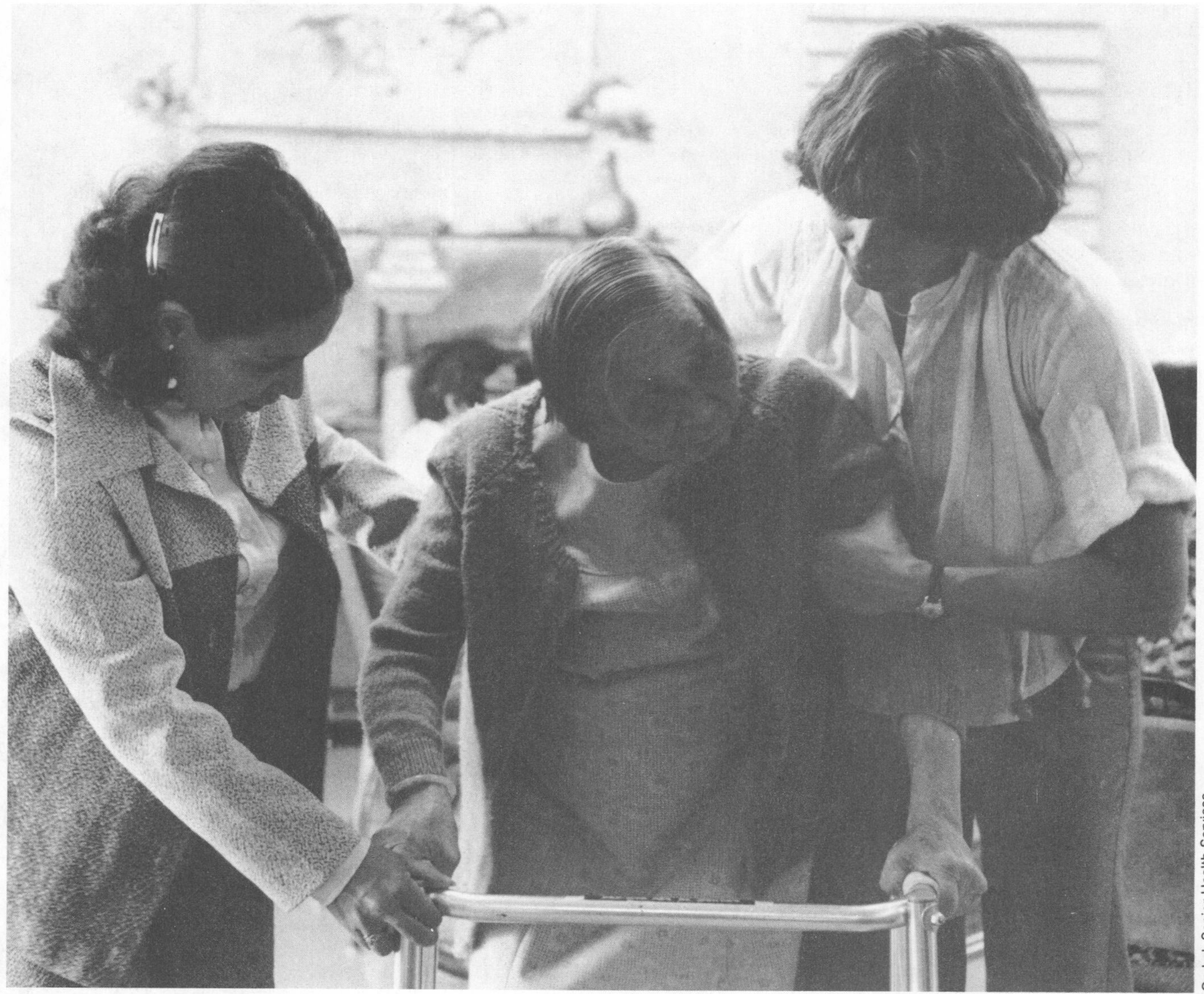

On Lok Senior Health Services

On Lok staffers help elderly lady use a walker.

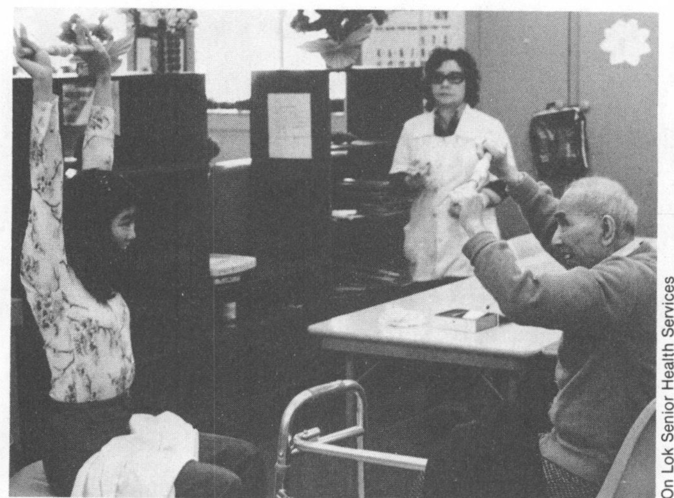

On Lok Senior Health Services

Therapy promotes physical advancement—and can be fun!

fer the best of all worlds—a place to visit daily for food, medical attention and social activities while still being able to return home at night.

Model Center

The successful On Lok Senior Health Services center, which serves San Francisco's Chinatown-North Beach area, opened in 1973. By 1979 its roster of clients—who are mostly Chinese, Filipino and Italian immigrants and are 55 years or older—had grown from two to 220.

On Lok staffers also visit the elderly in their homes and help them with difficult housekeeping chores as well as plan social outings for their clients. For those in need, On Lok has made arrangements for major medical treatment and surgery at two area hospitals. And the 54-unit On Lok house, slated for opening by the fall of 1980, will house 75 and also provide care to many other senior citizens who need only daytime medical attention.

Origins

It began in 1971 when a group of San Francisco health experts and residents became concerned about the shortage of health care facilities for the elderly in the Chinatown-North Beach area.

To remedy the problem the group formed a planning corporation to investigate the possibility of building an area nursing home. A study was launched which revealed that 10,000 area residents were over 65, but a nursing home proved not to be the answer. Many of the area's aging Chinese and other ethnic residents, fearing institutionalization when they became ill, preferred to go without needed medical attention. And most senior citizens did not need constant care.

"Too many people simply enter nursing homes prematurely," explains On Lok's Executive Director Marie-Louise Ansak, an early organizer.

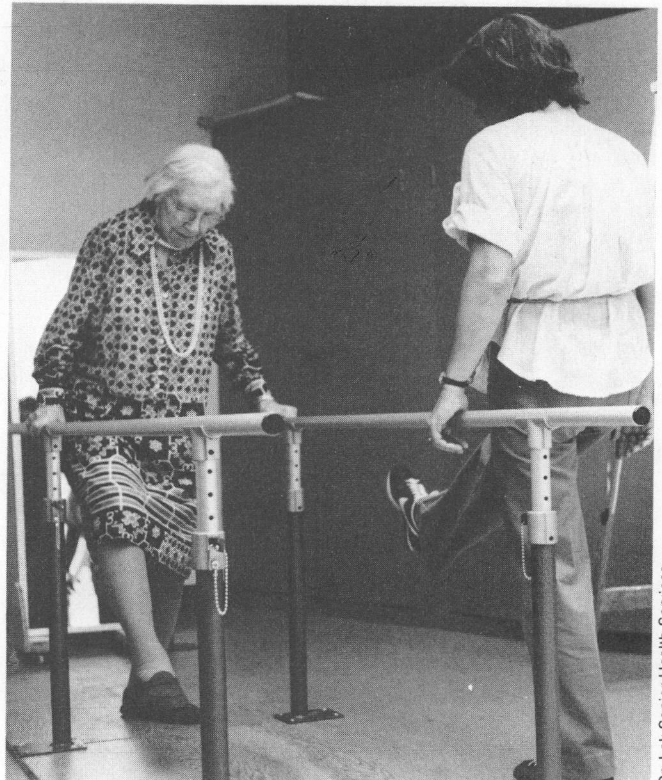

On Lok Senior Health Services

Everyday a little bit higher! On Lok therapist shows how and lends moral support.

Funding

Over the years On Lok has won funding from area businesses, civic organizations and government programs. For instance, a three-year Research and Demonstration Grant* from Title IV of the Older Americans Act,* administered by the Department of Health, Education and Welfare (HEW), allowed development of On Lok's day care facility in a building that once housed a nightclub. And a Model Projects Grant,* also under Title IV, enabled On Lok to include meals, housekeeping and housing assistance programs.

The On Lok House is being constructed with a $2.9 million mortgage and construction loan from the Department of Housing and Urban Development's (HUD) Direct Loans for Housing for the Elderly and Handicapped (Section 202) Program.*

Budget, Staff and Services

In 1979 On Lok's annual budget was $1 million, a dramatic increase over its 1973 budget of $180,000. Their main source of funding is Medicare,* a medical insurance program for the elderly, which is administered by HEW's Health Care Financing Administration. And On Lok's 80-strong paid staff is bolstered by 20 volunteers from area high schools and colleges.

In On Lok's day care facility a team of doctors and nurses provide examinations, physical therapy and laboratory tests. And at nearby Ping On, the social center, On Lok staffers offer games and exercises as well as Chinese and Western style meals which meet the dietary requirements of the senior citizens.

Executive Director Ansak would like to see more centers for the elderly. "I think the On Lok model can be replicated any place," she says. "We need to turn to community-based projects so older people can stay independent and in their own homes instead of being institutionalized right and left."

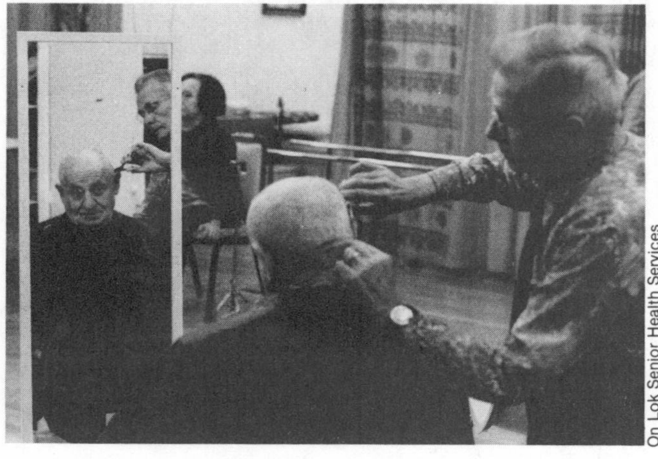

On Lok Senior Health Services

Senior citizens find comraderie and help each other at the On Lok social center.

Other Groups

Other public and private groups are also showing increased interest in adult day health care. The Massachusetts Department of Public Welfare's Adult Day Care Health Services Program funds day health programs across the state. And Massachusetts is currently testing a program which prescreens prospective nursing home patients to determine if alternative community care programs such as adult day health centers could be of greater help.

The Utah State Division of Aging, based in Salt Lake City, funds 29 programs—such as home meals and visiting nurses—that help 400 senior citizens statewide stay in their homes.

Groups Highlighted

Massachusetts Department of Public Welfare
Adult Day Care Health Services Program
Adult Day Care Unit
600 Washington Street, Room 740
Boston, Massachusetts 02111
(167) 727-5438

Utah State Division of Aging
150 West North Temple, Suite 326
Salt Lake City, Utah 84103
(801) 533-6422

*State and/or local government agencies are frequently responsible for administration of Federal program funds. For further information, see Appendix I under appropriate Federal agency.

Note: For a complete listing of groups featured throughout this book, see Index.

Hospices

The Connecticut Hospice, Inc.
Department of Public Information
765 Prospect Street
New Haven, Connecticut 06511
(203) 787-5871

Too often our medical establishment is not equipped, trained or even willing to deal with the dying and their families. The result is that many terminally ill patients spend their remaining days lonely and isolated in hospitals or nursing homes.

But attitudes about death and dying are beginning to change. Thanks to the hospice movement, many terminally ill Americans and their families are facing death more peacefully and comfortably and without the added burden of sky-high medical bills.

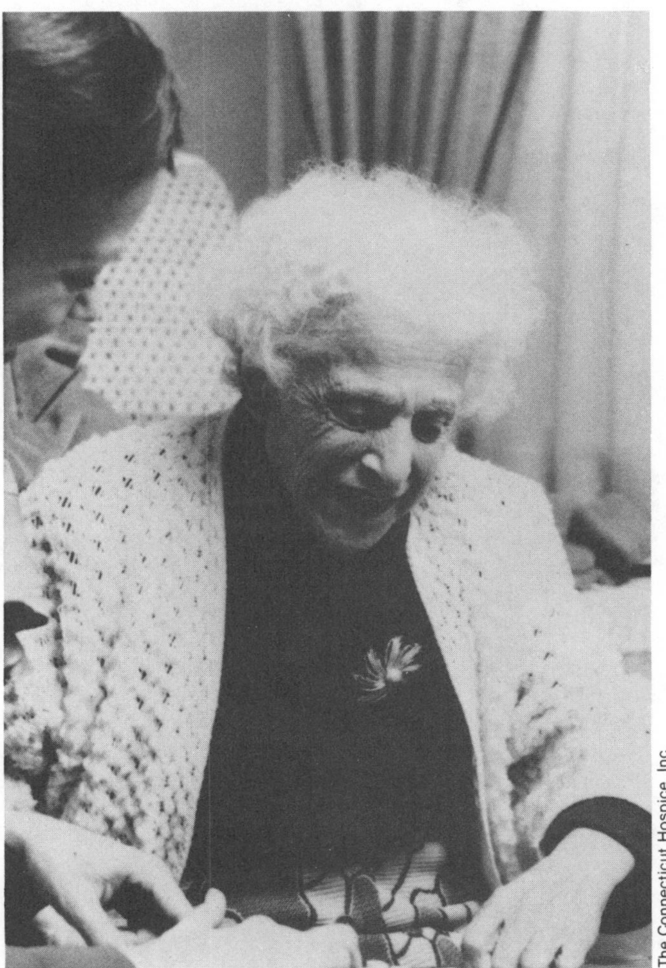

The Connecticut Hospice, Inc.

With guidance from the arts director of the Connecticut Hospice, a willing patient/student learns to play the autoharp.

Hospice programs encourage families to care for their dying relatives at home whenever possible. Medical care and essential emotional and spiritual help come from visiting nurses, doctors and others. Home care is the core of the program although some hospices have facilities where patients may be admitted for short treatment periods.

The American Pioneer

By 1979, according to the National Hospice Organization in Vienna, Virginia, there were more than 200 hospices in 40 states and the District of Columbia.[1]

The hospice movement began in England but was pioneered in this country by the nonprofit New Haven-based Connecticut Hospice, Inc. Since 1974 Connecticut Hospice's home care program has reached almost 1,000 terminally ill patients. In 1979 about 75 percent of the patients in the home program were able to die at home.

Irene Talburtt, a mother of three from North Branford, a suburb of New Haven, well remembers when her husband was ill with stomach cancer. ''After they operated on him,'' she says of her husband ''Tal'' who died in December 1974, ''they discovered there was nothing they could do. He would have to just stay in the hospital.''

She is grateful to the nurse who recommended the Connecticut Hospice home program. ''For Tal, being home was so great,'' she recalls. ''The kids would come home from school and tell him about their day, and they felt good because they could do things for him—little things, like fluff his pillow.''

Success Today

Connecticut Hospice, which operates out of an old house near Yale University, estimates that families are involved in the Hospice home program an average of 61 days at costs of about $19 per day—which contrasts sharply with the $325 average daily rate of area hospitals.

The Hospice home program will soon be supplemented by a 44-bed inpatient facility for those unable to stay at home or who need periodic hospitalization. The new complex in nearby Branford is scheduled for opening in the summer of 1980 and will offer ''like home'' patient rooms—large enough to permit visits by family members and friends who will be welcomed at all hours. The facility will serve residents statewide and will be the base for the home program. It will also include an outpatient clinic, administrative offices and a day care center for children of staff and volunteers.

Eligibility Requirements

With their physicians' consent, patients with a prognosis of six months or less to live are eligible for the Connecticut Hospice home program. Patients are admitted on the basis of health needs rather than ability to pay. And those without financial resources who are not covered by private or government medical plans are charged according to what they can afford.

Some of Connecticut Hospice's low-income and elderly patients receive financial help to enter the program from a number of Federal programs, including Title III of the Older Americans Act* and Title XX of the Social Security Act* as well as Medicare* and Medicaid.*[2]

How the Hospice Works

Treatment begins with a home visit by staffers and a host of volunteers that make up the Hospice team, including doctors, nurses, social workers and members of the clergy. Usually a nurse is assigned to each family to coordinate health services and, along with the rest of the Hospice team, is on call 24 hours a day.

The Connecticut Hospice, Inc.

Young twins are a special joy to their grandmother during a visit from a Connecticut Hospice volunteer physician.

Pain Free and Alert

The first step in Hospice home care is to free patients of their physical and emotional pain. A combination of drugs is given in careful around-the-clock doses, leaving patients comfortable but alert.

Dealing with Death

After the patient is comfortable the Hospice team turns its attention to helping the patient and family adjust to death, overcome anxieties and fears and live as fully as possible.

Family members are taught how to care for the patient by a physician, nurse and therapist who routinely visit the home. Volunteers also make frequent visits, helping with everything from household chores to transportation to drawing family members into relaxing conversation. As a sympathetic listener, the volunteer enables the patient and family to talk about fears, regrets, disappointments and grief.

"My initial reaction to the Hospice team was 'oh my goodness, who are these people,' but they turned out to be the answer to our prayers," Mrs. Talburtt says. "They kept reminding us that we had to talk about things like Tal's will and were things in order. They had a way of bringing things up so they didn't bother you."

And she adds, "They helped the children accept (his impending death) so much better . . . letting them know it was normal to have lots of feelings about what was going on."

When All is Said and Done

The Hospice program also aims to hasten the family's adjustment following death, and volunteers continue to provide support after the patient dies.

"When all was said and done, the children felt they had done everything they wanted to do for him," recalls Mrs. Talburtt. "They had been a part of everything up through the end, including picking out the casket. And without the Hospice program I would never have known that I could do what I did to care for him."

Origins

The Connecticut Hospice is modeled after Britain's St. Christopher's which opened in London in 1967 under the leadership of Dr. Cicely Saunders. Dr. Saunders visited health professionals in this country to promote hospices and inspired a group of medical, church and community leaders to look into the possibility of a program for the New Haven area. There was some initial skepticism but most community leaders and service agencies supported the concept. In November 1971 Connecticut Hospice was incorporated, and a handful of part-time volunteers began developing the program out of two rooms in a local church.

Winning Funds

By 1974 three foundations had provided major funding to get the program off the ground.[3] And the Connecticut General Assembly had pumped in $1.5 million—half the cost of building and equipping the planned inpatient facility. The action helped to spur Congressional approval of $1 million in Federal funds from the Department of Health, Education and Welfare's (HEW) National Center for Health Services Research.*

Meanwhile, the group entered a $790,000 three-year contract with HEW's National Cancer Institute's Division of Cancer Control and Rehabilitation* to launch the Hospice home care program.

Staff and Budget

In early 1980, with the planned opening of the new facility, the Connecticut Hospice's budget reached $2.5 million. And its 125 employees were supported by a roster of 300 volunteers.

Now the group's Hospice Institute for Education, Training and Research is helping others across the country to learn about the hospice concept and develop programs in their own areas.[4]

Religious Support for Hospices

Synagogues and churches across the country are supporting the hospice movement. For instance, volunteers from the Temple Emanuel congregation in Davenport, Iowa provide moral and spiritual support to patients of the local Hospice Care Group, Inc. and are prepared to assist with special needs such as providing kosher meals for Jewish patients wishing to continue their religious customs.

Other Groups

A hospice similar to that of Connecticut's is the Hospice of Marin (HOM) in San Rafael, California, which provides medical, psychological and social services to terminal cancer patients and their families. HOM offers seminars and training programs on patient care for individuals who wish to develop or work with hospice care teams across the country.[5]

The second hospice home care program to be developed in the United States, HOM's services began in February 1976. One unique feature of the HOM organization is the formation of an auxiliary called "Friends of Hospice." About 40 volunteers sponsor fundraising benefits to support HOM's work such as wine tastings, dinners and lectures.

And the Boulder County Hospice in Boulder, Colorado offers a slide presentation on hospices to groups across the country for a $25 rental fee.[6] The Boulder Hospice runs a home care program for the terminally ill and offers educational programs for those interested in caring for patients.

Groups Highlighted

Boulder County Hospice, Inc.
2118 14th Street
Boulder, Colorado 80302
(303) 449-7740

Hospice Care Group, Inc.
2501 East Pleasant Street
Davenport, Iowa 52803
(319) 326-6512

Hospice of Marin
77 Mark Drive, Suite 19
San Rafael, California 94903
(415) 472-0742

[1] For more information on the National Hospice Organization, see Resources at end of Health Section.

[2] The Medicare and Medicaid Programs,* as well as Title XX of the Social Security Act* are all administered by the Department of Health, Education and Welfare's (HEW) Health Care Financing Administration; Title III of the Older Americans Act* is administered by HEW's Administration on Aging's Office of Human Development Services. Medicare provides basic health benefits to elderly residents who are receiving Social Security while Medicaid, through grants to individual states, provides medical services to the needy.

[3] Initial funding for the Connecticut Hospice program came from the Commonwealth Fund, Sachem Fund and Kaiser Family Fund Foundations.

[4] For more information on the Hospice Institute for Education, Training and Research, see Resources at end of Health Section.

[5] For more information on the Hospice of Marin (HOM), see Resources at end of Health Section.

[6] The slide tape presentation of the Boulder County Hospice, Inc., is entitled "Hospice Care: An Alternative" and is available by writing the Boulder group at 2118 14th Street, Boulder, Colorado 80302.

*State and/or local government agencies are frequently responsible for administration of Federal program funds. For further information, see Appendix I under appropriate Federal agency.

Note: For a complete listing of groups featured throughout this book, see Index.

Specialized Cooperatives

Co-op Optical Service
Division of Cooperative Services, Inc.
7404 Woodward Avenue
Detroit, Michigan 48202
(313) 874-4000

It's not just hindsight that can provide 20/20 vision. A look at the heartening experience of Co-op Optical Services in Detroit, Michigan will prove otherwise. Co-op Optical has built a $4.3 million-a-year business by providing customers with high quality, low-cost eye service.

More than half of all United States citizens, or 120 million Americans, wear or need eyeglasses or other eye care services. Those customers support an optical industry with projected 1982 retail sales of $10 billion—which includes eye examinations, medical treatment, frames, lenses and eyeglass tints and coatings. And by the turn of the century 90 percent of the more than 43 million Americans over the age of 60 will need some type of eye care—a bonanza for the optical business.

Co-op Optical provides low-cost, high quality eye care.

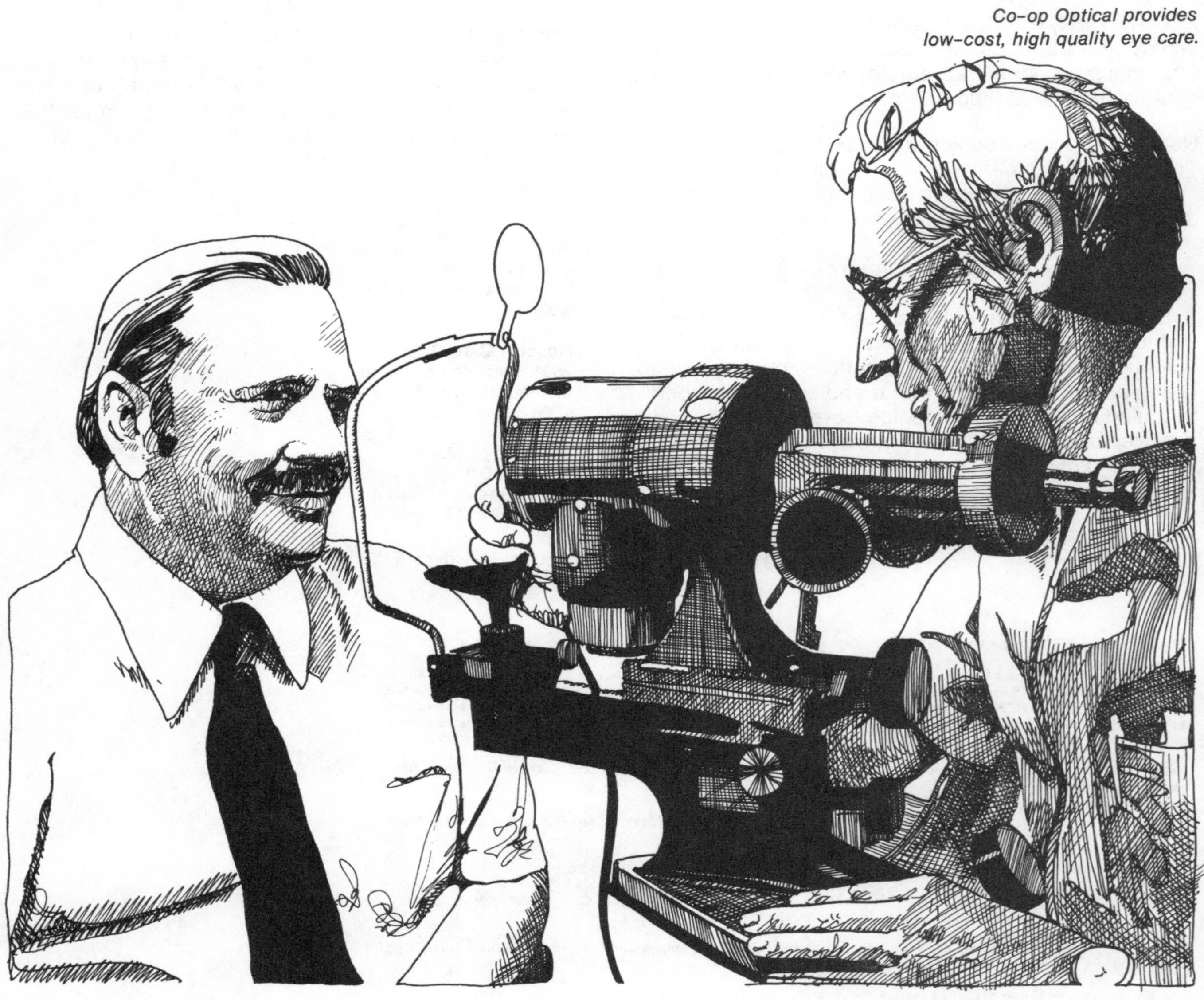

Eye Care Alternative

The nonprofit Co-op Optical is one of a small number of health co-ops around the country that is providing consumers with lower-cost health care alternatives. The Co-op, owned and operated by its members, estimates they save each of 100,000 customers a year at least $10 on eyeglasses.

In 1979 Co-op Optical had a staff of 81, a central laboratory and nine eye care centers which offer examinations at costs comparable to or lower than other facilities in the area.

Mr. and Mrs. Arthur Schaldenbrand, whose six children all wear glasses, have been Co-op Optical customers since 1971. ''I would say we get very good savings,'' says Mrs. Schaldenbrand. ''And the Co-op is also very good about repairs.''

Origins

The optical service is the brainchild of Cooperative Services, Inc. (CSI), a diversified cooperative organized in 1942.[1] By 1979 CSI's 4,000 members owned eight housing projects, an optical and dental service, a construction company, an architectural service and a credit union.

In 1960, to get Co-op Optical off the ground, CSI raised $15,000 from member contributions and borrowed $10,000 from its credit union.[2] An advisory council of labor and credit union representatives was formed and the group hired an optical services consultant to help determine needed equipment, inventory and personnel.

Co-op in the Red

But six months after Co-op Optical opened in April 1960 it was running in the red and had severely drained the resources of CSI. The group had difficulty finding optometrists to work for the Co-op and they had only a small pool of customers.

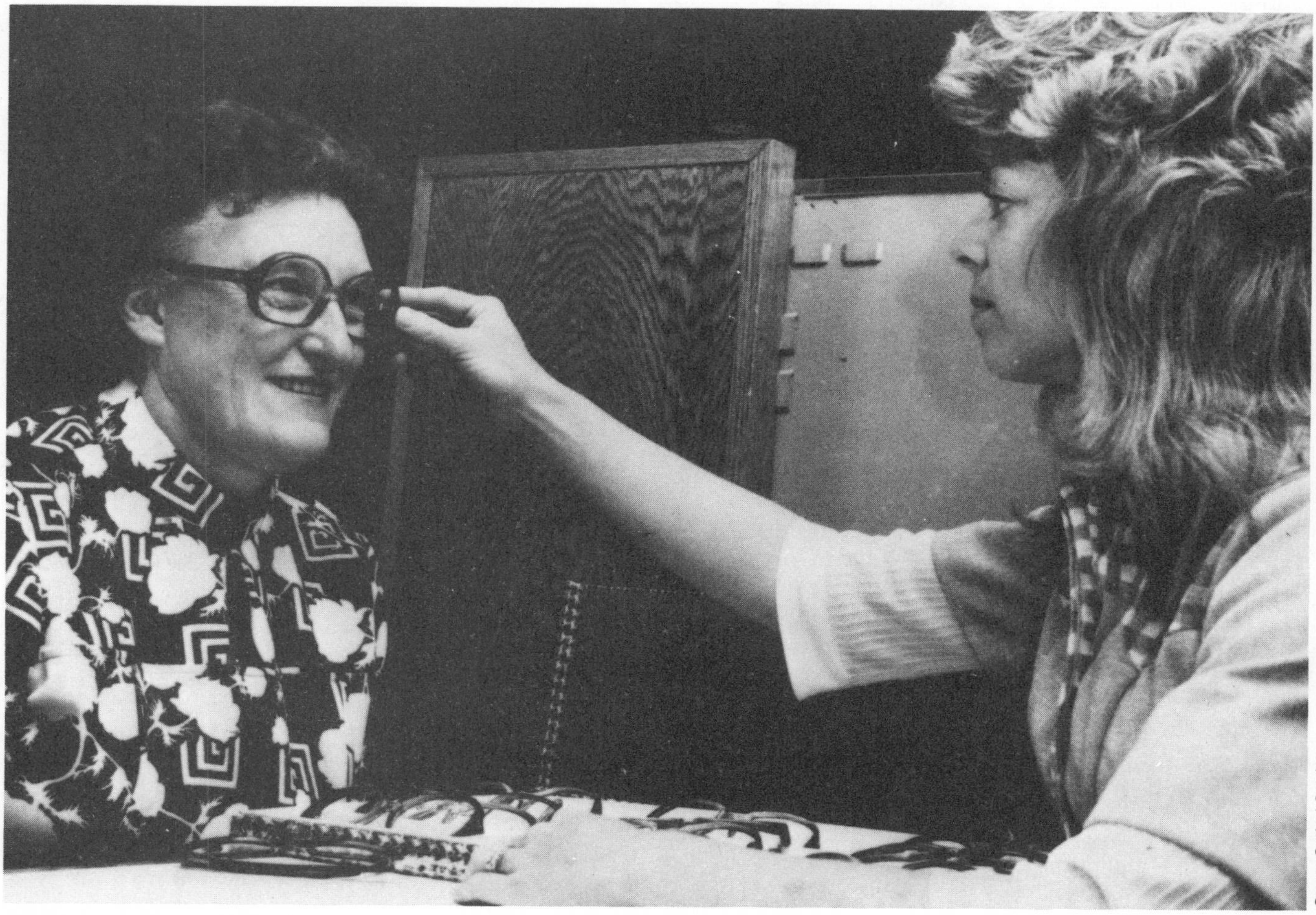

Co-op Optical Service

Selecting a frame at the Co-op

To overcome the shortage of professional staff the group hoped to attract optometrists from other states. But the State Licensing and Examining Board was approving few applications for reciprocity, an arrangement between states which allows professionals to transfer their licenses from one state to another. By marshaling public support and lobbying for enforcement of reciprocity, the Co-op was able to place one of its members on the State Licensing and Examining Board. Their lobbying efforts and representation on the Board led to more liberal consideration of reciprocity applicants.

Success Today

To reach a larger audience the group entered into eye care contracts with area labor unions and companies, the first of which was signed with the National Association of Machinists. Today the Co-op has 300 such contracts which serve 35,000 families and bring in more than half of the Co-op's annual receipts. A typical contract costs an employer $43 a year for each employee and his or her family. Contracts include eye exams, glasses and choices of frames. Contact lenses or special lense tints are extra.

The Co-op serves both CSI members and area residents, who become nonvoting members for a one-time $2 fee or voting members for $10. The fee entitles them to the services of Co-op Optical as well as CSI's dental cooperative and credit union.

New Competition Threatens Co-op

In 1980 Co-op Optical faces a new challenge: competition from chain stores and designer houses which have entered the eyeglass business. For instance, one chain store opened 20 stores simultaneously in the Detroit area, all offering eyeglass services. And chain stores attract high volume business with heavy television advertising—something the Co-op can't afford.

Moreover, chains and designer houses are boosting consumer interest in high-fashion glasses to counter the traditionally slow rate of repurchasing among wearers. "They treat glasses like hemlines," says Co-op Optical's manager Fred Thornthwaite. By ordering in large quantities chain stores can cut the costs of fashion eyeglasses. But the Co-op is unable to offer as much savings to customers on such items as upswept frames or oversized lenses because they are more expensive for the Co-op to buy.

However, the Co-op is determined to retain its competitive edge. The high fashion lines it offers are generally lower priced than those of chain stores. For instance, in 1979 the Co-op price for over-sized, tinted bifocals was $59, about $10 less than at most other stores. And the Co-op's $18 eye exam was comparable to or less than the $20 to $30 price charged by chain stores and private optometrists.

Price Survey Conducted by Co-op Optical Service, 1980.

Local Optical Centers	Exam	Tint		Single Vision Lens	Bifocal Lens (D-SEG)
Discount Chain Store	$ —	$ 5.00 - $12.00	glass	$20.00	$30.00
			plastic	20.00	45.00
Another Co-op	$18.00	8.00 - 13.50	glass	28.00	40.00
			plastic	28.00	50.00
Optical Company A	22.00	7.00	glass	33.00	36.00
			plastic	39.00	55.00
Optical Company B	20.00	10.00	glass	23.00	35.00
			plastic	26.00	55.00
Co-op Optical	18.00	5.00 - 8.00	glass	18.00	26.50
			plastic	21.50	44.50

Future Plans Include Expansion

Co-op Optical would like to establish more eye care clinics if they can find needed capital. (One potential funding source is the newly created National Consumer Cooperative Bank,** which provides technical and/or financial assistance to qualifying cooperatives.) Co-op Optical also hopes to increase business by forging strong alliances with more labor unions and other cooperatives.

Another Health Co-op

The co-op approach can be used for other health needs too. The Northwest Wisconsin Health Cooperative in Turtle Lake, Wisconsin was formed in response to the lack of low-cost dental care in the area, which caused residents to forego regular checkups.

The nonprofit co-op dental clinic opened in June 1977 after Dr. Michael Prusak, a local dentist, collected $6,000 from fundraising efforts and individual contributions. Word-of-mouth advertising and newspaper and magazine articles attracted patients to the clinic.

And by 1979 the clinic's small staff of one dentist, a receptionist/assistant and a part-time office manager was treating 500 to 700 patients a year at fees 25 to 50 percent below comparable rates in the area. Co-op membership is $5 per person and patients are charged according to ability to pay. Members elect the five-member Board of Directors.

Group Highlighted

Northwest Wisconsin Health Cooperative
Box 64
Turtle Lake, Wisconsin 54889
(715) 986-2599

[1] For more information on Cooperative Services, Inc. (CSI), see Housing Resources under "Building Together: How To Get Housing You Can Afford."

[2] For more information on credit unions, see Housing Section, p. 162.

**For further information, see Appendix II under "National Consumer Cooperative Bank."

Note: For a complete listing of groups featured throughout this book, see Index.

Chapter 3

Emphasizing Health Education and Self-Care

Introduction

It is said that knowledge is power. Without knowledge about our bodies or the medical resources available to us, we are more dependent on professionals and lose a certain amount of control over our lives. But as informed health consumers we can often avoid illness, stay healthy and save money.

Citizen groups across the country are bringing power to their neighbors by arming them with knowledge on a wide range of health subjects such as preventive medicine, low-cost alternative health care and community health care planning. Their educational approaches differ widely but the groups share a determination to help consumers make informed health decisions.

Some of our featured health care providers have spread the word through printed information. For instance, to help residents decide who will provide their medical care, an ambitious group in Cleveland, Ohio published a medical directory of area doctors and hospitals.

And an influential student controlled public interest group in New York decided to inform residents about the differences between brand name drugs and their chemically equivalent "generic" counterparts. The group unearthed startling variations in drug prices and successfully lobbied for significant reforms in state regulations, saving New York consumers millions of dollars.

Others are educating residents by listening first. We look at a Northern Virginia hotline which is staffed by volunteers who sympathetically respond to troubled callers and refer them to needed health resources.

In some instances people are avoiding unnecessary doctor visits by learning about their bodies and how to take care of themselves. For example, patients of a Minnesota clinic learn how—and when—to treat themselves by participating in examinations and laboratory tests.

And rural Alabama residents are learning through "health fairs" how to develop needed medical facilities with the help and inspiration of students at the University of Alabama. Residents are also offered a full range of free medical examinations and laboratory testing.

We end this chapter appropriately enough by highlighting a New York City group that helps residents become informed about a wide range of health issues. The organization's resources include a free medical library, a fact-filled newsletter on health topics and a telephone hotline containing taped information on over 100 health issues.

All of these programs show how knowledge can lead to better health. Establishing similar programs in your area is one of the best ways to contribute to your community's good health.

Directories

Cleveland Medical Directory
Cleveland Consumer Action Foundation
532 Terminal Tower
Cleveland, Ohio 44113
(216) 687-0525

You may be able to picture the doctor you want in your mind—a competent, old-fashioned general practitioner who offers convenient hours and reasonable prices. But often, finding the doctor that best suits your needs is not an easy task.

The two traditional sources of information on doctors, local medical societies and the Yellow Pages, give little more than names, addresses and specialties. Friends and neighbors are another source but their information is often sketchy, dated or based largely on personality. Being new to a town makes the problem just that much harder.

Some citizen groups have helped residents make responsible decisions about which doctors and other medical professionals to entrust with their health care by publishing medical directories which give a wide range of information on community health services.

The Cleveland Directory

In 1978, for instance, the Cleveland Consumer Action Foundation (CCAF), a nonprofit Ohio group, published the *Cleveland Medical Directory* which contains information on nearly 700 area doctors, 18 clinics, four Health Maintenance Organizations (HMOs) and 32 hospitals.[1]

The Directory lists doctors' hours, specialties, hospital affiliations, prescription practices and—in as many cases as possible—fees. And it also contains information on how to judge hospitals and read prescriptions, the difference between brand name and lower priced generic prescription drugs, profiles of local hospitals and a glossary of medical terms.[2]

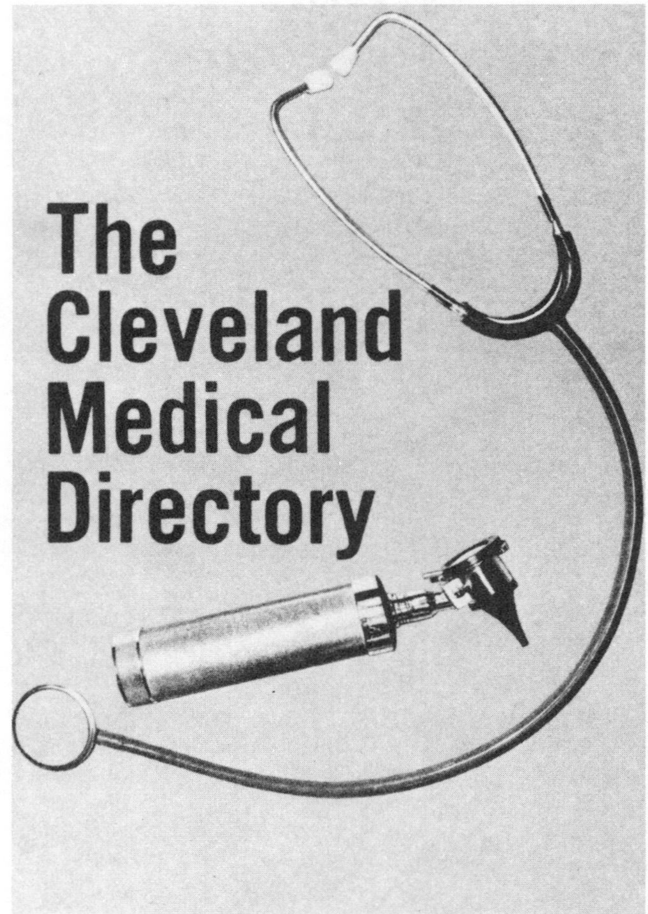

Planned and designed by a part-time staff of six volunteers and one paid person, the Directory was produced in a year. And by the end of 1979, 1,500 copies had been sold for $3.95 each, enabling the group to recoup $4,000 of the Directory's $6,000 production costs.

Reaching Buyers and Nonbuyers

CCAF was able to spur sales of the Directory and get the information to thousands of nonbuyers by launching a publicity campaign. A news conference announcing publication of the Directory was followed by radio and television talk shows. The group's publicity efforts were rewarded with an exhaustive summary of the Directory on the front page of the *Cleveland Press* and long articles in the *Cleveland Plain Dealer,* the local newspapers, as well as in *Cleveland Magazine.* Moreover, 100 Directories were purchased by area libraries.

Impetus for the Directory

CCAF knew that rising health care costs and lack of information on doctors and hospitals were major concerns of Cleveland consumers. The group's interest in producing a directory was sparked in the spring of 1977 by a *Consumer Reports* article on how to put a local medical directory together.[3] The group was also encouraged by a Federal Trade Commission (FTC) challenge to the American Medical Association's (AMA) ban on physician advertising which led AMA to relax its restrictions in 1975.

Getting Started

CCAF began by designing and sending questionnaires to 1,200 area physicians asking for a wide range of information on their practices.

After receiving replies from 670 doctors, the staff conducted phone interviews with clinic, hospital and Health Maintenance Organization personnel. Information was confirmed by those doctors and organizations responding to the questionnaires. Staffers then pasted up the Directory themselves to save on production costs.

Drawback

Unfortunately, only 190 doctors agreed to divulge fees. But since the Directory was published the stigma attached to doctors revealing fee information has considerably lessened. Doctors, dentists and other medical professionals are now encouraged to

The Cleveland Medical Directory boasts a wealth of health information.

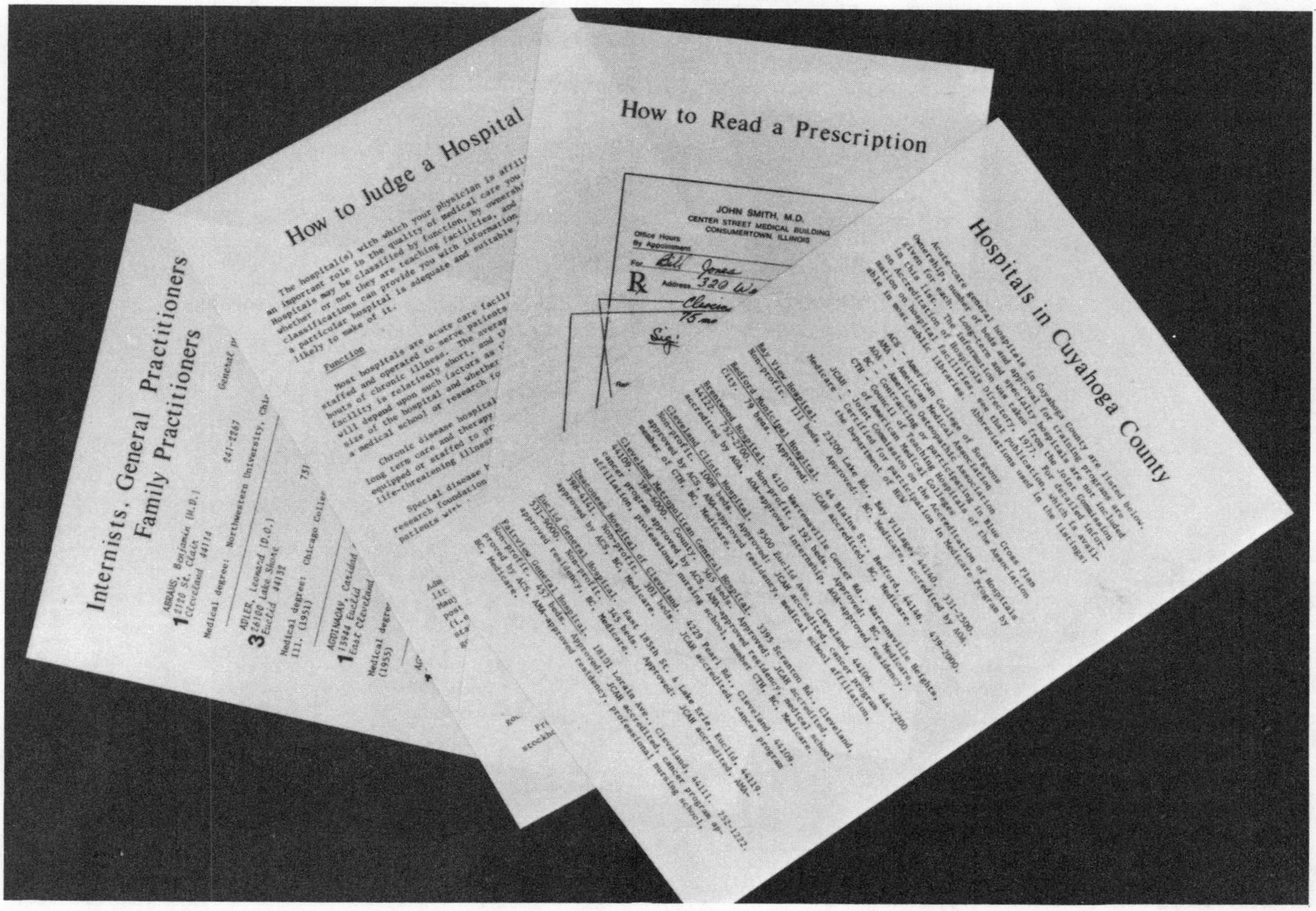

provide consumers with the price information they need to make informed choices, which should make future medical directories an even more valuable consumer tool.

Other Groups

Other consumer groups around the country are publishing directories and studies to help residents shop for medical care.

Community Advocates, Inc. published the *Consumer Guide to Hospitals in Nassau and Suffolk Counties* in 1979. With a foundation grant the group printed 5,000 copies of the guide which covers such topics as area hospital ownership and accreditation, medical school affiliation, emergency room service, special fees, billing practices and accessibility of hospitals to public transportation.

Taking a hospital survey one step further, the Maryland Public Interest Research Group (MaryPIRG), a nonprofit student-operated research and consumer advocacy group, published a study entitled *Acute Hospitalitis: A Consumer's Guide to Health Care Costs,* which focuses attention on extra hospital charges.[4] The group's survey revealed that low room rates don't guarantee low hospital bills. Hospitals aren't rated in the guide, but rising costs are reviewed and valuable hospital shopping advice is provided.

And in Washington D.C. the nonprofit Washington Center for the Study of Services publishes a quarterly directory for area residents. *Washington Consumers' Checkbook* compares prices and rates quality of area services.[5] The first issue, *Checkbook: Health,* for instance, covered area emergency rooms, HMOs, health insurance, drugs and nursing homes as well as practitioner fees for standard medical and dental procedures. Besides surveying service providers and consumers by mail and telephone, *Checkbook* staffers use unusual approaches to measure quality. For instance, they surveyed hospital emergency waiting rooms to determine waiting time before treatment. Now self-supporting, *Checkbook* has surveyed many other kinds of services such as credit and banking, auto repair and food retailing.

Some organizations have published directories for specific groups of consumers. For instance, the D.C. Public Interest Research Group (D.C. PIRG) recently compiled *Health Care for Women: A Guide to Services in the D.C. Area,* which lists women's clinics, obstetricians and gynecologists.[6]

Groups Highlighted

Community Advocates, Inc.
P.O. Box 71
Roslyn, New York 11576
(516) 487-0451

D.C. Public Interest Research Group
(D.C. PIRG)
P.O. Box 19542
Washington, D.C. 20036
(202) 676-7388

Maryland Public Interest Research Group
(MaryPIRG)
University of Maryland
3110 Main Dining Hall
College Park, Maryland 20742
(301) 454-5601

Washington Center for the Study of Services
1518 K Street, N.W., Suite 406
Washington, D.C. 20005
(202) 347-9612

[1] A Health Maintenance Organization (HMO) is a prepaid health care plan that delivers comprehensive, coordinated medical services to voluntarily enrolled members. HMOs are profiled in the Health Section, p. 290.

[2] For more information on generic versus brand name drugs, see profile in Health Section, p. 329.

[3] *Consumer Reports* is a monthly magazine published by the nonprofit Consumers Union. Subscriptions are $12 a year and can be obtained by writing *Consumer Reports,* Orangeburg, New York 10962.

[4] *Acute Hospitalitis: A Consumer's Guide to Health Care Costs* is available for $2 from MaryPIRG, 3110 Main Dining Hall, University of Maryland, College Park, Maryland 20742.

[5] The Washington Center for the Study of Services' *Washington Consumers' Checkbook* can be obtained for $16 per year by writing the group at 1518 K Street, N.W., Suite 406, Washington, D.C. 20005. (For more information on the Washington Center, see Resources at end of Basic Tools Section.)

[6] *Health Care for Women: A Guide to Services in the D.C. Area* is available for $1 from D.C. PIRG, P.O. Box 19542, Washington, D.C. 20036.

Note: For a complete listing of groups featured throughout this book, see Index.

Prescription Drug Surveys

New York Public Interest Research Group (NYPIRG)
5 Beekman Street
New York, New York 10038
(212) 349-6460

Many consumers don't bother to shop around and compare prescription drug prices. Unaware of huge price differences—sometimes as much as 200 or 300 percent in a single neighborhood—they don't question their doctors or their pharmacists about savings that could be realized by buying alternative drugs.

Brand Name Versus Generic

Each year consumers are paying hundreds of millions of dollars more for brand name prescription drugs when chemically equivalent "generic" drugs are available at lower prices. And according to the United States Food and Drug Administration, these lesser known drugs are as safe and effective as their higher priced counterparts.

To overcome this problem, more than 40 states have passed generic substitution laws that either allow or require pharmacists to substitute generic for brand name drugs if the treating physician has no objection.

One Group's Success

One private, nonprofit research and advocacy organization, the New York Public Interest Research Group (NYPIRG), studied the problem in New York and helped get a state generic law enacted that saves consumers millions of dollars each year and was heralded as the most important consumer measure passed by the New York State Legislature in 1977.

After the law was passed NYPIRG began a campaign to boost consumers' awareness of the law and help them get the maximum benefit from it.

Moreover, to monitor compliance with the legislation, NYPIRG conducted follow-up studies and launched a training program to teach consumers how to compare drug prices and determine if their pharmacists are complying with the law.

Drug Price Posting Violations

NYPIRG began tackling the generic drug issue in the winter of 1973-74 when student volunteers, working under a paid coordinator, decided to check reports that pharmacies were violating a 1973

Brooklyn College Drug Price Survey of Flatbush-Midwood Area
Partial survey compiled by NYPIRG and Brooklyn College Consumer Education Classes
April, 1979

Pharmacy Address	Brand Name: **Achromycin 250 mg/20 tabs**	Generic Equivalent: **Tetracycline hydrochloride 250 mg/20 tabs**	Brand Name: **Librium 10 mg/90 caps**	Generic Equivalent: **Chlordiazepoxide hydrochloride 10 mg/90 caps**	Brand Name: **V-Cillin K 250 mg/20 tabs**	Generic Equivalent: **Penicillin V Potassium 250 mg/20 tabs**
1066 Flatbush Ave.	$3.95	$2.95	$12.45	$ 4.95	$4.45	$2.95
1148 Flatbush Ave.	$3.60	$3.10	$11.50	$ 4.75	$4.50	$3.75
1258 Flatbush Ave.	$4.50	$3.50	$17.95	$ 9.95	$4.50	$3.95
1490 Flatbush Ave.	$5.00	$4.00	$12.95	$ 8.95	$5.04	$4.00
1830 Flatbush Ave.	$4.50	$2.75	$13.95	(didn't carry)	$4.50	(didn't carry)
2064 Flatbush Ave.	$3.45	$2.85	$ 8.10	$ 4.45	$4.30	$3.10
2472 Flatbush Ave.	$2.95	$2.50	$11.50	$10.50	$5.95	$3.95

Partial results of a NYPIRG survey as recorded by Project Director Carole Gould and student volunteers.

state law requiring drug prices to be visibly and clearly posted. The students surveyed more than 200 pharmacies in Queens and found widespread abuses—nearly 40 percent had either posted price lists in obscure corners or not at all.

NYPIRG Takes Action

While conducting the survey the students also became aware of large drug price differences. So NYPIRG—along with senior citizen and community groups, public organizations, government agencies and State Assembly committees—set out to win passage of the Generic Drug Law which was implemented in April 1978. Under this law, the placement of a doctor's signature on the right-hand side of a standard format prescription slip signifies that the doctor has no objection to generic substitution. Pharmacists are then required to substitute the lower-cost drug. This procedure makes it easy for doctors to prescribe generic drugs even if they are not familiar with the generic name.

Follow-Up Study and Results

A NYPIRG follow-up study conducted a year later revealed that 98 percent of the pharmacists surveyed were violating one or more provisions of the state law. And the study unearthed these startling facts:

- More than half of the pharmacists refused to dispense generic drugs even when doctors requested it.

- The average price of brand name drugs statewide was 29 percent higher than that of companion generic drugs. In a striking example, the lowest price in the state for one generic drug, 90 cents, was found in Syracuse and the highest price, found in Manhattan, for its brand name equivalent was $4.95 —a difference of 550 percent!

"Pharmacists across the state have demonstrated a pattern of lawlessness that in any other area of public life would be called a crime wave by editorialists," a NYPIRG staffer told a state legislative committee. The group called for tough action by the State Board of Pharmacy and greater integrity by pharmacy associations and individual pharmacists.

Based on this study and others, the Pharmacy Board fined 50 drug stores for noncompliance with the state law. "Most agree that the Board would never have acted had these studies not been conducted," says NYPIRG staffer Glen Gersmehl.

New York's Generic Drug Law

- New York's Generic Drug Law requires that patients receive prescriptions on slips containing two lines for doctors' signatures.
- Doctors fill in the top part of the prescription slips in the usual manner—name of patient, date, drug prescribed and how it is to be taken.
- By signing on the right-hand line over the statement "substitution permissible," doctors allow pharmacists to substitute generic for brand name drugs.
- Substitutions are forbidden when doctors sign on the left-hand side over the statement "dispense as written."

Rx

JOHN DOE, M.D.
MEDICAL BUILDING
OAK STREET
ANYTOWN, NEW YORK 00000

Jane Doe April 8 1980

John Doe, M.D.

· DISPENSE AS WRITTEN SUBSTITUTION PERMISSIBLE

Consumer Education Programs

Moreover, NYPIRG's consumer training program for senior citizen, social service, church and other community groups has reached 10,000 New York residents. "Our training program builds consumer skills in communication with doctors and pharmacists," says Gersmehl. "We help them to be more assertive and better informed. We train people to make price comparisons, for example."

Visual aids and role playing exercises are used to help individuals deal effectively with doctors and pharmacists. And technical assistance is offered to community leaders who wish to train others in their areas.

Mrs. Virginia Fenton, director of the Salem Senior Citizen Center in Harlem where NYPIRG conducted a series of training sessions, says, "The people who come here now know what drugs to ask for. The NYPIRG program offered our senior citizens an opportunity to learn how to get needed drugs for less money."

PIRG Staffing and Funding

Incorporated in 1973, NYPIRG began as a student organization with five staffers and two offices on three university campuses. By 1979 NYPIRG was the city's largest citizen/student action group with more than 100 paid staffers in 26 offices across the state. In 1979 NYPIRG's $1 million budget came from its 200,000 student members, most of whom pay dues of $2 a semester; door-to-door fundraising and other contributions; and publications sales. And grants from the Department of Health, Education and Welfare's (HEW) Office of Consumer Education have helped defray the cost of NYPIRG's community education programs.[1]

Other Surveys

Lynn Jordan, former president of the nonprofit Springfield-based Virginia Citizens Consumer Council (VCCC), was a driving force behind a drug pricing campaign that led to a landmark decision by the United States Supreme Court in 1976. The Court ruled that bans on pharmacist drug advertising blunt competition and violate consumer rights. With the decision, the problem for consumers is no longer to advocate state laws allowing drug price advertising—it is making sure the laws are obeyed and that consumers use the price information.

Background

The litigation arose in 1973 when Jordan and VCCC were asked by the Washington, D.C.-based, nonprofit Citizen Action Group to help challenge the legality of the Virginia Board of Pharmacy's advertising ban. VCCC conducted a study of pharmacies and found price variations as high as 100 percent—as well as discrepancies in prices quoted to consumers. Since the Supreme Court decision, VCCC has actively promoted drug advertising and has garnered newspaper, magazine and television attention nationwide.

University Study Supports Law

In August 1977 researchers from the University of Florida's Pharmacy College and the Health Services Research and Development Program of the Veterans Administration Medical Center launched a study of pharmacists' attitudes, drug selections and pricing policies. The group found that generic drugs could save consumers an average of one-third on prescription purchases. The group's findings helped persuade the State Legislature not to weaken or repeal Florida's 1976 generic drug law.

Groups Highlighted

Health Services Research and Development Program
Veterans Administration Medical Center
Gainesville, Florida 32602
(904) 376-6575

University of Florida
College of Pharmacy
Gainesville, Florida 32702
(904) 392-3541

Virginia Citizens Consumer Council
P.O. Box 777
Springfield, Virginia 22153
(703) 455-9515

[1] The Department of Health, Education and Welfare's (HEW) Office of Consumer Education provided NYPIRG with grants under the Consumer Education and Advocacy Training for Adults Program* and Community Services and Continuing Education Program.*

*State and/or local government agencies are frequently responsible for administration of Federal program funds. For further information, see Appendix I under appropriate Federal agency.

Note: For a complete listing of groups featured throughout this book, see Index.

Hotlines

Northern Virginia Hotline
P.O. Box 187
Arlington, Virginia 22210
(703) 522-4460

"People who need people," croons Barbra Streisand, "are the luckiest people in the world." But sometimes they can also be the loneliest—and even an anonymous voice at the other end of the phone can make a world of difference.

Volunteers at the nonprofit Northern Virginia Hotline in Arlington, Virginia know just how much a sympathetic human voice can mean to lonely or troubled callers. Around the clock, seven days a week, hotline "listeners" try to understand, help put tough problems in perspective and refer callers to needed professional help. It may be a simple, basic service but communities around the country are realizing what a valuable and cost effective health resource hotlines can be.

Success Today

Tom Geib, a former member of the Hotline's Board of Directors and now the director of the Arlington County Mental Health Center, credits the Hotline for easing the burden of area mental health facilities while linking those in need with organizations that can help them hurdle problems. "The Hotline has provided a first-rate prevention service to the community that could not be provided by a government agency," he says.

Hailed as one of the most successful operations in the country, Northern Virginia Hotline boasts a roster of over 175 trained volunteer listeners who helped over 50,000 lonely and troubled callers in 1979.

The names of callers and listeners are strictly confidential. And to prevent the Hotline from turning into a walk-in clinic, explains Hotline Director Bobbie Kuehn, even the location of the office is a secret.

Getting Started

The Hotline was targeted at teenagers when it began in 1969. Back then Kuehn was a church leader working with highschoolers. By talking with them about their problems, Kuehn realized there was a need in the rapidly growing Northern Virginia suburbs to provide anonymous help for troubled teens.

Kuehn formed a five-member task force to help rally support from probation officers, school guidance counselors and other experts. And with about $1,000 in donations from residents and area churches and service organizations, the Hotline was opened in December 1969. Located in tiny donated headquarters, the Hotline's two telephones and 70 rotating volunteers served about 50 callers a week.

Northern Virginia Hotline volunteers offer a sympathetic ear to troubled callers.

Growth

Today expanded office space in the same location accommodates seven telephone lines and serves 1,000 callers weekly—three out of four of whom are adults. In 1979 the Hotline's budget of $68,000 came from individual and community contributions and grants from Arlington and Fairfax Counties and the Virginia Department of Mental Hygiene.

Volunteers—A Diverse Group

Hotline volunteers represent a cross section of the community—college students, educators, housewives, business people, government employees and retired citizens. All volunteers receive at least 25 hours of instruction from experienced listeners and professionals in such fields as mental and physical health. Volunteers meet monthly to exchange information about their work and listen to a speaker or panel discuss problems such as rape, battered spouses and drugs.

Helping Callers

About one-third of Hotline callers are concerned about mental and physical health problems but many just want to hear an understanding voice. "Most calls fall into the loneliness category," Kuehn says, "and many other calls (about health and other problems) turn out to be loneliness calls."

To encourage relaxed conversations the volunteers sit in easy chairs listening to a range of problems that plague callers such as alcoholism and drugs, unwanted pregnancies, abortions, rapes and threatened suicides.

At hand are professionally prepared pamphlets on various medical problems which help listeners answer questions. Also at their side is a roster of mental health and social service organizations where callers can get help.

Helping Listeners

The listeners have a giant responsibility and sometimes "burn out" while calmly trying to convince callers not to commit suicide. It doesn't happen often but when it does, another volunteer takes over while the first listener gets counseling from colleagues.

"Above all," Kuehn stresses, "they are advised not to take calls home or to brood over them. Listeners are cautioned against feeling that they are responsible for the crises they are told about or for actions callers may take after the calls."

Advice to Others

Kuehn offers advice for other communities interested in establishing hotlines:

- determine that a genuine need exists;
- marshal support of community leaders;
- lobby area churches and service organizations for money and volunteers;
- and, most importantly, launch an ongoing publicity campaign using, for example, posters and radio announcements to advertise the hotline.

"It doesn't help to have phones and volunteers if people don't know about the service," Kuehn says.

And Hotline workers have prepared a 12-minute slide and tape show, funded by a grant from the Service League of Northern Virginia, which explains how the Hotline works. It is shown free of charge to interested groups.

Other Groups

While most hotlines serve the general public, some address specific problems. For example, the Women's Advocacy Center in Charleston, South Carolina provides abused and battered women in the area with 24-hour crisis counseling.

And for those seeking medical information the California-based TEL-MED, Inc., a nonprofit affiliate of the San Bernardino County Medical Society, serves residents in some 240 cities across the country. By dialing a local number consumers can hear tapes on one of 310 topics ranging from hiccups to heart attacks.[1]

Groups Highlighted

TEL-MED
22700 Cooley South Drive
Colton, California 92324
(714) 825-6034

Women's Advocacy Center of Charleston
P.O. Box 2054
Charleston, South Carolina 29403
(803) 723-1415

[1] For more information on TEL-MED, Inc., see Resources at end of Health Section.

Note: For a complete listing of groups featured throughout this book, see Index.

Health Education, Promotion and Self-Care

Helping Hand Health Center
506 West Seventh Street
St. Paul, Minnesota 55102
(612) 224-7561

Many don't know that the abdomen is different from the stomach or that the human body has over 200 bones. Yet the more we learn about our bodies, the better able we are to take care of ourselves and our families by properly treating minor ailments at home. Moreover, self-care reduces medical bills and frees doctors and nurses to treat patients with more serious problems.

Realizing this, medical facilities such as the non-profit, outpatient Helping Hand Health Clinic in St. Paul, Minnesota are teaching patients how to take care of their bodies and when to—and not to—treat themselves. Helping Hand patients are partners with the medical staff, learning about their bodies and participating in examinations.

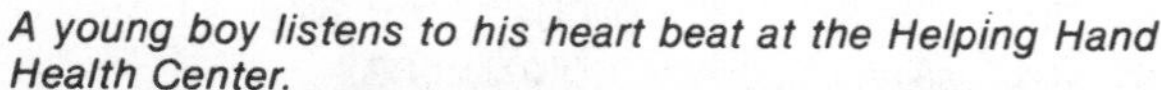

A young boy listens to his heart beat at the Helping Hand Health Center.

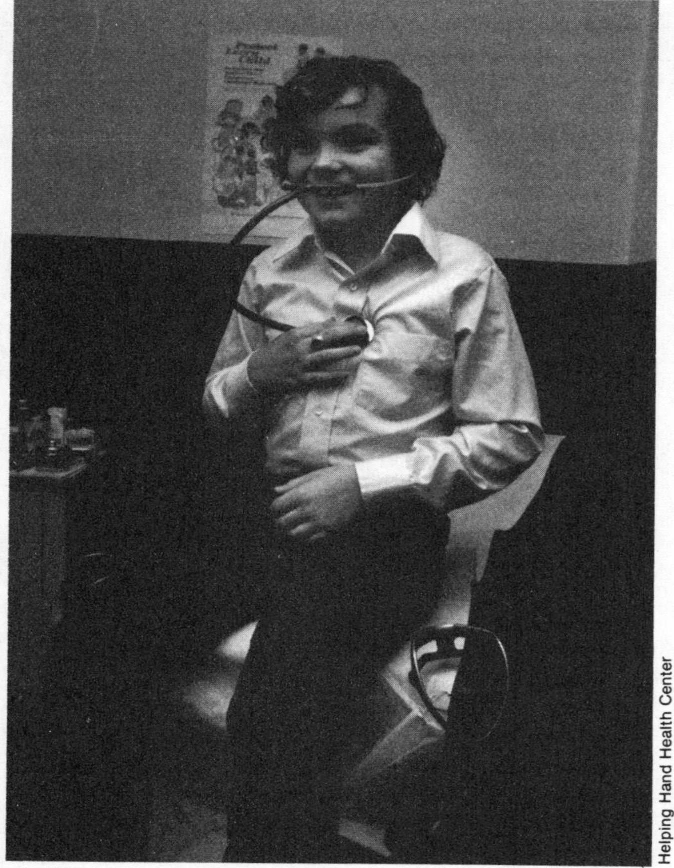

Helping Hand Health Center

Helping Hand Health Center

A mother learns to care for her child.

Dr. Tim Rumsey, medical director of Helping Hand, speaks of a patient in his 30s who at every visit pulls his own chart and takes his blood pressure, temperature and checks other vital signs before seeing the nurse. "This is what we call an activated patient," Rumsey says. "He is health-educated and takes personal responsibility for his health care."

Beginnings

It all began in 1976 when Rumsey and Helping Hand Executive Director Ellsworth Johnson, eager to cut unnecessary patient visits and free staff to treat more seriously ill patients, teamed up with Dr. Keith Sehnert, author of *How to Be Your Own Doctor, Sometimes,* to restructure the clinic. The new thrust was to promote self-help medical care and disease prevention by educating patients.

Budget and Staff

The Center, which was founded in 1971, has a staff of nine full-time and 10 part-time doctors, nurses and other personnel. About 10,000 low-income patients, who pay according to their income and ability, are treated each year. In 1979 about 45 percent of the clinic's $287,000 budget came from patient fees. City, county and private sources provided the balance.

Learning About Bodies

Education begins the moment the mostly low-income patients enter the clinic. The waiting room isn't stocked with movie star magazines. Rather, colorful bulletin boards feature a variety of health posters, flyers and tips on nutrition and racks of useful health literature encompass the area.

"But reading something worthwhile in the waiting room is just the beginning of our self-care approach," a Helping Hand nurse explains. "Once the patient goes into an examining room, the ball really gets rolling."

Helping Hand Health Center

Helping Hand patients can take their pick of reading material while waiting for doctor.

During examinations patients are told step-by-step what the medical staff is doing and why. For example, nurses discuss vital signs as patients participate in taking blood pressure, pulse and temperature. Doctors invite patients to listen to their heartbeats and let women watch their pelvic exams with mirrors. And parents are allowed to assist with their children's examinations by looking into ears, noses and throats while doctors explain what they are seeing.

Never a Missed Opportunity

Helping Hand's staff never misses a chance to teach. Health pictures and charts adorn clinic walls, doors and even ceilings. Patients peer through microscopes at their own specimens and closely review electrocardiogram test results with doctors.

Sixty-nine-year-old Bob Redman, a Helping Hand patient, learned to relieve his shoulder tension using techniques taught at the clinic. "I couldn't even turn my head," Redman says. "Now I can take care of myself and get rid of the pain myself."

A patient leaves the clinic with one of 50 individually tailored instruction sheets explaining how to care for problems such as sore throats, bladder infections, hypertension, fever or diarrhea. Also provided is a recommended reading list of books promoting the medical self-care concept with specific guidelines on when not to attempt self-treatment.

Reaching Out to The Community

Helping Hand's education efforts aren't confined to its building. Nurses serve as health teachers for the entire community, holding self-care seminars at preschool nurseries, elementary schools, senior citizen centers, half-way houses and other sites. The staff also writes a monthly health tips column for the community newspaper.

Health Concept Spreads

Hospitals, local Health Maintenance Organizations (HMOs), insurance companies and other institutions are becoming increasingly aware of the cost savings achievable through self-care, disease prevention and health promotion.[2]

For instance, an HMO in Latham, New York, the Capital Area Community Health Plan, Inc., offers an extensive health education program, including weight control and stop-smoking classes. And Audubon Area Community Services, Inc. of Owensboro, Kentucky, another HMO, has a consumer education project that includes blood pressure testing services.

Blue Cross and Blue Shield of Mississippi promotes physical fitness statewide through a "Fitness for Fun" program which features a speakers bureau, health fairs, "run for fun" contests, billboards, bumper stickers and even colorful T-shirts.[3] The St. Louis, Missouri Blue Cross Plan has a caravan of speakers to boost community awareness about preventive health care. And Blue Cross and Blue Shield of Atlanta, Georgia is also promoting health education and physical fitness programs.

Special Health Museum

An unusual health education setting is found at The Health Adventure, a nonprofit children's museum on the grounds of the Mountain Area Health Education Center in Asheville, North Carolina. The Buncombe County Medical Auxiliary, with the help of the local medical society and two hospitals, started Health Adventure in 1966 to help ease children's fears of hospitals. An average of 1,000 visitors a month learn about health concepts from volunteer instructors at the museum. Four-foot dinner plates and giant food models are used to teach visitors about proper nutrition and balanced meals. A skeleton mounted on a bicycle is used to explain bones. And dental care is taught with a three-foot toothbrush and equally large teeth.

Business and Industry

InterStudy, a Minneapolis, Minnesota-based health research firm, under contract with the National Chamber Foundation, an affiliate of the U.S. Chamber of Commerce, encourages businesses and industries to upgrade employees' health, thereby controlling spiraling medical costs. The group offers companies advice on programs such as physical fitness, stop smoking, alcohol abuse, nutrition and weight control.[4]

InterStudy's 1978 report, *A National Health Care Strategy: How Business Can Promote Good Health for Employees and Their Families,* highlights many ways businesses are helping employees maintain healthy bodies.[5] Some examples include Bonne Bell, a cosmetics manufacturing and distributing company based in Lakewood, Ohio, which offers employees an outdoor jogging path, exercise classes and tennis courts; Sentry Insurance in Stevens Point, Wisconsin, which has a swimming pool, gymnasium, racketball and handball courts as well as an indoor golf driving range and other facilities for their 1,000 employees; and the Speedcall Corporation, an electronics manufacturing plant in Hayward, California, which gives employees a $7 a week bonus for not smoking on the job. And the Kimberly-Clark Corporation in Neenah, Wisconsin offers employees a course on nutrition and diet taught by a local physician.

Groups Highlighted

Audubon Area Community Services, Inc.
731 Hall Street
Owensboro, Kentucky 42301
(502) 683-8267

Blue Cross/Blue Shield of Atlanta
3348 Peachtree Road, N.E.
Atlanta, Georgia 30326
(404) 262-8200

Blue Cross/Blue Shield of Mississippi, Inc.
P.O. Box 1043
Jackson, Mississippi 39205
(601) 932-3704

Blue Cross/Blue Shield of St. Louis
4444 Forest Park Boulevard
St. Louis, Missouri 63108
(314) 658-4444

Bonne Bell
185 19th Detroit Avenue
Lakewood, Ohio 44107
(216) 221-0800

Capital Area Community Health Plan, Inc.
1201 Troy-Schenectady Road
Latham, New York 12110
(518) 783-3110

The Health Adventure
Mountain Area Health Education Center
501 Biltmore Avenue
Asheville, North Carolina 28801
(704) 254-6373

Kimberly-Clark Corporation
Neenah, Wisconsin 54956
(414) 729-1212

Sentry Insurance Company
1800 North Point Drive
Stevens Point, Wisconsin 54481
(715) 346-6000

Speedcall Corporation
2020 National Avenue
Hayward, California 94545
(415) 783-5611

[1] Helping Hand Health Center publishes a 12-page pamphlet listing the names of health information resources. Self-care books on the body, adolescents, children, nutrition, first aid, prescription drugs, stress, etc. are listed by category. For information write to Helping Hand Health Center, 506 West Seventh Street, St. Paul, Minnesota 55102.

[2] A Health Maintenance Organization (HMO) is a prepaid health care plan that delivers comprehensive, coordinated medical services to voluntarily enrolled members. HMOs are profiled in the Health Section, p. 290.

[3] Health fairs are profiled in Health Section, p. 337.

[4] For more information on InterStudy, see Resouces at end of Health Section.

[5] A copy of *A National Health Care Strategy: How Business Can Promote Good Health for Employees and Their Families* can be obtained for $15.00 by writing: The National Chamber Foundation, 1615 H Street, N.W., Washington, D.C. 20062.

Note: For a complete listing of groups featured throughout this book, see Index.

Health Fairs

Student Coalition for Community Health
P.O. Box 435
Tuscaloosa, Alabama 35401
(205) 348-6432

Preventive health care is almost unheard of in many rural southern towns. Too often residents can't take care of their medical needs because health care facilities are either inadequate or nonexistent. And many rural residents don't realize how much convient community health facilities can improve their standard of living.

Health fair participants receive innoculations and other health services.

But in rural Alabama when the health fair—a kind of medical bazaar—comes to town, residents get a full range of medical examinations such as eye, blood pressure and laboratory testing. But more importantly, fair staffers are sparking interest in—and teaching local residents how to go about—planning needed health facilities for their areas.

It was the Cedar Bluff Health Fair that brought the town's lack of health facilities to the attention of Mayor ''Dude'' Meade. ''We do need something here . . . there aren't any doctors this side of the river. Now I know you can say that we can just go across the river to Centre—but that's not enough.''

Helping Residents Build Health Facilities

The rural fairs are the brainstorm of the nonprofit Student Coalition for Community Health (SCCH), based in Tuscaloosa, Alabama. SCCH members eagerly help the townsfolk determine community needs and help them develop plans for medical clinics or other health facilities. Residents learn how to form health councils to monitor plans and are led for more advice to such experts as their area health planning agency and other communities that have launched health facilities.[1] Fair leaders also give tips on how to raise funds and win grants from government assistance programs.

Success Today

From 1974 to 1979, 164 University of Alabama medical and education majors as well as other students have spent their summers treating community residents and learning the realities of rural health problems. The fairs, which are also staffed with medical professionals, have attracted more than 12,000 residents in rural Alabama towns. Fairgoers wander from station to station—manned by some 30 volunteers who explain preventive health care, community health planning and other subjects. A range of free medical services from full physical examinations to dental care is also available. And according to one participant, Daisy Hope of Henegar, "The health fair began to wake people up."

Nearly half of the 16 communities, including Cedar Bluff, that have hosted SCCH health fairs are now building community health clinics. Others are recruiting physicians to their areas or establishing nurse practitioner clinics to ensure decent health care for their residents.

Origins

The health fair idea originated in 1974 when several University of Alabama students wanted real opportunities to serve people in their state.

They organized the Student Coalition for Community Health (SCCH) under the guidance of faculty member Dr. John Shelton and began looking for a way to get practical experience in their chosen fields.

SCCH members and Dr. Shelton decided that community health fairs would be the best way to expose rural Alabama residents to a broad spectrum of health care programs, boost resident interest in community health facilities and allow students to learn what life would be like living and working in rural areas.

The group holds three fairs each summer in Alabama communities which have between 500 and 1,500 residents. Towns are chosen according to community interest and health care needs. Preparation for the health fairs begins with a course held in the spring semester. Physicians at the University of Alabama's Medical School in Birmingham train students in medical procedures such as performing lab tests and checking blood pressure.

Funding and Staff

The group's expenses run about $40,000 a year. And most of the fair team members volunteer their time.

The health fairs are funded by various private foundations and churches and by the Department of Labor's Comprehensive Employment and Training Act (CETA) Program.* The University of Alabama also contributes money and equipment. Supplies are provided by private companies, hospitals and individuals. To help defray fair expenses the staff stays with community residents whose lifestyles they share during the two-week period.

Keys to Success

A key element of the group's success has been its dedication to learning about the people they plan to treat and educate. Before staging a fair two SCCH workers move into each community for the summer. Working with local leaders they prepare for the health fair while learning about the community. They then impart their knowledge about the town's political and social structures, history and resident attitudes to the rest of the fair team.

The Fair Comes to Town

Finally, the caravan rolls into town with about three physicians, several medical and nursing students, two nurse practitioners, three optometry students, a nutritionist, a speech and hearing specialist, a counselor and 10 lab technicians—all eager to provide medical and educational services.

Urban Health Fairs

Health fairs are being held in large cities as well. In Bronx, New York, through the GUTS (Governmental Understanding for Today's Student: Growth Through Self-Help) Program, a group of junior high school students, teachers and administrators developed a community health fair to provide local residents with health information, testing and referrals. Students were taught how to screen residents and check blood pressure.

Students, teachers and administrators plan the GUTS health fair.

The fairs, which ran for two years, served approximately 600 residents at no charge. Testing was provided by community health institutions such as the Albert Einstein Medical Center and Lincoln Hospital.

Group Highlighted

Project GUTS
Intermediate School 19
345 Brook Avenue
Bronx, New York 10454
(212) 665-8448

Organizing a Health Fair

Seek Assistance
Contact professionals at local health departments, hospitals, etc. for information and technical assistance in planning and conducting a health fair.

Find Co-Sponsors
Approach local groups such as Parent Teacher Associations (PTAs), schools, churches, synagogues and service organizations that might be interested in co-sponsoring the fair.

Plan, Plan, Plan
Give your group time to plan. Experienced health fair sponsors estimate that advance planning takes two to 10 months.

Set Goals
Don't plan a fair simply to have one. Some realistic goals include providing community health education and early disease detection.

Target Audience
Plan activities for children and adults if your health fair is aimed at a cross section of the population. But if you have a specific group in mind, such as senior citizens, activities should be tailored to fit their interests and needs.

Decide and Plan Health Services
Decide if—and what —health care services will be offered. Then locate doctors, nurses and other health professionals willing to help or teach others how to perform such tasks as taking blood pressure and conducting eye and laboratory tests. You must also develop a list of referrals (doctors or health organizations) for those needing further attention. Also, obtain necessary insurance.

Decide Date and Time
Plan a date and time that will draw a good crowd. Fair veterans recommend springtime between the hours of 10:00 a.m. to 4:00 p.m.

Select Location
Pick a place that has a large, central room, such as a gymnasium, as well as smaller rooms for workshops. Restrooms and parking facilities are a must.

Garner Publicity
Make a list of the media in your area—television and radio stations as well as newspapers. Scout around for the best locations, such as schools, shopping centers, and community bulletin boards to display posters. (See Basic Tools Section.)

Invite Local Health Groups
Ask community organizations such as the local mental health center, Alcoholics Anonymous, the local heart, lung and diabetes associations, the Cancer Society, the La Leche League and the Red Cross to set up booths.

Solicit Contributions
Ask local businesses to contribute $10 to $20. Don't plan a fair as a fundraiser, however, because it is usually more effort than the proceeds justify. If you charge admission, clearly state how the money will be used.

Plan for Refreshments
Invite local health food stores to exhibit if you decide to have food. Remember, no junk food!

Get Feedback
Have suggestion forms available for fairgoers to complete.

Assess the Fair
Meet with your group following the fair to discuss results. Congratulate each other and make notes for improving future fairs.

Adapted from "A Health Fair for Your Community," Teaching and Learning Self Care, *by Tom Ferguson, M.D.; and "Planning a Community Health Fair,"* Public Health Reports, *by Daniel S. Blumenthal, M.D. and Henry S. Kahn, M.D., March-April 1979.*

[1] There are about 200 local health planning agencies, or Health Systems Agencies (HSAs), throughout the country which were created by a 1974 Federal law, the National Health Planning and Resources Development Act.* HSA Boards of Directors must be comprised of consumer majorities and are responsible for planning their areas' health future. (For more information on HSAs, see Health Section, p. 344 and 346.)

* State and/or local government agencies are frequently responsible for administration of Federal program funds. For further information, see Appendix I under appropriate Federal agency.

Note: For a complete listing of groups featured throughout this book, see Index.

Networks

Center for Medical Consumers and Health Care Information
237 Thompson Street
New York, New York 10012
(212) 674-7105

After taking a drug to treat hypertension for about a year, an elderly New York City man was told he had diabetes. When he went to the Center for Medical Consumers and Health Care Information in New York City, he learned diabetes was one of the drug's possible side effects—a detail his doctor failed to mention.

The nonprofit Center offers consumers an alternative to total reliance on doctors and other medical professionals for information necessary to make important decisions about their health care. Center services include a TEL-MED phone system which contains taped information on 150 topics such as arthritis, depression and cancer; a bimonthly newsletter that deals with a variety of health issues; and a library that boasts over 1,000 health books and magazines.[1]

While the organization does not recommend specific doctors, it does lead consumers to appropriate organizations that can help. For example, women with birth control questions would be referred to an organization such as Planned Parenthood. And the Center encourages residents to check doctors' credentials in the *Directory of Medical Specialists,* research drug side effects in the *Physicians' Desk Reference Guide* and browse through self-care guides and medical textbooks to better understand their illnesses.[2]

Consumers learn about health care at the Center's library.

Center for Medical Consumers and Health Care Information

"I knew of no other place where I could find information that my doctor should have given me," says a young woman whose doctor had recommended surgery. "Thanks to the Center I now have enough information to question my doctor."

Newsletter

In the Center's newsletter, *Health Facts,* various health topics are covered by several medical experts and alternative treatments are reviewed. The bimonthly newsletter is sent to 7,000 subscribers, including individuals, corporations and consumer groups.[3]

Origins

Opened in 1977, the Center was sponsored jointly by the Judson Memorial Church and Consumer Action Now (CAN), a nonprofit environmental group, and was aimed at enlightening consumers about the mysterious world of medical science. The sponsoring groups were eager to help consumers tackle the problems of unnecessary surgery, rampant prescription drug abuse and needless doctor visits.

Funding and Staff

In 1979 the Center's budget of about $60,000 came from church groups, foundations and newsletter subscription fees. And the Center's three-member full-time staff is reinforced by four volunteers.

Other Group

Another group finding innovative ways to get the latest, most comprehensive health information to consumers and health professionals is a hospital/library network in Massachusetts, the Community Health Information Network (CHIN), based in Mount Auburn Hospital in Cambridge.

The program was launched in 1977 by Lawrence M. Witte, Mount Auburn's associate administrator, who felt there was a growing need for "consumers to understand the process of health and disease so they may be more active participants in their health care." Witte persuaded officials of public libraries in the area to link their resources with those of the hospital library.

Medical Library Loans

The inter-library loan system gives public library patrons access to medical resources. And the program has spurred public libraries to increase their medical and health collections.

The network started with $100,000 in grants from the Massachusetts Board of Library Commissioners, the Federal Library and Construction Act and the National Library of Medicine.[4] The program trains all library staffers in the use of medical books so they can refer consumers to appropriate literature.

And CHIN staffers stand ready to answer consumer questions. The most common questions, according to staffers, are: which hospitals have programs to prepare children for surgery and how can bystanders help heart attack victims. Between January and August of 1978 over 400 questions were answered by CHIN's staff.

The network is now expanding into the public schools, enabling students and school health professionals to tap CHIN's resources.

Group Highlighted

Community Health Information Network
Mount Auburn Hospital
Department of Community Health Education
330 Mount Auburn Street
Cambridge, Massachusetts 02172
(617) 492-3500—Ext. 1788

[1] For more information on TEL-MED, see Resources at end of Health Section.

[2] *The Dictionary of Medical Specialists* and the *Physicians' Desk Reference Guide* are available at most public libraries.

[3] *Health Facts* can be obtained for $8.50/year by writing the Center for Medical Consumers and Health Care Information, 237 Thompson Street, New York, New York 10012.

[4] The Federal Library and Construction Act is administered by the Department of Health, Education and Welfare's (HEW) Office of Elementary and Secondary Education under the Library and Learning Resources Program.* The National Library of Medicine, part of HEW's National Institute of Health, administers grants under its Extramural Programs.*

*State and/or local government agencies are frequently responsible for administration of Federal program funds. For further information, see Appendix I under appropriate Federal agency.

Note: For a complete listing of groups featured throughout this book, see Index.

A Consumer Guide to Nursing Homes in Northern Virginia
LEXANDRIA
RSVP
ETIRED SENIOR VOLUNTEER PROGRAM

Increasing Citizen Participation in Health Planning

Introduction

Between 1977 and 1978 health care costs rose by over $22 billion—more than $2 million every hour, 24 hours a day, 365 days a year. Poor health planning is a major reason for these escalating costs, which are passed on to consumers in the form of higher medical bills and insurance rates.

But staggering health care costs can be, and are being, thwarted by citizens who are helping to prevent the creation of *needless* health facilities by learning how to effectively participate in their communities' health plans.

In this chapter we review a Federal law empowering health consumers with broad authority over their areas' health plans through the creation of a national network of some 200 consumer-controlled local health planning agencies.

We then see how the law works by glimpsing at a health planning agency that not only is preventing costly duplication of health services but also is making concerted efforts to bolster resident interest in participating in community health planning.

We move on to a group in California that conducted workshops arming consumers with the know-how to impact on local health planning agencies.

And we see how Marylanders, fed up with high hospital costs, formed the Maryland Health Services Cost Review Commission to keep hospital rates in check. And they've helped everyone in the process.

Instead of complaining about consumer helplessness in the health field, these groups are showing what consumer involvement can mean.

National Health Planning and Resources Development Act
(An Overview)

Instead of standing by helplessly as the third hospital within a three-mile area is built—each with identical expensive equipment—consumers can now participate at the local and state levels in decisions that determine how health care is meted out in their communities. This is crucial because we all pay for unnecessary health expenditures in the form of higher costs for insurance and medical care.

Most hospitals and other health facilities across the country are answerable to three major health planning bodies. Two of the three planning bodies—the local Health Systems Agency (HSA) and the Statewide Health Coordinating Council (SHCC)—must have boards with a majority of consumer members. These bodies, together with the State Health Planning and Development Agency (SHPDA), have broad authority over the allocation and development of health resources such as facilities, services and equipment. These three units aim to assure consumers of access to quality care while restraining health costs.

This nationwide multi-level network was created by the 1974 National Health Planning and Resources Development Act* and is funded through Federal grants.[1] Within this general framework, however, health care decisions are made at the local or state level and this is where consumers can have a real impact.

Local Level

Under the Act, the country is divided into more than 200 health service areas, each headed by the local planning unit, the Health Systems Agency (HSA).[2] Most HSAs are governed by 10 to 30 volunteer board members who are usually chosen either by local government officials or community groups. A majority of the board members (51 to 60 percent) must be consumers and represent the area's social, economic, linguistic, handicapped and racial populations.

In addition, each HSA employs 5 to 25 staffers with expertise in areas such as administration, health planning and financial and economic analysis. At least one staff person must provide assistance to consumers.

Consumer Impact

The powers of HSAs are substantial and far-reaching so consumers who are active in them and participate in their hearings can have a direct impact on the health care provided in their communities.

The HSA is charged with collecting information on and analyzing the health care delivery system in its area. After reviewing the strengths and weaknesses of the area's health resources, the HSA establishes a Health Systems Plan (HSP)—long-range goals that assure quality health care for the community. Each year the HSA develops an Annual Implementation Plan (AIP) which plots what the group plans to do the following year to reach these goals. Public hearings are required in the development of both plans.

Real Power

The influence of HSAs on their communities' health resources is great. For example, HSAs have the authority to approve or disapprove proposed Federally funded health projects such as community mental health centers and alcohol and drug abuse programs.

Consumer Impact on State Level

Consumers who are active in HSAs can also have an impact at the state level. The State Health Planning Development Agency (SHPDA), the governor-selected agency charged with preparing, revising and administering the state's health planning program—which is based on the collective goals of HSAs statewide—depends heavily on the local units for recommendations.

For instance, the SHPDA is charged with approving all requests by individuals or organizations within the state wishing to spend $150,000 or more for health facilities or additional equipment and medical services such as cardiac surgery for existing hospitals. And it depends on local experts, the HSAs, for advice when making decisions regarding facilities in their areas.

These powers enable HSAs to help prevent, for example, the expansion of a hospital when others in the area may have vacant beds—a decision which can save millions of dollars.

HSAs also assist the SHPDA in reviewing existing institutions to determine if they are still needed. And they recommend to the SHPDA new health projects or the conversion or modernization of older health facilities in their areas.

Consumers can also become involved in the Statewide Health Coordinating Council (SHCC), the advisory group for the SHPDA. The governor appoints all members, the majority of whom must be HSA representatives and consumers. A SHCC's principal responsibilities are the approval and revision of the state health plan and the approval of state plans for spending Federal health monies.

Evidence Indicates Consumer Gains

Since the national health planning program was launched, consumers have made a difference. The American Health Planning Association reports that between August 1976 and August 1978 the health planning program has prevented $3.4 billion of unnecessary expenditures for health facilities, services and equipment.[3]

Health Systems Agency (HSA)

What forms can an HSA take?
A Health Systems Agency can be either: 1) a nonprofit, private corporation; 2) a single or multi-purpose public regional planning body; or 3) a local government unit.

What are the responsibilities of an HSA?
The primary responsibilities of an HSA are to provide effective health planning and promote the development of health services, manpower and health facilities to meet the needs of its area.

How is an HSA formed?
An HSA is designated by the Secretary of Health, Education and Welfare (HEW) after consultation with the governor of each state in which a health service area is located.

How is an HSA designated?
An HSA is conditionally designated for up to two years. After that period, if it is determined that the HSA board has responsibly carried out all the functions outlined in the National Health Planning and Resources Development Act of 1974, the HSA receives full designation.

How often must an HSA hold meetings?
The governing body of the HSA must convene at least once in each calendar quarter and should have at least two additional meetings each year.

What are the required functions of an HSA?

- Assemble and analyze data concerning the health care delivery system in its area;
- Determine how area residents use that system;
- Determine the effect of the area's health care delivery system on the health of the residents;
- Locate the number, type and location of the area's health resources;
- Determine area patterns and occupational exposure factors (such as industrial pollution) affecting immediate and long-term health conditions;
- Establish, annually review and amend as necessary a health systems plan (HSP) which conforms to the goals, needs and resources of the area;
- Develop an annual implementation plan (AIP) describing the objectives which will achieve the goals of the HSP; and
- Develop and publish specific plans and projects for achieving the objectives established in the AIP.

Adapted from Membership on the Governing Body of a Health Systems Agency, *an orientation handbook of the U.S. Department of Health, Education and Welfare, Public Health Service, Health Resources Administration, Hyattsville, Maryland 20782. (Revised September 1976.)*

[1] The National Health Planning and Resources Development Act* is administered by the Department of Health, Education and Welfare (HEW).

[2] In some larger Health Systems Agencies (HSAs), sub-area councils (SACs) covering a smaller geographic area, have been established to advise the HSA.

[3] For more information on the American Health Planning Association, see Resources at end of Health Section.

* State and/or local government agencies are frequently responsible for administration of Federal program funds. For further information see Appendix I under appropriate Federal agency.

Note: For a complete listing of groups featured throughout this book, see Index.

Health Systems Agencies

Health Systems Agency of Northern Virginia
7245 Arlington Boulevard, Suite 300
Falls Church, Virginia 22042
(703) 573-3100

Great ideas that don't reach those who would benefit from them are useless.

In 1974 public leaders had a great idea. Eager to give more authority over community health plans to *users* of medical services, who pay for unneeded facilities through higher health and insurance rates, Congress created a national network of 200 Federally funded but independent local Health Systems Agencies (HSAs).[1]

Each HSA was to be headed by a board comprised mostly of consumers, Congress declared, who were charged with charting their area's health care future and making such important decisions as what Federally funded health facilities would grace their community.

All Residents Help With Health Planning

Congress further insisted that all residents be allowed to participate in HSA hearings and in the development of area health plans. Additionally, they mandated that HSA information on area health resources be made available to all residents. But Congress couldn't force residents to participate in—or care about—HSA activities.

Making A Great Idea Work

The Health Systems Agency of Northern Virginia (HSANV), based in Falls Church, is one group that is striving to make a great idea reach all of those whom it was meant to benefit by complying with the *spirit* as well as the letter of the 1974 law. The group, which serves nine jurisdictions and one million residents in the suburban area of Washington, D.C., is aggressively prodding citizens to become involved in their own health care and participate in their community's health plans.

Educating Residents

For instance, HSANV's speakers bureau eagerly accepts requests from area groups to lecture on community health issues and explain HSA operations. And the group boasts a huge mailing list of residents who receive free HSANV-published brochures and educational materials. Moreover, the group has published two directories on area physicians and nursing homes which contain information on fees, services offered, staff sizes and educational backgrounds of local health professionals. Patient rights are also outlined in the directories.

Reaching Out

And in 1979, to spur more resident participation in their activities, HSANV launched and funded the Northern Virginians for Health Planning (NVHP), a 100-strong independent group which is open to all area residents and includes representatives from community and civic groups, businesses and health care organizations. The advisory group is the vital link between resident ideas for health planning and responsible HSANV action.

"We absolutely need that kind of input," explains Edward Kelley, a member of the HSANV Board. "The 30 Board members are wonderful people, but they don't know everything. The one thing we needed most was to get a real pipeline going so we could learn what the community wanted and could tell the community what we were doing and get reactions to it."

And there is plenty for HSANV and its 16-member professional staff to do, including monitoring the community's health resources. In addition to approving Federally funded facilities, the National Health Planning and Resources Development Act,* which created HSAs, empowered HSA boards to recommend approval or disapproval of capital expenditures in their areas under state Certificate of Need (CON) laws. State CON laws require individuals or organizations wishing to build new or expanded health care facilities, buy medical equipment or add medical services costing $150,000 or more to submit requests to the local HSA. The HSA, after reviewing the needs of the community, recommends approval or disapproval of the project to the state health commissioner who gives heavy weight to the local group's views before making the final decision.

Saving Consumers Money

That power can mean real savings. From 1976 to 1979 HSANV estimates that Northern Virginia consumers were spared $20 to $50 million in unnecessary health care services.

In 1979, for instance, a hospital in Arlington applied for permission to construct a 30-bed psychiatric unit. After examining the needs of the community, HSANV recommended against the application and suggested that the hospital's existing building was large enough for the 12 beds which were needed.

The Virginia Commissioner of Health accepted HSANV's recommendation and vetoed the request. And the hospital subsequently submitted an amended application for the addition of the 12 beds recommended by HSANV. Thus the unnecessary construction of a new hospital unit was averted.

Planning For Future Health Facilities

But HSANV's responsibility doesn't end there. Like other HSAs across the country, the Northern Virginia group is responsible for planning and implementing short- and long-term goals for health facilities in their area; advising and helping the state government with statewide health planning goals; and approving or disapproving Federally funded health facilities in the Northern Virginia area.

To do this they must become experts on their community's health system, conducting exhaustive studies of area hospitals, drug abuse centers, child planning programs and other health resources.

Residents Help Decide Their Health Future

And to plan effectively, says Mary Grace Lintz, chairperson of the HSANV, resident support is essential. "It's not just doctors and administrators who should decide what kind of health care we should have," she says. "This is a social decision."

And when residents become involved in health planning, she adds, "providers (such as doctors and nurses) are forced to see consumers not only as pieces of human equipment that break down and have to be fixed, but as thinking human beings who can make intelligent decisions about health care and who have a very basic right to make those decisions."

Outreach Works

That's exactly why the advisory NVHP was created. By the end of 1979, after only six months, the group

Concerned citizens decide what kind of health care is needed in their community.

Health Systems Agency of Northern Virginia

had written bylaws, elected officers, launched membership drives and assigned members to "health issues" committees. Moreover, in 1980 the group plans to conduct workshops on a variety of health care issues for residents.

By providing forums for public reaction, Kelley says, the workshops might spur participants to come up with health ideas not thought of by HSANV.

So far HSANV hasn't been disappointed in its advisory group. "We fund them, provide staffing and review how they spend the money we give them. But the kind of people on NVHP are not the kind of people you can make perform as puppets," Kelley says. "For better or worse, this group has free rein so that they will have credibility . . . it's the best thing we could do."

A Rural HSA

The Greater Nevada Health Systems Agency in Reno (GNHSA) serves a population of more than 265,000 in a 102,000-square-mile, 16-county, largely rural area. Because GNHSA serves many isolated communities, its goals differ in some respects from those of HSANV.

For example, one of GNHSA's major goals is to increase the access of rural residents to primary care practitioners. Therefore, the HSA has approved a request by an area hospital wishing to construct an "Emergency Health Care Center" 25 miles away from its existing facility. The Center will provide primary and emergency care to those residents without regular physicians.

But GNHSA shares NVHSA's interest in consumer education. The agency has produced a handbook for residents wishing to participate in HSA activities; organized a speakers bureau for community groups; designed a display depicting HSA functions for circulation at area fairs and libraries; completed a slidetape presentation on GNHSA; and used public service announcements on local radio stations to advertise GNHSA activities.

Group Highlighted

Greater Nevada Health Systems Agency
P.O. Box 11795
Reno, Nevada 89510
(702) 323-1791

Health Systems Agency of Northern Virginia

Senior citizens volunteer to conduct studies of health facilities in Northern Virginia.

[1] For more information on Health Systems Agencies (HSAs), see Health Section, p. 344.

*State and/or local government agencies are frequently responsible for administration of Federal program funds. For further information, see Appendix I under appropriate Federal agency.

Note: For a complete listing of groups featured throughout this book, see Index.

Training for Consumer Power

Consumer Health Advocacy Training Institute
California Public Interest Research Group of San Diego
3000 E Street
San Diego, California 92102
(714) 236-1508

All consumers deserve and need adequate health facilities in their communities. But unfortunately, they often pay for unnecessary equipment and health services through higher medical and insurance costs.

Consumers around the country are learning how to fight for needed services and blunt unnecessary health expenditures by participating in local health planning. And some groups, such as the Consumer Health Advocacy Training Institute in San Diego, California, are showing them how.

Since 1979 the Institute, the creation of the California Public Interest Research Group (CalPIRG), has staged free 15-week workshops to give consumers in the San Diego area the technical expertise and skills necessary to become "advocates for their communities' health needs."

The workshops are aimed at creating competent consumers who will use their knowledge to increase the effectiveness of their local Health Systems Agencies (HSAs), which are responsible for community health planning and are charged with such awesome decisions as what new health facilities will be launched in their areas and which existing services can expand.[1] The results of the workshops have been impressive.

"The workshop gave me the information I needed to question the health system," says Joyce Zechter, co-chairperson of the San Diego Health Action Coalition, a nonprofit citizens group formed by workshop participants. "I also realized that my participation could make a difference." Coalition members learned their lessons well. In 1979 they successfully persuaded the area HSA to disapprove the purchase of $1.2 million worth of what they considered to be unneeded medical equipment for a local health facility.

Thanks to the Institute's workshops, consumers effectively participate in local health planning meetings.

Participation by Informed Consumers

The 200 local HSAs in the country are part of a nationwide Federally funded health planning program which aims to assure quality health care for consumers while restraining costs. According to Federal law, there must be a majority of consumers on HSA volunteer governing boards and all business must be conducted in public. But CalPIRG leaders know all too well that consumer representation on HSAs isn't enough. In short, effective health planning requires consumers on HSA boards and residents who participate in HSA hearings to be informed and knowledgeable.

Success Today

In 1979 the Institute conducted two workshop series, giving 160 area residents the expertise needed to help plan their communities' health futures. The Institute's first series, held in the spring, had immediate impact. Within five months:

- About a dozen participants began volunteering on San Diego HSA sub-area councils and task forces.
- A dramatic increase occurred in consumer participation and attendance at HSA public hearings on health planning.
- The San Diego Health Action Coalition was founded by workshop participants.
- The Institute published a comprehensive resource manual, containing a review of health issues and tips on how to participate in HSA hearings, which is available to consumers nationwide.[2]

And by the end of the year CalPIRG had received numerous requests from consumer health and labor groups around the country for technical assistance in setting up their own training workshops.

Origins

The Institute sent word of the workshops along with applications to more than 1,300 nearby community organizations and consumer groups. They also launched an intense media campaign which was rewarded with stories in local newspapers and public service announcements on radio and television stations.

Anxious to attract residents from all economic levels and ethnic backgrounds, CalPIRG offered the workshops free. In addition, many participants were reimbursed for transportation and for day care expenses if they had young children.

Applications came streaming in and staffers began selecting the 80 participants for the first workshop. Participants represented a cross section of the community and included senior, low-income, ethnic and minority, women and physically handicapped residents. Others concerned with health planning, such as labor union representatives and alternative health care providers, were also among those chosen to participate.

How the Workshops Work

To conduct the workshops the Institute recruited a staff of experts, including physicians, public health specialists, economists and attorneys. Participants learned about a wide range of health issues such as medical barriers facing the poor and the elderly, the economics of health care, HSA organization and medical technology. They were also taught how to use their knowledge. They learned about public speaking and how to debate and prepare testimony.

Funding

CalPIRG did its homework to win approval for the $73,000 grant from the National Science Foundation's Science for Citizens Program* which funded the Institute. Staffers sought advice from other health advocacy groups about similar training programs and kept in close touch with the area HSA to keep fully informed about its operation and plans for future area health services.

Institute Director Clare Lipschultz offers tips to other groups wishing to sponsor workshops in their areas:

- Make sure that participants understand why it is important to get involved in health planning and what their involvement can mean;
- Empower consumers by explaining health issues in understandable language and recruiting experts who can impart their knowledge to laypersons;
- Constantly encourage participant groups to form coalitions in order to have even greater impact on community health plans.

Other Groups

Other groups around the country are working to help consumers become health advocates. Some of the most effective are union-consumer coalitions.

For example, Cornell University's New York State School in Industrial and Labor Relations offers a series of nine credit courses for union health leaders and HSA board members across the state. The Health Studies Program is conducted in cooperation with Cornell Medical College's Department of Health and the Community Services Department of the New York City Central Labor Council, an affiliate of the American Federation of Labor and Congress of Industrial Organizations (AFL-CIO). By the end of 1979 over 700 people had been trained in the program, which offers 20 courses in areas such as work-related health hazards, nutrition and retirees' role in health care planning. Funding comes from Title I of the Higher Education Act,* administered by the Department of Health, Education and Welfare's (HEW) Community Services and Continuing Education Program* under the Bureau of Higher and Continuing Education.

The program has helped spark citizen participation, which has had an important impact on health care planning in New York. For example, many hospitals in the state have modified their record-keeping to pinpoint ineffective services and facilities. Some union members have won benefits such as the right to a second opinion when surgery is recommended. And many unions now negotiate directly with hospitals in an effort to keep costs down.

Health/PAC

In 1968 the Health Policy Advisory Center in New York City created Health/PAC. The program aims to inform consumers about the medical system and teach them how to help shape the quality of their health care by, for example, joining coalitions to help save needed local hospitals slated for closing because of financial crises.[3]

And the District League of Women Voters, which represents nine local Leagues in the District of Columbia, Maryland and Virginia, sponsor local debates and workshops on health issues for interested residents. League members frequently testify at HSA public hearings as well as monitor and inform residents about state and national legislation affecting the availability, quality and cost of health care services.

Groups Highlighted

Cornell University
New York State School of Industrial and Labor Relations
Health Studies Program
3 East 43rd Street
New York, New York 10017
(212) 599-4550

District League of Women Voters
1346 Connecticut Avenue, N.W., Room 718
Washington, D.C. 20036
(202) 785-2616

Health/PAC
Health Policy Advisory Center
17 Murray Street
New York, New York 10007
(212) 267-8890

[1] For more information on Health Systems Agencies (HSAs), see Health Section, p. 344 and p. 346.

[2] The Institute's resource manual, *Tools for Health Planning: A Consumer Workbook* is available for $5 by writing CalPIRG, 3000 E Street, San Diego, California 92102.

[3] Health/PAC also publishes an informative bimonthly *Health/PAC Bulletin* which can be obtained by writing to Health/PAC, Health Policy Advisory Center, 17 Murray Street, New York, New York 10007. Yearly subscriptions are $14 for individuals and $28 for institutions.

*State and/or local government agencies are frequently responsible for administration of Federal program funds. For further information, see Appendix I under appropriate Federal agency.

Note: For a complete listing of groups featured throughout this book, see Index.

Hospital Cost Review Commission

Maryland Health Services Cost Review Commission
201 West Preston Street, First Floor
Baltimore, Maryland 21201
(301) 383-6804

These days the bill from even a short hospital stay can cause health consumers to gasp in disbelief. And many feel helpless to do anything about spiraling inpatient costs. But in some states, such as Maryland, consumers are helping by serving on innovative commissions which effectively dampen hospital rate hikes.

Problems Yield Success

In the late 1960s two problems caused the Maryland Hospital Association, comprised of hospital professionals from around the state, to successfully push for increased state regulation. First, hospital costs were increasing by a whopping rate of 15 percent or more per year. Second, inner-city hospitals, which were shouldering 86 percent of the state's charity and bad debt cases, were uable to recover their losses and were on the verge of bankruptcy.

Enter the Maryland Health Services Cost Review Commission, an independent state agency created by the Maryland General Assembly in 1971 and charged with setting "reasonable" hospital rates and guaranteeing solvency of financially troubled hospitals that attempt to operate efficiently and effectively.

And enter the consumer who is at the heart of the Commission system. A majority of the governor-appointed, seven-member Commission must be medical users rather than health providers, and all residents are encouraged to participate in rate-setting hearings.

Collecting Data

So with a paid staff of seven and an annual budget of $180,000, the staff began conducting in-depth studies of each hospital's finances—considering patient loads, types of services offered, operating costs and other factors. Then the operating costs of different hospitals were compared and individual base budgets were established. Beginning in 1974, after collecting the needed data, rates were set for each hospital and adjusted annually to reflect inflation.

Hearings

Hospitals must request permission from the Commission to increase rates above the annual inflation adjustment. Public hearings are held after all information is collected; then the Commissioners make an initial decision. If the rate hike is denied the hospital can request a more formal public hearing. But once a final decision is made, hospitals must accept rates set by the Commission or appeal to the courts to overturn the ruling.

Other Duties

The Commission is also charged with producing annual reports for the public and the press which detail the financial condition of Maryland hospitals. And at monthly meetings the Commission presents a list of expected annual revenues of every hospital in the state and a computer printout of each approved rate.

Rate Setting and Consumer Involvement Spell Success

Commission member Carville Akehurst comments on the effect rate setting has had on containing Maryland's hospital costs: "It's like beefsteak went up 45 cents a pound nationwide while it only went up 20 cents in Maryland."

The figures bear his comment out. Since 1974—if hospital costs in Maryland had risen at the national rate—consumers across the state would have paid an additional $173 million in 1979 for hospital services. Daily per-patient costs in 1979 rose only 8.96 percent in Maryland compared to an 11.75 percent increase nationwide.

Making a Believer of Uncle Sam

At first the Federal government, which reimburses hospitals for services to citizens qualifying for Medicare* and Medicaid,* was leary of Maryland's untested system.[1] So the government continued to accept billings at rates set by Maryland hospitals. But in 1977, after watching the Commission work for several years, the government tipped its hat in approval, accepting Commission rates and making Maryland the only state in which rates are preset for all bill payers—individuals as well as private and government insurers. By 1979 the government had reaped the benefits of its decision, saving $52.5 million in Medicare and Medicaid payments.

Incentives to Economize

The system works because it offers strong incentives for hospitals to keep operating costs down. Traditionally, hospitals are paid after providing treatment, and the actual costs of goods and services used in treatment are reflected in patients' bills. So there is little incentive, for instance, to shop around for the best prices on towels, sheets and other needed supplies because costs are automatically passed on to consumers.

But the Commission predetermines reasonable rates designed to encourage cost cutting. So hospital administrators are eager to shop for the best prices, perform services economically and plan carefully because an efficient operation can mean a profit at the end of the year. But if expenses exceed revenues, the losses must somehow be absorbed or the hospital must request higher rates from the Commission.

What's Fair is Fair

The Commission and its 29-strong staff does its homework and knows well the reasons behind a hospital's financial woes. And it can be tough. For instance, a hospital in Laurel, Maryland had based its operating budget on an expected average 80 percent occupancy rate. By the end of the year, having realized a low 30 percent occupancy, the hospital was in financial hot water. The Commission turned down a request for a whopping rate hike.

"If you opened a McDonald's on the assumption that you'd be able to sell ten million hamburgers a week and you only could sell five million, you could hardly convince the public to pay twice as much per hamburger. The market just doesn't work that way," explains Harold Cohen, executive director of the Commission. "The Commission's view is that hospitals shouldn't be treated differently from any other enterprise."

The Commission can also be understanding and has helped several inner-city hospitals get back on their feet. For example, one 271-bed hospital, which was on the verge of bankruptcy in 1974, has shown slight operating surpluses for the last few years. The hospital administrators had made strong efforts to operate the facility efficiently and economically. The Commission rewarded their efforts by approving higher rates for several years until the hospital was once again operating in the black.

Staff and Budget

In 1979 the Commission's budget was $750,000, some $190,000 of which came from the Department of Health, Education and Welfare's (HEW) Medicare and Medicaid Programs. Staffers, which include health experts, accountants, attorneys and an economist, collect and analyze data, work closely with hospitals to keep abreast of costs and make recommendations to the Commission.

Hospital Cost Containment

Other states have also set up voluntary hospital cost containment programs. In addition, many private organizations have taken important steps to hold down hospital costs and curb waste.

In 1977 Blue Cross and Blue Shield of Southwestern Virginia launched a program to actively involve physicians in reviewing whether hospital admissions were needed. Thirty-six area hospitals formed utilization review commissions composed of hospital personnel. By estimating and closely monitoring patient length of stay, hospital admissions were cut 13 percent by the year's end, saving health consumers and their insurers $2.3 million.

The Greater Cleveland Coalition on Health Care Cost Effectiveness in Ohio, created in 1978 by several area groups interested in curbing health care costs, aims to boost hospital efficiency by helping each other and educating the public about health issues through workshops and publications. The Coalition's membership includes representatives of private companies, labor unions, hospitals, commercial insurance companies, local Health Systems Agencies (HSAs) and colleges.[2]

Groups Highlighted

Greater Cleveland Coalition on Health Care
Cost Effectiveness
900 Standard Building
Cleveland, Ohio 44113
(216) 771-6814

Utilization Review Program
Blue Cross/Blue Shield of Southwestern Virginia
P.O. Box 13047
3959 Electric Road, S.W.
Roanoke, Virginia 24045
(703) 989-4231

[1] The Medicare and Medicaid Programs* are administered by the Health Care Financing Administration of the Department of Health, Education and Welfare (HEW). Medicare provides basic health benefits to elderly residents on social security. Medicaid, through grants to individual states, provides medical services to the needy.

[2] For information on Health Systems Agencies (HSAs), see Health Section, p. 344 and p. 346.

*State and/or local government agencies are frequently responsible for administration of Federal program funds. For further information, see Appendix I under appropriate Federal agency.

Note: For a complete listing of groups featured throughout this book, see Index.

HEALTH CARE
IS
NO
LAUGHING
MATTER
HEALTH CARE
IS
NO
LAUGHING
MATTER
Cape Cod
Nursing
Home Council
We want
Access
SAVE
OUR
HOME
SAVE
OUR
HOME
SAVE
OUR
HOME
SAVE
OUR

Winning Health Care Power

Introduction

In this chapter we explore consumer groups that have discovered how to organize for power. By working together they have made a difference in the cost and quality of their health care.

We start with a savvy group of patients in Minnesota who actually help determine standards of patient care and office policy for their consumer-oriented doctor.

We then move on to a citizens group in Seattle that is monitoring area nursing homes to ensure quality service while teaching residents how to organize for more control over their lives.

We conclude this chapter with a dynamic Cape Cod group that has tackled a range of health issues, winning extraordinary health reforms for consumers nationwide.

The ideas presented here are worth studying and can be tailored to fit your community's needs. When consumers organize for health power, everyone wins!

Patient Participation

Patient Advisory Council
Milton H. Seifert Jr., M.D. & Associates, Ltd.
675 Water Street
Excelsior, Minnesota 55331
(612) 474-4167

Most of us have known the finger-tapping frustration of waiting for hours to see the doctor and the feeling of anger and resentment after receiving the bill. How, we wonder, could a 10 minute visit cost so much? Unaware of what is involved in running a medical office, we grumble in silence, fearful that criticizing would destroy our relationship with the doctor on whom we depend so much.

Some physicians are finding unique ways to overcome patient dissatisfaction. For example, in 1974 Dr. Milton Seifert, a family practitioner in Excelsior, Minnesota, formed a voluntary Patient Advisory Council (PAC) and gave members wide management responsibilities. Seifert's Council has increased patient awareness and understanding of his medical practice while relieving him of management pressures that divert him from treating the 5,000 patients he sees yearly.

Patient Advisory Council
Milton H. Seifert Jr., M.D. & Associates, Ltd.

Dr. Milton Seifert

Helping Staff

By handling such duties as collecting debts, resolving complaints and setting fees and salaries, Council members bolster Seifert's 10-member staff, which includes an associate doctor, a health educator, and a psychologist who helps patients cope with everyday stresses and strains.

"My concept reflects an understanding that not only does the individual patient share responsibility for his medical care, but patients collectively share responsibility for the way health care is delivered," Seifert says.

Working Together

Contributing their time on a rotating basis, Council members work closely with Seifert and operate through committees. "The doctor has to be present and involved in all Council deliberations," Seifert says, "to ensure that the best interest of all parties is considered."

The PAC committees are responsible for specific functions. For example, the financial committee handles debt collection and sets fees and salaries. A policy committee determines office procedures and sets general standards for patient care. And a patient committee investigates and evaluates patient complaints about fees and service.

Narrowing the Gap

Active Council members say that PAC has improved Seifert's relationship with his patients. "Although Dr. Seifert has been our family doctor for many years and our children went to school together and I felt as though we were good friends before," says PAC member Lu Lins, "I feel as though I know him better and feel more comfortable with him. As far as I can see, his patients are his top priority. That's why I call him a 'people doctor'."

Interest Grows

Speaking to the success of Seifert's patient-doctor management style, an increasing number of doctors and medical groups are inquiring about the program. And members of the Council's liaison committee are drawing up plans to package the PAC concept for distribution.[1]

Some Doubts

"However, some doctors are reluctant to try the system," Seifert explains, "fearing that patients will overstep their authority." But he adds, "The chances of this happening are slim because Council members experience first-hand the ups and downs of running a clinic, and their decisions reflect a sensitivity to the needs of patients and doctors. And patients make responsible decisions because they wouldn't want to harm their own practice."

Origins

In the early 1970s, after a decade of private and group practice in the Minneapolis suburbs, Dr. Seifert became concerned that office management was taking too much time and was diverting him from treating his patients.

So in 1973 he sent questionnaires to his patients proposing the creation of an advisory council. Many responded negatively, doubting their ability to contribute anything valuable. But enough patients responded favorably to justify trial meetings—the first taking place in May 1974.

"We were flying blind," Seifert recalls. "There were no precedents." The notion that a doctor would actually solicit advice from his patients was difficult for many people to swallow. "My biggest problem was convincing my patients that it was all right for them to tell me what to do and that what they had to say was useful," he says.

Any Patient Can Serve

Seifert's patients are all eligible to join the Advisory Council and attend its quarterly meetings at which committees report their progress on various studies and office matters are discussed. An "if-you-can" membership fee of $5 helps defray the Council's postage, mailing and duplicating costs. Membership is voluntary and no formal Council hierarchy exists.

"We've resisted laying down a lot of membership rules or becoming highly organized in order to make it easy for patients to participate," Seifert explains. Of the 50 Council members, about 25 or 30 attend each meeting. Those not attending receive copies of meeting minutes.

Key to Success—Working Together

The key to the success of a patient advisory council, says Seifert, is mutual respect and understanding and open communication between the council and the doctor.

Patient Advisory Council
Milton H. Seifert Jr., M.D. & Associates, Ltd.

Dr. Milton Seifert—His patient management style of practice has been a success.

And what happens when PAC members ask Seifert to do something that he doesn't believe reflects good medicine or good practice? He could handle it in one of two ways. "I could just say no," he explains, "but that's probably not the strategy I would use." Instead, Seifert says, he'd suggest testing the recommended practice to determine whose opinion was right.

Helping Others

PAC members also help their fellow patients. The services committee conducts health education forums for patients, giving them tips on how to maintain good health such as eating properly and exercising. And in 1979 they were busy compiling a list of patients willing to help others get to the doctor by providing such services as babysitting and transportation.

[1] The Patient Advisory Council's (PAC) package describing some of the procedures in setting up PACs, will be ready by late summer 1980. For information write Patient Advisory Council, 675 Water Street, Excelsior, Minnesota 55331.

Note: For a complete listing of groups featured throughout this book, see Index.

Stopping Nursing Home Neglect

Citizens For the Improvement of Nursing Homes
1305 Northeast 47th Street
Seattle, Washington 98105
(206) 634-2349

For many of our country's elderly, nursing homes provide the companionship of peers as well as the around-the-clock medical care needed for ailments that prevent them from living alone any longer.

Big Business

But too often that isn't the case. About one in five of America's elderly spend some time in nursing homes or other long-term institutions and over $8 billion is pumped into the industry each year. Yet according to the United States Senate Special Committee on Aging, half of the homes operating in this country fail to meet the government's minimum standards for cleanliness, quality of care and safety of building structure.

Over the years repeated Congressional investigations and newspaper exposes have revealed shocking treatment of residents in some nursing homes and have brought public attention to the problem. Residents have been victims of both physical and mental abuse. For example, investigators have found elderly patients unattended for hours, lacking adequate care. Along with poor hygiene, such as infrequent showers, shaving and teeth cleaning, many residents have been the targets of verbal abuse.

Unfortunately, profits rather than patient needs often determine what services nursing home residents will receive. Expensive nursing home care comes at an even higher price when services that should be included aren't provided. And residents, their families—or whoever pays the bill—don't get their money's worth. But more importantly, the residents are victimized. Isolated and often ill-equipped for leadership, many nursing home residents just live with poor conditions, either fearful of speaking up or unaware of how to go about winning reforms.

Citizen Group Takes Action

One nonprofit organization, Citizens for the Improvement of Nursing Homes (CINH) in Seattle, Washington, has shown how much a determined group can do to ensure quality care for nursing home residents.

Their efforts have led to legislative victories that have made nursing homes throughout the state more responsive to residents and to the public. In 1979 CINH members fought hard for and helped win state legislation requiring state inspection of nursing homes to specifically guard against misrepresentation, overcharging, duplicate billing and other activities that victimize residents. And that same year they successfully lobbied for legislation mandating that nursing assistants be trained and certified.

Moreover, the group is giving nursing home residents more control over their lives by teaching them how to form and operate resident councils. And CINH has organized support groups of friends and families to help nursing home residents overcome fears and speak out about abuses.

In 1979 CINH boasted 350 members in chapters throughout the state and affiliations with 14 other organizations whose members total 3,000. CINH's diverse membership includes rich and poor as well as elderly and young community residents. Members participate in civic meetings and work with allied organizations as well as with health and social service agencies to monitor nursing home conditions and determine needed reforms.

Origins

The organization was started in 1969 by five elderly women who had friends in area nursing homes and were concerned about the facilities' conditions. As one organizer recalls of the group's early meetings, "Had we known at that time the immensity of the problem and the complexity of the system, we might have been too discouraged to continue. By working together, however, we were able to interest other individuals with similar concerns."

Hesitant Residents

CINH members began by talking to nursing home residents, receiving and following up on complaints about abuse or lack of needed services. But many residents, dependent on nursing home personnel and services and fearing recrimination, were hesitant to report complaints.

Nevertheless, the group continued to help those residents willing to talk and, in the process, collected data that helped them determine what regulatory reforms were needed to correct abuses.

In 1971 CINH began sending out a newsletter and marshaling support from community groups, social service agencies and residents around the state. And within the year they were ready to launch their first strong lobbying effort.

Legislative Successes

That effort, which demonstrated the group's organizing skills, led to the passage in 1973 of a bill by the state legislature requiring nursing home financial disclosure and public access to state inspectors' reports.

The group then began a campaign for legislation creating a penalty system for those homes violating Federal and state nursing home regulations. CINH members, with the help of volunteer attorneys, were primarily responsible for drafting the bill, seeking out legislative sponsors and testifying at the hearings. After an intensive lobbying campaign the bill was passed in 1975.

Staff and Budget

In 1979 CINH's small $20,000 budget paid a full-time coordinator and other expenses. Three workers were provided by ACTION's Volunteers in Service to America (VISTA) Program.* In addition, a part-time secretary was funded by the American Association of Retired Persons (AARP).[1] VISTA workers received training in community organizing techniques and nursing home regulations from the nonprofit Washington, D.C.-based National Citizens Coalition for Nursing Home Reform, of which CINH is a charter member.[2] But CINH's real strength rests with the volunteer work of its many members.

A 20-member Board of Directors provides leadership, and dues are $3 a year for individuals and $10 for organizations. Private donations help defray the cost of publishing the monthly CINH newsletter which keeps members and nursing home residents up to date on such things as relevant legislation and CINH activities.

Giving Residents Their Own Voice

The past has been gratifying but the future for Seattle's nursing home residents looks even brighter—thanks to CINH.

In 1979 the group began forming support groups, comprised of CINH members and families of residents, to help diminish fears of recrimination among nursing home residents. Moreover, CINH spurred resident interest in protecting their own rights and monitoring the quality of care in their homes by establishing resident councils. Educational seminars are planned for council members who will learn about—and have input into—nursing home administration and policy as well as plans for such projects as nutrition programs and social activities.

Resident Power in Minnesota

Other groups are forming across the country to help nursing home residents. The Nursing Home Residents Advisory Council (NHRAC), an independent, nonprofit group in Minneapolis, Minnesota, has 96 resident councils in nursing homes throughout the state, representing 10,500 elderly residents. Also, the group's workshops, training programs and resource kits are helping nursing home residents across the country speak up within their homes and before regulatory and legislative bodies.[3]

Community Power in Greenwich Village

In April 1976, after private owners refused to make renovations necessary to meet state and Federal regulatory standards, the Village Nursing Home in New York City was scheduled to close. But residents of the city's Greenwich Village, whose interest was sparked by Caring Community, a nonprofit coalition of area churches and social agencies, came to the rescue of the elderly patients. Stunned by the Home's deteriorated condition, Greenwich Village residents banded together. And by distributing leaflets at area buildings explaining the plight of Home residents, they came up with enough money to buy the facility.

"The bulk of the money came in $5, $10 and $15 individual donations, not from foundations as we had expected," says Sister Bonnie Morrow, who was active in the fundraising efforts.

Since March 1979 the nonprofit Home has been owned and operated by Greenwich Village residents, and the future looks brighter for its patients. Renovations are slated to begin in March 1980 and will be made in phases over a two-year period to prevent patient displacement.

Groups Highlighted

Nursing Home Residents Advisory Council
3231 First Avenue South, Suite 210
Minneapolis, Minnesota 55408
(612) 827-8151

Village Nursing Home
607 Hudson Street
New York, New York 11014
(212) 255-3003

[1] For more information on the American Association of Retired Persons (AARP), see Resources at end of Health Section.

[2] For more information on the National Citizens Coalition for Nursing Home Reform, see Resources at end of Health Section.

[3] Packets explaining resident rights and showing how to form resident councils are available for $1 by writing: Nursing Home Residents Advisory Council, 3231 First Avenue, South, Minneapolis, Minnesota 55408.

* State and/or local government agencies are frequently responsible for administration of Federal program funds. For further information, see Appendix I under appropriate Federal agency.

Note: For a complete listing of groups featured throughout this book, see Index.

A Powerhouse Organization in Health Care Reform

Cape Cod Health Care Coalition
583 Main Street
Hyannis, Massachusetts 02601
(617) 771-0629

The popular seaside resort of Cape Cod, Massachusetts brings to mind images of building sand castles, digging for clams and running barefoot along the beach. But life is no vacation for one-fifth of the 120,000 year-round residents whose annual incomes are less than $5,000. Until recently, those eligible for Medicare* or Medicaid,* the Federal government's medical programs for elderly and low-income citizens respectively, were denied health care by some area doctors who preferred to treat the champagne set.[1]

Local Group Helps Health Consumers Nationwide

But since 1976 the Cape Cod Health Care Coalition (CCHCC), a nonprofit group in Hyannis, has tackled a wide range of health issues and successfully fought for reforms. The major goal of the Coalition, whose members include low-income residents, members of a hospital workers union and employees of social service agencies, is to assure Cape Cod residents access to a wide range of health care services, regardless of their ability to pay.

But in the process CCHCC has managed to chalk up victories for health consumers across the state and throughout the country. Within three short years, the group's impressive accomplishments included:

- The successful lobbying effort that helped win a Federal law amendment which assures citizens nationwide, regardless of their ability to pay, emergency treatment at Federally subsidized hospitals;
- The passage by the state legislature of a patient rights bill;
- The creation of a statewide health care coalition which monitors health issues for all Massachusetts residents;
- The representation of Coalition members on the influential local health planning board;
- The building of a much needed local medical clinic for low-income women;
- The end of a practice by a Cape Cod hospital of placing liens on the homes of patients unable to pay medical bills; and
- The creation of a council that oversees the operation of nursing homes to assure quality care for residents.

Origins

It began in 1976 when a Cape Cod mother was forced to drive her four-month-old son to Boston Hospital for emergency care because a local ophthalmologist refused to treat Medicaid patients. The delay caused by the 150-mile trip meant extensive treatment which might otherwise have been avoided. When the story hit the local paper an organizer for the Local 880 of the Massachusetts Hospital Workers Union mobilized public anger into what was to become a powerful force.[2]

"Unionization gave us a base of 500 people concerned about health care," says Bill Pastreich, the early organizer and current director of CCHCC. Noting that strength in numbers gave the Coalition the muscle to fight for needed changes, he explains, "With job security and the backing of their Union, they had the freedom to voice their concerns."

Pastreich began signing up interested Union members and in November 1976 the group formed the Coalition. They began surveying area hospitals and doctors and discovered that many were turning low-income residents away.

The group launched a lobbying effort, writing and calling on state leaders urging that reforms be implemented. In 1977 their efforts were rewarded when the state licensing board issued regulations requiring doctors to treat emergency cases regardless of patient ability to pay and forbidding discrimination against Medicare and Medicaid patients.

Cape Cod Health Care Coalition

Coalition members demonstrate for health reform.

National Impact

But Coalition members didn't stop at the state level. They launched another lobbying campaign—this time nationwide—to urge the amendment of a Federal law to better protect patients unable to pay for hospital services.

The Hill-Burton Act, enacted in 1946, authorized Federal loans and grants to hospitals nationwide for major capital improvements.[3] The Act also required the 80 percent of American hospitals that received Federal funding for construction to provide a "reasonable amount of (free) services to persons unable to pay." But the language of the act was vague and subject to interpretation by hospitals and clinics.

CCHCC's effort helped score a consumer victory that echoed across the nation in 1979 when Congress amended the legislation to *mandate* that emergency health care be provided to all citizens—even those unable to pay—by hospitals receiving Federal subsidies. In addition, the amendment forbids hospitals to discriminate against Medicare and Medicaid patients.

Meanwhile, Coalition members were busy working for health reforms at the local and state levels.

Cape Cod Health Care Coalition

Elderly Cape Cod Health Care Coalition demonstrators take time out to chat.

Statewide Impact

The Coalition's lobbying efforts helped win in 1977 a state patients' bill of rights which, among other things, requires Massachusetts hospitals and other health providers to offer patients explanations of all medical procedures. The law also gives patients the right to refuse examinations by medical students.

Working at the Local Level

Also in 1977 the Coalition sparked public interest in applying pressure on a local hospital to stop placing liens against the homes of patients who couldn't pay their bills. The hospital subsequently discontinued the practice, dropping action on 183 liens.

Cape Cod Health Care Coalition

Young and old deserve good health care.

That same year the group successfully campaigned for the election of numerous Coalition members to sub-area councils of the local Health Systems Agency (HSA), an influential board charged with community health planning and responsible for such important decisions as what Federally funded medical facilities will be built in the area.[4]

CCHCC representation on the local HSA helped spur the creation in 1979 of a much needed nonprofit Women's Health Clinic in Hyannis which provides medical treatment to 300 low-income Cape Cod women each month.

Staff and Funding

By 1979 the Coalition's membership numbered 800. Their $35,000 budget was raised from private sources. And their staff included four employees from ACTION's Volunteers in Service to America (VISTA) Program.*

Forming Other Groups to Help More Residents

In 1979 the Coalition formed two groups to further protect health consumers in their community and statewide.

To work for improved staffing and patient care at area nursing homes, the Coalition formed the non-profit Cape Cod Nursing Home Council. The Council includes members of the Massachusetts Hospital Workers Union, nursing home residents and other elderly citizens who stand guard over area nursing homes to ensure quality services for residents.

Launching a Statewide Group

And to help assure low-cost, quality health care for residents statewide, the group formed the Massachusetts Health Care Coalition (MHCC). The 200-member group also includes low-income and elderly residents and members of the Massachusetts Hospital Workers Union.

Besides monitoring hospitals to ensure adherence to state and Federal laws regarding patient rights, the group is tackling a range of health issues, including lobbying for more foreign language translators in hospitals. Its 1979 publication, *Opening Hospital Doors—Free Health Care for Community People,* which explains patient rights under the Hill-Burton Act, is available for interested residents nationwide.[5]

The Cape Cod Health Care Coalition has scored many other victories for area health consumers. Their dedication to ensuring quality, low-cost health care for all residents regardless of income stands as a model for other public and private groups across the country who are eager to win health reforms in their own areas.

Other Groups

In 1976, before Hill-Burton was amended, the Rhode Island Health Advocates (RIHA), part of the Roman Catholic Diocese of Providence, used pressure to spur Rhode Island hospitals to comply with provisions of the Act. Working with the Rhode Island Workers Association, a self-help organization, RIHA launched a publicity campaign to draw public attention to the problem and bring pressure on hospitals to treat those residents unable to pay. Their tactics worked and within a few months Rhode Island hospitals had provided an estimated $500,000 in free care to needy patients.

Since then RIHA has fought for patients' rights through a range of programs, including teaching community groups and health providers how to win private and government funding for health services and facilities; organizing citizens to fight proposed cutbacks for needed health facilities; and publishing a guidebook for Rhode Island residents listing health programs and relevant Federal and state health laws.

Group Highlighted

Rhode Island Health Advocates
Diocesan Community Affairs Office
Broad and Steward Streets
Providence, Rhode Island 02908
(401) 421-7833

[1] The Medicare and Medicaid Programs* are administered by the Health Care Financing Administration of the Department of Health, Education and Welfare (HEW). Medicare provides basic health benefits to elderly residents on social security. Medicaid, through grants to individual states, provides medical services to the needy.

[2] The Massachusetts Hospital Workers Union are members of the Service Employees International Union of the American Federation of Labor and Congress of Industrial Organizations (AFL-CIO).

[3] The Hill-Burton Act provided hospitals with Federal funds for construction and other capital improvements. Although still commonly referred to as the Hill-Burton Act, its provisions are now incorporated into the comprehensive National Health Planning and Resources Development Act,* which is administered by the Department of Health Education and Welfare (HEW). That Act was amended in 1979 to require that subsidized hospitals provide free health care to those patients unable to pay and not qualifying for government assistance and forbids discrimination against Medicaid and Medicare patients.

[4] Health Systems Agencies (HSAs) are part of a national health planning program created by Congress in 1974 by the National Health Planning and Resources Development Act.* For more information on HSAs, see Health Section, p. 344 and p. 346.

[5] A copy of *Opening Hospital Doors—Free Health Care for Community People* can be obtained by writing the Massachusetts Health Care Coalition (MHCC), 145 Tremont Street, Boston, Massachusetts 02111.

*State and/or local government agencies are frequently responsible for administration of Federal program funds. For further information, see Appendix I under appropriate Federal agency.

Note: For a complete listing of groups featured throughout this book, see Index.

Health Resources

The following resources contain descriptions of organizations and publications which can be of help to consumer groups across the country that wish to organize and launch community projects designed to combat high prices.

Those organizations offering assistance in a variety of areas are listed under "General" and are followed by a list of publications under the same heading. Other organizations and publications that provide help in specific areas are listed under corresponding chapter title headings.

Of course, it is not possible to list every organization and publication in the country that might prove helpful to you and your group, but we believe those we do mention are representative of the various kinds of assistance available. Chances are you'll hear of many other useful resources as you become involved in your own community project.

Space limitations made it extremely difficult to choose among the many fine groups considered, and we sincerely hope we haven't offended the many deserving organizations and/or authors of useful publications that have not been included.

General Health

Organizations

American Health Planning Association
1601 Connecticut Avenue, N.W., Suite 700
Washington, D.C. 20009
(202) 232-6390

Promotes policy changes in the health care industry by fostering dialogue among health planners and the public. Sponsors and promotes research, training and continuing education. Urges a health care system which is more rational, responsive and cost effective to consumers, providers, industry, labor and third party payers. Publishes weekly newsletter, *Today in Health Planning.* (Free to members of the Association, $30/year for non-members.) Also bimonthly, *Crosscurrents.* (Free.)

Consumer Commission on the Accreditation of Health Services, Inc.
377 Park Avenue South
New York, New York 10016
(212) 689-8959

Dual purpose is to educate consumers about current issues in health care delivery and to provide a perspective to the public on the needs and concerns of the health consumer. Publications include a newsletter, *Consumer Health Perspectives.* (8 issues/year, $10 to individuals, $25 to organizations.)

Government Research Corporation
1730 M Street, N.W.
Washington, D.C. 20036
(202) 857-1400

Provides managers of private and public institutions with independent analysis, forecasting and counseling services; areas include health care, consumer affairs and others. Maintains extensive collection of reference materials and publishes a number of periodic reports in subject areas covered.

Health Policy Advisory Center
17 Murray Street
New York, New York 10007
(212) 267-8890

Monitors and interprets the health system to change-oriented groups of health workers and consumers. Maintains a resource center and offers a network for sharing and analyzing the concerns and strategies of others with similar interests. Publishes bimonthly, *Bulletin.* ($14/year to individuals, $28/year to institutions, $8/year to students.)

Highlander Center
Route 3, Box 370
New Market, Tennessee 37820
(615) 933-3443

Residential education center and training facility for labor unions, local community leaders and low-income persons wishing to work in or learn about rural community health clinics. Coordinates efforts in finding common solutions to social and economic problems, specifically in the areas of occupational and environmental health. Oversees the functions of the Associated Clinics of Appalachia. Publishes quarterly newsletter, *Highlander Reports.* (Free.)

InterStudy
5715 Christmas Lake Road
Excelsior, Minnesota 55331
(612) 474-1176

Provides research, policy analysis, consultation and technical assistance in the delivery and financing of health care for business, labor, community and government leaders. Strives to find the most effective ways of delivering health care.

National Association of Community Health Centers, Inc. (NACHC)
1625 Eye Street, N.W., Suite 420
Washington, D.C. 20006
(202) 833-9280

National advocate for ambulatory health care delivery programs providing health services to the medically underserved. Through policy analysis, research, technical assistance, publications, and education and training, seeks to assure the continued growth and development of community health care programs. Interests span neighborhood and family health centers; migrant, rural and Indian health programs; and maternal and infant care programs. Publishes monthly newsletter, *NACHC News.* ($10/year, free to members.)

National Association of Farmworker Organizations
1332 New York Avenue, N.W.
Washington, D.C. 20005
(202) 347-2407

National coalition of organizations advocating farmworker rights and concerns. Sponsors programs on energy crisis assistance, food, housing, health and education. Publishes monthly newsletter, *National Farmworker,* which covers a variety of topics concerning farmworker rights and welfare; available in English or Spanish. ($15/year.)

National Center for Appropriate Technology
P.O. Box 3838
Butte, Montana 59701
(406) 494-4577

Offers assistance to low-income groups in areas of food, housing, energy and health care. Publishes monthly, *A.T. Times.* ($10/year to individuals, free to organizations working with the poor.)

National Health Law Program
2401 Main Street
Santa Monica, California 90405
(213) 392-4811

Provides specialized legal assistance to legal services attorneys and their clients in matters involving health programs. Assists with training, community education and coalition building. Acquires and shares information on health-related legislation, statutory or regulatory interpretation, location of experts in various health fields and policy positions of experts on delivery of health care to the poor. Publishes a number of health advocacy guides. Also publishes monthly, *Health Law Newsletter.* (Free.)

National Rural Center
1828 L Street, N.W.
Washington, D.C. 20036
(202) 331-0258

Develops and advocates health policy alternatives relating to rural needs by conducting demonstration programs, using the results of existing research, evaluating Federal programs and pursuing basic research. Monitors the writing of national legislation and program regulations. Provides information services and publications. Also monthly, *Rural Health Newsletter.* (Free.)

National Women's Health Network
2025 Eye Street, N.W., Suite 105
Washington, D.C. 20006
(202) 223-6886

Represents women as health care consumers. Provides community outreach and educational assistance for both health care providers and consumers. Monitors and disseminates information about legislative action relevant to women's well-being. Operates a national speakers bureau and a number of specialized information services such as a diethystilbestrol (DES) litigation service. Publishes bimonthly, *National Women's Health Network News.* (Free to members.)

Public Citizen Health Research Group
2000 P Street, N.W., Suite 708
Washington, D.C. 20036
(202) 872-0320

Informs consumers about issues that affect their health and monitors the work of health-related regulatory agencies. Primary areas of interest are health planning, health care financing, patients' rights and the safety of food, drugs and medical devices. Produces many health-related publications. Also a quarterly newspaper, *The Public Citizen.* (Free on a trial basis.)

Rural America
1346 Connecticut Avenue, N.W.
Washington, D.C. 20036
(202) 659-2800

Seeks to make certain that the needs of rural people are considered when public policies and programs are formulated, including those affecting rural health clinics. Serves as a national clearinghouse for health and other information and services to individuals and groups. Publishes monthly newspaper, *Rural America.* ($10/year to nonmembers.)

Publications

Catalog of Federal Health Resources. National Governors' Association, 444 North Capitol Street, Washington, D.C. 20001. 1979. ($2.) Provides information about (1) Federal programs that provide assistance for the delivery of health services, and (2) Federal programs that are not specific to the health care area but provide potential resources for assisting in the delivery of health services.

Frost, Shelley; Fearon, Zita; and Hymann, Herbert. ***A Consumer's Guide to Evaluating Medical Technology.*** Consumer Commission on the Accreditation of Health Services, Inc., 377 Park Avenue South, New York, New York 10016. 1979. ($7.) Designed to help consumers and health care professionals make informed judgments about costly medical equipment. Details the legal role of the consumer in health planning and facility board operations; suggests key questions to ask when confronted with decisions about acquisition and distribution of medical technology.

Health Resources Administration: Catalog of Publications. Health Resources Administration, Office of Communications, 3700 East-West Highway, Room 10-44, Hyattsville, Maryland 20782. 1979. (Free.) Lists most of the Administration's health publications, gives a brief description and includes an availability statement.

Healthy People: The Surgeon General's Report on Health Promotion and Disease Prevention. Superintendent of Documents, U.S. Government Printing Office, Washington, D.C. 20402. 1979. (Publication No. DHEW/PHS 79-55071, $5.) Details major risks to good health and outlines a national program for improving health. Health promotion and protection are addressed as are preventive health services.

Ittig, Peter T., ***Planning Health Care Delivery Systems.*** Program in Urban and Regional Studies, Room 209, West Sibley Hall, Cornell University, Ithaca, New York 14853. 1974. ($6.) Analyzes economic factors in planning health care delivery and presents current approaches to providing comprehensive ambulatory health care. Geared for Health Maintenance Organizations (HMOs), health planning agencies, ambulatory care facilities. Presents an optimum model and proposes implementation suggestions.

Prescription for Primary Health Care: A Community Guidebook. Program in Urban and Regional Studies, Room 209, West Sibley Hall, Cornell University, Ithaca, New York 14853. 1980. ($6.) Guide for organizing community residents; probes skills necessary for resident participation in community-based ambulatory care planning and delivery. Primary emphasis on rural settings. Produced by the Primary Care Development Project (Cornell University); funded by the University and the U.S. Public Health Service.

The following publications are available at no cost from the Bureau of Community Health Services, U.S. Public Health Service, 5600 Fishers Lane, Room 7-05, Rockville, Maryland 20857:

Ambulatory Health Care Standards. 1977. (Limited supply.) Gives standards to be used by health centers as a self-assessment tool.

Facility Planning Guidelines for Ambulatory Health Centers. 1978. Intended as a general guide for the planning and development of ambulatory health centers.

Hospital-Affiliated Primary Care Centers Program Guidance Material. 1979. Provides information to assist the Department of Health, Education and Welfare's regional offices in developing project grants for hospitals wishing to reorganize their outpatient care resources to provide primary care to medically underserved populations.

Clearinghouses

Clearinghouse for Adult Education and Lifelong Learning
6011 Executive Boulevard
Rockville, Maryland 20852
(800) 638-6628 (Toll-free).

Clearinghouse on Health Indexes
National Center for Health Statistics, Division of Analysis
Center Building, Room 2-27
3700 East-West Highway
Hyattsville, Maryland 20782
(301) 436-7035

National Clearinghouse on Aging
Office of Human Development Administration on Aging
330 Independence Avenue, S.W.
Washington, D.C. 20201
(202) 245-0188

National Clearinghouse for Alcohol Information
National Institute on Alcohol Abuse and Alcoholism
P.O. Box 2345
Rockville, Maryland 20852
(301) 468-2600

National Clearinghouse for Drug Abuse Information
National Institute on Drug Abuse
Parklawn Building, Room 10A53
5600 Fishers Lane
Rockville, Maryland 20857
(301) 443-6500

National Clearinghouse for Family Planning Information
Office for Family Planning
Bureau of Community Health Services
P.O. Box 2225
Rockville, Maryland 20852
(301) 881-9400

National Clearinghouse for Mental Health Information
National Institute of Mental Health
Parklawn Building, Room 11A33
5600 Fishers Lane
Rockville, Maryland 20857
(301) 443-4517

National Health Planning Information Center
Health Resources Administration
Center Building, Room 522
3700 East-West Highway
Hyattsville, Maryland 20782
(301) 436-6738

Office of Cancer Communications
National Cancer Institute
7910 Woodmont Avenue, Suite 1320
Bethesda, Maryland 20205
(301) 496-4070

Providing Alternative Health Care

Organizations

American Association of Retired Persons
1909 K Street, N.W.
Washington, D.C. 20049
(202) 872-4700

Operates the National Gerontology Resource Center. Furnishes information on aging and the elderly; maintains extensive library of materials on gerontology and retirement.

American Holistic Medical Association
Route 2, Welsh Coulee
La Crosse, Wisconsin 54601
(608) 786-2660

Serves as professional source of information for physicians and other health professionals interested in the principles of "medicine of the whole person." Holds national conferences. Publishes a directory of holistic physicians (available only to members, free); and a monthly newsletter, *Holistic Medicine* ($20/year for non-members, free to members.)

Bureau of Community Health Services
U.S. Public Health Service
5600 Fishers Lane, Room 7-05
Rockville, Maryland 20857
(301) 443-2320

Maintains programs on Appalachian health, community health, family planning, health in underserved rural areas, maternal and child health and migrant health. Operates the National Health Service Corps and several special programs. Publications available on all of the above programs.

National Council on Wholistic Therapeutics and Medicine
GPO, Box H
Brooklyn, New York 11202
(212) 683-4793

Federation of groups interested in an integrated system of healing. Explores new and innovative therapeutic techniques, promotes education in preventive medicine and disseminates information through a journal and a monthly newsletter for members. Conducts seminars and conferences.

Office of Health Maintenance Organizations (OHMOs)
U.S. Public Health Service
12420 Parklawn Drive
Rockville, Maryland 20857
(301) 443-2300

Administers the HMO Act of 1973. Fosters the expansion and growth of HMOs and enforces Federal laws and regulations relating to them. Publishes and distributes many publications on HMOs. (Free.)

Wholistic Health Centers, Inc.
137 South Garfield Street
Hinsdale, Illinois 60521
(312) 323-1920

Promotes treatment of social and spiritual problems along with physical and mental ailments. Provides technical assistance in establishing wholistic health centers. Distributes reprints of articles and news clippings on wholistic health care and publishes informative monographs as well as quarterly newsletter. (Free to members.)

Publications

Directory of Rural Health Care Programs. Department of Health, Education and Welfare, Assistant Secretary for Planning and Evaluation/Health, Humphrey Building, Room 442–E, 200 Independence Avenue, S.W., Washington, D.C. 20201. 1980. (Free.) Describes approximately 1,000 innovative primary health care programs (rural). Includes information on staffing, service area, basis for fees, etc.

Kaslov, Leslie J., ***Wholistic Dimensions in Healing: A Resource Guide.*** Doubleday & Company, Inc., Garden City, New York. 1978. ($7.95.) Covers the spectrum of the wholistic approach to health, with chapters devoted to a wide variety of subjects (e.g., childbirth programs, wholistic groups and centers). Lists numerous groups active in each field, with a short description of their activities.

The following publications are available at no cost from the Bureau of Community Health Services, U.S. Public Health Service, 5600 Fishers Lane, Room 7-05, Rockville, Maryland 20857:

Directory of Community Health Centers. 1978. (Limited supply.) Lists, by region, all community health centers which have received funding from the Bureau.

Equipment Guidelines for Ambulatory Health Centers. 1978.

Guide for Developing Nutrition Services in Community Health Programs. 1978. Provides technical guidance on how to plan, develop and evaluate nutrition services as an integral part of community health care programs.

Policy and Procedures Manual for Governing Board Members. 1979. Provides an overview of the functions of a Governing Board in a health facility and informs Board members of their role and responsibilities. Also available in Spanish. 1980.

Procurement Guidelines for Community Health Centers. 1976.

Publications of the Bureau of Community Health Services. 1979. Complete listing of the Bureau's publications, with a brief description of each.

Space Guidelines for Ambulatory Health Centers. 1977.

The following publications are available at no cost from the Office of Health Maintenance Organizations (OHMO), U.S. Public Health Service, 12420 Parklawn Drive, Rockville, Maryland 20857:

Federal Financial Assistance for HMOs. 1980. Describes the types of Federal assistance available under the HMO Act, and how it may be obtained.

HMO Feasibility Study Guide. 1974. Designed to assist potential HMO sponsors, their staff and consultants in conducting an HMO feasibility study. Addresses both objective data analysis and subjective determination of risk.

HMO Focus. Bimonthly newsletter on HMOs and the HMO program.

National HMO Development Strategy Through 1988. 1979. Outlines the goals, strategy, priorities and implementation plan for HMO development.

Publications on HMOs available from the Office of Health Maintenance Organizations. Bimonthly. Listing of publications, article reprints, laws and regulations, etc.

The following six publications comprise the "Rural Health Center Development Series," available from Ballinger Publishing Company, 17 Dunster Street, Cambridge, Massachusetts 02138. All 1979. Describes the achievements, problems and limitations of rural outpatient health centers. Set available in hardback ($60) or softcover ($31.75), or individually as priced below:

Alford, Terry W., ***Facility Planning, Design and Construction of Rural Health Centers.*** ($17.50, softcover $9.95.)

Bernstein, James D.; Hege, Frederick P.; and Farran, Christopher, ***Rural Health Centers in the United States.*** ($10, softcover $5.95.)

Denham, John W. and Pickard, C. Glenn, Jr., ***Clinical Roles in Rural Health Centers.*** ($10, softcover $5.95.)

Sullivan, Robert J., ***Medical Record and Index Systems for Community Practice.*** ($12.50, softcover $6.95.)

Wade, Torlen L. and Brooks, Edward F., ***Planning and Managing Rural Health Centers.*** ($15, softcover $7.95.)

Warren, David G., ***A Legal Guide for Rural Health Programs.*** ($15, softcover $7.95.)

NOTE: Also see Health Resources under "General."

Identifying Specialized Health Services

Organizations

Hospice Institute for Education, Training and Research
765 Prospect Street
New Haven, Connecticut 06511
(203) 789-1509 or 789-5871

Sponsors courses taught by nationally recognized faculty who specialize in the care of the terminally ill and their families. Continuing education credit for these courses is available. The Institute also provides technical assistance to develop hospice programs. Publishes semiannually, *Catolog of Courses.* (Free.)

Hospice of Marin
77 Mark Drive, #19
San Rafael, California 94903
(415) 472-6240

Offers broad range of services related to hospices, including five-day seminar on "Developing a Hospice Care Team," workshops, conferences, publications. Operates the second oldest hospice program in the United States.

Maternity Center Association
48 East 92nd Street
New York, New York 10028
(212) 369-7300

National voluntary health agency dedicated to the improvement of maternity care. Serves as maternity care information clearinghouse. Numerous publications available, including reprints of recent journal articles.

National Association of Parents and Professionals for Safe Alternatives in Childbirth (NAPSAC)
P.O. Box 267
Marble Hill, Missouri 63764
(314) 238-2010

Encourages and assists in implementing family-centered childbirth programs and in establishing childbearing centers. Maintains directories, including one on birth centers. Quarterly newsletter, *NAPSAC News.* (Free to members.)

National Council of Senior Citizens, Inc.
1511 K Street, N.W.
Washington, D.C. 20005
(202) 347-8800

Works to make certain that the rights and needs of senior citizens are addressed in legislation and government regulations; actively lobbies for national health insurance, social security issues, etc. Health is one of many areas addressed. Publishes monthly, *Senior Citizen News.* ($4/year.)

National Hospice Organization
301 Tower, Suite 506
301 Maple Avenue West
Vienna, Virginia 22180
(703) 938-4449

Promotes understanding of the hospice concept among health care professionals and the public, and provides technical assistance and evaluation services to hospice organizations in their formative years. Develops and maintains standards of care in program planning and implementation. Makes available basic training materials and a film on hospice care. Publishes monthly, *National Hospice Organization Newsletter.* ($8/year to nonmembers.)

National Institute of Mental Health
U.S. Public Health Service
5600 Fishers Lane
Rockville, Maryland 20857
(301) 443-3600

Provides leadership, policies and goals for the Federal effort in the promotion of mental health, the prevention and treatment of mental illness and the rehabilitation of affected individuals. Writes and distributes many publications on these topics.

Publications

Alternatives = Independence. Division of Aging, Utah State Department of Social Services, P.O. Box 2500, Salt Lake City, Utah 84110. 1977. (Free.) Report of a task force seeking alternatives to nursing home care. Addresses the problem of steadily increasing costs of nursing home care and the effectiveness of alternative support systems.

Directory of Adult Day Care Centers. Health Standards and Quality Bureau, Health Care Financing Administration, Department of Health, Education and Welfare, 1849 Gwynn Oak Drive, Baltimore, Maryland 21207. (Free.) Compiled by the Division of Long-Term Care, which is specifically concerned with the development of standards for long-term care as well as survey and certification activities. Adult day care programs included are restorative, maintenance or social.

First American Hospice: Three Years of Home Care. Hospice, Inc., 765 Prospect Street, New Haven, Connecticut 06511. 1978. ($15.75.) A comprehensive look into the theory and practice of hospice work. Provides guidance on the establishment of a home care program, utilization of community resources, selection of staff, etc.

Hospice: An Alternative Way to Care for the Dying. Billy Budd Films, Inc., 235 East 57th Street, New York, New York 10022. 1978. (May be rented or purchased. Write for prices.) A 16 mm documentary film intended to create community awareness, understanding and acceptance of the hospice movement. Developed by the National Hospice Organization. Also available on ¾ inch video cassette.

"Hospice Care: An Alternative." Boulder County Hospice, Inc., 2118 14th Street, Boulder, Colorado 80302. Revised 1980. (Rental fee, $25.) A 25-minute slide/tape presentation, with audio, that describes the organization of a hospice home care program and the essential characteristics of hospice care services.

Lubic, Ruth W. and Ernst, Eunice K., "The Childbearing Center: An Alternative to Conventional Care," ***Nursing Outlook,*** Volume 26, Issue 12. December 1978. (Reprints 35 cents each from Maternity Center Association, 48 East 92nd Street, New York, New York 10028.) Article reviews the operation and experience of the Maternity Center Association's Childbearing Center and sets forth some assumptions and general principles for the establishment of similar centers.

The Standards of a Hospice Program of Care. National Hospice Organization, 301 Tower, Suite 506, 301 Maple Avenue West, Vienna, Virginia 22180. 1979. ($12 to members; $20 to nonmembers.) Serves as the basis for future accrediting of hospice programs by the National Hospice Organization. Provides a description of a hospice care program and the hospice team.

NOTE: Also see Health Resources under "General."

Emphasizing Health Education and Self-Care

Organizations

Bureau of Health Education
Center for Disease Control
Atlanta, Georgia 30333
(404) 329-3235

Helps inform and educate individuals and families so they can make intelligent decisions and take knowledgeable action with respect to their health. Supports model and experimental programs to establish health education methodology. Assists state and local health agencies in initiating, strengthening and delivering health education programs.

Office of Professional Public Health Education
125 Worth Street
New York, New York 10013
(212) 566-5802

Offers technical assistance and advice on methods of providing community health education programs and outreach. Numerous publications on a variety of health education topics available at no cost.

Tel-Med, Inc.
22700 Cooley Drive
Colton, California 92324
(714) 825-6034

Will provide information on how to implement a Tel-Med phone-in tape program for organizations concerned with health care education. Publishes monthly, *Tel-Med Newsletter.* (Free.)

Publications

Acute Hospitalitis: A Consumer's Guide to Health Care Costs. The Maryland Public Interest Research Group, University of Maryland, College Park, Maryland 20742. 1977. ($2.) Analyzes the relationship between the hospital physician and insurance company as factors in health care costs. Illustrates how special services offered by hospitals contribute to inflated costs.

Anderson, Jack; Caftel, Brad; and Bryson, Anita, ***Implementing the EPSDT Program: A Step-By-Step Guide for Community Organizations.*** National Economic Development and Law Center, 2150 Shattuck Avenue, Suite 300, Berkeley, California 94704. 1978. (Free.) Reference guide to implementing Medicaid's Early and Periodic Screening, Diagnosis and Treatment Program (EPSDT), which is designed to identify low-income children with medical problems and provide early treatment.

Guide to Prescription Drug Prices. Health Care Financing Administration, Pharmaceutical and Medical Supplies Branch, East Low Rise Building, Room 1C5, 6401 Security Boulevard, Baltimore, Maryland 21235. 1980. (Free.) A comparative price list of 186 prescription drugs, intended to promote cost-conscious prescribing and dispensing of drugs.

New York State Prescription Drug Formulary. Health Education Service, P.O. Box 7126, Albany, New York 12224. 1979. ($1.) Published by the state Health Department. Lists approximately 700 prescription drugs by both generic and trade names.

Washington Consumers' Checkbook: Health. Washington Center for the Study of Services, 1910 K Street, N.W., Suite 303, Washington, D.C. 20006. 1976. ($4.95.) Comprehensive guide to health care in the metropolitan area of Washington, D.C. Serves as an example for others wishing to publish such a guide to health care in their communities.

The following publications are available at no cost from the Bureau of Community Health Services, U.S. Public Health Service, 5600 Fishers Lane, Room 7-05, Rockville, Maryland 20857:

A Guide to Health Education in Ambulatory Care Settings. 1979. Outlines ways in which health education strategies can be developed within an ambulatory care center and how they can be implemented effectively. Identifies and probes several of the most important opportunities for consumer health education.

An Interim Guide for Health Education in a Health Care System. 1978. (Limited supply available.) Outlines what should be specified in the health education portion of an application for Federal funding and other assistance for the initiation, development, monitoring and assessment of health care system projects.

The following publications are available on a subscription basis, at no cost, from the Bureau of Health Education, Center for Disease Control, Atlanta, Georgia 30333:

Current Awareness in Health Education. Monthly. Indexing and abstracting journal for providers of health education.

Focal Points. Monthly newsletter. Available to those interested and engaged in health education. Provides information on programs and projects being carried out on local, state, regional and national levels.

NOTE: Also see Health Resources under "General."

Increasing Citizen Participation in Health Planning and Winning Health Care Power

Organizations

Bureau of Health Planning
Health Resources Administration
3700 East-West Highway, Room 10-44
Hyattsville, Maryland 20782
(301) 436-6104

Administers the National Health Planning and Resources Development Act (Public Law 93-641) which created a system of local and state health planning agencies. Produces and distributes many publications.

Consumer Coalition for Health
1511 K Street, N.W., Suite 220
Washington, D.C. 20005
(202) 872-0670

Advocacy group composed of national and local organizations and individuals concerned about health policy. Works with Health Systems Agencies. Provides information, technical assistance and public education programs. Publishes newsletter, *CHAN* (Consumer Health Action Network). (6 issues/year, free to members.)

Gray Panthers
3635 Chestnut Street
Philadelphia, Pennsylvania 19104
(215) 382-3300

Works on issues relating to nursing homes and the aged. Maintains national network of offices. Publishes a manual for organizing. Also, bimonthly newsletter, *Network.* ($5/year.)

National Citizens' Coalition for Nursing Home Reform
1424 16th Street, N.W., Suite 204
Washington, D.C. 20036
(202) 797-8227

Activities based on collective work of member groups, including: monitoring the quality of service in nursing homes; providing public education regarding nursing home issues; organizing and promoting consumer involvement on important boards at community level. Serves as a clearinghouse for information on nursing home issues. Publishes newsletter, *Collation.* (8 issues/year, $15).

National League for Nursing
Council of Home Health Agencies and Community Health Services
10 Columbus Circle
New York, New York 10019
(212) 582-1022

Provides consultative services related to home and community health services (examples include surveying community health needs, marketing, organization structure, program planning and evaluation). Operates jointly with the American Public Health Association, a voluntary program for the accreditation of home health agencies and community nursing services. Produces a wide variety of publications on nursing services and education.

Nursing Home Residents Advisory Council
3231 First Avenue, South
Minneapolis, Minnesota 55408
(612) 827-8151

Represents more than 10,000 elderly people through resident councils in 96 nursing homes throughout Minnesota. Provides workshops, training programs and resource kits to help nursing home residents speak up within their homes and before regulatory and legislative bodies. Offers information packet explaining residents' rights and another showing how to form resident councils. ($1 each).

Office of Consumer Affairs
Food and Drug Administration (FDA)
5600 Fishers Lane, Room 1685
Rockville, Maryland 20857
(301) 443-5006

Sponsors (among others) the following two projects:
Consumer Advocacy Skills Training Project. Designed to give consumers the knowledge and skills essential to accurately and effectively represent the public interest through FDA advisory mechanisms, with special focus on advisory committee representation.
National Consumer Awareness and Access Project. Designed to raise a general awareness of the FDA and its statutory responsibilities. Purpose is to enable grassroots consumers to act on their own behalf in reaching the Administration through petitions, evidentiary hearings and direct comment on proposed rules and regulations.

Publications

Bogue, Ted and Wolfe, Sidney M., ***Trimming the Fat Off Health Care Costs: A Consumer's Guide to Taking Over Health Planning.*** Health Research Group, 2000 P Street, N.W., Washington, D.C. 20036. 1976. ($2.) Discusses the role of consumers in Health Systems Agencies (HSAs) and provides the rationale for consumer involvement in health planning. Gives background leading up to the HSA concept.

Consumer Health Action Network (CHAN) Newsletter. Sponsored by the Consumer Coalition for Health (CCH), 1751 N Street, N.W., Washington, D.C. 20036, and the Public Citizen Health Research Group, 2000 P Street, N.W., Suite 708, Washington, D.C. 20036. Bimonthly. (Free to members of CCH.) Broad coverage of health issues, including health planning, patients' rights and health care financing. Reports on Congressional activities, Department of Health, Education and Welfare actions and consumer organizations.

Cook, John S., ***A Health Services Cost Review Commission Staff Paper: A Discussion of the Causes of Hospital Cost Inflation.*** Maryland Health Services Cost Review Commission, 201 West Preston Street, Baltimore, Maryland 21201. 1977. (Free.) Examines the current health care financing system and outlines how its structure may prevent the success of rate setting, planning and Professional Standards Review Organization efforts. Discusses the relationship between planning and rate setting.

The First Annual Health Planning Directory: 1978. American Health Planning Association, 1601 Connecticut Avenue, N.W., Suite 700, Washington, D.C. 20009. 1978. (Free.) Lists more than 300 health-related information sources (organizations), with short descriptions of program services and publications.

A Handbook for Consumer Participation in Health Care Planning: Update #1. Blue Cross Association, 1700 Pennsylvania Avenue, N.W., Washington, D.C. 20006. 1979. (Free.) Describes how requirements of the Health Planning and Resources Development Act are being carried out and how local Health Systems Agencies are faring. Case studies from around the country are presented. The 1977 edition, which gives information about the enlarged consumer role in health planning as called for by the 1974 Act, is also available.

Horn, Linda and Griesal, Elmma, ***Nursing Homes: A Citizen's Action Guide.*** Gray Panthers, 3635 Chestnut Street, Philadelphia, Pennsylvania 19104. 1977. ($4.50.) Describes how nursing homes operate and gives strategies for bringing about reform. Suggests techniques for consumer organizing and presents several case studies. Includes extensive bibliography and list of other resources.

Opening Hospital Doors—Free Health Care for Community People. Massachusetts Health Care Coalition, 145 Tremont Street, Boston, Massachusetts 02111. 1979. (Free.) Details patients' legal rights to free hospital care.

Report on Coalitions to Contain Health Care Costs. Government Research Corporation, 1730 M Street, N.W., Washington, D.C. 20036. 1979. ($2.65.) A resource and guide for employers, unions, third-party payers and public policy makers interested in initiating or participating in community-based health care cost containment activities. Includes in-depth case studies of four coalitions, plus a discussion of types and sources of data available to gain an understanding of health care service and expenditure patterns.

Tools for Health Planning: A Consumer Workbook. Cal–PIRG, 3000 E Street, San Diego, California 92101. 1979. ($5.) Resource manual providing information on many health care issues, emphasizing citizen participation in the health planning process.

The following publications are available at no cost from the Bureau of Health Planning, Health Resources Administration, 3700 East-West Highway, Room 10-44, Hyattsville, Maryland 20782:

Catalog of Health Resources Administration Publications. 1979. Lists many of the publications produced by the three bureaus of the Health Resources Administration (Bureau of Health Planning, Bureau of Health Manpower and Bureau of Health Facilities Financing, Compliance and Conversion).

Health Planning in Action: Achieving Equal Access to Quality Health Care at a Reasonable Cost. 1979. Profiles the successful planning efforts of seven Health Systems Agencies and shows how these agencies are beginning to curb health costs.

Health Planning Newsletter for Governing Body Members. Monthly newsletter. Geared for participants in health planning activities authorized under the National Health Planning and Resources Development Act.

NOTE: Also see Health Resources under "General."

Appendices

Appendix I briefly describes Federal programs and/or administering offices which have provided technical or financial assistance to our featured groups. For more information about these as well as other government assistance programs for which your group might be eligible, we have included a listing of addresses and phone numbers for national and, where appropriate, agency regional offices.

Reminders: Sometimes Federal programs change. But authorities charged with implementing the programs can usually tell you if a discontinued program has been replaced or if another program can provide assistance for your particular needs. Also, Federal program funds are generally distributed through state and/or local government agencies where they are channeled to qualifying groups. Therefore, we suggest you first write to the appropriate regional office for additional information.

Appendix II explores the National Consumer Cooperative Bank, a new organization created by Congress that provides technical and financial assistance to those wishing to launch nonprofit cooperative ventures. The law creating it as well as the structure of the new bank is explained.

Appendix I

Federal Programs and Offices **Page**

Appendix II

ACTION

ACTION's purpose is to mobilize Americans for voluntary service throughout the United States and in developing countries through programs which help meet basic human needs and support the self-help efforts of low-income individuals and communities.

ACTION administers and coordinates the domestic and international volunteer programs sponsored by the Federal government, which foster self-reliance and utilize available human and economic resources to overcome conditions of poverty. Through special demonstration grants and programs, ACTION also tests new ways of bringing volunteer resources to bear on human, social and economic problems. It identifies and develops the widest possible range of volunteer service opportunities for Americans of all ages and backgrounds.

Special Volunteer Program

Tests new methods of encouraging the use of volunteers in programs specifically relating to human, social and environmental needs as they relate to the poor and near-poor. Administered by the Office of Policy Planning.

Volunteers in Service to America (VISTA) Program

Trains and places volunteers to supplement efforts of community organizations to eliminate poverty and poverty-related human, social and environmental problems. Provides limited grant awards to citizen organizations. Administered by the Domestic and Anti-Poverty Operations Office.

The following is a list of offices that will help you in locating further information about the programs highlighted as well as others for which your group might qualify. We suggest where appropriate to start with the regional office nearest you. (See Map)

National Office:

ACTION
General Information
806 Connecticut Avenue, N.W.
Washington, D.C. 20525
(202) 393-3111

ACTION
Regional Offices:

1. ACTION
   John W. McCormack Federal Building
   Room 1420, POCH
   Boston, Massachusetts 02109
   (617) 223-4501
2. ACTION
   26 Federal Plaza, Suite 1611
   New York, New York 10007
   (212) 264-5710
3. ACTION
   U.S. Customhouse, Room 112
   Second and Chestnut Streets
   Philadelphia, Pennsylvania 19106
   (215) 597-9972
4. ACTION
   101 Marietta Street, N.W.
   25th Floor
   Atlanta, Georgia 30303
   (404) 242-2859
5. ACTION
   1 North Wacker Drive, Room 322
   Chicago, Illinois 60606
   (312) 353-5107
6. ACTION
   Corrigan Tower Building, Suite 1600
   212 North St. Paul Street
   Dallas, Texas 75201
   (214) 749-1316
7. ACTION
   2 Gateway Center, Suite 330
   Fourth and State
   Kansas City, Kansas 66101
   (816) 374-4486
8. ACTION
   Columbine Building, Room 201
   1845 Sherman Street
   Denver, Colorado 80203
   (303) 327-2671
9. ACTION
   211 Main Street, Fifth Floor
   San Francisco, California 94105
   (415) 556-1736
10. ACTION
    1601 Second Avenue
    Seattle, Washington 98101
    (206) 399-4520

Standard Federal Regions

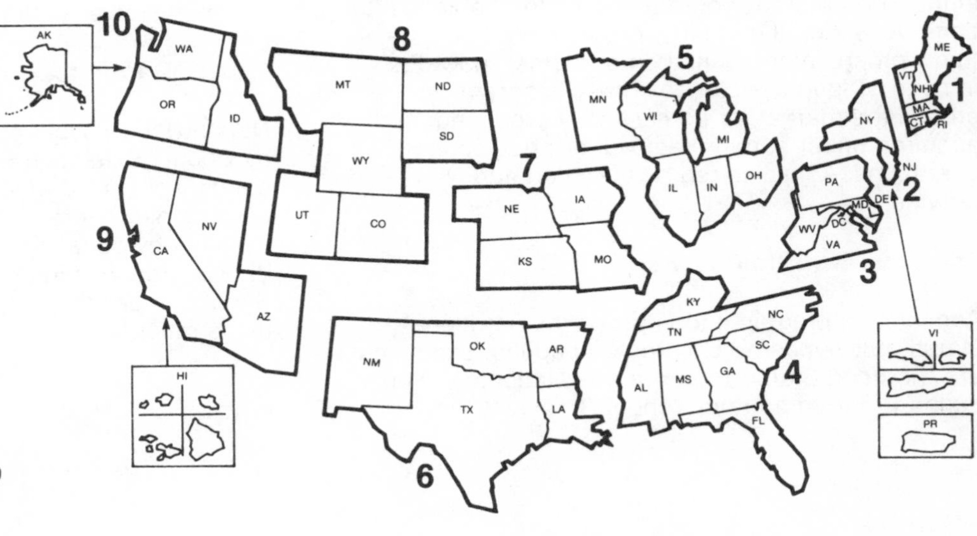

United States Department of Agriculture

The United States Department of Agriculture (USDA) works to improve and maintain farm income and to develop and expand markets abroad for agricultural products. USDA helps to curb poverty, hunger and malnutrition. It works to enhance the environment and to maintain our production capacity by helping landowners protect the soil, water, forests and other natural resources. Rural development, credit and conservation programs are key resources for carrying out national growth policies. The Department, through inspection and grading services, safeguards and assures standards of quality in the American food supply.

Child Care Food Program

Provides, through reimbursement and grants in aid, assistance to nonprofit child care institutions and other care centers. Designed to improve the diets of children 18 and under and certain handicapped people over 18 by providing nutritious, well-balanced meals. Administered by the Food and Nutrition Service.

Cooperative Extension Service

Provides educational programs based upon local needs in the broad fields of agricultural production and marketing, rural development, home economics and youth development. Operates as a three-way partnership comprised of the United States Department of Agriculture, state land grant universities and county governments. Activities are spearheaded by local County Extension Agents. Administered by the Extension Service of the Science and Education Administration.

Food Distribution Program

Provides funds and donates food to improve the diets of school children and needy persons in households, on Indian reservations not participating in the Food Stamp Program and in charitable institutions. Also aids the elderly, pregnant and post partum women, infants, children and other individuals in need of food assistance. These programs increase the market for domestically produced foods acquired under surplus removal or price-support operations. Administered by the Food and Nutrition Service.

Food and Nutrition Service

Administers programs to improve the nutritional status of low-income children and adults. Examples are the Food Stamp Program, the National School Lunch Program and the School Breakfast Program.

Food Stamp Program

Provides food coupons to help low-income households increase their food buying power. Coupons are exchanged for food at authorized stores. Administered by the Food and Nutrition Service.

4-H Youth Program

Provides nationwide program of informal, out-of-school learning designed to teach American youth how to enhance their own lives and development. Programs include day camps, club activities, instructional television series and special interest courses. Administered by the Cooperative Extension Service under the Science and Education Administration.

Low- to Moderate-Income Housing Loans (Section 502)

Designed to assist rural families obtain decent, safe and sanitary dwellings. Loans may be used for the construction, repair or purchase of housing; for necessary and adequate sewage disposal facilities; and for water supply, weatherization and other housing-related purposes. Administered by the Farmers Home Administration.

Master Gardener Program

Nationwide network of training programs conducted by County Extension Service Agents on the care of plants, soil, insect and disease control and all types of gardening. Persons completing the free program "repay" by donating time to other Extension Service efforts. Administered by the Cooperative Extension Service under the Science and Education Administration.

Rural Self-Help Housing Technical Assistance (Section 523)

Provides financial support for programs of technical and supervisory assistance which aid needy low-income individuals and their families in carrying out mutual self-help efforts in rural areas. Administered by the Farmers Home Administration.

School Breakfast Program

Funds nutritious breakfast programs for needy children in public and private schools and nonprofit child care institutions. Those eligible receive breakfast free or at a reduced price. Administered by the Food and Nutrition Service.

Technical and Supervisory Assistance Grant Program (Section 525)

Assists low-income rural families in obtaining adequate housing and provides guidance to promote continued occupancy of already adequate housing. Funds are made available to eligible organizations to provide competent counseling to Farmers Home Administration housing loan borrowers to prevent loan delinquency and foreclosure. Administered by the Farmers Home Administration.

Urban Gardening Demonstration Program

Designed to improve the general nutrition of low-income families in selected cities by helping them establish and maintain their own vegetable gardens. Funds are spent for educational purposes and staffing. Administered by the Cooperative Extension Services at the land grant universities in states where the cities are located.

Very Low-Income Housing Repair Loans and Grants (Section 504)

Enables very low-income rural homeowners to make essential minor repairs to their homes in order to eliminate safety and health hazards. Administered by the Farmers Home Administration.

The following is a list of offices that will help you in locating further information about the programs highlighted as well as others for which your group might qualify. We suggest where appropriate to start with the regional office nearest you. (See Map)

National Offices:

U.S. Department of Agriculture
General Information
14th Street and Independence Avenue, S.W.
Washington, D.C. 20250
(202) 655-4000

Food and Nutrition Service
General Information
U.S. Department of Agriculture
14th Street and Independence Avenue, S.W.
Washington, D.C. 20250
(202) 447-8384

Cooperative Extension Service:

Cooperative Extension Service
Publication Requests and Distribution
Science and Education Administration
U.S. Department of Agriculture
14th Street and Independence Avenue, S.W.
Washington, D.C. 20250
(202) 447-4111

or

Check with the State Extension Service located at the state land grant university

or

Look in phone directory under county government for Extension Service

Farmers Home Administration:

Farmers Home Administration
U.S. Department of Agriculture
14th Street and Independence Avenue, S.W.
Washington, D.C. 20250
(202) 447-4323

or

Look in phone directory under county government for Farmers Home Administration

Food and Nutrition Service Regional Offices:

Food and Nutrition Service
U.S. Department of Agriculture
New England Regional Office
33 North Avenue
Burlington, Massachusetts 01803
(617) 272-4272

Food and Nutrition Service
U.S. Department of Agriculture
Mid-Atlantic Regional Office
1 Vahlsing Center
Robbinsville, New Jersey 08691
(609) 259-3041

Food and Nutrition Service
U.S. Department of Agriculture
Southeast Regional Office
1100 Spring Street, N.W.
Atlanta, Georgia 30309
(404) 881-4131

Food and Nutrition Service
U.S. Department of Agriculture
Mountain Plains Regional Office
2420 West 26th Avenue, Suite 415-D
Denver, Colorado 80211
(303) 837-5339

Food and Nutrition Service
U.S. Department of Agriculture
Southwest Regional Office
1100 Commerce Street
Dallas, Texas 75242
(214) 767-0222

Food and Nutrition Service
U.S. Department of Agriculture
Western Regional Office
550 Kearney Street
San Francisco, California 94108
(415) 556-4950

Food and Nutrition Service
U.S. Department of Agriculture
Midwest Regional Office
536 South Clark Street
Chicago, Illinois 60605
(312) 353-6664

Food and Nutrition Service Regions

Department of Commerce

The Department of Commerce (DOC) encourages, serves and promotes the nation's economic development and technological advancement. It offers assistance and information to domestic and international business; provides research for and promotes the increased use of science and technology in the development of the economy; provides assistance to speed the development of the economically underdeveloped areas of the nation; assists in the growth of minority businesses; and seeks to prevent the loss of life and property from fire.

New England Regional Commission

Provides funds for technical assistance, research and development, planning and demonstration projects that will stimulate new growth and blunt conditions that stifle economic health. Programs are focused on energy, transportation and economic development. Authorized under Title V of the Public Works and Economic Development Act of 1965 as amended. (Other sections of the country have similar commissions.)

Public Works Grants Program

Provides assistance for the development of facilities which contribute to the creation or retention of long-term employment opportunities. Funds are provided for such activities as industrial park development, industrial expansion and the development of water and sewer facilities. Administered by the Economic Development Administration.

The following is a list of offices that will help you in locating further information about the programs highlighted as well as others for which your group might qualify. We suggest where appropriate to start with the regional office nearest you. (See Map)

National Offices:

Department of Commerce
General Information
14th Street and Constitution Avenue, N.W.
Washington, D.C. 20230
(202) 377-2000

Economic Development Administration
General Information
Department of Commerce
14th Street and Constitution Avenue, N.W.
Washington, D.C. 20230
(202) 377-5113

Economic Development Administration Regional Offices:

Economic Development Administration
Department of Commerce
Atlantic Regional Office
600 Arch Street
Philadelphia, Pennsylvania 19106
(215) 597-4603

Economic Development Administration
Department of Commerce
Southeastern Regional Office
1365 Peachtree Street, N.E., Suite 700
Atlanta, Georgia 30309
(404) 881-7401

Economic Development Administration
Department of Commerce
Midwestern Regional Office
175 West Jackson Boulevard
Chicago, Illinois 60604
(312) 353-7706

Economic Development Administration
Department of Commerce
Rocky Mountain Regional Office
909 17th Street
Denver, Colorado 80203
(303) 837-4714

Economic Development Administration
Department of Commerce
Southwestern Regional Office
221 West Sixth Street
Austin, Texas 78701
(512) 397-5461

Economic Development Administration
Department of Commerce
Western Regional Office
1700 Westlake Avenue, North
Seattle, Washington 98109
(206) 442-0596

Development Regions

Title V Regional Commissions:

Coastal Plains Regional Commission
Department of Commerce
215 East Bay Street
Charleston, South Carolina 29401
(803) 677-4250

Four Corners Regional Commission
Department of Commerce
2350 Alamo S.E., Suite 303
Albuquerque, New Mexico 87106
(505) 474-2991

New England Regional Commission
Department of Commerce
53 State Street, Suite 400
Boston, Massachusetts 02109
(617) 223-6330

Old West Regional Commission
Department of Commerce
201 Main Street, Suite B
Rapid City, South Dakota 57201
(605) 348-6310

Ozarks Regional Commission
Department of Commerce
1100 North University
Little Rock, Arkansas 72207
(501) 378-5905

Pacific Northwest Regional Commission
Department of Commerce
700 East Evergreen Boulevard
Vancouver, Washington 98661
(206) 696-7771

Southwest Border Regional Commission
Department of Commerce
100 North Stone Avenue, Suite 309
Tucson, Arizona 85701
(602) 792-6781

Upper Great Lakes Regional Commission
Department of Commerce
Hawkes Hall
2231 Catlin Avenue
Superior, Wisconsin 54880
(715) 392-7111

Title V Regional Commissions

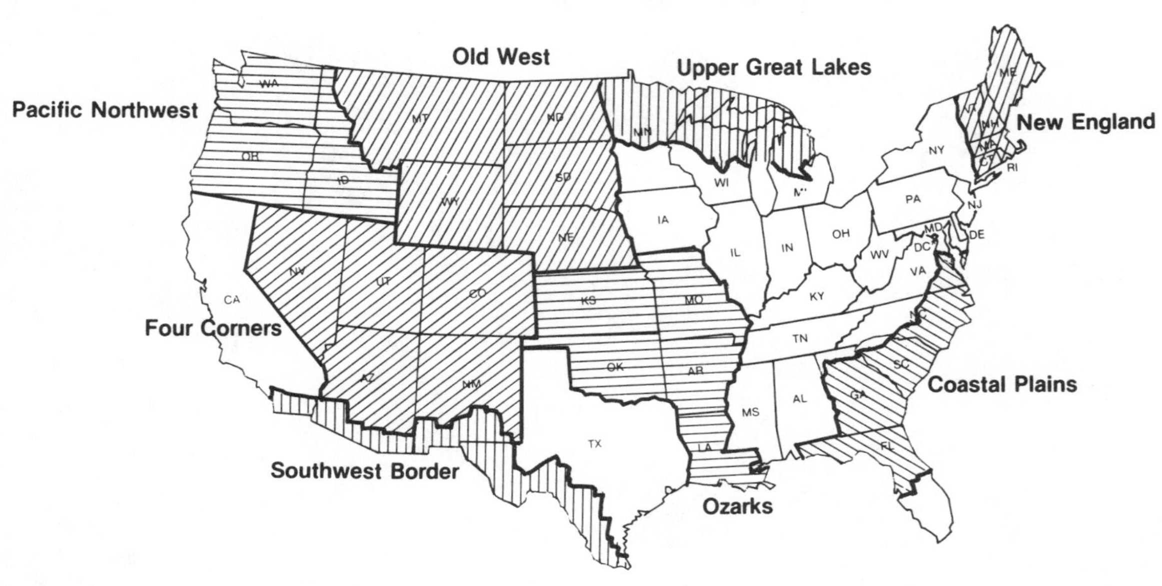

Community Services Administration

The Community Services Administration's (CSA) overall purpose is to combat poverty in America. It seeks to accomplish this goal by helping low-income families and individuals attain economic self-sufficiency.

The Agency's programs are available to all disadvantaged people in both urban and rural areas. The basic technique of CSA's antipoverty programs is the combined use of Federal, state and local funds in the organization and operation of Community Action Programs and other programs which are directed and overseen by locally selected boards. CSA seeks to help the disadvantaged help themselves by providing economic and educational opportunities and financial support.

Community Action Agency

Involves the entire community in combating poverty through special programs to meet the needs of the disadvantaged in food, housing, health care, energy and other areas. Goals are carried out through a variety of efforts, such as providing transportation for the elderly and gardening assistance for the urban and rural poor. Administered by the Community Action Program.

Community Action Program

Mobilizes and channels resources of private and public organizations into anti-poverty programs through the support of Community Action Agencies. Projects assisted include a wide range of activities such as job training and placement, health care, weatherizing and rehabilitating homes and providing meals for the elderly.

Community Development Corporation

Undertakes community business ventures using both private and public funding. Hires the poor and provides training where needed while seeking to establish profit-making businesses. Developed in low-income rural and urban areas. Administered by the Office of Economic Development.

Community Development Credit Union Initiative

Provides seed money for credit unions chartered by the National Credit Union Administration (NCUA) to undertake a broad range of community development programs. Administered by the Office of Economic Development in cooperation with NCUA, which provides technical assistance.

Community Economic Development Program

Provides special assistance, mainly through Community Development Corporations, to help alleviate unemployment and community deterioration by focusing on improved housing, job training and business opportunities for low-income residents of economically deprived rural and urban communities. Administered by the Office of Economic Development.

Community Food and Nutrition Program

Provides funds to local communities and agencies to help reduce hunger and malnutrition among the poor. Funds may be used to launch a broad range of food programs or to supplement, extend or broaden existing programs. Administered by the Office of Program Development.

Community Food and Nutrition Training and Technical Assistance Grant

Provides funds for training and organizing local residents to become self-sufficient in the areas of food and nutrition through such projects as constructing solar greenhouses and developing food-related businesses such as canneries. Also stresses nutrition education. Administered by the Office of Program Development.

Emergency Energy Conservation Services Program

Develops community-based programs to deal with energy-related problems. Mobilizes resources within states and communities to help the poor deal with the energy crisis. Conducts advocacy programs to assist the poor in public, administrative and legal proceedings involving energy costs, energy policy and rate regulations. Administered by the Office of Community Action.

Energy Demonstration Grant

Funds energy programs sponsored by nonprofit, public and private agencies. Examples include alternative energy and conservation education, rural energy development and weatherization research. Administered by the Energy Office under the Office of Program Development.

Appendix I

Local Initiative Program (Section 221)

Operates a variety of programs—such as food and nutrition, gardening and weatherization—which are directed at the poor and based on the needs of the community. Authorized under Section 221 of the Economic Opportunity Act as amended. Administered through Community Action Agencies.

Special Impact Program

Administered by Community Development Corporations. Includes activities in business and community development, training, public service employment and social service. Designed to help alleviate dependency and chronic unemployment and to help provide community ownership opportunities for the residents of targeted areas. Administered by the Office of Economic Development.

The following is a list of offices that will help you in locating further information about the programs highlighted as well as others for which your group might qualify. We suggest where appropriate to start with the regional office nearest you. (See Map)

National Office:

Community Services Administration
General Information
1200 19th Street, N.W.
Washington, D.C. 20506
(202) 254-5590

Community Services Administration Regional Offices:

1. Community Services Administration
John F. Kennedy Federal Building
Room E-400
Boston, Massachusetts 02203
(617) 223-4019
2. Community Services Administration
26 Federal Plaza, 32nd Floor
Room 3227
New York, New York 10007
(212) 264-3960
3. Community Services Administration
Gateway Building, Room 2400
3535 Market Street
Philadelphia, Pennsylvania 19104
(215) 596-6022
4. Community Services Administration
730 Peachtree Street, N.E.
Atlanta, Georgia 30308
(404) 881-3526
5. Community Services Administration
300 South Wacker Drive, 26th Floor
Chicago, Illinois 60606
(312) 353-5988
6. Community Services Administration
1200 Main Tower
Dallas, Texas 75202
(214) 749-1381
7. Community Services Administration
911 Walnut Street, Room 1600
Kansas City, Missouri 64106
(816) 374-3561
8. Community Services Administration
Federal Building, 12th Floor
1961 Stout Street
Denver, Colorado 80294
(303) 837-4923
9. Community Services Administration
450 Golden Gate Avenue
P.O. Box 36008
San Francisco, California 94102
(415) 556-5400
10. Community Services Administration
Arcade Plaza Building
1321 Second Avenue
Seattle, Washington 98101
(206) 442-0183

Standard Federal Regions

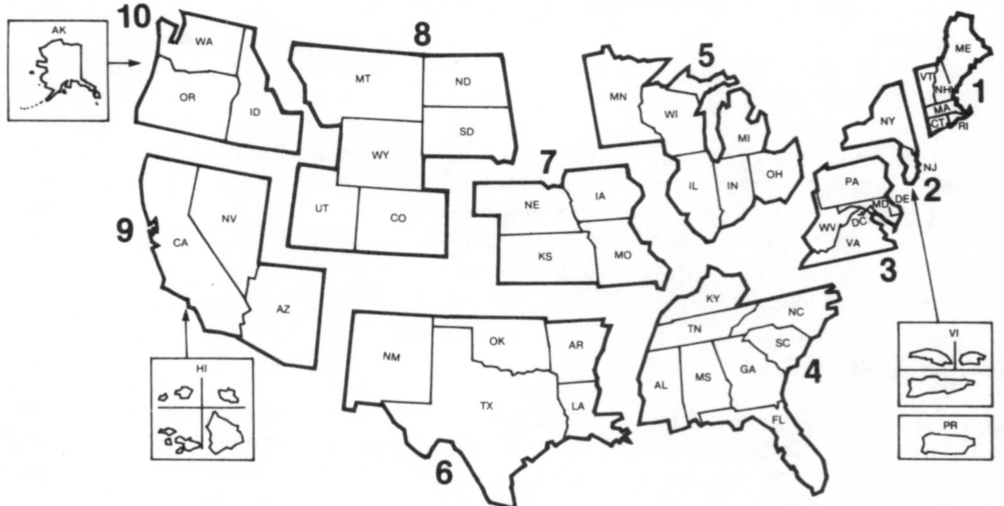

Department of Energy

The Department of Energy (DOE) provides the framework for a comprehensive and balanced national energy plan through the coordination and administration of the energy functions of the Federal government. DOE is responsible for the research, development and demonstration of energy technology; energy conservation; regulation of energy production and use; pricing and allocation; and a central energy data collection and analysis program.

Appropriate Technology Small Grants Program

Encourages the development of innovative, small-scale energy systems using local materials and skills to meet community needs. Provides grants to individuals and groups to develop and demonstrate new ideas in appropriate technology. Administered by the Office of Small Scale Technology under the Assistant Secretary for Conservation and Solar Applications.

Energy Conservation and Production Act

Authorizes grants to states to establish and operate State Offices of Consumer Services. Such offices are set up to support consumer representation in proceedings before utility commissions. The Act was subsequently expanded and extended by the Public Utilities Regulatory Policies Act of 1978 (PURPA). Administered by the Economic Regulatory Administration.

Energy Extension Service

Provides information on conservation and renewable energy sources to individuals. Encourages the reduction of energy consumption and the conversion to alternative energy sources. Assists states in building energy outreach programs which are responsive to local needs. Administered by the Office of State and Local Programs.

Fuels from Biomass Program

Provides financial and technical assistance to individuals and groups involved in the development of alternative energy sources. Develops conversion techniques to provide alternate fuels from biomass systems such as methane and gasohol. Administered by the Biomass Energy Systems Branch of the Division of Distributed Solar Technology.

Office of Solar Applications for Buildings

Administers grants and programs involved with the heating and cooling of buildings through solar applications. Focuses on research, development, demonstration and marketing of solar energy systems for buildings. Administered by the Assistant Secretary for Conservation and Solar Applications.

Public Utility Regulatory Policies Act (PURPA)

Sets forth innovative standards and regulations that public utility commissions must consider when setting rates. Provides for consumers, in certain cases, to recover the costs of their participation in regulatory hearings. Expanded upon the Energy Conservation and Production Act of 1976. Administered by the Economic Regulatory Administration.

Residential Conservation Service Program

Mandates large utilities to provide on-site audits to customers and in-home consultation regarding conservation, energy-saving alterations and their financing. Part of the National Energy Conservation Policy Act of 1978. Administered by the Office of Buildings and Community Systems under the Assistant Secretary for Conservation and Solar Applications.

Weatherization Assistance Program

Provides funds to local community action agencies to assist them in efforts to weatherize the homes of low-income families—particularly the handicapped and the elderly. Administered by the Office of State and Local Programs.

★ Appendix I

The following is a list of offices that will help you in locating further information about the programs highlighted as well as others for which your group might qualify. We suggest where appropriate to start with the regional office nearest you. (See Map)

National Office:

Department of Energy
General Information
1000 Independence Avenue, S.W.
Washington, D.C. 20545
(202) 252-5000

Department of Energy Regional Offices:

1. Department of Energy
   Analex Building, Room 700
   150 Causeway Street
   Boston, Massachusetts 02114
   (617) 223-3701
2. Department of Energy
   26 Federal Plaza, Room 3206
   New York, New York 10007
   (212) 264-1021
3. Department of Energy
   1421 Cherry Street, 10th Floor
   Philadelphia, Pennsylvania 19102
   (215) 597-3890
4. Department of Energy
   1655 Peachtree Street, N.E.; 8th Floor
   Atlanta, Georgia 30309
   (404) 881-2838
5. Department of Energy
   175 West Jackson Boulevard, Room A-333
   Chicago, Illinois 60604
   (312) 353-0540
6. Department of Energy
   P.O. Box 35228
   2626 West Mockingbird Lane
   Dallas, Texas 75235
   (214) 749-7345
7. Department of Energy
   324 East 11th Street
   Kansas City, Missouri 64106
   (816) 374-2061
8. Department of Energy
   P.O. Box 26247—Belmar Branch
   1075 South Yukon Street
   Lakewood, Colorado 80226
   (303) 234-2420
9. Department of Energy
   111 Pine Street, 3rd Floor
   San Francisco, California 94111
   (415) 566-7216
10. Department of Energy
    1992 Federal Building
    915 Second Avenue
    Seattle, Washington 98174
    (206) 442-7280

Standard Federal Regions

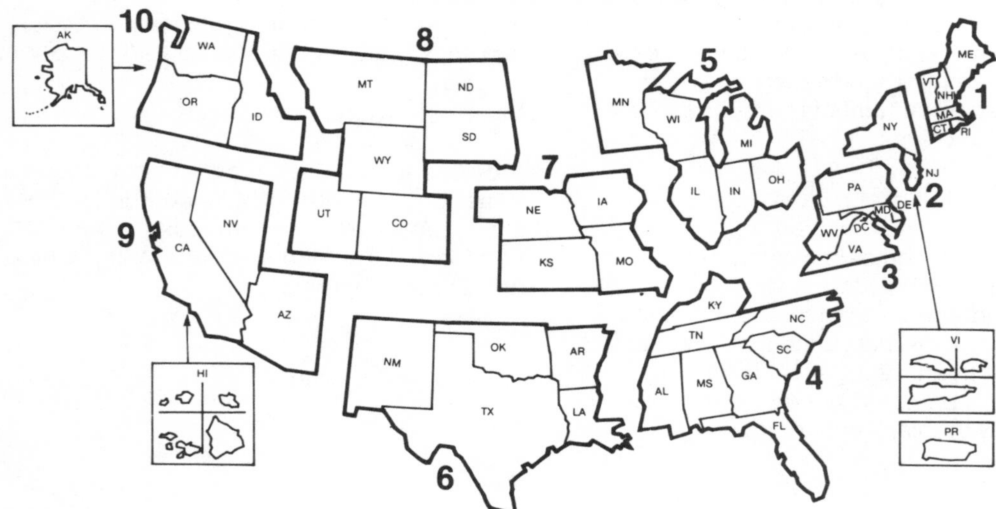

Environmental Protection Agency

The purpose of the Environmental Protection Agency (EPA) is to protect and enhance our environment today and for future generations to the fullest extent possible under the laws enacted by Congress. The Agency's mission is to control and abate pollution in the areas of air, water, solid waste, noise, radiation and toxic substances. EPA's mandate is to mount an integrated, coordinated attack on environmental pollution in cooperation with state and local governments.

National Water Demonstration Project

Plans and implements effective methods of preventing pollution of ground water, as mandated by Section 208 of the Clean Water Act. Administered by the Office of Water Planning and Standards under the Office of Water and Waste Management.

The following is a list of offices that will help you in locating further information about the programs highlighted as well as others for which your group might qualify. We suggest where appropriate to start with the regional office nearest you. (See Map)

National Office:

Environmental Protection Agency
Public Information Center
401 M Street, S.W.
Washington, D.C. 20460
(202) 755-0707

Environmental Protection Agency Regional Offices:

1. Environmental Protection Agency
   John F. Kennedy Federal Building
   Boston, Massachusetts 02203
   (617) 223-7210
2. Environmental Protection Agency
   26 Federal Plaza
   New York, New York 10007
   (212) 264-2525
3. Environmental Protection Agency
   Curtis Building
   Sixth and Walnut Streets
   Philadelphia, Pennsylvania 19106
   (215) 597-9814
4. Environmental Protection Agency
   345 Cortland Street, N.E.
   Atlanta, Georgia 30308
   (404) 881-4727
5. Environmental Protection Agency
   230 South Dearborn Street
   Chicago, Illinois 60604
   (312) 353-2000
6. Environmental Protection Agency
   1201 Elm Street
   Dallas, Texas 75270
   (214) 767-2600
7. Environmental Protection Agency
   324 East 11th Street
   Kansas City, Missouri 64106
   (816) 374-5493
8. Environmental Protection Agency
   1860 Lincoln Street
   Denver, Colorado 80203
   (303) 837-3895
9. Environmental Protection Agency
   215 Fremont Street
   San Francisco, California 94111
   (415) 556-2320
10. Environmental Protection Agency
    1200 Sixth Avenue
    Seattle, Washington 98101
    (206) 442-1220

Standard Federal Regions

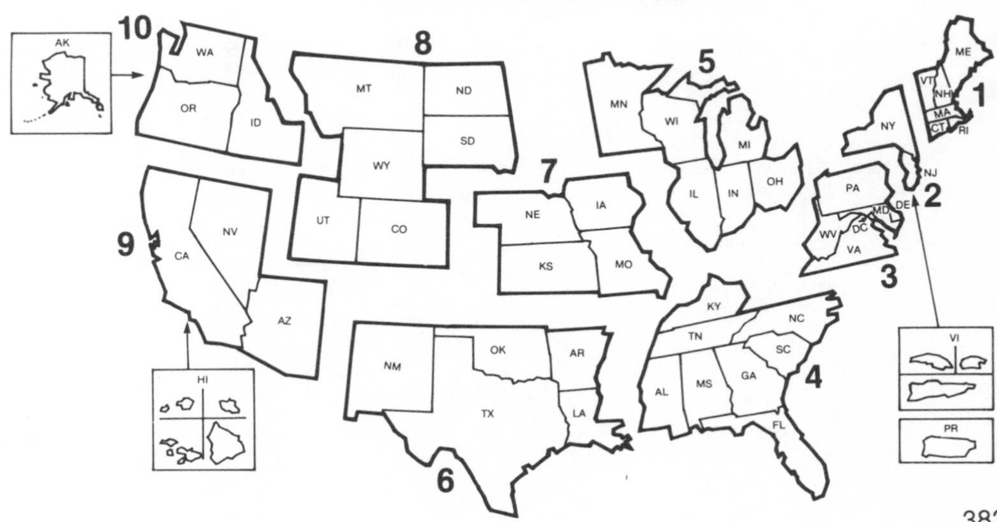

General Services Administration

The General Services Administration (GSA) establishes policy and provides for the government an economical and efficient system for the management of its property and records, including construction and operation of buildings; procurement and distribution of supplies; utilization and disposal of property; transportation, traffic and communications; stockpiling of strategic materials; and the government-wide automatic data processing resources program.

Community Gardens Program

Licenses civic associations, clubs, block organizations, horticultural societies, etc., to garden on Federal land. Administered by the Office of Buildings Management.

Living Buildings Program

Aims to make Federal buildings more accessible for citizens' use and enjoyment. Both individuals and groups can obtain space for meetings, exhibits, performances and classes. Administered by the Office of Buildings Management.

The following is a list of offices that will help you in locating further information about the programs highlighted as well as others for which your group might qualify. We suggest where appropriate to start with the regional office nearest you. (See Map)

National Office:

General Services Administration
General Information
General Services Building
18th and F Streets, N.W.
Washington, D.C. 20405
(202) 455-4000

General Services Administration Regional Offices:

1. General Services Administration
John W. McCormack Federal Building
Boston, Massachusetts 02109
(617) 223-2868
2. General Services Administration
26 Federal Plaza
New York, New York 10007
(212) 264-1234
3. General Services Administration
Seventh and D Streets, S.W.
Washington, D.C. 20407
(202) 472-1804
and
General Services Administration
600 Arch Street
Philadelphia, Pennsylvania 19106
(215) 597-9613
4. General Services Administration
1776 Peachtree Street, N.W.
Atlanta, Georgia 30309
(404) 881-4661
5. General Services Administration
230 South Dearborn Street
Chicago, Illinois 60606
(313) 353-5383
6. General Services Administration
819 Taylor Street
Fort Worth, Texas 76102
(817) 334-3284
and
General Services Administration
515 Rusk Street
Houston, Texas 77002
(713) 226-5783
7. General Services Administration
1500 East Bannister Road
Kansas City, Missouri 64131
(816) 926-7203
8. General Services Administration
Denver Federal Center
Denver, Colorado 80225
(303) 234-2216
9. General Services Administration
525 Market Street
San Francisco, California 94105
(415) 556-0877
and
General Services Administration
300 North Los Angeles
Los Angeles, California 90012
(213) 688-3210
10. General Services Administration
915 Second Avenue
Seattle, Washington 98174
(206) 442-5556

Department of Health, Education and Welfare

The Department of Health, Education and Welfare (HEW) has been cited throughout this book as being a source of assistance for many groups. However, HEW has been replaced by two Cabinet-level Agencies—the Department of Health and Human Services (HHS) and the Department of Education (ED). These two new Departments will be responsible (respectively) for the health and education programs formerly under HEW. (See end of program descriptions for proper administering agency.)

Community Health Centers Program

Supports the development and operation of community health centers which provide primary, supplemental and environmental health services to medically underserved populations. Administered by the Bureau of Community Health Services under the Health Services Administration. (HHS)

Community Mental Health Center Grant Applications Program

Provides aid to public and private nonprofit organizations to increase the availability of mental health services to individuals throughout the country. Requires that funded organizations supply a range of mental health services. Administered by the Alcohol, Drug Abuse and Mental Health Administration. (HHS)

Community Services and Continuing Education Program

Designed to strengthen and expand the community service and continuing education activities of colleges and universities and to promote community-wide sharing of educational resources. Administered by the Bureau of Higher and Continuing Education under the Office of Education. (ED)

Consumer Education and Advocacy Training for Adults

Provides instructional programs for adults with leadership potential to equip them with the skills needed to serve as consumer advocates and as organizers of consumer action projects. Administered by the Office of Consumer Education under the Office of Education. (ED)

Division of Cancer Control and Rehabilitation

Funds projects concerning the alleviation of pain associated with cancer, the investigation of psychological aspects of cancer and the development and use of devices for the rehabilitation of cancer victims. Supports outreach activities of cancer centers, and promotes professional education and training activities as a means of encouraging widespread application of practical procedures. Administered by the National Cancer Institute under the National Institutes of Health. (HHS)

Elementary and Secondary Education Act (Title IV)

Provides funds to states for school libraries and the improvement of guidance and counseling services within public school systems. Administered by the Office of Libraries and Learning Resources under the Office of Education. (ED)

Extramural Programs

Provides grants to improve information access for health professionals and to assist health care institutions in developing improved library services. Funds projects aimed at exploring new and innovative methods of handling information problems. Administered by the National Library of Medicine under the National Institutes of Health. (HHS)

Health Maintenance Organizations Act

Provides for the development of various models of prepaid, comprehensive health maintenance organizations throughout the country and the expansion of Federally qualified Health Maintenance Organizations. Administered by the Office of Health Maintenance Organizations under the Assistant Secretary for Health. (HHS)

Health Underserved Rural Areas Program

Designed to improve and increase the availability of rural health care service facilities accepting Medicaid patients. Funded by Title XIX (Medicaid) of the Social Security Act. Administered by the Bureau of Community Health Services under the Health Services Administration. (HHS)

Higher Education Act (Title I)

Provides funds to states for the improvement and continuation of community service and continuing education programs, the support of resource-sharing programs and the promotion of lifelong learning. Administered by the Office of Education. (ED)

Indian Controlled Schools Non-Local Education Agency Program

Provides financial assistance to Indian tribes or Indian organizations to plan for and establish Indian controlled schools. Also supports enrichment projects designed to meet special educational and cuturally related academic needs of Indian children in Indian controlled elementary and secondary schools. Administered by the Office of Indian Education under the Office of Education. (ED)

Library Services and Construction Act

Assists states in the extension and improvement of public library services, the construction of public libraries in areas without service or with inadequate service and the coordination of resources among libraries and information centers nationwide. Administered by the Office of Libraries and Learning Resources under the Office of Education. (ED)

Meals on Wheels Program

Provides a minimum of one meal a day to persons 60 years of age or older who are mobility impaired. Officially known as the Home Delivered Nutrition Service, the program is authorized by the Older Americans Act. Administered by the Administration on Aging (HHS) in cooperation with the United States Department of Agriculture's (USDA) Food Distribution Program.

Medicaid Program

Low-income people, those 65 or older, the blind and the disabled are eligible for medical services assistance financed by Federal, state and local governments. Each state designs its own program based on Federal guidelines. Administered by the Health Care Financing Administration under Title XIX of the Social Security Act. (HHS)

Medicare Program

Designed to provide basic health benefits to recipients of social security. Provisions include coverage of both hospital and medical insurance for people 65 or older and certain disabled persons. Administered by the Health Care Financing Administration under Title XVIII of the Social Security Act. (HHS)

Mental Health Formula Grant Program

Provides grants to state mental health authorities in carrying out their functions. Requires states to prescribe standards for programs and facilities and to provide assistance to courts and public agencies in determining alternatives to hospitalization. Administered by the Alcohol, Drug Abuse and Mental Health Administration. (HHS)

Model Projects Grant

Provides funding under Title IV of the Older Americans Act for innovative demonstration projects to help the elderly, especially in the area of social services such as home health care, senior citizen centers and adult day care facilities. Administered by the Office of Research, Demonstration and Evaluation under the Administration on Aging. (HHS)

National Center for Health Services Research

Provides funds for research, demonstration and evaluation of problems in organization, delivery and financing of health care services. Projects include health care planning and regulation; technology and computer use in health care; and health care costs. Administered by the Office of Health Research, Statistics and Technology in the Office of the Assistant Secretary for Health. (HHS)

National Health Planning and Resources Development Act

Mandates a comprehensive national program for health planning and resource development. Incorporates features of the Hill-Burton program, the Comprehensive Health Planning Program and the Regional Medical Program. Creates a network of Health Systems Agencies responsible for health planning and development. Administered by the Bureau of Health Planning and Resources Development under Health Resources Administration. (HHS)

Older Americans Act (Title III)

Provides funds to states to assist older persons in maintaining their independence as integrated members of the community. Authorizes state agencies to help eligible older persons meet their nutritional, housing and energy-related needs. Administered by the Administration on Aging under the Office of Human Development Services. (HHS)

Older Americans Act (Title IV)

Provides for research, development and training projects that promote innovative approaches for meeting the service needs of and improving conditions for older Americans. Authorizes Model Projects Grants and Research and Demonstration Grants. Administered by the Administration on Aging under the Office of Human Development Services. (HHS)

Research and Demonstration Grant

Provides research funds under Title IV of the Older Americans Act for alternative care projects for the elderly. Projects include community guides to area nursing homes, combating consumer fraud aimed at senior citizens and alternatives to long-term care. Administered by the Office of Research, Demonstration and Evaluation under the Administration on Aging. (HHS)

Social Security Act (Title XX)

Authorizes Federal-state social services programs, with each state designing and setting its own eligibility standards. Emphasis is placed on the provision of child day care services and the employment of welfare recipients in those day care programs. Also provides assistance for services for the aged, blind and disabled, in addition to many others. Administered by the Social Security Administration. (HHS)

Appendix I

The following is a list of offices that will help you in locating further information about the programs highlighted as well as others for which your group might qualify. We suggest where appropriate to start with the regional office nearest you. (See Map)

National Office:

Department of Health, Education and Welfare
General Information
200 Independence Avenue, S.W.
Washington, D.C. 20201
(202) 245-7000

Health, Education and Welfare Regional Offices:

1. Department of Health, Education and Welfare
John F. Kennedy Federal Building
Government Center
Boston, Massachusetts 02203
(617) 223-6827
2. Department of Health, Education and Welfare
Federal Building
26 Federal Plaza
New York, New York 10007
(212) 264-2560
3. Department of Health, Education and Welfare
P.O. Box 13716
Philadelphia, Pennsylvania 19101
(215) 596-6637
4. Department of Health, Education and Welfare
101 Marietta Tower, N.W., Suite 1203
Atlanta, Georgia 30323
(404) 221-2316
5. Department of Health, Education and Welfare
300 South Wacker Drive
Chicago, Illinois 60606
(312) 353-1385
6. Department of Health, Education and Welfare
1200 Main Tower Building
Dallas, Texas 75202
(214) 767-3879
7. Department of Health, Education and Welfare
601 East 12th Street
Kansas City, Missouri 64106
(816) 374-3291
8. Department of Health, Education and Welfare
Federal Office Building
1961 Stout Street
Denver, Colorado 80294
(303) 837-4461
9. Department of Health, Education and Welfare
Federal Office Building
50 United Nations Plaza
San Francisco, California 94102
(415) 556-5810
10. Department of Health, Education and Welfare
Arcade Plaza
1321 Second Avenue
Seattle, Washington 98101
(206) 442-0430

Standard Federal Regions

Department of Housing and Urban Development

The Department of Housing and Urban Development's (HUD) principal responsibility is to administer programs concerning housing needs, fair housing opportunities and the general improvement and development of the nation's communities.

To carry out the responsibility of improving and developing communities, HUD administers mortgage insurance programs and a rental subsidy program to help lower-income families to afford decent housing; promotes equity in housing activities; encourages programs aiding neighborhood rehabilitation and urban preservation; and fosters programs that stimulate and guide the housing industry to provide not only housing but a suitable living environment.

Community Development Block Grant Program

Awards block grants to local governments for a wide variety of community development activities. Local governments use the funds to provide adequate housing and expanded economic opportunities for low- and moderate-income groups and for neighborhood revitalization projects. Administered by the Office of Community Planning and Development.

Cycle II Residential Solar Research and Demonstration Grant

No longer available. Grants were awarded for the design and construction of residential solar energy projects to encourage the use of solar energy in housing. Program being replaced by HUD's Solar Energy Bank, which will provide loans at below-market interest rates for housing projects utilizing solar energy. Administered by the Division of Energy, Building Technology and Standards under the Office of Policy Development and Research.

Direct Loans for Housing for the Elderly or Handicapped (Section 202)

Provides long-term direct loans to eligible private, nonprofit sponsors to finance rental or cooperative housing facilities for elderly or handicapped persons. Administered by the Assistant Secretary for Housing.

Homeownership Assistance for Low- and Moderate-Income Families (Section 221)

Provides mortgage insurance to increase home-ownership opportunities for low- and moderate-income families, especially those displaced by neighborhood revitalization. Insures lenders against loss on mortgage loans for one to four-family housing. Administered by the Assistant Secretary for Housing.

Homeownership Assistance for Low- and Moderate-Income Families (Section 235)

Provides mortgage insurance and interest subsidies for low- and moderate-income home buyers. Enables eligible families to afford new homes which meet HUD standards. Administered by the Assistant Secretary for Housing.

Innovative Grants Program

Funds a variety of innovative community development demonstration projects for low- and moderate-income people. Provisions set forth as part of the Community Development Block Grant (CDBG) Program. Administered by the Office of Community Planning and Development (previously, by the Office of Policy Development and Research).

Low-Income Public Housing "Turnkey" Program

Provides aid to local public housing agencies to supply decent shelter for low-income residents at affordable rents. The public housing agency invites private developers to submit proposals, selects the best proposal and agrees to purchase the project on completion. A local public housing agency then operates it. Administered by the Assistant Secretary for Housing.

Lower-Income Rental Assistance Program (Section 8)

Provides rent subsidies for lower-income families to help them afford suitable housing in the private market. HUD makes up the difference between what is affordable to a household and the fair market rent. Administered by the Assistant Secretary for Housing.

Multifamily Homesteading Technical Assistance Project

Assists with the self-help rehabilitation of abandoned multifamily buildings that will be owned by the participating families upon completion of the rehabilitation. Project currently underway in five cities (Boston, Massachusetts; Chicago, Illinois; Cleveland, Ohio; Hartford, Connecticut; and Springfield, Massachusetts). Administered by the Office of Community Planning and Development.

Multifamily Rental Housing for Low- and Moderate-Income Families (Section 221)

Provides mortgage insurance and helps finance construction or substantial rehabilitation of multifamily rental or cooperative housing for low- and moderate-income or displaced families. Administered by the Assistant Secretary for Housing.

Neighborhood Development Program

Provides grants to neighborhood self-help development organizations to foster their development and self-reliance and to improve their ability to work with local governments and the private sector toward neighborhood revitalization. Administered by the Office of Neighborhoods, Voluntary Associations and Consumer Protection.

Neighborhood Housing Counseling Program

Approves and funds qualifying local agencies who counsel prospective home buyers and homeowners with respect to property maintenance, household budgeting, debt management and other related matters. Assists residents in improving their housing conditions and standards of living. Administered by the Office of Neighborhoods, Voluntary Associations and Consumer Protection.

Rehabilitation Loan Program (Section 312)

Authorizes direct Federal loans that finance rehabilitation of residential and nonresidential properties being revitalized under such programs as Urban Homesteading and Community Development Block Grants. Administered by the Office of Community Planning and Development.

Rental and Cooperative Housing Assistance for Lower-Income Families (Section 236)

Provides funds for mortgage insurance, interest reduction and operating subsidies to reduce rents for lower-income households. Subsidies cover the difference between the tenants' contribution and the actual costs of operating the project. Works in conjunction with the Lower-Income Rental Assistance (Section 8) Program. Administered by the Assistant Secretary for Housing.

Tandem Programs

Designed to expand housing investments by mostly low- and moderate-income families by providing a lower mortgage interest rate to qualifying individuals and groups through subsidizing the difference between current market prices and the rate at which the mortgage was bought.

Provides below-market rate financing for multifamily projects located in urban areas which meet HUD standards.

These Tandem Programs seek to provide affordable housing opportunities in urban areas and stem or reverse the outflow of middle-income residents. Administered by the Government National Mortgage Association.

The following is a list of offices that will help you in locating further information about the programs highlighted as well as others for which your group might qualify. We suggest where appropriate to start with the regional office nearest you. (See Map)

National Office:

Department of Housing and Urban Development
General Information
451 Seventh Street, S.W.
Washington, D.C. 20410
(202) 755-5111

Department of Housing and Urban Development Regional Offices:

1. Department of Housing and Urban Development
   John F. Kennedy Federal Building, Room 800
   Boston, Massachusetts 02203
   (617) 223-4066
2. Department of Housing and Urban Development
   26 Federal Plaza
   New York, New York 10007
   (212) 264-8068
3. Department of Housing and Urban Development
   Curtis Building
   Sixth and Walnut Streets
   Philadelphia, Pennsylvania 19106
   (215) 597-2560
4. Department of Housing and Urban Development
   Pershing Point Plaza
   1371 Peachtree Street, N.W.
   Atlanta, Georgia 30309
   (404) 881-4585
5. Department of Housing and Urban Development
   300 South Wacker Drive
   Chicago, Illinois 60606
   (312) 353-5680
6. Department of Housing and Urban Development
   Earle Cabell Federal Building
   1100 Commerce Street
   Dallas, Texas 75242
   (214) 749-7401
7. Department of Housing and Urban Development
   300 Federal Office Building
   911 Walnut Street
   Kansas City, Missouri 64106
   (816) 374-2661
8. Department of Housing and Urban Development
   Executive Towers
   1405 Curtis Street
   Denver, Colorado 80202
   (303) 837-4513
9. Department of Housing and Urban Development
   450 Golden Gate Avenue
   P.O. Box 36003
   San Francisco, California 94102
   (415) 556-4752
10. Department of Housing and Urban Development
    3003 Arcade Plaza Building
    1321 Second Avenue
    Seattle, Washington 98101
    (206) 442-5414

Standard Federal Regions

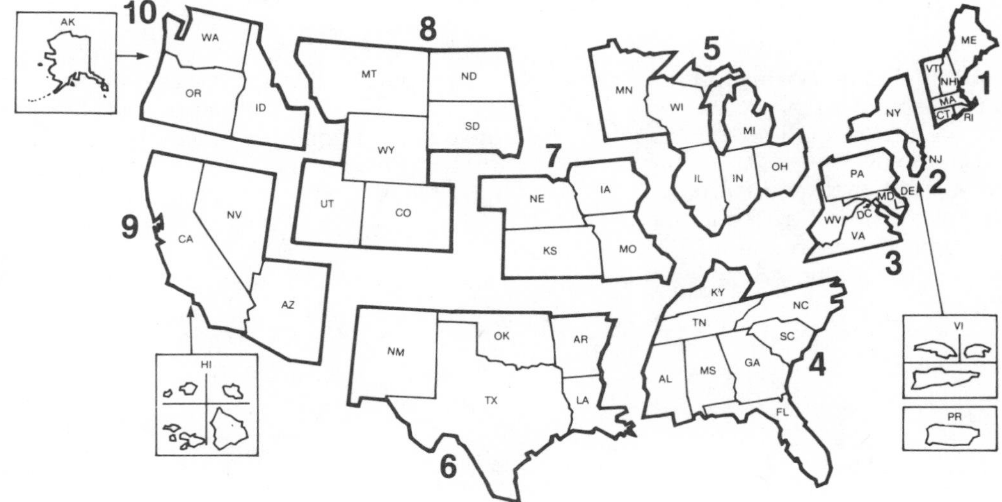

Department of Justice

The Department of Justice (DOJ) serves as counsel for the nation's citizens. It represents them in enforcing the law in the public interest. Through its thousands of lawyers, investigators and agents, the Department plays the key role in protection against criminals and subversion; ensuring healthy competition of business in our free enterprise system; safeguarding the consumer; and enforcing drug, immigration and naturalization laws. The Department also plays a significant role in protecting citizens through its efforts in effective law enforcement, crime prevention, crime detection and prosecution and rehabilitation of offenders.

Office of Juvenile Justice and Delinquency Prevention

Provides funding for groups and organizations with innovative programs for research and development, achieving career potential and alternative education. Administered by the Law Enforcement Assistance Administration.

Contact the following office for information about programs for which your group might qualify.

National Office:

Department of Justice
General Information
Constitution Avenue and 10th Street, N.W.
Washington, D.C. 20530
(202) 633-2000

Department of Labor

The purpose of the Department of Labor (DOL) is to foster, promote and develop the welfare of the wage earners of the United States, to improve their working conditions and to advance their opportunities for profitable employment. In carrying out this mission, the Department administers more than 130 Federal labor laws guaranteeing workers' rights to safe and healthful working conditions, a minimum hourly wage and overtime pay, unemployment insurance, workers' compensation and freedom from employment discrimination. The Department also protects workers' pension rights; sponsors job training programs; helps workers find jobs; works to strengthen free collective bargaining; and keeps track of changes in employment, prices and other national economic measurements. Through its programs, DOL seeks to meet the unique job market problems of older workers, youths, minority group members, women, the handicapped and other groups.

Comprehensive Employment and Training Act (CETA)

Provides funds to state and local agencies to design and administer comprehensive employment and training programs for their areas. Offers low-income, underemployed and unemployed persons of all ages help in obtaining a meaningful job and increasing their self-sufficiency. Administered by the Office of Comprehensive Employment Development Programs under the Employment and Training Administration.

Older Americans Act (Title V)

Provides funds to Federal and state agencies to operate employment programs for low-income citizens aged 55 or over who work part-time in public service jobs. Administered by the Office of National Programs under the Employment and Training Administration.

The following is a list of offices that will help you in locating further information about the programs highlighted as well as others for which your group might qualify. We suggest where appropriate to start with the regional office nearest you. (See Map)

National Offices:

Department of Labor
General Information
200 Constitution Avenue, N.W.
Washington, D.C. 20210
(202) 523-8165

Employment and Training Administration
General Information
Department of Labor
601 D Street, N.W.
Washington, D.C. 20214
(202) 376-6295

Employment and Training Administration Regional Offices:

1. Employment and Training Administration
   Department of Labor
   John F. Kennedy Federal Building
   Boston, Massachusetts 02203
   (617) 223-7328
2. Employment and Training Administration
   Department of Labor
   1515 Broadway
   New York, New York 10036
   (212) 339-5211
3. Employment and Training Administration
   Department of Labor
   P.O. Box 8796
   Philadelphia, Pennsylvania 19104
   (215) 596-6394
4. Employment and Training Administration
   Department of Labor
   1371 Peachtree Street, N.E.
   Atlanta, Georgia 30309
   (404) 881-3938
5. Employment and Training Administration
   Department of Labor
   230 South Dearborn Street
   Chicago, Illinois 60604
   (312) 353-1549
6. Employment and Training Administration
   Department of Labor
   555 Griffin Square Building, Room 317
   Dallas, Texas 75202
   (214) 767-6877
7. Employment and Training Administration
   Department of Labor
   911 Walnut Street
   Kansas City, Missouri 64106
   (816) 758-3101
8. Employment and Training Administration
   Department of Labor
   1961 Stout Street
   Denver, Colorado 80294
   (303) 837-3667
9. Employment and Training Administration
   Department of Labor
   450 Golden Gate Avenue
   San Francisco, California 94102
   (415) 556-5994
10. Employment and Training Administration
    Department of Labor
    909 First Avenue
    Seattle, Washington 98104
    (206) 399-5297

Standard Federal Regions

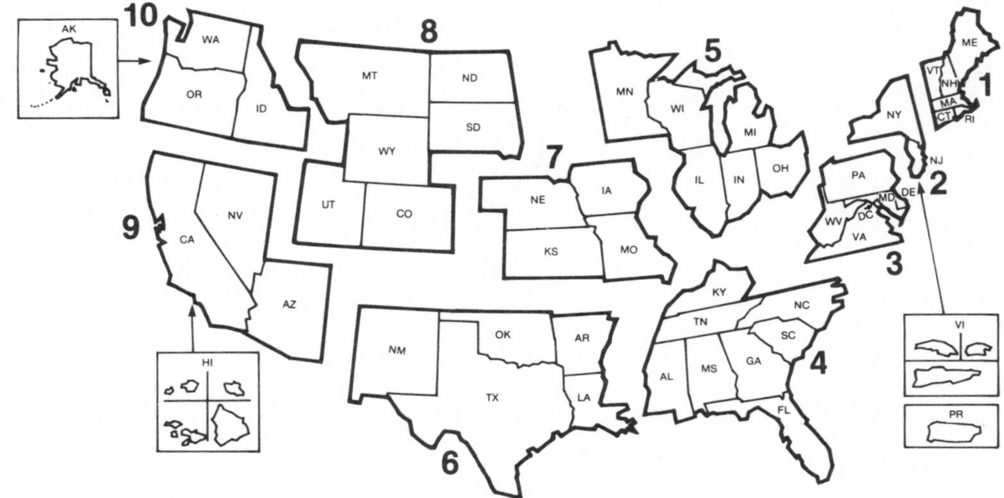

National Foundation on the Arts and the Humanities

The general purpose of the National Foundation on the Arts and the Humanities (NFAH) is to encourage and support national progress in humanities and the arts. The Foundation consists of a National Endowment for the Arts, National Endowment for the Humanities and a Federal Council on the Arts and Humanities.

Expansion Arts Program

Supports community-based organizations which produce, create or exhibit art, particularly for low-income, rural or ethnic segments of the population with little access to major art institutions. Use of grants includes providing for professional arts training and cross-cultural exchanges. Administered by the National Endowment for the Arts.

Contact the following office for information about programs for which your group might qualify.

National Office:

National Endowment for the Arts
General Information
2401 E Street, N.W.
Washington, D.C. 20506
(202) 634-6369

National Science Foundation

The National Science Foundation (NSF) promotes the progress of science through the support of research and education in the sciences. Its major emphasis is on basic research, the search for improved understanding of the fundamental laws of nature. The NSF is also involved in applied research directed toward the solution of more immediate problems of our society. Its educational programs are aimed at ensuring increased understanding of science at all educational levels and an adequate supply of scientists and engineers to meet our country's needs.

Science for Citizens Program

Encourages community-wide discussion of science-related issues. Provides grants for research and public education projects such as consumer health advocacy workshops and educational programs relating to alternative energy resources. Administered by the Office of Science and Society.

Contact the following office for information about programs for which your group might qualify.

National Office:

National Science Foundation
General Information
1800 G Street, N.W.
Washington, D.C. 20550
(202) 655-4000

Department of Transportation

The Department of Transportation (DOT) establishes the nation's overall transportation policy. Under its umbrella there are eight administrations whose jurisdictions include highway planning, development and construction; urban mass transit; railroads; aviation; the safety of waterways, ports, highways; and oil and gas pipelines. Decisions made by DOT in conjunction with the appropriate state and local officials strongly affect other programs such as land planning, energy conservation, scarce resource utilization and technological change.

Federal Aid to Urban Systems Program

Provides funds for improving transportation service within urban areas. Projects include modernized traffic signals and preferential bus lanes. Administered through the local offices of the Federal Highway Administration.

Highway Safety Act (Section 402)

Strives to reduce traffic accidents through grants to states for programs in such areas as driver education, highway desigr., identification and surveillance of potential accident locations and pedestrian and bicycle safety. Jointly administered by the National Highway Traffic Safety Administration and the Federal Highway Administration.

National Ridesharing Demonstration Program

No longer a demonstration program. Provides funds to state and local agencies for innovative approaches to ridesharing such as vanpooling, carpooling and computerized rider matching services. Ongoing ridesharing projects are funded by Federal highway funds. Administered by the Federal Highway Administration.

Rural and Small Urban Public Transportation Assistance Program

Provides capital equipment and operational assistance for rural and small urban transportation systems such as minibuses to transport rural residents to medical centers. Administered by the local offices of the Federal Highway Administration.

Urban Mass Transportation Act

Designed to plan, develop and improve public transportation systems. Provides assistance for the planning and implementation of urban transportation systems and grants for research, development and training. Administered by the Urban Mass Transportation Administration.

The following is a list of offices that will help you in locating further information about the programs highlighted as well as others for which your group might qualify. We suggest where appropriate to start with the regional office nearest you. (See Map)

National Offices:

Department of Transportation
General Information
400 Seventh Street, S.W.
Washington, D.C. 20590
(202) 426-4000

Federal Highway Administration
General Information
Department of Transportation
400 Seventh Street, S.W.
Washington, D.C. 20590
(202) 426-0677

Urban Mass Transportation Administration
General Information
Department of Transportation
400 Seventh Street, S.W.
Washington, D.C. 20590
(202) 426-1828

Federal Highway Administration Regional Offices:

1. Federal Highway Administration
   Department of Transportation
   Leo W. O'Brien Federal Building, Room 729
   Clinton Avenue and North Pearl Street
   Albany, New York 12207
   (518) 472-6476
2. (The Federal Highway Administration's Region 1 is a combination of the standard Federal Regions 1 and 2.)
3. Federal Highway Administration
   Department of Transportation
   31 Hopkins Plaza
   Baltimore, Maryland 21201
   (301) 962-2361
4. Federal Highway Administration
   Department of Transportation
   1720 Peachtree Road, N.W.
   Atlanta, Georgia 30309
   (404) 881-4078
5. Federal Highway Administration
   Department of Transportation
   18209 Dixie Highway
   Homewood, Illinois 60430
   (312) 370-9300

6. Federal Highway Administration
Department of Transportation
819 Taylor Street
Fort Worth, Texas 76102
(817) 334-3221
7. Federal Highway Administration
Department of Transportation
P.O. Box 19715
Kansas City, Missouri 64141
(816) 926-7565
8. Federal Highway Administration
Department of Transportation
Denver Federal Center, Building 40
Denver, Colorado 80225
(303) 234-4051
9. Federal Highway Administration
Department of Transportation
2 Embarcadero Center, Suite 530
San Francisco, California 94111
(415) 556-3850
10. Federal Highway Administration
Department of Transportation
222 Southwest Morrison Street
Portland, Oregon 97204
(503) 221-2052

Urban Mass Transportation Regional Offices:

1. Urban Mass Transportation
Department of Transportation
Transportation Systems Center
Kendall Square
55 Broadway
Cambridge, Massachusetts 02142
(617) 494-2055
2. Urban Mass Transportation
Department of Transportation
26 Federal Plaza, Suite 14-130
New York, New York 10007
(212) 264-8162
3. Urban Mass Transportation
Department of Transportation
434 Walnut Street, Suite 1010
Philadelphia, Pennsylvania 19106
(215) 597-8098
4. Urban Mass Transportation
Department of Transportation
1720 Peachtree Road, N.W., Suite 400
Atlanta, Georgia 30309
(404) 881-3948
5. Urban Mass Transportation
Department of Transportation
300 South Wacker Drive, Suite 1740
Chicago, Illinois 60606
(312) 353-2789
6. Urban Mass Transportation
Department of Transportation
819 Taylor Street, Suite 9A32
Fort Worth, Texas 76102
(817) 334-3787
7. Urban Mass Transportation
Department of Transportation
6301 Rock Hill Road, Room 303
Kansas City, Missouri 64131
(816) 926-5053
8. Urban Mass Transportation
Department of Transportation
Prudential Plaza, Suite 1822
1050 17th Street
Denver, Colorado 80265
(303) 837-3242
9. Urban Mass Transportation
Department of Transportation
Two Embarcadero Center, Suite 620
San Francisco, California 94111
(415) 556-2884
10. Urban Mass Transportation
Department of Transportation
Federal Building, Suite 3142
915 Second Avenue
Seattle, Washington 98174
(206) 442-4210

Standard Federal Regions

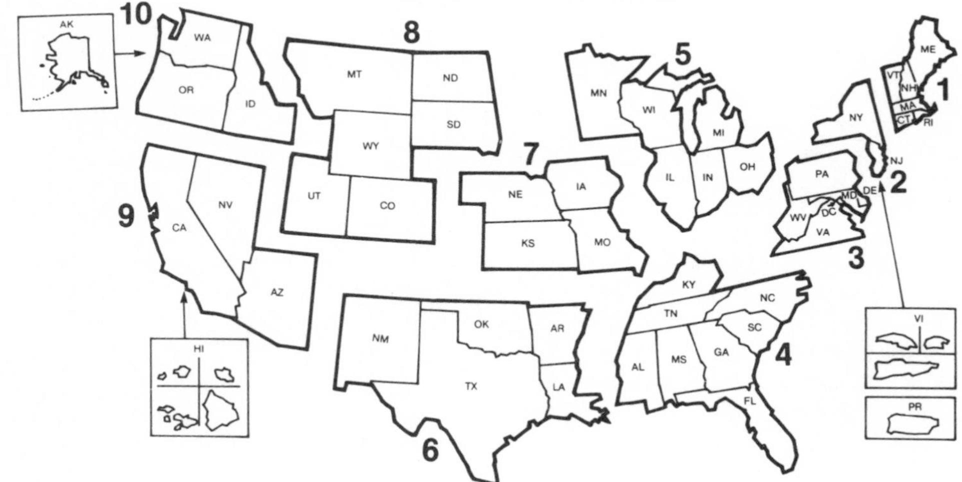

National Consumer Cooperative Bank

2001 S Street, N.W.
Washington, D.C. 20009
Toll Free: (800) 424-2481

"The Congress finds that user-owned cooperatives are a proven method for broadening ownership and control of the economic organizations, increasing the number of market participants, narrowing price spreads, raising the quality of goods and services available to their membership and building bridges between producers and consumers and their members and patrons. The Congress also finds that consumer and other types of self-help cooperatives have been hampered in their formation and growth by lack of access to adequate cooperative credit facilities and lack of technical assistance. Therefore, the Congress finds a need for the establishment of a National Consumer Cooperative Bank which will make available necessary financial and technical assistance to cooperative self-help endeavors as a means of strengthening the Nation's economy."

Public Law 95:351

What is the National Consumer Cooperative Bank?

The National Consumer Cooperative Bank (NCCB) is a major new national source of credit providing financial and technical assistance to existing and emerging consumer cooperatives. The NCCB consists of two parts: the Bank and the Office of Self-Help Development and Technical Assistance. The NCCB was established by an act of the 95th Congress and signed into law by President Carter on August 20, 1978.

What Will it Do?

The Bank will make loans to eligible cooperatives at prevailing interest rates. Initially, the Federal government (U.S. Treasury) will provide the capital for these loans. It is authorized to invest up to $300 million in the Bank over five years. The Bank may borrow up to ten times this amount, or $3 billion, from other capital sources.

The Office of Self-Help Development and Technical Assistance will provide capital advances and technical assistance to cooperatives that are just forming or expanding, especially those that serve or include low-income members. For the first three years of operation (1979–1981), the Self-Help Development Fund is authorized to receive up to $75 million from the U.S. Treasury.

Where Will the NCCB be Located?

The central Headquarters of the NCCB is located in Washington, D.C. As the NCCB develops, branch offices will be established in other parts of the country at the direction of the Board of Directors.

Who is Eligible to Borrow from the NCCB?

Consumer cooperatives will be eligible to borrow money from the NCCB if they:

- are chartered or operated on a cooperative, not-for-profit basis;
- produce or supply goods, services, or facilities for the benefit of their members as consumers;
- have a voluntary, open membership policy;
- observe one member, one vote principles.

A corporation owned by cooperatives (wholesale or federation of cooperatives) is also eligible to borrow from the NCCB if it meets the above requirements.

While credit unions are not eligible to borrow from NCCB, they may be eligible to receive technical assistance if their membership is mainly low-income.

How Will the NCCB Decide Who Will Receive Loans and/or Technical Assistance?

The Bank will decide whether to make a loan or provide technical assistance by looking at the following factors:

Organizational Structure.

For existing cooperatives, there must be competent management which is democratically controlled by the members. A new cooperative just getting organized will be judged on the likelihood of its developing an effective structure and on the experience of its leaders. The strength of membership support, education and participation will also be considered.

Financial Structure.

A cooperative must present enough financial information to allow the Bank to decide if the loan is sound and will be fully repaid. This normally includes balance sheets, income statements, future projections, etc. New cooperatives must submit a proposed financial plan. The experience of the cooperative's leadership must also be detailed.

Ability to Repay.

Loan requests are analyzed to make sure there is reasonable certainty that the cooperative can repay the loan and still have enough working capital to operate on a sound basis.

Expectation of Demand.

There should be reason to believe that there will be continuing demand for the cooperative's products or services.

Collateral.

Collateral may be required in order to get a loan. The type and amount required depends on the strength and weakness of other credit factors.

How Will the NCCB Help Eligible Organizations?

Under Title I, the NCCB will make loans at prevailing market rates. It will pay close attention to how well an organization meets the eligibility criteria.

The Board of Directors of the Bank must try to make sure that at least 35 percent of the loans go to:

a) cooperatives with a majority of low-income members, and/or

b) other cooperatives, if the loan will finance products or services used primarily by low-income persons.

No more than 10 percent of the loans may be made to cooperatives with products or services that are used by members who are also the primary producers. And after October 1, 1983, no more than 30 percent of the loans may be made for housing.

Under Title II, the Office of Self-Help Development and Technical Assistance may provide capital advances and technical assistance to cooperatives unable to meet the loan criteria under Title I. These cooperatives are likely to:

- serve low-income people
- have special needs or problems or
- be emerging cooperatives with no financial history.

The capital advances may be provided at lower interest rates than those charged under Title I. A capital advance from the Self-Help Development Fund will not require purchase of Bank stock, as does a loan from the Bank.

What Technical Assistance Will be Available?

The Office of Self-Help Development and Technical Assistance will make available information and services concerning the organization, financing and management of cooperatives. One of the many important functions of the technical assistance arm of the Office will be to act as a source of information regarding existing funding and technical assistance programs available through government agencies and other organizations. This will help the NCCB to extend its resources to serve more cooperatives.

It is anticipated that technical assistance will be available to all cooperatives on an ability-to-pay basis, and that those cooperatives unable to pay would still be eligible to receive technical assistance.

How Does the NCCB Operate?

The Board of Directors, consisting of 15 members appointed by the President of the United States and confirmed by the Senate, establishes operating policy for the Bank. The Board is charged with selecting a President for the Bank who will be responsible for day-to-day management of the Bank. The Director of the Office of Self-Help Development and Technical Assistance is appointed by the President of the United States, subject to Senate confirmation.

Who Owns the Bank?

The NCCB is a mixed-ownership government corporation. The U.S. Treasury, which will provide the initial capital for the NCCB, will share the ownership of the NCCB with cooperative shareholders until the government investment is repaid. Once this happens, the NCCB will be owned and operated by the cooperative shareholders.

How Will Cooperatives Assume Control of the Bank?

When a loan is made by the Bank to a cooperative, the cooperative will purchase stock in the Bank as part of the loan agreement. An eligible cooperative may also purchase stock in the Bank without taking out a loan.

When stock owned by cooperatives totals $3 million, three of the Board members will be replaced by members elected by cooperative shareholders. When stock owned by cooperatives totals $10 million, three more Board members will be replaced by shareholder-elected members. This process will continue until all but one Board member has been elected by shareholders. The remaining member will continue to be appointed by the President of the United States from among proprietors of small business concerns.

(Information taken from National Consumer Cooperative Bank brochure.)

Index

Following is a complete alphabetical listing of our *profiled* and *highlighted* groups. We have not indexed the many organizations that have provided financial and/or technical assistance to our featured groups. However, information on many of them can be found in the Resources which end each section.

Page

353 **Blue Cross/Blue Shield of Southwestern Virginia Utilization Review Program**
P.O. Box 13047
3959 Electric Road, S.W.
Roanoke, Virginia 24045
(703) 989-4231

34 **Blue Sky Alliance c/o New Mexico Federation of Cooperative Living**
632A Aqua Fria
Santa Fe, New Mexico 87501
(505) 988-5977

336 **Bonne Bell**
185 19th Detroit Avenue
Lakewood, Ohio 44107
(216) 221-0800

310 **Booth Maternity Center**
6051 Overbrook Avenue
Philadelphia, Pennsylvania 19131
(215) 878-7800

51 **Boston Urban Gardeners**
66 Hereford Street
Boston, Massachusetts 02115
(617) 267-4825

319 **Boulder County Hospice, Inc.**
2118 14th Street
Boulder, Colorado 80302
(303) 449-7740

25 **Broadway Local Food Co-op**
95 West 95th Street
New York, New York 10025
(212) 864-8165

56, **Bronx Frontier Development Corporation**
221 1080 Leggett Avenue
Bronx, New York 10474
(212) 542-4640

124 **Brothers Redevelopment, Inc.**
2519 West 11th Avenue
Denver, Colorado 80204
(303) 573-5107

157 **Buckeye-Woodland Community Congress**
10613 Lamontier Avenue
Cleveland, Ohio 44104
(216) 368-1070

34 **Bulk Commodities Exchange**
1432 Western Avenue
Seattle, Washington 98101
(206) 447-9516

C

42 **California Food Network**
942 Market Street
San Francisco, California 94102
(415) 421-8131

349 **California Public Interest Research Group of San Diego Consumer Health Advocacy Training Institute**
3000 E Street
San Diego, California 92102
(714) 236-1508

Page

63 **Cameron Chapter Farm Project**
P.O. Box 85
Cameron, Arizona 86020
(602) 679-2219

50 **Camphill Village, U.S.A., Inc.**
Copake, New York 12516
(518) 329-7924

361 **Cape Cod Health Care Coalition**
583 Main Street
Hyannis, Massachusetts 02601
(617) 771-0629

146 **Cape Cod and Islands Tenants Council**
Box 195
Hyannis, Massachusetts 02601
(617) 775-1070

335, **Capital Area Community Health Plan, Inc.**
336 1201 Troy-Schenectady Road
Latham, New York 12110
(518) 783-3110

192 **Casco Bank and Trust Company**
1 Monument Square
Portland, Maine 04101
(207) 774-8221

128 **Catholic Social Services, Inc.**
756 West Peachtree Street, N.W.
Atlanta, Georgia 30308
(404) 881-6571

340 **Center for Medical Consumers and Health Care Information**
237 Thompson Street
New York, New York 10012
(212) 674-7105

58 **Center for Neighborhood Technology The Sun Project**
570 West Randolph Street
Chicago, Illinois 60606
(312) 454-0126

216 **Center for Rural Affairs**
P.O. Box 405
Walthill, Nebraska 68067
(402) 846-5428

24 **Central Davenport Food Buying Club**
c/o Sue Wallinger
1318 Brown Street
Davenport, Iowa 52804
(319) 322-2386

226 **Central Senior High School**
200 Cabin Branch Road
Seat Pleasant, Maryland 20027
(301) 336-8200

157 **Cherry Hill Coalition**
810 18th Avenue
Seattle, Washington 98122
(206) 324-0980

65 **Cherry Hill Co-op**
MR # 1
Barre, Vermont 05641
(802) 476-8738

54 **Chicago Housing Authority Gardening Project**
22 West Madison Street
Chicago, Illinois 60602
(312) 791-8592

Page	
144	**Chicago Metropolitan Area Housing Alliance** 1123 West Washington Boulevard Chicago, Illinois 60607 (312) 243-5850
308	**The Childbearing Center** 48 East 92nd Street New York, New York 10028 (212) 369-7300
50	**Chittenden Community Correctional Center** 7 Farrell Street South Burlington, Vermont 05401 (802) 864-0344
58, 59, 60	**Christian Action Ministry** 5130 West Jackson Chicago, Illinois 60644 (312) 626-3300
273	**Citizens for a Better Environment** 59 East Van Buren Street, Suite 1600 Chicago, Illinois 60605 (312) 939-1984
157	**Citizens for Community Improvements of Waterloo** P.O. Box 875 Waterloo, Iowa 50704 (319) 232-8268
271	**Citizen Labor Energy Coalition** 600 West Fullerton Avenue Chicago, Illinois 60614 (312) 975-3680
266	**Citizen's Action League** 814 Mission Street San Francisco, California 94103 (415) 543-4101
358	**Citizens for the Improvement of Nursing Homes** 1305 Northeast 47th Street Seattle, Washington 98105 (206) 634-2349
273	**Citizens United for Responsive Energy** 3500 Kingman Boulevard Des Moines, Iowa 50311 (515) 277-0253
50	**Cleveland Board of Education** 1380 East Sixth Street Cleveland, Ohio 45202 (216) 696-2929
326	**Cleveland Consumer Action Foundation** **Cleveland Medical Directory** 532 Terminal Tower Cleveland, Ohio 44113 (216) 687-0525
271	**Coalition for Consumer Justice** 622 Charles Street Providence, Rhode Island 02904 (401) 521-1300
271	**Colorado ACORN** 1144 Cherokee Road Denver, Colorado 80218 (303) 831-1094
187, 188, 190	**Commission on Economic Opportunities of Luzerne County** 211-213 South Main Street Wilkes-Barre, Pennsylvania 18701 (717) 825-8571

Page	
185, 186	**Common Ground** c/o Mary Kumpula 2929 Bloomington Avenue, South Minneapolis, Minnesota 55407 (no phone)
156	**Communities Organized for Public Service** 122 East Durango San Antonio, Texas 78204 (515) 222-2367
204	**Community Action Program of Lancaster County, Inc.** **Solar Project** 630 Rockland Street Lancaster, Pennsylvania 17602 (717) 299-7301
328	**Community Advocates, Inc.** P.O. Box 71 Roslyn, New York 11576 (516) 487-0451
196	**Community Environmental Council** 924 Anacapa Street, Suite B-4 Santa Barbara, California 93101 (805) 962-2210
298	**Community Health Clinics, Inc.** 1503 Third Street North Nampa, Idaho 83651 (208) 466-7869
340, 341	**Community Health Information Network** **Mount Auburn Hospital** **Department of Community Health Education** 330 Mount Auburn Street Cambridge, Massachusetts 02172 (617) 492-3500—Ext. 1788
112, 113, 131	**Community Housing Education Corporation of Chicago** 2753 West Armitage Avenue Chicago, Illinois 60647 (312) 235-2144
311	**Community Mental Health Center South** 769 Tudor Road Lee's Summit, Missouri 64063 (816) 966-0900
64	**Community Self-Reliance, Inc.** 16 Armory Street Northampton, Massachusetts 01060 (413) 586-0543
110	**Community Training Dynamics, Inc.** 10 Fairway Street Boston, Massachusetts 02126 (617) 298-0825
117, 118	**Concerned Citizens of Butchers Hill** 2027 East Baltimore Street Baltimore, Maryland 21231 (301) 276-8827
273	**Connecticut Citizen Action Group** P.O. Box G Hartford, Connecticut 06106 (203) 527-7191
317	**The Connecticut Hospice, Inc.** **Department of Public Information** 765 Prospect Street New Haven, Connecticut 06511 (203) 787-5871

Page

37 **Connecticut Public Interest Research Group (ConnPIRG)**
FarmMarket
(Hartford Food System)
30 High Street, Room 108
Hartford, Connecticut 06103
(203) 525-8312

32 **Consumer Cooperative of Berkley, Inc.**
4805 Central Avenue
Richmond, California 94804
(415) 526-0440

28, **Consumer Cooperatives of Pittsburgh**
29 5474 Penn Avenue
Pittsburgh, Pennsylvania 15206
(412) 361-1521

292 **Control Data Corporation**
P.O. Box O-HQNO6U
Minneapolis, Minnesota 55440
(612) 853-3694

240 **Cooperative Auto, Inc.**
2232 South Industrial Highway
Ann Arbor, Michigan 48104
(313) 769-0220

242 **Cooperative Garage of Rockland County, Inc.**
14 Bobby Lane
West Nyack, New York 10994
(914) 358-9452

320 **Co-op Optical Service**
Division of Cooperative Services, Inc.
7404 Woodward Avenue
Detroit, Michigan 48202
(313) 874-4000

350, **Cornell University**
351 **New York State School of Industrial and Labor Relations**
Health Studies Program
3 East 43rd Street
New York, New York 10017
(212) 599-4550

295 **Country Doctor Community Clinic**
402 15th Avenue East
Seattle, Washington 98112
(206) 322-6698

D

197 **Davis, City of**
226 F Street
Davis, California 95616
(916) 756-3740

65 **Dekalb County Food Processing Center**
c/o Georgia Cooperative Extension Service
101 Court Square
Decatur, Georgia 30030
(404) 294-7449

298 **Delmarva Rural Ministries**
Blue Hen Mall
Dover, Delaware 19901
(302) 678-2000

105 **Delta Housing Development Corporation**
Box 847
Indianola, Mississippi 38751
(601) 887-4852

Page

107 **Detroit Shoreway Organization**
6516 Detroit Avenue, Room 242
Cleveland, Ohio 44102
(216) 961-4242

34 **Distributing Alliance of the Northcountry Cooperatives**
510 Kasota Avenue, S.E.
Minneapolis, Minnesota 55414
(612) 378-9774

328 **D.C. Public Interest Research Group**
(D.C. PIRG)
P.O. Box 19542
Washington, D.C. 20036
(202) 676-7388

351 **District League of Women Voters**
1346 Connecticut Avenue, N.W., Room 718
Washington, D.C. 20036
(202) 785-2616

237 **Domestic Technology Institute**
P.O. Box 2043
Evergreen, Colorado 80439
(303) 674-1597

E

27 **East End Food Co-op**
5472 Penn Avenue
Pittsburgh, Pennsylvania 15206
(412) 361-3598

218 **East River Electric Power Cooperative**
Locker Drawer E
Madison, South Dakota 57042
(605) 256-4536

295 **East of the River Health Center**
5929 East Capitol Street, S.E.
Washington, D.C. 20019
(202) 582-7700

122 **Eastside Community Investments, Inc.**
3228 East 10th Street
Indianapolis, Indiana 46201
(317) 633-7303

196 **Ecocycle**
P.O. Box 4193
Boulder, Colorado 80306
(303) 444-6634

218 **Ecotope Group**
2332 East Madison Avenue
Seattle, Washington 98112
(206) 322-3753

112, **Eighteenth Street Development Corporation**
113 1900 South Carpenter Street
Chicago, Illinois 60608
(312) 733-2287

60, **Eleventh Street Movement**
219 519 East 11th Street
New York, New York 10009
(212) 982-1460

196 **ENCORE**
2701 College Avenue
Berkeley, California 94705
(415) 849-2525

Page

221 **Energy Development Corporation**
3830 Dorney Park Road
Allentown, Pennsylvania 18104
(215) 395-3724

225 **Energy Management Center**
P.O. Box 190
Port Richey, Florida 33568
(813) 848-4870

185, 186, 219 **Energy Task Force**
156 Fifth Avenue
New York, New York 10010
(212) 675-1920

245 **Erving Paper Mills**
Vernon Road
Brattleboro, Vermont 05301
(802) 257-0511

167 **Exodus, Inc.**
355 Georgia Avenue, S.E.
Atlanta, Georgia 30312
(404) 622-1056

F

231 **Farallones Institute**
Integral Urban Housing
1516 Fifth Street
Berkeley, California 94710
(415) 525-1150

167 **Federation of Southern Cooperatives**
P.O. Box 95
Epes, Alabama 34560
(205) 652-9676

150 **Fifth City Human Development Project**
Chicago Mini-Zone Program
410 South Trumbull Street
Chicago, Illinois 60624
(312) 722-3444

144, 155 **Fillmore-Leroy Area Residents, Inc.**
307 Leroy Avenue
Buffalo, New York 14214
(716) 838-6740

138 **Flatbush Development Corporation**
1418 Cortelyou Road
Brooklyn, New York 11226
(212) 469-8990

331 **Florida, University of**
School of Pharmacy
Gainesville, Florida 32702
(904) 393-3541

81 **Food Advisory Service**
185 Valley Drive
Brisbane, California 94005
(415) 467-1343

42 **Food Bank, Inc. of Santa Clara County**
312 Brocaw Road
Santa Clara, California 95050
(408) 249-9170

Page

42 **Food Crisis Network**
1210 Locust Street
St. Louis, Missouri 63103
(314) 621-8840

76, 77 **Franklin Regional School Food Service**
3220 School Road
Murrysville, Pennsylvania 15668
(412) 325-1977

227 **Fulton County Cooperative Extension Service**
Pennsylvania State University
Courthouse Annex
McConnellsburg, Pennsylvania 17233
(717) 485-4111

G

66 **Gardens For All**
180 Flynn Avenue
Burlington, Vermont 05401
(802) 863-1308

292 **General Mills Corporation**
Employee Benefits Department
9200 Wayzata Boulevard
Minneapolis, Minnesota 55441
(612) 540-3677

271 **Georgia Action**
P.O. Box 7803
Atlanta, Georgia 30357
(404) 873-2223

234 **Glover's Mill Energy Center**
P.O. Box 202
Randolph, New York 14772
(716) 358-3306

268 **Granite State Alliance**
83 Hanover Street
Manchester, New Hampshire 03101
(603) 627-4439

353 **Greater Cleveland Coalition on Health Care Cost Effectiveness**
900 Standard Building
Cleveland, Ohio 44113
(216) 771-6814

348 **Greater Nevada Health Systems Agency**
P.O. Box 11795
Reno, Nevada 89510
(702) 323-1791

294 **Green Bay Area Free Clinic**
P.O. Box 2526
338 South Chestnut Avenue
Green Bay, Wisconsin 54303
(414) 437-9773

35 **Greenmarket**
24 West 40th Street
New York, New York 10007
(212) 840-7355

Page

256 **Green Mountain Stove Works**
Box 107, Westminister Station
Bellows Falls, Vermont 05158
(802) 463-9951

290 **Group Health Cooperative of Puget Sound**
200 15th Avenue, East
Seattle, Washington 98112
(206) 326-6262

292 **Group Health Plan, Inc.**
2500 Como Avenue
St. Paul, Minnesota 55108
(612) 641-3100

H

145 **Hartford Fair Rent Commission**
250 Main Street
Hartford, Connecticut 06103
(203) 566-6024

37, **The Hartford Food System**
86 **c/o Community Renewal Team**
3580 Main Street
Hartford, Connecticut 06120
(203) 278-9950

336 **The Health Adventure**
Mountain Area Health Education Center
501 Biltmore Avenue
Asheville, North Carolina 28801
(704) 254-6373

351 **Health Policy Advisory Center**
Health/PAC
17 Murray Street
New York, New York 10007
(212) 267-8890

346 **Health Systems Agency of Northern Virginia**
7245 Arlington Boulevard
Suite 300
Falls Church, Virginia 22042
(703) 573-3100

334 **Helping Hand Health Center**
506 West Seventh Street
St. Paul, Minnesota 55102
(612) 224-7561

298 **Hendry-Glades County Health Services, Inc.**
P.O. Box 278
133 Bridge Street
LaBelle, Florida 33935
(813) 675-0313

298 **Highlander Center**
Route 3, Box 370
New Market, Tennessee 37820
(615) 933-3443

137 **Home Loan Counseling Center**
2207 North Broadway
Los Angeles, California 90031
(213) 224-8011

102 **Homes in Partnership, Inc.**
8 East Fifth Street
Apopka, Florida 32702
(305) 886-2451

Page

292 **Honeywell, Inc.**
Honeywell Plaza
Mail Station MN12-6245
Minneapolis, Minnesota 55408
(612) 870-6220

318 **Hospice Care Group, Inc.**
2501 East Pleasant Street
Davenport, Iowa 52803
(319) 326-6512

319 **Hospice of Marin**
77 Mark Drive, Suite 19
San Rafael, California 94903
(415) 472-0742

125, **Housing Conservation Coordinators, Inc.**
193 777 10th Avenue
New York, New York 10019
(212) 541-5996

25 **Humphreys County Union for Progress**
Humphreys County Buying Club
513 Hayden Street
Belzoni, Mississippi 39038
(601) 247-1170

82 **Hunger Action Center**
Repeal of Sales Tax on Food in Washington State
2524 16th Avenue, South
Seattle, Washington 98144
(206) 324-5730

I

144, **Illinois Public Action Council**
266 59 East Van Buren Street
Chicago, Illinois 60605
(312) 427-6262

105, **Impact Seven**
159 Route 2, Box 8
Turtle Lake, Wisconsin 54889
(715) 986-4460

106 **Improved Dwellings for Altoona**
P.O. Box 705
Altoona, Pennsylvania 16603
(814) 944-9466

207, **Indian Development District of Arizona, Inc.**
209 1777 West Camelback Road, Suite A-108
Phoenix, Arizona 85015
(602) 248-0184

146 **Indiana Housing Coalition**
P.O. Box 44329
Indianapolis, Indiana 46244
(no phone)

72, **Indiana Nutrition Campaign, Inc.**
73 38 North Pennsylvania Avenue, Suite 312
Indianapolis, Indiana 46204
(317) 634-4172

170 **Inquilinos Boricuas en Accion**
Puerto Rican Tenants in Action
405 Shawmut Avenue
Boston, Massachusetts 02118
(617) 262-5274

Page

115 **Inter-Faith Adopt-a-Building**
605 East Ninth Street
New York, New York 10009
(212) 677-8700

34 **Intra-Community Cooperative**
1335 Gilson Street
Madison, Wisconsin 53715
(608) 257-6633

194 **Institute for Human Development**
718 West Norris Street
Philadelphia, Pennsylvania 19122
(215) 763-0742

184 **Institute for Local Self-Reliance**
Anacostia Energy Alliance
1717 18th Street, N.W.
Washington, D.C. 20009
(202) 889-7932

J

81 **Jefferson County Seniors' Resource Center**
1651-C Kendall Street
Lakewood, Colorado 80214
(303) 238-8151

152 **Jeff-Vander-Lou, Inc.**
2754 Bacon Street
St. Louis, Missouri 63106
(314) 534-3530

116 **Jubilee Housing, Inc.**
1750 Columbia Road, N.W.
Washington, D.C. 20009
(202) 332-4020

117, **Jubilee Housing, Inc. of Kentucky**
118 1125 West Burnett Avenue
Louisville, Kentucky 40208
(502) 637-4086

K

292 **Kaiser-Permanente Medical Care Program**
1 Kaiser Plaza
Oakland, California 94612
(415) 271-2604

100 **Kentucky Mountain Housing Development Corporation**
P.O. Box 431
Manchester, Kentucky 40962
(606) 598-5128

131 **Kenwood-Oakland Community Organization**
4618 South Lake Park
Chicago, Illinois 60653
(312) 548-7500

336 **Kimberly-Clark Corporation**
Neenah, Wisconsin 54956
(414) 729-1212

245 **Knoxville Commuter Pool**
South Stadium Hall
University of Tennessee
Knoxville, Tennessee 37916
(615) 637-7433

Page

L

264 **Labor Coalition on Public Utilities**
204 South Ashland Boulevard
Chicgo, Illinois 60607
(312) 738-4233

163 **La Casa Credit Union**
384 Plainfield Street
Springfield, Massachusetts 01107
(413) 734-8287

125 **Lake Braddock Good Neighbor Club**
c/o Ms. Judy Anderson
9509 Ashbourn Drive
Burke, Virginia 22015
(703) 978-0631

62 **Laramie County Community Action Agency**
Cheyenne Community Solar Greenhouse
1603 Central Avenue
Bell Building, Suite 400
Cheyenne, Wyoming 82001
(307) 635-9340

185, **League of Women Voters**
186 c/o Rhonda May Kriss
306 East Sixth Street
Northfield, Minnesota 55057
(507) 645-6914

50 **Lebanon in Service to Each Neighbor (LISTEN)**
P.O. Box 469
60 Hanover Street
Lebanon, New Hampshire 03766
(603) 448-4553

298 **Lee County Cooperative Clinic**
530 West Atkins Boulevard
Marianna, Arkansas 72360
(501) 295-5225

237 **Lehigh Valley Manpower Consortium**
Project Easton, Inc.
633 Ferry Street
Easton, Pennsylvania 18042
(215) 258-4361

273 **Light Brigade**
810 18th Avenue
Seattle, Washington 98122
(206) 329-9764

207 **Little Singer Community School**
Birdsprings, Navaho Nation
Star Route, Box 239
Winslow, Arizona 86047
(602) 774-7444

M

102 **Macon Programs for Progress**
P.O. Box 688
38½ East Main Street
Franklin, North Carolina 28734
(704) 524-4471

117, **Madison Community Cooperative**
118 254 West Gilman Street
Madison, Wisconsin 53707
(608) 251-2667

Page

192 **Maine Audubon Society**
Gilsland Farm
118 Old Route 1
Falmouth, Maine 04105
(207) 781-2330

126 **Maintenance Central for Seniors, Inc.**
3750 Woodward Avenue, Suite 32
Detroit, Michigan 48201
(313) 832-2134

172 **Manchester Citizens Corporation**
1120 Pennsylvania Avenue
Pittsburgh, Pennsylvania 15233
(412) 323-1743

230 **Manhattan, City of**
Department of Community Development
P.O. Box 748
Manhattan, Kansas 66502
(913) 537-0056

75 **MANNA**
School Breakfast Program Campaign
1502 Edgehill Avenue
Nashville, Tennessee 37212
(615) 242-3663

352 **Maryland Health Services**
Cost Review Commission
201 West Preston Street, First Floor
Baltimore, Maryland 21201
(301) 383-6804

328 **Maryland Public Interest Research Group**
(MaryPIRG)
University of Maryland
3110 Main Dining Hall
College Park, Maryland 20742
(301) 454-5601

37 **Massachusetts Department of Food and Agriculture**
Division of Agricultural Land Use
100 Cambridge Street
Boston, Massachusetts 02202
(617) 727-6633

316 **Massachusetts Department of Public Welfare**
Adult Day Care Health Services Program
Adult Day Care Unit
600 Washington Street, Room 740
Boston, Massachusetts 02111
(617) 727-5438

144, **Massachusetts Fair Share**
264 304 Boylston Street
Boston, Massachusetts 02116
(617) 266-7505

203, **Maui Economic Opportunity, Inc.**
204 189 Kaahumann Avenue
Kahului, Maui, Hawaii 96732
(808) 871-9591

292 **MedCenter Health Plan**
4951 Excelsior Boulevard
St. Louis Park, Minnesota 55416
(612) 927-3185

146 **Metropolitan Council on Housing**
24 West 30th Street
New York, New York 10001
(212) 725-4800

Page

118 **Metropolitan Washington Planning and Housing Association**
1225 K Street, N.W.
Washington, D.C. 20005
(202) 737-3700

249 **Michigan State Department of Transportation**
Dial-A-Ride
(DART—UPTRAN)
P.O. Box 30050
Lansing, Michigan 48909
(517) 374-9183

45 **Michigan, State of**
Office of Services to the Aging
300 East Michigan, Corr Building
P.O. Box 30026
Lansing, Michigan 48909
(517) 373-8230

117, **Michigan, University of**
118 **Inter-Cooperative Council**
Michigan Union, Room 4002, Box 66
Ann Arbor, Michigan 48109
(313) 662-4414

300 **Mid-County Medical Center, Inc.**
8190 Okeechobee Boulevard
West Palm Beach, Florida 33411
(305) 684-1119

125 **Milwaukee, City of**
Department of City Development
734 North Ninth Street
Milwaukee, Wisconsin 53233
(414) 278-2671

118 **Ministries United to Support Community Life Endeavors**
680 Eye Street, S.W.
Washington, D.C. 20024
(202) 554-1675

83 **Mississippi Legal Services Coalition**
P.O. Box 22887
Jackson, Mississippi 39205
(601) 944-0765

264 **Missouri Citizen Action**
393 North Euclid Avenue, Suite 203
St. Louis, Missouri 63108
(314) 361-0777

67 **Missouri, University of**
Extension Council, Urban Gardening Program
724 North Union Street
St. Louis, Missouri 63108
(314) 367-2585

123 **Monmouth County Board of Social Services**
P.O. Box 3000
Freehold, New Jersey 07728
(201) 431-6028

73 **Muskingum County Citizens for Nutrition**
333 Market Street
Zanesville, Ohio 43701
(614) 454-0161
(Program was short-term; no longer exists)

N

245 **Nabisco, Inc.**
East Hanover, New Jersey 07936
(201) 884-0500

Page

28, 29 **Natchitoches Area Action Association**
New Courthouse Building
P.O. Box 944
Natchitoches, Louisiana 71457
(318) 352-8085

42 **National Association of Farmworker Organizations**
1332 New York Avenue, N.W.
Washington, D.C. 20005
(202) 347-2407

132 **Neighborhood Housing Services, Inc.**
809 Middle Street
Pittsburgh, Pennsylvania 15212
(412) 321-2909

89 **Neighborhood Technology Coalition**
c/o Metro Center YMCA
909 Fourth Avenue
Seattle, Washington 98104
(206) 447-3625

30 **New Haven Food Co-op**
320 Whalley Avenue
New Haven, Connecticut 06511
(203) 777-9607

266 **New Jersey Federation of Senior Citizens**
20 East Hanover Street
Trenton, New Jersey 08608
(609) 394-0001

218 **New Life Farm**
Rural Gasification Project
Drury, Missouri 65638
(417) 261-2553

196 **New Paltz, Town of**
P.O. Box 550
New Paltz, New York 12561
(914) 255-0100

228 **New Western Energy Show**
226 Power Block
Helena, Montana 59601
(406) 443-7272

54, 55 **New York City Housing Authority Tenant Gardening Program**
250 Broadway
New York, New York 10007
(212) 433-4198

338, 339 **New York City Public School System**
Intermediate School 19
Project GUTS
345 Brook Avenue
Bronx, New York 10454
(212) 665-8448

329 **New York Public Interest Research Group (NYPIRG)**
5 Beekman Street
New York, New York 10038
(212) 349-6460

146 **New York State Tenant and Neighborhood Council**
198 Broadway, Room 1100
New York, New York 10038
(212) 964-7200

Page

250 **North Carolina Bicycle Program**
State Department of Transportation
Raleigh, North Carolina 27611
(919) 733-2804

245 **North Dakota State Vanpool Program**
Transportation Services
State Highway Department
Capitol Grounds
Bismarck, North Dakota 58505
(701) 224-2512

102 **Northeastern Connecticut Community Development Corporation**
P.O. Box 156
Danielson, Connecticut 06239
(203) 774-7020

332 **Northern Virginia Hotline**
P.O. Box 187
Arlington, Virginia 22210
(703) 522-4460

60 **North River Commission**
3440 West Lawrence
Chicago, Illinois 60625
(312) 463-5420

323 **Northwest Wisconsin Health Cooperative**
Box 64
Turtle Lake, Wisconsin 54889
(715) 986-2599

360 **Nursing Home Residents Advisory Council**
3231 First Avenue, South, Suite 210
Minneapolis, Minnesota 55408
(612) 827-8151

O

139 **Oak Park Housing Center**
1041 South Boulevard
Oak Park, Illinois 60302
(312) 848-7150

224 **Ocean County Youth Energy Conservation Corps**
127 Hooper Avenue
Toms River, New Jersey 08753
(201) 244-2121—Ext. 3250

115 **Oceanhill-Brownsville Tenants Association**
319 Rockway Avenue
Brooklyn, New York 11212
(212) 346-1588

68 **Oklahoma City Department of Economic and Community Affairs**
Division of Human Development
5500 Northwestern Avenue
Oklahoma City, Oklahoma 73118
(405) 840-2811

247 **Older Adults Transportation Service, Inc.**
601 Business Loop
70 West Parkade Plaza, Lower Level
Columbia, Missouri 65201
(314) 443-4516

P

R

Page

363 **Rhode Island Health Advocates**
Diocesan Community Affairs Office
Broad and Steward Streets
Providence, Rhode Island 02908
(401) 421-7833

185, **Rhode Islanders Saving Energy**
186 334 Westminster Mall
Providence, Rhode Island 02903
(401) 272-1040

25 **Riverdale Neighborhood House**
5521 Mosholu Avenue
Bronx, New York 10471
(212) 549-8100

110 **Ronan Neighborhood Associates**
252A Bowdoin Street
Boston, Massachusetts 02120
(no phone)

102 **Rural California Housing Corporation**
2007 O Street
Sacramento, California 95814
(916) 442-4731

158 **Rural Housing Improvements, Inc.**
218 Central Street
Winchendon, Massachusetts 01475
(617) 297-1376

39 **Rural Resources, Inc.**
Rural Route 1, Box 11
Loveland, Ohio 45140
(no phone)

S

136 **St. Ambrose Housing Aid Center**
321 East 25th Street
Baltimore, Maryland 21218
(301) 235-5770

102 **St. Landry Low-Income Housing**
P.O. Box 82
Palmetto, Louisiana 71358
(318) 623-5815

40 **St. Mary's Food Bank**
816 South Central Avenue
Phoenix, Arizona 85004
(602) 253-3407

107 **St. Nicholas Neighborhood Preservation and Housing Rehabilitation Corporation**
1129 Catherine Street
Brooklyn, New York 11211
(212) 388-4726

202 **San Bernardino West Side Community Development Corporation**
1736 West Highland Avenue
San Bernardino, California 92411
(714) 887-2546

Page

55 **San Jose Parks and Recreation Department**
151 West Mission Street, Room 203
San Jose, California 95110
(408) 277-4661

205 **San Luis Valley Solar Energy Association, Inc.**
512 Ross Street
Alamosa, Colorado 81101
(303) 589-2233

212 **Santa Clara, City of**
Santa Clara Water, Sewer and Solar Division
1500 Washington Avenue
Santa Clara, California 95050
(408) 984-3183

192 **Seattle City Light**
1015 Third Avenue
Seattle, Washington 98104
(206) 625-3738

195 **Seattle Recycling, Inc.**
5718 Empire Way South
Seattle, Washington 98118
(206) 723-2051

40 **Second Harvest**
1001 North Central
Phoenix, Arizona 85004
(602) 252-1777

44 **Senior Citizens Grocery, Inc.**
4707 North Lombard Street
Portland, Oregon 97203
(503) 285-4141

42 **Senior Gleaners**
2718 G Street
Sacramento, California 95816
(916) 448-1727

336 **Sentry Insurance Company**
1800 North Point Drive
Stevens Point, Wisconsin 54481
(715) 346-6000

117, **Settlement Housing Fund, Inc.**
118 1780 Broadway, Suite 600
New York, New York 10019
(212) 265-6530

207, **Shandiin Institute**
209 Route 3, Box 35
Flagstaff, Arizona 86011
(602) 526-4258

292 **SHARE Clinic**
555 Simpson Street
St. Paul, Minnesota 55104
(612) 645-0171

204 **Shelter Institute**
38 Center Street
Bath, Maine 04530
(207) 442-7938

216 **Small Farm Energy Project**
P.O. Box 736
Hartington, Nebraska 68739
(402) 254-6893

Page

273 **Solar Oregon Lobby**
720 Northeast Ainsworth Street
Portland, Oregon 97211
(503) 284-9320

235 **Solar Sustenance Team**
P.O. Box 733
El Rito, New Mexico 87530
(505) 471-1535

112, 113 **South Austin Realty Association**
5082 West Jackson Street
Chicago, Illinois 60644
(312) 378-3755

142 **South Brooklyn Against Investment Discrimination**
591 Third Street
Brooklyn, New York 11215
(212) 875-0835

112, 113 **South Bronx Community Housing Corporation**
391 East 149th Street, Room 520
Bronx, New York 10455
(212) 292-0800

266 **South Dakota ACORN**
611 South Second Avenue
Sioux Falls, South Dakota 57104
(605) 332-2328

76, 77 **Southeastern Tidewater Opportunity Project**
415 St. Paul's Boulevard
Norfolk, Virginia 23510
(804) 627-3541

256 **Southeastern Vermont Community Action**
P.O. Box 396
Bellows Falls, Vermont 05101
(802) 463-9951

210 **South Memphis Development Corporation**
Solar Resource Center
219 Madison Avenue
Memphis, Tennessee 38103
(901) 521-1031

162 **South Minneapolis Community**
Federal Credit Union
916 East 28th Street
Minneapolis, Minnesota 55407
(612) 871-2325

112, 113, 129 **Southside United Housing Development Fund Corporation**
238 South Second Street
Brooklyn, New York 11211
(212) 387-3600

213 **Southwest Alabama Farmers Cooperative Association**
Highway 80 West
Selma, Alabama 36701
(205) 872-6227

336 **Speedcall Corporation**
2020 National Avenue
Hayward, California 94545
(415) 783-5611

137 **Stop Wasting Abandoned Property**
439 Pine Street
Providence, Rhode Island 02907
(401) 272-0526

Page

337 **Student Coalition for Community Health**
P.O. Box 435
Tuscaloosa, Alabama 35401
(205) 348-6432

117, 118 **Swathmore Tenants Association**
1010 25th Street, N.W.
Washington, D.C. 20037
(no phone)

304, 305 **Swedish Wellness Center**
3444 South Emerson Street
Englewood, Colorado 80110
(303) 789-6940

T

333 **TEL-MED**
22700 Cooley South Drive
Colton, California 92324
(714) 825-6034

210 **Tennessee Valley Authority**
c/o Solar Memphis
240 Chestnut Street, Tower II
Chattanooga, Tennessee 37401
(615) 755-6851

244 **3M Company**
Central Engineering
Building 422E
St. Paul, Minnesota 55101
(612) 733-1110

292 **3M Company**
Group Insurance Department
Building 244-2E
3M Center
St. Paul, Minnesota 55144
(612) 736-1151

68, 72, 73 **Tompkins County Economic Opportunity Corporation**
318 North Albany Street
Ithaca, New York 14850
(607) 273-8816

237 **Total Environmental Action**
Church Hill
Harrisville, New Hampshire 03450
(603) 827-3374

264 **Toward Utility Rate Normalization**
693 Mission Street, Eighth Floor
San Francisco, California 94105
(415) 543-1576

105 **Town of Bolton Development Corporation**
P.O. Box 10
Bolton, Mississippi 39041
(601) 866-2221

42 **Tri-County Community Council Food Bank**
718 West Burnside Street
Portland, Oregon 97209
(503) 223-1030

Page

48 **Trust for Public Land**
39th Avenue Community Garden Windmill Project
82 Second Street
San Francisco, California 94105
(415) 495-4014

33 **Tucson Cooperative Warehouse**
1716 East Factory Avenue
Tucson, Arizona 85719
(602) 884-9951

U

316 **Utah State Division of Aging**
150 West North Temple, Suite 326
Salt Lake City, Utah 84103
(801) 533-6422

227 **Utah Technical College**
4600 South Redwood Road
Salt Lake City, Utah 84107
(801) 967-4111

268 **Utility Consumers Council of Missouri**
393 North Euclid, Suite 203
St. Louis, Missouri 63108
(314) 361-5725

V

268 **Vermont Public Interest Research Group (Vermont PIRG)**
26 State Street
Montpelier, Vermont 05602
(802) 223-5221

331 **Veterans Administration Medical Center**
Health Services Research and Development Program
Gainesville, Florida 32602
(904) 376-6575

249 **VIA TRANS**
P.O. Box 12489
San Antonio, Texas 78212
(512) 227-5371

360 **Village Nursing Home**
607 Hudson Street
New York, New York 11014
(212) 255-3003

331 **Virginia Citizens Consumer Council**
P.O. Box 777
Springfield, Virginia 22153
(703) 455-9515

111 **Voice of the People**
4927 North Kenmore Avenue
Chicago, Illinois 60640
(312) 769-2442

W

252 **The Walking Association**
4113 Lee Highway
Arlington, Virginia 22207
(703) 527-5374

Page

328 **Washington Center for the Study of Services**
1518 K Street, N.W., Suite 406
Washington, D.C. 20005
(202) 347-9612

72, **Watts Labor Community Action Committee**
102 11401 South Central Avenue
Los Angeles, California 90059
(213) 564-5901

28, **Weaver's Way**
29 559 Carpenter Lane
Philadelphia, Pennsylvania 19119
(215) 843-6945

304, **Wellness Associates**
305 42 Miller Avenue
Mill Valley, California 94941
(415) 383-3806

104 **Wesley Housing Development Corporation of Northern Virginia**
4701 Arlington Boulevard
Arlington, Virginia 22203
(703) 522-9432

68 **Western South Dakota Community Action Agency, Inc.**
1331 West Main Street
Rapid City, South Dakota 57701
(605) 348-1460

39 **West Virginia Department of Agriculture**
Produce Development Section
State Capitol Building
Charleston, West Virginia 25305
(304) 348-3708

199 **Wichita, City of**
Energy Commission
City Hall
455 North Main
Wichita, Kansas 67202
(316) 265-4193

303 **The Wholistic Health Center of Hinsdale, Inc.**
137 South Garfield Street
Hinsdale, Illinois 60521
(312) 323-1920

273 **Wisconsin's Environmental Decade**
114 East Mifflin Street, Third Floor
Madison, Wisconsin 53703
(608) 251-7020

333 **Women's Advocacy Center of Charleston**
P.O. Box 2054
Charleston, South Carolina 29403
(803) 723-1415

105, **The Woodlawn Organization**
112, 1180 East 63rd Street
113 Chicago, Illinois 60637
(312) 288-5840

221 **WTG Energy Systems, Inc.**
251 Elm Street
Buffalo, New York 14203
(716) 856-1620

266 **Wyoming Energy Advocacy Coalition**
1603 Central Avenue
Cheyenne, Wyoming 82001
(307) 635-9426